O9-ABI-384

COOKING

COOKING

JAMES PETERSON

ıne Art Institute Of Houston
Resource Center
1900 Yorktown
Housion Texas 77056

TEN SPEED PRESS
Berkeley | Toronto

Copyright © 2007 by James Peterson
Photography © 2007 by James Peterson

All rights reserved. No part of this book may be reproduced in any form, except brief excerpts for the purpose of review, without written permission of the publisher.

Ten Speed Press
PO Box 7123
Berkeley, California 94707
www.tenspeed.com

Distributed in Australia by Simon and Schuster Australia, in Canada by Ten Speed Press Canada, in New Zealand by Southern Publishers Group, in South Africa by Real Books, and in the United Kingdom and Europe by Publishers Group UK.

Book design by Nancy Austin

Library of Congress Cataloging-in-Publication Data

Peterson, James.
  Cooking / James Peterson.
    p. cm.
  ISBN 978-1-58008-789-6
  1. Cookery. I. Title.
  TX652.P455 2007
  641.5—dc22

                              2007021065
Printed in China
First printing, 2007

1 2 3 4 5 6 7 8 9 10 — 11 10 09 08 07

For my mother, Virginia

ACKOWLEDGMENTS

I'd like to thank all those who worked on developing and testing recipes, including Denise Michelson and Miranda Kany. Miranda Kany labored over the recipes to get them in shape; her hands also appear in some of the pictures. Laurie Knoop helped me keep organized during periods of impending chaos. Alice Piacenza, whose lovely hands grace these pages cannot be thanked enough for her hard work, support, and encouragement. It was often a team of only the two of us producing the photography for this book and she was my muse. I'd also like to thank the gentlemen at Fish Tales for their generosity and willingness to track down exotic seafood, and my butcher, Los Paisanos, who'll finally see what all my weird special requests were about. Thanks, too, to Eli Engelson-Mintz, whose hands also appear from time to time. Thanks to KitchenAid for supplying many of the pots and pans and one of the stoves that appear in the book. Converting a manuscript into a book takes an enormous effort by an almost alarming number of hard-working people. Lorena Jones, my editor, has worked immeasurably hard into the wee hours and has been agreeable even under enormous stress. Working with her has been a delight. Creative Director Nancy Austin is responsible for the book's brilliant design and is so quick and versatile that we were able to make changes to the text even at the last minute. I also want to thank copyeditor Sharon Silva, editor Amanda Berne, Publicity Manager Lisa Regul, Senior Marketing Manager Debra Matsumoto, Trade Sales Director Michele Crim, and Sales VP Patricia Kelly. And then of course there are the people I always thank because they stand behind me during all my projects, including the unsuccessful or impractical ones: my partner, Zelik, and my agents, Elise and Arnold Goodman. Thank you for being there for me.

CONTENTS

INTRODUCTION

A few months after my thirteenth birthday, I realized that my chemistry set didn't have all the chemicals I needed to satisfy my curiosity about what happened to various objects—coins, paperclips, flies—when they were submerged in different acids. The boiled-down battery acid I typically used for my favorite projects was no longer enough for me, so I convinced my mother to buy me nitric acid, and a whole new series of experiments ensued. When I read that hydrofluoric acid dissolved glass, it was a must-have, and Mom was dispatched, days before Christmas, to procure it. Because hydrofluoric acid is so deadly that the fumes alone can cause blindness, I had to bicycle down to the army surplus store (in those days army surplus really was army surplus) to buy a gas mask. On Saturday afternoons, Mom would regularly peek her head into the garage to tell me my peanut butter and jelly sandwich was ready, only to see me leaning over some boiling concoction, my voice garbled by the gas mask.

It's this same—and sometimes ill-advised—curiosity that gets me into the kitchen and keeps cooking exciting. Every time I cook, there's something a little new—something that makes the process interesting. Like my chemistry days, each dish has to involve a discovery, which means I rarely make the same thing exactly the same way twice. In other words, learning to cook well requires a willingness to experiment and to be less than perfect. It also demands repetition. Proficiency and, ultimately, perfection require trial and error in the kitchen until you get a feel for how dishes go together. Most cooking is based on a handful of basic techniques that, once understood, will allow you to discover your own cooking style and find confidence in the kitchen—much as my early chemistry self-education built on a growing body of experiments.

When college came, chemistry lost some of its charm because I could no longer soak cotton in sulfuric and nitric acids, dissolve it in ether, and paint it on things that I would then blow up. It boiled down, so to speak, to mathematics. I dropped out of college, worked in a laboratory to save money,

and, having determined that all life's nuisances were illusory, went to India to look for a guru. But India was a bust, so I worked my way by bus and train to Europe (in the 1970s you could go overland through Pakistan, Afghanistan, and Iran), ending up in Strasbourg on a sunny Sunday afternoon. The city was beautiful, with all the typical trappings of France at its best, but what impressed me was that everyone was eating, drinking, or smoking, or all three. The wisdom of this was immediately apparent. I had been ridiculed in the past for a more-than-usual interest in wine and fine dining, so I was ecstatic to discover a culture in which everyone was like me.

France was enchanting in those preglobalization days. Paris was alive with markets (there were no supermarkets) and everything was seasonal. A whole new flush of different vegetables, herbs, fruits, and fish would appear every couple of weeks. From noon to three in the afternoon, the streets would empty and seemingly hundreds of restaurants would fill with people eating multicourse meals and drinking wine. Back in America, most people were sipping coffee with their meals, few folks had ever seen a fresh tarragon sprig or a whole fish, and interest in food was considered effete and odd. Being effete and odd, I absorbed everything I could during my couple of months in France, and when I ran out of cash, I lived with a family near Carcassonne, where I worked tending the vineyards and picking grapes. We'd work from dawn until noon, spend three joyous hours at the table, and then return to the vineyards to finish the day's work.

I don't know the exact moment (I suspect it was while eating a Bresse chicken cooked in cream) that I decided to become a chef, but I do know it was sometime during that first stay in France. I returned to the United States and got a job as a short-order cook (good training for the rigors of the kitchen) and found I liked the frenzy of it, if not the food. I studied the few cookbooks then available—*Larousse Gastronomique* and Richard Olney's *Simple French Food* were the stars—and saved my pennies to return to France. I sold everything I owned except a suitcase of necessary clothes (including a sports jacket for restaurants) and set out for the south of France to find Richard Olney, who had become the mentor to Alice Waters and Jeremiah Tower at Berkeley's Chez Panisse—and eventually to me.

Richard Olney's reception is a whole other story, but in short he told me where to work to learn how to cook. I rented a room in Paris, sent out handwritten letters to every starred restaurant in town begging for work, and took classes at the Cordon Bleu until I was broke. Finally, after six months, I was hired by Vivarois, which boasted three Michelin stars. I was so intimidated during my first days at work that I was incompetent. I kept watching and waiting for the magic formulas to come out. True, there were a few unexpected tricks, like whisking pureed foie gras into the oxtail stew, but for the most part the cooking was straightforward.

Yet those months at Vivarois did transform me into a cook: they taught me that there are no secrets. I learned that good cooking is based on doing lots of little things correctly without taking shortcuts and by a profound reverence for ingredients—for letting them express their own character. The intense curiosity about what would happen to a silver coin in nitric acid translated into what happens to a piece of chicken as it sizzles in butter. When I left Vivarois I still wasn't a chef, but I had the confidence to become one, to gain a deeper understanding of food. During the decades that followed, I worked in many restaurants, from the disgusting to the divine, had my own restaurant in New York, taught cooking for some twenty years, and became a writer and photographer.

As a teacher, I always tell students, especially the ones who want to become chefs, to read, read, read. There's very little I've learned in my years as a cook that isn't written down somewhere. And if it wasn't written down before, it's written down now in this book. During forty years of cooking, I've acquired a keen feel for how foods react to heat or cold and how to bring out their best qualities. My cooking grows simpler over the years, as I feel less need to impress and realize that the finest foods are simple foods cooked in a way that suits them best.

With this book, I've tried to steer you away from the mistakes that my students and I have made, to instill a real passion for food that takes the dreariness out of having to cook every night. All of the basic cooking methods you need to know are explained in the beginning pages of the book, and you'll see that I rely on everyday equipment and don't think anyone needs a fancy outfitted kitchen to be a successful cook. Most of the recipes that follow are for everyday dishes (some of the pastries are a bit more complex) that either take little time or can be made ahead. I've included the foods I've learned to love (I admit to a bias toward France and Mexico) and the tricks I've learned from some of the world's great chefs, from four years of having my own restaurant (a kind of culinary laboratory), and from teaching how to make the same dishes year after year, in the process perfecting not only the dishes but also my explanation of how to make them. When every meal becomes a bit of an experiment, cooking is fun and interesting and far from dreary. Cook your way through this book and you will discover, as I have, the joy of cooking well.

ASSUMPTIONS

I don't believe in observing a lot of rules when I cook, but I do have strong preferences about what makes cooking taste best.

INGREDIENTS

Butter: All butter is unsalted. If you only have salted butter, don't worry, just cut down on the salt in the recipe. If you're trying to make clarified butter or ghee (see page 341), you'll have to use unsalted. And be aware that salted butter tends to burn a bit more easily than unsalted butter.

Salt: All salt is regular fine salt unless otherwise stated. If you have it, use fine sea salt as your basic salt, but otherwise regular "when it rains it pours" salt will be fine.

Cooking wine: Despite its virtues being extolled in many an old French cookbook, don't pour an expensive bottle of Bordeaux over a pot roast. True, a wine with bottle age gives wonderful flavor to anything braised, but unless you're set up with a cellar that guarantees you mature wine, don't buy aged wine for cooking unless you're very wealthy and don't care. In general, use white wine with a lot of acidity, which in general means French but not necessarily expensive; a generic sauvignon blanc is usually the right price and provides the requisite acidity and a bit of character you'll need for beurre blanc or for meats braised in white wine. For red, go for a lot of body. Red wines from South America are often a good value and wines that might be too soft to drink, such as a generic merlot, are perfect for the pot. Zinfandel was once a great value but no longer, unless you happen onto a sale. Wine that you've had around too long and that is a bit madeirized (white) or has lost its color (red) is perfect for cooking, and in fact the defects of wine gone "bad" can turn delicious when simmered with vegetables, meat, and herbs. Sherry, provided it's dry, is often delicious in place of "regular" white wine, and white vermouth is great to have around in a pinch when the only wine around is rare white Burgundy that friends brought to drink with dinner. When you are completely desperately out of wine, wine vinegar, especially your own homemade, will serve as a passable substitute.

Bay leaves: Use the imported European variety, not those from California where the leaves have an aggressive eucalyptus flavor and aroma.

Baking powder: All baking powder is double-acting; it's almost impossible to find any other version on grocery store shelves.

Nut oils: These are notoriously perishable and are often rancid before you even open the bottle. The best way to avoid rancidity is to buy oil made from roasted nuts; the roasting greatly slows down rancidity. These oils are expensive, but very little is needed to flavor foods, so you end up using less than you would of a less expensive oil.

Meat glaze: Use either homemade (take your best broth and reduce it to one-fifteenth its original volume, see page 177) or a commercially available glaze, which can be the equivalent of broth reduced to one-thirtieth of its original volume.

EQUIPMENT

Stoves: While all of us would like to have our kitchens equipped with 6-burner Vulcan ranges, most of us do with less and some of us with a lot less. Fortunately the best cooking isn't dependent on the best equipment. The only consistently annoying idiosyncrasy of most home stoves is a lack of heat, which makes it challenging to brown foods quickly enough. Recipes in this book often call for "medium to high heat," which sounds like a very wide range. It is, except that medium heat on a professional stove is the equivalent of high heat on many home kitchen ranges. If your stove is limited in this way, you may find yourself using the highest heat for all but the most gently simmered dishes.

Strainers and sieves: A drum sieve, a ring of steel or wood with a sheet of screen stretched over it, is the ideal gadget for straining solid mixtures, which are worked through the screen with the back of a large spoon or metal mixing bowl. Drum sieves, sometimes called by their French name *tamis*, are made in two forms: all metal with varying mesh screens and all wood with a fine mesh screen that requires replacing the whole device when worn out.

Benriner slicer: Plastic vegetable slicers are convenient and less expensive alternatives to professional-style metal mandolines. For some tasks, the Benriner works better than its pricey cousin. Be sure to buy the Benriner brand, which has adjustable nuts that enable you to control the thickness of the slices (some brands have set inserts for creating various thicknesses and these are rarely the right size).

Kitchen towels: These are indispensable and should be sturdy and made of cotton (polyester doesn't absorb liquids). Don't use terrycloth towels, which easily catch fire and leave lint on surfaces and foods.

Cooling racks: If you find a circular cake rack, nab it; they're perfect for improvising steamers. Otherwise just buy a large enough rack to cool at least a sheet pan full of cookies.

Sheet pans: The sheet pans I use are of standard size (professionals refer to them as "half sheet pans") and measure 17 by 13 inches. They fit in virtually all ovens.

Spider: A spider looks in fact like a spider web. The web part is made of wire and is attached to a long handle. Spiders are the best implements for frying because they allow you to remove ingredients quickly without bringing up a lot of oil as a slotted spoon does.

Much is made about the materials used to make cookware, but it doesn't make an enormous difference if you cook in a copper pot or an aluminum one. Just remember that the pots and pans should be heavy so they cook evenly and don't get too hot in the areas right over the heat source. The best bargains are iron skillets, commonly found in hardware stores. They're heavy and, once seasoned—heat a few tablespoons of vegetable oil in the pan until it smokes, then rub in the oil with a rag—can be used for just about anything. Aluminum pans, often found at restaurant supply stores, are also a good value; just keep in mind that aluminum sauté pans must be very hot—the oil in them should smoke—or food cooked in them will stick. Aluminum saucepans should never be used for sauces or soups containing egg yolks, or the liquid will turn gray.

Pots and pans: While a full collection of pots and pans looks great on the kitchen shelf, it's possible to cook with very few. A large pot is essential for boiling pasta and vegetables and for making broth. A saucepan is essential for soups and sauces and a frying pan is necessary for sautéing. A collection of sauté pans of different sizes is ideal, enabling you can match them to the amount of food you are cooking so that you just fill the pan, the perfect condition for sautéing. A medium pot with low sides is great to have for making soups in which vegetables are sweated in oil or butter before liquid is added. A saucepan with sloping sides is perfect for making egg-yolk based sauces such as hollandaise. A heavy sauté pan can often be improvised as a roasting pan, but if you're buying a roasting pan, try to find one that fits as closely as possible the shape of whatever it is you'll likely be roasting; oval pans are often just right.

The 10 Basic Cooking Methods

TECHNIQUES

Few cooking techniques require great skill or hours of practice. And even though lots of minor techniques and tricks are used in cooking, most dishes are prepared by one of ten basic methods: roasting, braising, poaching, sautéing, steaming, frying, grilling, smoking, barbecuing, and boiling. Once you have mastered these methods and understand how they work when applied to each basic food group, such as seafood, meats, and vegetables, you'll be able to alter recipes to suit your own taste or to take advantage of what's in the market—or you won't need a recipe at all.

Except for dishes served raw or marinated, such as ceviche or beef carpaccio, all cooking involves heat. Sometimes the heat is applied directly to the food, without moisture, as in roasting or grilling. Other times fats are involved, as in sautéing or frying, or water is used, as vapor when steaming and as liquid when poaching and braising. Sometimes the heat is intense, as when frying, or gentle, as when cooking a stew at just the hint of a simmer.

Some basic cooking methods include submethods, or techniques, such as peeling and shaping vegetables, glazing (really a form of braising), boning, filleting, and trimming all sorts of meats and seafood. As you learn to appreciate the role each of these so-called minor techniques plays in the basic methods, the details of cooking will make sense.

ROASTING

The word *roasting* comes from the French *rôtir*, which means "to roast." Traditionally, roasting was done in front of a roaring wood fire on a spit, a *broche*, that was rotated slowly to ensure the food cooked evenly. The result was a brown, savory crust concealing a properly cooked interior, and, if the cook was savvy, there was a pan or tray below the spit to catch the juices.

Nowadays, most of us don't have access to spits and roaring fires, so we use an oven. When foods are roasted in an oven, they are surrounded by the heat, as opposed to being under or over the heat source, as with broiling and grilling, respectively. Baking is simply the act of heating something through in the oven. Roasting, in the oven or on the spit, works by exposing the food to hot dry air. When done correctly, oven roasting yields almost the same delicious effect as spit roasting.

Convection Ovens

A convection oven is simply an oven that's very windy inside with the hot air blown around with a fan. The effect is analogous to the heat index in the summer or the wind chill in the winter, when the movement of air affects the way the air feels. Heated moving air behaves like still air that's fifty degrees hotter. If you have a convection oven, use it during the browning phase of roasting. If your oven only goes up to 500°F, you can make it function like 550°F by using the convection oven. This is useful when you need to brown small items such as chickens or squab.

How Hot to Roast?

To brown a roast without over- or undercooking it, you need to consider how large it is. If it's a turkey, you can roast it at a moderate temperature for the entire time. That's because it will be in the oven long enough to turn a beautiful golden brown even if the oven isn't very hot. On the other hand, if you're roasting a small chicken or other little birds, the oven needs to be hot enough for the brown crust to form before the bird overcooks. This is especially important for birds such as squabs, which have dark meat and are cooked to a relatively low internal temperature. A good rule is to start at the highest possible heat, roast until a golden crust is formed, and then turn the oven down for the rest of the roasting. If you're roasting something *very* small, such as a quail, you would need a 1500°F oven to get it to brown before it overcooked. In this case, or any time you think your oven might not be hot enough to brown whatever you're roasting, brown the food on the stove top before you slip it in the oven.

A hot oven at the beginning of roasting not only browns the roast, but also kills any bacteria on its surface. Once this has been accomplished, the oven temperature is not as critical. In fact, in some restaurants that serve prime rib, the roast is browned at a high temperature and then kept in a low oven—say, 130°F—for twenty-four hours. The meat can never overcook because it can't reach a temperature higher than 130°F, no matter how long it's left in the oven. The initial browning at a high temperature is essential, however. Starting the roast at 130°F wouldn't kill bacteria, which can cause the roast to go bad.

Don't try the twenty-four-hour method at home. Most ovens don't hold a temperature setting with sufficient accuracy, which makes the technique risky. In general, once the roast is browned, turn the oven down to 350°F. If the roast starts to get too brown before it is cooked through, turn the oven down again. If your guests are late, turn the oven down to 200°F. The lower the temperature and the longer the cooking, the more even the cooking will be.

Roasting Pointers

Roasts, especially large ones, should be brought to room temperature before they are roasted. While the actual length of time depends on the size of the roast, the time should never exceed 6 hours; leaving the roast out longer than 6 hours risks spoilage.

Start the roast in a hot oven until it browns and then finish it in a low to moderate oven.

Let the roast rest, loosely covered with aluminum foil, for at least 20 minutes before carving. How long it rests will depend on its size.

Testing for Doneness

The best way to determine if a roast is done is to stick an instant-read thermometer into the thickest part of a meat roast

or between the thigh and the breast of a bird. Don't slide the thermometer in so far that it touches bone, because the bone is always hotter than the surrounding meat. If it's ready, take it out of the oven, cover it loosely with aluminum foil—not tightly or it will steam—and let it rest in a warm place for 10 to 20 minutes for large birds (but not for squab or quail, which should rest for no more than a few minutes). Resting has two effects: it causes the heat to continue to penetrate to the middle of the roast, leaving the roast more evenly cooked, and it allows the meat to relax (remember meat is essentially muscle), so that when you cut into it the juices have redistributed evenly throughout the meat and don't come pouring out. When checking the temperature, keep in mind that it will rise 5° to 10°F during resting.

Basting

Students often ask me when they should baste a roast. Cooks originally basted roasts to keep their surface from drying out, but basting is unnecessary for birds, because the fat in the skin renders as the meat cooks, keeping the meat from drying out. A meat roast—a rib roast, a leg of lamb—should be left covered with a thin layer of its own fat, which will keep the meat from drying out. Some butchers, especially in Europe, trim all the fat off a roast and then tie a thin sheet of pork fat around the meat to keep it moist. The main problem home cooks face when it comes to basting is that repeatedly opening the oven door to baste allows heat to escape, which can prevent browning.

Stuffings

Many of us would regret forgoing the proverbial stuffed holiday turkey, but stuffings present a problem. When mixtures are stuffed into the cavities of birds or of meat roasts that have been split open, the roast usually has to be overcooked in order to cook the stuffing. Stuffings also absorb the juices released by the roast. They make the stuffing taste good, of course, but then there aren't enough juices for serving a jus or gravy. Yet another problem is the potential health risk: a stuffing can remain inside the roast at a warm, rather than hot, temperature long enough for bacteria to grow. If you do decide to opt for a stuffed bird or meat roast, always stuff it immediately before putting it in the oven so that there is less opportunity for bacteria to grow.

Gravy and Jus

This brings us to the question of whether to go with gravy or jus. Jus is just the drippings released by a roast, while gravy is the jus thickened, usually with flour. A jus is sometimes lightly thickened with cornstarch to give it a richer look, but it retains the sheen characteristic of a jus, rather than the more opaque look of a gravy. For example, in the United States turkey is usually served with a gravy and prime rib is usually serve with a jus.

A properly made jus or gravy has challenged cooks for centuries because roasts, at least when properly cooked, rarely provide enough drippings to go around. In times past, an extra roast was cooked well done so that it released all its juices, which were then used to supplement drippings from the roast being served. Some cooks, then and now, add broth to stretch a jus or a gravy. But even a concentrated broth doesn't have the pure, direct flavor of drippings. The problem is greatest with red-meat roasts that are cooked rare—the more cooked a roast, the more juices it releases— and with stuffed birds, because the stuffing absorbs a lot of the juices.

To prevent juices from burning, choose a heavy-bottomed roasting pan just large enough to hold the roast, with sides no higher than necessary, and don't use a rack. Roasting racks are useless. Rack partisans insist that racks allow the bottom of the roast to brown. But because the roast is not touching the pan, the juices from the roast drip down onto the bottom of the pan, which is at the same temperature as the oven, and then the drippings immediately burn, creating smoke that gives the roast a bad flavor and smells up the house. Any hope of using the juices to make a jus or gravy is lost. Cover the bottom of the roasting pan with pieces of onion and/or carrot (don't cut them too small or they'll burn too) to eliminate any exposed patches, to keep the roast from sticking to the pan, and to add flavor to the juices. To end up with more jus than the roast releases, you can also cover the bottom of the pan with a layer of meat trimmings that will release juices along with the roast. For smaller roasts, which roast in less time, you may want to put the meat trimmings in the pan with a carrot and an onion and roast them for 20 minutes or so to get them started before setting the roast on top.

Always keep an eye on the pan during roasting to make sure the juices aren't burning. If they threaten to burn before the roast is done, add about $1/2$ cup water to the pan to stop them from cooking. However, do this only as a last resort. Adding moisture can prevent browning.

When the roast is done, you need to analyze the contents of the pan. If it's covered with trimmings and the trimmings still look raw, put it on the stove top over high heat and stir the trimmings around to brown them, so they will release their juices. If the roast has released a lot of juices—this often happens with a turkey, especially if it's overcooked a bit—

you'll need only to separate the fat from the juices and serve the juices (the jus) as they are or make a gravy.

With a smaller roast, or with one that is cooked rare or medium-rare, you will probably see very few juices in the pan. The juices you do see may be emulsified with the fat into a cloudy, greasy-looking mixture, or they may have caramelized and formed a brown crust on the pan bottom. If the juices have formed a crust, just pour off and discard the fat. If the juices are emulsified with the fat, you need to separate them by putting the roasting pan on the stove top and boiling down the juices until they caramelize on the pan, leaving no liquid in the pan. You can then pour off the fat and proceed to make your gravy. For more about jus and gravy, and detailed directions, see pages 168 and 247.

BRAISING

One of the simplest cooking methods to describe, braising is nothing more than simmering foods in a small amount of liquid. In the process, the foods not only absorb flavor from the surrounding liquid but also contribute to it, creating a cycle of exchange that results in profoundly complex and satisfying tastes. What complicates braising is its many submethods, or techniques, and variations.

For example, short braising, which is what you are doing when you simmer a piece of fish or chicken in a little wine, is basically cooking food just long enough to heat it through to the temperature at which it is done. Long braising, typically used for stews and pot roasts, is when food is heated to a relatively high temperature—far higher than it would be if you were roasting or sautéing—and kept there long enough for proteins to break down, fats to melt, and other reactions to take place that leave the meat with the characteristic melting texture of a good stew. Brown braising, when foods are browned before they are simmered, and white braising, when they are simmered without browning, are two more techniques. Most braising variations are distinguished by the choice of liquid, aromatic ingredients, vegetables, and herbs; how the liquid is enriched and/or thickened; and how the finished dish is garnished. Despite these myriad options, the basic method itself varies little.

Long-Braised Stews

A stew is simply a braise in which meat has been cut into more or less bite-sized pieces. Older recipes recommend larding, which is the process of sliding strips of fatback, essentially bacon without any lean parts and that hasn't been smoked, into each cube of meat, which adds its own flavor and creates an impression of moistness, though nowadays this step is unusual. The meat is sometimes marinated, commonly with wine, herbs, and aromatic vegetables, and often it is browned before other ingredients—vegetables (often those used in the marinade) and liquid (wine, broth, or water)—are added. Usually a bouquet garni is slipped in at the beginning to add an herbaceous complexity. The stew is then brought to a gentle simmer, the froth is skimmed off with a ladle, the pot is covered, and its contents are left to cook at the slightest hint of a simmer until the meat is completely tender, usually in about four hours or so.

When a long-braised stew is presented in its most rudimentary form, the fat is simply skimmed off the top and the stew is served as it comes out of the pot, the aromatic vegetables left in. In more refined versions, the aromatic vegetables are picked out of the pot, the liquid is strained, degreased, and sometimes thickened (usually with a flour and butter paste called a beurre manié), and a garniture, such as the pearl onions, bacon, and mushrooms used for beef bourguignon, is prepared separately and combined with the meat just before serving. By changing the liquid, the aromatic vegetables, and the final garniture, a cook who has made one stew can make or invent another.

Pot Roasts

A pot roast is a relatively large cut of meat that is cooked like a stew. The meat should not be too lean, since it is fat, not liquid, that keeps meat moist. If the meat happens to be lean, like a shoulder of veal or a leg of lamb, you'll need to lard it well with strips of fatback (see page 193). The pot you use should match the size and shape of the meat as closely as possible to minimize the amount of liquid. The meat is usually browned, either in the oven or on the stove top, and then surrounded with aromatic vegetables and sometimes some meat trimmings or bones. You can add liquid right after browning, or you can first roast the meat until it releases all its juices and they caramelize on the bottom of the pan. Bring the liquid, which should usually come about halfway up the sides of the meat, to a simmer over medium heat on the stove top and then cover the pot. You need to invert the cover, or cover the pot with a sheet of aluminum foil, so that liquid condenses on the underside and drips down over the meat, effectively basting it from inside the pot.

You can then put the pot roast over low heat on the stove top or in a 300°F oven so that it cooks at the slightest simmer. Check it from time to time to make sure the liquid isn't boiling, which would dry out the meat and make the braising liquid cloudy and greasy. (Some cooks put a pot of water in the oven next to the braise, and then check it instead, to avoid uncovering the braising pot.) After a couple of hours, you can turn the meat over, so the top half is now submerged in the liquid, and continue braising until the meat is easily penetrated with a knife. Some older recipes even call for serving braised meats with a spoon. You can serve the meat as is, with the liquid perhaps reduced and degreased, or you can transfer the meat to a clean pot, pour the degreased liquid over the top, and put the uncovered pot in a 400°F oven. You then baste the pot roast until it is shiny and the braising liquid is syrupy and golden. The sliced or spooned meat is served with the braising liquid spooned over, or the braising liquid is finished with herbs, mushrooms, truffles, or various vegetables.

Short-Braised Stews

The best-known short-braised stew is beef stroganoff, in which cut-up pieces of tender meat are cooked just long enough to heat through and the braising liquid is finished with sour cream. Any tender cut of meat can be cooked this way, and the effect is dramatic when people expect the texture of stew and are instead greeted with the tenderness of a roast.

The inherent problem with this duplicity is that while the meat, provided it comes from a tender (and usually expensive) cut, will be properly cooked, the braising liquid will have had no time to develop flavor. For example, if you have decided to mimic a red wine stew but want your guests to find rare pieces of tenderloin instead of stewed chuck, you need to prepare the stewing liquid by making an authentic stew the night before and using the liquid, or you need to make a stock with beef bones and/or cheap cuts and red wine and then use that liquid.

What about Pressure Cookers?

For the same reason that foods cook more slowly at high altitude—because the lower atmospheric pressure allows water to boil at a lower temperature—a pressure cooker cooks foods under pressure at a much higher boiling point. In other words, foods can be braised at 300°F instead of 200°F, causing them to soften much faster. A pressure cooker is a good alternative to braising in a regular pot only if you're careful to keep it over low heat once it starts to release steam. This prevents rapid boiling, which can make stews greasy and dry.

Glazing Vegetables

Root and bulb vegetables, such as carrots and onions, are often braised in water or broth. The vegetables, sliced or shaped by rounding their edges, are placed in a straight-sided pan, ideally just big enough to hold them all in a single layer. Then water or broth is added to come halfway up their sides. They are then covered with a round of parchment paper, so the liquid will slowly evaporate while the vegetables are cooking, but partially covering the pan works just as well. The ideal is the complete evaporation of the liquid just as the vegetables have finished cooking. The liquid will have formed a glaze that covers the vegetables with their own natural sugars.

Sometimes a little butter and a pinch of sugar are added to the liquid to enhance the glaze. Onions are either brown glazed or white glazed, which is just as it sounds. When onions are white glazed, they are cooked just until they are coated with glaze. When they are brown glazed, they are cooked until the glaze is allowed to caramelize on the bottom of the pan. The pan is then deglazed with a little more water or broth and evaporated again so that a dark glaze covers the onions.

POACHING

Don't confuse poaching with boiling. Foods are rarely boiled—green vegetables are the exception—but meats and seafood are often poached in liquid that may approach a simmer but never boil. When we make broth, we poach meat, chicken, fish, or bones in water. If the water is allowed to boil, the churning action causes fat and proteins to emulsify into a cloudy, greasy mess. Gentle poaching, on the other hand, allows fats and proteins to accumulate on top of the broth, where we can skim them off with a ladle, or we can refrigerate the broth and wait for them to congeal and then lift them off, all at once, with a spoon.

Start with Cold Liquid or Hot?

When making broth, we always pour cold water over the meat and/or bones and bring it slowly to a simmer, so that the flavors of the ingredients are released into the liquid. If you start with hot water, the meat or seafood releases proteins in fine particles that cloud the broth, rather than form a froth that is easily skimmed off.

There are, however, exceptions to the cold-water rule. If you're poaching a large fish, say, a whole salmon, it's best to start with cold liquid and gradually heat it. If the liquid is hot from the beginning, the fish will overcook on the outside and still be raw on the inside. By slowly heating the poaching liquid with the fish in it, the heat has time to penetrate it. If you're poaching small fish, such as sardines or trout, it's best to start with simmering liquid. If you start with cold liquid and bring it to a simmer, the fish will be overcooked by the time the simmer is reached.

What Liquid to Use?

Depending on the dish, foods are usually poached in water, meat or fish broth, or a vegetable broth (called court bouillon). If you're poaching meats, it's best to poach them in broth, as it will leach out less of their flavor than water will. Seafood is usually poached in a fish broth or a court bouillon made with carrots, leeks or onions, a bouquet garni, and usually some white wine. When seafood is served surrounded with the court bouillon that was used to poach it and the vegetables used to make the court bouillon are left in, the dish is referred to as *à la nage,* which translates roughly to "in the swim." When a court bouillon is prepared for something cooked à la nage, the vegetables are often cut in a decorative way, such as in julienne, or at least are cut more carefully and evenly than they might be if they were being strained out and discarded. For more about cooking à la nage, see pages 160–162.

Poaching Meats

Sometimes the distinction between stewing and poaching is ambiguous. The French make a veal stew, or blanquette, by poaching strips of veal breast in broth or water. The poaching liquid is then thickened with a roux and finished with cream and egg yolks. But when the poaching liquid is kept to a minimum—just enough is used to cover the meat—the dish can also be considered a stew.

Three of the best-known poached dishes are Italian bollito misto, which often contains an assortment of meats from different animals; New England boiled dinner, which despite the name is poached, not boiled; and French pot-au-feu, made with assorted cuts of beef. All of these dishes are cooked for several hours to tenderize the tougher cuts of meat they utilize. When tender cuts, such as tenderloin or duck breast, are poached in broth (traditionally a pot-au-feu), the name of the dish sometimes ends with *à la ficelle,* which means "with string." The term refers to suspending the item being poached in the broth from a string tied to a spoon that spans the top of the pot, and it originates with a long-ago practice of French rural life in which villagers used a communal cauldron to cook their meats (tough, rather than tender, cuts), the string being the easiest way to retrieve their own meat without disturbing the supper of others. Poaching meats à la ficelle and serving them surrounded with broth and aromatic vegetables is a particularly lean and tender way to serve them.

SAUTÉING

Sauter means "to jump" and refers to tossing small items in a pan over high heat. The word has also come to mean the same as panfrying, in which foods are cooked in just enough fat to keep them from sticking to the pan. When you sauté a chop, steak, or chicken, for example, there's no tossing, just turning when one side is properly browned. Smaller items, such as mushrooms, sliced vegetables, or shrimp, can actually be sautéed in the original sense of the word by giving the pan handle a quick tug that causes the foods to hit the sloping sides of the pan and fly up above the rim—in other words, tossing them into the air—and then back onto the floor of the pan. For anyone afraid of making a mess, sautéed foods can be stirred, of course, but tossing is still the ideal method for delicate foods, such as certain mushrooms.

The primary purpose of sautéing is to create a brown crust on foods to accentuate their flavor and appearance. In the past, cooks believed this crust sealed in flavor, but that idea has been largely debunked. What does happen is this: Almost all foods release liquid as they cook. This liquid usually contains combinations of sugars and proteins but is mostly water. Ideally, when you're sautéing, the liquid evaporates the instant it is released, so that the sugars and proteins caramelize on the outside of the food when it comes in contact with the heat, forming a savory crust. If the heat is too low or the pan too crowded, the water won't evaporate fast enough and will create steam. The steam will cook whatever else is in the pan, causing it to release liquid. Simply put, you end up boiling instead of sautéing. When just creating a crust, it's called searing.

Anyone who has tried to sauté a pan full of mushrooms or tried to brown cubes of meat for a stew has probably encountered this phenomenon. To avoid it, get the fat in the pan almost smoking hot before adding the food. Then, when sautéing mushrooms, for example, add a handful, wait for them to sizzle and begin to brown, and then add more. When browning meat for a stew, sauté the cubes in relatively small batches, removing each batch before adding the next. Don't wipe the pan between additions, but add more fat when necessary. If you add too much to the pan at one time, the pan will cool down and the food won't brown.

Sometimes, especially when cooking meats and poultry, the pan is deglazed with liquid such as wine or broth, after sautéing. The liquid helps to dissolve the flavorful crust of caramelized juices stuck to the bottom of the pan, which are then used to form the base of a pan-deglazed sauce. To avoid burning the crust as you are sautéing, the pan should be just large enough to hold the sautéed foods in a single layer. If there's empty space, it overheats and the released juices from the food run onto it and burn.

STEAMING

The effect of steaming is similar to that of poaching, except that the liquid, usually plain water, is in the form of a gas. Many cooks prefer steaming to other techniques, especially for vegetables and seafood, because they feel it leaches out fewer nutrients than cooking in simmering liquid does. This is true, but only to a point. However they are cooked, foods release liquid. When they are steamed, this liquid drips down into the boiling liquid used to create the steam; when they are poached, it disperses into the surrounding liquid.

Some traditionalists argue that cooking green vegetables in a covered pan turns them a homely gray, and because steaming requires a covered vessel, it has this effect. For long cooking, this is true, but since most green vegetables cook quickly, in five minutes or so, they end up every bit as bright when steamed as they do when boiled uncovered in salted water.

When foods are braised or sautéed, the liquid they release is incorporated into a sauce, so no flavor is lost. But when foods are steamed, the liquid they release falls into the boiling water that is then discarded. You can avoid this by using a small amount of flavorful liquid, such as wine, court bouillon, or water scented with a small bouquet garni, for your steaming medium, watching carefully that it doesn't run dry and burn. The flavor of the liquid will concentrate as it boils, plus it will be enriched by the juices released from the steaming food. You can then use this tasty steaming liquid as the base for a sauce, broth, or soup. (See steamed mussels on page 108 for a good example of this technique.)

Selecting a Steamer

If you are shopping for a steamer, be sure to pick one that is large enough to hold a few pieces of fish and relatively large vegetables. Otherwise, they are all about the same: a pot for the liquid fitted with a perforated tray for the food—the steam travels upward through the holes—and a lid. Bamboo steamers also work well, and can be found at Asian markets. Even if you don't have a steamer, you can still steam. Just put a circular cake rack in the bottom of a large pan with a tight-fitting lid. Keep in mind, too, that some foods, such as mussels and clams, don't require a steamer for steaming. Their shells hold them above the liquid.

Cooking en Papillote

Cooking foods en papillote, in which food more or less simultaneously steams and braises inside a parchment-paper package, yields a particularly dramatic presentation when served. The food, usually fish, is sealed in parchment with wine and herbs and then baked. As it cooks, the food releases its own flavorful liquid, which is trapped in the bag. At the table, the diner cuts open the package and is greeted with a wonderful whiff of the aromatic steaming liquid scented with herbs or, sigh, truffles. (See tuna cooked en papillote on page 159 for a good example of this technique.)

FRYING

Despite its somewhat evil reputation as fattening and unhealthy, deep-frying seals in the flavor and nutrients of some foods better than any other method and introduces very little fat when done properly. Successful frying depends on the right kind of fat and the right temperature. Getting the food as quickly as possible from the hot fat into the diner's mouth is also important. Once fried foods cool off, much of the satisfying sizzling-hot effect is lost.

The most flavorful fat, long favored by connoisseurs and the traditional favorite for French fries, is beef suet made by rendering the white brittle fat that surrounds beef kidneys. Because it's highly saturated and contains cholesterol, it's rarely used today for cooking; vegetable oil is its most popular replacement. Any vegetable oil—canola, safflower, corn oil, peanut oil, or pure olive oil (versus extra virgin, which is expensive and loses its flavor when heated)—will work. But vegetable oil has little flavor or sometimes has an unpleasant fishy taste, so many cooks use pure olive oil for frying.

Determining the right frying temperature depends on what you're frying and how large it is. Larger pieces, such as chicken parts, need to be fried at lower temperatures so the heat has time to penetrate to the interior by the time the crust forms. Smaller items, such as sliced vegetables, are fried at higher temperatures, so a flavorful crust forms before they absorb too much oil. French fries must be fried in two stages: the first at a lower temperature to cook the potato through, the second at a higher temperature to form the crust.

Sometimes you'll encounter fried foods that are particularly rich because they are enrobed in a thick, absorbent batter. These same foods can be lightened up by using a simpler batter—a no-frills mixture of flour and water—or by just dredging them in flour and patting off the excess before frying.

Be careful when deep-frying, as hot oil in large amounts can easily cause serious burns if you don't exercise caution.

Electric skillets or deep fryers are convenient because they keep the oil temperature fairly constant without your having to fiddle with the controls. If you're frying on the stove top, use a heavy pot, never fill it more than half full of oil, and put it on a back burner so that no one bumps into it accidentally. When you're ready to fry, lower a piece or two of whatever you're frying into the hot oil to judge how much it is going to bubble up. If you add too much food at once, the oil can boil over. Have a large box of salt handy in case you need to douse the flames. Also, don't toss food into the oil with your hands, as the oil can splash up and burn you. Use a spider, which looks like a spider web with a handle, or a long-handled slotted spoon or strainer.

Stir-Frying

A stir-fry differs from a regular "fry" in that very little fat is used. Whereas fried foods are partially or completely immersed in fat, usually oil, stir-fried ingredients touch only enough oil to keep them from sticking to the pan, usually a wok. Stir-frying in fact is much more closely related to sautéing than it is to frying; the ingredients are kept in motion in the same way except that instead of being tossed, they are stirred, usually over very high heat.

GRILLING

Don't confuse grilling with barbecuing. Grilling simply means to cook over the heat source open to the air. Covering the grill will roast or bake the food but doesn't help it grill. The heat source can be a bed of charcoal or a row of gas jets or an indoor grill pan. The best grills allow you to adjust the distance of the grill rack from the fire. Thin foods, such as steaks or fish fillets, require intense heat to form a crust before the heat has a chance to penetrate and overcook the interior. The grill rack itself is ideally a heavy metal grid that is flat, not round like wire, which ensures attractive grill markets on steaks and chops. Gas grills have the advantage of requiring no fire building—a fire made with ordinary charcoal briquettes delivers no more flavor than a gas grill—and will still impart a grilled flavor.

Many cooks mistakenly think that a good grilled flavor comes from smoke and flame generated when fat from the grilling food drips down on the coals, causing flare-ups. But burnt fat gives grilled foods a sooty flavor and is best avoided. While many grills nowadays come with covers, authentic grilling is done uncovered in the open air. A cover does offer some advantages. If you're cooking something large—a leg of lamb, for example—grilling it for the entire time over hot coals can result in a burned exterior before the interior is ready. To solve this problem, you can build the fire on just one side of the grill bed, grill the meat directly over the fire just long enough to brown and flavor it, and then move the meat to the side with no fire, and cover the grill to finishing the cooking. However, during this final step, when you are using indirect heat, you are basically roasting or baking the meat, not grilling it.

A covered grill is also handy if you want your grilled food to have a smoky flavor. Again, build the fire to one side and use it to brown the food. Then sprinkle the coals with a handful of wood chips that have been soaked a couple of hours in water, or put a small sheet of aluminum foil over the coals and top it with a handful of sawdust. Put the food on the side of the rack away from the fire, cover the grill, and finish cooking the meat. The drill is essentially the same for gas grills, except that you don't soak the wood chips. Some gas grills come with a special smoker box to hold the chips. Otherwise, you will need to put the chips in a perforated foil packet and place the packet directly over the heat. The best woods for creating smoke are grapevine cuttings, fruit woods such as apple and cherry, hickory, and mesquite.

SMOKING

There are two ways to smoke—with hot smoke and with cold smoke. When hot smoking, the easier method of the two, the food smokes and cooks at the same time. Cold-smoked foods, such as smoked salmon, are cured but never actually cooked. The cold smoke adds flavor and acts as a preservative.

Hot smoking is relatively straightforward and can be done at home with a store-bought stove-top smoker or with a wok or sauté pan fitted with a round cake rack. Sawdust, wood chips from hardwoods or fruit woods or tea leaves (if wok smoking) provide the smoke. You can also smoke in a covered grill (see Grilling, opposite).

Cold smoking is more elaborate and requires more investment, but the results may be worth it when you compare the price of raw salmon with smoked salmon. You can make a cold smoker by investing in a hot smoker, which is essentially a metal box with an electric hot plate on the inside. On the top of the smoker is a small chimney. The trick is to take out the chimney and insert a length of stovepipe. Next, attach additional lengths of stovepipe that will direct the smoke sideways and then down into a cardboard box (the box the smoker comes in is the perfect size). Finally, hang the salmon in the cardboard box, seal the whole contraption up with duct tape, and start smoking.

BARBECUING

Barbecuing is basically a combination of grilling in a covered grill and smoking. Typically, a fire is built to one side of a grill, the meat is placed on the opposite side, and the grill is covered. Wood chips or sawdust are sometimes put on top of the coals to generate smoke (see Grilling, opposite), and usually the meat is brushed with a sauce to flavor it and keep it moist. Depending on the cut of meat, the meat is cooked—actually sort of roasted and smoked at the same time—either until it is just heated through (for tender cuts) or until it softens in the same way as meat that is braised. This softening of tougher cuts can take many hours, while the flavors of the meat, smoke, and sauce all mingle into a delicious melt-in-your-mouth finish.

BOILING

Blanching, the same as parboiling, is a preliminary cooking in hot water. Green vegetables are blanched by boiling in a large amount of salted water, whereas root vegetables are started out in cold water that's slowly brought to a gentle simmer and then maintained there until the vegetable cooks at least partially through. These terms often imply subsequent cooking using another method, such as sautéing, but often, especially when green vegetables are cooked and then creamed or served in a salad, the so-called blanching is their only cooking.

Protein-rich foods, such as meat and seafood, should never be boiled because it toughens them and clouds the surrounding liquid. Vegetables, however, are often blanched or boiled as a way of cooking them quickly to preserve their texture, flavor, and color (common candidates are green beans and asparagus). Root vegetables, such as turnips, celeriac, and potatoes, are sometimes blanched to cook them partially to fully through or to eliminate bitterness before they are fried, sautéed, or roasted. When blanching root vegetables, starting them out in cold water and bringing the water to a simmer helps the heat to penetrate the vegetable evenly, so it isn't more cooked on the outside than in the center. Pasta and some grains also need to be boiled.

These ten basic cooking methods are the underlying techniques that the following recipes are based upon. Once you have a good handle on the basic ten, the mystery of cooking gives way to the mechanics of cooking, achievable through the recipes in this book.

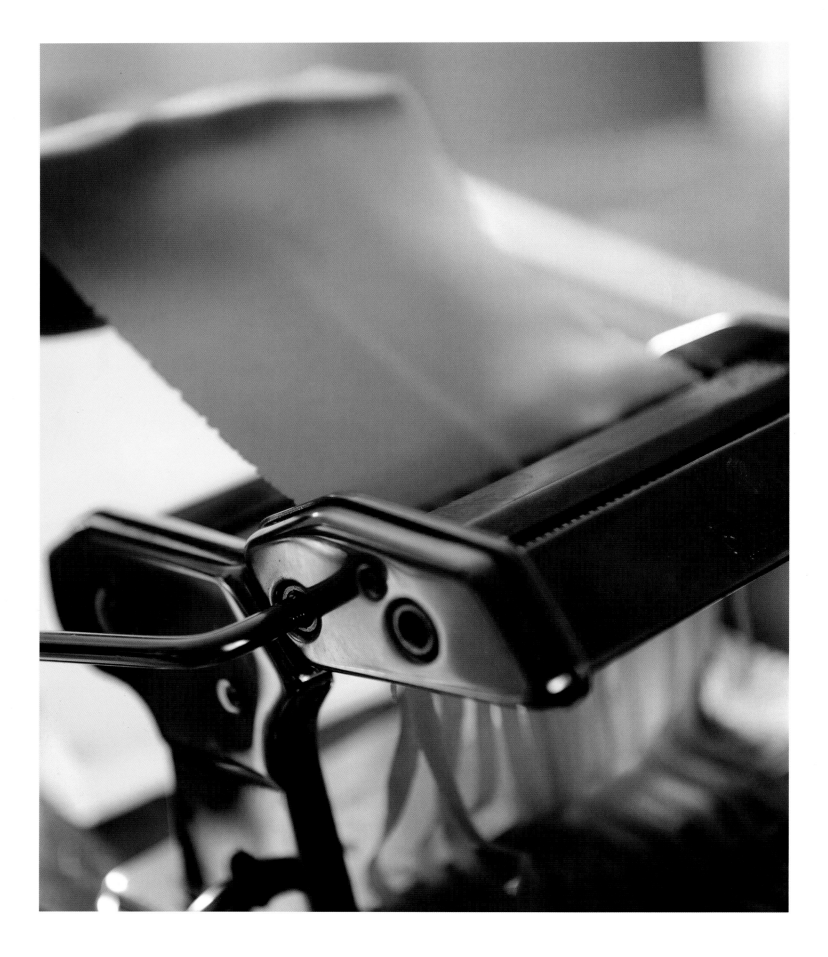

Recipes to Learn

STARTERS

Starters can be in the form of canapés or dips, miniature tartlets, or other savory pastries. They can also be as simple as a bowl of olives or nuts. Canapés and tartlets are the most versatile because the number of fillings for them is almost infinite. While some cooks get carried away and make platters of assorted starters, a single simple canapé is often just right. For additional simple starters, see the recipes for Guacamole (page 372), Tomato Salsa (page 371), and Breadsticks (page 415).

Cheese Straws

Once you've made or bought puff pastry, you can make these straws in just a few minutes. If you have pastry trimmings (see page 20), this is a perfect use for them. Keep the pastry dough cool so it stays manageable as you work with it, and shape the straws before you preheat the oven. Keep moving the pastry in and out of the freezer as needed to keep it firm.

MAKES 24 STRAWS

> 1 1/2 ounces hard aged cheese such as Parmigiano-Reggiano or aged Gouda
>
> 1 tablespoon paprika or Spanish pimentón
>
> Classic Puff Pastry (see page 476), Quick Puff Pastry (see page 478), or puff pastry trimmings
>
> Egg wash (opposite)

Grate the cheese; you should have about 1/2 cup when lightly pressed. Combine the cheese and paprika in a bowl.

On a lightly floured surface, roll out the puff pastry into a 12-by-16-inch rectangle. Brush the pastry with the egg wash, and sprinkle the cheese mixture evenly over the entire surface. Run the rolling pin over the surface to help the cheese stick to the pastry.

Fold the rectangle in half lengthwise, so it measures 8 by 12 inches, then roll it out again into a 12-by-16-inch rectangle. Place the rectangle of dough on a sheet pan lined with wax paper, and place in the freezer for 10 to 15 minutes, or until very firm but not hard and brittle.

Return the pastry rectangle to the work surface and, using a knife, trim the edges so they are even. Then, using the knife, cut the rectangle into strips 12 inches long and 1/2 inch wide. Working with 1 strip at a time, place a hand, palm down, on each end and roll in opposite directions until you see a distinct spiral pattern.

While it would seem that a 16-inch rectangle cut into 1/2-inch-wide strips would make 32 strips, it only makes 24 because of puff pastry's tendency to shrink. Place the straws on a sheet pan and freeze until solid.

Preheat the oven to 425°F. Bake the straws for about 12 minutes, or until pale brown. Serve within 24 hours.

Egg Wash

Most egg wash is made by beating whole egg with a healthy pinch of salt. The salt has the effect of loosening the egg and making it thinner so it's easier to apply. For a darker wash, use just the egg yolk; for a lighter egg wash add 1 teaspoon of cream or water to the whole egg.

Pastry Trimmings

Puff pastry trimmings can be used to make flaky pastries that don't require a dramatic rise. Save the rolled-flat scraps in the freezer, tightly wrapped in plastic—stack them on top of each other instead of just rolling them up into a ball—until you have enough to use for tarts, cheese sticks, or to cover ramekins for pot pies. Just thaw, roll out, and bake.

Cheese Puffs

These bite-size French cheese puffs, known as gougères, are perfect with a glass of wine or a cocktail. Most gougère recipes call for Gruyère cheese, but Gruyère contains a lot of moisture that can make the puffs heavy. You'll have more success with Parmigiano-Reggiano cheese, which is dry and flavorful and won't weigh down the pastry.

MAKES ABOUT 40 BITE-SIZED PUFFS

> **2 ounces hard aged cheese, preferably Parmigiano-Reggiano**
> **Cream Puff Pastry (see page 488)**
> **1 tablespoon paprika or Spanish pimentón (optional)**
> **Egg wash (see page 19)**

Preheat the oven to 500°F. Grate the cheese. You should have about 1 cup when lightly pressed. Reserve 1/4 cup of the cheese, and work the remaining 3/4 cup cheese into the pastry with a wooden spoon. Then work the paprika into the pastry.

Spoon the mixture into a pastry bag fitted with a 1/3 -inch plain tip. (See pages 438-441 for more about using pastry bags and decorating tips.)

If you have nonstick sheet pans, pipe the batter directly onto the pans. Or, line sheet pans with parchment paper, and anchor each corner of the paper with a tiny dollop of pastry. Pipe the pastry in dollops onto the prepared pan, spacing them about 1 inch apart. Each mound should be about 1 inch wide at the base and about 2/3 inch high. As you finish piping each mound, move the tip in a quick circular motion to disconnect it from the dollop, so no little thread of pastry is left in the middle.

Brush the mounds with the egg wash, smoothing the tops with the brush. Sprinkle with the reserved cheese. Slide the sheet pans into the oven and immediately lower the temperature to 400°F. Bake for about 15 minutes, or until puffed and golden brown. Turn the oven down to 300°F and bake for 10 minutes more. Don't open the oven at any point. Serve right away.

Puff Pastry Rectangles

Asparagus and other vegetables can be nicely presented by resting them on the bottom half of a puff pastry rectangle.

To make puff pastry rectangles, simply roll out the dough and cut to the dimensions you like. Brush with egg wash (see page 19) and bake in a 400° oven until fully puffed. Slice the rectangles horizontally in half, creating a top and bottom. Place blanched, cooled, and dried asparagus spears (see page 290) or other vegetables on the bottom half, cap with the top rectangle, and serve.

HOW TO MAKE CHEESE PUFFS

1. Stir the grated cheese into pastry.

2. Pipe into 1-inch mounds.

3. Bake until golden brown.

Canapés

While they may sound like a culinary cliché to some people, canapés are actually quick, versatile, and tasty ways to create a variety of hors d'oeuvres. With thin-sliced white or pumpernickel bread and a cookie cutter, you can make little open-faced sandwiches with almost anything that will stay attached to the bread. One tip: Use French butter for buttering the bread. It has a startlingly vibrant flavor—because it is made with crème fraîche—that will give your canapés a certain je ne sais quoi.

RADISH: One of the easiest and best toppings. Thinly slice radishes with a knife and arrange the slices on well-buttered bread rounds.

CUCUMBER: Peel, halve, and seed an English cucumber (also sold as hothouse cucumbers) and thinly slice each half into crescents. Place the crescents on well-buttered bread rounds.

SMOKED SALMON: Cut the salmon slices with the same cookie cutter you use to make the canapé bases. Butter the bases and top with the salmon. If you like, garnish with caviar.

PROSCIUTTO: Cut out thin slices of prosciutto and arrange on well-buttered bread rounds.

BRESAOLA: Use this air-cured beef in the same way as prosciutto.

CAVIAR

Some people consider caviar the ultimate hors d'oeuvre. Whether it is or not, you can be sure that if caviar is on your menu, you won't need to dress it up to impress your guests.

Just a handful of caviar tips will give you the assurance to serve it. First, American sturgeon caviar is much less expensive than Russian or Iranian and approaches the quality. Don't serve caviar with the classic accompaniments of egg and onion, and don't serve it with anything that is crunchy or has a distinctive texture. One of the great pleasures of eating caviar is feeling the eggs cave in under gentle pressure from your tongue. If there's something else crunchy on the plate, the effect is lost.

How Much to Buy?

Caviar is one of those foods that most of us never get enough of. But it's too expensive to allow your guests to eat it to their heart's content, so plan to buy $1/2$ ounce per guest. If you're serving it as an appetizer, put a heaping tablespoon (about $1/2$ ounce) on top of a small blini, or serve each $1/2$-ounce portion in an Asian porcelain soupspoon. It's possible to serve caviar as a main course if all reason has left you and your credit card has a high limit. Short of eating it with a spoon straight out of the can (the very best method), caviar is best with blini, which are soft buckwheat pancakes (see page 396). You can cook the blini on a hot plate next to the table or a hibachi (if you're outside), so they're piping hot as you hand them to your guests. If you offer smoked salmon at the same time, which will nicely round out the menu and help you from going broke, a 14-ounce can of caviar (what is called a pound despite being short 2 ounces) will be enough for blinis for four. The only garnish should be crème fraîche. Pour French champagne. Vodka gets everyone drunk too fast and anything else bubbly isn't complex enough.

Tartlets

The more tartlet molds you have, the more efficient you'll be when you bake these miniature pastry shells. Ideally, you need 40 molds for this recipe. Once you have the shells (they can be baked ahead and frozen for up to 3 months), you can fill them with all kinds of easy fillings (see below) for quick hors d'oeuvres.

MAKES TWENTY 2-INCH TARTLET SHELLS

> **Basic Pie and Tart Dough (page 445)**
> **2 ripe tomatoes, peeled and seeded (page 85)**
> **1 teaspoon wine vinegar**
> **Pinch of sugar**
> **Pinch of salt**
> **Pinch of pepper**
> **Splash of cream**
> **2 teaspoons minced tarragon or basil**

Preheat the oven to 400°F.

Roll out the dough as directed on page 448 into a thin rectangle measuring about 11 by 9 inches. Arrange fifteen 2-inch tartlet molds next to each other on a sheet pan, spacing the molds comfortably apart. Roll up the dough around the rolling pin and then unroll the dough evenly over the molds. Place a tartlet mold on top of the pastry draped over each mold on the sheet pan and press the top mold down to seat the pastry in the mold underneath. Trim around each set of tartlet molds with a knife. Gather together the trimmings, roll them out, and line 5 more tartlet molds in the same way.

Bake the tartlet crusts for 10 minutes, then remove the top molds. Bake for 15 minutes more, or until golden brown. Let cool completely on a rack before filling.

To make the filling, chop the tomatoes and cook them down with the cream and tarragon or basil over medium heat, stirring almost constantly, until thick. Flavor the mixture with the wine vinegar, sugar, salt, and pepper. Serve hot or at room temperature.

ALTERNATE TARTLET FILLINGS

MUSHROOMS: Finely chop 10 ounces cremini mushrooms, combine them with 1/2 cup heavy cream, and cook down over medium heat, stirring until thick. Season with salt and pepper. Use immediately, or reheat before filling tartlet shells.

OLIVES AND CAPERS: Pit a pint of green or black olives, combine with 3 tablespoons capers, and chop. Spoon into tartlets and sprinkle over chopped parsley. Use at room temperature.

ROE AND CAVIAR: Use 2 to 3 teaspoons of salmon roe or caviar per tartlet.

MUSSELS: Steam open 20 mussels, as directed on page 108, using just water for the steaming liquid. (Save the liquid they release for adding to a soup, sauce, or braising liquid.) Remove the steamed mussels from their shells. Fill the tartlet shells with the mushroom filling (above), top each one with a mussel, and then with a paper-thin square of raw bacon. Bake in a 400°F oven for about 10 minutes, or until the bacon is crisp.

CHEESE: Grate hard aged cheese, such as Parmigiano-Reggiano, or semi-hard cheese, such as aged Gouda, and mound it in the tartlet shells. Dribble over enough heavy cream to moisten, then bake in a 350°F oven for about 10 minutes, or until sizzling.

HOW TO MAKE TARTLET CRUSTS

1. Lay the rolled-out dough over the tartlet molds.

2. Set a second set of tartlet molds over the dough and press down to seat dough in bottom molds.

3. Cut between the molds to separate the tart shells.

4. Trim away the excess dough.

TARTLET FILLINGS

Tartlets filled with salmon roe.

Tartlets filled with caviar.

Tartlets filled with olives and capers.

Tartlets filled with tomatoes.

PÂTÉS AND TERRINES

Traditionally, a pâté has a crust, while a terrine is made by cooking forcemeat or a whole foie gras liver in a porcelain or metal terrine (the name doubles for both the dish and what is cooked in it). What used to be called a pâté (today pâté and terrine are used interchangeably) is now called, rather redundantly, pâté en croute. A pâté en croute is usually baked in an ovoid metal terrine that folds open and is often stamped with some decoration. Unfortunately, the dough used for making a pâté en croute is rarely worth eating and only absorbs flavorful juices released by the filling. For this reason, terrines are usually considered more flavorful than traditional pâtés.

Making your own terrine is a relatively simple matter of pressing raw whole duck foie gras livers into a terrine, baking it gently in a bain-marie (hot-water bath), and letting it cool. Ideally the baking dish is porcelain and rectangular, so the slices will be uniform. If you have a cooperative butcher, ask him to thinly slice fatback (not salt pork) or caul fat on his meat slicer to use for lining the baking dish. Caul fat consists of transparent fat held in a net-shaped substrate. It's useful for holding foods—especially forcemeats—in a shape while they're cooked in the oven or on the stove. The fat in caul fat renders as it cooks and leaves a flavorful delicate crust over the meat it encases. It's easier to use than sheets of fatback for making pâté. If you have a fancy delicatessen that sells Italian lardo (salt-and-herb-cured pork fat), you may use that to line the terrine instead. Short of that, skip the lining altogether or line the terrine with blanched leek leaves or prosciutto. If you don't have a terrine, an ovenproof porcelain bowl will work, though you'll have to serve the terrine in wedges rather than slices.

Nowadays, we can pick up pâté at many corner groceries, but the quality of any mass-produced pâté will never match that of homemade. One reason is because all the meats in a mass-produced pâté are chopped together to the same consistency. The result is a homogeneous flavor and texture that lacks the character found in a pâté in which ingredients have been chopped—or better, diced by hand—separately. The secret to making a good pâté is to use a variety of ingredients that contribute specific qualities, including pureed chicken livers for flavor and for binding; ground pork for body; diced prosciutto for color, flavor, and texture; pistachios for color and texture; and cubes of fatback for moistness and to form a checkerboard pattern on each slice that is absent in store-bought versions.

FOIE GRAS

Foie gras can turn up as a canapé at a cocktail party, as a stand-alone course at a dinner party, or as a component in a meat (or occasionally even fish) dish. It can be served hot or cold.

When buying foie gras, keep in mind that it is sold in a few different forms. First, there is the choice between duck and goose foie gras. Nowadays, most foie gras comes from ducks, but you can find French goose foie gras, which, though similar, is a bit more subtle. But more important than distinguishing the source is understanding the difference between raw whole foie gras and cooked foie gras terrine. Terrine is typically twice the price by weight. This is because the whole raw livers contain a large amount of water and some fat that are released during cooking. The terrine also has a more intense flavor and a richer texture. Foie gras is also sold fully cooked, in cans, or lightly cooked (mi-cuit), in jars. Check the label to see if it says *entier*, which means "whole liver" and is the best, or *bloc*, which is large chunks of the liver and is also very good, rather than *mousse*, which is made with trimmings and doesn't have the same superior texture. Mousse, which should be half the price of entier, offers good value for topping canapés or using in sauces. You can cut the cost even further by working mousse together with butter for canapés.

Foie Gras Terrine

This luxurious terrine can be made with one very large foie gras or two small foie gras and can be lined with fatback, lardo, or, as shown here, prosciutto.

MAKES ONE 10-BY-3-INCH TERRINE (ABOUT 12 SLICES)

> 5 ounces prosciutto, fatback, or lardo, sliced very thinly, or caul fat
>
> 2$\frac{1}{2}$ pounds fresh whole foie gras
>
> Salt
>
> Pepper

Line the terrine with the slices of prosciutto. Leave the excess hanging over the sides for covering the top.

Separate the two lobes that compose the foie gras liver. Pull out and discard any obvious veins from both lobes. It may seem like you are damaging the foie gras, but don't worry about appearance. Season generously with salt and pepper.

Press the foie gras firmly into the terrine, pressing it into the corners and sides.

Fold the excess prosciutto, hanging over the sides, over the top of the terrine. Hammer on the terrine with your fist to compact it. The foie gras should come up above the top rim of the terrine.

Place a rectangle of parchment paper on top of the terrine and then seal the terrine with a triple-thick layer of aluminum foil. Put a pan on top of the terrine to act as a weight.

Preheat the oven to 300°F. Put the terrine in a roasting pan with hot water coming halfway up the sides of the terrine, and bring to a simmer on top of the stove. Bake in the oven for approximately 1 hour or until the temperature in the center registers 140°F. Let cool at room temperature (leave the weight on) for 1 hour and then refrigerate overnight.

When the terrine is ready, peel away the foil and parchment and run a knife around the sides of the terrine. Slice the terrine.

HOW TO MAKE FOIE GRAS TERRINE

1. Line the terrine with prosciutto.

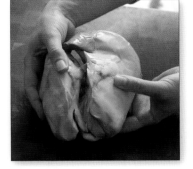
2. Separate the lobes.

3. Remove the veins.

4. Press the foie gras into the terrine.

5. Press the second lobe into the terrine.

6. Fold the prosciutto over the terrine. Pack down the terrine.

7. Weight down the terrine. Bake the terrine in a water bath.

8. When cool, peel away the foil and parchment. Run a knife around the edges of the terrine.

9. Slice the terrine.

1. Roll the foie gras into a parchment cylinder.

2. Roll the foie gras in a kitchen towel and tie securely.

3. Poach the torchon.

4. Hang the sausage. Here, it is hung from a roasting rack.

5. Cut away the string.

6. Peel away the towel.

Foie Gras au Torchon

A torchon *is French for a rag or kitchen towel, which is exactly what you need for poaching this foie gras. The raw livers are deveined, pressed into shape by being rolled in parchment paper, and then rolled up like a sausage in a kitchen towel. They are then poached for only 4 minutes, the towel tightened and the "sausage" hung overnight in the refrigerator.*

MAKES ONE 10-INCH "SAUSAGE" (ABOUT 12 SLICES)

> **2¹/₂ pounds fresh whole foie gras, composed of either one large or two small livers**
>
> **Salt**
>
> **Pepper**

Separate the lobes and devein the foie gras as shown on page 25. Season generously with salt and pepper.

Roll the pieces of foie gras together in a dampened sheet of parchment paper. Press firmly while rolling to help shape the foie gras and force it into the sausage shape.

Put the foie gras in a kitchen towel and roll it up. Twist together the two ends in opposing directions and tie each end closed with a piece of string. Tie about 10 loops of string along the length of the sausage to press it evenly into place.

Poach in simmering water for exactly 4 minutes. Twist the ends, which should now be loosened because the foie gras will have rendered fat and shrunk. Tie the ends again with string and make another series of loops along the length of the sausage to force it into its new position. As you tighten one loop, you'll notice the sausage swelling in another place. Tie a loop around the swelling and it will swell in another place. Continue in this way until the sausage is firm, after about 10 loops. Hang the sausage in the refrigerator overnight.

The next day, cut away the string and unpeel the towel. Serve in slices.

Foie Gras with Sautéed Apples

This recipe requires that you first make the foie gras au torchon, opposite. The short precooking required by cooking the foie gras in a towel causes it to render fat so it stays firmer in the pan when sautéed. The foie gras fat called for is the yellow fat that forms on the top of a terrine or that floats to the top when the foie gras is poached.

MAKES 4 FIRST-COURSE SERVINGS

> 2 tart apples
>
> 2 tablespoons butter for sautéing the apples
>
> 2 tablespoons foie gras fat (see above) or butter
>
> 4 slices foie gras au torchon, sliced ³/₄ inch thick

Peel and core the apples and cut them into 12 wedges each. Gently sauté the wedges over medium heat in butter until golden brown on both sides, turning as needed with a spatula.

Heat the foie gras fat or butter in a sauté pan over medium heat and cook the foie gras slices for about 2 minutes on each side or until golden brown. Arrange the apple slices around the foie gras slices on heated plates.

HOW TO MAKE FOIE GRAS WITH SAUTÉED APPLES

Sauté the apples.

Cook the foie gras slices until golden brown on each side. Serve with apples alongside.

Country Terrine

This "country" terrine is a bit more sophisticated than the usual versions because it contains ingredients cut by hand that are then layered into the forcemeat, the finely puréed meat. This creates a checkerboard effect and a complex flavor that makes this terrine beautiful to look at and delicious to eat. The version shown here contains lardo in the finely ground forcemeat and to line the terrine. You can also use fatback if you can find it and get it sliced thinly enough to line the terrine. If you use fatback instead of lardo, use more salt to compensate for the fact that fatback is unsalted.

MAKES ONE 12-BY-4-INCH TERRINE (ABOUT 15 SLICES)

> ²/₃ cup shelled pistachios
>
> Scant 8 ounces lardo, sliced very thinly
>
> 5 ounces rough cubes lardo or fatback for forcemeat
>
> 5 ounces chicken livers
>
> 4 slices white bread
>
> ²/₃ cup milk
>
> 2 whole eggs
>
> 2 pounds pork shoulder chops or 1¹/₂ pounds cubed pork shoulder meat
>
> 4 ounces lardo or fatback, sliced ¹/₈ to ¹/₄ inch thick
>
> 4 ounces prosciutto, sliced ¹/₈ to ¹/₄ inch thick
>
> 1 clove garlic, minced, crushed to a paste
>
> 1 teaspoon fresh thyme or ¹/₂ teaspoon dried thyme, chopped fine
>
> 1 teaspoon white pepper
>
> ¹/₈ teaspoon ground cloves
>
> ¹/₄ teaspoon ground ginger
>
> ¹/₈ teaspoon ground nutmeg
>
> ¹/₂ teaspoon fine salt
>
> 1 tablespoon olive oil

Plunge the pistachios in a quart of boiling water and simmer for 1 minute. Drain in a strainer and rinse with cold water. Rub the pistachios vigorously together in a towel to loosen the skins. Peel them by pinching between thumb and finger.

Line the terrine with the thin slices of lardo or fatback, leaving a couple of inches of excess hanging over the side.

Combine the cubes of lardo with the chicken livers and puree in a food processor for 1 minute until smooth.

Cut the crusts off the bread and work the bread with the milk to paste. Combine this with the eggs and chicken liver mixture until smooth.

Chop the pork shoulder meat in the food processor until

(continued)

1. Pinch the blanched pistachios to remove the skins.

2. Line the terrine with lardo.

3. Combine the lardo and livers.

4. Process until smooth.

7. Pork shoulder meat.

8. Process pork shoulder. Add to liver mixture to make forcemeat. Add seasonings. Fry small patty to taste seasonings. Adjust seasonings.

9. Slice the prosciutto into strips.

10. Slice the lardo into strips.

13. Arrange one-fourth of the prosciutto and lardo strips lengthwise in the terrine.

14. Layer another one-fifth of the forcemeat, one-fourth fat strips, and sprinkle in one-third of the pistachios.

15. Continue layering until all the fillings are used, finishing with a layer of forcemeat.

16. Fold the strips of lardo lining over the top of the terrine.

19. Bake the terrine in a water bath.

20. Run a knife around the edges of the cool terrine to loosen.

21. Unmold the terrine by placing a platter atop the mold and inverting the terrine onto the platter.

5. Cut the crusts off the bread.

6. Combine bread mashed with milk, eggs, and liver mixture.

11. Or instead of lardo, slice fatback into strips.

12. Spread one-fifth of the forcemeat in the terrine.

17. Cover the top of the terrine with parchment paper.

18. Seal the parchment with a triple layer of foil.

Country Terrine, continued

the consistency of coarse hamburger. Combine this mixture with the chicken liver mixture.

Slice the lardo or fatback and the prosciutto into $1/8$-inch- to $1/4$-inch-thick strips.

Stir the garlic, thyme, pepper, spices, and salt into the forcemeat mixture. Make a tiny hamburger and cook it in the olive oil in a sauté pan. Taste it to judge the seasoning and adjust accordingly, keeping in mind that the garnitures—the strips of prosciutto and lardo—are salty.

Spread one-fifth of the forcemeat mixture into the bottom of the lined terrine. Arrange one-fourth of the prosciutto and lardo in strips along the length of the terrine. Spread over another one-fifth of the forcemeat mixture and another one-fourth of the prosciutto and lardo and one-third of the nuts. Continue layering in this way, using the nuts for three of the layers, until you've filled the terrine. Finish with a layer of forcemeat.

Fold the overlapping strips of lardo over the top of the terrine and press in place.

Preheat the oven to 350°F. Place a rectangle of parchment paper on top of the terrine.

Fold a triple layer of aluminum foil into a rectangle 1 inch longer and wider than the terrine, and press this onto the terrine and fold it over the edges of the terrine.

Put the terrine in a roasting pan with hot tap water, and place the pan on the stove over high heat until the water comes to a simmer. Slide the roasting pan with the terrine into the oven. Bake for about 1 hour or until a thermometer inserted into the middle measures 150°F.

Take out of the roasting pan and let cool at room temperature for 1 hour and then in the refrigerator overnight. Remove the foil and parchment paper and slide a knife around the sides of the pâté. Serve the terrine by cutting slices from out of the mold or by unmolding the whole terrine and then slicing it.

Chicken Liver Mousse

Unlike most pâtés and terrines in which raw ingredients are cooked together in a mold, chicken liver mousse is made with cooked livers, shallots, and thyme pureed with butter, worked through a sieve, and then folded together with whipped cream. The delicate consistency and flavor puts chopped liver to shame, though any taboos about combining meat and dairy are obviously broken. Serve the mousse with little toasts.

MAKES 4 CUPS MOUSSE OR 20 HORS D'OEUVRE SERVINGS

3/4 pound chicken livers

Salt and pepper

2 tablespoons olive oil

2 shallots, minced

1 small clove garlic, minced

1/2 teaspoon chopped fresh thyme leaves
   or 1/4 teaspoon dried thyme

1/4 cup port or Madeira

2 tablespoons cognac (optional)

1/2 pound butter, cut into 1-inch pieces

1 cup heavy cream

Pat the livers dry and season with salt and pepper. Heat the olive oil in a large skillet over high heat until the oil is smoking hot. Add the livers and sauté, turning as needed, for about 10 minutes, or until browned on both sides and firm to the touch. Transfer the livers to paper towels to drain. Discard the oil in the pan.

With the pan still over high heat, add the shallots, garlic, and thyme and stir around for 30 seconds to toast and release their aroma. Add the port, boil it down until reduced by half, and then remove from the heat and add the cognac.

Add the livers, the contents of the pan, and the butter to a food processor and process until smooth. Using the back of a spoon or a plastic pastry scraper, work the mixture through a drum sieve (fine-mesh drum-shaped sieve, also known as a *tamis*) or regular fine-mesh sieve.

Whip the cream until medium-firm peaks form (peaks hold their shape but are not rigid when you stop and lift the whip out of the cream). Using a rubber spatula, fold the cream into the liver mixture just until combined. Season with salt and pepper. Cover with plastic wrap and refrigerate for 4 hours before serving.

Duck Rillettes

This spreadable yet chunky paste suffers from a public-relations problem because it calls for a lot of duck fat. While it is true that you can add much less fat than the amount used in traditional recipes, you still need some fat to achieve the desired moistness and a melting texture. The easiest way to make the rillettes is to shred the meat from duck confit, stir together the shredded meat and some fat, and season the mixture with spices. Serve chilled with little toasts and cornichons (small sour pickles).

MAKES 10 HORS D'OEUVRE SERVINGS
OR 4 FIRST-COURSE SERVINGS

4 confit Pekin duck thighs or 2 confit mullard duck thighs
   (see page 274)

1/3 cup rendered duck fat, cooled to room temperature

11/2 teaspoons quatre-épices (see right)

1 teaspoon salt, or to taste

Pull off and discard the skin from the duck thighs, then pull the meat from the bones and discard the bones. Shred the meat with your fingers or by piercing the pieces with 2 forks and pulling the forks in opposite directions. Place the meat in a bowl, pour in the fat, and add the quatre-épices and salt. Stir until combined. Cover with plastic wrap and chill well before serving. Serve in a small shallow serving bowl or 4-ounce ramekins for individual servings.

Slow-roasted duck thighs.

HOW TO MAKE DUCK RILLETTES

1. Peel the fat and skin off the duck thighs and discard.

2. Pull the meat into shreds.

3. Pour the fat over the meat.

4. Add the seasonings and stir until combined.

Quatre-Épices

Quatre-épices is the French term for a spice blend made from four spices, which can vary. Here's mine:

2½ teaspoons ground white pepper
¼ teaspoon ground cloves
¾ teaspoon powdered ginger
¾ teaspoon ground nutmeg

Chicken Skewers

These are very similar to the chicken "yakitori" that are so popular in Japanese restaurants.

MAKES 6 SKEWERS (6 FIRST COURSE SERVINGS)

½ cup Japanese soy sauce
1 tablespoon grated fresh ginger
1 large clove garlic, peeled, minced, crushed to a paste
1 teaspoon sesame oil
¼ cup sake or white wine (optional)
2 tablespoons sugar
6 tablespoons mirin
3 single boneless chicken breasts, trimmed, cut into ¾-inch dice

Boil all the ingredients, except the chicken, until reduced to ⅓ cup and lightly syrupy. Let cool. Marinate the chicken in the syrupy mixture for 4 hours.

Grill the chicken skewers for about 3 minutes over high heat while basting with the boiled-down marinade. Serve immediately.

Bruschette

Plural for "bruschetta," bruschette are essentially canapés with fresh, often raw, ingredients on top of toasted baguette slices. The most common toppings are an Italian-style tomato salsa and, in Tuscany, a chicken liver puree. The idea is transferable to just about anything you might otherwise serve as a dip for chips. If you're experimenting with bruschette for the first time, make a coarse-chopped tomato concassee (see page 367) and flavor it with shredded basil and chopped garlic and a little olive oil. As you get used to the idea, experiment with Mexican flavors, such as chiles and cilantro, and as you get bolder yet, try the essentially Thai bruschetta given here. To make these bruschette a little more substantial, consider topping them with grilled shrimp.

MAKES 24 BRUSCHETTE

1 long English cucumber, peeled

1 teaspoon sugar

2 dried chipotle chiles, soaked in hot water for 30 minutes to soften, seeded and chopped

2 tomatoes, peeled and seeded (see page 85), chopped, and drained for 30 minutes in a strainer

1 tablespoon Thai fish sauce

1 tablespoon rice wine vinegar or wine vinegar

2 tablespoons chopped cilantro

24 1/4-inch-thick baguette slices, toasted

24 cilantro leaves

Cut the cucumber in half lengthwise and scoop out the seeds. Slice and then chop in a food processor into 1/8- to 1/4-inch pieces. Combine with the sugar, chiles, tomatoes, fish sauce, vinegar, and cilantro. Just before serving, spoon the "salsa" on top of the baguettes, and garnish with the cilantro leaves.

Fried Squid

Because they have to be fried at the last minute, frying squid for a crowd can leave you isolated in the kitchen while your guests mix their own drinks. One good approach is to get the guests involved. Everyone likes to feel like they're helping, and getting someone to dredge and another to fry will keep everyone amused.

MAKES HORS D'OEUVRES FOR 8, OR 4 FIRST-COURSE SERVINGS

> **3 pounds squid or 2 pounds cleaned squid**
> **Vegetable oil or olive oil for deep-frying**
> **1 cup flour**
> **Salt**
> **Tartar Sauce (see page 361)**

Cut the squid into rings about 1/3 inch wide. If the clusters of tentacles are large, cut them in half through the top. Pat the squid with towels to make sure they are perfectly dry.

Pour vegetable oil to a depth of 4 inches into a heavy saucepan, skillet, or sauté pan, and heat over high heat until ripples are visible on the surface, about 360°F on a deep-frying thermometer. (The oil should not come more than halfway up the sides of the pan.) The oil is ready if when you drop in a cluster of tentacles it immediately rises to the surface and is surrounded with bubbles. While the oil is heating, spread the flour on a plate, dust the squid with the flour, and pat off the excess.

Lower one-fourth of the squid into the oil with a spider or with tongs—be careful not to let the oil splash on your hand—and fry for about 2 minutes, or until golden. Using the spider or a slotted spoon, transfer the squid to paper towels to drain. Salt immediately. Repeat in 3 more batches. Serve immediately with the sauce.

Crab Cakes

The ideal crab cake is made of big chunks of lump crabmeat held together with minimal bread crumbs and egg. While good-quality lump crabmeat, especially jumbo grade (see page 132 for more about crabmeat grades), has very little shell and cartilage, you should pick through it to be sure. To spot the cartilage, spread the meat on a sheet pan and slide it under the broiler for just a few seconds. The cartilage will turn red.

MAKES 8 CAKES (4 MAIN-COURSE SERVINGS OR 8 FIRST-COURSE SERVINGS)

> **1 pound lump crabmeat**
> **6 tablespoons fresh bread crumbs**
> **2 eggs**
> **2 teaspoons salt**
> **Pinch of pepper**
> **3 tablespoons finely chopped fresh parsley**
> **1/2 cup flour**
> **3 tablespoons butter**
> **Tartar Sauce (see page 361)**

Pick through the crabmeat and discard any bits of shell or cartilage. Work the bread crumbs through a fine-mesh strainer to make them very fine.

In a bowl, whisk together the eggs, salt, pepper, and parsley until blended. Add the crabmeat and bread crumbs. Gently work the mixture until you can form it into patties.

Form the mixture into 8 patties each about 1/2 inch thick. Spread the flour on a plate, dust the patties with the flour, and pat off the excess.

In a sauté pan, melt the butter over medium heat. Add the patties and cook for about 3 minutes on each side, or until firm to the touch and golden brown. Serve with the sauce.

BROTHS AND SOUPS

The word *stock* is used to describe a broth that is kept on hand as "stock" for making soups and sauces. All stocks are simply broths, but a broth is not necessarily a stock. Broth, which can be made from poultry, meat, fish, or vegetables, is soup at its most basic. There are white broths and brown broths. The latter are brown because whatever was used to make them was first browned in the oven or on the stove top. Brown broth is more savory than white and is easier to keep clear. White broth is most useful for making cream soups, when the color of the soup must be as pale as possible. Brown broth is better for reducing and making into sauces.

Some meats, especially young meats like veal, which contain large amounts of albumin, must be blanched before they can be used for making broth, or they will turn the liquid irreversibly gray. Meat, poultry, and fish broths almost always include carrots, onion, and celery, but may also include fennel, turnips, celeriac instead of branch celery, and other vegetables. Nearly every broth includes a bouquet garni (page 335), which is simmered along with everything else.

There is nothing mysterious about making a good broth, but there are a couple of tricks. Most important to remember is that the broth must never be allowed to come to a hard boil. Meats and seafood release proteins and sometimes fat as they cook. When the surrounding liquid, usually water, is kept at a gentle simmer, the proteins tangle up with one another and form froth that is easy to skim off the surface. If the liquid is boiling, these proteins and any fat released are churned into the broth, cloud it, and give it a greasy flavor. One frequent mistake made by beginning cooks is the addition of too much water. You need only add enough water to cover the ingredients. It is okay if the broth comes out too concentrated, as you

can always thin it. But if it comes out too thin because you used too much water, you will have to boil it down—a waste of time and energy.

MAKING DOUBLE AND TRIPLE BROTH

Unless we are feeling ill, we usually don't drink plain broth. Instead, we use it as a base for other soups or make it more substantial by adding vegetables, pasta, beans, rice, pieces of chicken or meat, and/or herbs.

You can also make a kind of superbroth by making broth using broth. For example, if when making chicken broth you simmer the chicken parts in chicken broth, you will create what is known as a double broth. You can even use this broth to simmer more chicken, thereby creating what is known as triple broth. The only time you will want to go to these lengths is if you are making concentrated broth for a sauce base (which can also be done by boiling down single-strength broth), or if you are making consommé, which is a double or triple broth that has been clarified, although any broth made carefully and strained properly won't need clarification.

What about Canned Broth?

Because many vegetable soups get their savor from meat or chicken broth, some cooks give up when confronted with the need to make two soups: first, the broth, and, second, the soup. This brings us to the question of whether canned broth is acceptable. Canned broth is fine for making soup because you don't boil it down, as you do when making a sauce. That means whatever salt it contains isn't concentrated, resulting in a too-salty finish. Chicken broth from a corner Chinese restaurant is another convenient broth source, as are some of the concentrated meat glazes (see box on page 177), which can be diluted with water until broth strength.

Some types of broth, such as beef broth, can be expensive. Restaurant cooks often get around this problem by using bones instead of meat, but bones never have the flavor of meat, so the results are rarely impressive. Another approach is to use meat and figure out a way to serve it so that it doesn't go to waste. You can make chicken broth, for example, by poaching a whole chicken in water with aromatic vegetables and then serving the chicken as soon as it is cooked through. The broth won't be very concentrated because you didn't cook all the savor out of the chicken, but you can repeat the process later in the week with another chicken ad infinitum and end up with what Chinese cooks call a master sauce base. As long as the broth comes to a boil every five days, it can be used indefinitely without freezing.

Vegetable Broth (Court Bouillon)

When making vegetable broth, cut the vegetables uniformly so they look attractive, or cut them into julienne. The bright tangle of vegetables on top of the seafood makes an attractive garnish. The time-consuming part of this dish—the julienned vegetables and the broth—can be done ahead of time. If you don't want to bother with the julienne, just slice the vegetables.

MAKES 4 MAIN-COURSE OR 6 FIRST-COURSE SERVINGS

> 1 large carrot
>
> 1 turnip
>
> 3 leeks
>
> Stalks from 1 fennel bulb (optional)
>
> 1/2 cup dry white wine
>
> 3 quarts cold water or more as needed to cover
>
> Bouquet garni
>
> 20 fresh tarragon leaves, chopped at the last minute (optional)
>
> Salt
>
> Pepper

Cut the carrot and turnip into fine julienne (page 298). Cut the greens off the leeks, rinse them, and use kitchen string to tie them together with the fennel stalks. Cut the whites of the leeks in half lengthwise, rinse out any grit, and cut into julienne. Peel apart the fennel blub and julienne each section. Simmer the vegetables and bouquet garni in the wine and water to cover for 25 minutes or until the vegetables are soft. Whisk in the tarragon and season to taste with salt and pepper. The broth keeps for up to 5 days in the refrigerator.

Straining

Broths and pureed soups are strained to eliminate lumps and to prevent cloudiness in broth. When straining broth, use the finest strainer you have, preferably a classic "chinois," a coned-shaped strainer with a very fine mesh. When straining puree soups, strain according to the consistency you like. If you like your soup thick, strain it through a regular household kitchen strainer; if you want it thin, strain it through a fine-mesh strainer or even a chinois. When straining broth, don't work it through the strainer with an implement such as a spoon or you'll cloud the broth. To help the broth through the strainer, tap on the edge of the strainer with a wooden spoon while straining. When straining purees or other opaque liquids, work the liquid through the strainer by moving a small ladle up and down in the strainer.

Brown Chicken Broth

This broth is best made with drumsticks or wings because they are the chicken parts with the most flavor and natural gelatin. But you can also cut up whole chickens, which are often less expensive than chicken parts, and use either all the parts or everything except the breasts, saving them for another use. As a general rule, a 3-pound whole chicken or 3 pounds of chicken parts will yield a quart of brown broth.

MAKES 2 1/2 QUARTS

> Two 3-pound chickens or 6 pounds chicken wings, drumsticks, and/or backs (backs should be chopped up into at least 3 pieces with a cleaver)
>
> 1 large onion, root end trimmed and then quartered without peeling
>
> 3 carrots, unpeeled, halved lengthwise, and sliced
>
> 1 stalk celery, sliced (optional)
>
> 1 handful of fennel stalks (optional)
>
> 3 quarts cold water or more as needed to cover
>
> Bouquet garni

If you are using whole chickens, cut them up as described on pages 248–249. Separate the drumsticks from the thighs, cut each of the single breasts in half, and cut the back into 3 pieces. If you are using only chicken backs, or backs combined with other parts, cut each back into 3 pieces with a cleaver.

Spread the chicken parts and all the vegetables in a heavy-bottomed roasting pan just large enough to hold them in a single layer. (If the pan is too large, the juices will burn; if it's too small, the chicken won't brown properly.) Slide the pan into the oven and turn the oven to 400°F. Roast, stirring the chicken and vegetables a couple of times as they cook so they brown evenly and thoroughly, for about 1¹/₂ hours.

Transfer the chicken and vegetables to a pot—ideally narrow and tall to facilitate skimming—and put the roasting pan on the stove top over high heat. Pour about 2 cups of water into the roasting pan, bring to a boil, and deglaze the pan, scraping up the browned-on juices from the bottom with a wooden spoon. Pour the liquid into the pot. Add enough water to the pot to cover the chicken and vegetables, and nestle the bouquet garni in the middle of the pot.

Bring to a gentle simmer and simmer uncovered for 1¹/₂ hours, skimming off the froth with a ladle every 15 minutes or so. Strain through a fine-mesh strainer into a clean container, let cool for 1 hour at room temperature, and then cover and refrigerate. Before using, pull off the fat that has congealed on top and discard. The broth will keep for up to 5 days in the refrigerator or 6 months in the freezer. If boiled every 5 days, it will keep indefinitely in the refrigerator.

HOW TO MAKE BROWN CHICKEN BROTH

1. Brown the chicken parts in the oven with the vegetables. Transfer the browned chicken and vegetables to a pot.

2. Pour water into the roasting pan over high heat and deglaze the pan, scraping up the browned-on juices.

3. Pour the liquid from the roasting pan into the pot. Add enough water to the pot just to cover the chicken and vegetables.

4. Nestle a bouquet garni in the pot and simmer the broth gently before straining.

White Chicken Broth

Brown chicken broth is more flavorful than white broth, but for cream soups and white sauces, you need a white broth, which takes less time to make. For a clear soup, make white broth with chicken parts that contain meat (not with backs or just wings) because the bones will cloud the broth.

MAKES ABOUT 1¹/₂ QUARTS

> Two 3¹/₂-pound chickens; one 5-pound stewing hen, 6 pounds chicken legs, drumsticks, and/or wings; or carcasses from three 4-pound roasted chickens; or any combination
>
> 1 large onion, root end trimmed and then quartered without peeling
>
> 2 carrots, unpeeled, halved lengthwise and sliced
>
> 1 stalk celery, sliced (optional)
>
> 1 handful of fennel stalks (optional)
>
> 3 quarts cold water or more as needed to cover
>
> Bouquet garni

If you are using whole chickens, cut them up as described on pages 248–249. Separate the drumsticks from the thighs and cut each of the single breasts in half. If you are using leftover chicken carcasses, break them up with a cleaver so they take up less room in the pot. Put the vegetables in the pot first—ideally tall and narrow to facilitate skimming—so they don't float up and interfere with skimming, and then add the chicken.

Add enough water to the pot to cover the chicken and vegetables, and nestle the bouquet garni in the middle.

Bring to a gentle simmer, starting on high heat and decreasing the heat to medium once the liquid is simmering. Move the pot slightly off center of the burner, and turn down the heat so the liquid bubbles gently on one side. Simmer uncovered for 2 hours, skimming off the froth with a ladle every 15 minutes or so. Strain through a fine-mesh strainer into a clean container, let cool for 1 hour at room temperature, and then cover and refrigerate. Before using, pull off the fat that has congealed on top and discard. The broth will keep for up to 5 days in the refrigerator or 6 months in the freezer. If boiled every 5 days, it will keep indefinitely in the refrigerator.

VARIATION

Prepare Brown Chicken Broth (opposite) as directed, let it cool, de-fat it, and then use it, instead of water, to make White Chicken Broth (above), omitting the vegetables. You can use this broth, which is chicken consommé, as the liquid for a second white chicken broth (to create a triple broth) and so on, depending on just how crazy and extravagant you want to get.

HOW TO MAKE WHITE VEAL BROTH

1. Trim off excess fat from the veal breast.

2. Cut between the bones to separate the meat into chunks.

3. Put the chunks in a pot with cold water to cover. Bring to a boil, then drain. Again, add cold water to cover.

4. Simmer gently for 5 hours, strain the broth, and eat the meat.

HOW TO MAKE BROWN VEAL BROTH

1. Brown the veal bones with carrots, onions, and celery in a roasting pan in a 500°F oven. Use 1 onion and 1 carrot for each 10 pounds of bones.

2. When the bones and vegetables are well browned, transfer them to a tall, narrow pot. Deglaze the roasting pan and add browned juices to the pot. Proceed as for white veal broth.

HOW TO MAKE MEAT GLAZE

1. Simmer veal broth, skimming off the fat and froth, until reduced to one-fifteenth of its original volume and syrupy.

BEEF BROTH

Most of the time you can avoid using beef broth in soup recipes, relying instead on something less expensive and time-consuming. French onion soup, for example, is delicious made with turkey broth fashioned from the leftover carcass of a roasted turkey.

Beef Broth and Pot-au-Feu

Most restaurants make beef broth out of beef bones and end up with a broth that lacks the subtle rich flavor of meat. Bones of course are cheap and meat is expensive, but if you serve the meat as a meal it's easier to justify using it to make broth. Roast knuckle bones for an hour or so until well browned and then simmer gently in just enough water to cover (about a pint per pound of bones) for 12 hours. The night you make your broth, plan on serving a pot-au-feu, which is the French equivalent of a New England boiled dinner—except that no corned beef is used and nothing ever gets boiled, just gently poached. For an authentic pot-au-feu, serve the broth as a first course or use it to surround the meat, served sliced and in deep soup plates. For variety, include three different cuts of beef, all of them tough, flavorful cuts meant for braising or, in this case, poaching.

MAKES 8 SERVINGS OF MEAT AND ABOUT 5 QUARTS OF BROTH

- **4 rounds of beef shank, tied widthwise and lengthwise with kitchen string**
- **3- to 4-pound chuck roast meant for pot roasting, tied widthwise and lengthwise with kitchen string**
- **4 pounds beef short ribs left in one piece**
- **5 quarts cold water or beef bone broth or more as needed to cover**
- **1 large onion, halved and peeled**
- **1 clove, stuck into the onion**
- **4 large carrots, peeled, cut into 3-inch sections**
- **2 turnips, peeled, each cut into 8 wedges**
- **8 small to medium leeks, greens removed, whites halved and rinsed, whites tied together with string**
- **Large bouquet garni**
- **Mustard**
- **French sour gherkins (cornichons)**
- **Coarse salt**
- **Pepper**

Put the meat in a large pot and pour over the broth or water to cover. Bring to a gentle simmer and skim off any scum that floats to the top. Simmer gently for about 2 hours, regularly skimming off and discarding fat. Add the vegetables and bouquet garni and simmer for 1 hour more. Lift the meat out of the broth and slice. Serve some of each kind of meat on heated plates and spoon some of the broth around the slices or reserve it all for another use. Pass the mustard, cornichons, salt, and pepper at the table. Keeps for up to 5 days in the refrigerator.

Beef Consommé

To make consommé, you must first make a basic beef broth with a tough, flavorful cuts such as the shank. Serve the shank with a little tomato sauce or horseradish-flavored mayonnaise. You can also use the broth from the pot-au-feu (opposite).

MAKES ABOUT 2¹/₂ QUARTS

  3 pounds beef shank, cut into 1-inch thick rounds
  2 large carrots, peeled, cut into sections
  1 large onion, peeled, quartered
  Bouquet garni
  3 quarts cold water or more as needed to cover
  2 pounds lean beef, such as round, trimmed
    of fat, ground
  3 egg whites
  3 egg shells
  5 sprigs fresh tarragon
  1 onion, peeled, chopped
  1 carrot, chopped

To prepare basic beef broth, put the beef shank, carrots, onion, and bouquet garni in a pot with enough water to cover and simmer gently for 6 hours. Strain and let cool.

To prepare the consommé, blend the ground meat with the egg whites, shells, tarragon, onion, and carrots in a food processor and pour into the cool broth. Stir with a whisk to combine all the ingredients. Bring to a gentle simmer in a small pot. Simmer until the liquid is clear and the egg has coagulated into a solid mass on the surface—called a "raft." Lift the raft out of the liquid and carefully discard. Strain the consommé through a fine-mesh strainer. Keeps for up to 5 days in the refrigerator.

SHRIMP BROTH

Shrimp is adaptable to a variety of soups and stewlike dishes, and for the most part can be simmered directly in the dish. Getting the soup or stew to take on the flavor of the shrimp, however, is trickier, since the most flavorful part of the shrimp is in the heads. When you want to make a shrimp broth, order shrimp with the heads—you will probably need to give a day's notice—and save up the heads and shells in the freezer.

Basic Shrimp Broth for Soups, Stews, and Sauces

The best way to extract the intense flavor carried in shrimp heads is to make a broth, which can then be used as the base for shrimp soups and stews. The broth can be frozen for months or kept refrigerated for up to 5 days (boiling every 5 days will allow you to keep it in the refrigerator indefinitely.)

MAKES ABOUT 2¹/₂ QUARTS

  1 small onion, coarsely chopped
  1 small fennel bulb or the stalks of a fennel bulb,
    coarsely chopped
  1 small carrot, coarsely chopped
  2 tablespoons olive oil
  4 quarts shrimp heads and/or shells
  3 quarts water or chicken broth (see pages 36–37)
  3 sprigs thyme (optional)

In a heavy-bottomed pot large enough to hold the broth, cook the onion, fennel, and carrot and cook in the oil over medium heat, stirring regularly, for about 10 minutes, or until the vegetables are softened but not browned. Add the shrimp heads and shells, raise the heat to high, stirring often, for about 4 minutes, or until the mixture smells fragrant and the heads and shells turn orange.

Let cool for a few minutes. Chop the whole mixture in a food processor for about 30 seconds, or until the shells and heads are broken up but not pureed. Rinse out the pot and return the chopped mixture to it. Add the water and thyme, bring to a gentle simmer, and simmer for 1 hour, skimming off any froth that forms on the surface. Don't let the broth come to a full boil, or the proteins the shrimp release will cloud the broth. Strain the broth through a fine-mesh strainer and discard the mixture that doesn't go through the strainer, reserving the shells and heads to make shrimp butter (see Crustacean Butters, page 351).

FISH BROTH

The inherent complication with making fish soups and stews is the need for fish bones and heads. In American supermarkets, it can be difficult to find whole fish, much less someone to fillet them for you. An alternative is to buy small, whole inexpensive fish at an ethnic market to use for the broth. You can then use meaty chunks of whatever kind of fish you find as the solid part of your soup. When you get your bag of fish home, you will usually need to clean them (see pages 146, 148, and 158), as ethnic markets are rarely willing to clean little inexpensive fish. You then just simmer the fish in water, perhaps with a little wine, and strain. You can also work the cooked fish through a food mill to make fish puree. Stir the puree into the fish broth to make a creamy base for your soup.

Fish Broth

The secret to fish broth is using fresh bones and heads and cooking them right away. The heads and bones are soaked to remove traces of blood, which turn the broth gray.

Don't cook fish broth more than 20 minutes or it will taste fishy instead of having a gentle sealike quality.

MAKES 3 QUARTS

> **5 pounds fish bones and heads, gills removed, heads and bones soaked in cold water, refrigerated, for 2 hours**
>
> **1 onion, peeled and sliced**
>
> **Bouquet garni**
>
> **Cold water to cover**
>
> **1/2 cup dry white wine**

Break up the bones and put them with the heads, onion, and bouquet garni in a small pot. Pour over enough cold water to cover. Bring to a gentle simmer, add the white wine, and skim off any froth that floats to the surface. Simmer for 20 minutes and strain. Keeps for up to 5 days in the refrigerator.

Dashi

For Japanese cooks, dashi is a universal solvent that ends up in all manner of sauces, soups, and stews. Once you get a hold of the requisite ingredients—which keep well—dashi is by far the easiest and quickest of all broths to make. You bring kombu (dried giant kelp) to a simmer in water, pick it out with tongs, and add a handful or two of dried bonito flakes. Bonito is a tunalike fish that the Japanese dry and smoke until it has the texture of wood and looks like an overripe banana. Traditionalists then shave the bonito as needed with a device that looks a little like a shoebox with a blade inserted into one side. However, most cooks, even purists, buy bonito already shaved.

Once you have your dashi in hand, think of it as you would any broth and use it to poach vegetables, pieces of seafood, or meat. Dashi is also the base for miso soup (following), which itself can be used as a base for more elaborate soups, especially those containing seafood.

MAKES 1 QUART

> **1 1/2 lengths kombu, or 18 inches total**
>
> **1 ounce (about 2 cups loosely packed) dried bonito flakes**

Wipe the kombu with a moist towel to wipe away any dust, and then fold it so you can get it into the pot. Pour in 1 quart cold water and set the pot on low to medium heat so the water takes about 15 minutes to come to a simmer.

Fish out the kombu with tongs—you can reuse it once if you save it in the freezer—and bring the infused water to a rapid boil over high heat.

Take the pot off the heat and immediately add the bonito flakes. Let the flakes infuse for 2 minutes and then strain through a fine-mesh strainer into a clean container. Let cool for 1 hour at room temperature, and then cover and refrigerate. The broth will keep for up to 5 days in the refrigerator or 6 months in the freezer. If boiled every 5 days, it will keep indefinitely in the refrigerator.

HOW TO MAKE DASHI

1. Wipe the kombu with a moist towel.

2. Put the kombu in a pot with cold water, place over low to medium heat, and remove the kombu as soon as the water comes to a simmer.

3. Bring the dashi to a boil, remove from the heat, and add the bonito flakes. Let infuse for 2 minutes.

4. Strain the dashi into a clean container.

Miso Soup

Miso (fermented soybean paste) comes in various colors and degrees of sweetness. White miso, which is relatively sweet and mild, is considered best for summer, while dark, salty red miso is more appropriate for winter. Brown miso falls between the two, and unless you start to appreciate the nuances, is a good all-purpose standby. Miso keeps for months—if not years—in the refrigerator.

MAKES 1 QUART OR 4 FIRST-COURSE SERVINGS

1 quart dashi

2 to 4 tablespoons miso (the lighter the miso, the more you need)

Bring the dashi to a simmer, scoop out 2 tablespoons, and mix with a little miso, working them together until smooth. Add a little more miso and work again until smooth. Work half of this paste into the gently simmering dashi and taste. If the dashi is salty enough, don't add any more miso. Otherwise, add as much as needed to make the dashi pleasantly salty and flavorful.

HOW TO MAKE MISO SOUP WITH COCKLES

1. Whisk some dashi into miso in a small bowl.

2. Put the cockles in a pot (see page 113 for more about cockles). Pour the miso soup over the cockles, bring to a simmer, and simmer until the cockles open.

3. Ladle the soup into bowls.

4. The finished soup.

Garnishes for Miso Soup

pieces of green vegetables • mushroom slices • raw mussels • clams, cockles, or scallops cooked right in the soup • meat cubes • tofu cubes • soba noodles • finely julienned root vegetables • shrimp • pieces of fish, lobster, or other seafood

GARNISHES FOR SIMPLE BROTHS AND CONSOMMÉS

Additions to a simple pot of chicken broth can be as simple as a few strands of angel hair pasta or as elaborate as the baroque concoctions—truffle slices cut into croissant shapes, tiny rounds of custard, miniature cheese puffs—added to consommé during the late nineteenth century. Here are a few ideas:

Pasta: Simmer $1/2$ cup dried pasta, such as elbow pasta, broken-up angel hair or spaghetti, or orecchiette, in the soup for the time indicated on the package. Miniature ravioli can be served surrounded with broth and, depending on the number of ravioli per serving, be a first or main course.

Rice: Simmer long-grain rice, about $1/2$ cup raw rice per quart of broth, in the broth for about 15 minutes.

Vegetables: Any vegetable can be diced or sliced and simmered in the broth until tender. The precision and care put into the cutting can range from extreme (such as the brunoise, shown on page 298) to simple slicing or sectioning.

Herbs: Chopped herbs both look attractive and can bring a plain broth to life. Some herbs, such as thyme or rosemary, are too aggressively flavored to be chopped and added at the end. Instead, they should go into the bouquet garni, so their flavor is released slowly into the broth. But delicate herbs, such as basil, tarragon, parsley, chervil, and chives, either alone or in combination, are an easy and eye-catching addition at the end of cooking.

Other Flavors: Finely chopped and crushed garlic, saffron threads, curry powder cooked in a little butter, grated fresh ginger, and citrus zests (which can be grated or finely julienned) are all excellent last-minute additions to a pot of broth.

SOUPS

A soup differs from a broth in that it implies there is something else in it. A chicken broth, for example, becomes chicken soup when pieces of chicken are added. In French cooking, a *soupe* is characterized and distinguished from a *potage* by being abundant and hearty, with a high proportion of solids to liquids. An onion soup made with croutons and lots of cheese is a perfect example of what the French call a *soupe*. A more refined offering—tiny croutons and a few curls of onions floating in a clear broth—is likely to be called a potage.

None of this is terribly important except that it helps get us thinking. For example, the abundant pistou on page 51, essentially a vegetable stew with pesto stirred into it, could be refinemened to match formality of the meal. An obvious approach would be to use clear broth, even consommé, and cut the vegetables carefully into a brunoise, macédoine (¹⁄₄-inch cubes), or julienne. The pesto can be passed at the table or swirled into each serving by the cook.

VEGETABLE CREAM SOUPS

Most cream soups are vegetable soups based on a single vegetable, with perhaps a leek or an onion in the background. Much of the time the soup is pureed until smooth and then some of the vegetable or just a part of it, such as asparagus tips, is added just before serving. Tiny croutons also make an attractive garnish and provide crunch.

Traditional cream soups are made by thickening broth or milk with flour, simmering the mixture with the vegetable, pureeing and straining, and then finishing with cream. When the soup is pureed, the cream can be left out, but even a small amount gives a soup a more luxurious taste. Another method, which works for almost any vegetable and is what I use here, is to use a basic leek and potato soup as a base for other vegetables. The vegetables—the leek, potato, and the third vegetable—can be left whole, in pieces, or pureed. Cold pureed leek and potato soup is vichyssoise.

Precautions

Immersion blenders are great conveniences because you don't need to dirty the blender—the immersion blender can just be rinsed off—and there's no transferring of hot liquids from one container to another. If you're pureeing hot soup in a regular blender, never fill the blender more than half full. Hold the lid on tightly with a kitchen towel and start by pulsing on the lowest speed. Gradually increase the duration and speed of the pulses until the air inside the blender has heated up and no longer threatens to burst out the top.

Leek and Potato Soup

This simple and satisfying soup can be put together in about the time it takes to open a can, and can be made as a smooth cream soup or left chunky. Different potatoes create different effects. If you want pieces of potato with texture in the soup, use white or red waxy potatoes and dice them. If you are pureeing the soup and want a smooth texture, use Yukon Gold potatoes.

MAKES 1 QUART OR 4 FIRST-COURSE SERVINGS

> **1 large Yukon Gold potato or white or red waxy potato, peeled**
> **3 leeks, cleaned and thinly sliced (page 293)**
> **1 quart milk, water, or chicken broth**
> **¹⁄₂ cup heavy cream or 4 tablespoons butter**
> **Salt**
> **Pepper**

If you are making a pureed soup, thinly slice the Yukon Gold potato lengthwise. If you are making a chunky soup, cut the waxy potato into ¹⁄₃-inch dice. In a pot, combine the potatoes, leeks, and milk and bring to a gentle simmer. Simmer for about 25 minutes, or until the potatoes and leeks are completely soft.

If you are serving a chunky soup, add the cream, bring to a simmer, and season with salt and pepper. Or, if using butter, cut the butter into pats and place a pat on each serving.

If you are serving a smooth soup, puree it with a blender (see precautions at left) and then strain it into a clean pot. Add the cream, bring to a simmer, and season with salt and pepper. Or, if using butter, cut the butter into pats and place a pat on each serving.

Soup Croutons

Tiny croutons in a bowl of soup float on the top, look attractive, and provide a delicate, buttery crunch. They must be cooked in butter and not just toasted, or they will get soggy in the soup. For 4 servings of soup, cut 2 thin slices dense-crumb white bread into small cubes, and cook them gently in 2 tablespoons of butter, preferably clarified, or olive oil until golden brown and crispy.

HOW TO MAKE LEEK AND POTATO SOUP

1. For pureed soup, thinly slice Yukon Gold potato lengthwise.

2. For chunky soup, slice potato into strips...

3. ...and then dice.

4. Combine potato, leeks, and milk and simmer until soft. Puree and strain for smooth soup; leave as is for chunky soup.

5. Add the cream and serve, or omit the cream and top each bowl with a pat of butter.

Cream of Asparagus Soup

This soup is a basic leek and potato soup to which cut-up asparagus stalks are added and simmered along with the vegetables. After pureeing this mixture, the asparagus tips are simmered in the soup for a few minutes before serving.

MAKES 1 QUART OR 4 FIRST-COURSE SERVINGS

1 large Yukon Gold potato, peeled and thinly sliced
3 leeks, cleaned and thinly sliced (see page 293)
1 quart milk, water, or chicken broth
1 pound asparagus
$1/2$ cup heavy cream
Salt
Pepper

In a pot, combine the potato, leeks, and milk and bring to a gentle simmer. Meanwhile, cut off the tips of the asparagus and reserve. Cut 1 inch off the bottom of each asparagus stalk and discard. Cut the stalks into 1-inch sections and add them to the simmering soup. Simmer for about 25 minutes, or until the potatoes, leeks, and asparagus are completely soft.

Puree the soup with a blender (see precautions on page 42) and then strain it into a clean pot. Add the cream and the asparagus tips, bring to a simmer, and simmer for about 4 minutes, or until the tips are just tender. Season with salt and pepper.

HOW TO MAKE CREAM OF ASPARAGUS SOUP

Cut the asparagus stalks into 1-inch sections and simmer them in a leek and potato soup before pureeing.

Cream of Pea Soup

Since fresh peas are usually starchy and tasteless, except for about two weeks in June, frozen peas are the one exception to the "fresh is always better" rule. If you want whole peas in the finished soup, keep a few out to add at the end.

MAKES 1 QUART OR 4 FIRST-COURSE SERVINGS

1 large Yukon Gold potato, peeled and thinly sliced

3 leeks, cleaned and thinly sliced (see page 293)

1 quart milk, water, or chicken broth

One 10-ounce package frozen petite peas or
  2 pounds fresh peas in the pod, shelled

1/2 cup heavy cream

Salt

Pepper

Soup Croutons (see page 42), optional

In a pot, combine the potato, leeks, and milk, bring to a gentle simmer, and simmer for about 25 minutes, or until the potatoes and leeks are completely soft. Add the peas and simmer for about 3 minutes.

Puree the soup with a blender (see precautions on page 42) and then strain it into a clean pot. Add the cream, bring to a simmer, and season with salt and pepper. Garnish with the croutons.

Cream of Mushroom Soup

This soup is best made with cremini mushrooms, instead of the more common cultivated white mushrooms. The dried porcini are expensive, but they give the soup depth and complexity.

MAKES 1 QUART OR 4 FIRST-COURSE SERVINGS

1 small Yukon Gold potato, peeled and thinly sliced

3 leeks, cleaned and thinly sliced (page 293)

1 quart milk, water, or chicken broth

1 1/2 pounds fresh cremini or cultivated white
  mushrooms, coarsely chopped or sliced

6 slices dried porcini mushrooms, soaked in
  1/2 cup warm water for 30 minutes (optional)

1/2 cup heavy cream

Salt

Pepper

Soup Croutons (see page 42), optional

In a pot, combine the potato, leeks, and milk, bring to a gentle simmer, and simmer for about 25 minutes, or until the potatoes and leeks are completely soft.

Add the fresh mushrooms to the soup. Lift the porcini out of their soaking water and squeeze them, releasing the liquid into the bowl. Carefully pour the soaking liquid into the soup, leaving any grit behind in the bowl. Then add the porcini to the pot and simmer for about 7 minutes.

Puree the soup with a blender (see precautions on page 42) and then strain it into a clean pot. Add the cream, bring to a simmer, and season with salt and pepper. Garnish with the croutons.

Cream of Spinach Soup

Even though this soup is strained, you have to stem the spinach. Otherwise, the fibers from the stems wrap around the blender blades and then end up in the soup bowls.

MAKES 1 QUART OR 4 FIRST-COURSE SERVINGS

1 large Yukon Gold potato, peeled and thinly sliced

3 leeks, cleaned and thinly sliced (see page 293)

1 quart milk, water, or chicken broth

Two 10-ounce bags spinach leaves or
  two 10-ounce bunches spinach, stemmed

1/2 cup heavy cream

Salt

Pepper

Soup Croutons (see page 42), optional

In a pot, combine the potato, leeks, and milk, bring to a gentle simmer, and simmer for about 25 minutes, or until the potatoes and leeks are completely soft.

Add the spinach, bring back to a simmer, and remove from the heat. Puree the soup with a blender (see precautions on page 42) and then strain it through a strainer into a clean pot. Add the cream, bring to a simmer, and season with salt and pepper. Garnish with the croutons.

Cream of Celeriac Soup

The trick to this soup is to use the knobby, brown celeriac, also known as celery root, instead of branch celery. The flavor is subtle and luxurious. You can make a cream of turnip soup by substituting 2 turnips for the celeriac, or a cream of carrot soup by substituting 2 large carrots for the celeriac.

MAKES 6 CUPS OR 6 FIRST-COURSE SERVINGS

    3 leeks, cleaned and thinly sliced (see page 293)
    1 large Yukon Gold potato, peeled and thinly sliced
    1 large celeriac, about 1 pound total, peeled and
        cut into rough cubes
    1 quart milk, water, or chicken broth plus more as
        needed to thin
    1/2 to 1 cup heavy cream (to taste)
    Salt
    Pepper
    Soup Croutons (see page 42)

In a pot, combine the leeks, potato, celeriac, and milk, bring to a gentle simmer, and simmer, covered, for about 30 minutes, or until the vegetables are completely soft.

Puree the soup with a blender (see precautions on page 42) and then strain it into a clean pot. Add the cream, bring to a simmer, and season with salt and pepper. If the soup is too thick, thin it with a little additional broth. Garnish with the croutons.

Cream of Cauliflower Soup

This soup calls for a whole cup of cream to balance the flavor of cauliflower, which can be a bit aggressive if not tempered. If you like, reserve a handful of tiny cauliflower "flowers," boil them for a minute or two, drain, and use to garnish the soup.

MAKES 6 CUPS 6 FIRST-COURSE SERVINGS

    1 head cauliflower
    3 leeks, cleaned and thiny sliced (see page 293)
    1 large Yukon Gold potato, peeled and thinly sliced
    1 quart milk, water, or chicken broth and more as
        needed to thin soup
    1/2 to 1 cup heavy cream (to taste)
    Salt
    Pepper
    Soup Croutons (page 42), optional

Take the little flowers off the cauliflower head as shown on page 325. In a pot, combine the cauliflower, leeks, potato, and milk, bring to a gentle simmer, and simmer, covered, for about 25 minutes, or until the vegetables are completely soft.

Puree the soup with a blender (see precautions on page 42) and then strain it into a clean pot. Add the cream, and bring to a simmer. Thin if necessary with additional broth or milk. Season with salt and pepper. Garnish with the croutons.

OTHER VEGETABLE SOUPS

Two of the greatest of all vegetable soups—tomato soup and onion soup—are made with just a single vegetable. Some cooks argue that tomatoes need the support of an onion and perhaps some herbs, but when tomatoes are at their best, the soup needs nothing more than the tomatoes themselves. French onion soup can be more solid than liquid, almost like a savory bread pudding, or it can be like a consommé, with just a small tangle of onion strands. It is usually somewhere in between, with a savory cheesy crust on top and plenty of onions and broth underneath.

Tomato Soup

The complexity of a tomato soup is inversely proportionate to the quality of the tomatoes. When you have perfect in-season ripe tomatoes, just peel, seed, and chop them and put them in a pot. Bring them to a simmer and they will release enough liquid to turn them into a soup. If you insist on being more decadent, chop some fresh tarragon or basil, combine it with a couple of tablespoons of heavy cream per serving, and swirl it on top of each bowl just before serving. If you are eating the last of the year's tomatoes and there is a nip in the air, here is something a little richer and warming.

MAKES 1 QUART OR 4 FIRST-COURSE SERVINGS

> Leaves from 10 sprigs tarragon
>
> 1 teaspoon olive oil
>
> 1 cup heavy cream
>
> 1/4 pound thick-cut bacon, cut crosswise into strips
>
> 12 tomatoes, peeled and seeded (see page 85), finely chopped
>
> Salt
>
> Pepper

Rub the tarragon leaves with the olive oil, finely chop the leaves, and combine them in a small bowl with 1/2 cup of the cream. Set aside.

In a pot large enough to hold the soup, cook the bacon over medium heat for about 10 minutes, or until it just begins to get crispy. Add the tomatoes and bring to a simmer. Add the remaining 1/2 cup cream and season with salt and pepper. Top each serving with a swirl of the tarragon cream.

French Onion Soup

Onion soup recipes usually call for beef broth, which puts some of us off or has us reaching for a can. Despite the fact that French onion soup can still be marvelous even made with indifferent canned broth, anemic cheese, and white bread, it is worth using a decent broth and the most savory cheese you can find. Because the onions are so flavorful, it makes little difference whether you use beef broth or something else. Some of the best onion soups use turkey broth made from the leftover holiday carcass, and the Brown Chicken Broth on page 36 is also a good choice. Traditional recipes call for Gruyère cheese, which is Swiss without the holes, but any sharp, semi-hard cheese, such as Cheddar, aged Gouda, or Fontina d'Aosta, work beautifully. The bread should have a dense crumb—don't use airy bread, which will get soggy—and is ideally cooked in butter ahead of time, which keeps it from absorbing liquid. If you run out of time and don't brown the bread in butter, your soup will still be a success. One warning: You are going to end up with what looks like a mountain of raw onions. Don't worry, as they will cook down to about one-tenth of their original volume. Don't use overly sweet onions, such as Vidalia; use a mild onion, such as a red onion.

MAKES 6 CUPS OR 6 FIRST-COURSE SERVINGS

> 5 pounds onions, preferably red Bermuda type, sliced as thinly as possible
>
> 3 tablespoons butter, plus 6 tablespoons (optional)
>
> 1 cup dry sherry or medium-sweet Madeira
>
> 1 cup water
>
> 1 quart broth, preferably brown beef, chicken, or turkey
>
> Salt
>
> Pepper
>
> 6 slices dense-crumb white bread, crusts removed and cut into 3/4-inch cubes
>
> 2 cups grated hard cheese such as Gruyère, Gouda, or Fontina (about 7 ounces)

In a heavy-bottomed pot large enough to hold the soup, cook the onions in 3 tablespoons butter over medium heat, stirring for about 10 minutes, or until they release some of their liquid. Raise the heat to high and cook, stirring often, for about 30 minutes, or until the liquid runs dry and caramelizes on the bottom of the pot and the onions are melted into a compact tangled mass. Keep a close eye on the onions as they cook so that the liquid doesn't run dry before it should and cause the onions to stick.

Add the sherry and water, bring to a boil, and cook, scraping the bottom of the pot with a wooden spoon to dissolve the browned-on juices, until the liquid is reduced by about half. Add the broth, season to taste, and simmer.

Meanwhile, preheat the oven to 350°F. Spread the bread cubes on a sheet pan and toast in the oven, turning them every few minutes, for about 15 minutes, or until evenly browned. Leave the oven on. Alternatively, melt the 6 tablespoons butter in a large sauté pan or skillet over medium heat and sauté the bread cubes for about 12 minutes, or until evenly browned on all sides.

Return the soup to a simmer if it has cooled. Put 6 soup crocks on a sheet pan (so the soup doesn't overflow onto your oven floor). Ladle the broth and onions into the crocks. Using half of the bread cubes, spread them evenly among the crocks. Top with half of the cheese. Spread the remaining bread cubes on top, and then the rest of the cheese. Bake for about 20 minutes, or until boiling broth starts to drip down the sides of the crocks.

Garlic Soup with Poached Eggs

You can skip the poached eggs and leave this Spanish soup lean (known as sopa de ajo), which makes it almost a tonic, but there is something about the egg yolks melting into the broth that makes the whole concoction especially satisfying. This version contains a lot of fresh marjoram, but a more traditional version would be made with thyme. A Mexican version could be made with oregano.

MAKES 6 CUPS OR 6 FIRST-COURSE SERVINGS

> **4 heads garlic**
> **1 bunch marjoram or thyme (about 30 sprigs)**
> **2 quarts chicken broth**
> **3 tablespoons fresh lemon juice**
> **One 1-inch strip orange zest (optional)**
> **Salt**
> **Pepper**
> **6 slices slightly stale French bread, toasted**
> **6 poached eggs (see pages 96–97), optional**
> **Extra virgin olive oil, for serving (optional)**

Break up the garlic heads into cloves and put the unpeeled cloves in a pot with the marjoram and the broth. Bring to a gentle simmer, cover, and simmer for about 45 minutes, or until the garlic is soft.

Work the soup through a food mill or through a strainer, pressing against the solids with the bottom of a ladle. Return the soup to the pot, bring to a simmer, and add the lemon juice and orange zest. Season with salt and pepper. Put a toast in each soup plate, top each toast with an egg, and ladle over the broth. Drizzle with the olive oil.

Fresh Corn and Chile Soup

Essentially a corn soup with dried and fresh chiles, this combination is magnificent. If you want to turn this soup into a meal, cook a chicken, cut it into quarters, and serve a quarter in each soup plate with the soup ladled around it. Make sure there is plenty of lime. The tang is important to balance the richness and heat of the soup.

MAKES 3 QUARTS (12 FIRST-COURSE SERVINGS OR 6–8 MAIN-COURSE SERVINGS

  6 cloves garlic, sliced

  1 onion, chopped

  9 tomatoes, chopped

  3 cups corn kernels from about 4 ears of corn

  1½ quarts chicken broth

  2 chipotle chiles, soaked in warm water for 30 minutes to soften if dried or rinsed if canned, or 2 jalapeño chiles, seeded and chopped

  18 assorted mild dried chiles such as guajillo, mulatto, ancho, chilhuacle negro, and pasilla, in any combination, soaked in hot water for 30 minutes to soften, seeded, stemmed, and chopped

  1½ cups heavy cream

  2 tablespoons chopped fresh cilantro

  3 tablespoons fresh lime juice

  Salt

  Pepper

  Sour cream and lime wedges for serving

In a pot, combine the garlic, onion, tomatoes, corn, broth, chipotle chiles, and assorted chiles, bring to a gentle simmer, and simmer for 30 minutes, or until everything has softened.

Puree the soup with a blender (see precautions on page 42) and then strain it into a clean pot. Add the cream, cilantro, and lime juice and bring to a simmer. Season with salt and pepper. Pass the sour cream and lime wedges at the table.

Gazpacho

Most gazpachos encountered in restaurants are sad affairs, pureed in some machine, with a few diced cucumbers floating around for effect. For a gazpacho to be at its best, the ingredients must be chopped by hand or very carefully in a food processor—small amounts, short pulses—or they will lose their identity. A gazpacho should be a study in contrasts—cool, hot, hard, soft—not homogenous. While the soul of the soup is tomatoes, the accent of a smoked chile, such as a chipotle or pasilla de Oaxaca, and the tang of lime make all the difference.

MAKES 6 CUPS OR 6 FIRST-COURSE SERVINGS

  1 red onion, very finely chopped

  2 cloves garlic, minced and then crushed with the flat side of the knife

  8 tomatoes, peeled, seeded, and finely chopped

  1 regular (not hothouse) cucumber, peeled and halved lengthwise

  1 bell pepper, preferably yellow (for color), charred, peeled, and seeded (see page 321) and then finely chopped

  1 or more chipotle chiles, soaked in hot water for 30 minutes to soften if dried or rinsed if canned, seeded, and finely chopped, or 2 jalapeño chiles, seeded and finely chopped

  1 poblano chile, charred, peeled, and seeded (see page 321) and then finely chopped

  2 tablespoons finely chopped fresh cilantro (optional)

  ¼ cup fresh lime juice

  Salt

  Pepper

In a bowl, combine the onion, garlic, and tomatoes, mix well, and refrigerate. Scoop the seeds out of the cucumber halves. Thinly slice each half lengthwise, cut each slice lengthwise to make narrow strips, and then cut the strips crosswise to make fine dice. Add the cucumber, bell pepper, chiles, cilantro, and lime juice to the tomato mixture, stir gently to combine, and then season with salt and pepper. Once the salt is added, the vegetables will begin to release their water, and the mixture will become more liquid. Cover and refrigerate until ice cold. Serve straight from the refrigerator in chilled bowls.

Borscht

You can approach borscht in two ways: The first is simply to simmer beets and other vegetables in broth and serve with sour cream. The second is to cook short ribs in broth, take the meat off the bones, and combine the meat and other vegetables in a substantial and irresistible soup-stew. Whichever version you do make, the central operation is dealing with the beets, which can be roasted in the oven, boiled, or cooked in the microwave before peeling and dicing. (See Roast Beets on pages 298–299 for general directions on roasting. Boiling takes about the same amount of time. Or, see page 306 for tips on microwaving.) Borscht can be made with canned beets, but something essential is lost.

MAKES 2 QUARTS (8 FIRST-COURSE SERVINGS FOR SIMPLE VERSION OR 6 MAIN-COURSE SERVINGS FOR COMPLEX VERSION)

Complex Version

4 beef short ribs, about 3 pounds total

1 onion, quartered

2 carrots, peeled and cut into 1-inch pieces

2 quarts chicken broth or water

Bouquet garni

Simple Version

2 quarts full-flavored broth

Both Versions

1 onion, chopped

4 leeks, white part only, cleaned and thinly sliced (see page 293)

3 cloves garlic, minced

4 beets, roasted in the oven, cooked in the microwave, or boiled until easily penetrated with a skewer, peeled and diced (see headnote)

6 tablespoons good wine vinegar, or more to taste

Salt

Pepper

Sour cream or crème fraîche for serving

4 tablespoons coarsely chopped fresh dill (optional)

To make the complex version, place the ribs, onion, and carrots in a roasting pan and roast in a 400°F oven for about 1 hour, or until well browned. Transfer the ribs and vegetables to a pot just large enough to hold the soup. Spoon or pour off the fat from the roasting pan, place the pan on the stove top over high heat, and add about a quart of the broth. Bring to a simmer and deglaze the pan, scraping up the browned-on juices from the bottom with a wooden spoon. Pour the liquid into the pot. Add the remaining broth and the bouquet garni, bring to a gentle simmer, cover, and simmer for 2 hours, or until the vegetables are soft and the meat is tender. Lift out the ribs and put aside, then strain the broth through a strainer into a clean container and discard the vegetables in the strainer. If you have time, let the broth cool, cover, and refrigerate until the fat congeals on the surface, and then lift off and discard the fat. If you are making the soup right away, use a large spoon to scoop off as much of the fat from the surface as possible. Pull the meat off the rib bones and shred; discard the bones.

To make the complex or the simple version, pour the broth into a pot and add the onion, leeks, garlic, and beets. Bring to a gentle simmer and simmer, uncovered, for 20 minutes, or until everything has softened. Add the vinegar to taste and the meat from the short ribs, if using. Season with salt and pepper. Pass the sour cream and dill at the table.

MIXED VEGETABLE SOUPS

Some of the world's best soups are hearty peasant affairs replete with an abundance of vegetables and flavored with herbs and often meat, especially preserved meats, such as pancetta, prosciutto, or confit. Minestrone is the best-known Italian version, pistou is a French vegetable soup finished with a pestolike basil paste, and a garbure is vegetable soup from southwestern France, which contains plenty of duck or goose confit. There is an amazing similarity in how all these soups are made, with the same commonsense thread running through all the methods.

Typically, aromatic or slow-cooking vegetables are sweated in a little fat, such as olive oil, pork fat, or duck fat, and then liquid, usually water or broth, is added and brought to a simmer. Vegetables and other ingredients, such as pasta or rice, are added according to their cooking times: beans and lentils first, green vegetables near the end, and such aromatic ingredients as basil, mint, or garlic mixed in just before the pot comes off the stove. Most of these hearty soups are left chunky, but they can also be partly pureed, just enough to give them a little body, something especially easy to do if you have an immersion blender. You can make these soups more or less hearty for main courses or first courses by varying the proportion of liquid to solids and the amount of meat. A slice of toasted bread placed in the middle of each soup plate—often rubbed with a little garlic—helps mound up the vegetables and creates a dramatic effect.

European Peasant-Style Vegetable Soup Model

This is a model for a soup, rather than a replica of something traditional. The list of ingredients is long, but you can use as few as three vegetables with good results.

MAKES ABOUT 3 QUARTS (12 FIRST-COURSE SERVINGS OR 8 MAIN-COURSE SERVINGS)

Meats (choose one)

4 confit Pekin duck thighs or 2 confit mullard duck thighs, meat pulled off the bone and coarsely chopped

$1/2$ pound prosciutto end, cut into $1/2$-inch dice

$1/2$ pound pancetta, cut into 1-inch strips

Fats (choose one)

3 tablespoons olive oil, rendered duck fat, or the fat rendered from the pancetta

Slow-Cooking Vegetables (choose one or more)

2 onions, chopped

1 large carrot, peeled, quartered lengthwise, and sliced crosswise

1 turnip, peeled and diced

2 cups dried beans, soaked for 4 hours in cold water and drained

Liquids, Tomatoes, and Slow-Cooking Herbs (choose one or more)

Broth or water

Tomatoes, peeled, seeded, and chopped

Bouquet garni

Starches (choose one)

1 cup long-grain rice such as basmati or jasmine

1 to 2 cups dried pasta such as macaroni, orecchiette, or ziti

Fast-Cooking Vegetables (choice of)

Green beans, ends trimmed and cut into 1-inch sections

Peas, shelled, or if frozen, thawed

Fresh shell beans such as fava or lima

Kale, stems removed and leaves shredded

Swiss chard, stems cut into cubes and leaves shredded

Spinach, chopped or cut into chiffonade

Sorrel, chopped

Flavorful Finishes (choose one or more)

Garlic, minced and then crushed with the flat side of the knife

Finely chopped fresh herbs such as mint, tarragon, or parsley

Pesto (see page 362) or pistou (right)

Herb butter (see page 349)

Choose one of the meats and cook it in your fat of choice with the slow-cooking vegetables (except the beans, which, if you are using, are added along with the liquid) for about 10 minutes, or until the onions are soft and shiny. Add the liquid to cover and the dried beans (if using), nestle the bouquet garni in the middle of the pot, and simmer partially covered gently until the vegetables and beans are almost done. Add any starch, cook until almost done, and then add whatever green vegetables you like and simmer until they are done.

Finally, decide on the finish. If you are using garlic or herbs, whisk them into the soup. If you are using pesto or pistou, whisk only half of it into the soup and pass the rest at the table. And if you are using herb butter, top each serving with a dollop.

Moroccan Lamb and Tomato Soup

This soup takes time. You have to find and cook lamb shanks (although lamb stew meat will do in a pinch) ahead of time, and then simmer the meat and broth with a trio of typical Moroccan spices: saffron, ginger, and cinnamon. This soup is marvelous ladled over couscous or rice and topped with a dollop of harissa.

MAKES 3 QUARTS (12 FIRST-COURSE SERVINGS OR 6–8 MAIN-COURSE SERVINGS)

4 lamb shanks (about 4 pounds total) or 2 pounds lamb stew meat, cut into 1-inch chunks

1 onion, finely chopped

2 carrots, peeled, quartered lengthwise, and sliced crosswise

4 cloves garlic, peeled but left whole

1 quart chicken broth or water, or more as needed

8 tomatoes, peeled, seeded, and chopped (see page 85)

2 tablespoons grated fresh ginger

1 teaspoon ground turmeric

1/2 teaspoon saffron threads, soaked in 1 tablespoon water for 30 minutes

1/2 teaspoon ground cinnamon

Salt

Pepper

Harissa

8 assorted mild dried chiles such as ancho, guajillo, and chilhuacle negro, in any combination, soaked in hot water for 30 minutes to soften, drained and seeded

2 cloves garlic

1 tomato, peeled, seeded, and finely chopped

In a pot just large enough to hold all the soup, combine the lamb, onion, carrots, garlic, and 1 quart broth, or as needed just to cover. Bring to a gentle simmer, cover, and simmer for about 3 hours, or until the meat offers no resistance when poked with a skewer. As the meat cooks, turn it every now and again so that it cooks evenly.

If you have used lamb shanks, remove them from the pot, pull away the meat from the bone, cut the meat into pieces and return the meat to the pot. Add the tomatoes, ginger, turmeric, saffron and its soaking water, and cinnamon and simmer for 10 minutes to blend the flavors. Season with salt and pepper.

To make the harissa, finely chop the chiles. Mince 2 cloves garlic with a chef's knife, and then crush them to a paste with the side of the knife. Combine the chiles, garlic, and tomato and season with salt and pepper. Pass the harissa at the table.

Pistou and Pesto

Pistou is both the name of the French version of the garlic-basil paste and of the soup into which the paste is traditionally stirred. Pesto, of course, is the well-known paste of garlic, basil, olive oil, pine nuts, and Parmigiano-Reggiano from Genoa. Pistou is similar to the Italian version except that it contains no pine nuts and includes tomatoes, which prove superfluous if there are already tomatoes in the soup.

To make enough pistou for 8 servings of soup, in a blender, combine the leaves from 2 large bunches of basil (about 100 leaves); 5 cloves garlic, minced and then crushed with the flat side of the knife; and 3/4 cup pure olive oil. Process on high for about 30 seconds. Transfer to a bowl, add 1/2 cup extra virgin olive oil and 1/4 pound Parmigiano-Reggiano cheese, grated (about 2 cups lightly packed), and stir to combine. To make a small amount of pesto, or pistou, grind the ingredients by hand in a mortar with a pestle. For pesto, add 1/2 cup of toasted pine nuts when processing.

SEAFOOD SOUPS

Wherever there is access to water, there are fish soups and stews made by simmering fish in flavorful liquid—sometimes seawater—along with indigenous herbs and vegetables that help give the soup its identity. Perhaps no dish, or family of dishes, more clearly reveals the combinations of ingredients that characterize a country's or a region's cooking.

Fish soups fall into two categories: those in which the fish is left in pieces and those in which the fish is pureed with the liquid. The easiest method is to toss the fish, whole or cut up, into a pot of simmering liquid and then to serve the whole thing, liquid and fish, in the same bowl. The only drawback to this plan is that eating fish with the bones still attached is messy at best, and for anyone unfamiliar with the anatomy of most fish, destined to end in frustration. One solution is to fillet the fish—or have it filleted—and then to make a flavorful broth with the bones and heads. This way, the heads and bones are strained out, the vegetables and other soup ingredients are added to the broth, and then, shortly before serving, the filleted fish is slipped in to cook.

Making Fish Soup

When you are cooking a soup with fish pieces, you need to add them to the simmering soup just a few minutes before the end of cooking, so they don't overcook. If you are serving a more complicated soup, such as a bouillabaisse, with an assortment of different types of fish, and you want everyone to have a bit of each type, sorting through the soup to divide the pieces evenly can be a nuisance. You can divide the soup into smaller pots, one for each kind of fish. But a better trick is to bake the fish: spread the fish pieces on sheet pans, or cluster them in portions, and if some of the pieces are of a different thickness, put pieces of like thickness on the same pan. This allows you to control the cooking of the fish.

What to Do with the Skin?

Fish skin gets rubbery and sticky when simmered in broth or served with hot broth ladled over, but if you like the effect of serving different-colored fish fillets and/or if you like crispy fish skin, there is a way to save the skin. Earlier the same day you are making the soup, check that the fillets are perfectly scaled and boned. Then heat some olive oil over high heat in a nonstick pan, add the fillets skin side down, and sauté for about 30 seconds while holding the pieces down firmly with the back of a spatula to prevent curling. Immediately transfer the fillets to an oiled sheet pan and refrigerate. When you are ready to serve the soup, bake the fillets in the oven as described above, arrange the fish in the soup plates, and ladle over the broth.

Seafood Soup Model

The stages for making most seafood soups are similar to the stages for vegetable soups: aromatic ingredients are first cooked in a little oil or fat, liquid such as water or wine is added, herbs and other aromatic ingredients are tossed in while the liquid simmers, the fish is poached in the liquid, and enrichers such as cream, coconut milk, peanut butter, or aioli are added near the end. All of the world's great seafood soups and stews can be made using these same methods by simply substituting different ingredients.

MAKES ABOUT 3 QUARTS (12 FIRST-COURSE SERVINGS OR 8 MAIN-COURSE SERVINGS)

Aromatic Ingredients

Onions, chopped

Garlic, peeled and minced

Carrots, peeled, quartered lengthwise, and sliced crosswise

Fennel, sliced and diced

Lemongrass, stalks crushed with the flat side of a knife

Fresh ginger, peeled and grated

Fresh chiles, stemmed and seeded

Fats

Olive oil

Butter

Palm oil

Peanut oil

Vegetable oil

Ghee

Starches

White beans, soaked for 4 hours in cold water and drained

Pasta

Wild rice

Potatoes

White Rice

Barley

Liquids and Moist Ingredients

Water (sometimes seawater)

Wine

Cider

Beer

Vermouth

Sake

Aromatic Herbs and Spices

Thyme

Parsley

Lemongrass

Galangal

Kaffir lime leaves

Mint

Basil

Cinnamon

Cumin

Dried chiles

Dried mushrooms

Saffron

Vegetables and Fruits

Crispy green vegetables such as green beans, snow peas, spinach, and Swiss chard

Mushrooms

Water chestnuts

Cucumbers

Pineapples

Shellfish Cooking Liquids

Tomatoes, peeled, seeded, and chopped

Tomatillos, husked, seeded, and chopped

Dashi (see page 40)

Fish broth made from bones (see page 40)

Crustacean broth (made from lobster or crab shells)

Rum

Pernod

Yogurt

Fish sauce

Fish and Shellfish

Fish fillets from red snapper, striped bass, sea bass, branzino, and/or sea bream, skinned or skin on

Shellfish such as shrimp, mussels, clams

Thickeners, Flavorful Finishers, Enrichers

Heavy cream

Coconut milk

Ground nuts

Corn puree

Flour

Ground seeds such as sesame seeds, pumpkin seeds, and poppy seeds

Bread

Aioli (see page 360)

Romesco (see page 363)

Rouille sauce (see page 363)

Butter

Herb Butter (see page 349)

Crustacean Butter (see page 351)

Cook aromatics of your choice in the fat in a stockpot over medium-high heat, for about 10 minutes, or until the onions are soft and shiny. Add the dried beans (if using), and the liquid to cover, and simmer gently, partially covered, until the beans are almost done.

Add the aromatic herbs and spices to the broth, and then add whatever green vegetables you like and simmer until they are done.

Heat the shellfish poaching liquid in a pan or pans (for poaching different kinds of fish and shellfish) on the stove, and slide the fish pieces and/or shellfish into the simmering liquid. Poach just until cooked, 4 to 8 minutes, depending on the thickness. Add the poaching liquid to the soup and reserve the cooked fish and/or shellfish.

Alternatively, cook the fish in the oven. Heat the oven to 400°F, arrange the fish on two sheet pans, placing the thickest pieces on one sheet and the thinner pieces on another. Slide the sheet pan holding the thickest pieces of fish into the oven, and bake about 10 minutes per inch. Slide sheet pans of thinner fish pieces into the oven, accordingly, so everything is done at once.

Decide on the finishes and whisk them into the soup, simmering for a few minutes to incorporate. If you are using herb butter, you will top each serving with a dollop. Arrange the pieces of fish and/or shellfish in heated soup plates. Ladle the soup over the fish and/or shellfish.

BOUILLABAISSE AND BOURRIDE

While not markedly different than many of its Mediterranean cousins, bouillabaisse has a reputation for luxury, probably because of the number of different fish varieties called for in the traditional recipe. The chances of finding them all at one time—there are seven to be exact—are small even within sight of the Mediterranean, and diminish with increasing distance to almost null on American shores. But while an authentic bouillabaisse may not be possible away from the Mediterranean, the spirit of the dish can be applied to any assortment of fresh, wholesome fish.

Bouillabaisse is best made for a crowd because you will be able to buy more kinds of fish. While the fish should be bought the same day the bouillabaisse is served, virtually all the work can be done earlier in the day, so that only the cooking of the fish is saved for the last minute.

Like many Mediterranean fish soups, bouillabaisse is finished with a flavorful sauce, in its case, rouille (see page 363), which means "rust" and is a paste of grilled peppers, saffron, and garlic. The version in this book also contains egg yolks, which turn the rouille into a mayonnaise like the aioli used in the bourride that follows.

A bourride is a less elaborate Provençal soup or stew, traditionally made with Mediterranean fish and thickened just before serving with aioli, a garlic mayonnaise made with plenty of olive oil. It is similar to a bouillabaisse, except that it doesn't have the same number of fish or the same implication of luxury.

The recipe shown here is a cross between the two: it has a variety of fish and is thickened with aioli containing saffron.

1. Gather an assortment of whole fish. Here are rougets (red mullet), pompano, dorade, irato, branzino, and whiting (Mediterranean sea bass).

2. Fillet the large fish. Reserve heads and bones for broth.

7. Soak the saffron in a small amount of water.

8. Make an aioli starting with pure olive oil.

13. Arrange on a sheet pan to finish cooking in a 400°F oven (10 minutes per inch of thickness).

14. Alternatively to baking fish in the oven, in a roasting pan on the stove, poach the fish fillets in some of the broth.

3. Take out the center strip from larger fillets.

4. Pull out any pin bones with needle-nosed pliers.

5. Cut the whiting into chunks, discarding the heads. Simmer the fish chunks in the broth until cooked.

6. Work the cooked fish and cooking liquid through a food mill.

9. Work in the extra virgin olive oil.

10. Add some of the broth to the saffron and add this mixture to the aioli.

11. Add some of the hot broth to half of the aioli and return this mixture to the pot. Stir over medium heat until silky smooth; do not let it boil.

12. To keep skin-on fillets from curling, hold them, skin side down, in a hot nonstick pan for 30 seconds.

15. Arrange the fish fillets in warmed soup plates.

16. Ladle the hot broth over the fish fillets.

17. Serve with toasts and the saffron aioli.

18. The finished bouillabaisse.

Bourride

You can make a bourride with any fish, but a combination of two or more is best, and you will need bones and heads to make the broth. You can also make the broth with little inexpensive fish sold in ethnic markets, but you may have to clean them yourself. When you buy your fish, have them cleaned and filleted, and explain that you need the bones and head for soup. If you like fish skin, have the fish scaled before it is filleted.

About half of the aioli called for here ends up in the soup, and the rest is passed at the table for guests to dollop into their soup or spread on little toasts. (If you are short on time, see also Quick Bottled Mayonnaise Fix, page 358.)

MAKES 3 QUARTS (12 FIRST-COURSE SERVINGS OR 8 MAIN-COURSE SERVINGS)

    1 pinch saffron in 1 tablespoon water

    Aioli (see page 360)

    Soup

    6 pounds whole fish such as red snapper, striped bass, sea bass, branzino, and/or sea bream, cleaned, filleted, fillets skinned if desired, and heads and bones reserved

    2 pounds small, inexpensive fish such as whiting, cleaned and cut into 2-inch sections

    1/2 cup dry white wine

    2 tablespoons Pernod (optional)

    8 tomatoes, coarsely chopped

    Bouquet garni

    Salt

    Pepper

    24 slices baguette, toasted on one side under the broiler

Add the saffron and its soaking water to the aioli and mix well. Taste and add more salt if needed.

To make the soup, begin by making the broth. In a large pot, combine the fish bones and heads, the whiting, wine, Pernod, tomatoes, bouquet garni, and 2 quarts water. Bring to a gentle simmer and simmer for 30 minutes. Work through a coarse strainer or a food mill and then through a fine-mesh strainer.

Cut the fish into pieces about 1 inch on each side. You want an even number of pieces, so that everyone gets the same number of pieces of each type of fish. If you are leaving the skin on, sauté the pieces as described in "What to Do with the Skin" (see page 42). Arrange the pieces on sheet pans, with thick pieces on one sheet pan, and thinner pieces on another, if they are not all the same thickness. Season with salt and pepper and refrigerate until needed.

About 20 minutes before serving, preheat the oven to 400°F. Bring the broth to a simmer in a stockpot. Put half of the aioli into a heatproof bowl large enough to hold at least half of the soup. Put the other half into a serving bowl and set it on the table with a spoon. Slide the fish pieces into the oven, giving them about 10 minutes per inch of thickness. Whisk about half of the simmering broth into the aioli. Pour this mixture back into the pot, turn the heat to very low, and stir for about 3 minutes, or until the soup thickens slightly. Don't let it boil, or the egg yolks in the aioli will curdle. Season with salt and pepper.

Arrange the fish on heated soup plates and ladle over the broth. Pass the toasts at the table to spread with aioli and dip in the soup.

VARIATION

Keep the tomatoes separate—cook them into a concassée (see page 367) and make a pesto (see page 362). Make the broth as directed, but don't add the aioli. Ladle the soup into soup plates and top each serving with a swirl each of the hot tomato mixture, the pesto, and the aioli. The effect is colorful and the juxtaposition of the flavors is striking.

Creamy Seafood Cider Soup
with Fresh Herbs

The idea for this rich soup comes from a method popular in northern France and in Belgium for cooking eels in a broth that is finished with cream and thickened with egg yolks. The cream can be kept to a minimum and the egg yolks can be left out entirely. It is the abundance of fresh herbs, chopped and added at the last minute, that makes this soup a revelation.

MAKES 2 QUARTS OR 8 FIRST-COURSE SERVINGS

- 4 leeks, white part only, cleaned and thinly sliced (see page 293)
- 2 tablespoons butter
- 4 pounds whole fish such as red snapper, sea bass, red mullet cleaned, filleted, fillets skinned, heads and bones reserved, and fillets cut into 1-inch cubes
- Bouquet garni
- 5 cups hard cider
- 1/2 to 1 cup heavy cream
- 6 egg yolks (optional)
- 1 bunch parsley, preferably flat-leaf, large stems removed and leaves finely chopped at the last minute
- 1 tablespoon finely chopped fresh tarragon, chopped at the last minute
- 1 tablespoon finely chopped fresh mint, chopped at the last minute
- 1 tablespoon finely chopped fresh chives, chopped at the last minute
- 1 bunch sorrel, stemmed (optional) and finely chopped at the last minute
- Salt
- Pepper

In a pot, cook the leeks in the butter over low to medium heat, stirring regularly, for about 10 minutes, or until they soften but do not brown. Add the fish bones and heads, bouquet garni, and cider and simmer gently for 30 minutes. Remove from the heat and work the mixture through a large-mesh strainer or a food mill fitted with the coarse disk into a clean pot. If using the egg yolks, don't use an aluminum pot, or the egg yolks will turn gray.

Stir the cream into the strained broth. If using the egg yolks, in a bowl, whisk them for 1 minute, or until they are slightly pale, and then whisk in about one-third of the broth. Pour this mixture back into the rest of the broth, and put the pot over medium heat. Stir with a wooden spoon for about 3 minutes, or until the soup is silky and smooth and the tiny ripples turn into smooth waves. Don't let it boil.

Stir in all the herbs and the fish and season with salt and pepper. Reduce the heat to low—again, don't let the mixture boil—and stir for about 3 minutes, or until the fish is cooked and the flavor of the herbs is infused.

Brazilian Coconut-Peanut
Fish Soup

The idea for this soup comes from the Brazilian vatapa, a hearty seafood stew flavored with peanuts and coconut milk.

MAKES 2 QUARTS (8 FIRST-COURSE SERVINGS OR 6 MAIN-COURSE SERVINGS)

- 1 large onion, finely chopped
- 8 cloves garlic, finely chopped
- 2 tablespoons olive oil or vegetable oil
- 5 pounds whole fish such as sea bass, black bass, black fish (tautog), red mullet, red snapper, and/or sea bream, cleaned, filleted, bones and heads reserved, and fillets cut into 12 or 16 pieces total (2 pieces per serving)
- 6 tomatoes, coarsely chopped
- 1/2 cup creamy peanut butter made with only peanuts and salt
- One 15-ounce can unsweetened coconut milk
- 3 jalapeño chiles, seeded and finely chopped
- 5 tablespoons fresh lime juice
- Salt
- Pepper

In a pot, cook the onion and garlic in the oil over medium heat, stirring regularly, for about 10 minutes, or until the onion softens and is shiny but does not brown. Add the fish bones and heads, tomatoes, and 2 quarts water and simmer gently for about 30 minutes. Remove from the heat and work the mixture through a large-mesh strainer or a food mill fitted with the coarse disk into a clean pot. If you want a thinner consistency, strain it again through a fine-mesh strainer.

Season the fish pieces with salt and pepper. In a small bowl, work about 1 cup of the broth into the peanut butter, a little at a time, until the mixture is smooth and well combined. Add the peanut mixture to the broth along with the fish pieces, coconut milk, chiles, and lime juice. Simmer for 2 to 4 minutes, or until the fish is cooked. Season with salt and pepper.

Corn and Shrimp Soup

This soup combines two flavors, corn and poblano chiles, that go especially well together and with shrimp. To get the most flavor out of the shrimp, use shrimp with their heads and make the broth on page 124.

MAKES 1½ QUARTS OR 6 FIRST-COURSE SERVINGS

- 1 white or yellow onion, finely chopped
- 2 cloves garlic, minced
- 2 tablespoons olive oil
- 3 ears of corn
- 4 tomatoes
- 1 quart chicken broth or shrimp broth
- 2 jalapeño chiles, seeded and finely chopped, or 2 chipotle chiles, soaked in hot water for 30 minutes to soften if dried or rinsed if canned, seeded and chopped
- 2 poblano chiles, charred, peeled, and seeded (see page 321) and then chopped
- 1 bunch cilantro, large stems removed
- 1 pound medium to large shrimp, peeled and then deveined if desired
- 3 tablespoons fresh lime juice
- 1 cup heavy cream (optional)
- Salt
- Pepper

In a pot large enough to hold the soup, cook the onion and garlic in the oil over medium heat, stirring regularly, for about 10 minutes, or until the onion softens and is shiny but does not brown.

Meanwhile, cut off the kernels from the ears of corn. If you want the soup perfectly smooth, you will need to strain it, so there is no point in peeling the tomatoes. If you are leaving the soup with some texture, peel and seed the tomatoes. In both cases, chop them, coarse if you are straining and fine if you are not.

Add the corn, tomatoes, broth, and jalapeño and poblano chiles to the onions. Raise the heat to high and bring to a boil, stirring with a wooden spoon to make sure the corn does not scorch on the pot bottom. Reduce the heat to medium and simmer for about 20 minutes from the time the broth is at a simmer.

Chop the cilantro—coarse if you are straining, fine if you are not—and add it to the soup. Puree the soup with a blender (see precautions on page 42) until smooth. If you want your soup perfectly smooth and creamy, work it through a coarse-mesh strainer or a food mill fitted with the coarse disk and return it to the pot.

Bring the soup to a simmer over medium heat and add the shrimp, lime juice, and cream. Simmer for 2 minutes, or until shrimp are cooked through. Season with salt and pepper. Ladle into warmed soup bowls and serve.

Shrimp and Tomatillo Soup

Don't confuse tomatillos with green tomatoes. Tomatillos are related to gooseberries—they have the same paperlike husk—and are relatively small and bright green. They are delightfully sour, which makes them a perfect foil for chiles, cilantro, cheese, and sour cream, and are the base for most versions of Mexican salsa verde.

MAKES 1½ QUARTS OR 6 FIRST-COURSE SERVINGS

- 1 white or yellow onion
- 2 cloves garlic, minced
- 2 tablespoons olive oil or canola oil
- 1 chipotle chile, soaked in hot water for 30 minutes to soften if dried or rinsed if canned, seeded and chopped, or 2 jalapeño chiles, seeded and finely chopped
- 2 poblano chiles, charred, peeled, and seeded (see page 321) and then chopped
- 2 pounds fresh tomatillos, husks removed, or three 13-ounce cans tomatillos, drained
- 2 cups shrimp broth, chicken broth, or water
- 18 or 24 large shrimp, peeled and then deveined if desired
- Salt
- Pepper
- 3 corn tortillas, optional
- Vegetable oil for deep-frying
- 1 pint sour cream
- ½ pound mild cheese such as Monterey Jack or mild Cheddar, coarsely grated

In a pot large enough to hold the soup, cook the onion and garlic in the oil over medium heat, stirring regularly, for about 10 minutes, or until the onion softens and is shiny but does not brown.

Add the chiles to the onion. If using fresh tomatillos, cut them in half before you add them to the pot. If using canned tomatillos, add them whole. Add the broth, cover, and simmer for 10 minutes for canned tomatillos or 15 minutes for fresh tomatillos, or until the tomatillos are completely soft and turn to mush when you stir them.

Puree the soup with a blender (see precautions on page 42) until smooth. If you want your soup perfectly smooth and creamy, work it through coarse-mesh strainer or a food mill fitted with the coarse disk and return it to the same pot.

Bring the soup to a simmer over medium heat, add the shrimp, and simmer for about 3 minutes, or until shrimp are cooked through. Season with salt and pepper.

To make the fried tortilla strips, cut 3 tortillas in half, and then cut each half on the diagonal into strips 1/3 inch wide. Pour vegetable oil to a depth of 2 inches into a heavy saucepan and heat over high heat until ripples are visible on the surface, about 375°F on a deep-frying thermometer. (The oil should not come more than halfway up the sides of the pan.) The oil is ready if when you drop in a tortilla strip, it stays on the surface and is immediately surrounded with bubbles. Add half of the tortilla strips and fry for about 1 minute, or until pale brown. Keep in mind that the strips continue to darken after you take them out of the oil. Using a spider or slotted spoon, transfer the strips to paper towels to drain. Repeat with the remaining strips.

Ladle the soup into warmed soup bowls and pass the tortilla strips, sour cream, and cheese at the table.

Thai Hot-and-Spicy Shrimp Soup

Once you track down the somewhat exotic ingredients for this soup—they keep in the freezer for months—this soup can be made in minutes. Best of all, it doesn't require broth, although shrimp broth (see page 124) would give it a wonderful flavor.

MAKES 1 1/2 QUARTS OR 6 FIRST-COURSE SERVINGS

- **2 green or red Thai chiles or 4 jalapeño chiles**
- **3 cloves garlic, finely chopped**
- **2 shallots, minced**
- **2 slices frozen or dried galangal root or fresh ginger, 1/4 inch thick**
- **4 kaffir lime leaves, cut into fine shreds**
- **1 stalk lemongrass, white bulb part only, tough outer layer discarded and very thinly sliced**
- **1 pound large shrimp, peeled and then deveined if desired**
- **1 small bunch cilantro, large stems removed**
- **1/4 cup fish sauce, or more to taste**
- **Juice of 3 limes**
- **Pepper**

In a pot, combine 6 cups water, the chiles, garlic, shallots, galangal, lime leaves, and lemongrass, bring to a simmer, and simmer gently for 12 minutes.

Add the shrimp and simmer for 1 minute. Add the cilantro, fish sauce, and lime juice and simmer for 1 minute, or until the shrimp are cooked. Season with pepper. Taste for salt and add more fish sauce—it is very salty and will contribute flavor—until the salt level is right.

HOW TO MAKE A FLAVOR BASE FOR THAI SOUPS

1. Here are Thai chiles, dried galangal soaking to soften, lemongrass, and kaffir lime leaves.

2. Chop the ingredients separately.

3. Complete initial chopping.

4. Chop all again until very finely chopped.

5. Cook the aromatic ingredients in oil in a pot over medium heat.

6. Add liquids such as broth, coconut milk, and fish sauce and simmer chicken, shrimp, or similar ingredients in the liquid.

CHICKEN SOUPS

The importance of chicken soup to our well-being is widely appreciated. Chicken soup is a medium for just about any flavor or texture. It can be spicy or mild, substantial or light, creamy or as clear as consommé.

In its most basic form, chicken soup is chicken broth with pieces of chicken in it, either the chicken from the parts used to make the broth or, in a more extravagant preparation, raw chicken cooked in the strained broth. For someone feeling sickly, this is perhaps as elaborate as the soup should get, but most of us usually crave something more robust.

Chicken soup can be given a national or regional identity by adding vegetables, herbs, or aromatic ingredients at various stages of simmering. It can be made more substantial by adding pasta, rice, matzo balls, or beans, and will take on a creamy richness when finished with coconut milk, cream, or a swirl of butter. It can also be finished with spices cooked in butter, pureed herbs, a sprinkle of cheese, or a dollop of sour cream.

Mexican-Style Tomatillo and Chicken Soup

The flavors of this soup are inspired by the enchiladas with green sauce found in virtually every Mexican restaurant in Southern California. The acidic tang of the tomatillos provides a perfect balance to the richness of the sour cream, chicken, and cheese.

MAKES 1¹/₂ QUARTS (6 FIRST-COURSE OR LIGHT MAIN-COURSE SERVINGS)

> Four 8-ounce boneless, skinless chicken breasts
> Salt
> Pepper
> 1 onion, finely chopped
> 3 cloves garlic, minced
> 3 tablespoons olive oil
> 1 pound fresh tomatillos, husks removed and coarsely chopped, or two 13-cans tomatillos, drained and coarsely chopped
> 2 jalapeño chiles, seeded and finely chopped, or more to taste
> 3 cups chicken broth or water
> 1 bunch cilantro, large stems removed and leaves finely chopped
> Sour cream and grated Monterey Jack cheese for serving

Cut the chicken on the diagonal into narrow 2-inch-long strips. Season with salt and pepper and reserve in the refrigerator.

In a pot, cook the onion and garlic in the oil over medium heat, stirring regularly, for about 10 minutes, or until the onion softens and is shiny but does not brown. Add the tomatillos, chiles, and broth and simmer gently for 10 minutes.

If you want to serve a pureed soup, puree it with a blender (see precautions on page 42) or work it through a food mill fitted with the medium disk and return it to the pot.

Bring the soup to a simmer, add the cilantro and chicken, and simmer for 3 to 4 minutes, or until the chicken is cooked. Season with salt and pepper. Pass the sour cream and cheese at the table.

Mexican-Style Chile and Chicken Soup

This exact recipe does not exist in the Mexican repertoire, but the flavors and methods produce a robust soup that has the character of many of Mexico's best soups and moles. Feel free to experiment with different dried chiles, as they each have their own delightful subtleties. If you get ahold of chilhuacle negro chiles—they look like wizened black bell peppers—use them. They are among the most flavorful and subtle of all the chiles.

MAKES 1¹/₂ QUARTS OR 6 FIRST-COURSE SERVINGS

> 2 ears of corn
> 6 assorted mild dried chiles such as guajillo, mulatto, ancho, chilhuacle negro, and/or pasilla, in any combination, soaked in hot water for 30 minutes to soften, seeded and coarsely chopped
> 1 or 2 hot dried chiles such as chipotle or pasilla de Oaxaca, soaked in hot water for 30 minutes to soften, seeded and coarsely chopped
> 2 poblano chiles, charred, peeled, and seeded (see page 321) and then chopped
> 5 cups chicken broth
> 2 teaspoons dried oregano
> 2 cups (¹/₂-inch) cubed cooked chicken or 2 raw boneless, skinless chicken breast halves, cut into ¹/₂-inch cubes
> 1 cup heavy cream (optional)
> Salt
> Pepper
> Sour cream and lime wedges for serving

Cut off the kernels from the ears of corn and then scrape the cobs with the back of the knife to extract the milky residue. In a pot large enough to hold the soup, combine the corn, chiles, and the oregano and simmer for 15 minutes, or until the corn kernels are soft when you bite into one.

Puree the soup with a blender (see precautions on page 42) until smooth. If you want your soup perfectly smooth and creamy, work it through a strainer or a food mill fitted with the fine disk and return it to the same pot.

Bring the soup to a simmer and add the cream; add the chicken. If the chicken is cooked, simmer just until heated through. For raw chicken, simmer for about 4 minutes, or until the chicken is cooked. Season with salt and pepper. Pass the sour cream and lime wedges at the table.

Thai-Style Coconut–Green Curry Chicken Soup

Thai cooks make curry pastes by slowly grinding herbs and aromatic ingredients in a mortar. Since making even a small amount can take as long as an hour, many cooks buy canned curry pastes, which never deliver the headiness of freshly made. To avoid this dilemma, simmer the same aromatic ingredients in broth and leave them chopped, sliced, or whole.

Thai soups and curries get their character from lemon- or lime-flavored ingredients, such as lemongrass and kaffir lime leaves or rind (regular lime zest can be used as a substitute); galangal, which looks a little like ginger but tastes like pine resin; chiles; cilantro; coconut milk; fish sauce for savor and saltiness; and lime juice or tamarind for tang. While some of these ingredients may require mail order or a trip to an Asian market, they will keep in the freezer for months.

MAKES 1¹/₂ QUARTS OR 6 FIRST-COURSE SERVINGS

  1 quart chicken broth

  3 shallots, minced

  5 cloves garlic, minced

  2 slices fresh, frozen, or dried galangal, ¹/₄ inch thick (optional)

  2 to 4 Thai chiles or 4 to 8 jalapeño chiles, seeded and finely chopped

  1 stalk lemongrass, white bulb part only, tough outer layer discarded and very thinly sliced

  3 kaffir lime leaves or zest of 1 lime, in strips

  ¹/₄ cup fish sauce, or more to taste

  Juice of 3 limes

  One 15-ounce can unsweetened coconut milk

  1 small bunch cilantro, large stems removed and leaves chopped

  1¹/₂ cups (¹/₂-inch) cubed cooked chicken or 2 raw boneless, skinless chicken breast halves, cut into ¹/₂-inch cubes

In a pot, combine the broth, shallots, garlic, galangal, chiles, lemongrass, and lime leaves and bring to a simmer. Simmer gently for 15 minutes.

Add the fish sauce, lime juice, coconut milk, cilantro, and chicken. If using cooked chicken, simmer for about 1 minute, or until the liquid is piping hot and the chicken is heated through. If using raw chicken, simmer for about 4 minutes, or until the chicken is cooked. Taste for salt and add more fish sauce—it is very salty and will contribute flavor—until the salt level is right.

Chicken, Tomato, and Tarragon Soup

When it is still summer and you have perfect tomatoes, this soup can do without the onion, bacon, and cream. But when there is a nip in the air, the bacon and cream will give it welcome substance. A slice of toasted bread, rubbed with a little garlic and placed in the bowl before ladling in the soup, makes a nice counterpoint by providing a contrasting texture.

MAKES 1¹/₂ QUARTS OR 6 FIRST-COURSE SERVINGS

  1 onion, finely chopped (optional)

  3 slices thick-cut bacon, cut into ¹/₄-inch dice (optional)

  1 quart chicken broth

  1¹/₂ pounds very ripe tomatoes, peeled and seeded (see page 85), and finely chopped

  1 cup (¹/₂ inch) cubed cooked chicken or 1 raw boneless, skinless chicken breast half, cut into ¹/₂-inch cubes

  1 cup heavy cream

  Leaves from 6 sprigs tarragon, chopped at the last minute

  Salt

  Pepper

If you are making the cool-weather version, in a pot, cook the onion and bacon over medium heat, stirring regularly, for about 10 minutes, or until the bacon just begins to get crispy. Add the broth and bring to a simmer. If you are making the warm-weather version, skip the onion and bacon step and just bring the broth to a simmer.

Add the tomatoes and simmer gently for about 15 minutes. Add the chicken, cream, and tarragon. If using cooked chicken, simmer for about 1 minute, or until the liquid is piping hot and the chicken is heated through. If using raw chicken, simmer for about 4 minutes, or until the chicken is cooked. Season with salt and pepper.

MEAT SOUPS

Virtually any meat stew can be converted into a soup by adding more liquid. Some dishes based on poached meats, such as New England boiled dinner and the French pot-au-feu (see page 38), are actually soups and solid dishes at the same time. (For more ideas, see under the specific meat and then poaching.)

Chinese Hot-and-Sour Soup

When made with the best ingredients, this soup is redolent of mushrooms, the pepper is aromatic but not biting, and the soup has a brothlike consistency, rather than gelatinous from too much cornstarch.

Traditionally, this soup is made with pork and pork broth, but any meat and any broth will work. In fact, it is particularly good with duck. For the best results, look for dried shiitake mushrooms with caps that have a network of fissures revealing white flesh. Depending on their size—and size seems to have little effect on flavor—these mushrooms will run anywhere from expensive to very expensive. Fortunately, a few go a long way, and it is worth buying a lot because they will keep for years. Some of the ingredients in this soup—the tree ears, tiger lily stems, and tofu—are more for texture than flavor and can be left out. I call specifically for Japanese tofu because I prefer its texture. If you are using raw meat, make sure it is from a tender cut, as tough cuts won't have time to tenderize. Use the finest wine vinegar you can find (sherry is often the best bet), and be sure to use dark Asian sesame oil made from toasted seeds (the Japanese brands are consistently superior). The cold-pressed sesame oil sold in health-food stores doesn't have the flavor you need.

MAKES 1 QUART OR 4 FIRST-COURSE SERVINGS

12 medium (about 3 ounces) dried or 10 ounces fresh shiitake mushrooms

1/2 cup dried tree ears (also called tree fungus or black fungus), optional

20 dried tiger lily stems (optional)

1 quart meat or poultry broth, preferably brown

1 cup (1/2-inch) cubed tender raw or cooked meat such as chicken, pork, duck, or beef (about 1/2 pound by weight)

3 tablespoons soy sauce

1 teaspoon Asian sesame oil

1 tablespoon cornstarch

One-half 10-ounce package firm Japanese tofu, cut into 1/3-inch cubes

1/4 cup sherry vinegar or other good wine vinegar, or more to taste

1 tablespoon freshly ground pepper

1 egg, beaten

1 green onion, white and 3 inches of the green, very thinly sliced

Salt

If using dried mushrooms, put them in a small heatproof bowl with boiling water to cover and soak for 1 hour. (You can also soak them overnight in cold water.) In separate bowls, soak the tree ears and lily stems in hot water for 10 minutes or until softened.

Lift the shiitake out of their soaking water and squeeze them, releasing the liquid into the bowl; discard liquid. Cut off the stems (save them for adding to broths) and slice the caps. Put the slices in a pot.

Drain the tree ears and lily stems; pull the tree ears into small pieces, discarding any hard parts, and pull the stems into shreds. Add to the pot with the mushrooms, and pour in the broth. Bring to a gentle simmer and add the meat. In a small bowl or cup, whisk together the soy sauce, sesame oil, and cornstarch until smooth, and then whisk the mixture into the soup. Add the tofu, vinegar, and pepper. With the soup still at a gentle simmer, and while stirring constantly, add the egg in a thin, steady stream, pouring it in a circle. You want it to set in thin wisps throughout the broth. Add the green onion and season with salt. If you added raw meat, make sure the soup simmers for at least 3 minutes before serving.

1. Place the dried shiitake mushrooms in a bowl and add hot water to soften them. Separately, soak the tree ears in hot water to soften them.

2. Soak the tiger lily stems in hot water to soften them.

3. Slice or quarter the mushrooms.

4. Cut the tofu into cubes.

5. Pull the lily stems into shreds.

6. Separate the tree ears into smaller pieces and pull off any hard parts, especially at the base of the stem.

7. Slice the green onion.

8. Simmer together the ingredients.

9. Add the beaten egg in a thin, steady stream, pouring it in a circle.

Oxtail Soup

Humble oxtails provide a tasty, gelatinous broth that can be served with the boned meat or with whole rounds of oxtails—guests will have to pick them up, since getting at the meat with a fork is nearly impossible. This soup requires no effort other than tracking down the oxtails, but it does take about 5 hours to cook. For an ultimate version, use beef broth or brown chicken broth. You can also use the rich broth and meat to make a terrine (following).

MAKES 3 QUARTS OR 6–8 MAIN-COURSE SERVINGS

> 5 pounds oxtails, cut into rounds
>
> Salt
>
> Pepper
>
> 2 tablespoons vegetable oil
>
> 2 tablespoons butter
>
> 1 onion, coarsely chopped
>
> 2 carrots, peeled and coarsely chopped
>
> 1 cup dry sherry or Madiera
>
> 4 quarts brown chicken broth or beef broth or
>   2 quarts each broth and water, or as needed
>
> Bouquet garni

Season the oxtails with salt and pepper. In a large pot, heat the oil over high heat. Working in batches so they brown well and don't steam, add the oxtails and brown well on all sides. This will take about 8 minutes for each batch. Take the oxtails out of the pot, and pour out the burnt oil. Let the pot cool for a minute or two.

Return the pot to medium heat and melt the butter. Add the onion and carrots and cook, stirring regularly, for about 10 minutes, or until the onion softens and is shiny. Add the sherry and cook until reduced by half. Return the oxtails to the pot and add enough broth just to cover them. Nestle the bouquet garni in the center of the pot and bring to a gentle simmer. Cover partially and simmer, skimming off the fat and froth every 20 minutes or so, for 5 hours.

As the liquid sinks below the level of the oxtails, add more to cover by about 1 inch. Check to see if the oxtails are done by taking out one of the larger pieces and pulling at the meat with your fingers. It should come away with absolutely no resistance. If it clings, simmer for another hour and test again.

At this point, you can season the soup with salt and pepper and serve everyone a few rounds of oxtail with the broth. Alternatively, carefully lift out the oxtails, strain the vegetables out of the soup, and then return the oxtails to the soup. Or, for the most refined version, you can lift out the oxtails, strain the vegetables out of the soup, and then pull the meat off the bones in shreds and return the meat to the soup. If you end up with less than 3 quarts, add broth or water to make up the difference. Season with salt and pepper as needed.

OXTAIL TERRINE

Strain the soup, take the meat off the oxtails, finely shred, and return the meat to the strained soup. Don't dilute the soup with additional broth or water. Measure out 1 quart soup and stir in 2 tablespoons finely chopped fresh flat-leaf parsley. Season with salt and pepper. Pour the mixture into a 1-quart rectangular porcelain terrine and cover and chill overnight. The next day, serve the terrine, sliced, with cornichons and mustard on the side. You will get about 12 first-course servings.

Indian Lentil Soup

Indian cooks are the masters of beans and lentils, and they draw on an overwhelming variety: pink, orange, bright red, and black. While Western cooks often enhance the flavor of bean and lentil soups with lamb, pork, or other meats, Indian cooks typically rely on spices and often on ghee, clarified butter with a wonderful butterscotch flavor (see page 341). Yogurt is often used in combination with other liquids and wet ingredients, such as coconut milk or even cream. The best approach is to simmer the lentils with spices, onions, water and, if you like, tomatoes—lentils absorb about triple their volume in liquid—then add whatever liquid suits you to bring the soup to the consistency you like. You can leave the lentils whole or puree them. If you want a fine, delicate soup, strain it through a fine-mesh strainer. A last-minute addition of chopped cilantro in a spicy soup balances the heat, while something else acidic, such as lime juice or vinegar, enhances a soup containing tomatoes.

1 onion, chopped

2 cloves garlic, minced

2 jalapeño chiles, seeded and minced, or 1 chipotle chile, soaked in hot water for 30 minutes to soften, seeded and minced

2 tablespoons butter

2 tablespoons grated fresh ginger, or 2 teaspoons ground

2 teaspoons ground cumin

1 tablespoon ground coriander

$1^1/_2$ cups red, pink, or yellow lentils, picked over for stones and grit and rinsed

6 tomatoes, peeled, seeded, and chopped, or 3 cups seeded and chopped canned tomatoes

12 curry leaves, tied into a bundle with string (optional)

1 tablespoon black mustard seeds (optional)

2 tablespoons ghee, or more to taste (optional)

$^1/_4$ cup fresh lemon juice, or more to taste

2 tablespoons chopped fresh cilantro

Salt

In a pot, cook the onion, garlic, and chiles in butter over medium heat, stirring regularly, for about 10 minutes, or until the onion softens but does not brown. Add the ginger, cumin, and coriander and cook for 1 minute.

Add the lentils, tomatoes, curry leaves, and 2 cups water and simmer gently for about 30 minutes, or until the lentils are soft. Remove and discard the curry leaves. Puree the soup with a blender (see precautions on page 42) until smooth.

Bring the soup to a gentle simmer. Meanwhile, in a small skillet, cook the mustard seeds in the ghee over medium-high for 1 minute, or until the seeds crackle. Stir the ghee mixture, lemon juice, and cilantro into the soup. Season with salt and simmer for 1 minute. If the soup is too thick, thin it with a little water before serving.

Basic Bean Soup

You can make this soup using virtually any bean, but the cooking times will vary accordingly; some beans cook faster than others, a phenomenon that results more from the age of the bean than the variety (see page 330). The secret to this soup is the smoke from the ham bone, ham hocks, or bacon. If you don't have all three, just use more of the one(s) you do have.

2 cups dried beans, soaked for 4 hours in cold water to cover

3 quarts broth or water and more as needed

Bouquet garni

1 ham bone or 2 ham hocks

2 teaspoons salt

$^1/_2$ pound bacon, preferably in one piece

1 large onion, peeled and chopped

2 garlic cloves, peeled and chopped

1 cup dry sherry

Tabasco sauce

Sour cream

Drain the beans and put them in a pot with the broth, bouquet garni, ham or hocks, salt, bacon, onion, and garlic and simmer, covered, until the beans are soft, about 2 hours. Add the sherry as soon as the beans begin to soften. Keep adding liquid as needed to keep the beans covered. Take the ham bone, hocks, and bacon out of the soup and pull the ham away from the bone, chop or shred into bite-size pieces, and put it back in the soup. Pull the rind away from the ham hocks and discard rind. Pull the meat away and add it to the soup. Slice the bacon into 8 slices. If you like, puree the soup for a moment with an immersion blender (see precautions on page 42) to give it a little richer consistency. Ladle the soup into serving bowls and place a slice of bacon on top of each one. Pass the Tabasco and sour cream at the table.

SALADS

Salads have come a long way from the days when they mostly meant a plate of chopped iceberg lettuce at the start of a meal. A generation ago we had access to three or four kinds of greens, but we now can find dozens. And today a salad is as likely to be a main course, or even a course served after the main.

Most salads fall into a few convenient categories. Green salads are simple mixtures of greens or a single green. There are also garnished green salads, in which chicken, grilled tuna, or a similar item is added to convert the salad into something more substantial. So-called simple salads showcase a single ingredient, such as carrots or beets, tossed with a sauce. What the French call American salads are made from various ingredients cut into pieces and tossed with a variety of dressings. Finally, composed salads are those in which two or more ingredients are presented separately on a single plate or platter.

GREEN SALADS

A simple green salad, made by tossing seasonal greens with olive oil and vinegar, can be served as a light opening to a meal, or after the main course, a European habit that many Americans are adopting. Some people find a first-course green salad a little austere, preferring the addition of something savory to make it more substantial. When served after a main course, though, the salad should be made with only greens, as the idea is to lighten the effect of a heavy meal, not add to it. Don't ask your guests if they want salad at this point in the meal. They are likely to say no, either because they are unaccustomed to the idea, or they are so full they don't want to eat another bite. But a green salad after the main course actually has the amazing effect of making people feel less full and more relaxed.

CHOOSING THE GREENS

In recent years, ready-made combinations of greens are often sold as mesclun mix. The word *mesclun* (pronounced mis-kla with the "a" pronounced as in "and") comes from the Provençal tradition of assembling salads from wild greens. Unfortunately, the makers of many of these contemporary mixes have gotten carried away, including such a dizzying assortment of greens that the mix ends up tasting too much like generic weeds. It is far wiser to select a few perfect greens and make your own combination, or simply to limit your green salads to a single green. A salad of perfect hearts of romaine is far more appealing than a profusion of unrecognizable leaves.

With so many greens grown in greenhouses, most types are available year-round. But fall and winter salads are traditionally made from the bitter greens of the chicory family, such as endive, frisée, and radicchio, while warm-weather greens might include basil, arugula (rocket), and nasturtium leaves or flowers.

A Few Favorite Greens

Arugula: Only in America is this spicy leaf called arugula. In England it is rocket, and in Italy it is sold as rucola. Nearly unknown in the United States as recently as the mid-1980s, it is now found virtually everywhere and has an addictive quality that makes it ideal in summer salads. It is delicious combined with an equal number of basil leaves.

Basil: Most of us think of basil as an herb, and use it sparingly to flavor salads or sauces or to put on pasta. But unless it is too mature and thus tough, it makes a wonderful summer salad green, especially combined with arugula, and is a great backdrop to such summery ingredients as tomatoes.

Belgian endive: Crisp, cool, and gently bitter, long, golden endive leaves, part of the chicory group, make an elegant green salad when used alone or in combination with other greens. They are delicious with mustard, citrus fruits such as orange or grapefruit, and with nuts or nut oils.

Bibb lettuce: Somewhat hard to find, this lettuce is sold in small heads that reveal fragile yellow-green leaves when broken apart. A Bibb lettuce salad is lovely to look at and light and refreshing to eat.

Boston lettuce: This has become one of the most popular greens, and even when fully grown, has delicate outer leaves, reducing waste to a minimum. A salad made with Boston lettuce alone is a perfect green salad.

Dandelion greens: Domesticated dandelion greens tend to be tough and very bitter, and are best used for cooking. The wild dandelion greens that show up in fancy markets in spring are younger, more tender, and not as sharp tasting. The long, jagged-edged leaves are a wonderful foil for strongly flavored foods such as sautéed sardines (see page 145).

Escarole: Another member of the chicory family, escarole is one of the most bitter greens. Be sure to cut off and discard any dark green parts, which tend to be tough and just too bitter. The pale green and yellow leaves are great dressed with a full-flavored vinaigrette, ideally one with a lot of mustard in it.

Frisée: A member of the chicory family, frisée (the word means "curled" in French) looks like a burst of sunshine, with a bright yellow center surrounded by green. Its delicate bitterness is a delightful accent to savory ingredients such as bacon. For salads, discard the hard, very bitter dark green outer leaves, and use only the pale green and yellow leaves. Frisée is sometimes sold as ricchia, its Italian name.

Iceberg lettuce: After decades of being unfashionable, iceberg lettuce is making a comeback. No lettuce is as cool and crunchy and nothing is better on a hamburger. Iceberg has a neutral refreshing flavor.

Mâche: This tiny, delicate green, also known as lamb's lettuce, is a standard winter salad item in France, where it is sold everywhere. In the United States, it seems to appear only in fancier groceries and is usually underdeveloped, so you don't get much for your money. It may be the most delicate green there is—it often has the faint scent of roses—so don't serve it with an aggressive dressing.

Romaine lettuce: De rigueur for a Caesar salad, romaine is almost always sold overgrown, with huge, tough outer leaves. In an ideal world, we would throw out the outer leaves and eat only the delicate, crisp yellow hearts. But most of us are put off by this kind of extravagance, especially since we no longer keep pigs or rabbits who can feast on the discards. Some stores sell hearts of romaine in little plastic bags—a perfect solution. Otherwise, throw out as much as you can bear.

Radicchio: This deep ruby Italian "green" is somewhat tough and bitter, so it is usually best in combination with more delicate greens. It always adds a delightful color to a simple salad. Round heads are the most common, but the elongated Treviso variety, which looks like Belgian endive except for being scarlet, is becoming more widely available.

Red leaf lettuce: This green with red-maroon fringed leaves has large, floppy leaves and a mild flavor.

Spinach: Americans are relatively new to eating raw spinach. It is extremely mild in a salad and needs to be accented with another, more flavorful green.

Watercress: Nearly always available and easy to clean, watercress makes a satisfying salad. It does not, however, mix well with other greens, so it is best to use it alone, with a few nuts or bacon for contrast.

PREPARING SALAD GREENS

A frequent mistake even the most accomplished cooks make is cutting salad greens into pieces that are too small. A better system is to tear the leaves gently with your fingers into manageable-sized pieces—pieces that won't end up hanging off a plate. There is nothing wrong with using a knife and fork to eat a salad, so don't aim to serve only bite-sized pieces. Besides, small pieces wilt more quickly and then their natural beauty in the bowl is lost.

Keep in mind that virtually all salad greens are fragile. If handled roughly, they crack in such a way that the vinaigrette gets into the leaves and makes them soggy. On the other hand, there is nothing worse than a sandy salad, so it's important to be thorough. Fill a large bowl with cold water, add the greens, and let them sit for a few minutes. Then, with your fingers splayed, lift them out and put them into an empty bowl. Feel the bottom of the first bowl. If there is sand, rinse it out, replace the water, and soak the leaves again. Two soakings is usually enough, but some greens—arugula is often a culprit—require three.

A lettuce spinner is good for drying greens, but don't get carried away. If you spin it too fast, the centrifugal force will crush the greens against the spinner's walls. Instead, spin gently, pour out any liquid released, toss the greens slightly in the spinner bowl, and spin again. Repeat several times until you no longer find any water after spinning. If you are not using the greens right away, wrap them gently in moist kitchen towels—don't use paper towels, which tear and stick to the greens—and keep them in the crisper of the refrigerator.

VINAIGRETTES AND SALAD SAUCES

Many cooks are needlessly intimidated when it comes to dressing a salad. Most of the time there is no need to make a vinaigrette. Instead, you just pour over some vinegar, sprinkle on some salt and pepper, and then pour over some oil. If you are unsure of the amounts, you can measure them, but there is no need to emulsify the oil and vinegar for a simple salad. A traditional vinaigrette is emulsified like a mayonnaise—the

oil gets distributed on a microscopic level in the vinegar—but instead of an egg yolk being the emulsifier, mustard is. However, the extra virgin olive oil that most of us like on our salads clashes with mustard. Also, extra virgin olive oil can turn bitter when beaten with a whisk. If you want to make a classic mustard vinaigrette, just whisk oil into a combination of mustard, salt, pepper, and wine vinegar until the mixture comes together. Vinaigrette is a less stable emulsion than mayonnaise and usually separates if you keep it overnight. But it is so easy to make, there is little point in doing it in advance.

Basic Vinaigrette

It's always convenient to know how to make a simple vinaigrette. This version can be used for virtually any combination of salad greens. If you're dressing bitter greens, consider replacing half the canola oil with a nut oil such as hazelnut oil or walnut oil. Make sure your nut oils are made from roasted nuts to prevent rancidity. If you're mixing spicy greens such as arugula and basil, replace the canola oil with extra virgin olive oil and leave out the mustard.

HOW TO MAKE BASIC VINAIGRETTE

1. Whisk vinegar into mustard and season with salt and pepper.

2. Whisk oil into mustard/vinegar mixture.

3. Gradually increase the amount of oil added until the vinaigrette thickens.

4. Finish vinaigrette by whisking until creamy.

MAKES ABOUT 5 TABLESPOONS, ENOUGH FOR A GREEN SALAD FOR 4

> 2 teaspoons Dijon mustard
> $1/2$ teaspoon fine salt
> $1/4$ teaspoon freshly ground black pepper
> 1 tablespoon red or white wine vinegar
> 3 tablespoons canola oil, peanut oil, or grape seed oil

In the salad bowl, whisk together the mustard, salt, pepper, and vinegar. Whisk in the oil about 1 teaspoon at a time. If you want to put the salad in the bowl ahead of time, place 2 long spoons in the bowl, crossing them so they will hold the greens above the vinaigrette. Place the greens on top of the spoons until you are ready to serve.

Toss just before serving.

VINAIGRETTE VARIATIONS

Chopped shallots, half of a crushed garlic clove, or an herb such as chervil, tarragon, or chives is often welcome in a vinaigrette. You can use cream or a vegetable puree, such as garlic puree, as an emulsifier in place of the mustard. An egg yolk will also pull the vinegar and oil together in an emulsion, but technically the sauce then becomes a mayonnaise. Lemon or lime juice can replace the vinegar.

Creamy Vinaigrette

This vinaigrette is lovely on vegetables and greens. The acidity of the lime juice or vinegar causes the cream to thicken to just the right consistency.

MAKES 1/2 CUP

> 3 tablespoons fresh lime juice or red or white wine vinegar or sherry wine vinegar
>
> 1/2 teaspoon fine salt
>
> Pepper
>
> 5 tablespoons heavy cream or crème fraîche
>
> 2 teaspoons chopped fresh herbs such as chives, tarragon, parsley, or chervil (optional)

In a small bowl, whisk together the lime juice, salt, and pepper to taste. Whisk in the cream and herbs. Let the herbs infuse in the sauce for at least 20 minutes before serving.

SERVING SALADS

One of the nicest familial rituals is to toss the salad at the dining table. Always use a bowl at least twice as large as needed for the greens so there is plenty of room to toss. Serve the salad on plates, which leaves excess vinaigrette in the bottom of the bowl, instead of on the salad. Restaurants in the United States have the odd habit of serving salads in individual bowls, with the idea that the diner should eat the salad directly out of the bowl. A better system, used in Europe, is to serve a plate and the bowl of salad on the side, so the diner can lift the salad out of the bowl, leaving extra vinaigrette behind. Whatever you do, don't toss the salad with any acidic ingredients—vinegar, citrus juices—until just before serving. Such acids cause green leaves to wilt and green vegetables, such as green beans, to turn gray.

VINEGARS AND OILS

The most important components in any salad are the acidic elements (usually vinegar) and the oil or fat. Extra virgin olive oil is usually the favorite oil and has many nuances depending on where it was made, what kinds of olives were used, the age of the olive trees, how ripe the olives were when they were pressed into oil, and the age of the oil itself. Because of the antioxidants extra virgin olive oil contains, it doesn't turn rancid as quickly as other oils. While very fine oils are the price of a good bottle of Burgundy, even the inexpensive brands found at the supermarket are of excellent quality, especially considering that a generation ago extra virgin olive oil was almost impossible to find in the United States.

Where most cooks go wrong is with the vinegar. First, it is imperative to use wine vinegar and not distilled white vinegar, which is often made from wood, corn, or rye and has an aggressive chemical taste. Good wine vinegar is hard to find, so unless you make your own, you will need to experiment with different brands. The best plain white wine vinegar is champagne vinegar. Sherry vinegar was of higher quality in the past than it is now, but more expensive long-aged brands are still among the best vinegars you can buy. Vinaigre de Banyuls, a vinegar made from the French portlike Banyuls, is of consistently very high quality. Balsamic vinegar ranges from the inexpensive bottles found at the supermarket to authentic traditionally made balsamic vinegar that costs a thousand dollars a liter. One trick for improving inexpensive store-bought balsamic vinegar is to boil it down to half its volume. Cider vinegar varies considerably in quality and can be aggressive, but a good artisan cider vinegar can be delicious.

Homemade Vinegar

The best way to ensure a supply of wine vinegar that is better than almost anything you can buy is to make your own. A small oak barrel and a little bit of living vinegar, or vinegar mother, is enough to get started. Begin by putting about a cup of mother in the barrel and adding a cup of leftover red wine. Cover the bunghole on top of the barrel with a towel—don't use the stopper, since the bacteria that make vinegar require air—and keep it in a warm place, next to a hot water heater, perhaps. After a couple of weeks, add 2 cups of wine. Wait another couple of weeks and add another 2 cups of wine. Continue in this way until the barrel is three-fourths full. (Don't fill the barrel all the way or the wine won't have access to enough air.) Depending on the temperature, the vinegar should be ready to use 2 weeks after you add the last of the wine. Tap off a few cups at a time and continue to add bottle ends to the barrel. As the vinegar matures in the barrel, it will develop a more complex flavor. Never drain off all the vinegar. Just keep tapping the barrel whenever you need vinegar, and replacing the vinegar with wine.

Infused Vinegars and Oils

It is easy to infuse herbs, aromatic ingredients such as garlic, truffles, dried porcini mushrooms, fruits, or citrus zests in your favorite vinegar to come up with different flavors. For example, raspberry vinegar is not made from raspberry wine, but instead by soaking raspberries in wine vinegar. Tarragon vinegar is one of the best types to have around and is easy to make: just cram a few sprigs of fresh tarragon into your bottle of white wine vinegar.

Oils can also be infused with herbs, such as thyme, rosemary, or marjoram. But remember that an herb infusion can distract from the subtleties of a particularly fine oil.

Nut Oils

Nut oils are delicious in vinaigrettes, mayonnaises, and even used alone as a sauce. Keep in mind that they are usually highly perishable, however, so that even the oil in unopened bottles is sometimes rancid. To avoid this, buy oils that are made from roasted nuts. The roasting accentuates the nutty flavor and extends the shelf life. For salads, nut oils can be combined with as much as $3/4$ cup canola oil, and the flavor of the nut oil will still shine through. When you are not using nut oils, keep them in the freezer.

HOW MUCH LETTUCE TO USE

If you are serving a salad as a first course or after a main course, you will need a couple of handfuls of leaves per serving. (For main courses, figure on about 3 handfuls.) One large head of lettuce, such as red leaf or Boston, is about right for 4 servings. For a combination of lettuces—such as Belgian endive, radicchio, and arugula—plan on a bunch of each for 4 servings. When buying escarole or frisée, look at the heads to gauge how much is actually usable. Since frisée, escarole, and other bitter greens are often best served in combination with other greens, buy 1 head of the bitter green and 1 small head of a milder green. Here are some possible greens combinations for salads to serve 4:

Bitter or Spicy Green Salad

1 Belgian endive, yellow leaves from 1 head escarole, or yellow and pale green leaves from 1 head frisée

1 bunch arugula

1 head round radicchio, the size of a small fist, or 1 small head Treviso

Mild Green Salad

1 head Boston lettuce or red leaf lettuce, 6 miniature heads Bibb lettuce, or 2 heads romaine lettuce, outer leaves removed

Summer Salad

2 bunches arugula

Leaves from 1 bunch basil

1 handful of nasturtium leaves or flowers (optional)

GARNISHED GREEN SALADS

The idea of adding savory ingredients to a green salad is a great way of lightening the effect of rich meats and seafood. Garnished salads can be served as first courses or main courses, depending on the amount of the greens and the garnishes, but as already noted, they should never be served after the main course, when the body wants relief from rich, savory foods. To make a garnished green salad, just make a green salad and arrange the other foods on top—if the foods are hot, add them at the last minute—and then toss just before serving.

Frisée and Bacon Salad

This salad, once only found in France, has become an American restaurant staple. The smokiness of the bacon balances beautifully with the bitterness of the greens, and good olive oil enhances the combination even more. If you can buy double-smoked slab bacon, use it for this. To keep the bacon, just wrap it in a kitchen towel and store it in the refrigerator, where it will hold for weeks. You just slice off the bacon as you need it. If you have slab bacon that still has the rind, cut between the rind and the bacon as you slice. This will provide you with a flap of rind you can fold over the rest of the bacon to keep it from drying out. If you are buying sliced bacon at the supermarket, buy the thickest slices and make sure it is labeled "naturally smoked."

MAKES 4 FIRST-COURSE OR LIGHT MAIN-COURSE SERVINGS

1 large head frisée

$1/2$ pound bacon, preferably double smoked, ideally in $1/4$-inch-thick slices

$1/4$ cup white wine vinegar

$1/4$ cup extra virgin olive oil

Pepper

Cut off the tough dark green leaves from the frisée and discard. Pull the leaves away from the yellow and pale green parts and wash and spin dry. Arrange in a salad bowl.

Cut the bacon slices crosswise into 1-inch-long strips. In a skillet, cook the bacon over medium heat for about 10 minutes, or until the fat is rendered and the pieces just begin to turn crispy. Don't be tempted to turn the heat up too high or you will burn the fat that is going into the salad.

When the bacon is ready, pour off all but about 2 tablespoons of the bacon fat. Add the vinegar to the skillet, put it over high heat, and boil the vinegar for a few seconds. Add the oil, heat for a few seconds, and pour the contents of the skillet over the salad. Toss right away.

Caesar Salad

While there is some dispute about who invented this salad, chef Cardini in Tijuana in the 1930s or chef Junia in Chicago in 1903, this is a purely American creation and one of the great salads of the world when properly prepared. In most restaurants, it is served with an indifferent sauce, bland cheese, stale croutons, and often without the anchovies. True, some people don't like anchovies, but a waiter should always ask, for a Caesar salad is defined by anchovies.

To make a great Caesar salad, you must be brutal about discarding the outer dark leaves of the romaine. If you can't stand the waste, save them for another salad the next day, but don't make your Caesar with huge, dark leaves. When you have reach the pale green, crisp hearts—you will need about ¹/₂ heart for each person—gently snap away the little leaves and leave them whole. Avoid store-bought croutons, instead make your own with good dense-crumb white bread. Use authentic Parmigiano-Reggiano cheese, and soft-boiled eggs instead of raw ones. The best anchovies are from Sicily and are packed in salt. If you can't find them, buy anchovies packed in olive oil. Drain the anchovies and taste one. If it seems strong or too salty, soak the anchovies in cold water for 5 minutes and pat them dry on paper towels.

MAKES 4 FIRST-COURSE SERVINGS

- 2 heads romaine lettuce or 3 hearts of romaine
- 1 clove garlic, peeled, crushed
- 2 eggs, soft-boiled for 2 minutes (see page 95)
- 2 teaspoons Dijon mustard
- ¹/₂ teaspoon salt
- 2 tablespoons red or white wine vinegar
- ¹/₂ cup (about 2 ounces) grated Parmigiano-Reggiano cheese
- 12 anchovy fillets (see headnote), optional
- ¹/₃ cup extra virgin olive oil
- 3 slices dense-crumb white bread, crusts removed, cut into ¹/₃-inch cubes
- Pepper

If using romaine heads, discard all of the large, dark green leaves. Separate the leaves of the heart, leave them whole, and wash and spin dry. Refrigerate until needed. If you want to hold them for more than 1 hour, keep them wrapped in a moist kitchen towel.

Just before you assemble the salad, rub the inside of the salad bowl with the garlic clove. Discard the garlic. Put the greens in the bowl. Cook the eggs as directed, then crack and scoop the eggs out of their shells and into the salad bowl. Add the mustard, salt, vinegar, cheese, and anchovies, and pour over about half of the oil.

In a skillet, heat the remaining oil over medium heat. Add the bread cubes and toss or stir every few minutes for about 12 minutes, or until evenly browned on all sides. Remove from the pan.

Sprinkle the croutons over greens, grind pepper over the top, and toss.

HOW TO MAKE CAESAR SALAD ———

1. Take the outer leaves off the heads of romaine and use only the hearts.

2. Add soft-boiled eggs, mustard, salt, wine vinegar, Parmigiano-Reggiano cheese, and anchovies.

3. Pour over olive oil.

4. Add the croutons, toss, and serve the salad on plates.

Chicken Caesar Salad

This popular salad provides a delightful way to use leftover chicken, or to serve freshly cooked chicken in a different guise.

MAKES 4 MAIN-COURSE SERVINGS

> **2 cooked chicken breast halves, torn into strips (see page 254)**
>
> **Salt**
>
> **Pepper**
>
> **Caesar Salad (opposite)**

Season the chicken with salt and pepper, and place it on top of the salad just before tossing and serving.

Tossed Winter Steak Salad

Toss the steak with the greens the instant before serving so the meat doesn't have a chance to compress the greens. The contrast of the savory meat and cool greens makes a salad that is light but richly satisfying at the same time.

MAKES 4 MAIN-COURSE SERVINGS

> **8 fingerling potatoes**
>
> **2 eggs**
>
> **$1/2$ pound haricots verts or small regular green beans, ends trimmed**
>
> **2 slices French coarse country bread, cut into $1/2$-inch cubes**
>
> **2 small heads frisée, about $1/2$ pound total**
>
> **1 head Belgian endive**
>
> **1 radicchio, about 5 ounces**
>
> **One 10-ounce package cremini mushrooms**
>
> **$11/2$ pounds strip steak or flank steak, seasoned with salt and pepper and rubbed with olive oil**
>
> **2 tablespoons pure olive oil**
>
> **2 ounces Roquefort, Stilton, Gorgonzola, or other high-quality blue cheese, crumbled**
>
> **6 tablespoons extra virgin olive oil**
>
> **3 tablespoons red wine vinegar**
>
> **Salt**
>
> **Pepper**

Preheat the oven to 350°F. Build a hot charcoal fire with the coals 3 to 4 inches away from the grill rack. Use enough charcoal to make a double layer large enough for all the steaks. Or, preheat a gas grill to high.

Meanwhile, in a saucepan, combine the potatoes, eggs, and water just to cover. Bring to a simmer over medium heat, and then turn the heat down to maintain at a gentle simmer. Ten minutes after the water first reached a simmer, remove the eggs with a slotted spoon and set aside to cool. Continue to simmer the potatoes for about 10 minutes, or until a knife slides easily through them. Drain the potatoes in a colander, rinse with cold water to make them easier to handle, and then pull away the peel in strips by pinching it between your thumb and a paring knife. Peel the eggs and cut them lengthwise into quarters.

Bring a saucepan filled with water to a boil, add the beans, and boil for 5 to 8 minutes, or until you feel only the slightest crunch when you bite into one. Drain in a colander and rinse with cold water.

(continued)

While the potatoes and beans are cooking, spread the bread cubes on a sheet pan and toast, stirring occasionally, for about 12 minutes, or until lightly browned on all sides.

Cut off the tough dark green leaves from the frisée and discard. Pull the leaves away from the yellow and pale green parts and wash and spin dry. Pull away the endive leaves and wash and spin dry. Pull away the leaves from the radicchio head, tear the larger ones in half, and wash and spin dry.

Wash and dry the mushrooms. Cut the end off the bottom of each mushroom stem if dried out or dirty. Unless they are very small, cut the mushrooms through the stem into quarters.

About 10 minutes before serving, grill the steak as directed in Basic Grilled Steak (see page 174). In a sauté pan, heat the pure olive oil over high heat. Add the mushrooms and sauté for about 5 minutes, or until brown and any liquid they release evaporates.

Put the greens in a large salad bowl and arrange the potatoes, eggs, beans, bread cubes, and cheese on top. When the mushrooms are ready, pour them out over the salad—this is dramatic done at the table—and then pour over the extra virgin olive oil and vinegar. At the table, cut the steak across the grain on the diagonal into thin slices, and place the slices on top of the salad. Sprinkle with salt and grind over pepper. Toss and serve.

Tossed Summer Steak Salad

Because you are slicing the meat, you don't have to use the most expensive cut. You can get by with London broil, which nowadays is usually chuck, flank, or sirloin steak. If you want to use a more luxurious cut, buy a New York steak, either a shell (with the bone) or a strip (without the bone).

MAKES 4 MAIN-COURSE SERVINGS

$1/2$ **pound haricots verts or small regular green beans, ends trimmed**

2 bunches arugula

1 bunch basil

$1/2$ **cup pitted dark olives such as Niçoise**

12 anchovy fillets, well drained (optional)

4 tomatoes, peeled if desired and each cut into 6 or 8 wedges

2 hard-boiled eggs (see page 95), peeled, and each cut into 4 wedges

Two $3/4$-pound strip steaks or flank steaks, seasoned with salt and pepper and rubbed with olive oil

1 handful of nasturtium flowers or other edible flowers (optional)

Salt

Pepper

Oil

Wine vinegar

Build a hot charcoal fire with the coals 3 to 4 inches away from the grill rack. Use enough charcoal to make a double layer large enough for both steaks. Or, preheat a gas grill to high.

Bring a saucepan filled with water to a boil, add the beans, and boil for 5 to 8 minutes, or until you feel only the slightest crunch when you bite into one. Drain in a colander and rinse with cold water.

Discard the larger stems from the arugula and all the stems from the basil. Wash and spin all the leaves dry, and place in a large salad bowl. Arrange the olives, anchovies, tomatoes, and eggs around the perimeter of the bowl.

About 10 minutes before serving, grill the steak by browning it over high heat and then cooking it over lower heat until it has the desired doneness, as directed in Basic Grilled Steak (page 174). At the table, cut the steak across the grain on the diagonal into thin slices, and place the slices on top of the salad. Scatter the flowers on top, and sprinkle with salt and grind over pepper. Toss with olive oil and wine vinegar and serve.

Mushroom and Duck Confit Salad

This is the kind of ultimate wilted salad that you can make luxurious by using wild mushrooms. I recommend assembling your own greens, instead of relying on the now-ubiquitous mesclun mixes that often taste like a collection of weeds. I have suggested some greens here, but use whatever looks good.

MAKES 4 FIRST-COURSE OR LIGHT MAIN-COURSE SERVINGS

- **1 bunch arugula, large stems removed**
- **1 small head radicchio, leaves pulled apart and large leaves torn in half**
- **1 Belgian endive, stem end trimmed and leaves cut crosswise into 1/2-inch-wide slices**
- **1 pound assorted mushrooms**
- **2 confit Pekin duck thighs or 1 confit mullard duck thigh (page 274)**
- **3 tablespoons duck fat**
- **Salt**
- **Pepper**
- **1/4 cup sherry vinegar**
- **3 tablespoons olive oil**

Wash and dry the salad greens and put them in a salad bowl large enough to leave plenty of room for tossing. Wash and dry the mushrooms. Cut the end off the bottom of each mushroom stem if dried out or dirty. If the mushrooms are large, cut them into smaller pieces. Set aside.

Pull off and discard the skin from the confit. Pull away the meat from the bones in shreds and reserve. In a large skillet, heat the duck fat over high heat. Add the mushrooms and sauté for about 7 minutes, or until fragrant and brown. Season with salt and pepper, scatter the confit over the mushrooms, and pour in the vinegar and oil. Stir or toss over high heat for about 30 seconds and then pour the contents of the skillet over the salad greens. Toss immediately and serve.

HOW TO MAKE MUSHROOM AND DUCK CONFIT SALAD

1. Prepare assorted greens and put them in the salad bowl.

2. Prepare assorted mushrooms and sauté them in duck fat. Season with salt and pepper. Scatter the confit over the mushrooms. Add olive oil and vinegar and toss over high heat.

3. Pour over the salad and toss at once.

Salade Niçoise

This almost ubiquitous salad has been upgraded in recent years by the addition of fresh tuna in place of the traditional canned. Either tuna is actually fine; each creates a different effect. You don't even need to use tuna. Other firm-fleshed fish are also good. Aficionados of salades niçoise are dogmatic about such things as green beans, potatoes, tomatoes, and eggs—some pro, some con. This version contains all of them, but if you leave out one or two, the salad will still be good. Slender French green beans, known as haricots verts, are lovely in this salad, but if you can't find them, you can quarter regular green beans lengthwise to achieve a similar profile.

MAKES 6 FIRST-COURSE OR 4 MAIN-COURSE SERVINGS

- 4 large handfuls of assorted lettuces such as Boston, Bibb, arugula, or frisée, washed and spun dry, or 10 ounces prewashed assorted greens such as mesclun mix
- 1 waxy potato, about $1/2$ pound
- 1 clove garlic, minced and then crushed with the flat side of the knife
- 2 tablespoons red or white wine vinegar
- Pinch of salt
- $2/3$ cup extra virgin olive oil
- $1/2$ pound green beans, preferably haricots verts, ends trimmed
- 2 tomatoes
- Two 6-ounce cans imported Italian tuna packed in olive oil, drained, or one $3/4$-pound fresh tuna steak, grilled or sautéed rare, sliced
- 1 red or yellow bell pepper, charred, peeled, and seeded (see page 321) and then cut lengthwise into $1/4$-inch-wide strips
- 3 eggs, hard-boiled (see page 95), peeled, and each cut into 4 wedges
- 8 anchovy fillets, or more to taste, well drained and cut in half crosswise
- $1/2$ cup Niçoise olives or other Mediterranean-style brine-cured black olives, drained

Reserve the greens in the refrigerator until you are ready to assemble the salad. Put the potato in a pot with cold water to cover and bring to a gentle simmer. Simmer for about 25 minutes, or until easily pierced with a paring knife. Meanwhile, in a small bowl, whisk together the garlic, vinegar, and salt until the salt dissolves. Pour in the olive oil.

When the potato is ready, drain and then peel away the skin in strips with a paring knife while still warm. Slice the potato thickly and place in a small bowl. Whisk the vinaigrette, add 3 tablespoons of it to the warm potato slices, and toss gently. (Each time before you use the vinaigrette, whisk it so the vinegar and oil are evenly distributed.)

Bring a large pot of salted water to a boil, add the beans, and boil for 5 to 8 minutes, or until you feel only the slightest crunch when you bite into one. Drain in a colander and immediately rinse with cold water. Pat dry or spin dry in a lettuce spinner. If you are serving the salad right away, toss the beans with 3 tablespoons of the vinaigrette. If not, toss them with the vinaigrette just before serving.

If you have perfect summer tomatoes, don't bother to peel them. If you don't, plunge them into boiling water for about 30 seconds, rinse them immediately with cold water, and pull away the skin in strips with a paring knife. Cut out the stem end, and cut each tomato into 8 wedges. Push the seeds out of each wedge with a fingertip. If using fresh grilled tuna, slice the tuna into rectangles.

You can serve the salad in a large bowl or on individual plates. If you are using a bowl, arrange the lettuces around the inside. If you are using salad plates, first toss the lettuces, tomatoes, bell pepper, and tuna separately with the remaining vinaigrette. Then arrange the lettuces on the salad plates. Arrange all the remaining ingredients—potato slices, beans, tomatoes, bell pepper, eggs, tuna, anchovies, and olives—decoratively on top of the lettuces in the bowl or on each plate. If serving at the table from the bowl, just before serving, pour the remaining vinaigrette over the salad and toss gently, then serve on plates.

1. Prepare all the ingredients, including the tomatoes shown here.

2. Grill the tuna for about 4 minutes on each side for a 2-inch-thick steak, as shown here.

3. Cut the tuna steak into rectangles.

4. Serve the salad in a large bowl or on large plates.

VEGETABLE SALADS

Most of us forget the delights of a simple salad made with a single vegetable, such as carrots, beets, or mushrooms. In France, these vegetable salads are often served together, sometimes as many as seven different ones on the same plate. Called a plate of crudités, it is deliciously light and satisfying and has nothing to do with the carrot or celery sticks that most Americans associate with the term.

If you are serving an assortment of these vegetable salads, use your imagination to come up with contrasting flavors. For example, you may decide to use different herbs, pairing tarragon and mushrooms, parsley and carrots, or basil and tomatoes. Or, you may want to use different oils, such as a neutral oil for carrots, walnut oil for beets, or olive oil for fennel. Vinegars can be varied, too, for even more contrast among the salads. Most of the recipes here serve 6 as a first course and 4 as a main. If you are serving more or fewer, adjust the amounts accordingly.

Clockwise: Cucumber Salad with Chiles and Yogurt (page 81), Celeriac Rémoulade (page 78), Artichoke and Toasted Walnut Salad (page 83), Shaved Fennel Salad (page 84), Tomato Salad (page 85), Grilled peppers (page 321), Roast Beets with nut oil (Variations, page 299), Marinated Mushrooms with Fresh Tarragon (page 80), (center) Grated Carrots with Parsley and Lemon (page 80).

EATING IN COURSES

With the exception of restaurant dining, most Americans aren't accustomed to eating in courses. On a weeknight, it is usually enough of a struggle to put together a dinner with meat or fish, a vegetable, and some kind of starch, much less to think about what to serve as a first course.

The trick is not to serve more food, but to deconstruct the main course so you are serving the same foods, just not all at once. For example, consider offering a green vegetable as a first course, and then you won't need to serve a vegetable with the main. Or, serve a small plate of risotto or pasta as a first course (as they do in Italy), and then skip the starch with the main course. Breaking a meal into courses makes everyone (including the cook) pay a little more attention to the food and spend more time at the table. The vegetable salads included here lose some of their charm if they are served at the same time as the main course. They should instead be showcased before the main, on a large plate so that their colors shine and their flavors bounce off of one another.

Serving Family Style

Nowadays, it seems like most restaurants, with the exception of Asian ones, plate all the dishes in the kitchen, rather than sending out a communal platter. It may mean dirtying an additional plate or two, but if you want to make your dinner more special, or you want to invite more interaction among your guests, send out your dishes on platters or in serving bowls and encourage everyone to pass them around. Some people will even catch on and hold the dish while their neighbor spoons out a portion. For more formal gatherings or when the platters are too hot to pass, serve the food from the end of the table and pass the plates. That way, everyone gets to see the dishes in the vessels in which they were cooked (especially if you have attractive cookware) or on platters before they are put onto the plates.

Celeriac Rémoulade

Given its appearance, it is no surprise that American cooks haven't experimented much with this subtle-tasting root vegetable. Also known as celery root, it is covered with various tuberlike growths and irregularities that seem strangely malevolent to some observers. The texture is reminiscent of a turnip, but the flavor is like celery, though more delicate and somehow more satisfying. It can be braised or roasted, but one of the most delightful ways to serve it is to cut it into thin matchsticks and toss them with mayonnaise. The name of this recipe is confusing, since it is not made with the classic French rémoulade sauce—mayonnaise flavored with shallots and herbs—but with a plain mayonnaise and extra mustard.

MAKES 6 FIRST-COURSE SERVINGS WHEN SERVED WITH 3 OTHER CRUDITÉ SALADS

1 celeriac
1 to 2 tablespoons fresh lemon juice
1 cup Basic Homemade Mayonnaise (see page 359)
2 tablespoons Dijon mustard, or more to taste
Salt
Pepper
1 tablespoon finely chopped fresh parsley

Peel the celeriac with a knife and then cut it in half lengthwise. Working with one half at a time, place it flat side down on a vegetable slicer (see page 292), and cut it into slices about as thick as a quarter. Stack 2 or 3 slices and cut the stack into sticks the width of a quarter. Repeat until all the slices are cut, place the sticks in a bowl, and toss with the lemon juice.

In a small bowl, stir together the mayonnaise and the 2 tablespoons mustard and season with salt and pepper. Taste and adjust with more mustard if needed. Pour the sauce over the celeriac, add the parsley, and stir to mix. Taste and adjust with more salt and pepper if needed.

HOW TO MAKE CELERIAC RÉMOULADE

1. Peel the celeriac and cut in half.

2. For 6 salad (crudité) servings, slice and julienne 1 celeriac.

3. Make a hazelnut mayonnaise (page 360).

4. Toss the celeriac with the mayonnaise.

Shredded Red Cabbage Salad with Pistachios

This is a little like coleslaw, but it is lighter and has a more interesting flavor. A nut oil is called for here—be sure to use one made from roasted nuts—but you can use olive oil if you like. You can also substitute another type of nut for the pistachios, but be sure to toast whatever you choose.

MAKES 6 FIRST-COURSE SERVINGS

- **1 cup pistachio nuts, whole pecans, or walnut halves**
- **1 small red cabbage, about 1¹/₂ pounds, loose or wilted outer leaves discarded**
- **2 tablespoons coarse salt**
- **¹/₃ cup sherry vinegar, balsamic vinegar, or other flavorful wine vinegar**
- **3 tablespoons walnut, hazelnut, or pistachio oil made from roasted nuts, or extra virgin olive oil**
- **¹/₂ cup canola oil**
- **Pepper**

Preheat the oven to 350°F. Spread the nuts on a sheet pan and toast in the oven, stirring occasionally, for 10 to 15 minutes, or until they are fragrant and have taken on color. Pour onto a plate and let cool. If using walnuts, chop coarsely (leave pistachios and pecans whole).

Quarter the cabbage through the bottom core, and then cut the core out of each quarter. Slice each quarter as finely as you can with a vegetable slicer (see page 292) or a chef's knife.

In a large bowl, sprinkle the salt over the cabbage and then toss and rub the salt into the cabbage for about 2 minutes, or until the salt dissolves and no longer feels gritty. Transfer the cabbage to a colander, set it in the sink or over a bowl, and let drain for about 30 minutes.

Working with a little at a time, squeeze the cabbage in your fists to extract as much liquid and salt as possible. Put the cabbage in a bowl, add the vinegar and both oils, and toss and stir to mix. Stir in the nuts just before serving so they don't get soggy. Season to taste with a few grinds of pepper.

HOW TO MAKE SHREDDED RED CABBAGE SALAD WITH PISTACHIOS

1. Peel off the outer wilted leaves from cabbage head. Cut the cabbage in half through the core.

2. Cut each half in half again lengthwise.

3. Cut away the strip of core from each quarter.

4. Thinly slice across the quarters to create fine shreds.

5. Add the coarse salt.

6. Rub the cabbage until you can no longer feel the salt. Let drain in a colander.

7. Squeeze the liquid out of the cabbage and dress with oil, vinegar, and pistachios.

Marinated Mushrooms
with Fresh Tarragon

These mushrooms may not look like much, especially after they have sat awhile and turned dark, but the darker they are, the better their flavor. For the best flavor, make them the day before serving.

MAKES 6 FIRST-COURSE SERVINGS WHEN SERVED WITH 3 OTHER CRUDITÉ SALADS

> **1 pound cultivated mushrooms, preferably cremini**
>
> **1/2 cup extra virgin olive oil, or more as needed**
>
> **1/4 cup sherry vinegar or aged balsamic vinegar, or more to taste**
>
> **2 tablespoons fresh tarragon leaves, coarsely chopped**
>
> **Salt**
>
> **Pepper**

Cut the end off the bottom of each mushroom stem if dried out or dirty. Rinse the mushrooms in a colander under running cold water while rubbing them together between your hands. Drain the mushrooms until dry, and then slice them as thinly as you can. You can use a vegetable slicer (see page 292) set to the thinnest setting, but be careful of your fingers.

In a large bowl, toss the mushrooms with the oil and 1/4 cup vinegar. Add the tarragon and toss to mix. Season with salt and pepper, cover, and refrigerate for at least 4 hours and up to 24 hours before serving.

As the mushrooms sit, they will darken and become more flavorful. Just before serving, taste the mushrooms again and add a little more oil if they seem dry, or more salt, pepper, and vinegar if needed.

HOW TO MAKE MARINATED MUSHROOMS WITH FRESH TARRAGON

1. Slice cremini mushrooms.

2. Combine with 20 tarragon leaves, aged balsamic vinegar, extra virgin olive oil, salt, and pepper.

Grated Carrots
with Parsley and Lemon

Served alone, this salad would be a little austere, but when served with other crudité salads, its lovely note of sweetness is welcome. You might assume that almost nothing could be easier than grating a carrot, but it actually requires considerable finesse. If you grate carrots too thickly, they will be hard and monotonous to chew. If you grate them too fine, they will be mushy. If you are grating just enough carrots for this recipe, the best tool to use is an old-fashioned box grater. But not all box graters are the same. The fine side— the side you need—of some of them consists of little punchouts (to be avoided), while others have little scoops (what you want). If you are making grated carrots for a crowd, grating by hand is impractical. Instead, cut the carrots into 3-inch lengths and put them on their sides in the food processor with the finest grater attachment.

MAKES 6 FIRST-COURSE SERVINGS WHEN SERVED WITH 3 OTHER CRUDITÉ SALADS

> **2 large or 4 medium carrots, peeled and cut into 3-inch lengths**
>
> **2 tablespoons fresh lemon juice**
>
> **5 tablespoons canola oil, pure olive oil, or extra virgin olive oil**
>
> **2 tablespoons finely chopped fresh parsley, chopped at the last minute**
>
> **Salt**
>
> **White pepper**
>
> **Small pinch sugar, optional**

HOW TO MAKE GRATED CARROTS WITH PARSLEY AND LEMON

1. Grate peeled carrot sections on the fine side of a box grater.

2. Combine with the olive oil, lemon juice, parsley, salt, and white pepper.

Grate the carrots by pushing them lengthwise along the fine grater teeth of a box grater. Grate each carrot by hand, or use the finest grater attachment on a food processor.

In a bowl, toss the grated carrots with the lemon juice, oil, parsley, salt, and a few grinds of white pepper. Taste the carrots and toss them with the sugar if they need to be sweeter.

Cucumber Salad with Chiles and Yogurt

Many of us have encountered this salad, made with yogurt and mint, in Indian restaurants, where it is called raita. If you make it with crème fraîche instead of yogurt, it can stand alone as a first course. If you make it with yogurt, it is best with other crudités.

MAKES 4 SIDE-DISH SERVINGS, 4 FIRST-COURSE SERVINGS, OR 6 FIRST-COURSE SERVINGS WHEN SERVED WITH 3 OTHER CRUDITÉ SALADS

> **2 cups whole-milk plain yogurt or 1 cup crème fraîche**
>
> **4 regular cucumbers or 2 English cucumbers, peeled (optional) and halved lengthwise**
>
> **2 teaspoons coarse salt**
>
> **3 Thai chiles, seeded and minced**
>
> **2 poblano chiles, charred, peeled, and seeded (see page 321) and then minced**
>
> **1 bunch mint or cilantro, large stems removed and leaves finely chopped at the last minute**
>
> **Pepper**

If using yogurt, scoop it into a strainer lined with cheesecloth or a coffee filter, place over a bowl, and let drain for at least 2 hours or up to overnight in the refrigerator.

Scrape out the seeds from the cucumber halves with a spoon, then slice the halves crosswise into crescents about 1/4 inch thick. Place the cucumbers in a bowl, sprinkle with the salt, and then toss and rub the slices for about 2 minutes, or until the salt dissolves and no longer feels gritty. Transfer the cucumbers to a colander, set it in the sink or over a bowl, and let drain for about 30 minutes.

Working with a little at a time, squeeze the cucumber slices in your fists to extract as much liquid and salt as possible. Put the cucumbers in a bowl. Add the drained yogurt or crème fraîche, chiles, mint, and a few grinds of pepper and stir to mix.

HOW TO MAKE CUCUMBER SALAD WITH CHILES AND YOGURT

1. Drain plain yogurt in a strainer lined with a coffee filter or cheesecloth.

2. Cut hothouse cucumbers in half lengthwise.

3. Scoop out the seeds from the halves with a spoon.

4. Thinly slice the halves crosswise.

5. Toss the slices with salt, and then drain in a colander over a bowl.

6. Squeeze small handfuls of the cucumbers in your fist to extract liquid.

7. Combine the cucumbers with the yogurt; charred, peeled, seeded, and chopped poblano chiles; seeded and chopped Thai chiles; and finely chopped cilantro; add a little pepper.

Japanese Cucumber Salad

One of the great things about Japanese salads is that they contain little or no fat. This one is more of a dipping sauce for cucumbers than it is a salad. It makes a great hors d'oeuvre with cocktails because it is savory and salty but won't fill anyone up.

**MAKES 8 HORS D'OEUVRE SERVINGS
OR 2 FIRST-COURSE SERVINGS**

   4 regular cucumbers or 2 English cucumbers, peeled and halved lengthwise

   2 teaspoons coarse salt

   1/4 cup rice vinegar

   2 tablespoons soy sauce

   1/4 teaspoon Asian sesame oil

   2 tablespoons fresh lime juice

   1 tablespoon sugar

   1/2 cup loosely packed dried bonito flakes (optional)

   1 green onion, white and 3 inches of the green, very thinly sliced

Scrape out the seeds from the cucumber halves with a spoon, then slice the halves crosswise into crescents about 1/8 inch thick. Place the cucumbers in a bowl, sprinkle with the salt, and then toss and rub the slices for about 2 minutes, or until the salt dissolves and no longer feels gritty. Transfer the cucumbers to a colander, set it in the sink or over a bowl, and let drain for about 30 minutes.

Working with a little at a time, squeeze the cucumber slices in your fists to extract as much liquid and salt as possible. Put the cucumbers in a serving bowl or in individual bowls.

If you are using the bonito flakes, combine the vinegar, soy sauce, sesame oil, lime juice, and sugar in a small saucepan, and bring to a boil. Remove from the heat, immediately add the bonito flakes, let steep for 5 minutes, and then strain through a fine-mesh strainer into a bowl and discard the bonito flakes. If you are not using the bonito flakes, just combine all the ingredients and stir to dissolve the sugar. Cover and chill the sauce.

Just before serving, stir the green onion into the sauce. Divide the sauce among small individual sauce bowls and serve with the cucumber. Give everyone chopsticks or little forks for dipping.

Thai Cucumber Salad

If you want to make this salad more substantial and serve it as a main course, toss it with shredded cold roast chicken or whole cooked shellfish such as shrimp.

MAKES 6 FIRST-COURSE SERVINGS

   4 regular cucumbers or 2 English cucumbers, peeled and halved lengthwise

   1 1/2 teaspoons coarse salt

   1/4 cup creamy peanut butter made with only peanuts and salt

   2 Thai or 4 jalapeño chiles, seeded and minced

   1 clove garlic, minced and then crushed with the flat side of the knife

   1/2 cup unsweetened coconut milk

   1 tablespoon plus 1 1/2 teaspoons sugar

   1/2 bunch cilantro, large stems removed and leaves finely chopped

   About 20 fresh basil leaves, preferably holy basil, each torn into about 3 pieces

   3 tablespoons fresh lime juice

   3 tablespoons rice vinegar or white wine vinegar

   2 to 3 tablespoons fish sauce, or more as needed

   6 sprigs mint or cilantro

Scrape out the seeds from the cucumber halves with a spoon, then slice the halves crosswise into crescents about 1/8 inch thick. Place the cucumbers in a bowl, sprinkle with the salt, and then toss and rub the slices for about 2 minutes, or until the salt dissolves and no longer feels gritty. Transfer the cucumbers to a colander, set it in the sink or over a bowl, and let drain for about 30 minutes.

Working with a little at a time, squeeze the cucumber slices in your fists to extract as much liquid and salt as possible. Set the cucumbers aside.

In a bowl, combine the peanut butter, chiles, garlic, coconut milk, and sugar and work the mixture with a whisk until smooth. Stir in the cilantro, basil, lime juice, vinegar, and fish sauce and mix well. Add the cucumbers and toss with the sauce. Chill for 1 hour. Serve on chilled plates, and decorate each serving with a mint sprig.

Artichoke and Toasted Walnut Salad

Because the choke remains undeveloped, once you remove the tough outer leaves from baby artichokes, you only need to simmer them for about 20 minutes and you can eat them whole—hot with olive oil or butter, or cold in a salad. Toasted walnuts or pecans make a delightful contrast of flavor and texture. If you can't find baby artichokes, "turn" large artichokes, simmer until easily penetrated with a skewer, and cut into wedges.

MAKES 6 SIDE-DISH OR FIRST-COURSE SERVINGS IF SERVED ALONE OR PROPORTIONATELY MORE WHEN SERVED WITH OTHER CRUDITÉ SALADS

> **30 baby artichokes, about 3 pounds, all the same size, (so they cook evenly) or 4 large artichokes**
>
> **3/4 cup walnut halves**
>
> **3 tablespoons walnut or hazelnut oil made from roasted nuts, or extra virgin olive oil, or more to taste**
>
> **1 tablespoon sherry vinegar or white wine vinegar, or more to taste**
>
> **Salt**
>
> **Pepper**

If using baby artichokes, prepare as shown on page 297. If using large artichokes, prepare as shown for artichoke bottoms on page 296. Put the artichokes in a nonaluminum pot with plenty of water to cover and bring to a gentle simmer. Simmer for 15 to 20 minutes, or until a paring knife poked into one of the artichokes goes through with just slight resistance.

Meanwhile, preheat the oven to 350°F. Spread the nuts on a sheet pan and toast in the oven, stirring occasionally, for 10 to 15 minutes, or until they are fragrant and have taken on color. Pour onto a plate and let cool.

Drain the artichokes. If you are using large artichokes, remove the chokes and cut into wedges. Immediately toss the artichokes with the oil, vinegar, and salt and pepper to taste. Just before serving, toss in the nuts (don't toss them in ahead of time or they will lose their crunch). This salad, except for adding the nuts, can be made 2 days in advance.

1. Scoop the choke out of large artichoke bottoms with a spoon.

2. Cut the bottoms into wedges.

3. Dress with walnut oil, vinegar, salt, and pepper and toss with the walnuts.

Shaved Fennel Salad

You can serve this salad as part of a crudité plate with other salads, or you can serve it alone as a first course. As a first course, it is enhanced by the addition of a few paper-thin strips of Parmigiano-Reggiano cheese. You can prepare the fennel a couple of hours ahead of time—keep it covered in the refrigerator—but don't add the salt until the last minute, or the fennel will lose its crunch.

HOW TO MAKE SHAVED FENNEL SALAD

1. Cut the stalks and fronds off of the fennel.

2. Trim off any stringy fibers from the bulb with a vegetable peeler.

3. Cut the conical core out of the bulb.

4. Shave the bulb crosswise on a vegetable slicer.

5. Season the fennel with olive oil, fresh lemon juice, salt, and pepper.

6. Shave off strips of Parmigiano-Reggiano cheese and top each serving. Decorate with a few little fennel fronds.

MAKES 4 GENEROUS FIRST-COURSE SERVINGS OR 6 FIRST-COURSE SERVINGS WHEN SERVED WITH 3 OTHER CRUDITÉ SALADS

> 1 large or 2 medium fennel bulbs
> 2 tablespoons fresh lemon juice
> 3 tablespoons extra virgin olive oil
> Salt
> Pepper
> 2-ounce wedge Parmigiano-Reggiano cheese (optional)

Cut the stalks off the fennel where they join the bulb. Pull off and reserve a small handful of the frizzy fronds. Discard the stalks or use them in broths or braised dishes to add a lovely subtle freshness. Pull off and discard any dark or dried-out layers from the bulb, and use a vegetable peeler to peel away the outermost stringy membrane, as you would peel a stalk of celery.

Using a vegetable slicer or a chef's knife, slice the fennel bulb crosswise as thinly as possible. Coarsely chop the reserved fronds. In a bowl, toss the fennel slices and fronds with the lemon juice, oil, and salt and pepper to taste.

If serving the salad alone as a first course, divide among plates and use a vegetable peeler to slice 3 or 4 thin strips of cheese over each serving. Decorate with the fronds.

1. Plunge the tomatoes into boiling water and boil for 30 seconds to loosen skins.

2. Lift the tomatoes out of the boiling water and rinse under cold running water.

3. Cut out the stem.

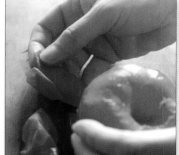

4. Pull away the peel.

5. To seed the tomatoes, cut them in half through the equator.

6. Squeeze the halves and pull out the seeds with your fingers.

Tomato Salad

When tomatoes are at the height of the season, serve this salad alone and make it with an assortment of heirloom varieties, preferably of different colors. Pushing the seeds out of the wedges with a finger helps prevent the juice from diluting the vinegar and oil.

MAKES 6 SIDE-DISH OR FIRST-COURSE SERVINGS IF SERVED ALONE OR PROPORTIONATELY MORE WHEN SERVED WITH OTHER CRUDITÉ SALADS

6 large ripe tomatoes, about $3/4$ pound each, or about $41/2$ pounds smaller tomatoes

$1/2$ cup extra virgin olive oil

2 tablespoons sherry vinegar or other wine vinegar, or more to taste

1 handful of fresh basil leaves; or 1 tablespoon chopped fresh marjoram; or 2 tablespoons chopped fresh tarragon leaves, chopped at the last minute (optional)

Salt

Pepper

If you have perfect summer tomatoes, don't bother to peel them. If you don't, plunge them into boiling water for about 30 seconds, rinse them immediately with cold water, and pull away the skin in strips with a paring knife. Cut out the stem end, and cut each large tomato into 12 wedges or smaller tomato into 6 wedges. Push the seeds out of each wedge with a fingertip.

Just before serving, combine the tomatoes, oil, vinegar, basil, and salt and pepper to taste in a bowl and toss to mix. Don't toss the salad any sooner. The salt will draw the water out of the tomatoes, which will dilute the vinegar and oil and make the dressing runny, and if you have included basil, it will wilt.

Bell Pepper and Anchovy Salad

You can serve this salad alone, as part of an antipasti platter, or as part of a selection of crudités.

MAKES 4 FIRST-COURSE SERVINGS IF SERVED ALONE OR 6 FIRST-COURSE SERVINGS WHEN PART OF A CRUDITÉ OR ANTIPASTI PLATTER

- 4 bell peppers, preferably of different colors except green, charred, peeled, and stemmed (see page 321)
- 1/4 cup extra virgin olive oil
- One 2-ounce bottle anchovies, drained
- 1 tablespoon chopped fresh marjoram, basil, or parsley
- 1 small clove garlic, peeled, crushed, and minced to a paste
- Salt
- Pepper

Cut the peppers lengthwise into 1/4-inch-wide strips and toss them with the rest of the ingredients.

POTATO SALAD

Many of us are familiar with the classic church-picnic potato salad made with mayonnaise and celery. But those classic components can be toyed with and expanded. You can use a classic vinaigrette (see Basic Vinaigrette, page 69, doubling the recipe) or homemade mayonnaise or a mayonnaise variation (see pages 359–361). You can also try different oils and vinegars and herbs. Savory ingredients such as capers, chopped shallots, mushrooms, charred and peeled bell peppers or poblano chiles (see page 321), and even truffle slices can be slipped between the layers. Or you can substitute cream for the oil. Heavy cream flavored with Dijon or whole-grain mustard, salt, and pepper makes an easy and delicious sauce. Crème fraîche is naturally thick and will cling to the potatoes, but heavy cream will thicken when combined with lime juice or vinegar (their acidity also provides a welcome note of tang). Plan on about 3 tablespoons fresh lime juice per cup of heavy cream, and then add mustard to taste. A potato salad can also include pieces of meat or seafood, making it substantial enough to serve as a main course.

White or red waxy potatoes are generally the best potatoes for potato salad because they hold their shape better than russets or Yukon Golds. Always start them in cold water to cook them. This allows the heat to penetrate evenly. If they are started in hot water, the outside cooks faster than the inside. The potatoes are done when they can easily be penetrated with a paring knife or skewer but still offer a little resistance. Don't cook them until they crack, or they will be overcooked.

French-Style Potato Salad

Here, the still-warm potato slices are dressed with a shallot vinaigrette, rather than mayonnaise. The combination produces a lighter result than the American version. Again, larger potatoes will mean less peeling time.

MAKES 6 SIDE-DISH OR FIRST-COURSE SERVINGS IF SERVED ALONE OR PROPORTIONATELY MORE WHEN SERVED WITH OTHER CRUDITÉ SALADS

- 3 pounds red or white waxy potatoes or fingerlings
- 2 tablespoons dry white wine
- $1/4$ cup white wine vinegar
- $1/2$ cup extra virgin olive oil
- 3 shallots, finely chopped
- 3 tablespoons coarsely chopped fresh parsley, preferably flat-leaf
- Salt
- Pepper

Put the potatoes in a pot with cold water to cover and bring to a gentle simmer. Simmer for about 35 minutes, or until the potatoes can be easily pierced with a paring knife. Drain in a colander and let cool for about 10 minutes, or until they can be handled. Don't let them cool for too long or they will be harder to peel, plus you want them warm when you combine them with the dressing. While the potatoes are cooling, in a small bowl, whisk together the wine, vinegar, oil, and shallots.

One at a time, peel the potatoes, holding them in a towel to protect your hand from the heat and pulling away the peel in strips by pinching it between your thumb and a paring knife. Slice the potatoes into $1/4$-inch-thick rounds.

Select a square or oval glass, earthenware, or porcelain gratin or baking dish large enough to hold the potatoes in

HOW TO MAKE FRENCH-STYLE POTATO SALAD ⎯⎯⎯

1. Layer the peeled and sliced potatoes, chopped shallots in a baking dish.

2. Sprinkle chopped parsley, vinaigrette, salt, and pepper over each layer.

about 4 layers. Arrange the still-warm potato slices in 4 layers, sprinkling each layer with one-fourth each of the vinaigrette (quickly stir the vinaigrette each time before adding it, so the ingredients are evenly distributed) and parsley and some salt and pepper.

Serve the salad at room temperature or slightly cooler but not directly out of the refrigerator. When serving the salad, be sure to reach all the way to the bottom of the dish, as the dressing tends to settle to the bottom.

American-Style Potato Salad

A so-called American potato salad is made with mayonnaise instead of the vinaigrette the French traditionally use, and a little diced celery is added for crunch. Buy large potatoes, to cut down on peeling time. This is usually tossed, but looks more elegant left layered.

MAKES 6 SIDE-DISH SERVINGS

- 3 pounds red or white waxy potatoes
- 3 tablespoons chopped fresh parsley, chopped at the last minute
- $3/4$ cup mayonnaise, homemade (see page 359) or purchased
- 1 tablespoon red or white wine vinegar if using bottled mayonnaise, or more as needed
- 1 red onion, minced
- 3 stalks celery, halved lengthwise and cut into $1/3$-inch cubes (about 1 cup)
- Salt
- Pepper

Put the potatoes in a pot with cold water to cover and bring to a gentle simmer. Simmer for about 35 minutes, or until potatoes can be easily pierced with a paring knife. Drain in a colander, rinse with cold water to make them easier to handle, and then pull away the peel in strips by pinching it between your thumb and a paring knife. Let the potatoes cool completely.

If using purchased mayonnaise, in a small bowl, stir together the mayonnaise and vinegar to taste. Slice the potatoes into $1/3$-inch-thick rounds. In a bowl, layer the potato slices with the mayonnaise, onion, celery, and salt and pepper to taste.

Indian-Style Potato Salad

Indian cooks make their own potato salads, seasoning them carefully with their own homemade combinations of roasted spices. Typically flavored with a mixture of cumin, various ground peppers, asafetida (a strong-flavored spice), mango powder, and a tangy seasoning called black salt, Indian potato salads fall into the large culinary category known as chaats, which are basically Indian snack foods. Onion can replace the asafetida, which gives the salad a similar dissonance, and lime juice can be substituted for the tangy mango powder. The black salt is optional, but it does offer a delicate smokiness, as does the chipotle, which is not traditional but is included here. The two favorite herbs are cilantro and mint, though not together. This recipe is adapted from one in Julie Sahni's important book, Classic Indian Cooking.

MAKES 6 FIRST-COURSE OR SIDE-DISH SERVINGS

- **2¹/₂ pounds white or red waxy potatoes**
- **1 teaspoon ground coriander**
- **1¹/₂ teaspoons ground cumin**
- **1¹/₂ tablespoons vegetable oil**
- **1 dried chipotle chile, soaked in hot water for 30 minutes to soften, seeded and chopped, or 2 jalapeño chiles, seeded and finely chopped**
- **¹/₄ teaspoon cayenne**
- **¹/₄ teaspoon black pepper**
- **¹/₄ teaspoon asafetida or ¹/₂ small onion, minced**
- **¹/₄ teaspoon mango powder or ¹/₄ cup fresh lime juice**
- **1 teaspoon black or regular salt**
- **3 tomatoes, peeled and seeded (see page 85) and coarsely chopped**
- **2 tablespoons chopped cilantro**

Put the potatoes in a pot with cold water to cover and bring to a gentle simmer. Simmer for about 35 minutes, or until potatoes can be easily pierced with a paring knife.

While the potatoes are cooking, in a small skillet or saucepan, cook the coriander and cumin in the oil over medium heat for about 1 minute, or until you smell the spices. Remove from the heat, let cool, and pour into a bowl large enough to hold the tomatoes and potatoes. Add the chile, both ground peppers, asafetida, mango powder, salt, and tomatoes and stir to mix.

Drain the potatoes in a colander, rinse with cold water to make them easier to handle, and then pull away the peel in strips by pinching it between your thumb and a paring knife. Let the potatoes cool completely.

Cut the potatoes into ¹/₃-inch-thick slices and gently stir them into the tomato mixture; add cilantro. Let stand for at least 3 hours or up to 5 hours before serving.

MIXED SALADS

Unlike so-called simple salads, which showcase a single ingredient, mixed salads contain two or more ingredients. The key to creating them is to use common sense, avoiding peculiar combinations. For example, tomatoes and beets don't marry well, but tomatoes do partner well with other root vegetables and green vegetables and can be dressed with a variety of different cold sauces. The addition of pieces of meat or seafood provides a central element and can make the salad substantial enough to serve as a main course.

A favorite mixed salad, with artichoke bottoms, yellow string beans, mushrooms, toasted walnuts, and beets.

Asparagus, Green Bean, Mushroom, and Chicken Salad

You can leave out the chicken and serve this salad as a first course. You can also substitute other ingredients, such as cooked shellfish or other seafood, for the chicken. Don't be scared off by the foie gras. It is completely optional, but it does take the salad to a new level.

MAKES 10 FIRST-COURSE SERVINGS OR 6 MAIN-COURSE SERVINGS

$1/2$ pound haricots verts or regular green beans, ends trimmed

1 pound white or green asparagus

$1/4$ cup sherry vinegar

$3/4$ cup heavy cream or crème fraîche

Salt

Pepper

1 small bunch chervil or fronds from a fennel bulb (optional)

10 ounces cultivated mushrooms, preferably cremini, sliced

$1/4$ pound terrine of foie gras (see pages 24–25), well chilled (optional)

Meat from 1 roast chicken (see pages 244–245), pulled off in strips and skin removed

Bring a large pot of salted water to a boil, add the beans, and boil for 5 to 8 minutes, or until you feel only the slightest crunch when you bite into one. Drain in a colander and immediately rinse under cold running water. Pat dry or spin dry in a lettuce spinner.

Trim and peel the asparagus spears as shown on page 290. Bring a large pot of salted water to a boil, add the asparagus, and boil for 4 to 8 minutes, depending on the size of the spears, or until just tender. Drain in a colander and immediately rinse under cold running water. Pat dry.

While the vegetables are cooking, in a small saucepan, combine the vinegar and cream, bring to a boil, and cook for about 2 minutes, or until reduced by one-third. Season with salt and pepper and let cool to room temperature.

Put the cream mixture in a bowl large enough to hold the salad. Reserve 4 to 6 nice sprigs of chervil and chop the rest. Stir the chopped chervil into the sauce.

Make sure the foie gras is very cold and then cut it into $1/4$-inch cubes. Separate the cubes from one another and add them to the sauce.

Just before serving, put the chicken, beans, and asparagus in the bowl with the sauce and foie gras. Season with salt and pepper, toss gently, and then divide among plates. Decorate each serving with a chervil sprig.

Chicken, Bell Pepper, Anchovy, and Tomato Salad

If you don't like anchovies, leave them out.

MAKES 4 MAIN-COURSE SERVINGS

3 slices crusty French coarse country bread or equivalent from a baguette, cut into 1-inch cubes

2 bell peppers, preferably 1 red and 1 yellow, charred, peeled, and seeded (see page 321)

2 poblano chiles, charred, peeled, and seeded (see page 321)

24 anchovy fillets, or to taste

4 tomatoes

Leaves from 1 bunch basil

$1/4$ cup extra virgin olive oil

3 tablespoons red wine vinegar or aged balsamic vinegar or 6 tablespoons inexpensive balsamic vinegar boiled down to 3 tablespoons

Meat from 1 roast chicken, pulled off in strips and skin removed

Salt

Pepper

Preheat the oven to 300°F. Spread the bread cubes on a sheet pan and toast for 10 to 15 minutes, or until lightly browned and crunchy. Let cool.

Cut the bell peppers and poblano chiles into $3/4$-inch-wide strips and then cut the strips crosswise into $3/4$-inch dice. Put into a bowl large enough to hold the salad. Soak the anchovies in enough water to cover for 5 minutes to remove some of their saltiness, drain well, pat dry, and add to the peppers and chiles.

Plunge the tomatoes into boiling water for about 30 seconds, rinse them immediately with cold water, and pull away the skin in strips with a paring knife. Cut out the stem end, and cut each tomato into 6 wedges. Push the seeds out of each wedge with a fingertip. Add the tomatoes to the peppers and other ingredients.

Just before serving, scatter the basil leaves and bread cubes over the salad. Pour over the oil and vinegar, add the chicken, and toss. Season with salt and pepper, keeping in mind that the anchovies are salty.

SEAFOOD SALADS

Cooked seafood, especially shellfish such as shrimp, lobster, or crab, is great combined with vegetables and salad greens. When buying shellfish don't be tempted to buy it already cooked, as fish markets often cook the lobsters that die in the tank or the shellfish that's getting a little stale in the case. Some shellfish, such as crab or lobster, provide roe and other innards (in lobster it is called tomalley, in crab it is called mustard) that can be incorporated into the dressing. Some shellfish, such as shrimp, is best left whole while a lobster tail should be sliced; crabmeat should be left chunky. For more about buying and handling shellfish, see pages 107–139.

Citrus and Endive Seafood Salad

Cool and slightly sweet citrus fruit contrasts well with the briny flavor of cooked shellfish.

MAKES 8 FIRST-COURSE OR LIGHT MAIN-COURSE SERVINGS

- 2 pounds cooked shrimp (out of the shell), crab, or lobster meat or scallops
- 4 navel oranges
- 2 grapefruits
- 2 avocados, preferably Hass
- 2 Belgian endives
- 2 bell peppers, preferably 1 yellow and 1 red, charred, peeled, and seeded (see page 321) and then cut lengthwise into 1/4-inch-wide strips
- 1/4 cup fresh lime juice
- 1/4 cup extra virgin olive oil
- 4 ounces bacon, cooked and crumbled
- 1 jalapeño chile, seeded and minced
- 1 tablespoon finely chopped fresh parsley
- Salt
- Pepper

Cut the shellfish in bite-sized pieces. Grate the zest off of 1/2 orange and set aside. Section the oranges and grapefruits (see right).

No more than 1 hour before serving, halve, pit, and peel the avocados and cut each avocado into 12 wedges. Trim the base of each endive, and then, starting from the bottom, cut half of the head into 1/2-inch-wide slices. Leave the top half of the leaves whole.

In a large bowl, combine citrus fruits, avocados, endive slices and leaves, pepper strips, lime juice, oil, bacon, the chile, parsley, and reserved zest. Toss gently, reaching to the bottom of the bowl with your hands or a pair of spoons and gently folding the ingredients over onto themselves. Season with salt and pepper.

Divide the citrus mixture among chilled plates, leaving the excess sauce behind in the bowl. Add the shellfish to the sauce that remains in the bottom of the bowl and toss gently. Arrange the shellfish on top of the citrus mixture.

HOW TO SECTION CITRUS

1. Slice off the top and bottom of the oranges' peels, creating a flat surface on both ends.

2. Resting one orange upright on its now-flat bottom, cut away the peel, slicing from top to bottom along the curvature of the fruit.

3. Holding the peeled fruit in your hand, cut along both sides of each exposed membrane to free the sections of the fruit, dropping them into the bowl.

HOW TO CUT A MANGO

1. Slice through the mango, skirting the side of the flat pit. Then slice along the other side of the pit to detach it.

2. Holding one side of the mango in one hand, make a series of slashes into the mango with the other. Repeat going in the other direction. Spoon out the flesh.

Tropical Fruit and Seafood Salad

When you make this salad, add the seafood to the other ingredients at the last minute, or the enzymes in the fruits will digest the proteins and turn the seafood into mush. The best approach is to assemble all the ingredients except the seafood, and then put the seafood (still warm if you just cooked it) into the salad just before serving.

MAKES 10 FIRST-COURSE OR 6 MAIN-COURSE SERVINGS

1 red onion, thinly sliced

Salt

1 mango, halved lengthwise, pitted, flesh scooped out with a spoon, and cut into 1/2-inch dice

2 Hawaiian papayas or 1 Mexican papaya (about 3 pounds total), peeled, seeded, and cut into lengthwise wedges

1 pineapple, peeled, quartered lengthwise, cored, and quarters sliced crosswise into 1/4-inch-thick wedges

2 avocados, preferably Hass, halved, pitted, peeled, and coarsely chopped

2 bell peppers, 1 yellow and 1 red, charred, peeled, and seeded (see page 321) and then cut lengthwise into 1/4-inch-wide strips

2 poblano chiles, charred, peeled, and seeded (see page 321) and then cut lengthwise into 1 1/4-inch-wide strips

2 jalapeño chiles, seeded and finely chopped

1 small bunch cilantro, large stems removed and leaves finely chopped

2/3 cup extra virgin olive oil

1/3 cup sherry vinegar

2 1/2 pounds cooked seafood such as lobster (see pages 127, 129), crab (see page 133), or shrimp meat (see page 123); sea or bay scallops (see page 119); or firm-fleshed fish such as tuna or swordfish (see page 163)

Pepper

Mint sprigs for garnish (optional)

In a bowl, sprinkle the onion slices liberally with salt and then toss and rub the salt into the slices for about 2 minutes, or until the salt dissolves and no longer feels gritty. Transfer the onion slices to a colander, set it in the sink or over a bowl, and let drain for about 15 minutes. Working with a little at a time, squeeze the onion slices in your fists to extract as much liquid and salt as possible.

Just before serving, in a large bowl, combine the mango, papayas, pineapple, avocados, peppers, chiles, onion, and cilantro. Pour over the oil and vinegar and toss gently. Season with salt and pepper. Add the seafood and toss to mix. Divide the salad among plates, grind pepper over each serving, and then garnish with a mint sprig.

GRAIN, PASTA, AND BEAN SALADS

Left-over cooked pasta, beans, and grains reheat uncertainly, but make great fillers for tossed salads. They can be combined with tomatoes, grilled and peeled peppers, chiles, herbs, cubes of chicken or turkey or other meats, or shellfish such as shrimp or lobster—the list goes on. Dress them with the best olive oil and a tablespoon or two of lemon juice or vinegar.

Tabbouleh

Most of us who have encountered this salad in restaurants haven't eaten it at its best because in restaurants it isn't usually realistic to chop the herbs at the last minute. Much of what gives this salad its flavor and punch is parsley, but the parsley has to be chopped just before it's incorporated into the salad or it will end up having a stale, grassy flavor.

MAKES 4 TO 6 SIDE-DISH SERVINGS

3/4 cup fine-grain bulgur

1 regular (not English) cucumber, peeled and halved lengthwise

1 1/2 teaspoons coarse salt

4 tomatoes

1/2 teaspoon salt

6 tablespoons extra virgin olive oil

1/2 teaspoon cayenne pepper

1/4 teaspoon ground allspice

1/4 teaspoon ground cinnamon

1/8 teaspoon ground cloves

1/8 teaspoon ground nutmeg

1/4 cup fresh lemon juice

Salt

Pepper

1 small bunch chives (about 30 blades)

1 large bunch flat-leaf parsley, stems removed

2 bunches mint, stems removed

Put the bulgur in a fine-mesh strainer and rinse under cold running water. Transfer to a kitchen towel and squeeze out the excess liquid.

Scrape out the seeds from the cucumber halves with a spoon, then cut the halves lengthwise into 1/4-inch-wide strips. Cut the strips crosswise into 1/4-inch dice. Place the cucumber dice in a bowl, sprinkle with the coarse salt, and then toss and rub the pieces for about 2 minutes, or until the salt dissolves and no longer feels gritty. Transfer the cucumbers to a colander, set it in the sink or over a bowl, and let drain for about 30 minutes.

(continued)

Working with a little at a time, squeeze the cucumber pieces in your fists to extract as much liquid and salt as possible.

Plunge the tomatoes into boiling water for about 30 seconds, rinse them immediately with cold water, and pull away the skin in strips with a paring knife. Cut the tomatoes in half through the stem end and gently squeeze each half to dislodge the seeds, pushing them out with your fingertip if necessary. Chop the tomatoes medium-fine, place in a fine-mesh strainer, toss with 1/2 teaspoon salt, and leave to drain over a bowl for 30 minutes.

In a bowl, combine the bulgur and 5 tablespoons of oil and stir gently.

In a separate bowl, combine the tomatoes, cucumber, cayenne, allspice, cinnamon, cloves, nutmeg, and lemon juice and stir gently. Add the tomato mixture to the bulgur mixture and stir gently to mix. Season with salt and pepper. Cover and refrigerate overnight.

The next day, sprinkle the chives, parsley, and mint with the remaining 1 tablespoon of the oil—the oil seals in their flavor and keeps the mint from blackening—and finely chop by hand. Stir the herbs into the bulgur.

Pasta or Rice Salad

Cold leftover pasta is a perfect medium for other ingredients, such as leftover chicken or seafood. The sauce for the salad can be as simple as some extra virgin olive oil and a little vinegar, or it can be slightly richer and contain an egg yolk (turning it into a mayonnaise) or crème fraîche. Celery provides contrasting crunch, and capers deliver notes of bright savor and tang. Here's an example of what you can do, but the idea is to improvise rather to than follow a recipe exactly.

MAKES 6 LIGHT MAIN-COURSE SERVINGS

- 4 tomatoes
- 3 cups leftover cooked elbow or other small shape pasta or cooked rice cool or at room temperature
- 3 tablespoons capers
- 3 stalks celery, diced
- 1 small red onion, minced
- 2 cups cooked cubed or shredded chicken, or cubed seafood
- 1/2 cup extra virgin olive oil
- 1/4 cup wine vinegar, or more to taste
- Salt
- Pepper

Plunge the tomatoes into boiling water for about 30 seconds, rinse them immediately with cold water, and pull away the skin in strips with a paring knife. Cut out the stem end, and cut each tomato into 8 wedges. Push the seeds out of each wedge with a fingertip.

In a large bowl, combine the tomatoes, pasta, capers, celery, onion, and chicken. Pour over the oil and vinegar and stir gently to mix. Season with salt and pepper.

Plain Beans with Butter or Olive Oil

Beans are best simply boiled and, if being served hot, lightly buttered or flavored with extra virgin olive oil. A nice variation is to toss the hot beans with herb butters, such as parsley butter or chervil or chive butter (see page 349). Virtually any dried bean will work for this recipe. Part of the fun of cooking beans is experimenting with all the (sometimes brightly colored) varieties.

MAKES 6 SIDE DISH SERVINGS

- 2 cups dried beans such as great Northern, navy, borlotti, or canellini
- 1 onion, peeled, split in two lengthwise
- Bouquet garni
- 1 teaspoon salt
- 8 tablespoons butter, herb butter, or extra virgin olive oil, to taste
- Salt
- Pepper

Soak the beans in enough cold water to cover by several inches for 4 hours and drain. Put them in a pot or pressure cooker with 2 quarts of water, the onion, bouquet garni, and salt and simmer for 30 minutes in the pressure cooker or 90 minutes to 3 hours (depending on the variety of bean and its age) in a regular pot. If using a regular pot, check them from time to time and add water as needed to keep it from running dry. Try to coordinate the beans being done with the pot running out of extra liquid. If the beans are done before the liquid has all evaporated, drain the beans in a colander over a pan, boil the liquid that runs through down to a couple of tablespoons, and add it back to the beans. Pick out the onion and bouquet garni and discard. Toss the beans with the butter or olive oil. Season to taste with salt and pepper.

Bean and Parsley Salad

Cooked beans make lovely salads, especially when seasoned with lots of fresh parsley and lemon juice. When olive oil is added such salads become distinctly Italian, but Mexican variations can be made by adding diced tomatoes, chopped chiles, lime juice, and cilantro.

MAKES 6 SIDE-DISH SERVINGS

> **Plain Beans with Butter (opposite)**
> **8 tablespoons extra virgin olive oil or more to taste**
> **Leaves from 1 bunch parsley, chopped very fine**
> **3 tablespoons lemon juice, or more to taste**
> **Salt**
> **Pepper**

Prepare the beans without the butter or olive oil. Let cool and toss with olive oil, parsley, and lemon juice. Season to taste with salt and pepper.

Bean and Mussel Salad

You can also make this salad with clams or cockles. The trick, which is what makes this salad outstanding, is to use the steaming liquid from the mussels to cook the beans. To turn this salad into a luxurious main course, add pieces of cooked lobster or crab or sections of octopus (see pages 126–129, 132, and 136–137).

MAKES 6 FIRST-COURSE SERVINGS

> **4 pounds small cultivated mussels**
> **2 shallots, peeled, minced**
> **1 cup dry white wine**
> **2 cups borlotti or cannellini beans, rinsed, soaked for 4 hours in cold water to cover, drained**
> **Leaves from 1 bunch parsley, chopped very fine just before using**
> **3 tablespoons lemon juice**
> **8 tablespoons extra virgin olive oil, or more or less to taste**
> **Salt**
> **Pepper**

Wash the mussels and drain in a colander.

Simmer the shallots in white wine in a pot large enough to hold the mussels for 5 minutes over medium heat and add the mussels. Cover the pot and steam until the mussels open, about 8 minutes. Make sure the mussels have completely opened and have lodged in one shell or the other—they're not clinging to both shells, which makes them tear when you remove them—before you take them off the heat. Take the mussels out of their shells and reserve, covered with plastic wrap, while you cook the beans. Discard the shells.

Pour the mussel cooking liquid into a large measuring cup, leaving any sand or grit behind in the pot. Add enough water to the liquid to make a total of 2 quarts, and use this liquid to cook the beans in a pot or pressure cooker, about 30 minutes in a pressure cooker, about 2 hours in a pot. Add water to the pot as needed if the liquid is running dry before the beans are cooked. Let cool.

Toss the cooked beans with the mussels, parsley, lemon juice, and olive oil and season to taste with salt and pepper.

EGGS AND CHEESE

It is hard to imagine life without eggs. They not only provide us with breakfast in so many forms that we rarely tire of them, but they also turn up in cakes and pastries, giving them airiness and flavor. When separated, they create soufflés, plus the yolks provide the base for hollandaise, mayonnaise, and sabayon sauces, while the whites give us fluffy frostings and meringues and clarify consommé. They give us eggnog and custards, pureelike French-style scrambled eggs or fluffy American scrambled eggs, and they are fried, poached, baked, and fashioned into omelets. They sustain us and rarely bore us.

BOILING EGGS

When boiling eggs, the trick is to stick to the same method and to learn exactly how long to cook hard-boiled eggs, soft-boiled eggs, and in-between eggs, what the French call *oeufs mollet*, to your liking. The best approach is to bring a pot of water to a rapid boil, put in the egg(s), maintain the water at a simmer, and watch the time. The reason for starting the eggs in boiling water is that the whites cook faster than the yolks. Most of us don't mind a runny yolk, but a runny white is something else entirely. Certain variables will change the cooking times, such as whether the eggs are straight from the refrigerator (cold eggs take longer), the amount of boiling water per egg (if the amount is small, the eggs cool the water, slowing the cooking), and the altitude (the higher the altitude, the slower they cook). Start out using a quart of water or so per egg. The times given here are approximations that are likely to need adjusting and are based on putting eggs

right out of the refrigerator into boiling water. If you want to prevent the shell from cracking, or at least make cracking less likely, insert a pin into the rounder end of the egg—this is the air sac—so the air is released as it expands with the heat, instead of pressing against the shell from the inside and cracking it. If you are making hard-boiled eggs or oeufs mollet eggs ahead of time, plunge them into cold water as soon as they are done to stop the cooking.

It is nice to serve soft-boiled eggs with strips of buttered toast onto which you can smear the eggs. Or, you can spoon the egg into a cup and add croutons (see page 42).

Stages of Doneness

2 minutes: very runny, both white and yolk; virtually raw

3 minutes: white starting to firm up but not completely, yolk very runny

4 minutes: white firm, yolk runny

5 minutes: white firm, yolk a thick liquid consistency

6 minutes: white firm, yolk thickening

7 minutes: white completely set, yolk starting to set but still runny

8 minutes: yolk starts to loose its sheen throughout

10 minutes: more of the edges of the yolk are opaque and the center is shiny yellow—perfect hard-boiled eggs

Add the eggs to rapidly boiling water and let the water return to a simmer over high heat.

3-minute egg

4-minute egg

5-minute egg

6-minute egg

7-minute egg

8-minute egg

10-minute egg

POACHING EGGS

There is no better curative when you are feeling queasy than a poached egg. Poached eggs go well with butter, so it is nice to make a piece of buttered toast to serve with the egg. If you are being more formal, cut round pieces of white bread and gently cook them in a skillet in butter until browned on both sides, and then set the poached egg on top. The butter both adds flavor and seals the bread, keeping it from getting soggy.

Poached eggs are best if made with the freshest eggs—because the white of a fresh egg holds closer to the yolk. The white of an older egg forms an amorphous foamy, unpleasant-tasting white mass around the egg that must be cut off. Some recipes suggest adding vinegar to the poaching liquid, but it doesn't seem to do much. Just bring about 3 inches of salted water to a gentle simmer in a skillet. Break the eggs as close to the surface as possible, and keep the water barely jiggling from the heat. If the yolks refuse to sink below the surface, baste them a couple of times with simmering water spooned over the top surface. The eggs should be ready in 5 minutes or so. Take them out with a skimmer, and use a knife to pare away the loose, foamy white, so the egg has a nice shape. Touch the bottom of the skimmer to a kitchen towel to absorb any water, before putting the egg on a heated plate.

Poached Eggs for a Crowd

If you are poaching eggs for a dozen people, you are going to have a hard time getting them out of the pan fast enough. Instead, poach the eggs ahead of time, trim off the unsightly part of the white, and immediately put the poached eggs in a heatproof bowl of ice water. You can keep the poached eggs cold this way for at least 24 hours in the refrigerator. When you are ready to serve, bring a few quarts of water to a boil, drain the cold water out of the bowl of eggs while holding the eggs back with your hand, and then carefully pour the boiling water over the eggs. Let stand for 45 seconds and then fish out the eggs with a skimmer, blot on a kitchen towel, and serve.

1. Use a cookie cutter to cut out rounds of thin white bread.

2. Cook gently in clarified butter (page 341).

3. Bring about 3 inches of salted water to a gentle simmer in a skillet. Crack the eggs as close to the surface as possible.

4. After about 5 minutes, lift out the eggs with a slotted spoon and cut away any spongy white, creating a perfectly neat egg.

POACHED EGGS FLORENTINE

Arrange lightly creamed spinach (page 295) on a round crouton, set a poached egg on top, and top with hollandaise sauce (page 345).

Prepare the Meurette Sauce on pages 354–355, place the poached eggs on buttered croutons, and spoon the sauce over the eggs.

Eggs Benedict Ideas

Eggs and butter have a wonderful affinity, and buttery hollandaise is the perfect topping for a poached egg. Eggs Benedict call for placing a slice of Canadian bacon (cured pork loin) between the poached egg and a round slice of bread that has been buttered or lightly fried in butter, but almost every neighborhood restaurant serving brunch has come up with variations, such as using creamed spinach or smoked salmon instead of the ham. Cut and fry the croutons ahead of time, make the hollandaise no more than an hour ahead of time (figure on about 3 tablespoons per serving), and poach the eggs at the last minute (see "Poached Eggs for a Crowd").

FRYING EGGS

When Americans talk about frying eggs, they mean panfrying. Some people, primarily the French, occasionally deep-fry eggs, but the result isn't worth the effort and danger—they spatter. Panfrying an egg is straightforward. Heat a thin film of butter or bacon fat in a skillet, preferably either a nonstick pan or a well-seasoned cast-iron one. If you like your fried eggs crispy, an effect that some find revolting and others adore, heat the butter until it is frothy and the froth subsides, or until the fat ripples on the surface. If you don't like your eggs crispy, heat the butter or fat less and cook your eggs more gently. If the white is setting and the yolk is more runny than you like, cover the pan for a minute or two to steam the yolk. Serve the eggs as soon as the white has set, or sunny-side up, or turn the eggs over, yolk down, cook for 30 seconds, and serve them over easy.

SCRAMBLING EGGS

Most of us are fussy about our eggs, especially scrambled eggs, and like them runny or stiff. If you order them runny in a diner, you will be guaranteed they are cooked to order, since it is impossible to keep runny eggs warm without them becoming fully cooked eggs. To ensure your scrambled eggs are tender, when you are beating them, add 1 tablespoon of milk, or even better, heavy cream, for each egg, and then season with salt and pepper. Melt the butter in a nonstick or well-seasoned skillet over medium heat until it is frothy. The more butter you melt, the tastier your eggs will be. Add the beaten eggs, wait until a thin layer of egg congeals on the bottom of the pan, and then scrape up the set layer with a spatula. Wait again, scrape again, and keep repeating this pair of actions until the eggs are how you like them. Keep in mind they will continue to cook once they are out of the pan, so lean a little toward runny.

BAKED EGGS

This is one of the neglected secrets of getting the most out of an egg. Select ramekins with a capacity of 4 to 6 ounces ($^1/_2$ to $^3/_4$ cup). Generously butter the ramekins. Baked eggs are good without any filling or sauce, but you can cover the bottom of each ramekin with a thin layer of creamed spinach (see page 295), some cooked-down tomato concassée (see page 367), diced leftover shrimp or other shellfish or seafood, a piece of smoked salmon, a few cubes of rendered bacon—whatever appeals—and then crack the egg into the ramekin. Add a tablespoon or two of heavy cream to each egg, and season with salt and pepper. Set the ramekins in a baking dish and pour in enough hot water to come one-third up the sides of the ramekins. Bake in a 375°F oven for about 15 minutes, or until the egg white is set. The cream allows the egg white to set without getting hard and gives it a custardlike consistency.

HOW TO MAKE BAKED EGGS

1. Put a thin layer of a mixture, such as creamed spinach (see page 295), cooked tomato concassée (see page 367), or mushroom duxelles (see page 318), into buttered ramekins.

2. Crack an egg into each ramekin, and pour in cream. Season with salt and pepper. Arrange in a baking pan and pour in water to come slightly up the sides of the ramekins.

3. Slide the pan into the oven and bake until the egg white is set and the yolks just begin to firm up.

4. Serve the ramekins on small plates with toast points.

OMELETS

Few preparations in the kitchen instill as much uncertainty in the cook as an omelet. This is due in part to the conflicting directions in cookbooks and magazines and to the so-called differences between a "French" omelet and an American one. The goal is simple: lightly scrambled eggs encased in a thin, tender crust, the whole thing shaped vaguely like an old-fashioned tapered cigar. There are a number of ways to go about cooking an omelet, with most of them designed to deal with the fact that when you put the beaten eggs in the pan of hot butter, the bottom sets and the eggs on top remain liquid. If you don't do something quickly, the egg on the bottom hardens, wrinkles, or even burns before the runny egg on top cooks. You can always slide the pan under a broiler, add any filling, and fold the eggs over. Or, you can lift up the edge of the set egg with a fork, so the liquid egg runs underneath, and then continue cooking until all the egg has set. Both methods will work, but to get a perfectly shaped omelet in about a minute, you need to use a specific technique.

If you are not experienced at making omelets, don't try making an omelet with more than 3 eggs. Begin by using a fork to beat the eggs with 1 tablespoon of milk or heavy cream and then season them with salt and pepper. The cream gives the omelet a melting, custardlike consistency and makes it harder to overcook and toughen the eggs.

Select a 9- to 10-inch (the bottom will be 7 to 8 inches) nonstick or well-seasoned cast-iron omelet pan. An omelet pan has curved sides that slope outward, making it easier to get the eggs to fold back over onto themselves. Heat the butter in the pan over high heat until the butter is frothy, the froth begins to subside, and the butter is on the verge of burning. Pour in the eggs in the nick of time and stir them with the back of a fork, held a fraction of an inch above the bottom of the pan but not actually touching it. This allows a thin layer of egg to set on the bottom while the eggs above the layer are being scrambled. When the eggs are scrambled and still runny, tilt the pan away from you and, using your fist, hit the handle where it touches the pan. This will cause the end of the omelet opposite you to fold inward. You can give it a little help with a fork. Use a fork to flip the end of the omelet nearest you (and nearest the handle), so the edge overlaps over the other fold. Hold the pan next to a warmed plate and flip the omelet out onto it.

1. Whisk 1 tablespoon of milk or cream per egg into the eggs.

2. Starting with a cold pan, melt 1 tablespoon of butter over high heat. When the butter froths and the froth starts to subside, add the eggs.

3. Stir the eggs but don't touch the bottom of the pan with the fork.

4. Pound on the pan handle with a fist to get the edge of the omelet farthest from the handle to flip inward.

5. Turn the part of the omelet nearest you in toward the middle.

6. Slide the omelet out onto a warmed plate.

Rolled Omelets

Some beginners find making a rolled omelet easier than making a traditional omelet. Start the same way: beat the eggs, melt the butter in the pan over high heat until the froth subsides, and pour in the eggs. Then hold the pan over the heat for 3 to 10 seconds, or until a thin layer of egg sets on the bottom. Pull the pan quickly toward you with a jerking motion until the layer of set egg folds over in toward the center of the omelet, leaving an area near the handle with no layer of set egg on it. Hold the pan over the stove again for several seconds until another layer forms and jerk again. Continue in this way until all the loose egg has cooked and the omelet is rolled up. Turn the omelet out onto a warmed plate.

HOW TO MAKE A ROLLED OMELET

1. Melt the butter over high heat, pour the eggs into the pan, and allow a thin membrane of egg to set on the pan. Pull the pan toward you, causing the omelet to fold in on itself, then let set again.

2. Jerk the pan toward you again. Repeat in this way until no raw egg remains.

3. Continue jerking the pan to roll the omelet up on itself.

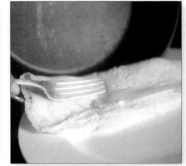

4. Turn the omelet out onto a warmed plate.

Omelet Flavorings and Fillings

You can add fillings and flavorings to omelets in three ways. You can whisk herbs, chopped truffles, wild mushrooms, and the like directly into the raw eggs; you can add cheese or cooked vegetables, meat, or seafood to the omelet before folding or rolling to seal the filling within; or you can make a plain omelet, cut a lengthwise slit along the top, spread open the slit slightly, and put a garnish such as lobster or caviar or other luxurious things on top. A few possibilities for customizing: adding 1 tablespoon mixed chopped fresh parsley, chervil, tarragon, and chives (the classic French *omelette aux fines herbes*); chopped reconstituted morels; or shaved fresh truffles. A couple of teaspoons of mustard whisked into the eggs wakes up their flavor, as do a couple of tablespoons of grated Parmigiano-Reggiano cheese. If using softer cheeses, fold them into the omelet—1/3 cup shredded is usually about the right amount—rather than beating them into the eggs, or the eggs may stick. Sautéed sliced mushrooms are always good folded up inside an omelet. So, too, is chicken or turkey in cream sauce (see page 343) when you are trying to make the most of leftovers. Luxurious foods that you don't have enough of, such as cooked crab, can be spooned over omelets. Or, caviar can be dolloped on a miniature one-egg omelet as a first course.

Fluffy Omelets

There is a famous restaurant on Mont Saint-Michel, a small island off the coast of Brittany, where they sell an equally famous fluffy omelet at an exorbitant price to tourists. The omelet is delicious, if not quite worth the price, and since the restaurant provides a window for gawkers to watch and analyze, it is easy to see how it is made. Anyone who says it is made by separating the eggs, the traditional approach to a soufflé omelet, has never stood at the window and watched. The secret to the omelet is extended beating of the eggs, which must be at room temperature or better warm, and a frightening amount of butter. At the restaurant, a copper pan with a handle the length of a spear is held in a wood fire for the final cooking, but this is more picturesque than any real culinary secret.

To make the fluffy omelet at home, you must have a powerful stand mixer with a whisk attachment or a great deal of patience. At the restaurant, the eggs are beaten in an unlined copper bowl, helpful certainly for beating egg whites but of questionable utility when beating whole eggs. But if you have a copper bowl attachment to your mixer, why not use it, in case it does do something extra. It is dramatic to make an

1. Warm the eggs in a bowl of hot tap water.

2. Beat warmed eggs until quadrupled in volume and pour them into the pan.

3. While the eggs are beating, melt a generous amount of butter in a nonstick pan.

4. Cook the omelet over low heat, repositioning it over the heat every 30 seconds or so.

5. The omelet will firm up and retain its loft.

6. Slide the omelet under the broiler just until the top is barely set.

7. Fold the omelet.

8. Serve on warmed plates.

omelet for two, using 5 eggs and a 12-inch skillet. Warm the eggs in their shells in a bowl of hot tap water, and then crack them into the mixer bowl and beat them on high speed for about 5 minutes, or until at least quadrupled in volume. Preheat the broiler. Heat about 4 tablespoons butter in a flameproof skillet (a paltry amount compared to the restaurant) until the butter is thoroughly frothy, and then pour in the beaten eggs. Cook the omelet over low heat until the bottom is golden brown, repositioning the pan over the heat several times to brown the omelet evenly. Once browned, slide the omelet under the broiler for 15 seconds, or just until the top is barely set. You don't want to dry out the inside. Fold the omelet and slide it out onto a warmed plate or platter.

SAVORY SOUFFLÉS

Other than sweet soufflés, which have their own charm, the best of all savory soufflés is the classic cheese soufflé made with good Gruyère cheese or something else sharp and well aged, such as Roquefort. Cooks are often frightened by the thought of making soufflés, because if they are overcooked, they fall within seconds of being removed from the oven. But they are less sensitive than usually thought. To judge their doneness, you have to move the dish back and forth in the oven, watching the motion of the soufflé, and then divine, by the subtleties of the movement, the consistency of the interior. This can be done but is hard to describe. Undercooked soufflés are amazingly forgiving. You can proudly bring one to the table, cut into it, find it underdone and runny on the inside, and just stick it back in the oven without it falling.

The only other real hazard that awaits the soufflé maker is getting a bit of yolk or some kind of fat into the whites, which will interfere with them beating to their full volume. The notion that you should beat egg whites in a copper bowl—a stainless-steel bowl and a pinch of cream of tartar are the next best thing—is not mistaken folklore. They don't fluff up more when beaten in copper, but they do hold better in the oven and rise a bit more, too. You will need a large bowl for beating by hand or the copper bowl insert for a stand mixer. If you are buying a copper bowl, buy the largest one you can find. Small ones don't give you enough room to move the whisk sufficiently. Before you use a copper bowl each time, clean it well with salt and vinegar, rinse it thoroughly, and then pat it dry with a clean kitchen towel. You have to re-clean the copper bowl each time to keep the copper reactive, so it gives off the chemical needed to make the whites rise.

Savory soufflés, including cheese soufflés, follow a standard formula: You make a stiff béchamel; you whisk some of the egg whites into it along with any savory ingredients, such as cheese; and then you fold this sauce into the beaten egg whites. You then transfer the mixture to a buttered and floured soufflé dish (or grated hard cheese can replace the flour).

Cheese Soufflés

If drama is important, the soufflé mixture should fill to the rim of the dish, and you will need to fit an aluminum foil collar, also buttered and floured or dusted with cheese, around the dish to prevent the expanding and still-liquid mass from spilling over the sides. Making a soufflé collar is a bit of a nuisance and can be avoided if you fill the soufflé dish no more than three-fourths full.

MAKES 4 INDIVIDUAL CHEESE SOUFFLÉS

> 2 tablespoons butter, room temperature, for dishes, plus 1 tablespoon if using collars
>
> 5 tablespoons grated Parmigiano-Reggiano, aged Gouda, or other hard cheese for dishes, plus 3 tablespoons if using collars

Béchamel Sauce Base

> 3 tablespoons butter
>
> 3 tablespoons flour
>
> 3/4 cup milk
>
> Tiny pinch of ground or freshly grated nutmeg
>
> 1/4 teaspoon salt
>
> Pepper
>
> 5 ounces Gruyère or other firm cheese, grated (about 1 cup)
>
> 4 egg yolks

Soufflés

> 7 egg whites
>
> Pinch of cream of tartar if not using a copper bowl
>
> 2 ounces Parmigiano-Reggiano, aged Gouda, or other hard cheese, grated (about 3/4 cup lightly packed)

To prepare the soufflé dishes or ramekins, brush the bottom and sides of four 8-, 10-, or 12-ounce soufflé dishes with the butter. Coat the bottom and sides of the dishes with the grated cheese, tapping out the excess. If using collars, cut 4 strips of aluminum foil wide enough to stand 2 to 3 inches above the rim of the dish when folded in half and long enough to wrap around the dish with a little overlap. Fold the foil in half lengthwise, butter one side and dust with cheese, and set aside until you are ready to bake the soufflés.

To make the sauce base, in a heavy-bottomed saucepan, melt the butter over medium heat. Add the flour and stir for about 2 minutes, or until the mixture is smooth. Slowly add the milk while whisking constantly, then continue to whisk for about 2 minutes, increase the heat to high, and continue whisking until it reaches a simmer, about 5 minutes, thickens, and is smooth. Take off the heat and whisk in the nutmeg, salt, and about 5 grinds of pepper. Add the Gruyère and stir until the sauce is smooth. It will be very stiff.

Stir the sauce for a minute to cool it slightly, then beat in the egg yolks one at a time.

Preheat the oven to 350°F. To finish the soufflés, put the eggs whites in a copper bowl, or in a stainless-steel bowl with the cream of tartar. Using a mixer on high speed or a whisk, beat until stiff peaks form. Stir about one-fourth of the beaten egg whites into the sauce to lighten it. Then gently fold the sauce base into the rest of the whites while sprinkling in the Parmigiano-Reggiano cheese with every stroke or two. Cut into the mixture and fold, don't press on the mixture, so as not to deflate the whites.

Divide the soufflé mixture evenly among the prepared dishes. If it rises slightly above the rim, smooth off the top with the back of a knife. Run your thumb around the rim of each dish to form a moat about 1/2 inch wide along the edge of the soufflé mixture. This keeps the top of the soufflé mixture from attaching to the rim. If using collars, wrap each one, buttered side in, around the rim of a dish, and pinch the ends together to hold the collar in place.

Put the soufflés on a sheet pan, place in the oven, and raise the oven heat to 375°F. Bake the soufflés for about 18 minutes, or until they have risen an inch or two above the rims. Stick a spoon into the center of one of the soufflés. It should be slightly runny in the very middle. Pull away the collars and serve.

1. Brush the molds with a thick layer of room temperature butter.

2. Fill one of the molds with grated Parmigiano-Reggiano cheese.

3. Rotate the mold over another mold to coat the sides.

4. Make a thick béchamel sauce.

5. Stir the cheese, here Roquefort, into the béchamel until smooth.

6. Beat the egg whites to stiff peaks.

7. Stir about one-fourth of the beaten egg whites into the béchamel.

8. Fold the béchamel into the remaining whites.

9. Pour the soufflé mixture into the molds.

10. Run your thumb around the rim of each dish to form a small moat in the soufflé mixture.

11. Bake the soufflé until well risen.

Twice-Baked Soufflés

The idea of baking a soufflé and letting it fall, or at least deflate slightly, before rebaking sounds oxymoronic. But in fact this method of making individual soufflés—on the small side, since they are so rich—and then rebaking them surrounded by a sauce creates a delightful first course. Here's how it goes: You make a basic soufflé mixture that is heavier than usual because of more béchamel. It bakes in individual ramekins until well risen, but is left a little underdone. All of this can be completed early in the day. You then turn the soufflés out of the molds, arrange them in a baking dish that holds them snugly, and pour a sauce over them—something as simple as a little cream with some diced tomatoes and minced tarragon in it. Then, you slide the dish into the oven and the soufflés repuff, absorb the delicious sauce like sponges, and end up wonderfully custardy yet light. The method is endlessly versatile, which means you can fold various ingredients into the soufflé mixture and infuse with any sauce that appeals.

MAKES 6 FIRST-COURSE SERVINGS

> 1 tablespoon butter, room temperature
>
> 1/4 cup grated Parmigiano-Reggiano or grana padano cheese
>
> **Soufflés**
>
> 4 tablespoons butter
>
> 4 1/2 tablespoons flour
>
> 1 1/2 cups milk
>
> 3 ounces Parmigiano-Reggiano or grana padano cheese, grated (about 1 cup lightly packed)
>
> Pinch of ground or freshly grated nutmeg
>
> Salt
>
> Pepper
>
> 4 eggs, separated
>
> Pinch of cream of tartar if not using a copper bowl
>
> 1 teaspoon butter, room temperature, for preparing the gratin dish
>
> 1 cup heavy cream
>
> 3 tomatoes, peeled, seeded, and chopped (see page 85)
>
> 1 tablespoon coarsely chopped fresh tarragon
>
> 1 cup grated Parmigiano-Reggiano or grana padano cheese

To prepare the soufflé dishes, brush the bottom and sides of six 5- or 6-ounce ramekins or custard cups with the butter. Coat the bottom and sides of the dishes with the grated cheese, tapping out the excess.

To make the soufflé mixture, in a heavy-bottomed saucepan, melt the butter over medium heat. Add the flour and stir for about 2 minutes, or until the mixture is smooth and smells toasty. Slowly add the milk while whisking constantly, then raise the heat to high and continue to whisk for about 5 minutes, or until the sauce boils, thickens, and is smooth. Remove from the heat and stir in the cheese until smooth, then season with the nutmeg and with salt and pepper to taste. Beat in the egg yolks one at a time and set aside.

Preheat the oven to 400°F. Put the eggs whites in a copper bowl, or in a stainless-steel bowl with the cream of tartar. Using a mixer on high speed or a whisk, beat until stiff peaks form. Stir about one-fourth of the beaten egg whites into the sauce to lighten it. Then gently fold the sauce base into the rest of the whites.

Divide the soufflé mixture evenly among the prepared dishes. Run your thumb around the rim of each dish to form a moat about 1/2 inch wide along the edge of the soufflé mixture. This keeps the top of the soufflé mixture from attaching to the rim. Put the soufflés in a baking pan or dish with sides at least as high as the ramekins and ideally just large enough to hold them. Pour enough hot water—the hottest water from the tap is fine—into the pan to come two-thirds up the sides of the ramekins, making a water bath (bain-marie).

Slide the baking dish into the oven and bake the soufflés for about 20 minutes, or until they have risen an inch or two above the rims. Take the pan out of the oven, remove the ramekins from the bain-marie, and let cool for 10 minutes. At this point, the soufflés will fall somewhat, but don't worry. They are going to puff again during the second baking. Rub a gratin dish or baking dish just large enough to hold the soufflés with the butter. Carefully turn the soufflés out of the ramekins and set them in the gratin dish. If you are not serving the soufflés right away, cover the dish with plastic wrap and refrigerate for up to 24 hours.

To finish the soufflés, preheat the oven (or raise the heat) to 450°F. In a small saucepan, combine the cream, tomatoes, and tarragon and bring to a simmer. Season with salt and pepper.

Pour the sauce over the soufflés and then sprinkle them with the cheese. Slide the dish into the oven and bake for about 20 to 25 minutes, or until the soufflés have risen again, turned golden brown on top, and the sauce in the bottom is bubbling. Use a spatula to transfer the soufflés to warmed plates, and spoon over any sauce left in the bottom of the baking dish.

FONDUE

After having fallen out of fashion, fondue sets are now being snapped up at yard sales, and the pleasures of sitting around a simmering pot of melted cheese and wine has been rediscovered. The secret to a successful fondue gathering is to do as the Swiss do and serve little glasses of frozen kirsch along with plenty of white wine. The kirsch isn't essential—it's expensive—but when it is authentic, which means imported from Switzerland, Germany, or France, it adds immeasurably to the experience. It's strong, especially when you are also drinking wine, so warn your guests.

Few dishes are easier to make than cheese fondue, as long as you don't scrimp on the cheese. Buy authentic Swiss Gruyère or French Comté and authentic Swiss Emmentaler (the Swiss cheese with the big holes). The packaging (or the cheese seller) must say "imported from Switzerland" or "imported from France," not just "imported," which can mean from anywhere outside the United States.

Use dry white wine, preferably something French like Muscadet that will guarantee plenty of tangy acidity to offset the richness of the cheese. Don't bother putting kirsch into the fondue itself. Its expensive aroma will cook off. Instead just drink it.

Cheese Fondue

This recipe includes a tiny bit of cornstarch to prevent the cheese from clumping up and separating from the wine.

MAKES 4 MAIN-COURSE SERVINGS

> 1 clove garlic, cut in half
> 2 cups dry white wine
> 2 teaspoons cornstarch
> 1/2 pound Swiss Emmentaler cheese, coarsely shredded
> 1/2 pound Swiss Gruyère cheese, coarsely shredded
> Salt
> Pepper
> Tiny pinch of ground or freshly grated nutmeg
> 2 crusty baguettes, cut in half lengthwise (or into quarters if especially thick) and then into bite-sized pieces

In a saucepan, combine the garlic and wine, bring to a boil, and boil for about 3 minutes to cook off most of the alcohol. Remove and discard the garlic. In a small bowl or cup, stir the cornstarch into 1 tablespoon cold water until smooth, and then whisk the mixture into the wine. Reduce the heat to low or medium-low, add both cheeses, and stir with a wooden spoon for about 3 minutes, or until they melt. At this point, the fondue may seem too thin, but it will thicken as it sits over the burner.

Position the metal cover on the Sterno burner so that it covers most of the flame, keeping the heat as low as possible to prevent scorching. Pour the fondue into the fondue pot and place it on the burner. Gather round and pass the bread. Use long fondue forks or regular kitchen forks to dip the bread into the fondue.

Quiche

A quiche is a savory custard baked in a prebaked tart shell. The most traditional quiche of all is a quiche Lorraine, made by pouring a custard mixture over pieces of bacon and sometimes cheese arranged in the tart shell. Because quiche is so versatile you can arrange almost anything you like in the shell before pouring over the custard mixture—the custard mixture stays the same. The quiche is then slowly baked until the custard sets. When making a quiche, or any tart filled with liquid, make sure that any holes or cracks in the tart shell have been sealed. For minor slits or cracks, you can brush them with a little beaten egg and bake for about 5 minutes to set the egg.

MAKES ONE 9- OR 10-INCH QUICHE

> Basic Pie and Tart Dough (page 445)
> 6 ounces bacon, preferably slab or thick-cut slices
> 2 eggs
> 1¼ cups milk
> Pepper
> Egg wash (page 19)
> 1/4 pound flavorful cheese such as Gruyère or Cheddar, finely shredded (about 1½ cups grated)

Roll out the dough and use it to line a 10-inch tart pan with a removable bottom or a porcelain quiche dish. Prebake the tart shell (page 458) and let cool completely.

Preheat the oven to 300°F. If using slab bacon, cut it into 1/3-inch-thick slices. Cut the bacon slices crosswise into strips about 1/4inch wide (called lardons). In a skillet, cook the bacon strips over medium heat, stirring often, for about 6 minutes, or until they render fat and barely begin to brown. Using a slotted spoon, transfer the bacon strips to paper towels to drain.

In a bowl, beat the eggs until blended, and then beat in the milk until well mixed. Grind in a little pepper.

If the tart shell has a crack or a hole, seal it with egg wash and put it in the oven for 5 minutes. Sprinkle the bacon over the tart shell and then spread the cheese over the bacon. Carefully pour in the egg mixture, trying not to disturb the cheese and bacon.

Put the quiche on a sheet pan—in case it leaks—and bake for about 40 minutes, or until set. Let cool on a rack.

SHELLFISH

Shellfish, big and small, are among the tastiest of edible things. While some are expensive, they all contribute wonderful flavor, even when only a small amount is used.

There are three kinds of shellfish: First are mollusks, which have hard shells made primarily of calcium compounds. Most mollusks are bivalves, meaning they have two shells, but some, such as limpets and sea snails, have only one. The second group is crustaceans, which have a series of legs to aid in crawling and also have shells, though softer than those of mollusks. Third are cephalopods, literally "foot-heads," which boast tentacles. The groups are cooked in fundamentally different ways, but members of the same family are often cooked in the same way as their relatives.

MOLLUSKS

Mussels, oysters, clams, scallops, and cockles are among the best-known mollusks. Numerous varieties exist of each one, but the cooking methods are so similar that you don't need to worry if you bought, for example, blue mussels or green-lipped mussels. Mussels, clams, and cockles are almost always steamed in the shell in a small amount of liquid, often wine or wine and water, and the liquid they release is turned along with their cooking liquid into a soup or sauce. Their liquid is the essence of the sea, and when used as a sauce base, it ensures that your sauces are as tasty as any in the finest restaurants. Oysters are usually shucked before cooking and most of the time gently heated in their own juices. While raw oysters may be the most flavorful of all shellfish, the liquid they release is less so. Scallops also are cooked out of their shell.

MUSSELS

You are likely to encounter three kinds of mussels: small blue cultivated mussels, large black wild mussels, and large green New Zealand mussels. They are all cooked in the same way, with the larger ones taking a minute or two longer. Cultivated mussels are the easiest to deal with because they don't have large beards—the tufts of hair that stick out one side of the shell, which they use to hold onto rocks or pilings. They can typically be ignored or pulled off each mussel after all the shellfish have been cooked and are open. The beards on wild mussels usually need to be pulled off before cooking—just grab it with your thumb and forefinger and tug. Wild mussels must be well scrubbed to eliminate any mud clinging to the shell. While cultivated mussels are cleaner and less likely to contain the grit commonly found in the wild mussels, their meats are sometimes disappointingly small and lack the complex flavor of their wild cousins. Some shellfish neophytes are put off by the size of wild mussels and the feeling of a large mussel in the mouth.

Cooks are regularly told that mussels are good only if they are tightly closed, or that if they gape slightly, they should close immediately when two are tapped against each other. Unfortunately, not all mussels, even the most robust, are so quick to respond, which means that many a healthy mussel has ended up in the garbage. First, give the mussel a little time to close. Then if it still doesn't close, give it a sniff. If it smells like anything other than a pristine beach, throw it out. Closed mussels are sometimes as likely to be dead as open ones, as you will discover when you encounter mud-filled mussels, more likely a problem with wild ones. These have to be sorted out right away, because if they open in the steaming liquid, all is lost. Scrub mussels with a stiff brush or scrape them with the back of a paring knife under cold running water. As you clean them, push the shells sideways in opposite directions. Any dead mussels will open and fall apart in your hand.

Mussels can be added in the shell (once scrubbed) to soups and seafood stews and allowed to open in the hot liquid. They open quickly, usually in 3 to 5 minutes, or they can be steamed in a small amount of liquid, which is then served with the mussels for mopping up with French bread. The liquid can also be reduced—but not too much since it is very salty—and turned into a sauce for the mussels or for other seafood, or it can be turned into soup. The inherent problem with mussel soup is that you need a large number of mussels to yield enough liquid. One solution is to prepare the salad on page 109 for the mussels and save the liquid for soup.

HOW TO STEAM MUSSELS

1. Brush the mussels under cold running water.

2. Simmer garlic, shallots, and thyme in the wine for 5 minutes, then put the mussels in the pot, cover, and cook over medium to high heat until they are wide open.

3. Drain in a colander set over a pan or bowl.

Mussels Steamed in White Wine

This is the archetypal mussel dish, and deservedly so since it is almost impossible to improve it. Variations involve only different herbs and flavorings in the steaming liquid. Serve this dish as a first course or light main course with plenty of crusty French bread for dipping. Pour a crisp, cool country white wine, such as a Muscadet or Sancerre.

MAKES 4 FIRST-COURSE SERVINGS

> **6 pounds mussels**
> **1 cup dry white wine**
> **3 shallots, minced**
> **1 clove garlic, minced and then crushed with the side of the knife (optional)**
> **Pinch of chopped fresh or dried thyme (optional)**
> **3 tablespoons finely chopped fresh parsley**
> **4 tablespoons butter (optional)**

Scrub the mussels, push the sides in opposite directions to eliminate dead ones, rinse thoroughly, and set aside.

Select a pot large enough so that the mussels will reach no higher than two-thirds up the sides. Combine the wine, shallots, garlic, and thyme in the pot, cover, bring to a simmer over low heat, and simmer for 5 minutes.

Add the mussels all at once, cover the pot, raise the heat to high, bring to a boil, and boil for 2 minutes. Holding the lid in place with a kitchen towel, shake the pot with a rotating motion to redistribute the mussels, so those that were on the bottom are now on the top. Steam for 2 minutes more, and then check to see if all the mussels have opened. They should be fully opened and each mussel meat should be in one shell, not stretched out between the two. If they are not fully cooked, they will tear as they are pulled out of the shells.

Use a spider or skimmer to transfer the mussels to warmed bowls. Check the liquid in the bottom of the pot. If it contains grit, carefully pour it into a saucepan, leaving the grit behind (don't worry about the shallots). Add the parsley to the steaming liquid, simmer for 1 minute, and whisk in the butter. Pour the liquid over the mussels in the bowls and serve.

VARIATIONS

Flavoring choices for the mussel steaming liquid are endless. Garlic and tomatoes are good additions. Chopped fresh basil or mint can replace the parsley, and $1/2$ cup to 1 cup heavy cream can replace the butter. A pinch of saffron simmered in the steaming liquid is irresistible, and curry powder—about 1 tablespoon cooked for 30 seconds to 1 minute in 1 tablespoon butter—imparts a welcome spiciness. You can give this dish a Thai accent by simmering a couple of kaffir lime leaves, some thinly sliced lemongrass, a few chiles, and some chopped fresh cilantro in the steaming liquid, with or without 1 cup or so unsweetened coconut milk. Or, for a Mexican note, add finely chopped reconstituted dried chiles, chopped tomatoes, fresh lime juice, and chopped fresh cilantro.

Mussel Saffron Soup

Mussels and saffron are destined to accompany each other. But curry powder is almost as good, as the popular seaside French mussel dish known as mouclade has long proven. The challenge when making shellfish soups is getting your hands on plenty of shellfish steaming liquid. You will need about 8 pounds mussels (which fortunately aren't expensive) to get the 4 cups of liquid called for here, leaving you with mussels for making the salad (right). Ideally, you will prepare the salad a few days ahead of time, and save the steaming liquid in the fridge or freezer. This soup contains cream that can be used sparingly, but don't leave it out completely. It is essential for pulling together the flavors of the sea and the saffron.

MAKES 4 FIRST-COURSE SERVINGS

 8 pounds mussels

 2 cups dry white wine

 3 shallots, minced

 1 clove garlic, minced and then crushed with the side of the knife

 3 sprigs thyme or 1/4 teaspoon dried thyme

 1 teaspoon saffron threads, soaked in 1 tablespoon water for 30 minutes, or 1 tablespoon curry powder

 1 tablespoon butter if using curry powder

 1 cup heavy cream

 Salt

 Pepper

Scrub the mussels, push the sides in opposite directions to eliminate dead ones, rinse thoroughly, and set aside.

Select a pot large enough so that the mussels will reach no higher than two-thirds up the sides. Combine the wine, shallots, garlic, and thyme in the pot, cover, bring to a simmer over low heat, and simmer for 5 minutes.

Add the mussels all at once, cover the pot, raise the heat to high, bring to a boil, and boil for 4 minutes. Holding the lid in place with a kitchen towel, shake the pot with a rotating motion to redistribute the mussels, so those that were on the bottom are now on the top. Steam for 4 to 6 minutes more, and

then check to see if all the mussels have opened. They should be fully opened and each mussel should be in one shell, not stretched out between the two. If they are not fully cooked, they will tear as they are pulled out of the shells.

Use a spider or skimmer to transfer the mussels to a large bowl, let them cool, and then remove them from their shells, discarding any beards you find. Pour the steaming liquid in the bottom of the pot into a storage container—or into a saucepan if you are making the soup right away—leaving any grit behind in the pot.

Bring the steaming liquid to a simmer and add the saffron and its soaking water. If you are using the curry powder, cook it in the butter in a small sauté pan or skillet over medium heat for about 1 minute, or until it smells fragrant, and then add it to the steaming liquid. Stir in the cream, season with salt—which may not be necessary, as the mussel liquid may already be salty enough—and pepper, and serve in warmed soup plates.

Cold Mussel Salad with Capers and Dill

This zesty salad is inspired by a recipe for a salad popular in Nantucket that appeared in Saveur magazine. It is a perfect way to use cooked mussels that have come about as a by-product of other dishes, such as soups and sauces. If you make the mayonnaise, you can experiment with the variations that accompany the basic recipe.

MAKES 8 FIRST-COURSE SERVINGS

 4 cups cooked mussel meats, from about 8 pounds mussels

 2 tablespoons olive oil

 2 cloves garlic, minced and then crushed with the side of the knife

 1/2 red onion, sliced paper-thin

 2 teaspoons coarse salt

 1 chipotle chile, soaked in hot water for 30 minutes to soften if dried or rinsed if canned, seeded and chopped, or 1 jalapeño chile, seeded and finely chopped

 1/2 cup mayonnaise, preferably homemade (see page 359)

 3 tablespoons fresh lemon juice

 4 tablespoons capers, drained

 1 bunch dill, minced (about 2 tablespoons)

 Leaves from 1 small bunch parsley, finely chopped

 Salt

 Pepper

(continued)

If the mussels feel gritty, rinse them under cold running water and drain. In a sauté pan, heat the olive oil over medium heat and add the garlic. Stir for 1 minute, add the mussels, and stir for 1 minute more. Remove from the heat and let cool.

In a bowl, sprinkle the onion slices with the coarse salt and then toss and rub the salt into the slices for about 2 minutes, or until the salt dissolves and no longer feels gritty. Transfer the onion slices to a colander, set it in the sink or over a bowl, and let drain for about 15 minutes. Working with a little at a time, squeeze the onion slices in your fists to extract as much liquid and salt as possible.

In a salad bowl, combine the mussels, onion, chile, mayonnaise, lemon juice, capers, dill, and parsley and stir gently to mix. Season with salt and pepper.

CLAMS

Clams come in several varieties, but the main categories are hard shell and soft shell. As their name implies, hard-shell clams have hard shells, like those of mussels or oysters. Soft-shell clams, also called steamers, have thinner, friable shells that crack relatively easily but are in no way soft. Steamers also have a little spout that sticks out of one side and prevents the clam from ever fully closing. Occasionally, you may encounter razor clams, soft-shell clams that are shaped like an old-fashioned straight razor and have sharp edges.

Several kinds of hard-shell clams are found on both the Pacific and Atlantic coasts of the United States. The most common Atlantic hard-shell clam is called a quahog (pronounced ko-hog), but it is rarely called that at fish markets. Instead, it is named according to its size. The smallest and most expensive by weight are littlenecks, larger are cherrystones, and the largest are chowder clams. Mahogany clams, sometimes called ocean quahogs because they are found in deeper water, are about the same size as cherrystones—about 2 inches across—and can be cooked the same way. Pacific clams include a variety called a littleneck, even though it is a different species than the Atlantic littleneck (it is cooked in the same way, however) and small Manila clams that can be cooked like littlenecks. You can occasionally find the less common Pismo and butter clams. Last is the geoduck clam (pronounced gooeyduck), which looks like a giant soft-shell clam—the shell is typically 8 to 10 inches long—with a long siphon that can grow as long as 3 feet. Geoducks are sometimes used in soups and stews, but they have such a remarkable briny subtlety when served raw that cooking seems a sacrilege.

When buying clams, remember that hard-shell clams, unlike mussels, must be fully closed. A soft-shell clam has no choice but to gape, but when you touch the end of its siphon, it should retract.

When clams are cooked in a little wine or water, they release the pure essence of the sea, which can be used to make sauces and soups. Many recipes suggest ridding clams of grit by storing them overnight in a tub of salt water, a system that works beautifully for steamers and razor clams, but does nothing for hard-shell clams. Hard-shell clams can be cooked directly in soups and stews, or they can be steamed in a little liquid, just like mussels, and the resulting liquid can be used for dipping French bread or as the base for sauces and soups. Clams take longer to steam open than mussels, usually about 10 minutes. Invariably, a few remain closed after all the others have opened, and despite the claims of many recipes, they are usually perfectly fine. Just slip a knife tip between the two shells and the clam usually snaps open. Don't do this over the rest of the clams, however, just in case the clam is dead and full of mud, which could ruin the rest of your dinner.

Soft-shell clams are typically steamed in a little seawater or white wine, just long enough to cook them through. They are then scooped out of the shells with a knife, dipped in sauce or melted butter using the spout as a handle, and the little membrane is peeled off the spout before it is eaten.

Clams can also be shucked and eaten raw. Recipes for stuffed clams that call for shucking the clams ahead of time can be simplified by steaming open the clams, thus bypassing the shucking. You can boil down the liquid released during the steaming and work it into the stuffing for more clam flavor.

Steamed Clams

Follow the recipe for steamed mussels on page 108, but substitute 2 dozen littleneck or cherrystone clams. If you are steaming open the clams to make linguine with clam sauce (opposite), use water instead of wine, or half water and half wine. Steam for 10 to 12 minutes, or until the clams open—slip a knife between the shells of any that don't, so they snap open—and serve in warmed soup plates with the steaming liquid spooned around them. Season with salt and pepper.

Linguine with Clam Sauce

In Italy, this dish is served with linguine or spaghetti, and the clam steaming liquid is combined with olive oil. In the eastern United States, cream is often added to the steaming liquid instead.

MAKES 6 FIRST-COURSE OR 4 MAIN-COURSE SERVINGS

> **Steamed Clams (see opposite)**
> **1/2 cup heavy cream or extra virgin olive oil**
> **Salt**
> **Pepper**
> **12 ounces dried linguine or spaghetti or 1 pound fresh linguine**

Cook the clams as directed. When all of them are open, scoop them out of the pot, put them into a bowl, and keep warm. Check the bottom of the pot for grit. If there is grit, pour the liquid into a clean bowl, leaving any grit behind in the pot, and then rinse out the pot and return the steaming liquid to it. Add the cream to the liquid and boil it down over high heat just until the sauce thickens slightly, just enough to coat the back of a spoon. If using oil, add it to the steaming liquid and bring it to a simmer. Season with salt (it may need just a little) and pepper.

Meanwhile, bring a large pot three-fourths full of water to a rapid boil, add the pasta, and cook according to the package directions or until al dente—the pasta has the slightest resistance to the bite but no rawness. Drain the pasta in a colander, and then pour it into the pot with the sauce, and stir and toss to coat the pasta evenly.

Divide the pasta among warmed pasta plates or soup plates and arrange the clams—6 per person for main courses, 4 per person for first courses—on top.

Clam Chowder

No two people agree on the best approach to clam chowder, so it is never safe to give a recipe for it. The greatest controversy surrounds the merits of the Manhattan type, made with tomatoes, and the New England tradition that dictates the use of milk and not a hint of tomato. It seems to make the greatest sense to include tomatoes in August and September and leave them out the rest of the year. Aficionados generally agree that chowder must include onions and potatoes and occasionally corn, and that bacon or butter can replace the more traditional salt pork. Most New England recipes call for milk, although cream, which can be used in smaller amounts, is a better carrier of flavor and is less likely to separate, eliminating the need for an excess of flour to hold the soup together. Recipes usually call for shucking the clams, but it is easier just to steam them and then incorporate their steaming liquid into the soup. The inherent problem encountered when cooking chowder is that the more clams used, the more flavorful the soup will be, but to base the soup on the steaming liquid from the clams alone would require an inordinate number of clams—more than the soup could hold. And unlike mussels, which are relatively cheap, using enough clams could drive you to financial ruin. It is possible, however, to use a little subterfuge and use the excess clams for something else, such as the stuffed baked clams, opposite. You can also stretch the liquid released by the clams with a little homemade fish broth. Avoid bottled clam juice, which has an aggressive fishy flavor.

This recipe calls for two kinds of potatoes, Yukon Gold to give the soup body and consistency, and waxy potatoes to provide solid pieces that are good to bite into.

MAKES 8 GENEROUS FIRST-COURSE SERVINGS

- 2 dozen chowder clams
- 2 cups water or fish broth (see page 40) for steaming clams
- 2 onions, finely chopped, or 4 leeks, white part only, cleaned and thinly sliced (see page 293)
- 2 tablespoons butter
- 1 quart fish broth, steaming liquid from clams or mussels saved from other recipes, or water, or a combination
- 1 Yukon Gold potato, peeled and thinly sliced
- 2 white or red waxy potatoes, peeled and cut into 1/2-inch dice
- 1 cup heavy cream
- Salt
- Pepper
- 2 tablespoons thinly sliced fresh chives (optional)

Scrub the clams energetically so any dead ones will fall apart in your hand, and rinse thoroughly. Select a pot large enough so that the clams will reach no higher than two-thirds up the sides. Pour the water into the pot, add the clams, cover the pot, place over low to medium heat, and steam for about 10 minutes, or until the clams open. Use a spider or skimmer to transfer the clams to a large bowl. Remove the clams from their shells, cut each clam into 2 or 3 pieces, and set aside. Set the pot with the liquid aside.

In a pot large enough to hold the soup, cook the onions in the butter over medium heat, stirring regularly, for about 10 minutes, or until they soften but do not brown. Carefully pour the clam steaming liquid into the pot, leaving any grit behind. Add the broth and Yukon Gold potato, bring to a gentle simmer, and simmer for about 25 minutes, or until the potato slices are completely soft.

Puree the soup with a blender (see precautions on page 42), or work it through a coarse-mesh strainer or a food mill fitted with the coarse disk into a clean pot.

Add the waxy potatoes and simmer for 10 minutes, or until soft. Add the clams and cream, bring to a gentle simmer, and season with salt and pepper. Add the chives just before serving.

VARIATIONS

You can depart from traditional chowder by omitting the cubed potatoes and/or by adding chopped herbs, such as parsley, chervil, or tarragon. Saffron is wonderful with clams, as is curry powder first cooked for about 1 minute in a little butter. Add them when you add the potatoes. You can also include assorted baby or sectioned root vegetables and pieces of green vegetables, all added according to their cooking times (see pages 289–305).

Baked Clams

Here is an example of steaming clams, rather than shucking them, for baking, and then using the steaming liquid in the stuffing for the recipe, or reserving it for another use. You can also make your own stuffing—actually a flavorful bed for the clams—with vegetables other than spinach, and use the steaming liquid to make a sauce for the clams (see variations).

MAKES 4 FIRST-COURSE SERVINGS

2 slices thick-cut bacon, cut into ¼-inch dice

1 onion, finely chopped

3 cloves garlic, minced and then crushed with the flat side of the knife

¼ teaspoon fresh or dried thyme leaves

1 cup tightly packed stemmed spinach leaves

24 littleneck clams

Salt

Pepper

¼ cup fine dried bread crumbs

3 tablespoons butter, melted

In a small sauté pan or skillet, cook the bacon over medium heat, stirring every minute or so, for about 12 minutes, or until it releases its fat and is lightly browned. Add the onion, garlic, and thyme and stir for about 10 minutes, or until the onion softens but does not brown. Remove from the heat.

In a small saucepan over high heat, combine the spinach with about 2 tablespoons of water, and stir for about 2 minutes, or until the spinach wilts and is tender. Let cool and squeeze out excess liquid. Chop the spinach and reserve.

Scrub the clams energetically so any dead ones fall apart in your hand, and rinse thoroughly. Select a pot large enough so that the clams will reach no higher than two-thirds up the sides. Pour ½ cup water into the pot, add the clams, cover, and steam over medium heat for about 12 minutes, or until all the clams open. Check every few minutes to make sure the liquid doesn't run dry, adding a little more if needed.

Use a spider or skimmer to transfer the clams to a bowl. Remove the clams from their shells and discard the top shells. Set the clams and the bottom shells aside separately. Carefully pour the steaming liquid into a storage container, leaving the grit behind, and reserve for another use. Or, pour it into a small clean saucepan, boil it down to 3 tablespoons, and stir it into the bacon mixture.

Stir the spinach into the bacon mixture and season with salt and pepper. Spoon the mixture into the reserved clam shells and top with a clam. Sprinkle with the bread crumbs, and drizzle evenly with butter. Arrange the clams on a sheet pan covered with a sheet of crumpled-up aluminum foil to create a net of hollows in which you can seat the clams. Preheat the oven to 400°F. Bake the clams for about 12 minutes, or until they are heated through and the bread crumbs have browned. Serve right away.

VARIATIONS

Almost any leftover vegetable—tomatoes, mushrooms, chard leaves—can be chopped and combined with the onion, garlic, and thyme and cooked with the bacon or in butter. You can also combine the steaming liquid with a little cream, boil it down to a saucelike consistency, and spoon the sauce over the clams, instead of drizzling with butter, before sprinkling them with the bread crumbs. An emulsified–egg yolk sauce, such as hollandaise (page 345), can be made by steaming the clams open in white wine and using the liquid for the sauce base. Omit the bread crumbs, spoon the sauce over the clams, and then broil them until the sauce bubbles and is lightly browned. A sprinkle of paprika looks dramatic on the browned sauce.

COCKLES

Most of the cockles we see in the United States are from New Zealand and have a little bit of green shading near the hinge. There isn't a whole lot of meat in a cockle, but the juices that cockles release when they are steamed or poached are perhaps the tastiest of all seafood juices and can be used as the base for sauces. To make a sensational seafood sauce, steam open a few handfuls of cockles in a little wine, use the liquid to cook a fish fillet, and then finish the liquid with some chopped herbs, a little butter, or a little cream, or all three. (For more about seafood sauces, see pages 344, 345, 350.) Serve the cockles around and over the fish. You can also include cockles in seafood "stews" (see page 157).

HOW TO COOK COCKLES

Put the cockles in a pan with white wine to come about one-fourth up the sides of the shellfish.

Bring to a boil and boil until they open, about 5 minutes.

1. Hold oyster in a towel to protect your hand, stick the tip of the knife into the hinge and twist the knife until you feel the hinge give.

2. With the knife blade against the underside of the top shell, slide the knife around the oyster to sever the muscle that holds the shells together. Pull off the top shell.

3. Ready to serve.

OYSTERS

Purists insist that oysters should only be eaten raw, others are squeamish about raw oysters and will only eat them cooked, and still others, in the words of M. F. K. Fisher, like them "hot, cold, thin, thick, dead, or alive." Some people worry about eating oysters because of past incidents regarding infection by a bacterium closely related to cholera, but no new cases have been reported in several years. Others hesitate to eat oysters in months that don't include the letter *r* for fear of contamination. In prerefrigeration days, there was justification for this concern, but nowadays oysters can be kept cold in the middle of August. While there is little health risk eating an oyster in the summer, it is true that oysters spawn during these months and become what oyster lovers call "milky." This milkiness does have a somewhat unpleasant texture in the mouth and obscures the clean brininess that makes the best oysters so good.

Many people have their favorite oysters, but the most logical stratagem is to search out the freshest oysters, rather than insisting on a particular variety. For the briniest, sometimes almost metallic-tasting specimens, buy oysters from cold water, such as northern Atlantic (Cape Cod, Prince Edward Island, Maine) or Pacific oysters. Unlike mussels that can gape and be perfectly fine, oysters should not be open, or their juice will run out and the oyster will be dry and flavorless. For this same reason, oysters should be stored flat, so no liquid oozes out the side.

If you are cooking your oysters and don't want to deal with shucking them, you can heat them on a grill or in an oven to loosen the top shell. Then all you need to do is slide a knife under the top shell to detach it, and then again along the bottom shell to detach the oyster. Once you have shucked your oysters, especially if you have heated them to speed the process, always eat them the same day, so they don't go bad.

Oysters on the Half Shell

It is hard to improve on what may be nature's most perfect food. Few foods—caviar, sea urchin roe—capture the pure briny essence of the sea better.

When serving raw oysters on the half shell, you can't shuck them by heating them first. You must open them raw, or ask the clerk at the fish market to do it, if you are serving them within a few hours. Shucking takes practice and a strong will to combat the tenacity of the oyster. If you are not yet skilled at it, get your guests involved. While disturbing to many who fear washing away the oysters' essence, oysters should be rinsed after shucking. They then release a second round of liquor.

Insert the tip of an oyster knife into the hinge at the pointed end of the oyster that holds the oyster shells together and twist. This may take several attempts until you find the right spot, but once you find it, you will feel the top shell give way. At this point, wipe off the oyster knife with a towel so you don't get grit inside the oyster, and then slide the knife along the underside of the top shell, pressing firmly and keeping the knife flush with the shell so you don't damage the meat. The top shell will come away. Next, hold the oyster—still attached to the bottom shell—under a slow, steady stream of cold water while running your finger around under the meat. This rinses out any grit. In French restaurants, oysters are served still attached to the bottom shell (a way of ensuring they haven't been shucked in advance and just scooped into shells), but it is easier on your guests if you slide the knife under the oyster to detach it from the bottom shell. Keep the knife flush with the bottom shell, so the tasty little abductor muscle stays attached to the oyster, not the shell.

As you shuck the oysters, put them on plates or a platter covered with cracked ice or seaweed. Don't put them on coarse salt, which gets everywhere, especially in the oyster. You can serve the usual condiments—lemon wedges, hot sauce, vinegar with a little chopped shallot and cracked pepper in it (mignonette sauce)—but purists usually eschew them all.

VARIATIONS

Little can be done to improve a raw oyster, but you can top them with dollops of caviar, sea urchin roe, or a single drop of Pernod.

COOKED OYSTERS

Cooked oysters can be presented in three ways: they can be placed in the washed and reheated bottom shells and then baked or broiled with various stuffings and sauces; they can be gently poached with other ingredients (including other shellfish) and served as oyster stew or oyster panfry, or they can be used to provide the sauce and garnish for fish or chicken. Oysters are so versatile that you can even have an all-oyster dinner, starting with raw on the half shell, followed by hot on the half shell, followed with a stew, and finishing with a piece of fish that has an oyster garnish.

Oysters shouldn't cook too long, only heated enough, usually in their own juices, to firm them up. If they are allowed to boil, they almost disappear into tiny bits reminiscent of chewing gum. Once heated through, they should be gently patted in a towel to eliminate grit, and then served with a sauce prepared with either the poaching liquid or another liquid, such as wine, mushroom cooking liquid, cooking liquid from other shellfish, or fish broth (see page 40). Cooked oysters are marvelous with cream and butter, which work wonders in even small amounts.

HOW TO MAKE BROILED OYSTERS WITH SAFFRON HOLLANDAISE SAUCE AND JULIENNED LEEKS ⸻⸻⸻⸻

1. Gently cook julienned leeks in butter. Place the shells on a sheet pan lined with aluminum foil, crumpled enough to create a net of hollows in which you can seat the oysters.

2. Spoon the leeks into the oyster shells. Set a cooked oyster on top and coat with saffron hollandaise sauce (see page 345).

3. Broil the oysters for a few seconds and sprinkle with paprika.

Oyster Panfry

This is really a stew more than a panfry—a panfry involves fat and high heat—but the name sticks because of the famous panfry at the oyster bar in New York City's Grand Central Station, where you can feast on dozens of oyster varieties, raw and cooked.

Oysters pack so much flavor that this dish requires nothing more than oysters, cream, and a grind of fresh pepper. Some people may want to have soda crackers available as a crunchy counterpoint or for crumbling into the dish, while others prefer crusty French bread. Or, you can serve croutons for sprinkling on top.

MAKES 6 FIRST-COURSE OR 4 MAIN-COURSE SERVINGS

HOW TO MAKE OYSTER PANFRY

1. Shuck oysters into a small sauté pan over medium heat.

2. Add a flavorful liquid, such as wine or beer.

3. Add some cream and gently heat.

4. Add chopped fresh herbs such as chives or parsley at the end of cooking.

2 dozen oysters, preferably from the north Atlantic or Pacific, shucked (see page 114)

$1/4$ cup white wine or beer (optional)

1 cup heavy cream

Salt

Pepper

Soup Croutons (see page 42), soda crackers, or French bread

Open, rinse, and shuck the oysters into a small sauté pan, put over medium heat, and pour over the wine or beer. When froth begins to form around the edges of the liquid, lightly swirl the pan on the burner to cook the oysters evenly, until they begin to curl around the edges.

Add the cream and bring to a simmer—the liquid should have a consistency of a light soup—and season with salt and pepper. Take the pan off the heat. Let the oysters sit in the sauce for 1 minute to warm them, and then transfer them to warmed soup plates. Pass the croutons at the table.

VARIATIONS

This rich and luxurious yet simple dish adapts well to all sorts of additions that transform it into a complete meal. The basic sauce flavor can be altered by simmering the poaching liquid (after taking out the oysters) with a little white wine and shallots. Vegetables can be cooked separately or directly in the sauce and combined with the stew at the end. Place creamed spinach (see page 295) or sorrel in the center of each bowl before spooning in the stew. Cultivated mushrooms (sliced or quartered) can be simmered in the poaching liquid before adding the oysters, fresh wild mushrooms can be sautéed and added to the stew, and dried wild mushrooms can be reconstituted and added to the stew. Truffles can be chopped or julienned and infused in the cream before it is added to the sauce. Baby root vegetables can be glazed and added to the stew whole, or larger root vegetables can be sliced or sectioned and turned (fashioned into little football shapes) and then glazed before adding. Blanched peas or haricots verts can be sprinkled over each serving, or chopped fresh chives, parsley, chervil, or other herbs can be chopped and added at the end. The finished stew, either the basic version or a variation, can be served over sautéed chicken or pieces of fish.

Oyster "Gazpacho"

This mildly spicy soup-stew gets its tang from lime juice and its spice from dried and fresh chiles. It draws additional savor from tiny cubes of prosciutto.

MAKES 8 FIRST-COURSE SERVINGS

3 tomatoes

$1/_2$ cup water

1 large mild dried chile such as guajillo, mulatto, ancho, chilhuacle negro, or pasilla, soaked in hot water for 30 minutes to soften, seeded and finely chopped

1 poblano chile, charred, peeled, and seeded (see page 321) and then cut into $1/_8$-inch dice

1 red bell pepper, charred, peeled, and seeded (see page 321) and then cut into $1/_8$-inch dice

Juice of 2 limes

Salt

Pepper

2 dozen oysters, shucked

Plunge the tomatoes into boiling water for about 30 seconds, rinse them immediately with cold water, and pull away the skin in strips with a paring knife (see page 85). Cut the outer pulp away from the sides of the tomatoes and cut into $1/_8$-inch dice. Chop the insides of the tomatoes and put them in a small saucepan with the water and the chopped dried chile. Simmer gently for 15 minutes, then strain, working the tomato pulp through a medium-mesh strainer placed over a bowl.

Add the poblano chile, bell pepper, lime juice, and diced tomatoes to the tomato mixture. Season with salt and pepper, cover, and chill well. Serve in small chilled bowls with 3 oysters on top of each serving.

Hot Oysters on the Half Shell

Hot oysters in the shell make an appealing first course or hors d'oeuvre. The various elements—the creamed spinach, the hollandaise, and the oysters themselves—can be prepared ahead of time and then broiled just before serving. You can also vary the topping and the vegetable bed on which the oysters sit (see variations). This is a rich dish, so 3 oysters are usually the right amount for a first course.

MAKES 6 HORS D'OEUVRE SERVINGS OR 4 FIRST-COURSE SERVINGS

>**12 oysters, shucked (see page 114)**
>**One 10-ounce bunch spinach, stems removed**
>**3 tablespoons heavy cream**
>**Salt**
>**Pepper**
>**1 tablespoon curry powder**
>**1 tablespoon butter**
>**1 cup Hollandaise Sauce (see page 345)**
>**Paprika**

Detach the oysters from the bottom shells and refrigerate until needed, collecting the liquor and storing the oysters in it. Scrub the bottom shells. Cover a sheet pan with a crumpled sheet of aluminum foil, and place the shells on it (the foil helps keep the oysters flat under the broiler).

Twenty minutes before serving, put the shells in the oven and turn the oven to 275°F.

In a saucepan, bring about 2 quarts water to a boil and stir in the spinach leaves. As soon as they wilt, after about 15 seconds, drain in a colander and rinse under cold running water. Squeeze out the excess liquid.

Ten minutes before serving, in a small saucepan, boil the cream for about 3 minutes, or until it is very thick—almost to the point of separation. Season with salt and pepper. Add the spinach and stir over medium heat until heated through.

Put the oysters in a small saucepan over medium heat. When froth begins to form around the edges, lightly swirl the pan on the burner to cook the oysters evenly. They should curl around the edges. Remove the oysters from the liquid with a slotted spoon and place them on a clean kitchen towel. Fold over the towel, or place another towel on top, so that any grit attached to the oysters clings to the towel.

In a small sauté pan or skillet, cook the curry powder in the butter over medium heat for about 1 minute, or until it smells fragrant. Stir the curry mixture into the hollandaise.

Preheat the broiler. Place a small spoonful of spinach into each oyster shell and place an oyster on top. Spoon a generous tablespoon of hollandaise over each oyster. Slide the oysters under the broiler and broil for about 1 minute, or until the sauce bubbles and is lightly browned. Sprinkle with paprika and serve right away.

VARIATIONS

The creamed spinach called for here can be replaced with sorrel (which gives everything a delightful tang), chopped onions or leeks cooked in butter, chopped mushrooms cooked down to eliminate the liquid they release and then lightly creamed (see duxelles, page 318), cooked tomatoes, creamed diced cucumbers, or peeled and diced fresh chiles, such as poblanos (see page 321). The sauce can be replaced by bread crumbs drizzled with a little melted butter, or by a sauce made by boiling down the oyster juices with a little white wine and shallots, adding heavy cream, and boiling the mixture until it is thick enough to coat the oysters. You can add finely chopped tomatoes, fresh herbs, or chiles to the sauce.

"Barbecued" Oysters

For a great party hors d'oeuvre, spread oysters in the shell on the hot grill. After 3 to 5 minutes, the oysters will gape and the tops are easily removed with fingers, so guests can pry open their own oysters. Serve with lemon wedges and hot sauce.

SCALLOPS

Three kinds of scallops are typically sold in American fish stores. The largest are sea scallops, considerably smaller are bay scallops, and the smallest of all—they look like miniature marshmallows—are calico scallops, which are usually sold as bay scallops but are quite different.

You can buy sea scallops in their shell, which have a little fluted base and are easy to recognize because they are the symbol of Shell gas stations. Buying any shellfish in the shell is ideal because it ensures freshness. But most scallops are shucked on the boat, making it harder to gauge their freshness. The best test is to smell them. You should detect only the sea and never sulfur.

Chemical soaking is another concern. Scallops are sometimes soaked in a solution that causes them to retain their water; otherwise, they would lose weight from the time they are harvested, and the fishermen, wholesalers, and retailers all would lose money. Instead, the cooks are the losers. When the scallops are put in a hot pan, they release all the liquid that was artificially retained. Sea scallops that have been soaked are a uniform white and are often sitting in a bit of milky liquid. They may also look a little sudsy, as though they contain soap. Scallops that haven't been soaked usually have variation in color and may include pale shades of pink, orange, or ivory. If you can't tell by looking, ask your fishmonger if the scallops have been soaked. Scallop containers are required by law to indicate if the shellfish were chemically treated.

Bay scallops, which have a subtle sheen and appear translucent, are usually sold out of the shell and look like miniature sea scallops. They tend to be expensive and are best when you can find them in their shells, which both guarantees freshness and provides little decorative vessels for serving.

Tiny calico scallops are opaque because they have been cooked as part of the process of getting them out of the shell. Because they have been steamed open, they don't have much flavor.

Sautéed Sea Scallops

Old cookbooks call for cooking scallops for 20 minutes and then covering them with a thick béchamel and broiling them. In fact, scallops need very little cooking—they are even delicious raw when freshly shucked—to bring out their delicate flavor, just enough to heat them through. When sautéing scallops, you need high heat to brown the two sides without overcooking the inside. Also, if the heat isn't high enough, the scallops will release liquid (especially if they have been soaked) into the pan and then boil in their own juices. Get your sauté pan very hot before you add the scallops, and then start sautéing them one at a time, waiting for the last one added to start browning before you add the next one. When they are ready to turn, after 2 to 3 minutes, turn them only one or two at a time. If you turn them all at once, the pan will cool and the scallops will release liquid. This is one time when you can use a pan larger than needed to hold the scallops in a single layer.

If you are serving scallops as a first course or as part of a multicourse dinner, serve a single very large scallop for a stunning presentation. If you are serving the scallops as the main course, make them in the White Wine–Herb Sauce (see page 120).

**MAKES 4 MAIN-COURSE SERVINGS OR
6 FIRST-COURSE SERVINGS**

> 16 large sea scallops for main courses, 18 small sea scallops or 6 very large sea scallops for first courses
>
> 3 tablespoons vegetable oil, olive oil, or grapeseed oil
>
> Salt, preferably fleur de sel
>
> Pepper

Don't season the scallops with salt and pepper ahead of time, because the salt will draw out their liquid and the flavor of the pepper will be destroyed by the heat. Pat the scallops perfectly dry.

Heat the oil in a large sauté pan over high heat until the oil smokes. Add 1 or 2 scallops, wait for about 30 seconds, and then add 2 more scallops. Continue in this way until the first scallops you added are well browned on one side. This should take 2 to 3 minutes. Then begin to turn the scallops, starting with those that are browned and turning 1 or 2 at a time. Sauté for 2 to 3 minutes on the second side, or until all the scallops have a brown crust on both sides. Remove from the pan, and place on a paper towel–covered plate to absorb the excess oil. Season with salt and pepper and serve on warmed plates. If you have fleur de sel, put a tiny pinch of it in the center of each scallop.

Scallops in White Wine–Herb Sauce

One of the easiest sauces for scallops and other shellfish is a white wine sauce with shallots, finished with a swirl of butter. You can add chopped herbs to the sauce, either at the beginning with the shallots if using oil-rich herbs, such as thyme or marjoram, or at the end if using delicate herbs, such as parsley or chervil. This sauce is fairly liquid, so you will need to serve the scallops in soup plates. If you want a thicker sauce, reduce the wine twice as much and double the butter.

MAKES ENOUGH FOR 4 MAIN-COURSE SCALLOP SERVINGS

> Sautéed Sea Scallops (see page 119)
>
> 1 large shallot, minced
>
> $1/2$ teaspoon fresh thyme or marjoram leaves, chopped (optional)
>
> $1/2$ cup dry white wine
>
> 1 tablespoon finely chopped fresh parsley, chervil, or chives, or a combination
>
> 6 tablespoons butter
>
> Salt
>
> Pepper

Wipe out the pan used to sauté the scallops with a paper towel to rid it of any burnt oil, add the shallot and thyme, and stir them around in the still-hot pan with a whisk for about 30 seconds, or until the shallot smells toasty (the heat retained in the pan is enough to bring out the flavor of the shallot and thyme). Pour in the wine and boil it down to about 2 table-spoons. Whisk in the parsley and the butter. Season with salt and pepper and spoon over the scallops.

VARIATIONS

Compound butters (see pages 348–350) can be used in two ways to top scallops and other seafood: Put it right on the scallops when they are served or melt it in the sauté pan, heat it until it is frothy, and then spoon it over the scallops. Some compound butters, such as escargot butter (garlic and parsley) are delicious when cooked in the pan until they break and turn frothy. More delicate butters, say, chervil or parsley butter, should be left emulsified, which is to say the pan should be deglazed with a liquid, such as wine, and the butter whisked into the liquid.

Sorrel Sauce for Sautéed Sea Scallops or Other Shellfish

Because of its tartness, sorrel is the perfect accompaniment to seafood. You can cream it as you would spinach, except that you don't blanch it first or it will melt into nothing. The leaves, which look very much like spinach, are cut into little strips, or chiffonade, and then swirled into a white wine sauce. Sorrel can be hard to track down, so when you see it, usually in the summer, buy it up for making soups, for creaming alone or with spinach, or for making sauces for accompanying seafood. To make the sauce, first prepare the White Wine–Herb Sauce (opposite), made without the herbs. Remove the stems of 8 large sorrel leaves and cut into chiffonade (see page 298). Whisk the sorrel into the warm sauce. The sorrel will immediately turn a sullen green. Serve immediately.

1. Brown the scallops over very high heat in a little oil.

2. Turn only 1 or 2 scallops at a time.

3. Transfer the scallops to a paper towel–covered plate and wipe out the sauté pan with a paper towel.

4. Add garlic and parsley compound butter (see page 349) to the sauté pan.

5. Cook over high heat until frothy.

6. Return the scallops to the pan and turn them around in the butter.

7. Arrange the scallops on plates with the butter sauce spooned on top.

BRAISED SCALLOPS, POACHED SCALLOPS

The advantage to braising scallops is that you can concentrate the sea-fragrant liquid they release and turn it into a sauce. The disadvantage, when compared with sautéing, is that the scallops won't have a savory brown crust. You can concentrate the braising liquid for the scallops—which can be fish broth, vegetable broth, white wine, or various combinations of all three—and finish it with cream and/or butter. Varying degrees of reduction and amounts of cream or butter will make the sauce thick or thin. If you are serving a thin sauce, serve the scallops in soup plates.

The only difference between poached and braised scallops is the amount of liquid used. When poaching, the scallops are completely covered with liquid.

Braised Scallops with Fennel

Here, the scallops are braised in a vegetable broth flavored with fennel stalks, and then the fennel bulb, cut into wedges and braised, is served as an accompaniment. The broth can be made ahead of time.

**MAKES 4 MAIN-COURSE SERVINGS OR
6 FIRST-COURSE SERVINGS**

> **1 fennel bulb, preferably with lots of stalks and fronds**
>
> **1/2 cup dry white wine**
>
> **1 teaspoon coriander seeds**
>
> **16 large sea scallops for main courses, 18 small sea scallops, or 6 very large sea scallops for first courses**
>
> **4 tablespoons butter, cut into four 1-tablespoon slices**
>
> **Salt, preferably fleur de sel**
>
> **Pepper**

Cut a few of the fronds off the fennel bulb and reserve for garnish. Cut the stalks into little pieces and put them into a pot with just enough water to cover. Cover the pot and simmer gently for 30 minutes, adding more water if needed to keep the fennel chunks covered.

Preheat the oven to 350°F. Cut the fennel bulb into 8 wedges for main courses or 6 wedges for first courses (see page 294), and arrange the wedges in a baking dish just large enough to hold them in a single layer. Pour the white wine over the wedges and sprinkle with the coriander. Cover loosely with aluminum foil or parchment paper, and bake for about 30 minutes, or until the fennel is easily penetrated with a knife.

Put the scallops in an ovenproof sauté pan just large enough to hold them in a single layer. Pour the fennel-stalk liquid through a fine-mesh strainer into the pan. If there is liquid in the baking dish with the braised fennel, tilt the dish over the scallops, adding the liquid to the pan as well. Cover the scallops loosely with aluminum foil and slide them into the oven. Bake for 10 to 15 minutes, depending on the size of the scallops, or until they are opaque on top and just start to feel firm to the touch.

Transfer the scallops to warmed soup plates, put a fennel wedge in each plate, and put the braising pan on high heat. Boil down the braising liquid to about 1/4 cup and whisk in the butter. Season the sauce with salt and pepper and pour over the scallops and fennel.

Sea Scallops à la Nage

Seafood is often poached in vegetable broth (court bouillon). When the broth is served with the poached seafood, and the vegetables used to make the broth are also served, the dish is referred to as à la nage.

**MAKES 4 MAIN-COURSE SERVINGS OR
6 FIRST-COURSE SERVINGS**

> **16 large sea scallops for main courses, 18 small sea scallops or 6 very large sea scallops for first courses**
>
> **2 quarts vegetable broth, including strained julienned vegetables (see page 36)**
>
> **1/2 cup heavy cream (optional)**
>
> **20 fresh tarragon leaves, chopped at the last minute (optional)**
>
> **Salt**
>
> **Pepper**

Put the scallops in a sauté pan, ideally one with straight sides, just large enough to hold them in a single layer, and pour in the strained broth. Bring to a gentle simmer and simmer for 5 to 7 minutes, depending on the size of the scallops, or until they are opaque on top and just start to feel firm to the touch.

Using a slotted spoon, transfer the scallops to warmed soup plates and reheat the julienned vegetables in the liquid in the pan. Use tongs to top the scallops with a tangle of julienne. Add the cream and tarragon, and season the broth with salt and pepper. Spoon about 1/3 cup of the broth over around each serving.

CRUSTACEANS

Unlike mollusks, which propel themselves around with jets of water, crustaceans have legs and flippers. Their shells are relatively soft and most of them turn red when cooked. More sophisticated recipes make use of the shell to provide flavor to sauces and soups.

SHRIMP

Of the hundreds of varieties of shrimp, we are likely to encounter only a dozen or so. Most shrimp nowadays are farmed, which has made them much less expensive than in years past. Depending on how they are farmed, they can be as flavorful as wild, but wild gulf shrimp, usually sold as "pinks," "whites," or "browns," are the most consistently tasty. Most U.S. markets, with the exception of Asian markets, sell shrimp with their heads removed. That's a pity, because the heads contain the tastiest parts, which can be sucked out when the heads are twisted off, or you can use the heads to flavor soups, stews, and sauces. The shrimp meat itself provides little flavor to any surrounding liquid.

Shrimp retains more of its flavor when cooked in the shell. But because this involves last-minute peeling by the cook or work for the guests, the shrimp are usually peeled ahead of time. Most recipes call for deveining, or taking out the little digestive tube that runs along the back of the shrimp. But now that most of the shrimp available are farmed, which means that their tubes are grit free, this isn't always necessary, although some people are bothered by the empty vein and remove it. If you are not sure, devein a few shrimp and look at the tube.

Shrimp is as versatile as chicken and can be cooked up in stews and soups or simply sautéed or grilled.

Sautéed Shrimp

Shrimp will have more flavor if sautéed in the shell, but your guests will then have to peel them while they are hot and oily. The choice is yours. Because they don't need to be cooked over the same extremely high heat that scallops demand, any oil or cooking fat can be used.

MAKES 6 FIRST-COURSE SERVINGS OR 4 MAIN-COURSE SERVINGS

> 1 1/2 to 2 pounds headless shrimp
> 2 tablespoons butter or olive oil
> Salt
> Pepper

Rinse the shrimp and, if you wish, peel and devein them In a sauté pan, melt the butter over high heat. Add the shrimp and toss and stir for about 3 minutes for medium shrimp in the shell to about 5 minutes for jumbo shrimp, or until the shrimp turn bright orange. Season with salt and pepper.

VARIATIONS

Cook the shrimp in escargot butter (parsley and garlic butter, see page 349), adding it 1 minute before the shrimp are done, add the butter to the pan and stir until it froths and the aroma of garlic fills the room. If you prefer to skip the butter, just sprinkle the shrimp with minced garlic, also about a minute before they're finished cooking.

HOW TO MAKE SAUTÉED WHOLE SHRIMP

Sauté shrimp with their heads intact in a little oil over high heat until bright orange.

How Many Shrimp to Serve

Shrimp are sold to the retailer according to the number per pound, usually expressed in a range such as 18/20. Unfortunately, this information doesn't get passed on to the consumer, who has to rely instead on arbitrary designations, such as jumbo, extra large, or medium. One retailer's jumbo is another retailer's extra large. In general, 3 extra-large to jumbo or 5 medium to large shrimp make a first-course serving, while 4 extra-large to jumbo or 7 medium to large shrimp are sufficient for a main course. If you buy shrimp by weight, count on about 4 ounces for a first course and 6 to 8 ounces for a main course.

Steamed or Poached Shrimp

If you are preparing shrimp for a salad or other recipe that calls for cooked shrimp, you can cook the shrimp ahead of time in simmering water or in a steamer for 2 to 4 minutes, depending on their size. Don't peel the shrimp until after you cook them, or too much flavor will be lost in the liquid.

Shrimp Tagine

Moroccan cooking is complex and underappreciated. This recipe is adapted from many similar recipes, but uses only the best flavors and components of each. Serve it with couscous or rice. To learn more about authentic Moroccan cooking, read Paula Wolfert's Couscous and Other Good Food from Morocco.

MAKES 6 MAIN-COURSE SERVINGS

- 3 tablespoons slivered blanched almonds
- 1 onion, finely chopped
- 4 carrots, peeled and sliced
- 3 cloves garlic, chopped
- 3 tablespoons butter
- 1-inch piece fresh ginger, peeled and grated (about 1 tablespoon)
- 1 teaspoon ground cumin
- 1/2 teaspoon ground cinnamon
- 1 teaspoon ground turmeric or 1 tablespoon grated fresh turmeric
- 1/4 teaspoon ground cloves
- 1/2 teaspoon saffron threads, soaked in 1 tablespoon water for 30 minutes
- 6 tomatoes, peeled, seeded (see page 85), and chopped
- 1 small bunch cilantro, large stems removed and chopped at the last minute
- Leaves from 1 small bunch mint and chopped at the last minute
- 3 tablespoons golden raisins (sultanas)
- 1/2 preserved lemon, cut into 1/4-inch dice (about 2 tablespoons) and rinsed in a strainer (at right), optional
- 18 jumbo or 30 large shrimp, peeled and then deveined if desired
- 3/4 to 1 cup harissa sauce, homemade (see page 50) or purchased

Preheat the oven to 350°F. Spread the almonds on a pie pan and toast in the oven, stirring occasionally, for about 12 minutes, or until they are fragrant and have taken on color. Pour onto a plate and let cool.

In a heavy-bottomed pot large enough to hold the tagine, cook the onion, carrots, and garlic in the butter over medium heat, stirring regularly, for about 15 minutes, or until the onion and carrots are softened but not browned. Add the ginger, cumin, cinnamon, turmeric, cloves, and saffron and its soaking water and reduce the heat to medium-low. Cook, stirring gently to avoid breaking up the carrots, for about 2 minutes more.

Add the tomatoes, cover, and simmer over low heat for 10 minutes, or until the liquid released by the tomatoes evaporates. Stir in the cilantro, mint, raisins, lemon, shrimp, and almonds and simmer, stirring over low heat for 3 minutes, until the shrimp has turned bright orange. Pass the harissa at the table.

HOW TO MAKE PRESERVED LEMONS

Cut 4 lemons into wedges and stack them in a jar with 6 tablespoons coarse salt. Pour over enough lemon juice to cover, usually the juice of the 4 lemons plus juice from 5 additional lemons. Cover tightly, and let sit for 3 weeks before using.

Indian Shrimp Stews

Nearly every region has a version of shrimp simmered in curry and yogurt, cream, or coconut milk. Authentic Indian recipes often call for some obscure ingredients, but most can be replaced with easier-to-find items that can be purchased by mail order.

What distinguishes all authentic Indian recipes is the absence of curry powder. An Indian cook using a premixed curry powder is akin to a French cook using a premixed dried herb blend for every dish. Typically, onion and garlic are lightly panfried in vegetable oil or ghee (see below), and ginger and hot chiles are added along with various freshly ground spices. The stew is then finished with coconut milk, cream, or yogurt, or a combination, and is often given a sour tang with tamarind pulp and a sunny color with turmeric. Many Goan recipes—Goa is a former Portuguese colony on India's west coast—include a spice paste that is made in advance and preserved with vinegar. It gives a delightful tangy complexity to many stews, not just those made with shrimp, and once you have it on hand, you can throw together a dish in minutes. While in Indian restaurants we often eat stewlike dishes with various traditional breads, simple steamed or boiled basmati rice is a perfect foil for these saucy dishes.

Goan-Style Shrimp Curry

This dish is a snap to make, once you have the curry paste on hand. The paste recipe makes about 2 cups—enough to help you get in the habit of making shrimp curry on weeknights.

MAKES 4 MAIN-COURSE SERVINGS

Goan Red Spice Paste

2 onions, finely chopped

6 cloves garlic, minced and then crushed with the flat side of the knife

4 tablespoons ghee (see page 341) or vegetable oil

8 red Thai chiles, seeded and finely chopped

2 teaspoons ground cumin

2 teaspoons ground cardamom

1 teaspoon ground cinnamon

4 teaspoons ground turmeric

4 teaspoons ground coriander

1 teaspoon ground cloves

4 teaspoons freshly ground black pepper

3 tablespoons paprika

Two 4-inch pieces fresh ginger, peeled and grated

1 cup red or white wine vinegar

One 15-ounce can unsweetened coconut milk

1 bunch cilantro, large stems removed and leaves finely chopped

1¹/₂ pounds large shrimp, peeled and then deveined if desired

Salt

2 tablespoons fresh lime juice

To make the curry paste, in a small sauté pan, cook the onion and garlic in the ghee over low to medium heat, stirring regularly, for about 7 minutes, or until the onion is softened but not browned. Add the chiles, cumin, cardamom, cinnamon, turmeric, coriander, cloves, pepper, paprika, and ginger and cook, stirring, for about 3 minutes, to bring out the flavor of the spices. Pour in the vinegar and remove from the heat.

Let the mixture cool, then puree in a blender for about 1 minute, or until smooth. Transfer to a tightly covered container and store in the refrigerator. It will keep for several months.

In a medium saucepan, combine 3 tablespoons spice paste, the coconut milk, and the cilantro and bring to a gentle simmer. Add the shrimp and simmer for 2 to 3 minutes, or until the shrimp has turned bright orange. Season with salt and sprinkle with the lime juice.

LOBSTER

Almost everyone seems to like lobster and think of it as a special treat, but most of the time its delicate texture is lost, along with a lot of its flavor, by overcooking.

Several lobster varieties are found in U.S. markets, but the most popular variety, and what most people think of when they hear the word *lobster,* is Maine lobster. Maine lobster, which is caught off of our north Atlantic coast (a similar species is found on the European side), should always be bought live. When buying lobster, purchase it in a popular place with a lot of turnover, which gives you the best odds that you will end up with a lobster that has been caught recently, rather than one that has sat too long in the tank. The lobster should be frantically flapping its various claws and flippers, rather than hanging limp. When you get your lobster home, wrap it in a wet towel and keep it in the refrigerator. In Florida and California, you may also encounter rock lobster, which does indeed look a little like a rock. It has a flavor similar to Maine lobster, but it has no claws. Lobster tails are available frozen and can be baked or sautéed.

Cooks, especially those confronting a live lobster for the first time, want to know the most humane way to kill it. There is, of course, no way of really knowing, but the recipes here suggest using a chef's knife to cut its head in half—grisly but no doubt instantaneous.

HOW TO TELL THE SEX OF A LOBSTER

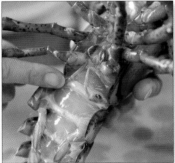 

Look at the little flipper closest to the front part of the lobster. The female's flippers (left) are thin and flexible while the male's flippers (right) are hard and bony.

The usual cooking method—plunging the living creature in a big pot of boiling water—is effective and quick but not ideal. That's because the flavorful juices released by the lobster are lost into the surrounding water. Equally easy is steaming, which allows you to capture the briny lobster juices and use them to make a sauce. Some recipes call for cutting up the live lobster and cooking it in pieces, usually by sautéing.

Lobster dishes can be as simple as a boiled lobster, or they can be relatively complex, depending on how committed you are to extracting the most flavor from the crustacean. To get the flavor and color out of the shells, the cut-up lobster is sautéed long enough to cook it partially, and then the shells are removed and cooked with aromatic vegetables and sometimes cream. The cream draws out color, which is soluble in fat and not in water. The most flavorful parts of the lobster are the roe, which is so dark green that it looks almost black, and the paler green tomalley, which is basically the liver. These can be left in the lobster or extracted and worked into a sauce.

Boiled Lobster

Bring enough water to a boil to cover the lobster(s) and throw in a handful of salt. Kill the lobster(s) first with the knife technique (see right), if decapitation seems more humane to you than dropping the live lobster(s) into the boiling water. Immerse the lobster(s) in the water (if cooking more than one, add them all at once), and boil until bright orange, 5 minutes for 1¼- to 1½-pound lobsters, and 1 minute more for each additional ½ pound per lobster.

Drain the lobster(s) and serve. If you want to make it easier on your guests, take the meat out of the claws, cut the lobsters lengthwise in half, and put the claw meat on top of the tails. Serve the lobster with melted butter.

1. Turn the lobster back side down, and insert a knife into the head, but not all the way through. Then bring the knife forward, effectively cutting the head, but not the outer shell, in half.

2. Put a strainer over a bowl containing 1 teaspoon vinegar or brandy (to prevent the juices from congealing), and twist off the lobster's tail while holding it over the strainer.

3. Reach into the head and tail and pull out the tomalley and any roe. Leave them in the strainer.

4. Twist off the pinchers.

5. Finish cutting the head in half.

6. Pull out the grain sacs in each half of the head and discard.

7. Work the roe and tomalley through the strainer with a ladle and your fingers. Refrigerate until needed for adding to a sauce (see page 350).

1. Take the skewer out of the tail if you used it (opposite).

2. Break off the flipper at the end of the tail.

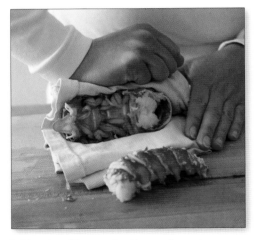

3. Wrap the tail in a towel and lean on it, pressing together the sides, until you feel a crack.

4. Pull the shell away from the sides of the tail.

5. Gently fold down the pincher on the claw, leaving the meat attached to the lobster, not the shell.

6. With the lobster claw thorny side up, give it a quick whack with a knife to crack the shell. Twist the knife to separate the shell in two.

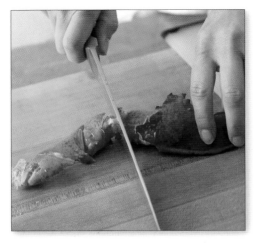

7. Give the hinge a whack on both sides to break it.

8. Use scissors to cut through the shells of the small articulations that lead to the claw. Gently pull out the claw meat.

9. Use whole claws in recipes or serve with sauce.

Steamed Lobster

Steaming lobster allows you to cook it more slowly than boiling it, which leaves it more tender. It also allows you to make a little sauce from the lobsters' juices. The sauce is rich, but much less rich than the customary drawn butter.

MAKES 4 MAIN-COURSE SERVINGS

> **4 live lobsters**
> **$1/2$ cup dry white wine**
> **1 shallot, minced**
> **2 tablespoons finely chopped fresh parsley**
> **6 tablespoons cold butter, cut into 6 slices**
> **Salt**
> **Pepper**

Kill the lobsters as shown on page 127 and hold them over a bowl to catch their juices.

Put the juices in a pot large enough to hold the lobsters, add the wine and shallot, and bring to a gentle simmer.

Put the lobsters in the pot, cover, and steam for 12 to 15 minutes, or until the lobsters have turned bright orange all over. About halfway through the steaming, redistribute the lobsters so that those that were on the bottom are now on top. Check the liquid in the pot every few minutes to make sure it isn't running dry; if it runs low, add $1/2$ cup water.

When the lobsters are done, take them from the pot and set aside. Strain the liquid in the pot through a fine-mesh strainer into a saucepan and boil the juices down to about $1/4$ cup. Add the parsley and whisk in the butter a piece at a time. Season with salt and pepper. Pass the sauce at the table.

You can serve your guests whole lobsters and pass the sauce at the table or make life easier for everyone by snapping off the claws and removing the claw meat as shown. Then cut the tails in half lengthwise with a large chef's knife, place the tail halves flesh side up on heated plates, put the claw meat on top of the tails, and spoon over the sauce.

HOW TO SAUTÉ A CUT-UP LOBSTER

1. To keep the tail from curling, slide a skewer between the membrane and the flesh along the bottom of the tail.

2. Heat oil in a pan over high heat and put in the lobster parts. Turn them around until they start to turn red.

3. Cover the pan and let the lobster steam over medium heat.

4. When the lobster is red, take it out and add chopped onion, carrot, and celery to the pan. Cook over medium heat until the vegetables begin to brown.

5. If the lobster needs more cooking, put it in the pan with the vegetables. Add liquid such as wine, cover, and cook for 5 minutes.

LOBSTER STEWS AND SOUPS

One of the best-known lobster stews is lobster à l'américaine, made by cooking cut-up lobster with tomatoes and wine. The lobster is served surrounded with sauce, making the dish, as good as it is, disturbingly messy to eat. Also, because the shells are only cooked as long as the meat, they don't contribute much flavor.

To make life easier for your guests, take the meat out of the shells ahead of time and very gently reheat it just before serving. In this way, only the sauce needs to be finished at the last minute, whisking in the roe and tomalley scooped out of the lobsters.

To make a lobster soup, use the crab soup recipe on page 133, but substitute 3 cut-up lobsters for the crab.

Nouvelle Lobster à l'Américaine

This version is easier to eat than the traditional recipe, because the lobster is taken out of the shell. Most of the hard work can be done earlier the same day.

MAKES 4 MAIN-COURSE SERVINGS OR 6 FIRST-COURSE SERVINGS

> **1 teaspoon white wine vinegar**
> **4 live lobsters, including at least 1 female**
> **1/4 cup olive oil**
> **1 onion, finely chopped**
> **1 carrot, finely chopped**
> **4 tomatoes, chopped**
> **1/2 cup dry white wine**
> **3 sprigs thyme or 1/2 teaspoon dried thyme**
> **3 sprigs tarragon, coarsely chopped (optional)**

> **1 cup heavy cream**
> **Salt**
> **Pepper**
> **4 or 6 sprigs chervil (optional)**

Have a small bowl ready containing the vinegar, with a fine-mesh strainer resting over the bowl. Cut up the lobsters as shown on page 127. Pull the tomalley and roe out of the heads and tails and work them through the strainer into the bowl (the vinegar prevents congealing). Cover the bowl and refrigerate until needed.

In a skillet, sauté the lobster pieces in the oil, with the lid on the pan, over high heat for about 5 minutes, or until they turn orange. Set the lobster aside on a plate and add the onion and carrot to the sauté pan. Lower the heat to medium and cook, stirring regularly, for about 12 minutes, or until the onion and carrot are softened but not browned. Add the tomatoes, wine, thyme, and tarragon to the pan, cover, and simmer gently while you grind up the shells.

Remove the lobster meat from the shells (see page 128) and set the meat aside. Discard the claw shells, which are too hard for the food processor, and put the tail shells in the processor. Grind for about 1 minute, or until coarsely ground.

Add the ground shells to the tomato mixture and simmer covered for 5 minutes, or until the shells release their flavor. Pour in the cream, bring back to a simmer, and strain through a coarse-mesh strainer, and then through a fine-mesh strainer into a small saucepan. Push down on the contents of the strainer with the back of a ladle or wooden spoon to release as much liquid from the shell mixture as possible.

Cut the lobster meat in pieces so that everyone gets the same amount. You can cut the tail in half lengthwise or into medallions, and if you are serving first courses, you can cut the

HOW TO MAKE SAUCES OR SOUPS WITH LOBSTER SHELLS

1. Put the lobster shells, except the hard claw shells, into the food processor and grind.

2. Add chopped tomatoes (optional).

3. Cook onions, carrots, and celery in butter until soft.

4. Add the ground shells.

claw meat in half horizontally. Put the lobster, in portions, on a sheet pan, and cover it tightly with plastic wrap. Refrigerate until just before serving.

Thirty minutes before serving, put the lobster in the oven and turn on the oven to its lowest setting. Warm the soup plates.

Remove the strained roe from the refrigerator. Bring the sauce to a simmer and slowly pour it into the roe while whisking constantly. Pour this mixture back into the saucepan and whisk over medium-low heat until the sauce turns bright orange. Don't let it boil or it will curdle. Season with salt and pepper.

Arrange the lobster in the warmed soup plates and pour the hot sauce over the top. Decorate each serving with a chervil sprig.

VARIATIONS

You can vary this recipe by substituting sherry or Madeira for the white wine, using reduced chicken or mushroom broth instead of the cream as the base for the sauce, leaving out the tomatoes, and/or finishing the sauce with finely chopped fresh chervil, parsley, or chives. Garnishes, such as lightly blanched peas, fava beans, or haricots verts; mushrooms (wild

or cultivated, reconstituted dried or fresh); shaved or chopped truffles; or braised fennel wedges (see page 294), glazed pearl onions (see page 302), baby turnips (see page 305), or carrots (see page 301) can be added for color and to make the dish a complete meal.

This "stew" can also be used as a sauce and garnish for other seafood, such as pieces of sautéed or braised fish. In this way, you get more servings out of the lobsters (see Bass Fillets with Lobster and Lobster Sauce, below).

Bass Fillets with Lobster and Lobster Sauce

You can cook the fish fillets for this dish using any basic method, such as sautéing, steaming, or braising. If you are braising, incorporate the braising liquid into the sauce.

MAKES 8 MAIN-COURSE SERVINGS

> **Nouvelle Lobster à l'Américaine (opposite)**
> **Eight 6- to 8-ounce fish fillets such as sea bass, striped bass, red snapper, or other white-flesh fish, with or without skin**

Prepare the lobster recipe just to the point where the roe is to be added. Preheat the oven to 350°F. Place the fish fillets in a single layer in a baking dish and pour the sauce over the top. Braise the fish in the oven for about 15 to 20 minutes, or until opaque throughout and firm to the touch.

Transfer the fillets, skin side up if the skin is still on, to warmed soup plates and keep warm. Warm the lobster meat in the turned-off oven. Pour the braising liquid into a small saucepan and whisk in the roe as directed in the lobster recipe. Spoon the sauce over the fish. Arrange the lobster pieces around each serving.

5. Add fresh tarragon and cream and simmer.

6. Thin as needed with broth or shellfish steaming liquid.

7. Work through a fine-mesh strainer with the bottom of a ladle.

8. Put the sauce in a saucepan, add the strained lobster roe to it. Heat gently—don't allow it to boil. Whisk constantly.

CRAB

In the United States, you will find Dungeness crab on the West Coast and blue crab (both hard and soft shell), Jonah crab, and peekytoe crab on the East Coast. Because most snow crab and king crab are frozen where they are caught (in Alaska), you will find them nearly everywhere. Occasionally, however, you will find them fresh at a sushi bar (the crab is cooked), which is a delight not to be missed.

Most crab is simply boiled in a big pot of water and the meat picked out at the table. Soft-shell crabs are almost always sautéed to enhance their crispiness. King crab and snow crab legs are sometimes split lengthwise and broiled with butter.

Blue Crabs

The blue crab is the most common East Coast crab and is usually served simply boiled. Extracting the meat from blue crabs is frustrating for anyone not brought up eating them, so unless you know what you are doing, hesitate to extract your own crabmeat when cooking for a crowd. At certain stages in their life cycles, blue crabs shed their outer hard shell and for a few days are surrounded with a soft shell that gets harder each day. The trick, of course, is to catch the crabs as soon after this shedding as possible.

Soft-Shell Crabs

These are whole blue crabs with soft shells that require no tedious picking out of the meat: they are eaten whole. Clean the crabs as shown on page 134, and flour and sauté them in butter or olive oil for a few minutes on each side.

Dungeness Crabs

In many West Coast markets, Dungeness crabs are sold already cooked, but crab is so perishable that they are rarely as fresh as you want. You are better off buying a live crab and boiling it yourself, or buying a cooked crab in a place where it is boiled in front of you, such as on the docks of Fisherman's Wharf in San Francisco. To extract the meat, see below. Serve the crab with plain or flavored mayonnaise (page 359).

King Crab and Snow Crab

Because these long-legged creatures are harvested for only a relatively short period, competition is frantic and prices are high, especially for king crab. Their legs are usually sold frozen.

Jonah Crabs

Most Jonah crabs come from Maine and are fairly large, almost as large as Dungeness crabs and with similar sweet meat. Meat from Jonahs is usually labeled "Maine crabmeat."

Peekytoe Crabs

Also known as rock or sand crabs and once considered trash, peekytoe crabs are now prized by high-end restaurants for their meat, which is particularly good in crab cakes and salads.

Stone Crabs

In what to some sounds like a sadistic process, stone crabs are harvested, their large claw is snapped off, and they are immediately tossed back into the water. The action doesn't kill them and they grow a new claw. Each claw provides a thick chunk of meat.

HOW TO REMOVE THE MEAT FROM DUNGENESS CRABS

1. Whole cooked Dungeoness crab.

2. Turn the crab over and unfold the "apron". Twist off and discard the apron.

3. Snap off and reserve the legs.

4. Pull off the large top shell. Spoon out the mustard and serve it or use it in sauces.

CRABMEAT

Sold "fresh," frozen, pasteurized, or canned, crabmeat is always cooked in order to get it out of the shell. Pasteurized crabmeat is cooked again to increase its shelf life. Most canned crabmeat is imported and is usually of lower quality than crabmeat sold in plastic tubs. The best crabmeat is fresh and unpasteurized and is kept on ice until it is sold. Frozen crabmeat can also be good, since it is frozen immediately after picking.

Meat from blue crabs, the most common type available, is labeled according to its source on the crab. Meat from other crabs, such as Dungeness or Maine, is usually a mixture of claw and fin meat.

Jumbo Lump Backfin: This is the best—which is to say it has the largest and whitest chunks—and most expensive crabmeat.

Backfin or Lump Backfin: Almost as good as jumbo lump backfin, this is the meat to use when you don't have jumbo lump backfin and need large chunks, such as for a soup.

Claw Meat: Very tasty, this is just the meat from the claws. It is darker than backfin meat, which makes it less attractive.

Cocktail Claw Meat: This is claw meat with all but the meat from the pinchers removed. It is designed for dipping.

Flaked or Special: Smaller pieces, rather than lumps, this crabmeat can come from any part of the crab.

Blue Crab Soup

Blue crabs are perfect candidates for soup because they are inexpensive and you don't have to extract the meat, unless you want crabmeat in the soup and you don't want to buy it already out of the shell.

12 live blue crabs, rinsed and cleaned

$1/4$ cup olive oil

1 onion, minced

1 carrot, peeled and finely chopped

3 sprigs thyme or $1/2$ teaspoon dried thyme

8 tomatoes, chopped

2 cups Brown Chicken Broth (page 36) or other flavorful broth

$1/2$ cup dry white wine

1 cup heavy cream

2 cups (1 pound) crabmeat (optional)

Salt

Pepper

In a sauté pan, preferably straight sided, sauté the crabs on both sides in the oil over high heat for about 4 minutes, or until bright orange. Remove from the pan and let cool. Meanwhile, add the onion, carrot, and thyme to the pan and cook over medium heat for about 12 minutes, or until the onion is softened but not browned.

Pull the hard top shell off the crabs and discard it. If you have the energy, pick out as much crabmeat as you can and save all the shells. Cut the bottom half of the crab with the legs into 4 pieces. Put these crab pieces into a food processor and chop for about 1 minute, or until it has a coarse, mealy consistency. Add them to the onion mixture.

Add the tomatoes and pour in the broth and wine. Cover the pan and simmer gently for 15 minutes, or until the tomatoes soften. Work the mixture through a coarse-mesh strainer, and then through a fine-mesh strainer into a pot. Reheat gently, add the cream and crabmeat, and season with salt and pepper.

5. Pull off and discard the gills.

6. Cut the bottom section in half from front to back and then cut each half crosswise in half again.

7. Crack the legs with a cracker or by whacking them with a rolling pin.

8. Pull out the meat with an oyster fork.

Sautéed Soft-Shell Crabs

Soft-shell crabs are surprisingly rich, such that one is usually enough for a first course and two or three for a main course. They are best just sautéed and served as they are. One of the mayonnaises on pages 359–361 makes a great accompaniment. The crabs are also great in a sandwich.

**MAKES 4 MAIN-COURSE SERVINGS OR
6 FIRST-COURSE SERVINGS**

8 large or 12 small soft-shell crabs for main courses
  or 6 medium crabs for first courses
Flour
3 tablespoons olive oil or butter
Salt
Pepper

Clean the crabs as shown below. Pat them with flour, pat off excess. In a large sauté pan, heat the oil over high heat if using olive oil, and over medium heat if using butter. Add the crabs, top side down first, and sauté for 2 to 4 minutes on each side, depending on their size, or until deep orange. Season well and serve immediately.

HOW TO CLEAN SOFT-SHELL CRABS

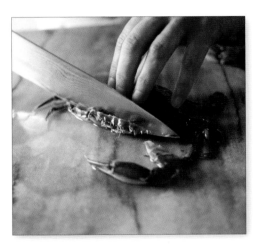

1. Cut off the eyes.

2. Unfold and pull off the "apron."

3. Pull back the top shell on one side, and pull away the gills that cling to the crab.

HOW TO SAUTÉ SOFT-SHELL CRABS

1. Clean the crabs as shown (above) and pat them with flour.

2. Cook them, top side down in butter or olive oil over medium heat for a few minutes on each side, or until deep orange.

3. Serve immediately.

CRAYFISH

If you say crayfish in the South, where everyone says "crawfish," you will be labeled a Yankee. Regardless, crayfish are sold whole and live, or just their tail meat is sold. The advantage of buying them live is that you are sure of their freshness and you can use the shells and heads to make sauces and soups or to add flavor to seafood stews. To make a crawfish soup, follow the recipe for Blue Crab Soup (see page 133), substituting 40 live crayfish for the crabs, removing the tail meat before cooking the soup and adding it at the end.

HOW TO REMOVE MEAT FROM COOKED CRAYFISH ⎯

1. Buy crayfish that are visibly alive and moving around.

2. Kill the crayfish by boiling them or sautéing in hot oil until they turn orange all over.

3. Take the intestine out of the crayfish by pinching on the little flipper at the end of the tail and gently pulling.

4. Twist the tail away from the head section.

5. Pinch the tail so the shell cracks.

6. Pull the shell from both sides until the meat pops out.

CEPHALOPODS

A generation ago, many Americans wouldn't get near a piece of squid, much less an octopus. But now both of them have become relatively common fare. Squid and octopus are the two cephalopods (cephalopod means "head foot") most often encountered in American markets. In Europe, and in fancy markets in the United States, you may find cuttlefish, which is like large squid. It has thicker, meatier flesh, but its flavor is much the same. Its one distinct advantage over squid is its ink sack, which contains about a tablespoon of smooth, very black paste, enough to impart a dramatic color to a stew, risotto, soup, or pasta dish.

SQUID

Squid must be cooked for very little time or for a fairly long time. Any amount of time in between leaves them tough. Usually, the tentacles are cut away from the head, the innards discarded, and the hood cut into rings. Most recipes say to peel away the purple membrane covering the hoods, but others argue that this contains a lot of flavor. The fact is it makes no difference. The squid is then either sautéed, stir-fried, deep-fried, or braised. The first three methods take 2 to 3 minutes, while braising takes about 1 hour.

CLEANED SQUID ⎯⎯⎯⎯⎯⎯⎯⎯⎯⎯⎯⎯

1. Clockwise: tentacles, innards (to discard), hood.

2. Hoods and tentacles ready to slice for cooking.

Squid Braised in Red Wine

The secret to this recipe is to boil down the liquid released by the squid before adding the red wine. Serve with French bread and aioli, ideally flavored with saffron.

MAKES 4 MAIN-COURSE SERVINGS

> 3 pounds squid, cleaned, hoods cut into 1/2-inch rings, tentacles left whole
>
> 1 medium onion, chopped
>
> 1 large carrot, peeled and chopped
>
> 3 cloves garlic, minced
>
> 2 tablespoons olive oil
>
> 2 cups full-bodied red wine
>
> Bouquet garni
>
> Salt
>
> Pepper
>
> Aioli (see page 360)
>
> French bread

Rinse the squid and let drain in a colander. Gently cook the onion, carrot, and garlic in the olive oil in a pot large enough to hold the squid. When the onion turns translucent, after about 10 minutes, add the squid and stir over high heat. Continue stirring until the liquid released by the squid completely evaporates. Add the red wine and the bouquet garni and simmer gently, partially covered, for 45 minutes. Remove the lid and simmer until the sauce cooks down and thickens slightly but still remains soup-like. Season with salt and pepper and serve in heated soup plates. Pass the aioli and bread at the table.

OCTOPUS

Octopus is meaty and tough and needs to be cooked almost as long as stew meat to tenderize it. Once cooked, it can be grilled or used in salads. It can also be stewed in red wine and served like a meat stew, with rice, noodles, or potatoes.

Red Wine Octopus Stew

When octopus is simmered gently for an hour or so, it loses all toughness and becomes meltingly tender.

MAKES 4 MAIN-COURSE SERVINGS

> 1 octopus
>
> 1 onion, chopped
>
> 1 carrot, peeled and chopped
>
> 3 cloves garlic, chopped
>
> 2 tablespoons olive oil
>
> 2 cups full-bodied red wine, such as Zinfandel
>
> Bouquet garni
>
> 2 tablespoons concentrated meat glaze (see page 177), optional
>
> 4 slices crusty French bread, toasted and rubbed with a garlic clove (optional)
>
> 2 tablespoons chopped parsley
>
> Aioli Sauce (page 360)

If you have tracked down a whole octopus, cut it up as shown and cut the tentacles into 1-inch sections. Cut the head into pieces about the same size as the tentacle sections.

In a pot large enough to hold the octopus, cook the onion, carrot, and garlic in the oil over medium heat for about 12 minutes, or until the onion is softened but not browned. Add the octopus pieces, pour in the red wine, and nestle the bouquet garni in the center of the pot. Bring to a gentle simmer and simmer covered for about 1 1/2 hours, or until a skewer slides easily in and out of a large piece of the octopus.

Add the meat glaze and simmer until the liquid is reduced to about 1 cup. Meanwhile, discard the bouquet garni.

Sprinkle in the parsley. Put a piece of toasted French bread in each soup plate and spoon the octopus and sauce over the top. Pass the aioli and baguette toasts at the table.

Whole octopus. Cut between the tentacles to where they join in the middle so they are each detached. Cut the tentacles into 3-inch sections.

Cook the onion, carrot, garlic, and octopus pieces in olive oil. Add the wine and bouquet garni. Simmer until octopus is tender.

MIXED SHELLFISH STEWS

Some of the most elaborate seafood dishes are made by cooking different shellfish, each in the optimum way, and then extracting and combining their flavors. A variety of shellfish prepared this way creates deeply complex flavors redolent of the sea but not of any single creature.

Some combinations are simpler than others because the cooking methods are the same or similar. Mussels, clams, and cockles, for example, can all be steamed together; they are just added to the pot at different times. Combining mollusks with crustaceans is more complex, since the cooking methods are different. But it is still fairly easy to steam open the mollusks and then use the liquid they release to steam or stew crustaceans, such as lobster or crayfish.

Because of the complexity of these dishes, you will need to cook some of the shellfish ahead of time and then reheat it at the last minute. The important thing is not to overcook it and to keep it well covered, with the plastic wrap touching the meat to keep it from drying out. Then when it is time to reheat it, you must do it gently, again covered with plastic wrap, in a warm oven.

Mixed Shellfish Stew with Wild Mushrooms

This recipe is purposely complex to show the various possibilities, but many of the ingredients are optional, including the mushrooms.

MAKES 4 MAIN-COURSE SERVINGS

$1/2$ cup dry white wine

1 shallot, minced

8 littleneck clams, rinsed

1 pound small cultivated mussels, rinsed

$1/2$ pound New Zealand cockles, rinsed (optional)

1 teaspoon wine vinegar

Two $11/4$-pound live lobsters, at least 1 female

2 dozen live crayfish (optional)

4 tomatoes, chopped

$1/2$ cup heavy cream

1 ounce dried morels, soaked in $1/2$ cup hot water for about 30 minutes (optional)

1 tablespoon sea urchin roe (optional)

2 tablespoons finely chopped fresh parsley or chervil

Salt

Pepper

4 sprigs chervil or fennel fronds (optional)

In a pot large enough to hold the lobsters, combine the wine and shallot, bring to a gentle simmer, and simmer for 5 minutes. Add the clams, cover the pot, and steam over medium heat for 5 minutes. Add the mussels, re-cover, and steam for 2 minutes. Add the cockles, re-cover, and steam for about 5 minutes, or until all the shellfish open. If a few refuse to open, open them with a knife. If any of the mussels don't open, throw them out. Using a spider or skimmer, transfer the shellfish to a large bowl. Leave the shellfish juices in the pot.

Have a small bowl ready containing the vinegar, with a fine-mesh strainer resting over the bowl. Cut up the lobsters as shown on page 127. Pull the tomalley and roe out of the heads and tails and work them through the strainer into the bowl (the vinegar prevents congealing). Cover the bowl and refrigerate until needed.

Put the lobster pieces in the pot, cover, and steam over medium heat for about 10 minutes, or until bright orange all over.

Meanwhile, take the meats out of the mussels, clams, and cockles, reserving 12 mussels in the shell, 4 clams in the shell, and half of the cockles in the shell. Cover the meats tightly with plastic wrap and refrigerate.

When the lobster pieces are ready, take them out of the pot with a spider, and put the crayfish in the shellfish juices in the pot. Cover, raise the heat to high, and steam for 4 minutes, or until bright orange. Again using the spider, take the crayfish out of the pot and let cool. Reserve the liquid in the pot.

Take the meat out of the crayfish tails as shown on page 135, reserving the shells, and then snap the claws off the bodies and crush with the end of a rolling pin or discard. (The claw shells are hard and can damage a food processor.) Take the lobster meat out of the shells (see page 128) and discard the claw shells. Grind the lobster and crayfish shells in a food processor for 1 minute, or until the mixture has a coarse, mealy consistency.

Add the ground shells, crushed claws (if using), tomatoes, and cream to the shellfish cooking liquid in the pot and bring a gentle simmer. Lift the morels out of their soaking liquid, squeezing them over the bowl. Set the morels aside. Carefully pour the liquid into the tomato mixture, leaving any grit behind in the bowl. Simmer gently for 15 minutes, and strain through a coarse-mesh strainer, and then through a fine-mesh strainer into a small saucepan.

Work the sea urchin roe through the fine-mesh strainer into the lobster roe. Cut the lobster tails in half lengthwise or into medallions so everyone gets the same amount. Arrange the portions of lobster, crayfish, and mollusks (including those still in the shell) on a sheet pan and cover with plastic wrap. Put into the oven set to the lowest setting and heat for 15 to 20 minutes. Don't keep the shellfish in the oven any longer than necessary.

Just before serving, bring the sauce to a simmer, whisk in the parsley, and add the morels. Whisk the sauce into the lobster roe. Return the mixture to the saucepan, and whisk over medium heat for about 2 minutes, or until the sauce turns bright orange. Don't let it boil.

Arrange the warmed shellfish in warmed soup plates, and spoon the sauce and morels over the shellfish. Decorate each serving with a chervil sprig.

FISH

Many of us are intimidated by fish for fear of encountering bones, cooking it too little or too much, or being sold something old. Once you know how to choose a fish and how long to cook it, your problems are few.

There are two basic types of fish: flatfish and round fish. Flatfish, like sole and flounder, usually have white skin on the bottom and gray skin on the top. They swim typically on the bottom of the sea, spread flat. Round fish are symmetrical and swim belly down.

Most fish comes in one of three forms: steaks, fillets, or whole fish. Steaks are made by cutting across the fish, fillets are removed from the spine and ribs of the fish by cutting parallel with the spine between the flesh and bone, and whole fish are cleaned and usually scaled. Flatfish fillets are sold as double fillets, which are made up of one-half of the whole fish and are two single fillets attached to each other with a thin membrane, or the double fillets are separated and sold as two single fillets.

BUYING FISH

Many cooks are afraid of buying fish because they don't know if what they are getting is fresh. True, knowing what is fresh takes some knowledge and practice, but once you discover what to look for, you will recognize fresh fish immediately. First, a fresh whole fish is shiny, and almost always has bright eyes (some exceptions exist, such as the walleye). The irises should be clear, shiny, and translucent. It is also stiff and has no fishy smell—just an ocean smell. Choosing fillets and steaks is a little harder, because they have usually been skinned and, of course, have no eyes. White-fleshed fish commonly has pink or red pigmentation running the length of the fillet. If the fillets show any hint of brown or chocolate coloration, pass them up.

Buy your fish in a market that enjoys a lot of turnover of stock and preferably has sashimi quality fish. The shop should look and smell clean. Fish neatly organized in the case also signals care and attention. Fish fillets and steaks should not be directly on ice, but on paper placed over ice. The people at the fish market should show some enthusiasm and knowledge about what they're selling.

How Much to Serve

If serving fish fillets, plan on 4 ounces for a first course and 6 to 8 ounces for a main course. If serving steaks, plan on 1 ounce more. Whole fish are about half bone, head, and innards by weight, so double the amounts when buying whole fish.

COOKING FISH

The second most intimidating factor, after the act of buying the fish, is how long to cook it. It can go from undercooked to overcooked in a heartbeat. In general, fish cooks in 9 minutes per inch of total thickness (in the case of whole fish, at the thickest part, near the base of the head), but this can vary depending on the shape and size of the fish. The species, in contrast, makes little difference, and most can be cooked in the same way.

Unlike meat, which is cooked to different degrees depending on the type and the cut, fish is almost always cooked to about 135°F, the point at which it loses its translucency. Cooking it beyond this point will only dry it out.

Despite what many recipes say, don't cook fish until it flakes, or it will be overcooked.

An instant-read thermometer is a useful tool for judging doneness of whole fish and thick steaks. To take the reading, slide it through the side into the center of the fish. When it registers 130°F, the fish is ready. The internal temperature of the fish will continue to rise another few degrees away from the heat. Rare tuna is the exception to this rule. You can also stick a metal skewer into the fish, leave it there for a few seconds, and then withdraw it and immediately touch it to your bottom lip. When it feels distinctly warm, the fish is done. (You can also practice this technique by reading the thermometer and immediately touching it to your lip.) Last, fish becomes firm to the touch such that with a little practice you can know when it's ready by pressing on it with your forefinger.

THE TECHNIQUES

Regardless of how you cook your fish—sauté, fry, steam, poach—and regardless of its form—whole, fillets, or steaks—the internal temperature of all fish correctly cooked will be the same. The cooking technique will affect the skin—sautéing or frying will leave it crispy, while poaching or steaming will leave it rubbery, so it should be removed—and the exterior of the fish, but the flavor inside will be much the same.

Keep in mind that however you cook your fish, the temperature of the heat source should be related to its thickness and/or size. Cook a large fish or piece of fish at a lower temperature than a small fish. If a small fish is cooked at too low a temperature, it will overcook inside by the time it browns on the outside, while a large fish cooked at too high a temperature will dry out or even burn on the outside before the heat reaches the center.

HOW TO CLEAN AND FILLET A ROUND FISH FOR COOKING

1. Cut off the fins from the back, tail, belly, and side (pectoral) of the fish (striped bass is shown here).

2. Slide a flexible knife along the back of the fish, on top and against the bones.

3. Continue, pressing the knife against bone, until you separate the fillet.

4. Cut off the fillet. Turn the fish over and slide the knife against the bones under the second fillet.

5. Cut around the base of the head to detach the fillet.

6. Continue cutting, over the ribs, until you detach the fillet.

7. If you wish, skin the fillets (see opposite page).

1. Trim off the fins all around the fish (shown here is a Dover sole).

2. With a long, flexible knife, cut around the head, separating the fillet from the base.

3. Slide the knife along the centerline of the fish, pushing all the way down to the bone.

4. Cut around the base of the head on the other side.

5. Pushing firmly on the knife so it lies flat against the bones, slide it under the first fillet.

6. Continue working the knife against the bones, separating the fillet.

7. Cut away the fillet.

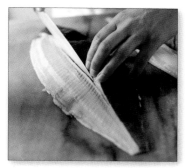

8. Cut down to the spine along the side of the other fillet.

9. Press the knife against the bone and slide it under the fillet.

10. Separate the fillet.

11. Turn the fish over, cut around the base of the head, and then down the center.

12. Draw the knife along the length of the fillet, running it along the bone.

13. Separate the fillet.

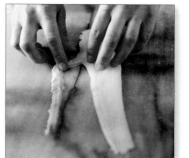

14. Separate the frill (the thin strip along the side of the fillet) from the fillet.

HOW TO SKIN FISH FILLETS

With a flexible knife, make a slit at the base of the fillet, between the skin and the flesh.

With the knife flat against the work surface, pull on the skin while moving it from side to side.

SAUTÉED FISH

Whole fish, fish fillets, and fish steaks can all be sautéed in hot fat. The main risk, other than overcooking, is the fish sticking to the pan, so that it tears when you try to turn it or remove it. Nonstick pans are always good for sautéing fish, although some fish, especially with the skin on, can even stick to them. To prevent sticking, heat the fat until it just begins to smoke before you put the fish in the pan. The heat can then be turned down according to the thickness of the fish. Fish fillets and steaks can also be floured and cooked over medium heat, but again, use a nonstick pan.

You can sauté fish fillets with the skin off or on, since the skin turns delightfully crispy, has a good flavor, and looks attractive. Most experienced cooks leave it on. To keep the skin from contracting when it hits the hot fat, which will cause the fillet to curl, press down on the fillets with the back of a spatula for the first 30 seconds of sautéing.

Experienced cooks usually know when a piece of fish is done by pressing on it with a fingertip to see if it feels firm to the touch. Since this takes practice, another method that works for relatively thick fillets and steaks is to use an instant-read thermometer (see "Cooking Fish," pages 141–142).

Once the fish is cooked, you can make a sauce, either in a separate pan or in the pan used for sautéing. In the case of the latter, don't expect much in the way of juices to deglaze. If you used a nonstick pan, none will adhere, and if you used a regular pan, the high heat probably prevented them from forming.

Sautéing Fish Steaks

Fish steaks can be sautéed exactly the same way as fillets, but since the skin won't have been in contact with the hot oil and turned crispy, it can be pulled away once the fish is cooked. Steaks can also be boned to form attractive medallions.

Sautéed Thick, Firm-Fleshed Fish Fillets

Use salmon, striped bass, sea bass, or similar fish for this recipe. If you are buying fillets with the skin on, make sure the skin has been scaled.

MAKES 4 MAIN-COURSE SERVINGS

>   Four 6- to 8-ounce fillets
>   Salt
>   Pepper
>   3 tablespoons olive oil, vegetable oil, whole butter, or clarified butter (see page 341)

Season the fillets on both sides with salt and pepper. In a sauté pan, preferably nonstick, heat the oil over high heat until it just begins to smoke. (If you are using an aluminum or stainless-steel pan, the oil should be even hotter—it should be distinctly smoking; if using whole butter, sauté over medium heat.) Place the fillets in the pan. Put skin-on fillets skin side down and immediately press down on them with the back of a spatula, moving from fillet to fillet every few seconds, for a total of about 30 seconds.

When the skin is crispy and brown and about half of the estimated cooking time has elapsed (plan on about 9 minutes total per inch of thickness), turn the fillets over. If the skin is brown and crispy long before it is time to turn the fillets, turn down the heat. If at any point the fillets seem to be sticking, rapidly move the pan back and forth on the burner—this often dislodges them—rather than trying to turn them with a spatula, which can tear the skin. Turn over the fillets and cook to an internal temperature of 130°F, or until the fillets just begin to feel firm to the touch.

Sautéed Flatfish Fillets

Except for authentic Dover sole, from the European side of the Atlantic, flatfish fillets are fragile once cooked. Since their skin isn't very savory, it is best to remove it. Because they are thin, there is no point in trying to brown them using high heat. They will cook through in a minute. Instead, cook them in butter in a nonstick pan over medium heat. They can also be dusted with flour or coated with flour, beaten egg, and fresh bread crumbs (the same way as the chicken breasts on page 255) and cooked over medium to high heat in clarified butter. A long offset spatula is useful for turning the fillets.

Four 6- to 8-ounce double fillets of sole, flounder,
fluke, or skate or eight 3- to 4-ounce single fillets,
skin removed

Salt

Pepper

3 tablespoons butter or clarified butter

Season the fillets on both sides with salt and pepper. In
a nonstick sauté pan just large enough to hold the fillets in a
single layer, melt the butter over medium heat until it froths.
Add the fillets, attractive side down, and turn up the heat. The
idea is to keep the heat hot enough to evaporate any liquid
released by the fish, but not so hot as to burn the butter. If you
use clarified butter, you can turn the heat to high.

As soon as you add the fillets, move the pan gently back
and forth on the burner for 30 seconds to keep the fish from
sticking. Cook the fillets for 1 to 2 minutes, depending on their
thickness. Then turn them over gently with an offset spatula,
and cook for 1 to 2 minutes more, or until they feel firm to the
touch. Serve immediately on warmed plates.

SAUTÉED WHOLE FISH

Many of us are afraid to cook a whole fish because we don't
know how to eat it without ending up with a mouthful of
bones. (To learn, see page 147.) This is a pity, because a whole
fish always retains its flavor better than fillets or steaks. It is
also fun for each person to have his or her own fish to fillet.
(After you learn, you can teach your guests right at the table.)

The main danger, the fish sticking to the pan, can be
avoided by using a nonstick pan, by moving the pan back
and forth on the burner for the first 2 minutes of sautéing, by
leaving the scales on the fish, or by flouring the fish. (If you
leave the scales on, be sure to tell your guests to peel off the
skin.) You should start sautéing over very high heat, but then
turn the heat down so the fish will have time to cook through
without the skin burning. (Small fish, such as sardines, can
be cooked the entire time on high heat.) A fish knife is handy
for filleting and carving fish because it's possible to slide the
blade, which is angled, under the fillet while easily gripping
the handle.

Sautéed Fresh Sardines

*Fresh sardines, difficult to find until recently, are a revelation to anyone who has only eaten their canned cousins. The
fresh ones are easy to clean and scale and are inexpensive.
To eat, nibble them like corn-on-the-cob.*

MAKES 6 FIRST-COURSE OR 4 MAIN-COURSE SERVINGS

Twelve 4-ounce sardines

Salt

Pepper

3 tablespoons olive oil

Clean the sardines by running your thumb along the belly
and pushing out the innards. It is easiest to do this in the sink
with cold running water. Remove the scales by rubbing the fish
under running water. Pat dry with paper towels, but don't leave
the paper towels on the fish or they will stick.

Season the sardines on both sides with salt and pepper. In
a large nonstick sauté pan, heat the oil over high heat until it
just begins to smoke. Add the sardines and cook for 3 minutes,
or until they begin to develop a crust. Turn them with tongs
and cook for 3 minutes longer, or until crispy on the other side.
Serve immediately on warmed plates.

HOW TO CLEAN AND COOK SARDINES ——————

After removing the innards and scales, sauté until the sardines develop a crust. Turn and
cook on the other side until crispy.

1. Cut off the side fins.

2. Cut off the top fins.

3. Remove the gills.

4. Cut the fish open through the belly.

5. Pull out the innards.

Sautéed Whole Round Fish

Look for fish that weigh about 1 pound each. If you don't have a nonstick pan, you can prevent the fish from sticking by leaving the scales on (though some fish, like mackerel, don't have scales), by flouring the fish, or by cooking the fish over very high heat for the first minute on both sides. Rapidly moving the sauté pan back and forth on the burner during the first minute of sautéing on each side also prevents sticking.

MAKES 4 MAIN-COURSE SERVINGS

> **Four 1-pound whole round fish such as sea bass, striped bass, mackerel, trout, or red snapper, cleaned and then scaled if desired (see headnote)**
>
> **Salt**
>
> **Pepper**
>
> **Flour (for fish without scales)**
>
> **3 tablespoons olive oil**

Season the fish on both sides with salt and pepper. If you are using flour, spread it on a plate, dust the fish with the flour, and pat off the excess.

In a large nonstick sauté pan, heat the oil over high heat until it just begins to smoke. Slide the fish into the pan and rapidly move the pan back and forth on the burner for 1 minute to help prevent sticking. Then lower the heat, depending on the thickness of the fish. If the fish are very thick, the heat should be between low and medium; for smaller fish, the heat can be higher. Cook the fish on the first side for about 5 minutes per inch of thickness, or until browned. Raise the heat to high, turn the fish with an offset spatula, and sauté for a minute or two. Lower the heat and continue to cook for about 5 minutes per inch of thickness, or until the fish test done. To check for doneness, stick an instant-read thermometer into the back of the fish, in the center between the top fillet and the spine. The temperature should read 130°F. Serve immediately on warmed plates.

1. Slide a fish knife along the back, between the bone and the top fillet.

2. Slide the knife under the base of the head all the way down to the bone.

3. Pull off the bony cartilage from the belly flap near the head.

4. Slide the knife under the top fillet.

5. Fold back the fillet.

6. Slide the knife under any bones that remain attached to the fillet and remove them.

7. Lift away the spinal bones and head.

8. Separate the bones that remain attached to the bottom fillet.

9. Transfer the fillets to warmed plates.

HOW TO PREPARE A FLATFISH FOR COOKING WHOLE

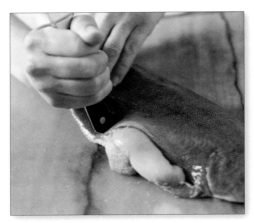

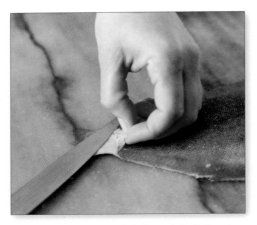

1. Make a slit along the belly, but not deep enough to cut into the viscera and/or roe.

2. With a knife handle, working from the back of the fish, push the viscera out through the belly.

3. Make a slit between the dark skin and the flesh and separate about an inch of skin.

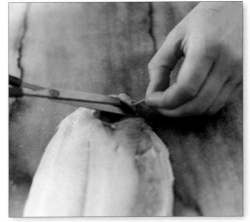

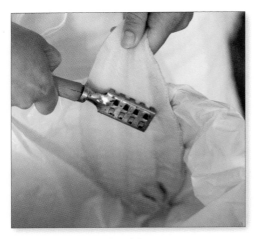

4. Hold the base of the fish in one hand and the end of the skin in the other, using a kitchen towel for grip, and peel away the skin. (This works only for Dover sole; leave skin on, scales on, for other fish.)

5. Cut out the gills with scissors.

6. Scale the white side of the fish.

HOW TO FILLET A COOKED WHOLE FLATFISH FOR EATING

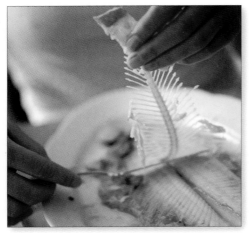

1. Slide a fish knife or large spoon under the fillet to your left.

2. Rotate the fish 180 degrees and repeat with the other fillet.

3. Lift off the bones and head to reveal the bottom two fillets.

Sautéed Whole Flatfish

Most flatfish are cleaned and scaled before sautéing. Dover sole traditionally has the top gray skin pulled off, but the flesh of American flatfish is softer and tears when you try to pull off the skin. Sautéing flatfish for a crowd takes a lot of pans and stove space, so unless you are equipped, don't try cooking whole flatfish for more than four.

MAKES 4 MAIN-COURSE SERVINGS

> **Four 1-pound flatfish such as sole, flounder, or fluke, or eight 8-ounce flatfish such as rex sole, cleaned (opposite)**
>
> **Salt**
>
> **Pepper**
>
> **3 tablespoons butter**

Season the fish on both sides with salt and pepper. In 2 or more nonstick sauté pans (enough to hold the fish in a single layer), melt the butter over medium heat. Place the fish, top (gray) side down, in the butter and cook for 5 to 7 minutes, depending on the thickness of the fish, or until the fish is golden brown. Using a large offset spatula, gently turn the fish over and cook for 3 to 5 minutes longer, or until the fish feels firm to the touch. Pat off the cooked butter with a paper towel and serve immediately on warmed plates.

Salmon Teriyaki

Salmon has a delicious skin that turns crispy and juicy when sautéed. The trick is to buy salmon fillets with the skin on—make sure the fish has been scaled—and sauté them, mostly skin side down, to render the fat out of the skin and make it crispy. To treat the skin to a teriyaki glaze, pour out the burnt fat when the fish is done, add mirin (sweetened sake) and soy sauce, and put the fish back in the pan, skin side down. The sauce is then boiled down to a glaze that adheres to the skin. Salmon is sometimes sold with the pin bones still in. They are easily extracted with tweezers—you just have to remember to check for them. Shichimi togorashi is a versatile blend of seven seasonings, sold in a narrow bottle with a shake-top.

MAKES 4 MAIN-COURSE SERVINGS

> **Four 6-ounce salmon fillets, skin on, scaled**
>
> **2 tablespoons canola oil**
>
> **6 tablespoons Japanese dark soy sauce**
>
> **9 tablespoons mirin**
>
> **1/2 teaspoon Asian sesame oil**
>
> **4 teaspoons Shichimi togorashi (optional)**

Pull out any bones in the fillets with tweezers or needle-nosed pliers. In a nonstick sauté pan, preferably nonstick, heat the oil over high heat until it ripples. Put the fillets, skin side down, in the pan and immediately press down on them with the back of a spatula, moving from fillet to fillet every few seconds, for a total of 30 seconds. When the skin is crispy and brown and about half of the estimated cooking time has elapsed (plan on about 9 minutes total per inch of thickness), turn the fillets over. If the skin is brown and crispy long before it is time to turn the fillets, turn down the heat. If at any point the fillets seem to be sticking, rapidly move the pan back and forth on the burner—this often dislodges them—rather than trying to turn them with a spatula, which can tear the skin. Cook until brown and crispy on the second side and firm to the touch.

Take the fillets out of the pan and pat with paper towels to absorb the burnt oil. Wipe out the pan with a paper towel and add the soy sauce, mirin, and sesame oil. Boil until the sauce thickens and is syrupy, about 1 minute and then return the fillets, skin side down, to the pan. Turn the salmon in the pan to coat both sides with the syrup in the pan. Then sprinkle with the togorashi; turn and sprinkle the other side of the fillets. Serve the fillets skin side up on warmed plates.

(continued)

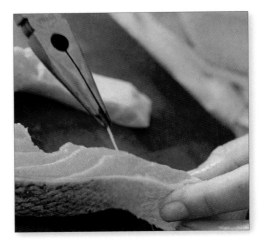

1. Remove the pin bones.

2. Brown the salmon in oil over high heat. Hold down the fillets to prevent curling while browning the skin side.

3. Turn fillets and brown the other side.

5. Take the cooked salmon out of the pan, pour out the burnt oil, and wipe out the pan. Add mirin, soy sauce, and sesame oil and bring to a gentle boil.

5. Boil down the sauce and return the salmon fillets, skin side down, to the pan. Turn the salmon over to coat both sides.

6. Sprinkle with Japanese 7-spice mixture or sesame seeds (optional) and serve.

Fish Meunière

A standard of the French repertory, sole meunière is usually made in the United States with flounder fillets. Authentic sole meunière served in Europe is made with whole Dover sole, which has had the bottom scaled and the gray top skin peeled off (see page 143). But what defines the process, which can be used for almost any fish, whole or filleted, is that the fish is coated with flour (optional) and sautéed in clarified butter or oil. When the fish is done, the cooked butter in the pan is discarded, fresh butter is added to the pan, the pan is put on the fire until the butter froths, and lemon juice is added to the frothing butter. The butter is then poured over the fish. Since fish cooked à la meunière is served with butter poured over it, the clarified butter can be replaced with oil, and the fish can be floured and sautéed as it is for other sautéed fish recipes.

This recipe is for 2 Dover sole; making more requires 2 huge sauté pans or 4 large sauté pans.

MAKES 4 MAIN-COURSE SERVINGS

Sautéed Whole Round Fish (see page 146), Sautéed Whole Flatfish (see page 149), Sautéed Thick, Firm-Fleshed Fish Fillets (see page 144), or Sautéed Flatfish Fillets (see pages 144–145), dusted with flour (optional)

$1/2$ cup butter

3 tablespoons fresh lemon juice

Cook the fish as directed, remove from the pan, and pat with paper towels to eliminate the taste of cooked oil or burnt butter. Wipe out the sauté pan and let cool slightly.

Add the butter to the pan and place over medium to medium-high heat until the butter melts and is frothy. Remove from the heat, let cool for 30 seconds, pour or squeeze the lemon juice over the fillets. Pour the frothy butter over the fish.

VARIATIONS

The French have put names on every possible coating for fish. When simply floured and served with lemon butter, the fish is said to be cooked à la meunière. When the fish is floured and then dipped in beaten egg before it is sautéed, it is cooked à la parisiennne; when then dipped in bread crumbs it is cooked à l'anglaise. The frothing lemon butter can be made with wine vinegar instead of lemon juice, and chopped fresh herbs, such as parsley, can be added to the pan with the butter. When capers, miniature croutons, little pieces of lemon, and parsley are added to the butter, the fish is cooked à la grenobloise, a preparation especially popular for skate.

HOW TO COOK A WHOLE FLATFISH MEUNIÈRE

1. Prepare the whole fish for cooking (see page 148) and dust it with flour.

2. Cook the fish in butter over medium heat until well browned.

3. Carefully turn the fish and cook the other side until browned.

4. Transfer the fish to a plate. Squeeze over lemon juice. Pour over hot frothing butter.

Skate with Capers and Lemon

A generation ago, skate was rarely served in the United States except in French restaurants, and with few exceptions could only be purchased in Asian markets. Now, no doubt in part because the old standbys cod and haddock have been fished out, skate has become popular. If you are buying whole skate wings, the only way they come in many Asian markets, you will have to fillet them yourself (opposite).

MAKES 4 MAIN-COURSE SERVINGS

> **Four 6- to 8-ounce skate or other white fish fillets**
>
> **Salt**
>
> **Pepper**
>
> **Flour**
>
> **3 tablespoons olive oil or vegetable oil**
>
> **$1/2$ cup butter**
>
> **1 lemon, cut into skinless wedges (see page 51) and cut into $1/4$-inch dice**
>
> **Soup Croutons (see page 42)**
>
> **2 tablespoons fresh lemon juice**
>
> **2 tablespoons capers, drained**
>
> **2 tablespoons finely chopped fresh parsley**

Season the fish on both sides with salt and pepper. Spread the flour on a plate, dust the fish with the flour, and pat off the excess.

In a sauté pan large enough to hold all the fillets in a single layer, heat the oil over high heat until it just begins to smoke. Add the fillets (skin side down if skin on, bone side down if skin off), and immediately press down on them with the back of a spatula to prevent curling. Curling happens with or without the skin on because there is a thick membrane covering the fillets that contracts when it comes into contact with the heat. Sauté for 2 minutes for thin fillets or up to 4 minutes for thick fillets. Carefully turn and sauté the same amount of time on the second side, or until the fish is firm to the touch. Remove from the pan and pat with paper towels to remove the taste of cooked oil.

Wipe out the sauté pan and let cool slightly. Add the butter to the pan and place over medium to medium-high heat until the butter melts and is frothy. Add the lemon dice, croutons, lemon juice, capers, and parsley and heat for about 15 seconds. Pour the frothy lemon butter over the fish.

1. Cut through the skin down to the bone all around the top fillet.

2. Slide a flexible knife under the first fillet flush against the bones until it comes away.

3. Repeat on the other side.

4. Season and flour the skate and sauté in butter until browned on both sides. Hold down with a spatula to prevent curling.

5. Transfer to a serving dish, and top with frothy lemon butter with croutons and capers.

Sautéed Thick Fish Fillets with Miso Soup

This dish is most dramatic if the fillets are cut into squares or rectangles and then served in soup plates surrounded with the broth. Here, the soup contains only a little chopped green onion, but you can add sliced shiitake mushrooms, julienned leeks (blanched for 5 minutes), a few snow peas, thin green beans, or cockles, mussels, or other shellfish.

MAKES 4 MAIN-COURSE SERVINGS

> Four 6- to 8-ounce wild striped bass, tilefish, red snapper, or other thick white fish fillets, skin on and scaled
>
> 2 green onions, white and 2 inches of green tops, very thinly sliced
>
> 2 cups Miso Soup (see page 41), heated to serving temperature

Cook the fillets as directed for Sautéed Thick, Firm-Fleshed Fish Fillets (see page 144). Remove from the pan and pat off the cooked oil with paper towels. Place the fillets in warmed soup plates. Add the green onions to the hot soup, let them infuse for 1 minute, and spoon the soup around the fish.

BRAISED FISH

Whole fish, fish fillets, and steaks can be braised in various liquids in the oven or on the stove top. The great advantage to braising is that the fish contributes its juices to the surrounding liquid, which in turn can be used as a sauce or as a base for a more elaborate sauce.

Use a baking dish or sauté pan just large enough to accommodate the fish, so that a minimum of liquid is needed to surround the fish. The surrounding liquid can be fish broth (made from the head and bones of the fish), vegetable broth (see page 36), white wine, sherry, water, cooking liquid from steamed mussels or clams, vegetable broth with vinegar, red wine broth made from salmon (see page 39) or chicken (see page 36), hard cider, or beer. Aromatic ingredients, such as garlic, shallots, tomatoes, mushrooms, chiles, herbs, or lemongrass, can be added to the liquid.

When the fish is cooked through, transfer it to plates or soup plates (soup plates allow you to keep the sauce more liquid and lighter) and make a sauce out of the liquid or serve the liquid as is. The easiest way to convert the liquid to a sauce is to reduce it slightly and whisk in a little butter or add a little cream.

Fillets of Sea Bass with Mushrooms

Here, fillets of sea bass or another lean white fish are braised in white wine or in fish broth made with white wine, shallots, and mushrooms. The sauce is finished with a little cream and served around and over the fillets.

MAKES 4 MAIN-COURSE SERVINGS

> Two 1-pound whole Atlantic sea bass, striped bass, sole, flounder, fluke, skate, or blackfish or four 6- to 8-ounce fillets of the same fish, skin removed
>
> 1/2 cup dry white wine, if not using whole fish
>
> 1 cup water
>
> 1 shallot, minced
>
> Salt
>
> Pepper
>
> 8 cremini or cultivated white mushrooms, thinly sliced
>
> 2 tablespoons finely chopped fresh parsley
>
> 1/2 cup heavy cream

If you are using whole fish, fillet the fish (see pages 142–143) and put the bones—break the spine in two—and heads in a pot with the white wine, the water, and the shallot. Bring to a gentle simmer and simmer for 20 minutes. Strain through a fine-mesh sieve and discard the contents of the sieve.

Preheat the oven to 350°F. Season the fillets on both sides with salt and pepper. Put them, attractive side up, in a baking dish that can go on the stove top or a sauté pan that can go in the oven. Pour in the fish broth or white wine and water. If using white wine, sprinkle the shallot over the fish along with the mushrooms.

Put the fish over high heat on the stove top until the surrounding liquid comes to a simmer, cover loosely with aluminum foil, and slide it into the oven. Bake for about 9 minutes per inch of thickness—you can check the fish by cutting into the center of a fillet—or until the fish is cooked through. Using a slotted spatula, transfer the fish to warmed plates or soup plates.

Put the baking dish or sauté pan on the stove top over high heat. Boil down the liquid until reduced by about one-half. Add the parsley and cream and boil down to the consistency you like. If you are serving the fish in soup plates, the sauce can be more souplike. Season with salt and pepper and spoon over the fish.

(continued)

VARIATIONS

The steaming liquid from mussels or clams makes a delicious braising liquid. Just steam the shellfish ahead of time (see pages 108–113), take them out of the shell (or leave some in the shell to be decorative), and reheat the shellfish in the braising liquid at the last minute and serve with the fillets. The cooking liquid can also be transformed into a classic white wine sauce by whisking in egg yolks (see page 344).

Baked Fillets of Sole or Scrod with Sherry

One of the delights of this dish is that there is no last-minute conversion of the braising liquid into a sauce. You just spoon the braising juices over the fish.

MAKES 4 MAIN-COURSE SERVINGS

Eight 6- to 8-ounce sole, scrod, or other mild white fillets
Salt
Pepper
1/2 cup dry sherry
4 tablespoons butter, cut into small pieces

Preheat the oven to 400°F. Season the fish on both sides with salt and pepper. Arrange the fillets in a buttered baking dish just large enough to hold them in a single layer.

Pour in the sherry and dot with the butter. Cover loosely with aluminum foil and bake for about 15 minutes, depending on thickness, or until the fish is just cooked through—you can check the fish by cutting into the center of a fillet. Using a long offset spatula, carefully transfer the fillets to warmed plates. Spoon the braising liquid over the fish.

Fillets of Striped Bass with Cockles and Oysters

This dish is especially dramatic if you can track down thick fillets of wild striped bass, cod, tilefish, or red snapper. The cockles impart a wonderful flavor to the braising liquid, and the oysters are a luxurious garnish for topping or surrounding the fish. The sauce can be kept very light with a minimum of cream and butter or made as rich as you like. The cockles or mussels can be steamed earlier the same day, saving you a step at dinnertime.

MAKES 4 MAIN-COURSE SERVINGS

1/2 cup white wine
1 shallot, minced
1 pound New Zealand cockles or cultivated mussels, scrubbed
Four 6- to 8-ounce striped bass, tilefish, blackfish, or other thick white-fleshed fish fillets or sections of fillets, skin removed
Salt
Pepper
1 dozen oysters, shucked (see page 114)
1/4 to 1/2 cup heavy cream
2 to 4 tablespoons butter

Preheat the oven to 350°F. In a pot, combine the wine and shallot and bring to a simmer. Add the cockles, cover, and steam over high heat for about 3 minutes, or until all the shells open. Using a spider or skimmer, transfer the shellfish to a bowl. Remove the meats from half of the cockles, and set aside the shelled meats and the cockles in the shell.

Season the fish fillets on both sides with salt and pepper. Put them, attractive side up, in a baking dish that can go on the stove top or a sauté pan that can go in the oven. Pour in the steaming liquid, leaving any grit behind in the pot. Put the fish over high heat on the stove top until the surrounding liquid comes to a simmer, cover loosely with aluminum foil, and slide it into the oven. Bake for about 9 minutes per inch of thickness—you can check the fish by cutting into the center of a fillet—or until the fish is cooked through.

While the fish is in the oven, put the oysters in a small saucepan over medium heat. When they begin to curl around the edges and the liquid gets frothy, take them out of the liquid with a slotted spoon and put them on a kitchen towel.

When the fillets are ready, transfer them to warmed plates or soup plates. Put the baking dish or sauté pan on the stove top over high heat. Boil down the liquid until reduced to about one-half. Add the cream and boil down to the consistency you like. Whisk in the butter a tablespoon at a time and season with salt and pepper. If the fish fillets have released liquid while you prepared the sauce, hold the fillets in place and tilt the plates over the sauce to capture the liquid. Add the shelled meats and the cockles in the shell to the sauce, including any liquid that has collected while they have been resting.

Reheat the oysters for just a few seconds in the sauce. Spoon the sauce over the fillets and place 3 oysters over or around each fillet.

FISH STEWS AND SOUPS

The only differences between a fish stew and a fish soup are the proportion of liquid to solids and the fact that some soups are pureed, which makes the cooking time almost irrelevant. Stews are trickier to make because the cooking liquid has to have the correct consistency and flavor at the same time the fish is perfectly cooked.

For fish stews of a more rustic character, whole fish are thrown into a pot of water—often seawater—or water combined with a little shallot or onion and sometimes red or white wine, and then the liquid is boiled until the fish are done. The result isn't bad if the fish are fresh. But such a concoction also requires dissecting the fish at the table and often leaves the cooking liquid without much flavor or with the flavor of raw wine. A solution to both these problems is to fillet the fish (or buy it filleted and ask for the head and bones), make the cooking liquid ahead of time, and then cook the fillets in the cooking liquid at the last minute. If you make a fish stew with fillets that have different thicknesses, you may need to add them at different times or bake them in the oven as described below.

Red Wine Fish Stew

Despite the fact that Europeans have been boiling up fish in red wine for centuries, such as the matelote of France, there is an inherent problem in many of these traditional dishes: the red wine doesn't cook enough to lose its harsh acidity and astringent tannins. You can bypass this problem by making a red wine fish broth from the fish heads and bones well in advance, giving it plenty of time to cook, and then using it to simmer chunks of fish at the last minute.

Traditional recipes for fish broth warn against using strong-flavored fatty fish such as salmon or mackerel, but red wine is so assertive that these are the fish you want here. You can make a deeply flavored brown sauce, richly complex and analogous to a meat sauce, with a couple of salmon heads and a bottle of red wine. The sauce base can be made earlier the same day.

MAKES 6 MAIN-COURSE SERVINGS

- 1 salmon head, gills removed
- 1 onion, chopped
- 2 tablespoons olive oil or butter
- One 750-ml bottle full-bodied red wine
- Bouquet garni
- 3 pounds assorted fish fillets such as salmon, monkfish, striped bass, swordfish, and halibut, in any combination, skin removed and cut into 1-inch cubes
- 1 tablespoon butter, room temperature
- 2 teaspoons flour
- Salt
- Pepper

In a saucepan, combine the salmon head, onion, and oil over medium heat. Cook, stirring every few minutes, for about 30 minutes, or until the head falls apart and the juices it releases caramelize on the bottom of the pan. Pour in the red wine, add the bouquet garni, and simmer gently for 30 minutes.

Strain the broth through a fine-mesh strainer into a clean saucepan. Put the saucepan over medium heat, placing off center on the burner so that the liquid simmers on only one side. Simmer until reduced to 1 cup, regularly skimming off any fat or froth.

Twenty minutes before serving, preheat the oven to 350°F. Put the fish fillets, attractive side up, in a baking dish that can go on the stove top or a sauté pan that can go in the oven. The fillets should just fit in a single layer. Pour in the red wine broth and put the fish over high heat on the stove top until the surrounding liquid comes to a simmer. Cover loosely with aluminum foil, slide it into the oven, and bake for about 9 minutes per inch of thickness—you can check the fish by cutting into the center of a fillet—or until the fish is cooked through.

While the fillets are cooking, in a small bowl or cup, work the butter and flour together with a fork to form a smooth paste. When the fillets are ready, using a slotted spatula, transfer them to warmed soup plates. Put the baking dish on the stove top over high heat and whisk in the butter-flour paste a third at a time, bringing the liquid to a boil after each addition. Add only as much paste as needed to make the liquid the consistency you like. Season with salt and pepper, and pour over the fish.

1. Arrange the fillets in a flameproof baking dish just large enough to hold them in a single layer. Pour in liquid such as fish broth, shellfish steaming liquid, wine, or water.

2. Put the baking dish over high heat and bring the liquid to a simmer. Cover loosely with aluminum foil and maintain over low heat on the stove top or put in a 350°F oven.

3. When the fillets are ready, transfer them to plates, soup plates, or a platter.

4. Boil down the braising liquid until reduced by one-half and add cream.

5. Whisk in parsley.

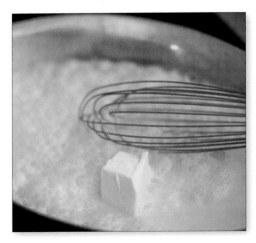

6. Whisk in butter and lemon juice.

7. Pour the sauce over the fillets.

8. If you steamed shellfish to make the braising liquid, you can serve the shellfish on or around the fish.

Thai-Style Braised Fillets of Striped Bass or Other White Fish

Season the fillets as directed in Fillets of Sea Bass with Mushrooms (see page 153), but omit all the remaining ingredients. Braise the fillets in 1½ cups of the curry sauce used in Thai Chicken Curry (see page 253).

Indian-Style Braised Fillets of Striped Bass or Other White Fish

Season the fillets as directed in Fillets of Sea Bass with Mushrooms (see page 153), but omit all the remaining ingredients. Braise the fillets in ½ cup unsweetened coconut milk mixed with 1 cup of the korma sauce used in Chicken Korma (see page 261).

Braised Fillets of Striped Bass with Curry

Season the fillets as directed in Fillets of Sea Bass with Mushrooms (see page 153), but omit all the remaining ingredients. Braise the fillets in 1 cup unsweetened coconut milk. Cook 1 tablespoon good-quality curry powder in 1 tablespoon butter for 1 minute. When the fillets are ready, remove them from the coconut milk, boil down the liquid by one-half, and whisk in the curry-butter mixture.

Braised Fillets of Striped Bass or Other White Fish with Tomato Sauce

Season the fillets as directed in Fillets of Sea Bass with Mushrooms (see page 153), but omit all the remaining ingredients. Braise the fillets in 1½ cups coulis (see page 366). When the fillets are ready, remove them from the sauce. Spoon the sauce over them, or finish the sauce by whisking in 1 tablespoon chopped fresh tarragon or other herb, 2 tablespoons tarragon butter (see page 349), or swirl in 2 tablespoons pesto (see page 362).

Braised Fillets of Striped Bass with Mole Sauce

Season the fillets as directed in Fillets of Sea Bass with Mushrooms (see page 153), but omit all the remaining ingredients. Braise the fillets in 1½ cups mole sauce (page 252).

Baked Whole Fish

One of the easiest ways to come up with a special meal is to bake whole fish in a hot oven. The effect is most dramatic if everyone gets their own fish, but you can also roast a much larger fish, bring it to the table, and fillet it before your guests. It is sometimes hard to find a variety of whole fish to choose from. Many people don't know how to cook or eat them, so fish sellers usually don't have a lot of whole fish on hand. They fear if they did, they would end up filleting most of them at the last minute.

Bake the whole fish in a hot oven so the skin gets nice and crispy. (You can also leave the scales on and have your guests peel off the skin, but then the crispy skin is lost.) To keep the fish from sticking, rub it with olive oil and use an ovenproof nonstick pan.

MAKES 4 MAIN-COURSE SERVINGS

Four 1-pound whole round fish such as sea bass, striped bass, red snapper, branzino (Mediterranean sea bass), porgy, or bream, cleaned and scaled or not scaled (see headnote)

3 tablespoons olive oil

Salt

Pepper

Preheat the oven to 450°F. Rub the fish and the baking dish with the oil and season with salt and pepper. Bake for about 12 minutes per inch of thickness at the thickest part, or until cooked to an internal temperature of 130°F.

1. Slide a long, flexible knife along the inside of the belly of the fish (a red snapper is shown here), and along the top of the bones in the tail. Slide the knife all the way to the end of the tail, but leave the flesh attached at the tail. Repeat on the other side.

2. Continue to slide the knife along the bones between the flesh and the ribs.

3. Starting near the spine and working outward, slide the knife under the ribs.

 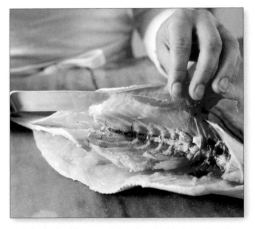 

4. Slide the knife inward all the way to the back of the fish without cutting through. Repeat on the other side.

5. Slide the knife outward, keeping the blade against the bones.

6. Slide the knife along the center bones all the way to the back without cutting through.

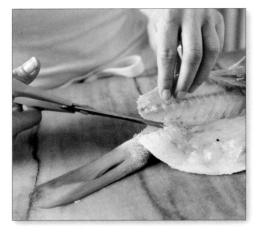  

7. Cut the bone away where it joins the tail.

8. Cut the bone away where it joins the head.

9. If you like, stuff the fish.

BAKING FISH STEAKS AND FISH FILLETS

There are two ways to bake fish steaks and fillets: relatively slowly with liquid, which is the same as braising (see page 154), or in a very hot oven, which allows no liquid to accumulate and is closer to broiling.

Baking in a Paper Bag

The idea of sealing fish in parchment paper for baking (en papillote) has been around for years but is oddly neglected, especially considering how versatile it is and how dramatic it is at the table. It also has the advantage of being something you assemble in advance and bake just before serving.

The basic method is to place an individual serving of firm-fleshed fish, such as tuna or salmon, on a sheet of parchment paper, sprinkle some aromatic ingredients, such as chopped shallots, ginger, garlic, herbs, mushrooms (cultivated or wild), or truffles or chopped or julienned vegetables (precooked slightly if necessary), on top, and then drizzle over a little

HOW TO MAKE TUNA EN PAPILLOTE ———————

1. Julienne carrots, leeks, and celeriac and cook in butter. Season the tuna on both sides with salt and pepper and brown in oil over high heat. Place in the center of a rectangle of parchment, put the julienne on top, add a slice of herb butter (see page 349), and drizzle with white wine.

2. Brush the edges of the parchment with lightly beaten egg white.

3. Fold over the edges to seal.

4. Bake until the bags puff, then open at the table.

wine, vegetable broth, or shellfish broth. The paper is folded over and sealed, and then the "bag" is baked just before serving. The effect is essentially the same as braising, except that the liquid released by the fish is not fashioned into a sauce at the last minute. Always remove the skin from fish that will be cooked en papillote, as it will end up rubbery and unattractive.

Salmon en Papillote with Saffron, Garlic, Julienned Vegetables, and White Wine

The only time-consuming step of this dish is julienning the vegetables. If you are pressed for time, you can leave them out.

MAKES 4 MAIN-COURSE SERVINGS

> Four 6- to 8-ounce salmon or other firm-fleshed fish fillets or steaks, skin removed
>
> Salt
>
> Pepper
>
> 1 leek, white part only, julienned (see page 293)
>
> 1 small celeriac or turnip, peeled and julienned (see pages 299 and 305, respectively)
>
> 1 carrot, peeled and julienned
>
> 6 tablespoons butter
>
> 3/4 cup dry white wine
>
> About 20 fresh tarragon leaves
>
> 1 egg white, lightly beaten

Season the fillets liberally on both sides with salt and pepper. Set aside.

In a small pot or medium saucepan, cook all the julienned vegetables in 2 tablespoons of the butter over medium heat, stirring regularly, for about 15 minutes, or until softened but not browned.

Place each fillet on a sheet of parchment paper as shown. Mound an equal amount of the vegetables on top of each fillet. Put 1 tablespoon of butter on each mound of vegetables, and then top each mound with 2 tablespoons of the wine and 5 tarragon leaves. Brush the edges of the parchment paper with the egg white. Fold the paper over the fish and roll and crimp the edges together to seal in the fish; reserve in the refrigerator, up to several hours, until needed.

Preheat the oven to 375°F. Arrange the parchment bags on a sheet pan, and bake for about 10 minutes per inch of thickness of the fish, or until the bags are puffed.

To serve, put each bag on a warmed plate with a rim or a soup plate, to catch any liquid that spills out of the bag. Pass a pair of scissors around the table.

POACHING WHOLE FISH

There are few dishes more dramatic than a whole salmon served at a long table of guests. Large fish such as salmon or Arctic char have to be poached in a fish poacher with a rack. Wrestling with them in any other way will result in disaster. Large flatfish such as authentic turbot, rarely seen in the United States and expensive, are poached in a diamond-shaped fish poacher called a *turbotière*. However, smaller fish, such as trout, don't require a specialized pan and can be gently lifted out of a pot of poaching liquid with a long spatula. Or, you can wrap the fish in cheesecloth and then pull it out of the liquid with the help of tongs and a spatula.

Small fish, such as sardines and trout, should be plunged into simmering liquid, while large fish, such as salmon, should be started in cool liquid and heated. If a large fish is plunged in hot liquid, the outside will overcook before the heat penetrates the center. If, on the other hand, a small fish is started in cold liquid, the fish will overcook by the time the liquid gets hot.

While some cooks fuss over the liquid used to poach fish, little of its flavor actually penetrates the fish. Water simmered with a little wine, a bay leaf, some salt, and a sprig of thyme will more than do the trick. Even plain salted water will do in a pinch. If you want to serve the fish à la nage, you will have to cut vegetables into decorative slices or julienne and use them to make a vegetable broth (see page 36).

HOW TO MAKE POACHED WHOLE RED SNAPPER

1. Put the snapper in a fish poacher and ladle over enough cold vegetable broth (see page 36) or other flavorful liquid to cover. Bring to a simmer.

2. When the fish is done, take it out of the liquid and peel away the skin while the fish is still hot.

3. Fillet and serve the fish as shown on page 147.

4. Lift and pull away the back bone.

5. Serve with olive oil and lemon wedges.

Poached Whole Trout

The most famous version of poached trout is truite au bleu—blue trout—named after the blue tint it takes on when it is poached. Blue trout can only be made with a trout that has recently been caught (or pulled out of a tank) and carefully handled (wrap it in waxed paper if you buy it from a fish-market tank). What turns the trout blue is the shiny layer of slime (but good slime) that covers only truly fresh trout. Most of us will have to be content with trout that doesn't turn blue. But if you do have access to freshly caught trout, include the vinegar in the poaching liquid to accentuate the fish's blue color. Vegetable broth (see page 36) or salted water can be used in place of the simple poaching liquid.

MAKES 4 MAIN-COURSE SERVINGS

> **Four 14-ounce trout or other small fish, cleaned**
> **1 cup dry white wine**
> **1 onion, chopped**
> **1 bay leaf**
> **¼ cup white wine vinegar, if your trout is freshly caught**

In a wide pot large enough to hold the trout, combine the wine, onion, bay leaf, vinegar, and 4 quarts water and bring to a simmer. (If you are worried about the trout falling apart when you remove it from the poaching liquid—which can easily happen if you don't have a nice long metal spatula—wrap each fish in cheesecloth.)

Slide the trout into the pot and poach at a bare simmer for about 12 minutes. To check if the trout are done, slide a spatula along one of the back (dorsal) fins to see if the flesh is no longer shiny and raw. Using a long metal spatula (or tongs and a spatula if the trout are wrapped in cheesecloth), transfer the trout to a serving platter.

HOW TO MAKE POACHED TROUT FILLETS

1. Poach trout in simmering vegetable broth (see page 36). If the trout float to the surface, press them down into the liquid.

2. Slide a spatula along a dorsal fin to check for doneness.

3. Transfer the trout to a platter and pull the skin off both sides.

4. Pull out the bones between the fillets that were connected to the dorsal fin.

5. Cut the trout in half, spoon over the vegetables used to make the vegetable broth, and ladle over the broth.

Poached Whole Salmon

When you buy your salmon, make sure it is not too large for your fish poacher. If you get it home and it is, you will have to cut off the head and trim the tail, a pity since they are part of the drama. If you want to serve the salmon à la nage, see page 160. Strain the vegetables out of the broth before using it for the salmon, and then reheat them in the poaching liquid and serve them spooned over the fish.

MAKES 10 MAIN-COURSE SERVINGS

> **1 cup dry white wine**
> **1 bay leaf**
> **5 sprigs thyme**
> **5 quarts vegetable broth**
> **One 8- to10-pound whole salmon, cleaned**
> **2 tablespoons sea salt**

In a pot, combine the wine, bay leaf, thyme, and broth. Bring to a simmer and simmer for 10 minutes. Strain through a fine-mesh strainer and let cool.

Put the fish on a rack in a fish poacher and pour over the cooled broth. It should just cover the fish. If it doesn't, add water as needed. Sprinkle the salt into the broth. Place the fish poacher over 2 burners on the stove top, and turn the heat to medium.

When the liquid comes to a simmer, after about 25 minutes, check the doneness of the salmon by inserting an instant-read thermometer into the back, parallel with the spine. When it reads 130°F, the salmon is done. You can also slide a knife in along the back fin (dorsal fin) to see if the flesh looks cooked: pink and opaque instead of shiny orange.

Lift the rack to remove the salmon from the liquid and place the fish on a platter. Present the salmon at the table, peel off the skin, and serve.

VARIATIONS

A whole poached salmon, served cold with Tartar Sauce (see page 361) or Green Sauce, or Gribiche Sauce (see page 360), makes a lovely buffet dish. Be sure to peel the skin off the salmon while it is still warm, or it will stick.

GRILLING FISH

Grilling fish would be as straightforward as cooking chicken if it were not for its tendency to stick to the grill. While there is no foolproof way to avoid this, some precautions will help most of the time. If you are grilling whole fish, you can leave the scales on and just have the guests peel off the skin, scales and all. But this of course means you don't get the crispy skin. Or, you can also flour the scaled fish and wipe or spray the grill (remove the grill grate from the fire to spray), which should be immaculate, with nonstick cooking spray.

Turning a whole grilled fish can be awkward, especially if the fish is large. If you grill fish a lot, you may want to invest in a few fish baskets. Baskets for larger fish are fish-shaped metal cages with handles that allow you to turn the basket instead of the fish. However, sometimes the fish sticks to the basket. One solution is to wrap the fish in grape leaves, fresh or bottled, so that when the fish comes out of the basket the skin sticks to the leaves and can just be peeled off—but again the crispy skin is lost. Or, the fish can be floured and the inside of the basket can be sprayed with nonstick cooking spray. Baskets for smaller fish look like a pair of cake racks, with a hinge on one end and handles on the other for easy turning.

When grilling fish, whole or otherwise, make sure the grill rack is hot before you put the fish on it. If you are not using a basket, use a long-handled, two-pronged kitchen fork to reach under the grilling fish, between the grill bars, and lift it gently off the grill a tiny bit every now and again. This will help to keep it from sticking.

Grilling thick fish steaks, such as shark, swordfish, or tuna, is easier because they tend to stick less. Even if they do stick a bit, they are so sturdy that they won't fall apart when you turn them. Thin steaks are trickier because they are fragile. Avoid grilling these delicate fish, especially flatfish fillets such as sole or flounder, as they fall apart too easily.

The Best Fish to Grill

The ideal fish for grilling are somewhat oily and have firm flesh, such as mackerel, Spanish mackerel, and kingfish. But round fish with scales will also work. American flatfish are difficult to grill because they can fall apart so easily, but Dover sole is delicious floured and grilled whole and basted with butter. The very best grilling fish may be pompano, which has smooth skin and no scales, and if first rubbed with a little olive oil, rarely sticks to the grill.

Grilled Whole Red Snapper

If this is your first time grilling a whole fish, you may want to leave the scales on to prevent sticking (see "Grilling Fish," opposite).

MAKES 4 MAIN-COURSE SERVINGS

> Four 1-pound whole red snapper, Atlantic sea bass, striped bass, pompano, mackerel, or Spanish mackerel, cleaned, scaled or not, and floured if scaled

Prepare a medium-hot fire in the grill. Grill the fish for about 15 minutes per inch of thickness at the thickest part, turning once halfway through the grilling. Serve as shown on page 147.

Sauces for Grilled Fish

In Italy and France, grilled fish is served with extra virgin olive oil, lemon wedges, or sometimes wine vinegar. High-quality balsamic vinegar served with a coffee spoon or even an eye dropper (so your guests get the hint not to pour over half the bottle) is also a luxurious seasoning (see page 70 for more about infused vinegars and oils). You can also serve one or more assorted mayonnaises (see pages 359–361), hollandaise (see page 345), chutneys (see pages 372–373), salsas (see pages 370–371), or compound butters (see pages 348–349).

Grilled Tuna, Swordfish, or Shark

All three of these fish are grilled in much the same way except for tuna, which is best cooked like a steak, rare or medium-rare. Swordfish and shark, however, are ready when they reach an internal temperature of 130°F. If you are serving rare tuna, try to buy 2 large steaks instead of 4 smaller ones because thin, small steaks dry out before they develop nice grill marks.

MAKES 4 MAIN-COURSE SERVINGS

> Four 8-ounce swordfish, shark, or tuna steaks or two 1-pound tuna steaks
>
> 2 tablespoons olive oil
>
> Salt
>
> Pepper

Prepare a medium-hot fire in the grill. Rub the steaks with the oil and season on both sides with salt and pepper.

Grill the fish for 2 minutes, give them a 90-degree turn (this makes the attractive crosshatch pattern), and cook for 1 to 3 minutes, depending on the thickness and whether you are serving rare tuna. Turn the fish over and cook for 1 to 5 minutes on the second side, again depending on thickness and whether you are serving rare tuna. It's difficult to judge the doneness of tuna by touch and appearance. You can judge somewhat by looking at the side of the piece, but you need to cut into the center of the tuna to be sure.

Serve on warmed plates. If you have cooked 2 large tuna steaks, cut them against the grain into 1/4-inch-thick slices and arrange on warmed plates.

BEEF

Whether you want to cook a thick, juicy cheeseburger or a fancy rib roast, you need to know which cut is the best to buy. A good understanding of how a steer—a castrated bull—is put together helps you to purchase the right cut for the cooking method, a situation made difficult by the fact that naming conventions differ around the country and can differ even within the same city.

The basic cuts, similar to the primal cuts used by butchers and wholesalers, are the shoulder, known as the chuck; the rib, which includes part of the shoulder, rib steaks, and rib roasts; the loin, which is the source of strip steaks, shell steaks, the tenderloin, and porterhouse steaks; the sirloin, which is the continuation of the muscles on the back that connect to the leg and the rump; and the leg, which includes the bottom and top round, the eye of the round, and the shank.

THE CHUCK (SHOULDER)

The chuck section of the steer—the shoulder—includes the least expensive cuts that, paradoxically, are also the most flavorful. They are inexpensive because they are tough, so they must be braised in pot roasts or stews. The chuck can also be ground into the best hamburger meat. The whole chuck, as it is sold to the butcher, weighs between 75 and 100 pounds, but you will be buying something much smaller and more manageable.

When shopping for chuck roasts for cooking a pot roast or for cubing for stew, look for fat, preferably fat marbled within the muscle. This fat is what keeps braised dishes moist. The best cuts for pot roasts and stews come from the top blade roast—the piece lifted off the shoulder blade—also known as the chuck arm roast, chuck eye roast, or sometimes just chuck roast. Bone-in cuts of the chuck are good for pot roasting, such as the section of the foremost ribs. The brisket, which is a large flap of muscle and fat that hangs down off the ribs, is usually cut into two sections, each weighing about 5 pounds, but there is nothing wrong with braising a whole brisket, since the weight of the meat decreases almost by half when you braise it. Of the two halves, the thick cut or front cut is the best for braising. Because it is the less regular of the two cuts and contains more fat, it is usually less expensive than the so-called flat half, thin cut, or first cut, which is prettier but less juicy and flavorful. Since brisket is rather flat, you need to tie it for braising.

THE RIBS AND MIDSECTION

The area directly behind the shoulder contains the ribs. It yields tender rib roasts when cut in larger sections and steaks when sliced between the ribs.

Between the front legs and back legs—the chuck and round—is the animal's torso and abdomen. The muscles running along the back, to each side of the spinal column, are the most tender and most expensive cuts and are the best for roasts and steaks. The front part of the animal, the rib section, is cut into the primal rib section, which contains 7 ribs, 6 through 12. Ribs 1 through 5 are left attached to the chuck. Depending on which end you are looking at, there should be 3 to 4 inches between the main interior loin muscle and the end of the rib bone. If you like, you can trim off some of this meat and fat to expose the ends of the bones, a technique known as frenching (see pages 212–213) that is a dramatic effect for steaks, chops, and roasts.

THE LOIN

Behind the ribs, along the back, is the most expensive part of the steer, the loin. In its primitive state, the primal loin cut includes the last, or thirteenth, rib, but it is almost always cut out by the time this section reaches the customer. If you look at the loin from the rib end, you will see only one large muscle, the loin. But if you look from the opposite end—the sirloin end—you will see the classic porterhouse shape, with both the loin and tenderloin muscles. You will also see that the porterhouse is just a giant version of a veal or lamb loin chop. The small round is a cross section of the filet or tenderloin, and the larger cross section is from the strip steak, sometimes called a New York cut.

THE LEG

The leg provides us with various muscles, including the bottom round and top round. While these two cuts are tempting to the eye—they are nicely shaped—they are too lean for braising and too tough to serve as you would prime rib, in thick meaty slices. Cuts from the round can be roasted and then thinly sliced for sandwiches, but if you want to serve an elegant roast that you can carve at the table, avoid the round. Some people like the round for hamburger meat because it is so lean, but the fattier chuck produces a tastier burger. Beware of the eye of the round, which looks almost identical to a tenderloin but is tough as nails; it's suitable for slicing thin and using in sandwiches or for grinding into ground round.

On the top of the leg, are the sirloin (connecting to the back) and rump. While not as tender and conveniently shaped as cuts from the loin and rib sections, the sirloin is tender enough to serve as a roast or slice into steaks. It is often a good value, especially if you buy it from a butcher who dry-ages his or her meat.

Aging Beef

Good butchers continue the tradition of aging certain cuts of meat to get them to develop flavor, often an intense nutty flavor, and to tenderize them. To be effective, meat must be dry aged, not aged in the cryovac bags that meat now so often comes in. Dry aging allows for the formation of microorganisms that break down the meat and give it flavor without causing it to turn bad. Aficionados often fail to agree on the optimum length of time to age beef, but most concur that around 6 weeks is optimum. Don't try dry-aging steaks at home—only large primal cuts should be dry aged while well refrigerated in well-ventilated refrigerators.

BEEF ROASTS

The steer offers lots of possibilities for roasting. Choosing the best cut to roast depends on how you are serving it, to how many people, and, of course, your budget. If it is a special occasion and you want to stand triumphantly at the end of the table cutting thick slices of rare meat, you will need a roast cut from the rib or loin section of the steer. If it is a family affair, or you are cooking for a crowd, you can get by with a roast taken from the sirloin, often called the sirloin butt, which is tender enough to serve in somewhat thick slices. If you want an inexpensive roast, consider one of the cuts from the leg, such as top round, bottom round, eye of round, or rump. Don't overcook these roasts—they are lean and can dry out easily—and slice them as thinly as you can, so they aren't tough. They are great for sandwiches.

Stew meat from chuck (shoulder)

Shoulder roast

Beef short ribs

Flank steak

Beef porterhouse

Rib eye

Strip steak

Prime rib roast (standing rib roast)

Chateaubriand

Tenderloin

HOW TO CARVE A RIB ROAST

1. Slide a long knife along the inside of the first rib so the meat is detached.

2. Continue slicing slices of equal thickness.

3. To get a whole rib, slice at each side of the rib, creating a slice about 1 inch thick.

4. Serve the sliced roast with the jus.

HOW TO MAKE MEAT JUS

1. Spread a heavy bottom pan large enough to hold the roast with a cut-up peeled onion, a carrot cut into sections, and 2 pounds of stew meat cut into small pieces. Cook over high heat until the meat releases its liquid. Boil the liquid down by about half.

2. Tie the roast in two or three places to make it compact and help it cook evenly. Put the roast on top of the meat and vegetables and slide into a 400°F degree oven.

3. When the roast is done transfer it to a platter and cover it loosely with aluminum foil.

4. Boil down the juices in the pan until they caramelize in a crust on the pan.

5. Pour out and discard the liquid fat.

6. Deglaze the pan with a cup of water.

7. Put the juices over medium heat and stir, scraping up the crusted bits.

8. Strain the juices.

Prime Rib

Arguably the best piece of meat for roasting, the prime rib contains 7 ribs, 6 through 12. When you buy the roast, the butcher will probably try to sell you the ribs from the shoulder end, which are fattier and less presentable than those from the loin end. Insist on ribs from the loin end, and count on one rib for every two people—a 3-rib roast serves six nicely—which may yield some leftovers. Have the butcher remove the chine bone to make the roast easier to carve. For more drama and more leftovers, buy a bigger roast. Anticipate spending a lot of cash. The stew meat and broth included in this recipe are for the jus, and are especially important if you like your meat rare, because a rare roast doesn't release many juices. If you like your meat closer to medium, there will be plenty of juices in the pan. A prime rib is also sometimes called a standing rib roast. The roast needs to sit for 4 hours at room temperature before cooking (see page 170).

MAKES 6 MAIN-COURSE SERVINGS WITH LEFTOVERS

- 3-rib prime rib roast cut from the loin end, frenched if you wish (opposite)
- Salt
- Pepper
- 1 pound stew meat, cut into 1/2-inch cubes
- 1 carrot, peeled, quartered lengthwise, and cut into 1-inch sections
- 1 onion, quartered
- 3 cups beef broth or water

For a classy effect, but one that does nothing to affect the cooking, french the ribs: trim off about 1 inch of meat and fat from the end of each rib, and then scrape away connective tissue so the ribs are nice and clean (see pages 212–213). Season the meat liberally with salt and pepper and let sit at room temperature for 4 hours before roasting (see page 170).

Forty minutes before roasting, spread the stew meat, carrot, and onion in the roasting pan you are using for the roast, and slide the pan into the oven. Turn the oven to 500°F. When the meat starts to brown, after about 25 minutes, stir it around in the pan so it browns on all sides. When the stew meat is nicely browned, after about 40 minutes, put the roast on top.

Roast the meat at this high temperature for 20 minutes, which will kill any bacteria on its surface. Then turn down the heat to 275°F. Try to avoid opening the oven door for the next hour, so the temperature will drop slowly. However, if you know your oven holds its temperature well, open the oven door every 5 minutes for a second, so the temperature will drop. Roast the meat at this low temperature for about 1 hour, and then start checking for doneness with an instant-read thermometer. If the juices in the pan threaten to burn at any point, pour in 1 cup of the broth.

Roast the meat until the thermometer reads 5 degrees less than the desired temperature. Be sure that you insert the tip of the thermometer into the very center of the roast, not touching bone, which can skew the reading. When the roast is ready, transfer it to a warmed platter, cover it loosely with aluminum foil, and keep it in a warm place while you prepare the jus. It should rest for at least 20 minutes before you carve it.

If you have not cooked your roast rare, you may see plenty of juices in the pan. If there are enough to go around—figure about 1/4 cup per serving—just pour them into a pitcher and skim off the fat with a ladle, or pour them into a degreasing measuring cup and pour off the fat.

If the juices are sparse, say, less than 1 cup total, but they haven't all caramelized into a crust, put the pan on the stove top and boil down the juices until they caramelize, and then pour or spoon off the fat. Deglaze the pan with 1 cup of the broth, stirring and scraping with a wooden spoon to dissolve the juices, and then boil down the liquid again until the juices caramelize. Add 2 cups broth (or part water, if you have used up all the broth) and simmer, stirring constantly, for about 5 minutes, and then strain through a fine-mesh strainer into a warmed sauceboat. (For more about making jus, see opposite page.)

To show off your financial ruin, carve the roast at the table. If you like, you can transfer it to a cutting board, ideally one with a moat to catch the juices. Carve it using one of two approaches: The most spectacular approach is to slice between the ribs. Keep the knife flush against the rib so the meat you are slicing is only as thick as the rib, and then serve the meat on a warmed plate with the rib. Then slice with the knife flush against the next rib, so you have a slice of meat as thick as the last one but with no rib. This way, only every other person gets meat with a bone attached. The second approach is simply to cut against the ribs and remove the bones entirely, leaving you with the whole loin muscle which you then simply slice.

"Fake" Meat Jus

You can fake a good-tasting jus to augment the juices your roast releases by roasting meat trimmings, or browning them on the stove top, and then treating the drippings to a succession of deglazings and caramelizations. You can do this with trimmings you've put in the roasting pan with the roast (see Prime Rib, page 169), or you can do it separately and make the jus completely in advance, which is what some restaurants do.

MAKES 1 CUP

> **1 pound meat or poultry trimmings, depending on the type of roast you are serving, cut into about 3/4-inch cubes**
>
> **1 onion, quartered**
>
> **1 small carrot, peeled and sliced**
>
> **4 cups broth (preferably the same meat or poultry you are serving)**

Put the meat trimmings, onion, and carrot in a heavy-bottomed pan or skillet or other shallow pan and slide it into a 450°F oven—there's no need for preheating—for about 30 minutes or until the meat is well browned and a crust has formed on the bottom of the pan.

Alternatively, place the pan on the stove top over medium-high heat until a caramelized crust forms on the bottom of the pan. Pour off and discard any fat floating on top of the crust.

Add about 1 cup of broth to the pan, put the pan back on the burner, and as the broth is boiling down scrape against the crust with a wooden spoon to dissolve it. Repeat this process as needed until only 1 cup or so of broth remains. Use this remaining cup to deglaze for the final time. Scrape the pan of broth over the heat just long enough to dissolve the crust. (Don't simmer for more than a minute or two, or the jus will lose vitality and end up tasting like concentrated broth.) Strain through a fine-mesh sieve to remove the caramelized vegetables and bits, cool, and store in an airtight container in the refrigerator until ready to use.

ROAST SIRLOIN STRIP OR SHELL

In some parts of the country, the word *sirloin* is used, in conjunction with shell, strip, or even New York cut, to describe the loin meat below the rib section. Don't confuse this cut, which comes from the back of the animal, with the less expensive sirloin cuts that come from the leg. The difference between a shell steak and a strip steak is that the shell contains the bone. If you are buying a section of the shell to roast, buy it from the neater, more compact rib end.

Roast these cuts as described for prime rib, counting on about 8 ounces of strip or 10 ounces of shell per serving.

Less Expensive Beef Roasts

Sirloin roasts from a good butcher are often the best value and are tender enough to serve in thick slices. Cuts such as eye of the round, top round, and bottom round should not be roasted more than medium-rare, or they will be dry, and should be served in very thin slices. Roast these cuts as described for prime rib. The broth and stew meat are optional.

Letting Roasts and Steaks Sit at Room Temperature

A roast or steak should be allowed to come to room temperature before it is roasted, grilled, or sautéed, so it cooks evenly and doesn't end up raw in the middle and dry and overcooked on the outside. The USDA recommends never leaving meat out for more than 2 hours, but unless you're dealing with thin steaks, 2 hours is not enough time for the meat to come to room temperature. It takes 4 hours for a large roast to come to room temperature and 3 hours for a thick porterhouse. If you're worried about bacteria, rub the steak or roast liberally with salt before letting it come to room temperature.

STEAKS

Great steaks come from the same cuts as great roasts, as well as from other cuts. As with selecting roasts, choose steaks according to how you will be serving them, the size of your guest list, and your budget. One of the best ways to serve steak is to buy a steak large enough for two, four, or even six people, and then carve it at the table. The effect is not only memorable and elegant, but the meat also tastes better.

Grilled or Broiled Porterhouse

The porterhouse, equivalent to a loin chop, is sliced across the whole bone-in loin from the leg end. It includes both the large loin muscle (the sirloin strip) and the tenderloin (the fillet), separated by the bones that surround the spine. High-end supermarkets often sell a porterhouse cut into single steaks. But they are so thin that they are hard to brown without overcooking. Ask your butcher to cut a porterhouse that allows for about $1/2$ inch per person, or 4 inches thick for eight people. Don't tell the butcher you are grilling or sautéing the meat—say it is a roast—or he will think you are crazy.

When grilling, broiling, or sautéing an especially thick steak, you need to cook it in two stages: hot for browning at the beginning, and then moderately, so the heat penetrates the meat. A covered grill or an oven handles the second stage nicely.

MAKES 6 MAIN-COURSE SERVINGS

>   **One 3-inch-thick porterhouse steak**
>   **Salt**
>   **Pepper**
>   **2 tablespoons olive oil**

Rub the steak liberally on both sides with salt and pepper and let sit at room temperature for at least 3 hours before cooking.

Build a hot charcoal fire with the coals 3 to 4 inches away from the grill rack under about half of the rack. The charcoal should be in a double layer and large enough so that the whole steak rests over it. Or, preheat a gas grill to high, or preheat the broiler.

Pat the meat dry—the salt will have drawn out liquid—and rub on both sides with the oil. Put the steak directly over the hot coals or gas burners, or under the broiler, 4 inches from the heat source. Grill or broil the steak, turning once, for about 2 to 5 minutes on each side, or until well browned on both sides. If you don't have a covered grill or you are broiling, preheat the oven to 250°F. If your oven is very hot from broiling, turn it off completely for the second cooking stage. Move the steak to the cool side of the charcoal grill, or a part of the gas grill not over the heat source. Test for desired doneness (pages 174–175) with an instant-read thermometer. Let the meat rest for 10 minutes in a warm place before carving and serving.

How to Grill a Steak

While a sizzling steak right off the grill is hard to resist, many of us are afraid of looking like an amateur and ruining a sizable investment in red meat. Keep in mind that the only thing that can go wrong is drastic overcooking, and fortunately a steak provides plenty of warning (see pages 174–175) before it gets near that point. Still, knowing when a steak is cooked just right takes experience—there is no way to fake it—and until you have the experience, the only way to know for sure is to stick a thermometer through the side or to cut into it. If you can be covert about it, fine, but don't just guess.

HOW TO MAKE SAUTÉED PORTERHOUSE

1. Trim off excess fat and membranes from the outside of the steak.

2. Cook in very hot oil in a sauté pan just large enough to accommodate the steak.

3. Press on the steak to ensure it is touching the hot oil.

4. Put the sliced steak on a platter and pour a pan-deglazed sauce over the top.

HOW TO CARVE A PORTERHOUSE

Cut along the bone that separates the large loin muscle and remove the muscle.

Do the same with the smaller tenderloin. Slice both the loin and the tenderloin.

Eight Tips for the Perfect Grilled Steak

1. THE BEST CUTS

Some of the most flavorful steaks, such as flank or chuck (shoulder), are tough and must be thinly sliced for serving. There is nothing wrong with serving sliced steaks, and slicing them at the table adds some welcome ritual to the meal. More tender (and expensive) steaks, such as sirloin strip, tenderloin, small T-bone, or hangar, are just the right size for a single serving, and nowadays most people opt for grilling individual steaks.

But carving a very large, tender steak at the table allows for big, luxurious slices. The best choice is a porterhouse that serves four to six. A variety of T-bone, the porterhouse includes both the tenderloin and the sirloin strip (sometimes called the New York cut), so that when you carve it, you can give everyone a little of both. When you take the steak off the grill, transfer it to a cutting board—with a moat so the juices don't escape—and cut away the sirloin and tenderloin, always

HOW TO MAKE A PAN-DEGLAZED RED WINE MEAT SAUCE

1. Pour the fat out of the pan. While the pan is still hot, add chopped shallots and stir.

2. When the shallots smell toasty, pour in red wine.

3. Boil down the wine until reduced by half and add a teaspoon of meat glaze per serving.

4. When the sauce is the consistency you like, thin it with broth or water or thicken it by boiling it down. Whisk in cold butter.

keeping the knife against the bone. Slice these two sections and serve them on warmed plates. A large section of the sirloin strip is also a beautiful steak to serve for up to eight.

Like sparsely populated Caribbean islands, underappreciated cuts of beef are ever harder to find. Flank steak was "discovered" twenty years ago, but is still a good value. Hangar steak has been around for a decade or so and is one of the tastiest cuts. Perhaps least appreciated are top blade steaks, which are taken from the chuck above the shoulder blades. Despite being chuck, they are very tender. Depending on what the butcher has or has not done to them, they may have a strip of gristle running down the middle. Slide a knife along one side of the gristle and pull it out. Sirloin steaks (not sirloin strip) from a good butcher are also a good value.

2. THE KIND OF GRILL TO USE

The best grills for individual steaks are ones that allow you to adjust the distance of the grill rack from the coals. Steaks, especially thin ones, require intense heat to form

a good crust on the exterior, before the heat can penetrate and overcook the interior. The rack itself should be made of heavy metal—and flat, not round, bars—to make attractive grill marks. To achieve the classic crosshatch, give the steak a 90-degree turn after a minute or two of grilling. If you are cooking a large, thick steak that yields multiple servings, intense heat is less critical and a covered grill works best. It allows you to move the steak away from the coals, cover the grill, and finish the steak in an ovenlike environment.

Gas grills have the advantage of imparting a grilled flavor without having to build a fire. Indeed, a fire made with ordinary charcoal briquettes delivers no more flavor than a gas grill. To give your meat the flavor of wood, you must create smoke. For tips on generating smoke, see page 15.

3. THE NEED FOR STEAK KNIVES

More expensive steak cuts, such as tenderloin, sirloin, and porterhouse, are tender enough that the slightly serrated edge of an ordinary table knife will do the trick. Serve tougher cuts, such as flank or round, in slices so the diner only has to slice the slices. If the slices are thin enough, a regular knife should work fine. If you are in doubt and you have them, use your steak knives.

4. HOW MUCH MEAT TO BUY

Steak lovers are often big eaters and expect generous portions. In general, count on 8 ounces of pure steak per person. So if the steak is on the bone, you need to buy about 20 percent more (about 10 ounces per person), and if there is fat on the steak, another 10 percent more (about 11 ounces per person). If you are serving some kind of rich first course, such as seafood or a substantial soup, or you are serving other grilled foods at the same time, you will need less meat.

5. HOW TO BE SURE THE STEAK IS EVENLY COOKED

Three steps will ensure evenly cooked steaks. First, let the steak come to room temperature before grilling. Depending on the thickness of the steak, this may take the whole afternoon (see page 170).

Second, adjust the distance between the coals and the steak according to the thickness of the steak: 3 inches or less for a steak no more than 1 inch thick, 3 to 6 inches for thicker steaks. The thinner the steak, the hotter the fire should be because you need to create a dark, crispy crust quickly, without overcooking the center. If you are cooking a very large steak—say, a porterhouse big enough to serve six, making it almost a roast—you can cook it over lower heat because the outside will have plenty of time to brown. Or, you can brown it over the coals, move it to a cooler part of the fire, and cover the grill to finish.

HOW TO MAKE GRILLED FLANK STEAK ———————

1. Rub flank steak with chopped garlic, fresh thyme, and balsamic vinegar or soy sauce. Poke it in two directions with the tip of a paring knife.

2. Prepare a hot fire in a grill or preheat a grill pan over high heat and brown the steak for 2 minutes on the first side. Give it a 90-degree turn to create crosshatch marks and brown it for 2 minutes more on the same side.

3. Turn the steak over and brown it on the other side.

4. Let the steak rest for 5 minutes, and then slice it on the diagonal on a cutting board with a moat to catch the juices.

Third, let the steaks rest on a warmed platter before serving. Make sure they are in a single layer, loosely cover them with aluminum foil—they steam if you wrap them too tight—and let rest for 5 minutes per inch of thickness. The internal temperature of the steak will rise from 5 to 10 degrees during resting.

6. HOW LONG TO COOK A STEAK AND HOW TO KNOW WHEN IT IS DONE

It is hard to give exact cooking times. Everyone's fire is different, and steaks come in all sizes and shapes. As a loose rule, count about 5 minutes per inch of thickness for black and blue (essentially raw but browned on the outside), 7 to 10 minutes per inch for rare (the thicker the steak, the less time per inch), 12 minutes for medium-rare, and 13 to 15 minutes for medium, not including resting time.

There are four ways to test a steak for doneness. You can cut into it (in an unobtrusive place) with a knife. Or, you can slide an instant-read thermometer through its side into the center, keeping in mind that the temperature will increase from 5 to 10 degrees after resting. The pictures below show the meat *after* resting, so if you want your meat to look like the slice labeled 110°F, take it off the grill when the thermometer reads 105°F.

Pressing the steak with your fingertip is another good test. A rare steak will feel fleshy, like an unflexed muscle; a rare to medium-rare steak will just begin to bounce back to the touch; and a medium-rare to medium steak will feel firm to the touch. Finally, you can tell by looking at the steak. A rare steak doesn't release any juices. As the steak approaches medium-rare, you see red juices beginning to form on the surface (you might also hear them dripping over the coals). As the steak approaches medium, there will be more juices. And as it approaches greater doneness, the juices will turn brown.

7. HOW TO AVOID FLARE-UPS

Flames shooting up under the steaks leave an oily, sooty taste on the meat. To avoid them, trim off the fat that surrounds the meat (the only time this is worth eating is on the best dry-aged beef), then once on the grill, move the steaks around as soon as you see any flames. You can finish a very thick steak in a covered grill over an area with no coals and therefore no flare-ups. If flare-ups persisted despite these precautions, wipe off the steaks with a paper towel—the oily soot will cling to the towel—as soon as they are off the grill.

8. HOW TO SEASON A STEAK

When you sprinkle salt on a steak, the salt draws out moisture and makes the surface of the meat moist, which in turn makes it hard to brown. This isn't a problem for a big steak, because there is plenty of time for browning. Otherwise, season the meat a couple of hours before it goes on the grill, and then pat it dry with a paper towel just before you put it over the fire. This allows the salt to seep into the steak and eliminates any beads of water that are drawn out by it.

Basic Grilled Steak

Very few foods are as satisfying as a perfectly grilled steak. Grilling steaks also offers an occasion to gather guests around the grill and give opinions about when the steaks are ready. Remember, if you're in doubt, there's no shame in cutting into a steak to see whether it's done (see left, "How Long to Cook a Steak," for determining doneness).

MAKES 4 MAIN-COURSE SERVINGS

> Four 3/4-pound New York strip steaks, about 1 inch thick
> Salt
> Pepper
> Olive oil

DEGREES OF DONENESS

Blue (90°F)

Very Rare (110°F)

Rare (120°F)

Medium-rare (125°F)

Season the steaks with salt and pepper and let them rest at room temperature for 2 to 4 hours.

Build a hot charcoal fire with the coals 3 to 4 inches away from the grill rack. Use enough charcoal to make a double layer large enough for all the steaks. Or, preheat a gas grill to high.

Pat the steaks dry with paper towels and rub them with oil. Estimate the total cooking time following the guidelines in tip 6 of "Eight Tips for the Perfect Grilled Steak" (see page 172), then put the steaks on the grill. Grill for 2 minutes, rotate the steaks 90 degrees to create a crosshatch pattern, and then continue grilling for half the estimated cooking time. Using tongs, turn the steaks over, grill for 2 minutes, rotate them 90 degrees, and then continue grilling until done to your liking. (Don't turn them more than once or you will loose the attractive crosshatch and leave them with random markings instead.)

Transfer the steaks to a warmed platter, arranging them in a single layer. Cover loosely with aluminum foil and let rest for 5 to 10 minutes before serving.

Tenderloin Sandwich

This ultimate steak sandwich is made with the most expensive cut of the steer, the tenderloin, the only cut tender enough that it doesn't need to be sliced for a sandwich. One caveat: If you like well-done meat, don't make this sandwich. Because it is so lean, tenderloin dries out as soon as it reaches the temperature needed to cook it beyond medium-rare. Each sandwich contains only a small amount of meat— you may want to offer 2 sandwiches per person.

MAKES 8 SMALL SANDWICHES, OR 4 MAIN-COURSE SERVINGS

One 6-inch center-cut beef tenderloin section, about 1¼ pounds

2 tablespoons olive oil

Salt

Pepper

16 slices white bread, or 8 English muffins or hamburger buns, split

4 tablespoons butter, melted, or olive oil (optional)

Assorted condiments such as tomatoes, onion slices, relish, ketchup, mustard, aioli, mayonnaise variations (see pages 359–361)

Ask your butcher to remove the chain, or small muscle that runs along the side of the tenderloin and the shiny tissue, or silver skin, that covers the meat. If you bought your meat at the supermarket and there were no butchers in sight, you will need to do the trimming yourself with a sharp knife.

Slice the tenderloin into 8 perfectly round steaks, each about ¾ inch thick. Rub the steaks with olive oil and season both sides with salt and pepper.

Build a very hot fire in a charcoal grill with the coals 2 to 3 inches away from the grill rack. Use enough charcoal to make a double layer large enough for all the steaks. Or, preheat a gas grill to high.

Meanwhile, if using bread slices for the sandwiches, use a cookie cutter or small bowl to cut the slices into rounds the exact size of the steaks. Brush the bread rounds on one side or the muffins or buns on the cut side with butter on one side.

Grill the steaks for 1 minute, rotate them 90 degrees, and grill for 1 minute more. Using tongs, turn the steaks over and grill for 2 minutes more.

Grill the bread, muffins, or buns on both sides just long enough to brown them. Transfer the steaks to a warmed platter. Serve with the bread and condiments, and let diners assemble their own sandwiches.

Medium-rare to medium (130°F)

Medium (135°F)

Medium to medium-well (140°F)

Medium-well (145°F)

The Best Burgers

The best meat for hamburgers is ground chuck—get it from a good butcher if you can—and there is nothing you need to do to it other than shape it into patties the size you like and grill over a hot fire, broil, or sauté to the doneness you like, keeping in mind that hamburgers are usually better slightly more done than steaks so some of the fat they contain can render. Serve buns and condiments and let everyone serve themselves.

CONDIMENTS FOR TENDERLOIN SANDWICHES AND BURGERS

TOMATOES Ideally, use beefsteak tomatoes cut into 1/4-inch-thick slices. If the slices are wider than the steaks or burgers, you can use a cookie cutter to match them to the meat. Otherwise, just slice good in-season tomatoes. If you can find them, an assortment of different heirloom tomatoes makes a great impression. Figure on 1 to 2 slices per sandwich.

LETTUCE Here is an opportunity to be retro and use iceberg lettuce, which has the cool, crisp crunch you need to balance the texture of a burger or steak. If you like, cut out steak-sized rounds with a cookie cutter.

ONIONS Thinly sliced red onions provide crunch and help cut the richness of the meat. If possible, slice them on a vegetable slicer. To tenderize them, sprinkle the slices liberally with salt—1 teaspoon coarse salt per onion—and then toss and rub the salt into the slices for about 2 minutes, or until the salt dissolves and no longer feels gritty. Transfer the onion slices to a colander, set it in the sink or over a bowl, and let drain for about 15 minutes. Working with a little at a time, squeeze the onion slices in your fists to extract as much liquid and salt as possible. Or, for a more wintry feel, thinly slice the onions and cook them gently in a little butter for about 30 minutes, or until they caramelize, and then serve warm. Plan on 1 raw red onion for every 4 sandwiches, or 2 caramelized onions for every 4 sandwiches.

CHEESE Steaks cook so quickly that there is no time for cheese to melt on top. Because of this, use softer cheeses such as Camembert or a good blue, like Stilton, Roquefort, or Gorgonzola (avoid generic blue cheese and Danish blue, which have an aggressive sour flavor). For your burgers, experiment with any good-melting cheese, such as Gruyère, Cheddar, Gorgonzola, or Roquefort.

PICKLES You can stick with standard dill pickles, thinly sliced, or try sour gherkins (cornichons) sliced lengthwise. Sweet gherkins provide a sweet-and-sour taste that helps break up the richness of the meat.

RED, YELLOW, AND ORANGE BELL PEPPERS Char, peel, and seed bell peppers (see page 321) and then cut lengthwise into strips. Count on 1 bell pepper for every 4 sandwiches.

CUCUMBERS Because raw cucumbers contain a lot of water, you need to salt them and squeeze out some of their moisture. Peel the cucumbers, cut them in half lengthwise, and scoop out the seeds with a spoon. Salt, squeeze, and drain as directed for Cucumber Salad, page 81. Count on 1 English (hothouse) cucumber for every 2 sandwiches, or 1 regular cucumber for every 4 sandwiches.

BACON Cook the bacon separately just until it begins to get crispy (see page 234).

MUSHROOMS Slice and sauté in olive oil (see page 318).

POT ROAST POSSIBILITIES

Red wine goes particularly well with braised beef, but you can use almost any liquid you like: white wine, beer, hard cider, broth, even rum. You can also shape the flavor of the braising liquid with herbs, either cooked with the meat in a bouquet garni (slow-cooking herbs such as thyme and bay leaves) or chopped and added to the pot at the last minute to impart a fresh note (chervil, parsley, chives, basil, or tarragon, or a combination). The garnish can be the aromatic vegetables included at the beginning, or you can strain out those vegetables and cook new vegetables, either separately or with the roast, during the last 30 minutes to 1 hour of braising.

Classic Garnishes

Most of us think of a garnish as the sprig of parsley or the orange wedge alongside an omelet. French-trained cooks give garnishes a more important distinction and describe them much as American cooks describe accompaniments. Stews or sautéed meats or seafood are often served with an accompanying vegetable, but when the vegetable(s) is spooned over the meat or fish along with the sauce, it is more integral to the dish and is formally called a garniture, or more colloquially, a garnish.

One of the best examples is the Burgundian garnish of sautéed mushrooms, glazed pearl onions, and strips of bacon. It is used for stew—boeuf à la bourguignonne—for coq au vin, and for any stewlike dish made with red wine. A printanier garnish (from the French *printemps,* or "spring"), which is baby or shaped root vegetables and green vegetables, can be used for any meat or seafood stew or braised dish. If you look at a French cookbook full of stew recipes, or full of sautéed chicken recipes, the basic recipe is the same for all of them and only the garnish changes.

The natural way to think about a garnish is to select what looks pretty at the market. Depending on what it contains, a garnish can be cooked separately and added to the dish just before serving, or it can be added to a stew or braised dish so that it cooks with the meat or fish.

To add to the confusion, cooks sometimes talk about the aromatic garniture. This refers to the ingredients, usually vegetables, that go into a pot roast or stew at the beginning of cooking. In homespun stews and pot roasts, these ingredients can be left in, so they become the garnish. In more refined versions, they are picked or strained out and one or more freshly prepared garnishes are added near or at the end.

Here are some possible garnishes for meat or seafood stews. They can be used alone or in combination:

Baby green beans (boiled or steamed as on page 292)

Peas (boiled for 1 minute if fresh, or heated in the sauce if frozen as on page 294)

Asparagus tips (boiled or steamed as on page 290)

Leeks (greens removed, whites halved or quartered lengthwise, and boiled until tender as on page 293)

Mushrooms (cultivated or wild, cut into pieces or thick slices if large, and sautéed as on page 319)

Tomatoes (peeled, outer pulp cut off in wedges as on page 85, and heated in braising sauce)

Pearl or boiling onions (glazed as on page 302)

Carrots or baby carrots (braised as on page 301, or glazed as on page 300)

Turnips or baby turnips (glazed as on page 305)

Celeriac (glazed as on page 299)

Bacon (slices cut crosswise into strips 1 inch long and $1/4$ inch wide and thick and cooked until lightly crisped)

Bell peppers (charred, peeled, and seeded as on page 321 and then cut into strips)

Dried beans (soaked and cooked as on page 330)

Fresh shell beans such as cranberry beans (blanched and simmered in the braising liquid)

Potatoes (sliced, shaped into balls, or cut into sticks or cubes and sautéed as on pages 309 or 314)

Meat Glaze

The best-known brand of commercial meat glaze, More-than-Gourmet, is extremely concentrated. Whereas homemade meat glaze is made by concentrating good broth down to one-fifteenth of its original volume, commercial meat glaze behaves almost as though it has been cooked down to one-thirtieth. Use very sparingly when making sauces, about 1 teaspoon per serving, which is equivalent to 1 tablespoon of homemade meat glaze.

Larding and Barding

Unless you are a fanatic who loves spending time in the kitchen in pursuit of perfection, skip this little text block. Larding and barding are the antitrends of the modern diet. Larding simply means to insert strips of fat into meat. The fat, from the belly of a pig, increases the impression of moistness when you braise meat that is too lean. In the eighteenth century, everything, including roasts, was larded, but a roast is better barded—wrapped with a thin sheet of fat—than larded. That's because the strips don't cook through and you end up chomping on little hard bits of fat. The sheet of fat used for barding protects the surface of the roast from drying out, essentially basting the meat as it roasts or braises.

There are two ways to lard: with a tubular larding needle (for big pieces of meat) or with a device reminiscent of a knitting needle, but hinged and with a jagged clamp, that allows you to sew strips of fat into the meat.

Stew Components

THE MEAT
Chuck roasts in various sizes.

MARINADES FOR THE MEAT
Usually the braising liquid, such as wine, and aromatic ingredients, such as onions, carrots, and sometimes garlic.

MARINADES FOR THE FAT STRIPS FOR LARDING
Minced parsley, cognac, and minced garlic, combined into a marinade for the strips of lard.

BRAISING LIQUIDS
Red wine, white wine, sweet wine (Sauternes, Muscat de Beaumes-de-Venise), dry or sweet Madeira, Marsala, broth, beer such as sweet Belgian bière brune, hard cider, apple juice, rum (pot stilled from Martinique is best), tomato (coulis or concassée, pages 366 and 367, respectively).

AROMATIC VEGETABLES FOR BRAISING
Onions, carrots, garlic, fennel (the branches are great), turnips, celery.

HERBS FOR BOUQUET GARNI
Thyme, parsley, bay leaves, marjoram, oregano, very small amount of rosemary.

GARNISHES
Carrots (sectioned, cored, and/or turned), pearl or walnut-sized onions, turnips (wedges, rounded), fennel wedges, leeks (whites cut in half, held together with kitchen string), mushrooms (cultivated cooked in the braising liquid or wild sautéed and added at the end). See pages 289–319 for more information on preparing these vegetables.

HERBS FOR FINISHING BRAISING LIQUID OR GARNISHES
Finely chopped fresh parsley, chervil, tarragon, or chives.

OTHER FINISHES FOR BRAISING LIQUID
Butter (whisked into the reduced liquid just before serving), cognac (a tablespoon or so simmered in the liquid for 30 seconds), vinegar (for a note of tang).

How to Thicken the Braising Liquid

In a perfect world, the braising liquid is naturally thick from the gelatin it contains. If you have used concentrated broth or meat glaze in your pot roast, the braising liquid will have enough body of its own. But if not, you may want to thicken it slightly. If it has reduced down to the minimum amount of about 3 tablespoons per serving and still seems watery, thicken it with flour or cornstarch. To thicken with flour, prepare what is called a beurre manié, which is a term for a little paste made by using the back of a fork to work together equal amounts of flour and room-temperature butter until the mixture has no lumps. If you want the braising liquid to have a shiny look, dissolve 1 tablespoon cornstarch in 2 tablespoons cold water to create what is known as a slurry. Just before serving, bring the braising liquid to a simmer and whisk in half of the beurre manié or the slurry. Make sure the braising liquid is simmering or the cornstarch or flour won't thicken it. Judge the thickness and whisk in more flour paste or slurry as needed.

Red Wine Beef Daube

Like most braised beef dishes, the liquid for a daube can be almost anything you wouldn't mind drinking, except maybe for Coke or coffee. You can even use a mixture of liquids: the ends of bottles of red and white wines, sherry, Madeira, full-bodied beer (though not with the wine), chopped peeled tomatoes, hard cider, apple juice, wine vinegar, broth, concentrated broth and meat glaze, leftover roasting juices, or even chic verjuice, the juice of underripe grapes popular in the Middle Ages and again now. The vegetables you cook along with the meat to flavor the braising liquid can be the usual suspects, including onions, carrots, a little celery, maybe a turnip, and/or some garlic. Or, you can emphasize one vegetable and use an abundance of it, such as sliced, sectioned, or turned carrots or pearl or walnut-sized onions, adding them three-fourths of the way through the cooking, rather than at the beginning, so they function as both aromatic ingredients and the final garnish. Yet another alternative is to use one or more of the garnishes suggested for Red Wine Pot Roast (see page 180).

MAKES 6 MAIN-COURSE SERVINGS

> 4 pounds boneless beef chuck or other stew meat, cut into 1-inch cubes
>
> One 750-ml bottle full-bodied red wine or a mixture of bottle ends
>
> 1 cup concentrated (1 quart simmered down to 1 cup) broth or 2 tablespoons commercial meat glaze, or $1/_4$ cup homemade meat glaze (see page 177), optional
>
> 2 carrots, peeled, quartered lengthwise, and cut into 1-inch sections
>
> 2 onions, quartered
>
> Bouquet garni
>
> 1 tablespoon flour (optional)
>
> 1 tablespoon butter, at room temperature (optional)
>
> Garnish for Red Wine Pot Roast (see page 177), optional

Select a tall, narrow pot. Put the beef, wine, broth, carrots, and onions in the pot, and then nestle the bouquet garni in the center. Bring to a simmer and skim off any froth. Adjust the heat so the liquid is at a gentle simmer—you want a bubble or two to break on the surface about every second—cover, and cook on the stove top or in a 325°F oven. Check every 10 minutes or so and adjust the burner heat or oven temperature as needed to maintain the gentle simmer. Cook for about 2½ hours, or until a skewer easily slides into a cube of meat. Serve as is, or go on to the refinements:

Refinement one: Pour the daube into a strainer placed over a saucepan, and then simmer the braising liquid over medium heat for about 30 minutes, with the pan off center over the heat, to concentrate its flavor and thicken it, regularly skimming off any fat or froth. If you end up with less than 1½ cups and the liquid is too thin, use the back of a fork to make a smooth paste with the flour and butter in a small bowl, and then whisk half of the paste into the simmering liquid. Simmer the liquid briefly, check the consistency, and add more paste if needed.

Refinement two: Sort through the contents of the strainer and remove and discard the bouquet garni and the onions and carrots (they will have given up all of their flavor to the liquid and meat) and then spoon the meat into soup plates and spoon the braising liquid around the meat.

Refinement three: Add one or more of the garnishes to the stew or to each serving. This makes it necessary to strain the stew and pick out the vegetables that were used for braising before you add the additional ingredients.

Red Wine Pot Roast

This is the classic red wine pot roast served all over Europe. If you decide to include more or fewer than three additional ingredients, decrease or increase the amount of each garnish you use accordingly.

MAKE 6 TO 8 MAIN-COURSE SERVINGS

One 3- to 4-pound chuck or beef shoulder roast

One 750-ml bottle full-bodied red wine

Bouquet garni

2 onions, quartered

2 carrots, peeled, quartered lengthwise, and cut into 1-inch sections

Salt

Pepper

1 cup concentrated (1 quart simmered down to 1 cup) broth or 2 tablespoons commercial meat glaze or 1/4 cup homemade meat glaze (see page 177), optional

2 tablespoons finely chopped fresh parsley or chervil (optional)

Garnish (choose 3)

3 carrots, peeled, cut into sections, cored, rounded, and then glazed (see page 300) or added to the braising liquid the last 20 minutes

11/2 pounds cultivated white or other small mushrooms, larger mushrooms quartered through the stem, cooked in the braising liquid for the last 15 minutes or sautéed in olive oil and seasoned with salt and pepper

11/2 pounds wild mushrooms, sautéed in olive oil and seasoned with salt and pepper

1 cup thawed, frozen petite peas, added to braising liquid 5 minutes before serving, or fresh peas, boiled for 2 minutes and added to braising liquid 5 minutes before serving

1 pound haricots verts or small regular green beans, ends trimmed, boiled or steamed, and served over each serving

2 turnips, peeled, cut into sections, rounded, and then glazed (page 305) or added to the braising liquid the last 20 minutes

1 celeriac, peeled, sectioned, rounded, and then glazed (page 299) or added to the braising liquid the last 30 minutes

1 pint pearl onions, small shallots, or walnut-sized boiling onions, glazed (see page 302) or added to the braising liquid the last 20 to 30 minutes

4 slices thick-cut bacon, cut crosswise into strips 1 inch long and 1/4 inch wide and thick, cooked until barely crispy and added at the end

4 leeks, greens removed, whites halved lengthwise, blanched, and added to the braising liquid the last 10 minutes

1 cup fava beans (from 2 pounds unshelled), blanched and added to the braising liquid a minute before serving

2 fennel bulbs, prepared for braising (see page 294) and added to the braising liquid 5 minutes before serving

If the roast is flat and needs tying with kitchen string, marinate it first—if you are bothering with that step—with the wine, bouquet garni, onions, and carrots for 3 hours at room temperature or overnight in the refrigerator. Remove the meat from the marinade, reserving the marinade. Season the meat on the inside with salt and pepper and tie it with string to keep it compact.

Turn on the oven to 450°F (there is no need for preheating) and put the roast in a pot as close to its size (and shape, if you are lucky enough to have an oval pot) as possible. Surround it with the vegetables reserved from the marinade, if you made a marinade, and roast uncovered for 30 minutes. Turn the roast over in the pot and continue roasting for about 11/2 hours for a 3-pound roast, or until the meat releases liquid and all the liquid caramelizes on the bottom of the pot. Be careful not to let the juices burn.

Pour in the wine and broth, which should come about halfway up the side. Cover the pot with a sheet of aluminum foil, pressing it down so the middle hangs over the roast. (This causes moisture that condenses within the pot to baste the roast from the inside.) Cover the pot and bring to a gentle simmer—you want a bubble or two to break on the surface about every second—over low heat on the stove top or in a 325°F oven, or first bring to a simmer on the stove top and then move to a 325°F oven. Check every 10 minutes or so and adjust the burner heat or oven temperature as needed to maintain the slow simmer.

After 11/2 hours, turn the roast over in the liquid—be gentle, it may be fragile—so the part that was submerged is now on top. Re-cover with the foil and lid and braise for another hour, or until a skewer slides easily in and out of the meat without the meat clinging to it and pulling up when the skewer is drawn out of the meat.

Transfer the meat to a clean pot—you can clean out the same pot—and strain the braising liquid into a saucepan, discarding the onions and carrots. Place the pan of braising liquid off center on the burner so that the liquid simmers on only one side and pushes the fat to the other. Simmer for 10 minutes, regularly skimming off any fat or froth. Ladle about one-third of the braising liquid over the roast, put the uncovered roast in the oven, and turn the oven to 400°F.

If adding garnishes, ready them, so you can add them as directed.

When the roast has been in the oven for 15 minutes, pour the rest of the braising liquid over the roast.

Baste the roast every 5 to 10 minutes with the surrounding liquid for about 30 minutes, or until the meat is covered with a shiny glaze. You should have about 2 cups lightly syrupy liquid. Add the parsley.

Remove the roast from the pot and slice it thickly. Place the slices in warmed soup plates. Taste the cooking liquid and adjust the seasoning with salt and pepper. Ladle the braising liquid—3 to 4 tablespoons per serving—over the meat, and then spoon the garnishes around the slices.

VARIATIONS

For those of us who like cold leftover meat, there is nothing like leftover pot roast. Some folks are squeamish about the jelled braising liquid—it recalls the horrible aspic salads popular a few decades ago—but once this fear is conquered, wide vistas of leftover possibilities are revealed. Try slicing the pot roast and layering it in a terrine. Stir plenty of chopped fresh parsley into the barely melted gelée and then pour it over the meat. Chill well and serve sliced, as you would pâté, with little pickles and mustard. You can also spread the slices out in an oval dish and pour the gelée over the meat. Or, turn your pot roast into a pasta sauce: shred the meat and simmer it with the braising liquid. Or into a filling for ravioli or cannelloni: Reduce the liquid to a thick syrup, mix it with the shredded meat, chopped mushrooms, blanched chopped spinach, and fresh marjoram. Seal up the mixture into large or little squares, or roll up into cannelloni. If making cannelloni, cover with tomato sauce, bake in a moderate oven, and serve with lots of grated Parmigiano-Reggiano cheese.

HOW TO MAKE A BEEF POT ROAST

1. Surround the pot roast with sliced carrots and onions and season with salt and pepper.

2. Roast in a 450°F oven for 30 minutes, then turn and roast until all the juices are released and caramelize on the bottom of the pan.

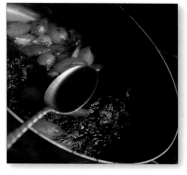

3. Add enough broth or other liquid to come halfway up the side of the roast. Cover with foil and braise at 325°F for 1¹/₂ hours. Turn and braise until easily penetrated with a skewer.

4. Put the pot roast in a clean pot. Strain and degrease the braising liquid. Add any new vegetables, and baste in the oven. After repeated basting, the pot roast surface will develop a shiny glaze.

5. Serve the meat surrounded with vegetables and braising liquid. You can also serve it on a bed of spinach (page 295).

Beef à la Mode

This pot roast is made much like Red Wine Pot Roast (see page 180), except that carrots and parsley are the only garnishes. You can serve this meat hot—you may want to add a teaspoon or two of vinegar to the braising liquid to balance the sweetness of the carrots—or you can serve it chilled in an oval gratin or other baking dish.

MAKES 6 TO 8 MAIN-COURSE SERVINGS

Red Wine Pot Roast (see page 180), without garnishes, cooked just until the meat tests done with a skewer

4 carrots, peeled and cut into 1/8-inch-thick slices

3 tablespoons very finely chopped fresh parsley, chopped at the last minute

Salt

Pepper

When you strain the braising liquid and put the pot roast in a clean pot, put the carrots in the pot with the roast. Pour half of the degreased braising liquid over the roast, cover the pot, and put it in a 400°F oven for 15 minutes.

Remove the lid, add the rest of the braising liquid, return to the oven, and baste the roast every 5 to 10 minutes with the surrounding liquid for 30 minutes, or until the meat is covered with a shiny glaze and the liquid is lightly syrupy. Add the parsley and season to taste with salt and pepper.

Slice the meat and serve surrounded with the carrots and braising liquid as directed for Red Wine Pot Roast. Or, slice the meat, layer the slices in an oval or square gratin dish or other baking dish, and ladle the carrots and braising liquid over the slices. Ideally, all the solids will be completely submerged in liquid. Chill thoroughly until set and then turn out onto a platter. If the beef won't come out of the dish, put the base of the dish in a bowl of hot water for 30 seconds and then invert again. Slice with a long thin knife into square slices.

Beef Stew

Many people don't make stews because they don't think of them in time and they associate them with messy prep, overnight marinades, and long cooking. The first thing you should know is that you can make a beef stew without marinating or browning the meat (the French have a whole family of such stews, called daubes). As soon as you come home and take off your coat, just put the meat in a pot with some onions, carrots, and a bouquet garni, pour over enough liquid to cover, bring to a simmer, and cook for 2 to 3 hours. You can then serve as is, or you can reduce and/or thicken the stewing liquid. Serve the onions and carrots used from the beginning, or strain them out and use one of the garnishes suggested for the pot roast on page 180. If you know how to use a pressure cooker (see page 11), you can make the stew in an hour.

The beef stew presented here uses all the steps: marinating, flouring, browning. If you don't have the time, you can skip them.

MAKES 4 TO 6 MAIN-COURSE SERVINGS

3 pounds boneless beef chuck

1 large onion, chopped

1/2 head garlic

2 carrots, peeled and chopped

Bouquet garni

2 cups full-bodied red wine, or more as needed

Salt

Pepper

Flour for patting cubes (optional)

3 tablespoons olive oil or canola oil (optional)

2 tablespoons butter (optional)

2 cups broth, or as needed

Cut the chuck roast into 1 1/2 -inch cubes. Combine the onion, garlic, carrots, bouquet garni, and wine in large bowl. Add the cubes of chuck and, if you have time, marinate for 1 to 12 hours.

Remove the meat cubes from the marinade, pat dry, and season with salt and pepper. Place the flour in a shallow dish. Coat the meat cubes with the flour and shake off the excess.

In a heavy-bottomed stew pot over high heat, brown the meat in the oil, adding only a few pieces at a time so the temperature of the pan remains hot enough to sear each meat cube as it is added. Using tongs, turn the cubes until all the cubes are seared and browned on all sides. Transfer the cubes to a plate.

Strain the marinade, reserving the wine, bouquet garni, and vegetables separately. Add the butter to the pan used to brown the meat, and heat over medium heat until the butter melts and begins to foam. Add the vegetables and gently cook until softened. Add the meat cubes, wine, broth, and bouquet garni, adding more wine and/or broth, if needed, to cover the meat. Cover and cook over low heat on the stove top or in a 325°F oven, or start on the stove top and transfer to the 325°F oven, for 2½ hours or until a knife blade easily slides into the meat. Spoon portions of stew into shallow bowls and serve.

HOW TO MAKE A BEEF STEW

1. Cut meat into large chunks of equal size.

2. Marinate meat in a bowl with onions, garlic, carrots, bouquet garni, and wine (optional).

3. Remove meat from marinade and pat dry. Season with salt and pepper.

4. Coat meat cubes with flour and shake off the excess (optional).

5. Brown the meat, a few pieces at a time, in oil over high heat.

6. Strain the marinade, reserving the wine, bouquet garni, and vegetables separately. Cook the vegetables in a little butter in the pan used to brown the meat.

7. Combine the browned meat, vegetables, wine, broth, and the bouquet garni in the pot used to brown the meat. Add more wine and/or broth to cover the meat. Cook over a low heat on the stove top or in the oven until the meat is done.

Braised Short Ribs

Short ribs are a perfect cut for braising, because they contain a lot of fat that keeps them moist. Approach them like any braise: brown the meat with vegetables in the oven, simmer gently with wine and broth, strain and degrease the braising liquid, and use the liquid to baste the meat for the final glazing. Keep in mind that short ribs come in two forms. Sometimes they are cut crosswise into strips containing 4 ribs or so and about 2 inches long. The alternative, and the one called for here, are 4-rib pieces with ribs about 6 inches long and covered with meat.

This recipe will satisfy eight normal appetites or four hungry people with little else to eat. You can get by serving six people, too, some hungrier than others.

MAKES 4 TO 8 MAIN-COURSE SERVINGS

>   Two 4-rib pieces, with ribs about 6 inches long
>   (about 7 pounds total)
>   Salt
>   Pepper
>   2 large carrots, peeled and cut into 2-inch sections
>   1 large onion, sliced
>   1 head garlic, halved crosswise
>   1 bottle full-bodied red wine
>   2 cups chicken broth, or as needed
>   Bouquet garni

Season the short ribs with salt and pepper and put them in a pot just large enough to accommodate them. Surround with the carrots, onion, and garlic, and roast uncovered in a 400°F oven for about 1½ hours, or until browned and any juices released have caramelized on the bottom of the pot.

Transfer the ribs to a pot that holds them as compactly as possible, pour over the wine and broth, and add the bouquet garni. Cover the pot with aluminum foil, pressing it down so it hangs just above the meat. (This causes moisture that condenses within the pot to baste the meat from the inside.) Top with the lid and simmer very gently for 1 hour. Rearrange the ribs so any that were protruding above the liquid are now submerged. Re-cover and simmer in the same way for about 1 hour more, or until a knife slides easily through the meat.

Put the short ribs in a clean pot. Strain the braising liquid and skim off any fat. Pour the braising liquid over the ribs. Return the ribs to the 400°F oven and cook, basting every 5 to 10 minutes with the liquid, for about 30 minutes, or until the ribs are covered with a shiny glaze and the liquid is syrupy.

Carve the ribs and serve each person 1 or 2 ribs, surrounded with the braising liquid.

1. Season short ribs with salt and pepper and put them in a roasting pan or pot surrounded with carrots, onion, and garlic. Roast until browned and the juices have caramelized.

2. Transfer the ribs to a pot that holds them as compactly as possible, add the wine, broth, and the bouquet garni. Cover the pot with aluminum foil, and then the lid. Simmer very gently for 1 hour. Rearrange the ribs, re-cover, and simmer in the same way for about 1 hour more.

3. Put the short ribs in a clean pot. Strain the braising liquid and skim off fat. Pour the braising liquid over the ribs. Return the ribs to the oven and cook, basting until the ribs are covered with a shiny glaze.

4. Carve the ribs and serve with the braising liquid.

Irish Beef Stew

Not surprisingly, Irish stew is all about potatoes. The secret is to use two kinds: Yukon Gold, which will dissolve and give the stew a silky body, and waxy potatoes, which will keep their shape and give the stew texture. Most recipes call for slicing the waxy potatoes, but you can also shape them into ovals. If you have sliced the Yukon Gold potato in advance, keep it immersed in a bowl of water to prevent darkening. Like a daube, the meat for Irish stew isn't browned. (Hurrah.) Usually, Irish stew is made with lamb, but this version made with beef is delicious.

MAKES 6 MAIN-COURSE SERVINGS

- 4 pounds boneless beef chuck or other stew meat, cut into 1-inch cubes
- 2 onions, minced
- 3 cups beef broth, chicken broth, or water, or more as needed
- Bouquet garni
- 1 large Yukon Gold potato, peeled and thinly sliced with a vegetable slicer
- 3 large white or red waxy potatoes
- 1 pint pearl onions or walnut-sized boiling onions, peeled, optional
- 1/4 to 1 cup heavy cream (optional)
- Salt
- Pepper

Select a tall, narrow pot. Put the beef, minced onions, and enough broth to cover in the pot, and then nestle the bouquet garni in the center. Bring to a simmer and skim off any froth. Add the sliced potato and return to a gentle simmer—you want a bubble or two to break on the surface about every second—cover, and cook on the stove top or in a 325°F oven. Check every 10 minutes or so and adjust the burner heat or oven temperature as needed to maintain the gentle simmer.

After the stew simmers for 1 hour, stir it with a wooden spoon to dissolve the sliced potato and continue to simmer. Just before the stew has finished simmering for its second hour, peel the waxy potatoes, and then cut into 1/4-inch-thick rounds, yielding 4 or 8 ovals from each potato. Add the potatoes and pearl onions to the stew and continue to simmer gently for about 25 minutes, or until the meat and potatoes are easily penetrated with a skewer.

Stir in the cream, bring back to a simmer, and season with salt and pepper. Serve in warmed soup plates.

WHY BROWN MEAT?

In the past, browning meat was thought to create a kind of semi-hermetic seal on the surface, so that when the center of the meat got hot and the steam produced began to push outward, the brown crust would keep it sealed inside. Plus, that same pressure was thought to cause the meat fibers to loosen and separate. Unfortunately, this handy hypothesis doesn't really apply. The seal is by no means hermetic, and when the meat is submerged in liquid, the crust becomes soft enough that steam and liquid alike easily pass through. So what is the point?

First, browning caramelizes juices that adhere to the meat and pan as a savory crust that ultimately dissolves into the braising liquid, making it more flavorful. Meat from a young animal, say, a lamb, chicken, or calf, should always be cooked in some way before it is poached or braised, so that the albumin it contains coagulates into long strands that tangle with one another and form froth and scum that is either skimmed off or rinsed off, such as when making the Creamy Veal Stew on page 195. This is why brown chicken broth is clear (as long as it didn't boil) and white chicken broth (unless you blanched the chicken first or made it with whole chicken and not bones) is cloudy.

A second advantage to thorough browning of meat cubes for a stew is that the meat contracts, so you need less liquid to cover. The result is a more concentrated braising liquid.

Third, if you brown the meat long enough, so that the heat thoroughly penetrates it, the meat will release all its juices, which then caramelize, delivering great flavor. Of course, getting the heat just right is tricky. If it is too hot, the meat will burn. If it is not hot enough, the juices won't caramelize and will instead flood the pan, leaving you with a pot of boiled, not browned, meat.

For stews, such as Boeuf à la Bourguignonne, we brown the meat in the oven, which causes it to release its juices. The juices end up caramelizing and browning on the bottom of the pan. Just be careful not to let the juices burn. When the juices are caramelized, pour out the fat, deglaze the pan, and make your stew.

Boeuf à la Bourguignonne

Like so many fancy-sounding French specialties, this dish gets its identity from a relatively small component—the garnish typical of most things served à la bourguignonne: glazed pearl onions, mushrooms, and little strips of lightly crisped bacon, known as lardoons. Also, unlike Irish Beef Stew (see page 185) and Red Wine Beef Daube (see page 179), the meat here must be browned before it is stewed.

MAKES 8 MAIN-COURSE SERVINGS

- 6 pounds boneless beef chuck or other stew meat, cut into 1-inch cubes
- Salt
- Pepper
- 4 carrots, peeled and cut into 1/2-inch-thick slices
- 2 onions, halved
- 1 cup broth or water, if needed
- One 750-ml bottle full-bodied red wine
- Bouquet garni
- 1 cup concentrated (1 quart simmered down to 1 cup) chicken, veal, or beef broth (see page 38), 3 tablespoons commercial meat glaze, or 6 tablespoons homemade meat glaze (see page 177), optional
- Glazed Pearl or Boiling Onions (see page 302)
- 2 tablespoons butter or olive oil
- 10 ounces mushrooms, preferably cremini, quartered through the stem unless very small
- 4 slices thick-cut bacon, cut crosswise into strips 1 inch long and 1/4 inch wide and thick
- 2 tablespoons flour, if needed for thickening
- 2 tablespoons butter, at room temperature, if needed for thickening
- 1 teaspoon wine vinegar, or to taste

Preheat the oven to 500°F. Season the meat cubes with salt and pepper. Spread the meat, carrots, and onions in a roasting pan just large enough to hold everything in a single layer. Roast, turning the meat and vegetables with tongs every 5 to 10 minutes, for about 40 minutes, or until well browned. If the meat has released liquid on the bottom of the pan, continue roasting until the juices caramelize into a crust. If a crust has formed before the meat is browned and it threatens to burn, add the 1 cup broth.

When the meat is browned and all the juices have caramelized on the bottom of the pan—don't confuse the clear fat floating on top with caramelized juices—remove the pan from the oven, and use the tongs to transfer the meat and vegetables to a tall, narrow pot. Spoon or pour out the clear liquid fat from the roasting pan and place the pan on the stove top over medium-high heat. Deglaze the pan with 2 cups of the wine, stirring for about 5 minutes, or until the caramelized juices have fully dissolved in the wine.

If you are braising the stew in the oven, turn the oven down to 325°F. Otherwise, turn it off.

Pour the deglazed juices over the meat and vegetables. Nestle the bouquet garni in the center, and add the remaining 2 cups wine and the concentrated broth. The meat should be completely covered. If it isn't, add more wine or broth if you have it or add water.

Bring the stew to a gentle simmer on the stove top and maintain it at a gentle simmer for at least 10 minutes, even if you will be cooking it in the oven. Then cover and cook at a gentle simmer—you want a bubble or two to break on the surface about every second—on the stove top or in the oven. Check every 10 minutes or so and adjust the burner heat or oven temperature as needed to maintain the gentle simmer. Continue to cook the stew in this way for about 3 hours or as many as 5 hours, or until a cube of meat poked through with a skewer just falls off without clinging. Strain the stew into a saucepan and discard the carrot and onions. Gently simmer the braising liquid over medium heat and skim off any scum and fat that floats to the top. Simmer down to about 1 1/2 cups.

About 30 minutes before the stew is ready, prepare the pearl onions. In a large sauté pan, melt the butter over high heat. Add the mushrooms and sauté for about 5 minutes, or until they're well browned and any liquid they release evaporates, then set aside. In a separate sauté pan, cook the bacon gently over medium heat for about 12 minutes, or until lightly crispy. Using a slotted spoon, transfer to paper towels to drain.

If the liquid is too thin, use the back of a fork to make a smooth paste with the flour and butter in a small bowl, and then whisk half of the paste into the simmering stew. Simmer briefly, check the consistency, and whisk in the remaining paste if needed. Season the liquid with a little salt and pepper. Add the vinegar a tiny bit at a time, tasting as you go. You may add up to a few tablespoons. Pour the liquid over the meat.

Add the onions, mushrooms, and bacon to the stew and then serve in warmed soup plates, or you can spoon the stew into the plates and arrange the garnishes on each serving.

1. Make the stew as directed on page 186, pour through a strainer, and remove and discard the braising vegetables. Return the meat to the braising liquid.

2. Cut the bacon into strips.

3. Cook the bacon strips gently until barely crispy.

4. Assemble the bacon, glazed pearl onions, and sautéed mushrooms.

5. Combine the garnishes with the stew and serve.

VEAL

Veal is generally perceived of as a luxurious meat, even though some lesser-known cuts are relatively inexpensive. It is extremely versatile and lends itself to nearly every cooking method, from braising and roasting to grilling and sautéing. None of these techniques is difficult, but you do need to know the structure of the animal to know which cuts are best for which dishes.

The most high-priced cuts come from the back of the animal, the muscles that run parallel to the spine. These cuts can be bought in large pieces and roasted—a large veal roast is an expensive and elegant purchase that usually has to be special ordered—or cut into smaller pieces for grilling or sautéing. Tougher cuts from the shoulder are usually sold as stew meat, but the shoulder also makes a perfect pot roast. The leg is a bit more complicated, since it contains both tender and tough muscles. The most tender muscle, the round, is indeed round, almost spherical, but sags a little like a large water balloon resting on a counter. Other muscles in the leg can be braised gently in stews or sliced and pounded.

ROASTING VEAL

Roasting veal is a straightforward affair. But like many of the simplest things, it can also be a bit tricky. Unlike beef or other red meats, which are cooked to varying degrees according to taste, veal is done at what for beef would be the equivalent of medium. Only in the most pretentious restaurants do waiters ask you if you want your veal rare. You don't. You want it cooked to the point at which it is pink and moist inside, with only a trace of the translucence of raw meat. The exact temperature of perfect roast veal, after resting, is 137°F. As with all roasts, the internal temperature continues to rise after the meat is removed from the oven. If you anticipate a rise of

7 degrees, and take the roast out at 130°F, your veal will be perfectly cooked.

Four cuts of the calf are suitable for roasting: the clod, a compact piece of meat, usually weighing about five pounds, taken from the shoulder; the rack, a section with as few as 3 ribs or as many as 9 ribs; the saddle, the section that contains the loin chops, which is back of the animal below the rib; and the whole round. None of these cuts is cheap, but the shoulder clod is reasonable. Rack and saddle are exorbitant but are justifiable for holiday dinners.

Buy a rack of veal with as many ribs as people you will be serving. If you are serving fewer than four, it makes more sense to sauté veal chops. If you are serving more than eight, you will need another roast. Keep in mind when calculating the roasting time that it doesn't increase proportionately with the weight of the rack. The thickness of the rack is the critical measure, and it remains the same except in very small roasts.

A rack includes the beginning of the ribs and the muscles that run along the spine of the animal. The ribs are sawed off 2 or 3 inches from where the muscle begins. Don't let the butcher break them off. Tell the butcher that you want the section of rack closest to the loin end, not the shoulder end, and ask the butcher to french the roast for you. If the butcher won't, or if you would rather do it yourself, scrape the meat and tissue off the ends of the ribs as shown on pages 212–213. Also, have the butcher make cuts through the chine bone (the vertebral column), or trim it off completely (keep it and cook it with the roast to add flavor to the jus), so the roast will be easier to carve.

A roast requires you to do nothing in advance except that you take it out of the refrigerator about 4 hours before you put it in the oven (see page 170). If you put a cold roast in the oven, it will overcook on the outside before the inside reaches the right temperature.

Roasted Rack of Veal

If you want to make a jus to go with your roast, surround the roast with about a pound of veal trimmings or veal stew meat to add extra flavor (you can nibble on the stew meat the next day). To simplify your meal, surround the roast with sections of carrots, turnips, parsnips, walnut-sized onions, and/or shaped potatoes, all tossed with a little olive oil or butter ahead of time to prevent them from drying out. (See the Vegetables chapter for tips on roasting these vegetables.)

MAKES 6 MAIN-COURSE SERVINGS

> One 6-rib rack of veal, frenched (see pages 212–213), frenching optional
>
> Salt
>
> Pepper
>
> 1 pound veal stew meat, cut into rough ¹/₂-inch cubes (optional)
>
> 2 cups veal broth, chicken broth, or water

Take the roast out of the refrigerator 4 hours before roasting and rub with salt and pepper (see page 170).

Preheat the oven to 375°F. Put the veal stew meat in a roasting pan just large enough to hold it in a single layer and brown it in the oven for about 30 minutes. Place the roast on top and roast for about 50 minutes, or until an instant-read thermometer inserted into the center of the roast not touching bone reads 130°F. Transfer the roast to a warmed platter, cover it loosely with aluminum foil, and let rest while you make the jus.

Place the roasting pan on the stove top over high and boil down any juices until they congeal and caramelize. Pour in 1 cup of the broth and boil it down, stirring and scraping with a wooden spoon until all the liquid caramelizes. Add the remaining 1 cup broth and boil it down, again while stirring, until reduced by about one-quarter. Strain through a fine-mesh strainer into a warmed sauceboat.

Carve the roast and serve. Pass the sauce at the table.

HOW TO MAKE ROASTED RACK OF VEAL

1. French the roast by trimming an inch or so of meat off the ends of the ribs.

2. If you want a smaller roast, cut the rack in half so each smaller roast has 4 ribs.

3. Season the roast.

4. Place the rack over a roasting pan of the trimmings that have been roasted. Cover loosely and let rest.

5. Pour off the jus.

6. Carve by slicing between the ribs.

7. Serve with the jus.

Roast Saddle of Veal

This is a special cut—the whole lower back of the animal— that contains all the loin chops. Its anatomy matches that of a saddle of lamb (see pages 214–215). If your butcher doesn't know what you are talking about, tell him or her that the number of the cut is 331 (from the meat buyer's guide butchers use). The saddle will come with its flaps (the equivalent of flank steaks, which you can use to surround the roast, so they contribute to the jus) and may even come with its kidneys and their surrounding fat. The whole saddle will likely weigh around 35 pounds, but after trimming will weigh closer to 15 pounds, 5 pounds of which will be bone. In short, you are getting 10 pounds of pure meat, enough for a big crowd.

MAKES 20 MAIN-COURSE SERVINGS

> 1 saddle of veal, about 35 pounds
>
> 4 onions, quartered
>
> 5 carrots, peeled and cut into 1-inch sections
>
> Salt
>
> Pepper
>
> 4 cups veal or chicken broth, or as needed

Let the roast sit at room temperature for about 4 hours before roasting (see page 170).

Pull out the suet—the white fat on the inside—and the kidneys, if they have been left in. (If you like kidneys, see the recipe on page 203.) Being careful not to cut into the loin meat, cut off the flaps where they join the loin muscles. Slide the knife along the inside of the ribs, detaching them from the meat without cutting into it. Twist off the ribs and save. Trim most of the fat off the back of the saddle, leaving only a thin layer and the silver skin. Trim the meat off the flaps, and then cut it into 1/2-inch-wide strips.

Put the strips of flap meat, the ribs, and the vegetables in the roasting pan and put the pan in the oven. Turn the oven to 400°F (no need to preheat) and roast for about 1 1/2 hours, or until the juices from the meat have released into the pan and are beginning to caramelize.

Season the roast with salt and pepper and tie it up to keep it compact. Place it in the roasting pan on top of the meat and vegetables. Roast for about 2 hours, or until an instant-read thermometer inserted into the center of the roast away from bone reads 130°F. If at any point the juices in the roasting pan start to darken and threaten to burn, add 2 cups of the broth. Transfer the roast to a warmed platter, cover it loosely with aluminum foil, and let it rest while you make the jus.

Place the roasting pan on the stove top over high heat and boil down any juices until they congeal and caramelize. Pour out or ladle out the fat, and add the remaining 2 cups broth. Boil while stirring and scraping the bottom of the pan with a wooden spoon until all the caramelized juices dissolve and the liquid has reduced by half. Strain through a fine-mesh strainer in a warmed sauceboat.

Carve the roast in the same way as for the saddle of lamb (see page 215) and serve. Pass the jus at the table.

BRAISING VEAL

Veal can be braised in large pieces as a pot roast or small pieces as a veal stew. The best piece of veal for braising is the veal shoulder "clod," a particularly meaty part of the shoulder that's easy to tie up into a cylinder. The veal breast can also be boned and braised.

Roast Veal Round

This dramatic and unusual roast will no doubt be a first for all or most of your guests. The roasting is straightfor- ward, but the timing is critical. The round is so lean that it becomes dry when overcooked even slightly.

MAKES 6 MAIN-COURSE SERVINGS

> One 3-pound top round of veal, cap removed
>
> Salt
>
> Pepper
>
> 4 tablespoons clarified butter (see page 341)
>
> 2 cups veal or chicken broth, as needed

Season the roast with salt and pepper and leave it at room temperature for at least 3 hours before roasting (see page 170).

Preheat the oven to 400°F. In a pan just large enough to hold the roast, heat the butter over high heat and brown the roast on all sides until golden. Put the pan in the oven and roast for 15 minutes. Turn the oven down to 375°F and continue to roast for about 30 minutes, or until the roast starts to feel firm to the touch instead of fleshy and an instant-read thermometer inserted into the center reads 130°F. Transfer the roast to a warmed platter, cover it loosely with aluminum foil, and let rest for 15 minutes before carving.

Place the roasting pan on the stove top, add the broth, and simmer gently, stirring and scraping up any caramelized juices on the pan bottom with a wooden spoon, for about 2 minutes. Strain through a fine-mesh strainer into a warmed sauceboat.

Carve the roast and serve. Pass the jus at the table.

1. If the round still has the cap, a sheath of meat covering most of the top, trim it off.

2. Follow the natural seam in the meat to completely remove the cap.

3. Use the cap for stew meat or trim it, pound it, and tie it up for braising (page 194).

4. Tie the rolled cap with kitchen string and braise separately.

5. Season the round roast with salt and pepper, heat the butter in a pan that will fit the roast as closely as possible, and brown the roast on all sides. Roast in a 400°F oven for 15 minutes, turn the temperature down to 375°F.

6. Surround the roast with turned carrots and turnips and pearl onions. Cook to an internal temperature of 130°F and let rest before carving. If the vegetables need more cooking, cook them in the veal juices on the stove top.

1. Use a long, flexible knife to cut the fat away from the rind of a piece of fatback.

2. Cut the fatback into strips about ¼ inch on each side.

3. With a hinged larding needle, pull the strips through the veal and out the other side. Cut off the excess.

4. Tie the veal lengthwise and then around the sides.

5. Place the clod, in a pot as close to its size as possible, over a bed of thickly sliced carrots and onions.

6. When the liquid released by the veal has caramelized on the bottom of the pot, add broth to come halfway up the sides of the veal. Cover and simmer.

7. Baste the roast until the liquid is syrupy and the roast is shiny.

8. Serve in warmed soup plates with braising liquid.

Veal Pot Roast

In eighteenth-century France, a veal pot roast, called a fricandeau, represented the height of luxury. Nowadays, we think of roasts and grilled or sautéed tender cuts as the most desirable, but in past centuries, braised dishes were preferred. In fact, a pot roast develops a more complex flavor than a roast. The final texture is quite different, of course, having the bite of stew meat or even softer. French cooks call pot roast braised almost to the point of falling apart à la cuil-lière, or "with a spoon," and indeed serve it with one.

For this roast, you will need to order a veal shoulder clod, not a whole shoulder. (Tell your butcher that the number of the cut is 310 in the meat buyer's guide.) The roast usually comes tied with string, which you will need to cut off if you are larding the meat. Larding the meat keeps it moist, but it requires a larding needle, fatback, and 20 minutes. The roast is cooked with aromatic vegetables in the oven until it releases its juices into the pot, and then it is braised on the stove top in broth, the liquid is reduced, and the roast is treated to a rich glaze.

MAKES 8 TO 10 MAIN-COURSE SERVINGS

> One 5-pound veal shoulder clod
>
> 4 pounds fatback (optional)
>
> Salt
>
> Pepper
>
> 1 large carrot, peeled and cut into 1-inch sections
>
> 1 large onion, quartered
>
> 3 cloves garlic, crushed
>
> Stalks from 1 fennel bulb, cut into 1-inch sections (optional)
>
> 1 turnip, peeled and quartered (optional)
>
> 4 cups veal broth, chicken broth, or water, or as needed
>
> Bouquet garni

Preheat the oven to 375°F. Cut the string off the clod. Cut the rind off the fatback. Cut the fatback into strips ¼ inch wide and thick and as long as you can make them. Lard the inside of the clod with the fatback as shown on page 193. Season the inside with salt and pepper. Turn the meat over, lard the outside, and season with salt and pepper. Tie the roast with kitchen string.

Put the roast in a pot just large enough to hold it and deep enough that the roast doesn't extend above the rim. Surround the roast with the carrot, onion, garlic, fennel, and turnip and roast for about 1½ hours, or until the meat releases its juices and they caramelize on the bottom of the pot. Check the roast often, so the juices don't burn on the bottom of the pot.

Put the pot on the stove top, pour in enough broth to come halfway up the sides of the roast, and bring to a simmer over high heat. Turn the heat down to maintain the gentlest simmer, and nestle the bouquet garni in the center of the pot. Cover the pot with a sheet of aluminum foil, pressing it down so the middle hangs over the roast. (This causes moisture that condenses within the pot to baste the roast from the inside.) Top with the lid and simmer over very low heat for 1 hour.

Turn the roast over in the liquid—be gentle, it may be fragile—so the part that was submerged is now on top. Re-cover with the foil and lid and braise for 1 hour more. To test for doneness, slide a skewer into the roast and lift. If the roast clings to the skewer and rises up out of the pot as you lift, braise for 30 minutes more and check again. Keep braising until there is no resistance when you pull out the skewer. The braising can take as long as 4 hours.

Transfer the roast to a clean pot or straight-sided pan—you can clean out the same pot—and strain the braising liquid into a saucepan. Discard the vegetables in the strainer. Place the pan of braising liquid off center on the burner so that the liquid simmers on only one side and pushes the fat to the other. Simmer for about 10 minutes, regularly skimming off any fat or froth. Then ladle about one-third of the braising liquid over the roast, put the uncovered roast back in the oven, and turn the oven down to 325°F. Continue simmering, skimming, and reducing the braising liquid. When the roast has been in the oven for 15 minutes, ladle over half of the reduced braising liquid. Simmer and skim the braising liquid for 10 minutes more, and then pour all of it over the roast. Baste the roast every 10 minutes for about 40 minutes, or until the braising liquid takes on a lightly syrupy consistency and the roast is shiny.

Remove the roast from the pot. Spoon out portions or slice it thickly, and place the servings in warmed soup plates. Ladle the braising liquid over the meat.

VARIATIONS

You can braise with red wine instead of broth or water. Or, if you are a real fanatic, you can make a veal broth with red wine and use it for the braising liquid. Hard cider is also a good choice for braising. Most other variations consist of additions to the braising liquid at the end. Chopped fresh herbs such as parsley, chervil, chives, or tarragon add interesting notes, as do reconstituted dried morels or porcini simmered in the braising liquid or sautéed fresh wild mushrooms spooned over the veal slices. You can swirl butter into the braising liquid to give it a more complex and subtle flavor, but don't overdo it. The liquid and meat are very rich. Compound butters, especially Truffle Butter (see page 350), make great additions.

Creamy Veal Stew

This satisfying stew, a blanquette de veau, has almost legendary status in France as a grandmother's dish par excellence. Nowadays, you are more likely to encounter it in restaurants.

Because veal stew is made from stew meat taken from the shoulder, leg, or breast, it is the least expensive way to serve veal. The best (but more arduous) way to go about acquiring stew meat is to buy a whole breast of veal. It will be large—and will consist primarily of bones. You will wonder what you have gotten yourself into. Ideally, you will get it home and separate the meat from the bones, make a veal broth with the bones, and use this broth to make the stew a day or two later.

The easier approach is to buy veal stew meat and braise it in water or whatever meat broth you can find. Button mushrooms and glazed pearl onions are the classic garnishes, but you can improvise your own—see page 177 for more ideas. Serve the stew with rice to absorb the abundant sauce.

MAKES 8 MAIN-COURSE SERVINGS

- 1 breast of veal, about 15 pounds, or
  5 pounds veal stew meat
- 1 large carrot, peeled, quartered lengthwise,
  and cut into 1-inch sections
- 2 onions
- 2 whole cloves
- Bouquet garni
- 4 cups veal broth, chicken broth, or water
- 1 pint pearl onions, boiled for 1 minute, rinsed with
  cold water, and peeled
- One 10-ounce package cultivated white mushrooms
- 2 tablespoons butter
- 2 tablespoons flour
- 1/2 cup heavy cream, or to taste
- Salt
- Pepper

If using the veal breast, trim it and cut the meat into 1-inch cubes, discarding the fat and gristle. Put the bones and meat in a large pot and cover with cold water. Put on the stove over high heat, bring to a boil, and simmer for 5 minutes. This step eliminates the scum that would turn the stew gray and give it a soapy flavor. Drain in a colander and rinse the bones and meat thoroughly with cold water to rid them of any clinging scum. If you have the time, put the bones in a pot, cover them with water (or some broth if you have it), and simmer gently, skimming off the froth and fat occasionally, for 6 hours, adding water as needed to keep the bones covered with liquid. Then strain through a fine-mesh strainer into a clean container and use as the broth for the stew.

In a pot, combine the meat (and the bones if you are using veal breast and have not made a broth with them) and carrot. Peel the onions but leave them whole, stick 1 clove into each onion, and add the onions to the pot along with the bouquet garni. Pour in enough broth (ideally, the broth you made from the bones) just to cover the meat. Bring to a gentle simmer and simmer gently, regularly skimming off any froth and fat from the surface, for 1 1/2 hours, or until the meat crushes easily when you squeeze a piece.

Strain the stew through a fine-mesh strainer placed over a pot large enough to hold the finished stew. Pick out the vegetables, and the bones if you cooked them with the meat, and discard them. Set the meat aside.

Bring the stewing liquid to a simmer and cook until reduced to about 2 cups. Add the pearl onions, cover, and simmer gently for about 12 minutes. Add the mushrooms, re-cover, and simmer gently for 5 minutes, or until the onions and mushrooms are tender.

In a small saucepan, melt the butter over medium heat, whisk in the flour, and cook, whisking constantly, for about 2 minutes, or until the butter bubbles up and smells nutty. Whisk about half of the braising liquid into the butter mixture until smooth, and then bring to a simmer. Pour the butter mixture into the pot with the rest of the braising liquid, onions, and mushrooms and stir to mix. Add the cream and bring to a simmer. If the liquid is too thick, add broth, water, or more cream. If it is too thin, boil it down for a couple of minutes. The sauce should not be too thick.

Stir the meat into the sauce and simmer gently for about 5 minutes to heat through. Season with salt and pepper and serve.

VARIATIONS

Any of the garnishes on page 177 can replace or be added to the mushrooms and pearl onions. If you use wild mushrooms in place of the cultivated mushrooms, sauté them in butter to bring out their flavor and then add them at the last minute just to heat through. Truffles, sliced or julienned, would be lovely, as would tarragon, chervil, or parsley, either chopped and added directly or whisked in as part of an herb butter. The braising liquid can be flavored with curry powder (first cooked in butter for 1 minute) or saffron threads (first soaked in 1 tablespoon water for 30 minutes). For veal Marengo, cut the cream in half, and add tomatoes that have been cooked down and strained to make a coulis (see page 366). For veal chasseur, omit the cream, add sautéed mushrooms, and whisk in a little butter.

Osso Buco with Julienned Vegetables

Just a fancy name for veal shanks, osso buco usually comes in thick, meaty slices that have a marrowbone in the middle. If you were to sauté them like a steak, they would be unbearably tough. But when they are braised, they soften and release their delicious flavor. Virtually all braised meat dishes—stews and pot roasts—include aromatic vegetables for flavor that are often strained out before serving. In this version of osso buco, the vegetables are julienned, added midway during cooking, and then served in a melting tangle on top of each serving. If you don't want to bother with julienning the vegetables, you can dice or slice them.

MAKES 6 MAIN-COURSE SERVINGS

> **Six 12- to 14-ounce, 3-inch-thick osso buco**
> **Salt**
> **Pepper**
> **3 tablespoons olive oil**
> **1 cup dry white wine**
> **3 cups veal broth, chicken broth, or water**
> **Bouquet garni**
> **3 leeks**
> **2 turnips**
> **1 celeriac (optional)**
> **3 large carrots**
> **1 fennel bulb (optional)**

Season the veal on both sides with salt and pepper. Select a sauté pan with high, straight sides just large enough to hold the osso buco in a single layer. Heat the oil in the pan over high heat, add the osso buco, and brown well on both sides. Remove the veal from the pan and pour out the burnt oil.

Return the veal to the pan, pour in the wine, bring to a simmer, and simmer for 5 minutes. Add the broth and bouquet garni and adjust the heat to maintain at a very gentle simmer. Cover the pan with a sheet of aluminum foil, pressing it down so the middle hangs over the meat. (This causes moisture that condenses within the pot to baste the veal from the inside.) Top with the lid and simmer over very low heat for 1 hour.

While the veal is braising, julienne the leeks, turnips, celeriac, carrots, and fennel as shown on pages 293–305. After the veal has simmered for 1 hour, pile the vegetables on top of it, replace the foil and lid, and simmer for 1 hour more.

HOW TO MAKE OSSO BUCO WITH JULIENNED VEGETABLES

1. Season the osso buco with salt and pepper.

2. Brown the osso buco over high heat on both sides.

3. Take out the meat, pour out the burnt oil, add wine, put the meat back in, and add broth to come halfway up the sides of the meat.

4. Add a bouquet garni, cover the pot with aluminum foil.

5. Cover the pot with the lid and simmer gently for 1 hour.

6. Add julienned vegetables, cover again with foil and the lid, and simmer gently for 1 to 2 hours, or until a skewer slides easily in and out of the meat and the vegetables are tender. Serve them on top of the veal in a soup plate with the braising liquid.

To check if the meat is done, slide a paring knife into it and lift straight up. When the meat no longer clings to the knife as you lift, it is ready. Using tongs, remove the vegetables from the pan and set aside, and then discard the bouquet garni. Put the osso buco in warmed soup plates, ladle over the braising liquid, and place a tangle of vegetables on top of each serving.

1. Make sure the cap has been removed from the veal round (page 192).

2. Slide a sharp knife along the veal at an angle, slicing across the grain.

3. Press against the veal with your other hand to keep it firm and the slices even.

4. To coat with cheese, finely grate Parmigiano-Reggiano cheese.

5. Work the cheese (or bread crumbs) through a drum sieve or fine-mesh strainer.

6. Season the scaloppine with salt and pepper and coat with flour, patting off the excess.

7. Dip in beaten egg.

8. Dip in cheese or bread crumbs.

SAUTÉING VEAL

The best cuts for sautéing are taken from the rack, saddle, or round and are never inexpensive. There is nothing tricky about cooking veal rib chops (from the rack) or loin chops (from the saddle), because they are thick enough that you can brown them without their releasing water or overcooking. The round, however, is larger and has to be thinly sliced into scallops (scaloppine) for serving. It is almost impossible to brown or seal thin veal slices without their releasing water and boiling (and toughening) in their own juices. A better approach is to bread them as shown here and cook them relatively gently in clarified butter. The result is weinerschnitzel, which is more or less what the French call à la viennoise. If you have a good butcher or buy a whole veal top round, which typically weighs 3 to 4 pounds, you can cut the scallops yourself, across the grain, and relatively thick as shown. Be sure to specify that you want the round "cap off," so you are left with only one solid muscle.

Sautéed Veal Cutlets

In many Italian restaurants, veal dishes are made with thin, wide slices called scaloppine. Unfortunately, these slices aren't always taken from the top round. Instead, they often come from the tougher muscles of the leg and are then pounded to tenderize them and make them wide and thin.

Veal Piccata

Maybe a cliché, but this classic is easy to make and always good. You can bread the veal slices as shown for chicken on page 255, or you can simply flour them. If using only flour, sauté the veal in clarified butter or olive oil, not whole butter, which won't get hot enough. The pan should be very hot and the veal cooked literally for only seconds on each side.

MAKES 4 MAIN-COURSE SERVINGS

Four 6-ounce slices veal top round, about $1/4$ inch thick

Salt

Pepper

$1/2$ cup flour

3 tablespoons clarified butter (page 341) or olive oil

$1/4$ cup dry white wine

3 tablespoons fresh lemon juice

1 tablespoon commercial meat glaze or 2 tablespoons homemade meat glaze (see page 177), softened in 3 tablespoons hot water (optional)

1 tablespoon finely chopped fresh parsley

3 tablespoons cold butter, sliced

Just before sautéing, season the veal slices on both sides with salt and pepper and then coat with the flour and pat off the excess.

In a large, heavy-bottomed sauté pan, heat the butter over very high heat until it begins to smoke. Add the veal slices one at a time, waiting about 15 seconds after each slice is added before adding the next one, so the pan stays hot. Cook each slice for about 30 seconds on the first side, or until golden. Then turn the slices, again one at a time, and cook for about 30 seconds on the second side, or until golden. As the slices are ready—they will feel firm to the touch—transfer them to a warmed platter.

Pour the burnt butter out of the pan, add the wine and lemon juice, and place over high heat. Boil down until reduced by half. If using the meat glaze, add it and its soaking liquid and boil down until a lightly syrupy consistency forms. Add the parsley and then whisk in the butter, 1 slice at a time.

Transfer the veal slices to warmed plates and spoon the sauce over them.

VARIATIONS

You can make veal Marsala by substituting Marsala (or Malmsey Madeira for similar results) for the white wine. Veal Francese is much like veal piccata, except the veal is breaded with flour, eggs, and bread crumbs. Veal à la Milanese is breaded just like veal Francese except that finely grated Parmigiano-Reggiano cheese replaces the bread crumbs. For veal à la parmigiana, bread the cutlets as for veal Francese, layer the sautéed cutlets with Parmigiano-Reggiano cheese, mozzarella cheese, and tomato sauce in a baking dish, and bake in a 350°F oven. For veal saltimbocca, proceed as directed for veal piccata, but add 4 fresh sage leaves to the sauce at the same time as the wine and omit the parsley. As you serve the veal slices, place a thin slice of prosciutto on top of each one, pick the sage leaves out of the sauce and put 1 leaf on each prosciutto slice, and then spoon the sauce over the top.

HOW TO MAKE VEAL PICCATA

1. Dust the veal with flour and brown in clarified butter on both sides.

2. Squeeze lemon juice over the veal and spoon over hot frothy butter.

HOW TO MAKE VEAL MARSALA

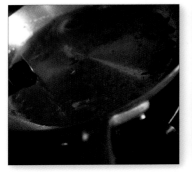
1. Cook the floured veal as for Veal Piccata. Remove the veal from the pan, pour out the cooked butter, and add 1/2 cup Marsala.

2. Boil down the Marsala until reduced by half and add meat glaze (page 177) or broth.

3. Simmer down to a syrupy consistency, and then thin if necessary with broth or water.

4. Whisk in butter.

1. Cook in clarified butter over medium heat until brown on both sides.

2. Cook sage leaves in clarified butter until wilted.

3. Arrange prosciutto slices over the veal and sage leaves on top. Spoon over the butter used for cooking the sage.

Sautéed Veal Chops

Buy rib chops or loin chops, whichever cut is cheaper, because there is no difference in the quality of the meat. A loin chop is like a miniature porterhouse steak and has both the loin muscle (which in beef would be the New York cut) and the tenderloin. Rib chops have only the loin.

Sauté veal chops over medium-high heat in clarified butter, whole butter, or pure olive oil so they brown and their juices caramelize before they overcook. The most reliable test for doneness is to push on a chop with your finger. When it stops feeling like flaccid flesh and more like a flexed muscle, it is done. If this approach seems utterly mysterious, stick an instant-read thermometer through the side of the chop into the center and wait until it reads slightly over 130°F.

The only variations for sautéed veal chops have to do with making a sauce from the pan drippings. This can be as easy as adding a few tablespoons of white wine, or it can be a complicated structured sauce made with aromatic vegetables, meat glaze, wine, herbs, and butter. (For sauce ideas, see pages 340–355.)

Sautéed Veal Chops with Madeira Sauce

If you don't have Madeira, use a slightly sweet or dry sherry or even white wine. Meat glaze or reduced broth will give the sauce a silky consistency and deep flavor, but you can still make a lovely little sauce without it.

MAKES 4 MAIN-COURSE SERVINGS

> **Four 10-ounce veal rib or loin chops**
>
> **Salt**
>
> **Pepper**
>
> **3 tablespoons olive oil or clarified butter (page 341)**
>
> **1 shallot, minced**
>
> **$^1/_3$ cup Rainwater or Malmsey Madeira**
>
> **1 tablespoon commercial meat glaze or 2 tablespoons homemade meat glaze (page 177), softened in 3 tablespoons hot water, more broth or water as needed**
>
> **2 tablespoons cold butter, cut into slices**

Season the chops on both sides with salt and pepper and leave at room temperature for 1 to 2 hours before sautéing.

In a sauté pan just large enough to hold the chops—preferably neither nonstick nor with a dark bottom—heat the oil over medium-high heat until it ripples and barely begins to smoke. Add the chops and sauté, turning once, for about

5 minutes on each side, or until an instant-read thermometer inserted through the side into the center reads 130°F or the meat bounces back when pressed with your finger. Transfer the chops to a warmed platter and cover loosely with aluminum foil.

Pour the burnt oil out of the pan. If the juices on the bottom have burned, add a tablespoon or two of water to the pan while it is still hot to dissolve them, and then pour out the water and wipe the pan with a paper towel. If the juices are brown and haven't burned, just pour out the fat, add the shallot, and stir with a whisk over medium heat for about 30 seconds, or until fragrant. Add the Madeira, raise the heat to high, stand back, and if you have a gas stove, tilt the pan backward toward the flame. The Madeira should catch fire. Boil down the Madeira until reduced by about half, and certainly until it stops flaming. If you don't have a gas stove or feel unsure about your ability to manage the flame, don't bother igniting the Madeira and just boil off the alcohol. Whisk in the meat glaze and its soaking water until it dissolves.

At this point, the sauce should have a lightly syrupy consistency. If it is too thick, add a tablespoon or two of water or broth. If it is too thin, boil it down for a minute. When it has the consistency you like, pour in any juices released by the chops—this may thin the sauce, so you will have to boil it again for a minute—and when whisk in the butter, a slice a time. Season with salt and pepper.

Transfer the chops to warmed plates and spoon the sauce over them.

GRILLING VEAL

While you can grill a veal roast, most of the time the only veal we grill is the same chops we would sauté except for thin cuts we use for scaloppine. The cooking times are similar, and the only real difference is that there are no juices for making a sauce. But the flavor of grilled veal is so hearty on its own that most of us can forgo a sauce. Sometimes a sauce can be a welcome treat, however. Consider serving a round of compound butter (see pages 348–350) on top of each chop, or Bordelaise Sauce (see page 353), Madeira Sauce (opposite), or an emulsified egg sauce (see page 346) on the side. One of the most festive approaches is to make several different mayonnaises and salsas and pass them around at the table.

VEAL ORGAN MEATS

While in this country a lot of veal parts no doubt end up disguised in other foods—many folks who won't eat sweetbreads will devour a hot dog that is laced with them—elsewhere organ meats are considered among the tastiest parts of the animal. Here, veal kidneys almost never show up on menus, but in Europe they are likely to be the most expensive choice. Sweetbreads, which are the thymus gland near the throat of the animal, have a refined milky flavor and melting texture that make them a true delicacy to the French and others. People who have eaten only stronger-flavored baby beef liver, rather than authentic veal liver, are convinced they don't like liver without ever giving it another chance. And brains send many diners screaming in terror, when in fact they are among the most treasured of all the organ meats.

CALF'S LIVER

Buy real calf's liver or veal liver, not beef liver, unless you have eaten it before and don't mind its assertiveness. The trick to cooking slices of liver (whole liver can also be roasted) is to get a crust to form without overcooking the interior. This requires very high heat and a dusting of flour. The flour helps the slices brown and the juices to caramelize on the outside, instead of flowing out and boiling.

Sautéed Calf's Liver

Remember, successfully sautéed liver demands extremely high heat, so be sure the oil is smoking before you add the liver slices. Liver is best served with a sauce containing some vinegar, such as the one that follows.

MAKES 4 MAIN-COURSE SERVINGS

> **Four 6- to 8-ounce slices calf's liver, about 1/2 inch thick**
> **Salt**
> **Pepper**
> **1/2 cup flour**
> **3 tablespoons olive oil**

Make a series of slits through the thin membrane that surrounds the liver slices. This prevents the membrane, which contracts when hot, from causing the slices to curl. Just before sautéing, dry the liver slices with paper towels, season with salt and pepper, coat with flour, and pat off the excess.

(continued)

Sautéed Calf's Liver, continued

If you don't have a sauté pan large enough to hold the slices in a single layer, use 2 pans or work in batches, keeping the first 2 slices warm in the oven while sautéing the second 2 slices. To make sure that at least one side is well browned for serving, sauté the first side longer than the second side and serve the slice with the well-browned side up.

Place a heavy sauté pan over high heat and add the olive oil. When the oil begins to smoke, gently place a slice of liver in the pan. Wait about 30 seconds and then add the second slice. Wait again for about 30 seconds—the waiting allows the pan to regain heat lost to the meat—and add another slice. Repeat with the last slice. Sauté for about 4 minutes on the first side, or until well browned. Turn the slices and sauté for about 2 minutes, or until the liver barely begins to feel firm to the touch. Again wait for about 30 seconds after turning each slice before turning the next one.

As the liver slices are done, transfer them to a plate lined with paper towels to absorb the oil, and then serve.

Calf's Liver with Onions

The trick to calf's liver with onions is to incorporate vinegar into the onions to create a sweet-and-sour effect. If the onions are slowly cooked down, their natural sugars concentrate and provide the necessary sweetness.

MAKES 4 MAIN-COURSE SERVINGS

Sautéed Calf's Liver (see page 201)
6 tablespoons cold butter
4 large red onions, sliced paper-thin
1/4 cup wine vinegar, or to taste
1 tablespoon commercial meat glaze or 2 tablespoons homemade meat glaze (see page 177), softened in 3 tablespoons hot water
Salt
Pepper

Assemble the ingredients for the sautéed liver.

In a heavy-bottomed pot, melt 2 tablespoons of the butter over medium heat. Add the onions and cook, stirring every couple of minutes so they don't burn. After about 10 minutes, they will have released liquid. At this point, turn the heat up to high until the liquid evaporates, and then reduce the heat to medium-low and continue to cook the onions, stirring them every few minutes and scraping up any caramelized juices on the bottom of the pot. When the onions are soft and have no crunch, after about 30 minutes, they are ready.

Sauté the liver as directed, transfer to a plate lined with paper towels to absorb the oil, and cover loosely with aluminum foil. Rinse out the sauté pan and return it to the stove top. Add the 1/4 cup vinegar, the meat glaze and its soaking liquid, and the cooked onions and bring to a simmer. Taste and adjust with more vinegar if the mixture needs more tang. The sauce should be lightly syrupy. If it is too thin, boil it down for a minute. If it is too thick, add a little broth or water.

Slice the remaining 4 tablespoons butter and whisk into the sauce, a slice at a time. Season with salt and pepper. Serve the sauce over and around the liver slices.

Calf's Liver with Madeira Sauce

The nutty flavor of Madeira has a natural affinity for liver. This recipe also contains wine vinegar to balance the sweetness of the Madeira.

MAKES 4 MAIN-COURSE SERVINGS

Sautéed Calf's Liver (see page 201)
1/4 cup Rainwater or Malmsey Madeira or medium-sweet sherry such as cream sherry
3 tablespoons red, white, or sherry wine vinegar, or to taste
1 tablespoon commercial meat glaze or 2 tablespoons homemade meat glaze (see page 177), softened in 3 tablespoons hot water
3 tablespoons cold butter, sliced
Salt
Pepper

While the liver is cooking, combine the Madeira, 3 tablespoons vinegar, and the meat glaze and its soaking liquid in a small saucepan and bring to a simmer. The sauce should be lightly syrupy. If it is too thin, boil it down for a minute. If it is too thick, add a little broth or water. Taste the sauce and adjust with vinegar if it needs more tang. If it is too acidic, boil it down until it is very thick and then thin it with water or broth to the consistency you like. Whisk in the butter, a slice at a time, and season with salt and pepper.

When the liver is ready, transfer it to a plate lined with paper towels to absorb the oil and then place on warmed plates. Serve the sauce over the liver slices.

VEAL KIDNEYS

For anyone who likes them, veal kidneys have a lot of flavor. But that same robust flavor turns off anyone who doesn't like them. One of the interesting things about kidneys is that, unlike most meats, cooking them lightens their flavor, rather than concentrates it. You should never make a jus from kidneys or deglaze the sauté pan to make a sauce. However, kidneys are delicious when paired with a mustard sauce that carries a sweet-and-sour accent.

Veal Kidneys with Mustard and Port

The juxtaposition of the hot, savory flavor of mustard with the gentle sweetness of port makes the perfect contrast to the forthright flavor of kidneys. It is worth experimenting with herbs, such as marjoram, oregano, or sage, either sprinkled on the meat or added to the sauce.

MAKES 4 MAIN-COURSE SERVINGS

> 4 veal kidneys
>
> Salt
>
> Pepper
>
> 2 tablespoons olive oil
>
> 1¹/₂ cups ruby or tawny port
>
> 1 tablespoon commercial meat glaze or 2 tablespoons homemade meat glaze (see page 177), softened in 3 tablespoons hot water
>
> 2 tablespoons Dijon mustard
>
> 1 tablespoon wine vinegar, or more to taste
>
> 4 tablespoons cold butter, sliced

Preheat the oven to 400°F. Pull and cut off any fat clinging to the kidneys. Cut out any inside membranes that hold the kidneys together (as shown), but don't cut so much out that the kidney comes apart. Season with salt and pepper.

In an ovenproof sauté pan, heat the oil over high heat until it barely begins to smoke, add the kidneys, and brown well on all sides. Slide the sauté pan into the oven and roast until the kidneys bounce back to the touch or an instant-read thermometer inserted into the center reads 135°F after about 25 minutes in the oven.

Take the sauté pan out of the oven, cover loosely with aluminum foil, and keep warm for 15 minutes. In a saucepan, boil down the port until it is reduced by half. Add the meat glaze and its soaking liquid and simmer for about 2 minutes, or until the mixture is lightly syrupy. Whisk in the mustard and 1 tablespoon vinegar and simmer again until syrupy. Taste and add vinegar if the sauce needs more tang. Whisk in the butter, a slice at a time, then turn the heat down to low.

Slice the kidneys crosswise as shown below and put the slices in the sauce. Season with salt and pepper.

VARIATIONS

Mixing sautéed sliced mushrooms into the sauce adds interesting texture. If your budget allows, add thick slices of sautéed porcini and/or other wild mushrooms. Madeira, white wine, or red wine can replace the port. To make a mellower sauce, replace the meat glaze with a cup of concentrated (quadruple-strength) meat broth, and simmer the broth with the wine gently until the mixture becomes syrupy. This reduction of the wine and broth together removes acids and tannins from the wine. You can also use heavy cream—about twice the amount——in place of the butter. Add a little lemon juice to sharpen the flavor of the creamy sauce, and then finish it with chopped fresh tarragon, chervil, chives, and/or parsley.

HOW TO MAKE VEAL KIDNEYS ——————————

1. Locate the membrane inside the kidney that holds it together. Cut off any excess without causing the kidney to come apart.

2. Heat oil in a sauté pan, add the kidneys, and brown well.

3. Move sauté pan to the oven and roast the kidneys until done.

4. Slice the kidneys.

5. Spoon over sauce and serve.

VEAL SWEETBREADS

Sweetbreads are never cheap, even in the United States where they are underappreciated. But in Europe, where they are generally prized, they are exorbitant. They come as two attached parts, one long and a bit ragged (in French *la gorge*, meaning "throat") and the other a neat round (in French *la noix*, meaning "nut"). If your butcher or supermarket will sell you just the nut, go for it. Both sections have the same flavor, but the noix is easier to manage and slice.

Sweetbreads are cooked in one of two ways: they are braised just long enough for their internal temperature to reach medium (137°F) or they are sautéed. Classic recipes always call for a preliminary blanching of the sweetbreads and then topping them with a weight. The latter compacts them, making them neater to look at and easier to slice.

Braised Sweetbreads with Root Vegetable Macédoine

Macédoine is used to describe vegetables that are diced into relatively large (1/4-inch) cubes instead of brunoise, which are tiny cubes (see page 298). If you are a fanatic, you can cut your vegetables into brunoise. If you are making this dish on a whim, skip the weighting process or just weight the sweetbreads for an hour or so.

MAKES 4 MAIN-COURSE SERVINGS

2 1/2 pounds veal sweetbreads

2 large carrots, peeled and cut into 1/4-inch cubes

1 turnip, peeled and cut into 1/4-inch cubes

2 leeks, white part only, cleaned and julienned and then sliced crosswise 1/16 inch thick

1 small celeriac, peeled and cut into 1/4-inch dice (optional)

2 tablespoons butter

3 cups chicken broth or veal broth

Bouquet garni

1/2 cup heavy cream

2 tablespoons finely chopped fresh parsley

Salt

Pepper

1 tablespoon fresh lemon juice, or to taste

Put the sweetbreads in a pot with cold water to cover and place the pot over high heat. As soon as the water comes to a boil, drain the sweetbreads in a colander and discard the liquid. Put the sweetbreads on a sheet pan, top them with a cutting board, and then weight the board with a couple of cans or saucepans. Refrigerate the whole contraption for at least 6 hours or up to overnight.

Preheat the oven to 350°F. Select a sauté pan with straight sides, just large enough to hold the sweetbreads in a single layer. Put the carrots, turnip, leeks, celeriac, and butter in the pan and cook over low to medium heat, stirring every few minutes, for about 15 minutes, or until the vegetables are soft. Add 1 cup of the broth, raise the heat to high, and boil it down until it caramelizes on the bottom of the pan. As the broth reduces, stir the vegetables constantly so they don't stick to the bottom of the pan.

Pour the remaining 2 cups broth into the pan and add the bouquet garni. Put the sweetbreads in the pan and bring to a gentle simmer. Cover the pan loosely with aluminum foil and slide it into the oven. Bake for about 15 minutes, or until the sweetbreads bounce back to the touch or a thermometer inserted into the center of one reads 135°F. Using a slotted spoon, transfer the sweetbreads to a plate, cover loosely with the foil you used to cover the pan, and keep warm.

Put the pan on the stove top and boil down the liquid until reduced to about 1/2 cup, or until it is lightly syrupy. Add the cream and simmer, stirring occasionally, for about 2 minutes, or until the sauce coats the back of the spoon. Pull out the bouquet garni. Add the parsley, season with salt and pepper, and then add the lemon juice to taste.

Slice the sweetbreads on the diagonal and arrange them on warmed plates. Spoon the sauce and vegetables on top.

VARIATIONS

The vegetables can be julienned as for the osso buco on page 196, and different herbs—chives, chervil, tarragon—can replace or join the parsley. You can add Tomato Coulis (see page 366), garlic puree (see page 332), or sorrel puree (see page 121). (Creamed sorrel also makes a nice accompaniment.) A few wild mushrooms, especially reconstituted dried morels or porcini, are a delicious addition when simmered in the sauce, as are truffles. The sauce can be turned into a brown sauce by using brown broth and whisking in butter, instead of cream, at the end. Madeira or white wine can be added along with the broth.

Sautéed Sweetbreads with Lemon and Parsley

The delicate milky flavor of sweetbreads comes into its own when sweetbread slices are gently cooked in butter. As long as the slices are cooked just until they start to firm up to the touch, they will have an irresistible melting consistency. They are excellent floured or lightly breaded. A little brown butter with a spot of lemon makes the perfect sauce.

MAKES 4 MAIN-COURSE SERVINGS

- **2¹/₂ pounds veal sweetbreads, preferably the noix parts**
- **Salt**
- **Pepper**
- **¹/₂ cup flour**
- **3 tablespoons clarified butter (see page 341) or whole butter**
- **4 tablespoons butter**
- **1 tablespoon finely chopped fresh parsley**
- **1 tablespoon fresh lemon juice**

Put the sweetbreads in a pot with cold water to cover and place the pot over high heat. As soon as the water comes to a boil, drain the sweetbreads in a colander and discard the liquid. Put the sweetbreads on a sheet pan, top them with a cutting board, and then weight the board with a couple of cans or saucepans. Refrigerate the whole contraption for 6 hours or up to overnight.

Cut the sweetbreads lengthwise on the diagonal into ¹/₂-inch-thick slices. Season the slices on both sides with salt and pepper, coat them with flour, and pat gently to remove the excess.

Select a sauté pan, preferably nonstick, just large enough to hold the sweetbread slices in a single layer, place over medium heat, and add the clarified butter. When the clarified butter ripples slightly or the whole butter is frothy, add the sweetbread slices and cook for about 3 minutes, or until browned on the first side. Turn the slices over and cook for about 3 minutes more, or until browned on the second side and the slices just begin to feel firm to the touch. Transfer them to a plate covered with paper towels to absorb the butter, then arrange the slices on heated plates.

Pour the cooked butter out of the pan, add the 4 tablespoons butter, parsley, and lemon juice, and heat over medium-high heat for about 2 minutes, or until the butter froths, the froth diminishes, and brown specks appear. Spoon the sauce over the slices and serve.

VARIATIONS

Nearly any sauce can be used for sautéed sweetbreads, though it shouldn't be too rich or complicated, as the sweetbreads are quite rich on their own. For example, a light bouillon, infused with herbs and maybe finely diced prosciutto, would work nicely. The breading can be varied as well, with the floured slices dipped in egg (à la Parisienne) and then in bread crumbs (à l'anglaise), in grated Parmigiano-Reggiano cheese (à la Milanese), or even in chopped truffles, as at one well-known Parisian restaurant. Ground dried porcini or morels can also replace the flour.

Veal Brains

It is hard to imagine that our aversion to brains is anything but psychological. Unlike kidneys or liver with their forthright flavor, brains are the most delicately flavored organ meat of all. Their texture is like gently scrambled eggs, and in fact the two are often served together. Traditionally, brains are poached in a vinegary vegetable broth, sautéed in butter, and then served with brown butter—sometimes with capers added—in the same way as the sautéed sweetbreads.

LAMB

A lamb roast, such as a leg or rack, is often the ideal choice for a simple dinner that you don't want to cost a fortune. Lamb is available year-round, and most of the lamb in American markets is domestic or imported from New Zealand. New Zealand lamb is a lot smaller than its American counterpart and is most often seen in the form of Cryovac-wrapped racks. American lamb tends to be relatively large and dark, especially compared to the lamb available in Europe, where so-called baby lamb is most commonly sold. Baby lamb, sometimes called milk-fed lamb, is available around Easter. It typically weighs about 10 pounds and is roasted whole.

LAMB ROASTS

Lamb provides three roasts: the leg, which is the least expensive but not really cheap; the rack; and the saddle. The saddle is just lower down on the back—it is the small of the back—than the rack. Because people are unfamiliar with the saddle and its meat is nearly identical to the meat on the rack, it is often a good value.

A good standby roast, a bone-in leg of lamb commonly weighs about 8 pounds. Usually, it is sold with a section of the lower vertebrae and pelvic bone attached, which can make it awkward to carve. If you have a nice butcher, ask him or her to remove this section and tie up the roast. You can also do it yourself, following the contours of the bone until you reveal the round ball joint. Cut into the joint and separate the bone. Season the inside of the meat, fold over the meat at the end of the roast, and tie it up with string.

While considered the height of luxury, a rack of lamb is nothing more than eight lamb chops left attached to one another. In recent years, the lamb racks in our markets are mostly from New Zealand, and they are so small that a whole rack is only enough for two servings. An American rack is considerably larger and will serve four (two chops per person).

When the saddle is sliced, it is made up of the loin chops, which, like porterhouse steaks, contain both the loin muscle (the larger piece of meat that runs along the back on the outside) and the tenderloin (the small round). On the saddle, the two loin muscles run parallel along the top, and the two tenderloin muscles run parallel along the bottom.

Crown Roast

A crown roast is made of two or more racks that are bent around each other, with the ribs sticking up and out in the shape of a crown. But there is an inherent problem with this: it requires cutting between the individual rib chops to get the rack to bend, and this allows juices to escape and prevents the meat from browning properly. A more elegant and sensible approach is to french your rack (see pages 212–213) and serve it as is.

Braised Lamb Shanks with Garlic

It wasn't too long ago that such cuts as lamb shanks—the shin, including the meat and bone—were relegated to antiquated cookbooks on the traditional cuisines of old Europe. Now, lamb shanks find their place in the chicest restaurants. When braised with plenty of wine and then glazed with their gelatinous braising liquid, they are one of the best braised dishes. Like stews, they can be garnished with mushrooms or assorted vegetables, but one particularly popular method calls for a large amount of garlic.

MAKES 6 MAIN-COURSE SERVINGS

6 lamb shanks, about 14 ounces each

Salt

Pepper

6 tablespoons olive oil

1 large carrot, peeled and sliced

1 large onion, sliced

2 cups full-bodied red wine

2 cups broth

Bouquet garni

2 heads garlic, cloves separated and peeled

Season the shanks with salt and pepper. In a sauté pan large enough to hold the shanks in a single layer, heat 3 tablespoons of the oil over high heat. When the oil begins to smoke, add the shanks and brown them on all sides. Remove the shanks from the pan and pour out the burnt oil.

Add the remaining 3 tablespoons oil to the pan over medium heat. Add the carrot and onion and cook, stirring every few minutes, for about 20 minutes, or until the vegetables are soft.

Return the shanks to the pan, add the wine and broth, and nestle the bouquet garni in the center. Bring to the barest simmer, cover, and cook for about 2 hours, or until the shank meat offers little or no resistance when poked with a small knife. Then preheat the oven to 375°F.

Gently lift the shanks out of the liquid and transfer them to a plate. Strain the braising liquid into a saucepan and simmer it gently, skimming off any froth or fat, for about 15 minutes or until the liquid is clear and greaseless. Put the shanks back into the empty sauté pan or an oval gratin dish, add the braising liquid, and sprinkle the garlic cloves over the top.

Cover the pan and slide it into the oven for 15 minutes. Uncover and continue to cook, basting every few minutes, for about 30 minutes, or until the braising liquid has a syrupy consistency, the shanks are covered with a dark sheen, and the garlic cloves crush when squeezed with your fingers. Season to taste with salt and pepper.

Leg of lamb, bone in

Leg of lamb, boned and tied

Lamb shoulder chop, boned

Lamb shoulder, bone in

Lamb shoulder

Rack of lamb

Rack of lamb, frenched

Lamb rib chop

Lamb shank

Lamb loin chop

Lamb saddle

Leg of Lamb

A satisfying and affordable roast, a leg of lamb is often the perfect option. It's less expensive than a rack, and the cooking time is less critical than for both a rack and a saddle. You can buy a half leg of lamb, the shank or butt end, or you can buy it whole. If you buy the butt end or a whole leg of lamb, you're best off boning out the pelvic bone and chine bone at the wide end of the leg, both of which make it hard to carve. To describe the rather intricate system of bones is impossible, but if you start cutting, keeping the knife against bone, you'll finally arrive at the joint where the whole assembly connects to the shank bone; cut through the joint and remove the set of bones.

Leg of lamb comes from the wholesaler covered with a thin, papery membrane called the fell, which should be trimmed off along with any thick sections of fat. Leave a thin layer of fat covering the meat, which will make the roast self-basting and keep it from drying out. Tie the leg with long lengths of string that reach from one end to the other to keep the loose flaps (generated from the boning) tightly against the rest of the meat. Leg of lamb tastes best when roasted rare to medium-rare.

MAKES 8 TO 10 MAIN-COURSE SERVINGS

> **One 8-pound bone-in leg of lamb**
>
> **Salt**
>
> **Pepper**
>
> **1 pound lamb stew meat, cut into 1-inch cubes or strips (optional)**
>
> **1/2 cup water or broth**

Preheat the oven to 400°F. Cut the vertebrae and pelvic bone out of the leg of lamb as shown. If the fell has been left on the lamb, trim it away, along with any excess fat. Season the lamb inside and out with salt and pepper and tie up the roast as shown. Leave the lamb out of the refrigerator a couple of hours before you roast it so it comes to room temperature and roasts more evenly (see page 170).

Place the lamb in a roasting pan just large enough to hold it and the stew meat. Surround the leg with the bone and any meat (not fat) trimmings and the stew meat. Roast the lamb for about 1 hour, or until an instant-read thermometer inserted into the thickest part reads 125°F for rare or 130°F for medium-rare. After the first 30 minutes of cooking, check the juices in the pan. If they appear to be burning, add 1/4 cup water to the pan. If after an hour the lamb needs more browning, continue to roast at 400°F for another 30 minutes. If it does not need more browning, but it still has not reached 125°F inside, turn the heat down to 300°F and continue roasting.

When the lamb is done, set it on a cutting board or platter, cut away the string, and cover it loosely with aluminum foil. Let it rest for 20 minutes. If the stew meat in the roasting pan looks raw, put the pan back in the oven until the juices caramelize and form a crust on the bottom of the pan. Pour off any fat or grease that has formed on top of the crust. Add the remaining water to the pan and bring to a simmer on the stove top, stirring and scraping to dissolve any caramelized juices. Pour the juices into a small pitcher and skim off the fat with a spoon, or strain through a fine-mesh strainer into a degreasing cup and pour off the fat. You don't need to be fastidious about this step. A little fat in the jus is tasty.

Cut the strings off the roast, carve as shown, and serve on a warmed platter. Pass the jus in a sauceboat at the table.

1. Cut along the underside of the pelvic bone, keeping the knife against the bone.

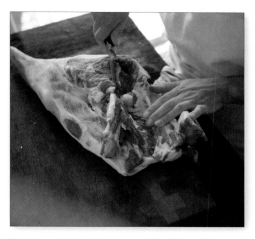

2. Cut into the joint that connects the whole pelvic section to the rest of the leg and detach the pelvic bones.

3. Trim off the thin skin that covers the outside of the leg.

4. Spread flavorful mixtures such as the garlic and thyme shown here over the exposed meat of the leg.

5. Tie the leg lengthwise with string, folding the exposed meat over the joint.

6. Season the leg and place it in a roasting pan with trimmings, bones, and aromatic vegetables. Roast at 400°F until the internal temperature reaches 125°F. Let the leg rest, loosely covered with foil, for 15 minutes.

7. Hold the leg by the bone and carve lengthwise along the thick side of the leg.

8. When you reach the bone, turn the leg around and carve along the other side.

9. Continue slicing until you have cut as much as you plan to serve. The inner slices will be rarer than the first slices you cut.

Rack of Lamb

Most of the time the racks come already trimmed, but the effort to french the ribs—trim the meat off the last two inches or so of bone—is well compensated by the drama of presenting and carving the rack at the table. If your rack is untrimmed, trim it as shown.

Because a rack of lamb cooks quickly, usually in about 25 minutes, it produces little in the way of a jus. You can make a fake jus with lamb trimmings (see page 170), or you can buy a pound of lamb stew meat (or take the meat off of lamb shoulder chops) and brown it in the roasting pan with the rack. Because a rack cooks so quickly, you will need to get the trimmings roasting before you put in the rack.

MAKES 4 MAIN-COURSE SERVINGS

> **1 pound lamb stew meat, cut into 1/2-inch cubes (optional)**
>
> **One 8-chop American rack of lamb or two 4-chop New Zealand racks of lamb, chine bone removed**
>
> **Salt**
>
> **Pepper**
>
> **1 cup lamb, veal, or chicken broth or water**

Preheat the oven to 450°F. Spread the stew meat in a roasting pan just large enough to hold the rack(s) and roast for about 20 minutes, or until the meat browns.

Put the rack(s) on top of the stew meat, season the rack(s) with salt and pepper, and roast for about 25 minutes, or until the meat feels firm when you press both ends at once or an instant-read thermometer inserted into the center reads 125°F for rare or 130°F for medium-rare. After the first 15 minutes of cooking, check the juices in the pan. If they appear to be burning, add 1/2 cup of the broth to the pan.

When the lamb is done, transfer the rack(s) to a platter and cover loosely with aluminum foil. Let it rest for 15 minutes. If you have not added any broth to the pan, add 1/2 cup of it now. Put the pan on the stove top and bring to a simmer, stirring and scraping with a wooden spoon and boiling down the liquid until it caramelizes on the bottom of the pan. Add the rest of the broth and simmer, stirring, for 1 to 2 minutes. Strain the juices through a fine-mesh strainer into a small pitcher and skim off the fat with a spoon, or strain into a degreasing cup and pour off the fat.

Carve the rack(s) as shown. Pass the jus in a sauceboat at the table.

1. Be sure to have the butcher cut off the chine bone to make carving easier.

2. Find the small muscle at one end of the large loin muscle and make a line, about 1/2 inch out from this muscle.

7. Follow the line you made and cut all the way down to and between the ribs. Scrape the knife against the ribs to loosen the tissue.

8. Cut through the membrane along the center of the ribs and push the membrane to the sides with the knife. Don't cut through it.

13. Trim excess fat off the loin end, but don't cut all the way down to the meat.

14. Cut away the long cordlike nerve that runs along the back of the rack.

3. Cut down to the bone.

4. Draw the knife all the way across the length of the rack.

5. Pull back the flaps of meat and fat on the shoulder end.

6. Cut out the shoulder blade.

9. Push the meat to the side and back around the bone with a spoon handle.

10. Pull away any meat and fat clinging to the bones.

11. Scrape off any membrane clinging to the ribs.

12. Cut down through the center of the rack and pull away the thick layer of fat and meat that covers the shoulder end. This ensures that both ends cook in the same amount of time.

15. Trim the meat away from the fat on the trimmings, and put the meat, cut into strips, in the roasting pan with the stew meat and chine bone.

16. Assemble the trimmings, stew meat, and chine bone in the roasting pan.

17. Arrange the seasoned rack, meat side up, on the trimmings. Roast until the ends spring back when you push on them or until an instant-read thermometer inserted into the center of the rack reads 125°F.

18. Cover the meat loosely with aluminum foil and let rest before carving. Cut between the bones in even slices.

Saddle of Lamb

This roast needs to be turned over during roasting so the tenderloin muscles cook in the same amount of time as the loin muscles. If you order a whole saddle from the butcher, it may arrive with the flaps still attached—it in fact looks a little like a saddle with stirrups hanging on both sides—which are the equivalent to flank steaks. Trim these off where they approach the loin muscles, and then trim the meat away from the fat, cut it into strips, and use it in the roasting pan to add to the jus.

A saddle of lamb can be carved in two ways. You can carve it lengthwise into strips by first slicing the loin muscles on top and then turning the roast over and carving the tenderloins in the same way. Or, you can cut under and next to the loin muscles, and then cut them crosswise into rounds, or noisettes, before turning over the saddle, cutting out the tenderloins, and then slicing them.

MAKES 4 TO 6 MAIN-COURSE SERVINGS

> **One 8-pound saddle of lamb, including flaps, or one 5-pound saddle of lamb without flaps**
>
> **1 pound lamb stew meat, cut into ¹/₂-inch cubes or strips, if you don't have the flaps**
>
> **Salt**
>
> **Pepper**
>
> **1 cup broth or water**

If the saddle has flaps, cut them off and trim them as shown. Cut them into strips.

Preheat the oven to 400°F. Spread the flap trimmings or stew meat in a roasting pan just large enough to hold the saddle and roast for about 20 minutes, or until the meat browns. Season the saddle with salt and pepper.

Put the saddle on top of the stew meat and roast for about 25 minutes, or until the meat feels firm when you press both ends at once or an instant-read thermometer inserted into the center reads 120°F for rare or 125°F for medium-rare. After the first 15 minutes of cooking, check the juices in the pan. If they appear to be burning, add ¹/₂ cup of the broth to the pan.

1. Notice how the saddle of lamb has two loin muscles and flaps on each side. If this were a steer, these flaps would be where the flank steaks are found.

2. Cut the flaps right next to the loin muscles down to the rib.

7. Season the roast and put it on top of the roast trimmings.

8. Roast until firm to the touch or 130°F in the center. Transfer the saddle to a platter and let rest.

When the saddle is done, transfer it to a platter and cover loosely with aluminum foil. Let it rest for 15 minutes. If you have not added any broth to the pan, add ¹/₂ cup of it now. Put the pan on the stove top and bring to a simmer, stirring and scraping with a wooden spoon and boiling down the liquid until it caramelizes on the bottom of the pan. Add the rest of the broth and simmer, stirring, for 1 to 2 minutes. Strain the juices through a fine-mesh strainer into a small pitcher and skim off the fat with a spoon, or strain into a degreasing cup and pour off the fat.

Carve the saddle as shown. Pass the jus in a sauceboat at the table.

3. Cut out the rib on each side where it adheres to the flaps.

4. Cut out the meat in the flaps—discard the fat—and cut it into thin strips.

5. Trim off excess fat from the top of the saddle. Leave a thin layer of fat covering the meat.

6. Spread the meat from the trimmings in the roasting pan with sliced carrot and onion. Roast these for about 20 minutes in a 400°F oven.

9. Put the pan on the stove top, remove the trimmings and vegetables, and bring to a simmer, stirring and scraping and boiling down the liquid until it caramelizes. Add the remaining broth and simmer. Strain and skim off the fat.

10. To carve the saddle lengthwise, cut along the top of the loin muscles with the knife parallel to the cutting surface.

11. Separate the loin muscle from the chine bone by sliding a knife between the two.

12. Continue slicing all the way down to the bone.

ALTERNATE WAY TO CARVE

13. Turn the roast over and slice the tenderloins lengthwise.

14. Serve on heated plates or platter.

To serve the roast in rounds, cut away one of the loin muscles.

Slice the loin muscle in rounds.

SAUTÉED LAMB

The same parts of the lamb that are good for roasting are also good for sautéing and grilling. The roasts are just cut into chops. A rack of lamb is sliced into rib chops, a saddle into loin chops, and occasionally the round of the leg is sold as a small roast or sliced into small steaks. The shoulder is also cut into less expensive chops, but they usually contain a lot of fat, with the meat unevenly distributed instead of being in small, neat rounds. In general, the shoulder meat is better for stews and pot roasts.

HOW TO MAKE SAUTÉED LOIN LAMB CHOPS ────

1. Trim excess fat off the chops.

2. Season the chops with salt and pepper.

3. Brown the chops over high heat in a pan just large enough to hold them in a single layer.

4. Turn the chops after 2 to 3 minutes, depending on their thickness.

5. Notice how the chop is made of two muscles: the loin and tenderloin.

6. Here, chops are shown with the oregano, shallot, and white wine brown sauce.

How to Cook a Lamb Chop

A lamb chop is cooked much like a steak and is usually served between rare and medium-rare. To cook a chop rare, make sure it's at room temperature to start and then brown both sides for 2 to 4 minutes each. To cook a chop slightly more, to between rare and medium-rare, cook it on the first side until beads of blood form on the raw surface (on top). Turn it over and cook for about the same length of time on the other side or until the chop just begins to spring back to the touch. To cook a chop more, say, to between medium-rare and medium, wait until the beads of blood quadruple in number from when they first appear, and if you want your meat medium or more, until they turn from red to brown, turn the chop and sauté for the same amount of time on the other side or until the chop is firm to the touch.

Sautéed Lamb Chops

Loin chops and rib chops are sautéed in the same way, in a little oil over high heat. The thinner the chop, the higher the heat needs to be. That way, the chop browns before it overcooks. For an elegant effect, french the bones on rib chops the same way you french the ribs on a rack of lamb (see pages 212–213).

MAKES 4 MAIN-COURSE SERVINGS

> **8 loin lamb chops or rib lamb chops, trimmed of excess fat**
>
> **Salt**
>
> **Pepper**
>
> **3 tablespoons olive oil**

Season the chops on both sides with salt and pepper. In a sauté pan just large enough to hold the chops in a single layer, heat the oil over high heat. When the oil starts to smoke, add the chops. If the chops are thin, leave the heat on high; if they are thick, turn it down slightly. Cook for about 2 minutes on each side for thin chops and up to 5 minutes on each side for thick chops, or until beads of blood form on top.

Transfer the chops to a plate lined with sheets of paper towels to absorb the burnt fat. Pour the burnt fat out of the pan, wipe the pan out with a paper towel, or rinse it out if the juices are burned, and then make a pan-deglazed sauce (opposite) to accompany the chops.

PAN-DEGLAZED SAUCES FOR SAUTÉED LAMB CHOPS

A basic pan-deglazed sauce for lamb chops usually includes from one to five components. The first ingredient added to the still-hot pan is typically finely chopped shallots or garlic; the second is wine, usually white wine; and the third is a chopped herb, such as oregano or marjoram. Meat glaze or broth is often added and boiled down with the other ingredients to give the sauce a lightly syrupy consistency. Butter will impart a silky consistency to the sauce. But don't use too much, as lamb is already very rich.

White Wine–Marjoram Sauce for Lamb Chops

This sauce is a model for any pan-deglazed sauce for lamb. Tarragon, chives, parsley, oregano, or chervil can replace the marjoram, or you can leave out the herb entirely. The butter and meat glaze are optional, too. Indeed, the sauce can be as simple as a little wine and butter.

MAKES ENOUGH FOR 4 MAIN-COURSE SERVINGS OF LAMB CHOPS

- **1 shallot, finely chopped**
- **1/4 cup dry white wine**
- **2 tablespoons commercial meat glaze or 4 tablespoons homemade meat glaze (see page 177), softened in 1/4 cup water or 1 cup broth**
- **2 teaspoons finely chopped fresh marjoram**
- **2 tablespoons cold butter**
- **Salt**
- **Pepper**

Put the shallot in the pan used to sauté the chops and stir with a whisk over medium heat for about 30 seconds, or until fragrant. Add the wine and boil for 30 seconds, or until reduced by three-quarters. Add the meat glaze and its soaking liquid or the broth and simmer until the sauce has a lightly syrupy consistency. If you're using meat glaze, you'll need to thin the sauce with water to the consistency you like. If you're not using meat glaze, only reduce the wine by half. (If you are not using meat glaze or broth, just boil down the sauce to about 3 tablespoons, though it won't get syrupy.)

Whisk in the marjoram and the butter and season with salt and pepper. Pour the sauce over the chops.

HOW TO MAKE A PAN-DEGLAZED SAUCE WITH OREGANO AND SHALLOTS

1. Sprinkle a little olive oil over the fresh oregano to keep it from turning black, and then finely chop.

2. Pour the fat out of the sauté pan used to cook the lamb and put in finely chopped shallots and oregano. Stir over medium heat for about 30 seconds, or until fragrant.

3. Pour in wine and reduce by half.

4. Add some meat glaze (optional).

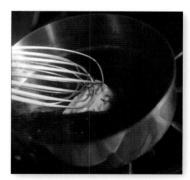

5. Whisk in butter.

BRAISED LAMB

The best part of the lamb for stewing and braising is the shoulder. The leg can also be used, but because it is so lean, it can become dry unless it is well larded, a process that most of us don't want to bother with.

Because most butchers and supermarkets cut the lamb shoulder into chops, you may have to special-order a half shoulder (the whole shoulder has both shoulders of the animal) and bone it yourself (opposite). The meat can then be cut up for stewing, or you can tie the half shoulder with string and braise it as a pot roast.

Lamb Pot Roast

Here we use the shoulder to make a delicious pot roast. The pot roast is tied up into a spherical shape, what the French call en ballon.

MAKES 4 TO 6 MAIN-COURSE SERVINGS

    1 boned half lamb shoulder, about 4 pounds
    1/2 cup dry white wine
    3 cloves garlic, minced and then crushed with the
        flat side of the knife
    2 tablespoons finely chopped fresh parsley
    2 teaspoons finely chopped fresh marjoram (optional)
    Salt
    Pepper
    1 carrot, peeled and thinly sliced
    1 large onion, chopped
    1 turnip, peeled and thinly sliced
    4 cups chicken broth, lamb broth, or water, or as needed
    Bouquet garni

Spread the shoulder out on the work surface with the "inside" up, as shown. Scatter the garlic, parsley, and marjoram over the lamb. Season with salt and pepper and roll and tie into a balloon shape.

Preheat the oven to 375°F. Put the carrot, onion, and turnip in a pot just large enough to hold the roast, and put the roast on top. Roast the shoulder for 1 1/2 hours, or until it releases its juices into the bottom of the pan.

Put the roast on a plate. Put the pot on the stove top and boil down the juices until they caramelize and the fat separates. Be very careful at this point not to burn the juices. Pour off and discard the fat floating on top of the caramelized juices. Put the roast back in the pot and pour over the wine.

Pour enough broth over the roast to reach halfway up the sides of the meat. Nestle the bouquet garni, and cover the pot with a sheet of aluminum foil, pressing it down so the middle hangs over the meat. (This causes moisture that condenses within the pot to baste the meat from the inside.) Bring to a simmer, cover with the lid, and slide the pot into the oven. Turn the oven down to 350°F. Check the lamb after 30 minutes to make sure the liquid isn't boiling—you want a bubble or two to break on the surface about every second—and adjust the oven temperature if necessary.

After an additional 30 minutes, turn the shoulder over in the liquid so the part that was submerged is now on top. Re-cover with the foil and lid and braise for another hour, or until a skewer slides easily in and out of the meat without the meat clinging to it and getting pulled up with it.

Transfer the lamb to a clean pot—you can clean out the same pot—and strain the braising liquid into a saucepan. Bring the liquid to a simmer and skim off any fat and froth with a ladle. Ladle about 2 cups of the braising liquid over the lamb, put the lamb in the oven, uncovered, and baste about every 10 minutes.

Meanwhile, place the pan of braising liquid off center on the burner so that the liquid boils on only one side and pushes the fat to the other. Simmer, regularly skimming off any fat or froth, for about 20 minutes, or until the liquid has a lightly syrupy consistency. Pour the liquid over the roast.

Continue basting the roast every 5 to 10 minutes, or until all the surrounding liquid is lightly syrupy and the meat is covered with a shiny glaze.

Remove the roast from the pot and cut it into wedges. Place the wedges in warmed soup plates and ladle the braising liquid over and around each serving.

GARNISHES AND VARIATIONS FOR LAMB POT ROAST

The braising liquid can be red wine or white wine combined with an equal amount of broth, or all beer or hard cider. You can simmer root and bulb vegetables in the braising liquid along with the pot roast during the last hour of cooking; you can add glazed root vegetables just before serving; or you can top each serving with boiled or steamed green vegetables. Sautéed mushrooms, wild or cultivated, can also be served over each portion.

HOW TO BONE A HALF LAMB SHOULDER

1. Notice both halves of the shoulder.

2. Trim off the excess fat from the outside of the shoulder.

3. Slide the knife along both sides of the shoulder blade, detaching it from the meat.

4. Cut the meat away from the top of the shoulder blade.

5. Cut down to the joint, and then insert the knife between the ball joint and the end of the shoulder blade.

6. Detach the shoulder blade.

7. Slide a knife along the outside of the ribs and detach the meat.

8. Slide the knife along the neck and detach the meat.

1. Spread crushed garlic and parsley over the inside of the meat.

2. Tie the meat up into a spherical packet with string. Season with salt and pepper.

3. Put the roast on a bed of aromatic vegetables in a pot just large enough to hold the roast.

4. Roast until well browned and the juices are released in the bottom of the pot.

5. Boil down the juices over high heat until they separate and are covered with a clear layer of fat. Pour off and discard the fat.

6. Deglaze the pot with white wine.

7. Scrape the bottom of the pot with a spoon.

8. Put the meat back in the pot and add liquid to come at least halfway up the side of the meat.

9. Cover with aluminum foil and the pot lid and braise gently in the oven or on the stove.

10. Braise for 1 hour, turn the roast over, and continue to braise until a small knife easily slides in and out of the meat.

11. If you have time, chill the liquid overnight and remove the fat with a spoon.

12. Put the lamb back in a smaller pot with the degreased (and/or reduced) hot braising liquid and roast while basting until well glazed.

LAMB STEWS

When you cook a lamb stew or other stew with raw meat, the stew generates its own broth, which you then reduce and thicken. But if you want to make a stew from pieces of left-over roast leg of lamb, you will need to use a flavorful broth, thickened perhaps with a little roux of flour and butter, and simmer the lamb in it just long enough to heat it through.

There is also a family of stewlike dishes that the French call *sautés*. They are made by heating tender pieces of meat in liquid just long enough to warm the meat through. Beef stroganoff, in which cubes from a tender cut are heated in broth and the liquid is finished with sour cream, is an example of this method of preparation. You can make this type of dish with tender parts of the lamb—the leg is the most likely candidate, since meat from the rack or saddle is very expensive—but the best approach is to make a lamb broth with inexpensive lamb taken from the shoulder and then use it for heating the meat.

Lamb Stew

The best meat for lamb stew comes from the shoulder or the shanks. Most butchers and supermarkets sell already-cubed lamb stew meat, but if you can't find it, you can buy lamb shoulder chops or shanks and bone them. You will need about twice the weight of chops or shanks to get the necessary weight of stew meat. Once you have made the basic stew, you can serve it as it is—leave the carrots, onion, and garlic in or pick them out—or you can finish it as described in the variations that follow. Flouring and browning the meat in a pan coated with hot oil will give the stew a deeper color and the flour will thicken the braising liquid, but this is a time-consuming step and not at all necessary.

MAKES 6 MAIN-COURSE SERVINGS

> 4 pounds lamb stew meat or 8 pounds lamb shoulder
> chops or lamb shanks
> Salt
> Pepper

1/2 cup flour
3 tablespoons olive oil
4 cloves garlic, crushed
1 large carrot, peeled, halved lengthwise, and sliced
1 large onion, sliced
1 cup dry white wine
3 cups broth or water
Bouquet garni
1 tablespoon flour for thickening (optional)
1 tablespoon room-temperature butter for thickening
 (optional)

If you are using lamb shoulder chops or lamb shanks, take the meat off the bone and cut it into 3/4-inch cubes. Season the meat with salt and pepper and then coat with the flour and pat off the excess.

In a large, heavy-bottomed sauté pan, heat the oil over high heat. When the oil begins to smoke, add half of the meat. When the meat begins to brown, after a minute or two, add the rest of the meat. As the meat browns, turn it over with tongs and continue to cook until it is browned on all sides. Put the meat in a bowl and pour the burnt fat out of the pan.

Put the meat in a pot with the garlic, carrot, and onion. Add the wine and broth to the sauté pan and deglaze. Bring to a gentle simmer, pour the deglazing liquid over the meat, and nestle the bouquet garni in the center. Simmer for about 2 hours, or until the meat crushes easily when you squeeze a piece.

If the braising liquid needs to be thicker, strain the liquid into a clean saucepan and set the meat and vegetables aside. Bring the liquid to a simmer and simmer gently, skimming off any froth and fat, until it thickens. If you have reduced it to 2 cups and it still isn't thick enough, use the back of a fork to make a smooth paste with the flour and butter in a small bowl, and then whisk half of the paste into the simmering liquid. Simmer the liquid briefly, check the consistency, and add more paste if needed.

Pick the meat out of the vegetables, discard the vegetables and reheat meat in the thickened liquid, and serve.

Spring-Style Lamb Stew

This colorful version of lamb stew is made by adding vegetables to the basic stew recipe. The root vegetables can be glazed and added to the stew or they can be cooked in the stew, while the green vegetables are boiled or steamed and added to the stew just before serving.

MAKES 6 MAIN-COURSE SERVINGS

> Lamb Stew (see page 221)
>
> 1 large carrot, peeled
>
> 1 pint pearl onions, boiled for 1 minute, rinsed with cold water, and peeled
>
> 1/2 pound haricots verts or regular green beans or 1/2 cup fresh peas or frozen petite peas

Cook the stew as directed. While it simmers, cut the carrot into wedges. Then add the carrots and onions to the stew during the last 30 minutes of cooking, or glaze the carrots and onions as directed on pages 300 and 302, respectively, and add them to the stew just before serving. If using beans or fresh peas, boil or steam them, and place on top of each serving. Or, if using frozen peas, heat them for a minute in the braising liquid just before serving.

Lamb Stew with Indian Spices, Cream, and Yogurt

In its most basic form, lamb curry is lamb stew with curry powder cooked in a little butter added to the braising liquid. If you want to stay with this simple approach, cook 2 tablespoons curry powder in 2 tablespoons butter in a small pan over low to medium heat for about 1 minute, or until the curry is fragrant, and then whisk half of the mixture into the finished stew, taste, and add more of the mixture to taste. If you want to attempt a more elaborate dish, prepare this or the Lamb Korma (see page 224).

This delicately flavored stew is a refined alternative to a basic curry. You can apply this same treatment to the lamb pot roast on page 218.

MAKES 6 MAIN-COURSE SERVINGS

> Lamb Stew (see page 221)
>
> 1/2 cup slivered blanched almonds
>
> 3 tablespoons butter
>
> 1 large onion, very thinly sliced
>
> 2 tablespoons ground coriander
>
> 2 teaspoons ground cardamom
>
> 1 cup heavy cream
>
> 1 tablespoon grated fresh ginger
>
> 2 tablespoons finely chopped fresh cilantro
>
> 1 cup plain yogurt
>
> Salt
>
> Pepper

Cook the stew as directed. About 30 minutes before the stew is ready, preheat the oven to 350°F. Spread the almonds on a small shallow pan and toast in the oven, stirring occasionally, for 10 to 15 minutes, or until they are fragrant and have taken on color. Pour onto a plate and let cool.

Meanwhile, in a sauté pan, melt the butter over medium heat. Add the onion and cook, stirring occasionally, for about 15 minutes, or until all the liquid it releases evaporates. Add the coriander and cardamom and stir over medium heat for about 2 minutes, or until the spices are fragrant. Pour in the cream and boil down for about 5 minutes, or until the mixture thickens.

Stir the onion mixture into the stew along with the ginger, cilantro, and yogurt, mixing well. Season with salt and pepper. Serve in warmed soup plates and garnish each serving with the almonds.

1. Add half of the meat cubes to the hot oil and begin to brown them.

2. As the meat heats, add the rest of the meat cubes to fill the pan and cook until browned on all sides.

3. Transfer the meat to a pot, pour out the burnt fat, and deglaze the pan with white wine or other liquid.

4. Pour the wine over the meat.

5. Add aromatic vegetables, a bouquet garni, and enough liquid just to cover, and cover and simmer very gently until tender.

6. Spoon into bowls and serve. Shown here is Lamb Stew with Indian Spices (opposite).

Fall-Style Lamb Stew with Wild Mushrooms

This is a great lamb stew variation in the fall when wild mushrooms are available. Be sure to spoon the mushrooms over each serving, rather than add them to the stew, or they will be soggy. You can combine this version of lamb stew with the spring version (opposite) and use only $1/2$ pound mushrooms.

MAKES 6 MAIN-COURSE SERVINGS

Lamb Stew (see page 221)

1 pound assorted wild mushrooms such as morel, chanterelle, porcini, lamb's foot, and/or black trumpet, in any combination

4 tablespoons butter or olive oil

2 cloves garlic, minced and then crushed with the flat side of the knife

2 tablespoons finely chopped fresh parsley

Salt

Pepper

Cook the stew as directed. Just before the stew is ready, trim the mushrooms, cutting away tough or dried stem ends and very dirty parts. Rinse the mushrooms in a colander and pat them dry with paper towels. If the mushrooms are very large, such as porcini, slice them or cut them into sections.

In a sauté pan, heat 3 tablespoons of the butter or oil over high heat. When the butter froths and the froth begins to subside, or the oil begins to ripple, add the mushrooms and sauté for about 5 minutes, or until they are fragrant. Use a large spoon to move the mushrooms to one side of the pan, and then tilt the pan so the empty half is in contact with the burner. Add the remaining 1 tablespoon butter or oil to the pan. It will accumulate in a pool. Add the garlic and parsley to the pool, and when the mixture begins to froth, toss or stir the mushrooms over the heat with the parsley mixture for a minute or so. Season with salt and pepper.

Serve the stew in warmed soup plates and spoon the mushrooms over each serving.

VARIATION

To make lamb stew with morels, heat reconstituted dried or sautéed fresh morels in the braising liquid along with cooked spring vegetables just before serving.

Lamb Korma

This curry includes an assortment of fragrant spices, cream, yogurt, and a rather shocking amount of ghee, which is butter that has been cooked until it takes on a nutty flavor (see page 341). In deference to the fat-conscious, the ghee can be replaced with a small amount of butter.

MAKES 6 MAIN-COURSE SERVINGS

> Lamb Stew (see page 221)
> 1/2 cup ghee or 2 tablespoons butter
> 1 large onion, very thinly sliced
> 2 tablespoons grated fresh ginger
> 2 teaspoons ground cumin
> 1/2 teaspoon ground nutmeg
> 1 teaspoon ground cinnamon
> 1 teaspoon ground cardamom
> 1/4 teaspoon ground cloves
> 1 cup heavy cream
> 1 cup plain yogurt
> Salt
> Pepper

Cook the stew as directed. About 30 minutes before the stew is ready, melt the ghee in a sauté pan over medium heat, add the onion, and cook, stirring occasionally, for about 15 minutes, or until all the liquid it releases evaporates. Add the ginger, cumin, nutmeg, cinnamon, cardamom, and cloves and stir over medium heat for about 2 minutes, or until the spices are fragrant. Pour in the cream and boil down for about 5 minutes, or until the mixture thickens.

Add the strained braising liquid from the stew and simmer until the liquid thickens. Stir in the yogurt and season with salt and pepper. Return the stew meat to the liquid and heat through. Serve in warmed soup plates.

VARIATIONS

In Julie Sahni's definitive book on Indian cooking, *Classic Indian Cooking,* she presents a similar dish but adds a considerable amount of garlic. To make something like her version, add 3 cloves garlic, minced and crushed to a paste with the side of the knife, to the onions at the same time as the spices. Another addition that gives this curry its own special character is 1/2 teaspoon saffron threads, soaked in 1 tablespoon water for 30 minutes and added to the stew just before serving.

Irish Stew

Potatoes and the absence of wine are what give Irish stew its identity. Strangely, Irish stew is particularly popular in France, where the cooks include two kinds of potatoes—a fragile potato, like a russet or Yukon Gold, that will fall apart and thicken the stewing liquid, and a firmer waxy potato that will hold its shape until serving.

MAKES 6 MAIN-COURSE SERVINGS

> Lamb Stew (see page 221)
> 1 large Yukon Gold or russet potato, about 3/4 pound, peeled and thinly sliced
> 2 pounds white or red waxy potatoes, peeled and shaped into elongated ovals or the same amount of baby fingerling potatoes, peeled and left whole

Prepare the stew as directed, omitting the wine and adding an additional cup of broth, and adding the sliced potato at the same time as the broth. When the stew has been simmering for about 1 1/2 hours, stir it vigorously to break up the potato slices. Add the shaped potatoes and continue to simmer until both the potatoes and the stew are done.

PORK

Pork is one of the most savory and least expensive of all the meats. It can be prepared much like veal, though unlike veal, which provides cuts from the leg, pork legs are generally used to make ham. When most people prepare pork, they cook chops or perhaps roast or grill a loin. But they are missing out on the superb rack of pork—essentially the loin with the rib bones still attached—which looks more dramatic at the table than a loin and has more flavor. Many also forget the delights of fresh roast ham, which is just a leg of pork, a large cut that is ideal for serving a crowd.

Unlike lamb, which is cut crosswise into sections that make up the primal cuts, pork is cut in half lengthwise and then separated into two shoulder parts, one called simply the shoulder or picnic ham, and another, farther back, called the Boston butt. Farther back still is the loin, which includes the muscles running next to the ribs and also those farther down. This is equivalent to a saddle of lamb, a New York cut on beef, or the small of our backs. Last is the pork leg or fresh ham.

PORK ROASTS

The pig offers a lovely assortment of delicious roasts, from a sautéed tenderloin quickly finished in the oven, to a giant ham for twenty hungry souls. The simplest roast is a boneless pork loin cooked in the oven until it is heated through. More tasty is the rack, with the rib bones left on and roasted in the same way.

Boneless Pork Loin

The easiest and most common pork roast is a boneless pork loin, always available at the butcher's and usually at the supermarket. Despite the recent trend toward restaurant waiters asking you how you want your pork done, there is only one correct degree of doneness, the point at which the first pink translucence turns wet and rosy. Any more cooking will dry out the meat, and any less will leave the center raw. The only additional complication depends on how dedicated you are to serving a deeply flavored and colored jus. Overcooked meat yields a lot more jus than properly cooked meat, which produces relatively little (see page 170 for more about this). To augment the jus, you can spread a handful of pork trimmings—not fat, just lean meat—around the loin in the roasting pan. This addition also ensures that the surface of the roasting pan is completely covered, which prevents hot spots that could cause the jus to burn.

An instant-read thermometer is a good way to judge doneness. It should read 130°F when you take the loin out of the oven, since the internal temperature of the meat will rise to 135°F, the perfect temperature, as it rests. Another easy test is to press on the center of the meat. As soon as it loses its fleshy feel that gives under pressure and starts to firm up, take it out of the oven. Transfer the loin to a warmed platter and cover it loosely with aluminum foil to keep it warm while you make the jus. Don't wrap it tightly, or it will steam and the brown crust will get soggy and lose some of its savor.

Leg of Pork (Fresh Ham)

A whole fresh ham is a leg of pork (its typical label in super-markets) with nothing done to it—no smoking, curing, or aging. It weighs at least 12 pounds and often as much as 20 pounds, with most of it meat. The leg is also sold in halves, either the butt end or the shank end. If you like challenging yourself with meat preparation, you can buy a whole fresh ham and break it down into various roasts and cutlets just as you might do with veal.

MAKES ABOUT 8 MAIN-COURSE SERVINGS

> **1 fresh ham, shank or butt end, about 6 pounds**
> **Salt**
> **Pepper**

Rub the ham with salt and pepper and let it rest at room temperature for a couple of hours before roasting.

Preheat the oven to 350°F. Place the ham in a roasting pan just large enough to hold it and roast for about 2 hours, or until an instant-read thermometer inserted into the center reads 135°F (its internal temperature will rise to 140°F while it rests). If the juices threaten to burn, add a few tablespoons of water or broth to the pan from time to time. When the roast is ready, transfer to a warmed platter, cover loosely with aluminum foil, and let rest for at least 20 minutes before carving.

Cured Hams

Some hams are cured by soaking in brine or rubbing with salt and usually a little saltpeter. These hams, like the famous prosciutto of Italy, our fully cured Virginia hams (of which Smithfield ham is the best known), and the serrano ham of Spain, are meant to be eaten raw, thinly sliced. Other hams are only partially cured and must be cooked before they are eaten. If you are cooking a fully cured ham, such as a Smithfield, you will need to soak it first to eliminate some of the salt. Some hams are sold already cooked and simply need to be heated to an internal temperature of 130°F.

When buying a ham, don't mistake the so-called picnic ham, which comes from the fattier shoulder section of the pig, with a ham from the leg.

Country Ham

Buy a whole or half (a shank or rump end; the shank end is easier to carve) Virginia, Kentucky, or Tennessee ham (Smithfield ham is the most famous, but other hams are often at least as good). Soak a whole ham in cold water for at least 2 days—in the bathtub is good—changing the water twice a day. If you have only a half ham, you can get by with a day's soaking. You then simmer the ham in water with some thyme, bay leaves, and juniper berries (although none of these is essential), which flavors the ham and leaches out the salt. After simmering, the ham is roasted and glazed in the oven.

Roast Country Ham

Perfect for a feast, the secret to success of this country ham is the long soaking.

MAKES 20 MAIN-COURSE SERVINGS

> **1 fully cured whole country ham, about 15 pounds**
> **12 juniper berries, crushed**
> **Bouquet garni**
> **2 tablespoons commercial meat glaze or homemade meat glaze (see page 177), dissolved in 1/3 cup hot water (optional)**

Soak the ham in cold water to cover for 2 days, changing the water twice a day. (Or, follow the directions that come with the ham.) Put it in a pot with cold water to cover and bring the water to a simmer. Simmer for 5 minutes and drain off the water. Add more cold water to cover, the juniper, and the bouquet garni, and bring to a gentle simmer over high heat. Lower the heat so that a bubble or two breaks on the surface every second or so and simmer gently for about 1 1/2 hours, or an instant-read thermometer inserted into the center reads 140°F. Finish the ham by baking it in a 375°F degree oven for about 30 minutes until the surface browns. Brush with the meat glaze to give the ham a shiny finished glaze.

Pork rib roast

Pork shoulder

Pork tenderloin

Noisettes from tenderloin

Pork loin chop

Pork rib chops

Pork shoulder chop

HOW TO FRENCH A RACK OF PORK

1. Notice the small muscle next to the rib and loin muscle. Leaving this intact, slide a knife along the length of the rack all the way down to the bone.

2. Pull away the flap of meat that covers the bones.

3. Slide a knife between the bones with the blade right up against the bone. Scrape the bone to detach the membrane.

4. Scrape along the bones and detach the flap of meat.

5. Turn the rack over and cut through the membrane on the back of the bones.

6. Scrape the membrane away from the bone.

7. Using a kitchen towel or paper towel for grip, peel away the meat attached to the bone.

PREPARING AND ROASTING A RACK OF PORK

1. Tie up the roast so it cooks more evenly. Season with salt and pepper.

2. Have the butcher cut away the chine bone (the spinal bones) to make the rack easy to cut up. If you like, place a chopped carrot and onion in the pan you are using to roast the pork and put the chine bone and any other trimmings or meat on top.

3. Roast the trimmings and vegetables until browned, and then place the rack on top.

4. If at any point the juices in the bottom of the pan threaten to burn, pour in about 1/2 cup broth or water.

5. Roast until the meat bounces back to the touch and has an internal temperature of 130°F.

Rack of Pork

The rack of pork contains the same meat as the center part of the loin except that the ribs are left attached. This makes for a much more dramatic roast, especially if you french the rack (see pages 212–213). If you have a friendly butcher, let him or her do this for you. Whatever you do, don't let the butcher break the bones, which many butchers like to do for some inexplicable reason. Do have the butcher cut out the chine bone, which is the spinal column. If it is left in place, the roast becomes impossible to carve.

When you buy your roast, ask for the rib section nearest the loin and for as many ribs as you need servings, from four to eight. When the chine bone has been removed, the ribs will be attached to the meat as well as to a series of flat bones along the bottom of the roast. You can leave these in place, but carving will be easier if you slide a knife underneath, remove, and then tie them back on with string. Then when the roast is ready to serve, you can remove these easily by snipping the string. If the butcher offers to remove them for you, have him or her tie them back on—or at the least make sure you end up leaving the shop with them so you can put them in the roasting pan to contribute to the jus. As with any other roast, a pound or so of lean meat trimmings cooked along with the roast will do wonders for the jus. If you can't find pork trimmings, buy 2 pounds of pork shoulder chops, bone them, and put both the bones and meat in the pan.

MAKES 4 TO 8 MAIN-COURSE SERVINGS

> 1 rack of lamb, taken from the loin end, with as many ribs as servings
> Salt
> Pepper
> 1 pound pork shoulder meat, cut into 1/2-inch-wide strips

Ideally, leave the rack at room temperature for a couple of hours before roasting (see page 170).

Preheat the oven to 400°F. If the butcher didn't do it, french the rack as shown on pages 212–213. Season the rack with salt and pepper. Put the pork pieces in a roasting pan—spread them around to cover the surface completely—and put the pan in the oven for about 20 minutes, or until they start to brown.

Put the rack on top of the trimmings and roast until the meat feels firm to the touch or an instant-read thermometer inserted into the center reads 130°F. Transfer to a warmed platter, cover loosely with aluminum foil, and let rest (the internal temperature will rise to 135°F) while you prepare the jus.

If the roasting pan contains liquid juices, put the pan on the stove top and boil down the juices until they caramelize into a brown crust on the bottom of the pan. If the juices have already caramelized, skip this step. Add about 3 tablespoons water per serving and simmer over medium heat while stirring and scraping the bottom of the pan with a wooden spoon to extract all the savor from the caramelized juices. After about 3 minutes, strain the jus through a fine-mesh strainer into a warmed bowl for serving.

Carve the rack and serve with the jus.

Boneless Pork Loin Roast

You can buy a piece of pork loin for four to ten people. If you shop for meat for a smaller crowd, the loin just becomes a thick pork chop.

MAKES 4 TO 10 MAIN-COURSE SERVINGS

> 1 boneless pork loin, 6 to 8 ounces per serving
> Salt
> Pepper
> 1 pound pork shoulder meat or 2 pounds pork shoulder chops (optional)

Preheat the oven to 400°F. If the butcher has not removed the silver skin from the loin, take it off as shown on page 237. Season the loin with salt and pepper. If using pork shoulder meat, cut into 1/2-inch-wide strips. If using chops, bone them, cut the meat into strips, and use both the meat and the bones. Put the pork pieces (and bones) in a roasting pan—spread them around to cover the surface completely—and put the pan in the oven for about 20 minutes, or until they start to brown.

Put the loin on top of the trimmings and roast until the meat feels firm to the touch or an instant-read thermometer inserted into the center reads 130°F. Transfer to a warmed platter, cover loosely with aluminum foil, and let rest while you prepare the jus.

If the roasting pan contains liquid juices—there won't be much fat from a boneless loin—put the pan on the stove top and boil down the juices until they caramelize into a brown crust on the bottom of the pan. If the juices have already caramelized, skip this step. Add about 3 tablespoons water per serving and simmer over medium heat while stirring and scraping the bottom of the pan with a wooden spoon to extract all the savor from the caramelized juices. After about 3 minutes, strain the jus through a fine-mesh strainer into a warmed bowl for serving.

Carve the loin and serve with the jus.

BRAISED PORK

Many pork cuts contain quite a bit of fat and tissue, especially the shoulder. This makes them perfect for braising, because it eliminates the need for any preliminary larding. The Boston butt is the best cut for pot roast. Shoulder pork chops, which many people eschew because of their fattiness, are also excellent braised.

Braised Pork Shoulder

A whole pork shoulder makes a lovely pork pot roast, tender and melting in the mouth. You can get the well-marbled meat of the shoulder by getting the butcher to cut off the last four ribs from the loin, or you can buy a boneless Boston butt and cook it in the same way.

MAKES 4 (RIBS FROM A LOIN) TO 6 (FROM A BOSTON BUTT) MAIN-COURSE SERVINGS

> **4 ribs from the shoulder end of a pork loin or 1 boneless Boston butt, about 4 pounds, rind removed**
>
> **Salt**
>
> **Pepper**
>
> **1 onion, sliced**
>
> **1 large carrot, peeled and sliced**
>
> **1 cup dry white wine**
>
> **4 cups brown chicken broth or veal broth, or as needed**
>
> **Bouquet garni**

Preheat the oven to 375°F. Season the meat with salt and pepper and tie it up with string. Put the onion and carrot in a pot just large enough to hold the meat, and put the meat on top. Put the pot, uncovered, in the oven for about 1 hour, or until the meat releases its juices into the bottom of the pot and then the juices boil down to a thick syrup. Be very careful at this stage not to burn the juices.

Pour the wine into the pot and then enough broth to reach halfway up the sides of the meat. Bring to a simmer, and nestle the bouquet garni in the center. Cover the pot with a sheet of aluminum foil, pressing it down so the middle hangs over the meat. (This causes moisture that condenses within the pot to baste the meat from the inside.) Then cover with the lid and slide the pot into the oven or simmer on top of the stove. Simmer very gently for 1 hour, checking the meat after 30 minutes to make sure the liquid isn't boiling—you want a bubble or two to break on the surface every second or so—and

HOW TO MAKE PORK SHOULDER POT ROAST

1. Notice the shoulder end (above) is less neat than the loin end (above, right) and has the shoulder blade.

2. Loin end.

3. Cut all around the shoulder blade and remove it.

4. Cut off as many ribs as you need from the shoulder end. Here, 4 ribs have been removed.

9. Cover the pot with aluminum foil, sagging in the middle so it bastes the roast, and put on the lid.

10. Braise in the oven or on the stove top for about 1 hour, and then turn the roast over.

11. Braise until the roast is easy to penetrate with a skewer.

12. Take the roast out of the pot and strain the braising liquid into a saucepan.

adjusting the oven temperature if necessary. Then carefully turn the meat over so the part that was submerged is now on top. Re-cover with the foil and lid and braise for another hour, or until a skewer slides easily in and out of the meat without the meat clinging to it.

Transfer the meat to a platter and turn down the oven to 350°F. Strain the braising liquid into a saucepan, and place the pan off center on a burner over medium heat so the liquid boils on only one side and pushes the fat to the other. Simmer, regularly skimming off any fat and froth until the liquid is clear and free of fat.

Clean out the pot or use a new one (a smaller one, since the meat will have shrunk) and put the meat in the pot. Pour half of the braising liquid over the meat, put the pot in the oven, and cook the meat, basting every 5 to 10 minutes with the surrounding liquid, until the liquid in the pot looks slightly syrupy. At this point, pour the remaining braising liquid into the pot and continue basting the meat until the liquid again looks like a light syrup and the meat is nicely glazed. This final cooking and glazing step will take about 45 minutes.

Use a spoon or a knife to serve the pork in soup plates, with the braising liquid ladled on top.

5. Tie up the shoulder to make it more compact.

6. Put the pot roast in a pot with chopped carrots and onions and roast until well browned and all the juices have caramelized on the bottom of the pot.

7. Pour in enough wine, broth, or other liquid to come halfway up the sides of the roast.

8. Put in a bouquet garni.

13. Clean the pot and put the roast back into it, or use a new same size or smaller pot.

14. Put the pot roast in the oven with the degreased braising liquid and baste it.

15. Continue basting until the liquid becomes syrupy and the roast is covered with a shiny red glaze.

Braised Shoulder Pork Chops with White Wine and Prunes

This dish calls out for shoulder chops, instead of the leaner, more expensive center-cut rib or loin chops. The fat and tissue in shoulder chops give a moist melting consistency to the meat during the braising. This dish cooks for about 2 hours.

MAKES 6 MAIN-COURSE SERVINGS

> 1 cup prunes, pitted
>
> 1 cup dry or semidry white wine
>
> 6 large shoulder pork chops
>
> Salt
>
> Pepper
>
> 3 tablespoons pure olive oil
>
> 1 carrot, peeled and chopped
>
> 1 onion, peeled and chopped
>
> 3 tablespoons butter
>
> 1 cup chicken broth or water
>
> 1 tablespoon commercial meat glaze or homemade meat glaze (see page 177)
>
> Bouquet garni
>
> 1/2 cup heavy cream (optional)

In a bowl, soak the prunes in the white wine for an hour or so until plumped.

Season the chops on both sides with salt and pepper. In a heavy-bottomed sauté pan, heat the oil over high heat. When the oil begins to smoke, add the chops and brown well on both sides. Transfer the chops to a plate and pour the burnt oil out of the pan. Return the pan to medium heat, add the carrot, onion, and butter, and cook gently for about 10 minutes, or until the vegetables soften and brown slightly.

Return the chops to the pan and pour in the wine from the prunes and broth or water and the meat glaze. Bring to a gentle simmer, and nestle the bouquet garni in the center. Cover the pot with a sheet of aluminum foil, pressing it down so the middle hangs over the meat. (This causes moisture that condenses within the pot to baste the meat from the inside.) Cover with the lid and simmer gently—you want a bubble or two to break on the surface every second or so—for about 2 hours, or until a knife stuck into one of the chops slips in and out with no resistance.

Gently transfer the chops to a plate and keep them warm in a low oven while you make the sauce. Take out the bouquet garni and strain the braising liquid into a saucepan. Place the pan off center on a burner over medium heat so the liquid boils on only one side and pushes the fat to the other side. Simmer, regularly skimming off any fat and froth with a ladle, until reduced to a lightly syrupy consistency. Add the cream and simmer again until the sauce thickens just slightly. You want it to be light. Add the prunes, simmer for about 1 minute to soften and heat through, and season with salt and pepper. Reheat the chops in the sauce.

Arrange the chops on warmed plates and spoon the prunes and sauce over them.

VARIATIONS

The braising liquid can undergo all the usual possibilities. Leave out the prunes and add tomato puree, cooked down until thick, to the sauce to give the dish a southern French taste. You can add pureed dried chiles and spices (see the chicken with simple mole sauce on page 252) to the braising liquid to give it a Mexican character. Any vegetable, such as shaped or sectioned glazed root vegetables or boiled or steamed green vegetables (see Vegetables chapter, pages 289–305), can be used instead of the prunes.

Cooking Bacon

The trick to cooking bacon is using slow, gentle heat so that the fat has time to render before the bacon becomes too brown. Use a small heavy-bottomed sauté pan that's just the size of the bacon you're cooking and place it over low to medium-low heat. You can save the bacon fat for a future use, provided the bacon never got too hot which would have caused the fat to burn. Most bacon has so much of its own fat that you can put the slices directly in the pan without using any other oil or fat to cook it in.

If you can find it, buy double-smoked slab bacon and cut it yourself, which enables you to slice it to the thickness you want, such as the rather thick lardon slices for Boeuf à la Bourguignonne on page 186. Fresh slab bacon will keep for weeks, in the refrigerator, wrapped in a kitchen towel. Always buy bacon labeled as "naturally smoked," not "smoke-flavored."

1. Season the chops and then brown on both sides over high heat. Transfer the chops to a plate.

2. Add chopped carrots and onions to the pan with a little butter and stir over medium heat until well caramelized.

3. Arrange the chops over the cooked vegetables.

4. Pour in liquid such as wine and/or broth to come halfway up the sides of the chops.

5. Braise the chops until a knife slides in and out easily.

6. Gently take the chops out of the pan and strain the braising liquid.

7. Degrease the braising liquid. Here, it has been chilled and the congealed fat has been removed.

8. Put the chops back in the pan. Here, prunes, softened in hot broth and cream, are added to the strained and degreased braising liquid.

SAUTÉED PORK

Pork has so many tender muscles that virtually any part can be sautéed just long enough for the heat to penetrate the middle. While less than ideal because of their fat and gristle, shoulder pork chops can be sautéed and paired with a simple pan sauce. Any of the chops from the loin, including center-cut rib chops or loin chops, sauté beautifully. As you approach the leg, you may sometimes find ham steaks that, as their name implies, can be sautéed in the same way as their bovine cousins.

Medallions, Noisettes, and Pork Tenderloin

Boneless rounds of meat are often called medallions when they are at least 3 inches in diameter and noisettes (French for hazelnuts) when they are smaller. One of the best cuts for making pork noisettes—in fact the only cut that yields suitable noisettes—is the tenderloin. Pork tenderloins are usually about 8 inches long and 2 inches wide and are tapered at one end. Their meat is the most tender of all the pork cuts, and if you are careful not to overcook them, they stay moist and delicate. They are surprisingly inexpensive, too, maybe because people don't know how to cook them, and the only preparation they require is the removing of the silver skin, as shown. They can then be sliced into neat 1-inch-thick rounds, or noisettes. Tenderloins should be sautéed, not braised, since braising will dry them out.

Pork Tenderloins with Mushroom Sauce

The sauce for these tenderloins is made by pureeing mushrooms in a blender. This is just one example of how vegetable purees can be used as thickeners and flavorings for sauces. You can also sauté mushrooms and scatter them around and over the noisettes. Wild mushrooms make this an especially elegant dish.

MAKES 4 MAIN-COURSE SERVINGS

> 2 pork tenderloins, 12 to 14 ounces each
>
> Salt
>
> Pepper
>
> 10 ounces cremini or cultivated white mushrooms, or 5 ounces cremini for the sauce and 5 ounces cremini or wild mushrooms for the garnish

> 2 tablespoons homemade meat glaze or 1 tablespoon commercial meat glaze (see page 177), softened in 3 tablespoons hot water (optional)
>
> 1/2 cup heavy cream
>
> 4 tablespoons clarified butter (see page 341) or olive oil
>
> 1 teaspoon wine vinegar, or as needed

If the butcher didn't do it, take the silver skin off the tenderloins, as shown. Cut the tenderloins into 1-inch-thick rounds, or the thickness needed to give you 3 noisettes per serving. Season the noisetttes on both sides with salt and pepper and, if you have the time, let sit at room temperature for 1 hour before sautéing.

Wash and dry the mushrooms. Cut the end off the bottom of each mushroom stem if dried out or dirty. Chop half the mushrooms coarsely and cut the other half through the stem into quarters. If you are using wild mushrooms, leave them whole or cut them in ways that preserve their shapes. Put the chopped mushrooms in a saucepan with the meat glaze and its soaking liquid and the heavy cream, bring to a simmer, and simmer gently for about 5 minutes. Remove from the heat, pour into a blender, and process for about 1 minute—hold the blender lid on tight with a towel so the hot mixture doesn't shoot out and burn you—or until smooth. Rinse out the saucepan, strain the puree into the pan, and simmer gently until it thickens to the consistency you like, but don't make it too thick. Set aside.

In a sauté pan or skillet, heat half of the butter over high heat. When it ripples, add the remaining mushrooms and sauté for about 7 minutes, or until well browned. Season with salt and pepper and place in a low oven to keep warm.

In a sauté pan just large enough to hold the noisettes, heat the remaining butter over high heat. When it ripples, add the noisettes a few at a time and brown for about 2 minutes. Turn the heat down to medium and continue browning for about 1 minute longer. Turn the noisettes over, raise the heat to high, and brown for about 2 minutes more, or until the noisettes bounce back to the touch. Transfer them to a plate covered with paper towels and pat them with paper towels to eliminate the cooked fat.

Reheat the sauce gently, season with salt and pepper, and add the vinegar. Taste and adjust with more vinegar, salt, and pepper.

Arrange the noisettes on warmed plates, and spoon the sauce and sautéed mushrooms over the top.

Pork Tenderloin with Apples

To make this dish, you prepare and sauté the pork noisettes in the same way as for Pork Tenderloins with Mushroom Sauce (opposite), but apples and apple juice replace the sautéed mushrooms and pureed mushroom sauce. The Calvados, apple brandy from Normandy, adds a note of authentic flavor, but it can be omitted.

MAKES 4 MAIN-COURSE SERVINGS

2 pork tenderloins, 12 to 14 ounces each

Salt

Pepper

3 tart apples such as Granny Smith

6 tablespoons butter

2 teaspoons sugar

2 tablespoons clarified butter or olive oil

1/2 cup apple cider or 3/4 cup hard cider

2 tablespoons concentrated homemade meat glaze or 1 tablespoon commercial meat glaze (see page 177), softened in 3 tablespoons hot water (optional)

2 tablespoons Calvados (optional)

1 teaspoon wine or cider vinegar, or as needed

If the butcher didn't do it, take the silver skin off the tenderloins, as shown. Cut the tenderloins into 1-inch-thick rounds, or the thickness needed to give you 3 noisettes per serving. Season the noisettes on both sides with salt and pepper and let them rest at room temperature while you prepare the apples.

Peel, halve, and core the apples, and then cut each apple into 8 or more wedges, depending on its size. In a nonstick skillet or sauté pan large enough to hold the apples in a single layer, melt 3 tablespoons of the butter over medium heat. Add the apple wedges, sprinkle with the sugar, and cook for about 12 minutes, or until browned on the first side. Gently turn the wedges over and cook for about 7 minutes longer, or until browned on the second side and soft when poked with a knife. Keep warm in a low oven while you cook the noisettes and make the sauce.

In a sauté pan just large enough to hold the noisettes, heat the clarified butter over high heat. When it ripples, add the noisettes a few at a time and brown for about 2 minutes. Turn

(continued)

HOW TO MAKE SAUTÉED PORK NOISETTES FROM THE TENDERLOIN

1. Trim off the silver skin that covers the tenderloins.

2. Cut the tenderloins into slices about 1 inch thick.

3. Heat oil in a heavy-bottomed sauté pan just large enough to hold the noisettes in a single layer. Add only 2 or 3 noisettes for the first minute.

4. When you have added all the noisettes, keep the pan over the highest heat until well browned. Turn the noisettes two or three at a time and wait for 30 seconds before turning more.

5. Take the noisettes out of the pan and pour out the burnt oil. Deglaze the pan with whatever you choose. Here, broth is used.

6. To give the sauce more body, add a little meat glaze. Simmer the sauce until it is lightly syrupy.

7. Whisk in butter. Season with salt and pepper.

8. Spoon the sauce over the noisettes and serve.

Pork Tenderloin, continued

the heat down to medium and continue browning for about 1 minute longer. Turn the noisettes over, raise the heat to high, and brown for about 2 minutes more, or until the noisettes bounce back to the touch. Transfer them to a plate covered with paper towels and pat them with paper towels to eliminate the cooked fat. Keep them warm in the low oven.

Pour the burnt oil out of the pan, add the apple cider, and boil it down by about half, stirring and scraping the pan bottom with a wooden spoon to loosen any caramelized meat juices. Add the meat glaze and simmer the sauce until it takes on a lightly syrupy consistency. Or, if you haven't used the broth or glaze, simmer the sauce until reduced to about 1/3 cup. Whisk in the remaining 3 tablespoons butter, season with salt and pepper, and add the Calvados and the vinegar. Bring to a simmer and simmer for 30 seconds. Taste and adjust the seasoning with vinegar, salt, and pepper.

Spoon the sauce over the noisettes and the apple wedges on warmed plates.

Sautéed Pork Chops

In recent years, pork chops have become so lean that they dry out easily if you overcook them even slightly. Fattier shoulder chops will stay moister than leaner—and more expensive—rib and loin chops, but they taste best when braised (see page 234), which softens their tissues and releases their fat.

Sautéing pork chops is straightforward, and as is true with all white meats, there is an exact temperature at which the chops are perfect, 135°F. Beyond that they will toughen and dry out.

All the variations on the sautéed pork chop theme have to do with what you do in the way of a pan sauce and whether you surround the chops with vegetables or fruits, included or separate from the sauce. The variations are limitless, but the sauce here made with mustard and little pickles is tangy and bright and cuts through the richness of the chops.

> 4 loin pork chops or center-cut rib pork chops
>
> Salt
>
> Pepper
>
> 3 tablespoons olive oil
>
> 1/3 cup dry white wine or white vermouth
>
> 6 sour gherkins, drained and chopped to the consistency of relish
>
> 1 tablespoon Dijon mustard
>
> 1 tablespoon commercial meat glaze or 2 tablespoons homemade meat glaze (see page 177), softened in 3 tablespoons hot water
>
> 3 tablespoons butter (optional, if using the meat glaze or broth)
>
> 1 tablespoon wine vinegar, or as needed

Season the chops on both sides with salt and pepper and let come to room temperature.

In a sauté pan just large enough to hold the chops, heat the oil over high heat. When it ripples, add the chops and brown for about 3 minutes. Turn the heat down to medium and continue browning for about 1 minute longer. Turn the chops over, raise the heat to high, and brown for about 2 minutes more, or until the chops are firm to the touch or an instant-read thermometer inserted through the side to the center reads 130°F. Transfer the chops to a plate covered with paper towels and pat them with paper towels to blot away the cooked fat.

Pour the burnt oil out of the pan, add the wine, and boil it down by about half, stirring and scraping the pan bottom with a wooden spoon to loosen any caramelized meat juices. Add the gherkins and mustard and the glaze with its soaking liquid, and boil the sauce until it takes on a lightly syrupy consistency. (If you haven't used the meat glaze, it will still turn syrupy, thickened by the mustard.) Whisk in the butter, season with salt and pepper, and add the vinegar. Taste and adjust the seasoning with vinegar, salt, and pepper.

Arrange the chops on warmed plates and spoon the sauce over the top.

1. Ideally, french a rack as described on pages 212–213 and slice it into chops.

2. Put the chops on a hot grill or a hot grill pan. After 2 minutes, give them a 90-degree turn to make grid marks. Grill for 1 to 2 minutes longer.

3. Turn chops and grill on other side for about 2 minutes, then give them a 90-degree turn to make grill marks. Chops are done when firm to the touch and 130°F inside.

4. Serve the grilled chops with gherkin-mustard sauce.

GRILLING AND BARBECUING

Remember, grilling and barbecuing aren't the same thing. Grilling is cooking on a grill over a coal or gas fire until the heat penetrates the meat. Barbecuing implies long, slow cooking, usually with smoke. Authentic barbecuing is, in fact, slow braising, with the juices in the meat and the barbecue sauce that are brushed on it serving as the braising liquid.

Barbecued Pork Spareribs

Regular spareribs are tougher and require longer cooking than baby back ribs, which, as the name implies, are smaller. But regular spareribs have more flavor and are worth the extra time spent brushing and spraying.

MAKES 4 TO 6 MAIN-COURSE SERVINGS

2 cups balsamic vinegar

3 tablespoons sugar

3 cups wood chips, soaked in cold water for 3 hours and drained, or 2 cups sawdust

4 racks of spareribs, about 1½ pounds each, inside membrane trimmed off (see page 218, step 8)

Barbecue Sauce (see page 367)

Build a hot charcoal fire with the coals to one side in a grill with a cover, or preheat a gas grill to high.

In a saucepan, bring the vinegar to a simmer, add the sugar, and stir until the sugar dissolves. Put this mixture into a clean spray bottle (or brush on).

Spread the coals slightly, but still keep them to one side of the grill. If using a gas grill, turn off half of the burners.

Sprinkle the coals with a small handful of the wood chips. If using a gas grill, make a small sawdust-filled packet out of aluminum foil, and place the packet on one of the burners. Brown the spareribs over the coals on both sides and move them to the cool side of the grill. Spray the ribs with the vinegar mixture and cover the grill.

Continue cooking in this way, spraying the ribs every 5 to 10 minutes and brushing them with the sauce every 10 minutes. Turn the ribs every hour or so and add more hot coals, chips, or a new sawdust packet as the originals become spent. Cook for about 3 hours, or until one of the ribs pulls away easily.

Inventing Your Own Stir-Fries

This technique is very similar to sautéing, except that a wok is usually used instead of a sauté pan. A wok makes it easy to keep ingredients in motion over high heat and prevent burning. In most stir-fries, ingredients are cut into small pieces so they cook quickly (originally to minimize the use of costly firewood), and the sauce, if any, is made directly in the wok with the meat, seafood, and/or vegetables that comprise the dish. Often cornstarch is used as a thickener. When inventing stir-fries, keep in mind that certain ingredients always contribute flavor and excitement: garlic (minced), ginger (grated), sesame oil (the dark Asian kind), hoisin sauce, fresh chiles (minced), pineapple juice, and orange zest (grated or julienned). All or some of these ingredients can be used to marinate meat or seafood and the marinade then brought to a boil and used as the sauce for the ingredients you're stir-frying.

PORK STIR-FRIES

Pork is especially well suited to stir-frying because tender cuts are inexpensive and don't dry out. The best cut for a stir-fry is the tenderloin, which should be cut into narrow 3-inch-long strips. The premise of a stir-fry is to brown the meat quickly—stir-frying is essentially sautéing—and then add flavorings and other ingredients that are also cooked relatively quickly. Sometimes a stir-fry is finished with liquid, such as broth, or with cornstarch mixed with a little broth to thicken the sauce. Stir-fries are easy to improvise with what you have on hand, but certain stir-fry staples, such as snow peas, pineapple, cashews, and tofu, are particularly good additions for texture.

Sweet-and-Sour Pork

We never seem to tire of this satisfying classic. This recipe is typical except for the cashews, which add an essential crunch, and the dark sesame oil, which lends a deep complexity. Once you have prepped all the ingredients—which you can do earlier the same day—it only takes 5 minutes or so to cook the dish.

MAKES 6 MAIN-COURSE SERVINGS WHEN SERVED WITH 4 TO 5 OTHER MAIN-COURSE DISHES

1 pound pork loin, cut into $3/4$-inch cubes

1 teaspoon dark sesame oil

2 tablespoons grated ginger

1 clove garlic, minced, and then crushed to a paste with the flat side of the knife

Two 8-ounce cans cubed pineapple

4 tablespoons balsamic vinegar

1 cup plus 1 tablespoon vegetable oil

Flour for dredging

$1/2$ cup cashews, toasted for 10 minutes in a 300°F oven or until pale brown

1 bell pepper, cut into 1-inch squares

Combine the pork with the sesame oil, ginger, and garlic. Open the cans of pineapple and drain the liquid over the pork. Sprinkle the vinegar over. Toss the pork and let marinate for 5 minutes (if you're in a mad rush) to overnight (if you've had some foresight).

When ready to serve, heat 1 cup of the vegetable oil in a wok or heavy skillet until it ripples and just begins to smoke. Drain the pork, saving the liquid, and dredge it in flour. Using a spider or slotted spoon, gently lower one-third of the pork into the hot oil. Fry for about 30 seconds, and then transfer it to paper towels to drain. Repeat with the next third and then the last third of the pork. Discard the hot oil in the wok and add the remaining 1 tablespoon of fresh oil. Over high heat, stir the cashews and bell pepper in the hot oil for about 1 minute. Add the pork, pineapple, and the reserved marinade and stir until the sauce thickens, about 1 minute. Serve immediately.

HOW TO MAKE SWEET-AND-SOUR PORK

1. Marinate the pork.

2. Stir-fry the pork quickly in hot oil, cooking in small batches and transferring to paper towels to drain.

3. Add the rest of the ingredients and a little fresh oil to the wok and stir-fry briefly. Stir in the pork, pineapple, and reserved marinade and serve.

CHICKEN AND TURKEY

Chicken is truly versatile. Almost any technique can be used to cook it, and because its flavor is relatively neutral, it adapts well to countless flavor combinations. However you prepare chicken and turkey, one secret to success remains: don't overcook them. Most cooks follow recipes that call for cooking the bird to a temperature of 160°F or higher for fear of salmonella. But in fact, a whole chicken or turkey is done when the innermost part—where the thigh joint lodges in the back—reaches 140°F. The salmonella organism dies at a temperature of 137°F, and since the bacteria is found not in the meat, but only on the surface and in the cavity, both of which become much hotter than 137°F by the time the chicken is cooked to an internal temperature of 140°F, there is no need to overcook the chicken. If you are cooking chicken parts, they are done when the breast and thigh meat bounce back to the touch. When you cut the thigh away from the breast of a roast chicken or turkey, the thigh meat near the joint should still be pink or have red streaks. The meat is only undercooked when it is shiny and translucent looking.

ROAST CHICKEN

Inexplicably, roasting a chicken intimidates even experienced cooks, which is strange only because it is almost impossible to go wrong. If you overcook your chicken, the breast meat will be a little dry and if your oven isn't hot enough initially the skin may not brown, but in either case your chicken will still be perfectly delicious. Here are some tips that guarantee a perfectly roasted chicken:

1. **START THE CHICKEN IN A VERY HOT OVEN.**
   This ensures that the chicken will brown. If it starts to get too brown, you can always turn the oven down, but if the bird starts out in too low an oven, it may not brown by the time it cooks through.

2. **ROAST THE CHICKEN IN A HEAVY-BOTTOMED VESSEL AS CLOSE TO THE SIZE OF THE CHICKEN AS POSSIBLE.**
   Cast-iron skillets are often just the right size. Spread the giblets around the chicken so there is no space in the pan that is not covered. This prevents the juices from the chicken from burning on the pan bottom.

3. **DON'T USE A ROASTING RACK.**
   A rack keeps the chicken above the roasting pan. The roasting pan gets very hot, and as the juices from the chicken drip down onto it, they burn and smoke up the kitchen.

4. **TRUSS THE BIRD.**
   For even cooking and a prettier finished bird, truss the chicken as shown on page 245. Let the chicken rest for about 10 minutes, covered loosely with aluminum foil, before serving. This allows the heat to continue to penetrate to the inside of the chicken and leaves it cooked more evenly.

5. **COVER THE BREAST WITH ALUMINUM FOIL.**
   There is the inherent problem of the breasts cooking faster than the thighs, so they dry out by the time the thighs are done. Fold a sheet of foil into a triple-thick layer, butter one side, and use it to cover the breast meat for the first 20 to 30 minutes of roasting, to slow down the cooking of the breast meat.

Roast Chicken

The rite of carving makes a roast chicken seem like a special occasion, and with a little practice, any cook can look like an expert. The photos on page 246 show the basic way to carve a chicken: into 2 breasts and 2 thighs with the drumsticks attached.

MAKES 4 MAIN-COURSE SERVINGS

> **One 4-pound chicken**
> **Salt**
> **Pepper**
> **1 tablespoon butter, room-temperature**

Jus or Gravy (optional)

> **2 pounds chicken drumsticks, wings, or backs, chopped into 2-inch pieces with a cleaver**
> **1 large carrot, cut into 1-inch sections**
> **1 onion, quartered**
> **2 teaspoons flour if making gravy**
> **1 cup chicken jus from roasting pan or chicken broth or water**

Preheat the oven to 450°F. Truss the chicken if you want to go to the trouble and season the chicken on the outside with salt and pepper. Take a sheet of aluminum foil about 18 inches long and fold it to create a triple thickness. It will need to be vaguely trapezoidal to cover the breasts and not the thighs. Smear one side with the butter and place it, buttered side down, over the chicken breasts.

If you are making a jus or gravy, spread the chicken parts, carrot, and onion in a roasting pan or skillet just large enough to hold them in a single layer and roast for 20 minutes.

Place the chicken in a pan just large enough to hold it or in the pan with the chicken parts. Roast the chicken for 25 minutes, take off the foil, and roast for 15 minutes more. Check the temperature by sticking an instant-read thermometer about 3 inches in through the skin between the breast and the thigh. When it reads 140°F, take the chicken out of the pan. If you don't have a thermometer, judge the doneness by lifting the chicken and tilting it so some of the juices run out of the cavity. If the juices are pink and cloudy, the chicken isn't done. If they are clear but streaked with red, it is done. If they are perfectly clear, with no red, the chicken is overdone. Lift the chicken out of the roasting pan by inserting a wooden spoon into the cavity. Tilt the chicken so any juice in the cavity runs into the pan. Let the chicken rest in a warm place loosely covered with aluminum foil for 10 minutes before serving.

If you are making a jus or gravy, look in the roasting pan to see if the juices have caramelized. If they have, the bottom of the pan will be coated with brown and a layer of clear fat will be floating on top. Just pour or spoon off the fat and discard it. If they haven't caramelized, you will see brown liquid combined with the fat. The mixture of fat and juices may even be cloudy, meaning the juices have emulsified with the fat, which you want to avoid. If the juices haven't caramelized, put the roasting pan on the stove top and boil the juices until they caramelize on the bottom and separate from the fat, and then pour off the fat. You now have a roasting pan with a layer of caramelized juices and no or very little fat. Add a small amount of water or chicken broth, put the pan on the stove, and scrape the bottom with a wooden spoon for a couple of minutes to dissolve the caramelized juices. Strain the juices and serve in a warmed sauceboat.

If you want to thicken the juices into a gravy—not usually worth the bother with a roast chicken—leave about a tablespoon of fat in with the juices, add 2 teaspoons flour, stir it in the fat over the heat for a minute, and then whisk in the water or chicken broth.

Carve the chicken (see page 246). If you need to divide the meat more equitably, cut the breasts crosswise in half and cut the thighs away from the drumsticks. Give everyone half of a breast and a thigh or a drumstick. Pass the jus or gravy in a sauceboat.

(continued)

Safety

If not handled carefully, raw chicken can contaminate other foods with salmonella. Never, for example, cut up a chicken on a cutting board and then use the same cutting board, unwashed, to cut other ingredients that you will be serving raw or to later carve the cooked chicken. Cutting boards used for raw chicken should be well washed with hot water mixed with a little bleach to disinfect them. When working with raw chicken, wash your hands constantly.

1. Slide a length of string under the tail and about an inch farther back.

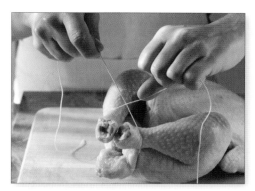

2. Cross the string over the drumsticks, and then tuck it under the drumsticks on the opposite side. Bring the string along the sides of the chicken over the unfolded wings and flip the chicken over.

3. Pull the string over the back of the chicken.

4. Tie a knot and tuck under the wings.

5. Butter a triple thickness of foil for each chicken.

6. Lay the foil over the chicken breasts; don't cover the thighs.

7. Arrange the chickens on a bed of vegetables and chicken parts.

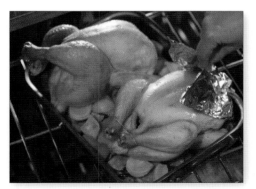

8. Roast for 25 minutes and remove the foil.

9. Roast until golden brown and internal temperature is 140°F.

Roast Chicken, continued

VARIATIONS

A lot of roast chicken recipes call for putting something in the cavity—often a lemon—but since a membrane separates the cavity from the meat, this does little to enhance the flavor of the chicken. Other recipes call for stuffing the chicken, often with elaborate mixtures, but in order to cook through the stuffing and make sure it is hot enough to kill bacteria, you have to overcook the chicken. A better solution is to slide flavorful ingredients under the skin, such as wonderfully aromatic tarragon or sage leaves. You can also slice large mushrooms, such as porcini or portobellos, about 1/4 inch thick, sauté them in butter or olive oil, and then slide these under the breast skin. Or, you can chop mushrooms, cook them down on the stove top until the water they release evaporates,

season with salt and pepper, and stuff this mixture under the breast skin. When you do this, don't bother with the buttered aluminum foil, since the stuffing protects the breast meat from the heat. If you want to serve your dinner guests a whole breast each with the stuffing, roast 2 chickens and serve the thighs after or save them for leftovers.

Perhaps the earliest recipe that recommends stuffing aromatic ingredients under the skin is one that calls for truffles. The chicken, which looks like it has been in a fight, is covered with black spots, a dish the French call chicken in half mourning. If you decide to embark on such an extravagant project, slide the truffles under the skin the night before you plan on roasting and wrap the chicken in aluminum foil. Leave it wrapped in the foil when you roast it. It won't come out of the oven brown and crispy, but all of the truffle aroma will be intact and the juice that collects in the foil will be celestial.

HOW TO CARVE A ROAST CHICKEN

1. Slide the carving knife under the thigh, and begin detaching it from the breast.

2. Cut through the joint and detach the thigh.

3. Slide the knife into the joint connecting the wing and detach the wing.

4. Slide the knife along one side of the breastbone, detaching the breast meat.

5. Repeat on the other side.

1. Put the roasting pan with the vegetables and juices over high heat and cook until you only see clear fat.

2. Pour the fat out of the tilted pan.

3. Deglaze the pan with broth or water.

4. Over medium heat, scrape the pan with a wooden spoon to dissolve the carmelized juices.

5. Strain into a saucepan or sauceboat.

CHICKEN JUS OR GRAVY

It is perfectly fine to serve a roast chicken with no sauce at all, but a light gravy or jus will enhance its flavor. A jus is simply a gravy that hasn't been thickened. In its purest form, it is just the drippings from the chicken. In authentic roasting—cooking on a spit—a pan is placed under the chicken to catch the juices, and that's it. When roasting in the oven, the pan that catches the juices is the roasting pan itself, and because this pan is hot, the juices often dry and caramelize on the pan bottom. If the pan isn't completely covered with the chicken and pieces of chicken, the juices can even burn. The chicken also releases fat that has to be separated from the juices.

Because a properly roasted chicken doesn't release much in the way of juices—an overcooked chicken releases lots of juices—it is helpful to augment the juices by adding chicken parts, like wings or drumsticks, to the pan along with an onion and a carrot. To get the chicken parts started, put the roasting pan with the chicken parts and vegetables in the hot oven about 20 minutes before adding the chicken.

When you have established that your chicken has reached the correct doneness temperature, cover it loosely with aluminum foil and keep it in a warm place while you figure out what to do about the jus.

1. Turn the chicken breast-side down and cut through the wing joints, detaching the wings.

2. Cut the wing off at the second joint, so you leave a little still attached to the breast.

3. Pull a thigh forward and cut through the skin that runs along the side of the thigh.

4. Continue cutting until you reach the back, and then slide the knife along the back, under the oyster, the tiny nugget of meat nestled in the back.

9. Turn the chicken so the pointed end of the breasts is facing up. Whack through the bone with a knife to cut through the ribs and separate them from the back.

10. Pull the ribs away from the breasts.

11. Snap off the section with the ribs. Cut around the inside of the collarbone to detach the rib section.

12. Pull the skin over the breasts so they are both well covered.

HOW TO BONE CHICKEN BREASTS

1. Pull the skin off the breasts.

2. Cut along the bone.

3. Completely cut away the bone.

4. Hack off the knob at the end of the wing joint.

5. Continue in this way until you have completely detached the thigh.

6. Rotate the chicken around and repeat on the other side.

7. Cut through the skin that connects the other thigh to the back.

8. Completely remove the second thigh.

13. Turn the breasts skin side down, and slice a knife through the cartilage that separates them.

14. Draw the knife forward through the breast.

15. Cut all the way through the double breast.

16. Separated breasts.

HOW TO PREPARE CHICKEN THIGHS

1. Cut the joint and separate the thigh and drumstick.

2. Hack off the joint at the end of the thigh.

3. Slide a knife under the bone in the thigh, and cut through the joint that attaches it to the drumstick. This allows the thighs to cook at the same rate as the breasts.

4. Detach the thigh bone from the drumstick bone.

SAUTÉED CHICKEN

The tastiest way to sauté a whole chicken is to cut it up into 2 breasts and 2 thighs and sauté it in butter or olive oil. Always use a pan just large enough to hold the pieces. If the pan is too big, the juices run into the exposed parts and burn. Cover any spaces with the chicken giblets and the chicken back. Start the chicken skin side down so that the skin renders its fat and turns crispy. A nonstick pan is handy, since chicken skin can stick. If you don't have a nonstick pan, move the pan quickly back and forth on the burner during the first few minutes of cooking. If the chicken is sticking when you try to turn it, cook it for a few minutes more. It will often come loose when the skin cooks a bit longer.

Chicken Sautéed in Butter

The amount of butter in this recipe often puts off cooks and guests, but very little of it is actually absorbed by the chicken. In fact, if you measure both the fat that goes into the dish and the fat that comes out, you will discover more fat comes out. That's because the butter causes the fat in the skin to render and liquefy. And even though very little butter is absorbed, the chicken has an intensely buttery flavor because the proteins in the butter cling to the skin and flavor it. Many guests have declared this simple dish the best chicken they have ever eaten. If you are dead set against the butter, substitute olive oil.

MAKES 4 MAIN-COURSE SERVINGS

> **One 4-pound chicken**
> **Salt**
> **Pepper**
> **4 tablespoons butter or pure olive oil**

Cut up the chicken as shown on pages 248–249 and season the pieces on both sides with salt and pepper.

In a skillet just large enough to hold the chicken, heat the butter or olive oil over medium to high heat. Put the chicken pieces, skin side down, in the pan and cook for about 12 minutes, or until the skin is golden brown. Turn the pieces over and cook for about 7 minutes longer, or until the thighs and breasts are firm to the touch. Serve immediately.

VARIATIONS

Nearly every country in the world has simple sautéed chicken recipes such as this one. European recipes, especially French ones, tell you to pour out and discard the fat in the pan, and then put together some kind of sauce or garnish in the pan used to cook the chicken. This makes sense if you have used a traditional pan (not nonstick), which will have savory juices clinging to it. But if you have used a nonstick pan, there will be no clinging juices, so you can just as easily put together a sauce or garnish in another pan or saucepan while the chicken is cooking.

Chicken with Tomatoes and Tarragon or Basil

Make this dish near the end of the summer, when perfect tomatoes are in season.

MAKES 4 MAIN-COURSE SERVINGS

> **Sautéed Chicken in Butter (opposite)**
> **1/2 cup dry white wine or white vermouth**
> **4 large or 6 medium tomatoes, peeled, seeded, and finely chopped**
> **1/3 cup heavy cream (optional)**
> **Leaves from 10 sprigs tarragon or 20 fresh basil leaves, chopped at the last minute**
> **Salt**
> **Pepper**

Prepare the chicken as directed, and then transfer to warmed plates or a platter and pour the fat out of the pan. Pour the wine into the pan and boil over high heat until reduced by about half. Add the tomatoes and continue boiling, stirring every minute or two, for about 15 minutes, or until the sauce thickens.

Add the cream, boil for about 2 minutes more—don't overdo it, or the sauce will be too thick and gloppy—and add the herbs. Simmer for 30 seconds, season with salt and pepper, and serve over the chicken.

Chicken with Red Wine Sauce

This abbreviated version of coq au vin is best made with red wine chicken stock, which is broth made exactly like brown chicken broth, except that red wine is used instead of water (but you can get by without it). Use a soft, low-tannin, low-acidic wine, such as a Merlot from Argentina. If you want to make this dish more like an authentic coq au vin, add the Burgundian garnish—the pearl onions, bacon, and mushrooms.

MAKES 4 MAIN-COURSE SERVINGS

> Sautéed Chicken in Butter (opposite)
>
> 1 cup red wine or red wine chicken stock (brown broth made with wine, see page 36)
>
> 2 tablespoons homemade meat glaze or 1 tablespoon commercial meat glaze (see page 177), dissolved in 3 tablespoons hot water (optional)
>
> 1 tablespoon balsamic vinegar
>
> 2 tablespoons butter
>
> 1 tablespoon heavy cream, broth, or water, or more as needed (optional)
>
> Salt
>
> Pepper

Prepare the chicken as directed, and then transfer to warmed plates or a platter and pour the fat out of the pan. Pour the wine and the reduced stock or glaze into the pan and boil down until lightly syrupy. This will happen faster if you are using meat glaze and will not happen if you do not use the stock or glaze. Add the vinegar, boil for 30 seconds, and whisk in the butter. If the sauce gets too thick, thin it with a little heavy cream, broth, or water.

Season with salt and pepper and pour over the chicken or pass in a sauceboat at the table.

Chicken Cacciatore

This combination of mushrooms and tomatoes is traditional and hard to resist. Try to find cremini mushrooms, which have much more flavor than their cultivated white cousins. For the best result, be sure to sauté the mushrooms over high heat so they brown rather than stew. The recipe calls for using unpeeled tomatoes and then straining out the peels, but you can also peel and seed the tomatoes or use canned tomatoes and avoid the straining step. If you don't strain the sauce, remember to pick out and discard the bay leaves.

MAKES 4 MAIN-COURSE SERVINGS

> 2 tablespoons butter or olive oil
>
> 1 onion, chopped
>
> 2 cloves garlic, minced
>
> 1 teaspoon fresh thyme leaves or $^1/_2$ teaspoon dried thyme
>
> 4 large or 6 medium tomatoes, coarsely chopped
>
> 1 cup chicken broth or water
>
> 2 bay leaves
>
> 1 pound cremini or cultivated white mushrooms
>
> 2 tablespoons olive oil
>
> Sautéed Chicken in Butter (see page 250)
>
> Salt
>
> Pepper

In a medium saucepan, melt the butter over medium to high heat. Add the onion, garlic, and thyme and cook, stirring occasionally, for about 10 minutes, or until the onion is translucent. Add the tomatoes, broth, and bay leaves and simmer gently for about 15 minutes, or until the mixture thickens. Use the back of a ladle to work the mixture through a strainer into a bowl (or into the cooked mushrooms, if they are ready).

Meanwhile, wash and dry the mushrooms. Cut the end off the bottom of each mushroom stem if dried out or dirty, and then cut through the stem into quarters. In a large sauté pan, heat the oil over high heat until it begins to smoke. Add half of the mushrooms and toss and stir for 2 to 3 minutes, or until they start to brown. Add the rest of the mushrooms and continuing sautéing for about 6 minutes, or until all the mushrooms are well browned and fragrant. If the mushrooms release water—something to avoid—continue cooking until all the water evaporates. Stir the mushrooms into the tomato sauce (or strain the tomato sauce into the mushrooms).

While the sauce is cooking, cook the chicken as directed and then transfer to warmed plates or a platter. Season the sauce with salt and pepper and serve over the chicken.

Chicken with Simplified Mole Sauce

Traditional mole sauces contain a frightening number of ingredients—although not always chocolate—but an excellent mole can be made with far fewer. A mix that includes all four dried chile varieties makes the flavor of the sauce more complex and intriguing, though it will still be satisfying with only one type. Serve this dish with rice or warm tortillas.

MAKES 4 MAIN-COURSE SERVINGS

12 dried chiles such as mulatto, ancho, pasilla, and/or chilhuacle negro, preferably a mix

1 chipotle chile, soaked in warm water for 30 minutes to soften, then drained

2 tablespoons vegetable oil

1 teaspoon ground coriander

1/4 cup almonds

1 onion, chopped

2 cloves garlic, chopped

2 tomatoes, chopped

2 cups chicken broth or water

1/4 cup raisins

1/4 teaspoon ground cloves

1/2 teaspoon ground cinnamon

1 teaspoon sugar

1 tablespoon sherry vinegar, or to taste

Salt

Pepper

Sautéed Chicken in Butter (see page 250)

Put all the chiles, except the chipotle, in a cast-iron skillet over medium heat and toast for about 5 minutes. Rearrange them every couple of minutes and turn them over so they are all roasted the same amount. Put them in a bowl with warm water to cover and move them around every 10 minutes for about 30 minutes total, or until they are soft and pliable.

Drain the chiles, cut off the stems, and rinse out the seeds. Stem and seed the chipotle chile. Cut all the chiles into several pieces each.

In a saucepan, heat the oil over medium to high heat. Add the coriander, almonds, onion, and garlic and cook gently for about 12 minutes, or until the onion is translucent. Add the tomatoes and broth and simmer for about 5 minutes, or until the sauce thickens.

Remove from the heat, let cool slightly, pour into a blender (see precautions on page 42), and add the raisins, chiles, cloves, and cinnamon. Process for 1 minute, or until smooth, and then strain through a medium-mesh strainer into a clean pot. Bring the mixture back to a simmer, add the sugar and vinegar, and season with salt and pepper. Taste and add more vinegar if needed.

While the sauce is cooking, cook the chicken as directed and then transfer to a warmed platter. Spoon the sauce over the top.

Provençal Chicken with Aioli, Tomatoes, and Basil

The trick to this dish comes from a Provençal fish stew called a bourride (see page 56), in which the stewing liquid for the fish is thickened with aioli. Remember when chopping basil to sprinkle it with a little olive oil and chop it at the last minute so it doesn't turn black. You can be more or less refined about the tomatoes as you like: peel and trim away the inner pulp as shown on page 85, so you end up with perfect dice, or just peel, seed, and coarsely chop.

MAKES 4 MAIN-COURSE SERVINGS

Sautéed Chicken in Butter (see page 250)

1 cup chicken broth, preferably brown chicken broth

4 tomatoes, peeled, seeded, and diced or coarsely chopped (see headnote)

1/2 cup aioli (see page 360)

1/2 teaspoon saffron threads, soaked in 1 tablespoon water for 30 minutes

20 fresh basil leaves, finely chopped

Salt

Pepper

Cook the chicken as directed and transfer to warmed soup plates. Just before the chicken is ready, bring the broth to a simmer in a saucepan and add the tomatoes. Put the aioli in a bowl and slowly pour in half of the broth while whisking constantly. Pour this mixture into the broth remaining in the saucepan and whisk over low heat for just a minute or two to make sure the broth is nice and hot. Don't let it boil or the aioli will curdle.

Whisk in the saffron and its soaking water and the basil and season with salt and pepper. Pour the brothlike sauce over the chicken and serve.

Moroccan Chicken Tagine

Moroccan cooks have a light touch with the spices—ginger, cinnamon, cumin—that give their cuisine its identity. This dish calls for saffron, which you should buy in a relatively large amount, such as an ounce, to make it more affordable. If you decide to add the olives, be sure to use good-quality ones, rather than bland canned ripe olives. Serve the chicken and its wonderfully light sauce with rice or couscous in warmed soup plates.

MAKES 4 MAIN-COURSE SERVINGS

- 1/2 cup sliced almonds
- Sautéed Chicken in Butter (see page 250)
- 2 tablespoons olive oil
- 4 cloves garlic, finely chopped
- 2 jalapeño chiles, seeded and finely chopped
- 1 onion, finely chopped
- 1-inch piece fresh ginger, peeled and grated
- 1/2 teaspoon ground cinnamon
- 1 teaspoon ground cumin
- 1 teaspoon paprika
- 1/4 teaspoon ground cloves
- 2 chipotle chiles, soaked in warm water for 30 minutes, drained, seeded, and finely chopped
- 2 cups chicken broth, preferably brown chicken broth
- 4 tomatoes, peeled, seeded, and chopped
- 1/2 teaspoon saffron threads, soaked in 1 tablespoon water for 30 minutes
- 1/2 cup pitted black olives (optional)
- 2 tablespoons diced preserved lemon, homemade (see page 124) or store-bought
- Salt
- Pepper
- Harissa sauce, homemade (see page 50) or store-bought

Preheat the oven to 350°F. Spread the almonds on a pie pan and toast in the oven, stirring occasionally, for about 12 minutes, or until they are fragrant and have taken on color. Pour onto a plate and let cool.

Cook the chicken as directed. While the chicken is cooking, in a sauté pan, heat the oil over medium-high heat. Add the garlic, jalapeño chiles, and onion and cook, stirring occasionally, for 10 minutes, or until the onion is translucent. Add the ginger, cinnamon, cumin, paprika, cloves, and chipotle chiles and cook for 1 minute more. Add the broth, tomatoes, and the saffron and its soaking water and bring to a simmer.

Just before serving, add the olives and lemons to the sauce and simmer for about 2 minutes. Season with salt (it may not need any because of the lemons and olives) and pepper. When the chicken is ready, place in warmed soup plates and ladle the sauce over the top. Sprinkle almonds over each serving. Pass the harissa at the table.

Coconut Curry Chicken

You can make this dish with heavy cream, instead of coconut milk—use 1 cup cream in place of the coconut milk—but it will be substantially richer. This dish is great served with jasmine or basmati rice.

MAKES 4 MAIN-COURSE SERVINGS

- Sautéed Chicken in Butter (see page 250)
- 2 tablespoons butter
- 2 teaspoons flour
- 1 tablespoon curry powder
- One 15-ounce can unsweetened coconut milk, preferably Thai
- 2 jalapeño chiles, seeded and finely chopped
- Leaves from 1 small bunch cilantro, chopped at the last minute
- Salt
- Pepper

Prepare the chicken as directed, and then transfer to a warmed shallow serving platter. Just before the chicken is ready, in a small saucepan, melt the butter over medium heat and add the flour and curry powder. Stir with a whisk for about 1 minute, or until the curry smells fragrant, then pour in the coconut milk and add the chiles. Bring to a simmer and simmer gently for 5 minutes, or until the sauce has the consistency you like.

Add the cilantro, simmer for 1 minute more, and season with salt and pepper. Pour the sauce over the chicken and serve right away.

Sautéed Boneless, Skinless Chicken Breasts

Chicken breasts are a lot tastier cooked with their bone and skin intact, but there are ways to enhance the flavor of boneless, skinless breasts. You can always serve them with a sauce—the sauces served with bone-in, skin-on sautéed chicken breasts on pages 250 to 253 work for boneless breasts, too—or you can coat them. If you are cooking a boneless breast with no flour or breading, sauté it over the highest heat possible so that it browns, which will accentuate its flavor.

Keep in mind that the oil you use to sauté the breasts is not absorbed by the chicken, so you don't need to count the calories.

MAKES 4 MAIN-COURSE SERVINGS

> **3 tablespoons olive oil or canola oil**
> **4 boneless, skinless chicken breasts**
> **Salt**
> **Pepper**

In a skillet just large enough to hold the breasts, heat the oil over high heat. Season the breasts on both sides with salt and pepper. When the oil begins to smoke, add the breasts and cook, turning once, for about 4 to 6 minutes on each side, or until they bounce back to the touch. Pat the breasts with paper towels to remove any burnt oil before serving.

Sautéed Boneless Chicken Breasts with Madeira Sauce

Since the main reason for cooking boneless, skinless chicken breasts is speed, it is handy to have an all-purpose sauce to liven them up a little. (You will find more ideas in the Sauces chapter.) The butter in this sauce gives it a silky texture, but it can also be left out. Any sweet wine, such as Marsala or port, can be substituted for the Madeira.

MAKES 4 MAIN-COURSE SERVINGS

> **Sautéed Boneless, skinless Chicken Breasts (above)**
> **1 shallot, finely chopped**
> **1/2 cup Rainwater or Malmsey Madeira**
> **1 cup brown chicken broth boiled down**
>   **to 1/4 cup, or 1 tablespoon commercial meat glaze**
>   **or 2 tablespoons homemade meat glaze (page 177),**
>   **softened with 1 tablespoon hot water (optional)**
> **1 tablespoon finely chopped fresh parsley**
> **2 tablespoons butter (optional)**
> **Salt**
> **Pepper**

Cook the chicken breasts as directed and transfer to warmed plates. Pour the burnt fat out of the pan, add the shallot to the still-hot pan, and whisk over medium heat for about 1 minute, or until the shallot smells toasty. Add the Madeira—stand back in case it ignites—and boil down until reduced by about half. Add the broth or glaze—if you are using the glaze, you will have to stir it around until it dissolves and perhaps add a little water if the mixture gets too thick—and simmer the sauce until it has a lightly syrupy consistency.

Stir in the parsley, whisk in the butter, and season with salt and pepper. If the sauce is too thick, add a teaspoon or two of broth, water, or heavy cream. Spoon the sauce over the chicken breasts and serve right away.

BREADED AND FLOURED BONELESS CHICKEN BREASTS

You can also coat boneless, skinless chicken breasts with flour, egg, or bread crumbs, or all three, which will give the breasts more texture and, depending on what you sauté them in, more flavor. A simple dredging in flour will make the chicken breast a bit crispier and will allow you to sauté it on a slightly lower heat than if you were cooking it with no coating at all. If you then dip it in egg, a treatment the French call à la parisienne, you can cook it on relatively low heat. You will have made it richer but also more flavorful. Last, if you decide to give it a final coating with bread crumbs after you have dipped it in egg, or à l'anglaise, you must cook it gently so the breading doesn't burn. Here are the tricks for magnificent breaded chicken:

1. **USE FRESH BREAD CRUMBS.**
   Use only fresh bread crumbs (not store-bought), made from fresh fine-crumb white bread, such as Pepperidge Farm Original White Bread, rather than a foam-textured white bread. Panko crumbs work well in a pinch.

2. **USE FINELY TEXTURED BREAD CRUMBS.**
   Pass the bread crumbs through a fine-mesh strainer or a drum sieve so they are uniformly fine. This ensures they will absorb only minimal fat.

3. **USE BUTTER.**
   Cook the breaded breasts in butter, preferably clarified butter so the milk solids don't cling to the breading and burn. The bread crumbs absorb the fat, so the fat must have a good flavor.

4. USE A LOT OF BUTTER.

The breading won't absorb it all—you end up actually eating very little—and you need a generous amount so the breading browns evenly.

5. STRAIN FAT BETWEEN PANFULS.

If you are cooking a lot of breaded breasts, you can keep using the same butter in the pan, but strain it between each use to rid it of crumbs, which can burn and ruin the taste of your butter.

6. DON'T OVERFLATTEN THE CHICKEN.

Flatten the breasts by whacking them with the side of a cleaver, but don't overdo it or the meat will dry out. Just flatten the thicker side enough so that the breast is of even thickness.

7. BREAD THE BREASTS JUST BEFORE YOU COOK THEM.

If you coat the breasts and then let them sit while you work on another task, the coating becomes partially absorbed and the breading will peel away from the meat while it is in the pan.

8. SERVE SAUCE ON THE SIDE.

If you want to serve a sauce with a breaded chicken breast, don't pour the sauce over the breasts, which will make the breading soggy. Instead, serve the sauce around the breasts. If you want to lighten the dish and prevent the bottom of the breasts from getting soggy, bread them on one side—the top side—only.

HOW TO MAKE FRESH BREAD CRUMBS

1. Cut the crusts off white bread.

2. Cut the bread into cubes, and process in a food processor.

3. Work the bread crumbs through a fine-mesh strainer.

4. Or work bread crumbs through a drum sieve.

HOW TO BREAD CHICKEN BREASTS WITH FRESH BREAD CRUMBS

1. Pound the chicken breasts on the thicker side so they are an even thickness.

2. Dredge the chicken in flour. Pat off the excess flour.

3. Dip the chicken in egg beaten with salt and pepper. Wipe off the excess egg.

4. Dip in the bread crumbs, coating evenly.

HOW TO SAUTÉ BREADED CHICKEN

1. Put the chicken, most attractive side down, in clarified butter in a nonstick pan over medium heat.

2. Turn after about 3 minutes, or when golden brown. Cook on the second side until firm to the touch.

3. Put on paper towels to absorb the excess butter.

Breaded Boneless and Skinless Chicken Breasts

Breaded chicken and veal have a bad name because most of us have tasted indifferent weinerschnitzel or some version of veal scaloppine overcooked in burnt vegetable oil. In fact, a properly breaded chicken breast cooked in clarified butter is one of the most satisfying ways to cook chicken.

MAKES 4 MAIN-COURSE SERVINGS

> 4 slices dense-crumb white bread such as Pepperidge Farm, crusts removed
>
> 1/3 cup flour
>
> 1 egg
>
> 2 teaspoons salt
>
> Pepper
>
> 4 boneless, skinless chicken breasts
>
> 4 tablespoons clarified butter (see page 341)

Cut the bread slices into quarters, place on a sheet pan, and heat in a 200°F oven for about 10 minutes, or just long enough to eliminate some of their moisture but not dry them out. Let cool. Process the bread in a food processor for about 1 minute, or until finely ground, then pass the crumbs through a fine-mesh strainer or a drum sieve so they are fine and uniform.

Put the bread crumbs and the flour on 2 separate plates. In a soup plate or small baking dish, beat the egg with the salt and a few grinds of pepper. Flatten each breast by pounding the thicker end with the side of a cleaver until the breast is of even thickness.

Working with 1 breast at a time, coat the breast with flour, pat off the excess, and dip it in the egg. Hold the breast above the egg by pinching one end, and then with the thumb and index finger of your other hand, wipe off any excess egg. Lay the breast down on the bread crumbs, wipe your hands to avoid getting egg into the crumbs, and carefully turn the breast over to coat it on the other side. As the breasts are coated, place them on a plate.

In a skillet (preferably nonstick), heat the clarified butter over medium to high heat. Gently add the breasts, most attractive side down, and cook, turning once, for 3 to 6 minutes on each side, or until evenly golden brown and firm to the touch. Don't use tongs to turn the breasts, as they will tear the coating. Instead, use a spatula and your hand. Drain briefly on paper towels and serve immediately.

VARIATIONS

One of the best variations is to replace the bread crumbs in this recipe with very finely grated Parmigiano-Reggiano or other hard dry cheese. You can also replace the bread crumbs with finely chopped mushrooms, or you can grind dried porcini or morel mushrooms, strain to obtain a fine powder, and use the powder in place of the flour. The breasts can then be sautéed with just the mushroom powder, or they can also be dipped in egg and bread crumbs.

BRAISED CHICKEN

Old-fashioned recipes for long-cooked chicken stews, such as authentic coq au vin or poule au pot, were made with a mature rooster (a coq) or hen (a poule) that was cooked for hours to soften its tough flesh. Since nowadays it is rare to encounter a hen, and almost impossible to find a rooster, most modern equivalents to these traditional recipes call for an ordinary chicken and cook it just long enough to heat it through (for more about braising, see pages 10–11).

A fricassee is a specific French dish served with mushrooms and baby onions, but the term also refers to a technique in which a cut-up chicken is lightly browned, as you do when sautéing chicken, and then liquid is added and the chicken is braised. The difference between a fricassee and sautéed chicken with a sauce is somewhat subtle, but fricassees often serve as the model for more refined and complicated (and rich) dishes in which the sauce contains cream and the chicken is served with more elaborate garnishes, such as wild mushrooms or an assortment of spring vegetables.

Chicken Fricassee with Morels

You can make this recipe with ordinary mushrooms or other wild mushrooms, either fresh mushrooms that you sauté at the last minute or dried mushrooms reconstituted in water. Dried morels and porcini are the tastiest of all the dried mushrooms—in fact, dried morels have more flavor than fresh—but dried porcini can sometimes be tough, so that you have to chop them or at least cut them into small pieces. Peeling the pearl onions is the most timing-consuming part of this dish—something to do the night before in front of the television.

One 4-pound chicken

Salt

Pepper

2 tablespoons butter

2 cups chicken broth

1 cup pearl onions or walnut-sized boiling onions, peeled (page 302)

1 ounce dried morels, soaked in $1/4$ cup water for 30 minutes

$1/2$ cup heavy cream

Cut up the chicken as shown on pages 248–249 and season the pieces on both sides with salt and pepper. In a skillet just large enough to hold the chicken, melt the butter over medium heat. Add the chicken pieces, skin side down.

While the chicken is cooking, bring the broth to a simmer and add the pearl onions. Simmer for 10 minutes, and then lift the morels out of their soaking water, squeeze them gently to release the water into the bowl, and add the morels to the broth. Then carefully pour the soaking water into the broth, leaving any grit behind in the bowl.

When the chicken has cooked for about 10 minutes, turn it over and cook for about 5 minutes more. Pour the onions and morels over the chicken and cover the pan. Simmer gently for about 5 minutes, or until the chicken is firm to the touch. Transfer the chicken pieces to a plate and keep them warm.

Put the sauté pan over high heat and boil down the broth for about 15 minutes or until it is lightly syrupy. You may end up with as much as $1/2$ cup or as little as a few tablespoons. Add the cream and continue to boil for about 3 to 5 minutes or until the sauce is just thick enough to coat the back of a spoon. Season with salt and pepper.

Put the chicken pieces on warmed plates and spoon the sauce, onions, and morels over them.

Chicken Fricassee with Spring Vegetables

Authentic baby peas seem to be in season for only a week or two in June, but frozen peas are the one frozen vegetable that is better than fresh most of the year. Just don't follow the directions on the package and boil them. They have already been boiled at the factory, so all you need to do is heat them through.

One 4-pound chicken

Salt

Pepper

2 tablespoons butter

6 ounces green beans, preferably haricots verts, ends trimmed

8 baby carrots, peeled, or 2 small carrots, peeled and cut into 8 equal pieces

8 baby turnips, peeled (optional)

1 cup pearl onions or walnut-sized boiling onions, peeled (see page 302)

2 cups chicken broth

$1/2$ cup heavy cream

1 cup fresh baby peas or frozen petite peas

2 tablespoons chopped fresh parsley, tarragon, or chives, or a mixture

In a large saucepan, bring 3 quarts water to a rapid boil.

While the water is heating, cut up the chicken as shown on pages 248–249 and season the pieces on both sides with salt and pepper. In a skillet just large enough to hold the chicken, melt the butter over medium heat. Add the chicken pieces, skin side down. While the chicken is cooking, ready the vegetables for cooking. Turn the chicken over after about 10 minutes and cook for 5 minutes more.

Add a small handful of salt to the boiling water and add the beans. Boil for about 5 minutes, or until they lose all but the slightest crunch. Drain in a colander and rinse with cold water. While the beans are cooking, put the carrots, turnips, and onions in a small saucepan with the broth, bring to a gentle simmer, and simmer for about 20 minutes, or until the vegetables are almost cooked through but still retain a little resistance when you poke at them with a knife. Remove from the heat.

Pour the vegetables and their broth over the chicken and cover the pan. Simmer gently for about 5 minutes, or until the chicken is firm to the touch. Transfer the chicken pieces to a plate and keep them warm.

Put the sauté pan over high heat and boil down the broth for about 15 minutes or until it is a light syrup. Add the cream, green beans, and peas and herbs and boil for about 2 minutes, or until the sauce is just thick enough to coat the back of a spoon and the green beans and peas are heated through. Season with salt and pepper.

Put the chicken pieces on warmed plates and spoon the vegetables and sauce over them.

Vegetable-Lover's Chicken Fricassee

This dish may seem complicated, but it really involves only fixing an assortment of vegetables and then serving them over the chicken. You can cut out some of the vegetables, if you like, or you can trade some of them out for whatever looks good at the market.

MAKES 6 FIRST-COURSE OR 4 MAIN-COURSE SERVINGS

- 12 thick spears green or white asparagus
- One 10-ounce package cultivated mushrooms, preferably cremini
- 1/2 cup fresh baby peas or frozen petite peas
- 2/3 pound fava beans in the shell, shucked (optional)
- 1 ounce dried morel mushrooms (optional)
- 2 large artichokes (optional)
- 1/2 lemon if using artichokes
- Salt
- 1/3 pound green beans, preferably haricots verts, ends trimmed
- 2 cups spinach leaves
- 18 or 24 pearl onions or walnut-sized boiling onions (optional)
- One 4-pound chicken, or 2 thighs and 2 breasts, or 4 thighs or breasts
- Pepper
- 3 tablespoons butter or olive oil
- 3 cups chicken broth or water if using onions, or 3 1/4 cups if not
- 1 small bunch chives
- 1 small bunch parsley, large stems removed
- 1 small bunch chervil (optional)
- Leaves from 2 sprigs tarragon
- 1/2 cup heavy cream

Early on the day you will be serving the fricassee, trim and peel the asparagus spears as shown on page 290. Cut each spear into 3 sections about 3 inches long.

Wash and dry the mushrooms. Cut the end off the bottom of each mushroom stem if dried out or dirty. Shuck or thaw the peas and fava beans.

Place the morels in a very small bowl with just enough water to reach one-third up their sides. Soak them for about 30 minutes, pressing down on them, and move them around every 10 minutes until they are completely soft. Lift them out of the water, squeeze them, capturing the water in the bowl, and put the morels in a separate small bowl.

Prepare the artichokes as shown on page 297 for artichoke bottoms. Put the artichokes in a nonaluminum pot with plenty of water to cover and bring to a gentle simmer. Simmer for about 15 minutes, or until a paring knife poked into one of the artichokes goes through with moderate resistance. Drain the artichokes, rub with the lemon half, and set the artichokes and lemon aside.

Select a pot that you can reach into with a large strainer or spider, so you can fish out the vegetables as they are ready. Fill with about 6 quarts water, bring to a rapid boil, and add a small handful of salt. Add the green beans and boil for about 5 minutes, or until they lose all but the slightest crunch. Scoop them out into a colander, rinse with cold water until cool, and transfer to a bowl. Add the asparagus to the boiling water and boil for about 3 minutes, or until tender. Scoop out with tongs into the colander, rinse with cold water until cool, and add to the bowl. If using fresh peas, boil them for about 1 minute, scoop them out and rinse them with cold water, and add them to the bowl. If using frozen peas, reserve them until you are ready to assemble the dish. Add the fava beans to the boiling water, boil for 1 minute, scoop them out into the colander, rinse them with cold water, and set aside in a separate bowl. Add the spinach to the boiling water, stir it around for just a few seconds until it goes limp, and scoop it out into the colander and rinse it with cold water. Squeeze out the water and reserve on a plate. Finally, add the pearl onions to the boiling water, boil for 2 minutes, and then drain into the colander and rinse with cold water.

Peel the fava beans, using a paring knife and your thumbnail to remove the tough skin. Trim and peel the pearl onions and place in a separate bowl. Scoop the chokes out of the artichoke bottoms, and cut each bottom into 6 wedges. If you are not finishing the fricassee right away, put the artichoke bottoms in a bowl, squeeze in the juice from the lemon half, and toss to coat. Cover all the vegetables and refrigerate until you are ready to finish the dish.

About 1 hour before serving, if using a whole chicken, cut up as shown on page 000. Season the chicken pieces on both sides with salt and pepper. In a sauté pan large enough to hold the chicken, sauté in the butter over medium heat. Add the chicken pieces skin side down and cook gently for about 15 minutes. Turn the chicken over, cook for about 5 minutes longer, pour off and discard the fat in the pan, and pour in 2 cups of the chicken broth.

Meanwhile, in a saucepan large enough to hold all the sauce and vegetables, combine the pearl onions and 1 cup broth, bring to a simmer over low to medium heat, and cook for 15 minutes. Slice the cultivated mushrooms and add to the pan with the onions. (Or, if not using the onions, combine the mushrooms with 1/4 cup chicken broth in a saucepan large enough to hold the sauce and the vegetables.) Cover the pan and cook over low heat for 5 minutes.

While the mushrooms are cooking, chop the herbs, reserving 4 chervil sprigs for garnish. Stir the herbs into the saucepan, add to the onions and/or mushrooms, and pour in the cream. Heat the spinach in the microwave or in a small saucepan. Put all the other vegetables—asparagus, peas, favas, morels, artichokes, and green beans—on top of the mushrooms. As you add the vegetables, season them with salt and pepper. Cover the pan and cook gently over medium heat for 3 minutes.

Arrange the spinach in warmed soup plates and place a piece of cooked chicken on top of each mound. Spoon the sauce and vegetables over. Decorate with a chervil sprigs.

BONELESS CHICKEN STEWS

A chicken stew is an example of short braising in which the meat is cooked just long enough to heat it through. This is different than long-braised stews made with lamb, veal, or beef that cook for hours to tenderize the meat.

Because the cooking time for the chicken is short, it does little to contribute flavor to the surrounding stewing liquid, so the liquid has to be manufactured from flavorful ingredients, such as broth, herbs, spices, or cream. Some of the best chicken stews are Indian, made with spices and yogurt, but Mexican mole-style dishes and Moroccan and Thai stews are also delicious.

Thai Chicken Curry

Thai curries, of which there are several types—yellow, red, green, and mussaman—are actually pastes traditionally made by grinding herbs and aromatic ingredients in a mortar. A food processor can be used instead, but it won't make a smooth enough paste, so you have to strain the mixture before you use it. You can buy premade Thai curry pastes, but they never have the same flavor as freshly made ones.

A variety of flavor-packed ingredients go into Thai curry pastes, including cilantro (ideally the root), chiles, lemongrass (citronella, the same thing used to make candles), kaffir lime (zest or leaves or both), galangal (which looks a little like ginger but has a very different, pinelike flavor), and fish sauce, among others. Traditional recipes also call for shrimp paste, a heady ingredient made by fermenting shrimp in the sun. It is so pungent that many Western cooks leave it out of dishes for fear of the house smelling like an Asian fish stall on a hot day.

The pastes are notoriously hot—green is hotter than red—and require a shocking number of chiles. This recipe strays from traditional versions in its use of poblano chiles, normally associated with Mexican cooking. They are a good choice because they provide plenty of flavor without overwhelming the dish with heat. Thai curries are best served with jasmine or basmati rice that has been simply boiled or steamed.

MAKES 6 MAIN-COURSE SERVINGS

> 3 poblano chiles, charred, peeled, and seeded (see page 321) and then chopped
>
> 2 jalapeño or Thai chiles, seeded and chopped (optional)
>
> 1 stalk lemongrass, 6 inches of white bulb part only, tough outer layer discarded and very thinly sliced
>
> 3 shallots, chopped
>
> 3 cloves garlic, chopped
>
> 1 bunch cilantro, including stems, coarsely chopped
>
> 6 kaffir lime leaves
>
> 1-inch piece galangal, peeled and sliced thin (optional)
>
> 1 teaspoon ground coriander
>
> 1/2 teaspoon ground cumin
>
> 1/2 teaspoon ground white pepper
>
> 2 cups chicken broth or water
>
> 1/4 cup Thai fish sauce
>
> 1/2 cup fresh basil leaves, preferably small holy basil leaves
>
> One 15-ounce can unsweetened coconut milk, preferably Thai
>
> 3 tablespoons fresh lime juice
>
> 2 1/2 pounds boneless, skinless chicken breasts, cut on an angle into strips 2 to 3 inches long and 1/2 inch wide

In a food processor, combine the chiles, lemongrass, shallots, garlic, cilantro, 2 of the kaffir lime leaves, the galangal, coriander, cumin, white pepper, and 1 cup of the broth. Process for 1 minute. If the mixture gets too stiff and the blades can't turn, add a little more of the broth. Transfer the mixture to a saucepan, bring to a simmer, and simmer gently for 5 minutes to infuse the ingredients in the liquid. Work the mixture through a fine-mesh strainer into a clean pot large enough to hold the whole finished curry.

Add the remaining 1 cup broth and 4 kaffir lime leaves along with the fish sauce, basil, coconut milk, and lime juice and bring to a simmer. Simmer for 5 to 10 minutes, or until slightly thickened. If the curry needs salt, add more fish sauce, which will provide both salt and savor.

Add the chicken, simmer for 3 to 4 minutes, or until just cooked through, and serve.

Velvet Chicken with Spices, Cashews, and Ghee

This is a somewhat rich dish because of the ghee. If you want to lighten it, replace the cream with plain yogurt (drained as directed) and leave the ghee out entirely. But the rich nuttiness of the ghee, combined with the nuttiness of the cashews, is hard to beat. Serve with basmati rice.

MAKES 4 MAIN-COURSE SERVINGS

- 1/3 cup ghee or 2 tablespoons vegetable oil
- 1 onion, finely chopped
- 2 cloves garlic, chopped
- 1-inch piece fresh ginger, peeled and grated
- 3 tablespoons Goan Red Spice Paste (see page 125), or to taste
- 1 cup roasted cashews
- 1 1/2 cups heavy cream or 2 cups plain yogurt, drained in a cheesecloth-lined strainer for 1 hour to overnight or 1 cup plain Greek-style yogurt
- 1 1/2 pounds boneless, skinless chicken breasts, cut on an angle into strips 2 to 3 inches long and 1/2 inch wide
- Salt
- Pepper

In a pan large enough to hold the stew, heat 2 tablespoons of the ghee or the 2 tablespoons oil over medium to medium-high heat. Add the onion, garlic, and ginger and cook, stirring occasionally, for 6 to 8 minutes, or until the onion is translucent. Stir in the spice paste and cook for 3 minutes more.

Add half of the cashews and the cream and cook just long enough to heat the cream to the temperature of a hot bath. (If the cream is cold, it will turn to butter in the blender; if it is too hot, it will try to shoot out from under the blender lid.)

Pour the cream mixture into a blender and process for about 1 minute, or until smooth. Strain the puree back into the pan and bring to a gentle simmer. Stir in the remaining cashews, the chicken, and the remaining ghee, if using. Simmer for about 3 minutes, or until the chicken is just cooked through.

Season with salt and pepper and serve in warmed soup plates.

Chicken with Shrimp

Poulet aux écrevisses—chicken with crayfish—is one of the great dishes of France, or more specifically of Lyon. Two hundred years ago, there were more such dishes—seafood combined with chicken—that provided a means of extending the flavor of rare and expensive ingredients with something relatively neutral, such as chicken. The same method used for crayfish works for shrimp. Be sure to buy wild gulf shrimp with heads for this dish, as you will need the heads to make the creamy broth. Or, if you have shrimp heads reserved in the freezer, you can use them to make the broth.

MAKES 4 MAIN-COURSE SERVINGS

- 24 shrimp with heads intact, peeled and deveined, with heads reserved
- 2 tablespoons olive oil
- 4 tomatoes, chopped
- 1/2 teaspoon fresh thyme leaves or dried thyme
- 1 cup heavy cream
- One 4-pound chicken or 2 chicken breasts and 2 chicken thighs with drumsticks
- Salt
- Pepper
- 5 or 6 tablespoons butter
- 1 onion, finely chopped
- 1/2 teaspoon saffron threads, soaked in 1 tablespoon water (optional)
- Leaves from 4 sprigs tarragon, chopped at the last minute
- 1 cup pearl onions or walnut-sized boiling onions, peeled (see page 302), optional
- One 10-ounce package cultivated mushrooms, preferably cremini

In a heavy skillet, heat the oil over high heat until it ripples. Toss in the shrimp heads and stir for about 5 minutes, or until red and fragrant. Remove from the heat, let cool, and then process in a food processor for 1 minute, or until finely ground.

In a saucepan, combine the ground shrimp heads, tomatoes, thyme, and cream, bring to a gentle simmer, and simmer for 20 minutes. Remove from the heat, strain through a coarse-mesh strainer, and then again through a fine-mesh strainer. Set aside.

If using a whole chicken, cut up as shown on pages 248–249. Season the chicken pieces on both sides with salt and pepper.

In a sauté pan just large enough to hold the chicken, melt 3 tablespoons of the butter over medium heat. Add the chicken pieces skin side down and cook for about 10 minutes, or until lightly browned. Turn and cook on the other side for about 5 minutes more, or until lightly browned. The chicken shouldn't be completely cooked at this point. Transfer the chicken pieces to a plate and discard all but 1 tablespoon of the fat from the pan. If the fat is burnt, discard all of it and replace it with 1 tablespoon fresh butter.

Return the pan to medium heat, add the chopped onion, and cook gently for about 10 minutes, or until translucent. Add the reserved shrimp head mixture, the saffron and its soaking liquid, and the tarragon, and let the sauce sit off the heat until close to serving.

While the chicken is cooking, put the pearl onions in a pan large enough to hold them in a single layer and add enough water to come halfway up their sides. Partly cover the pan, bring to a medium simmer, and simmer for about 15 minutes—watch closely and add a little more water if it begins to boil away—or until the onions are easily penetrated with a knife. If there is still water left in the pan, turn the heat to high and boil away the water. Then add 1 tablespoon of the butter to the pan and sauté the onions for about 5 minutes, or until lightly browned. Remove from the heat.

Cut the end off the bottom of each mushroom stem if dried out or dirty. If the caps are larger than 1 inch across, cut through the stem into quarters. In a sauté pan, melt the remaining 1 tablespoon butter over high heat. Add half of the mushrooms and toss and stir for 2 to 3 minutes, or until they start to brown. Add the rest of the mushrooms and continue sautéing for about 6 minutes, or until all the mushrooms are well browned and fragrant. If the mushrooms release water—something to avoid—continue cooking until all the water evaporates. Remove from the heat.

About 10 minutes before serving, return the chicken, skin side up, to the sauté pan, add the sauce, pearl onions, and mushrooms, and cover the pan. Bring to a gentle simmer and simmer for 5 to 10 minutes, or until the chicken is firm to the touch. Season the sauce with salt and pepper.

Put the chicken on warmed plates. Add the shrimp to the sauce and simmer for 2 minutes, or until it turns orange. Spoon the shrimp and sauce over the chicken.

Chicken Korma

Once you have chicken broth or concentrated broth and Greek yogurt, you can throw this stew together in minutes. Serve it with plenty of rice, preferably basmati.

MAKES 4 MAIN-COURSE SERVINGS

- 1 cup plain yogurt or $1/2$ cup Greek-style yogurt
- 4 boneless, skinless chicken breasts, cut into strips 2 inches long by $1/2$ inch wide
- Salt
- Pepper
- $1/2$ cup ghee or 4 tablespoons butter
- 1 large onion, very thinly sliced
- 2 tablespoons grated fresh ginger
- 2 teaspoons ground cumin
- $1/2$ teaspoon ground nutmeg
- 1 teaspoon ground cinnamon
- 1 teaspoon ground cardamom
- $1/4$ teaspoon ground cloves
- 2 cups brown chicken broth
- $1/2$ cup heavy cream

If you're using regular yogurt, drain it in a cheesecloth-lined strainer placed over a bowl and let drain for at least 1 hour or up to overnight in the refrigerator. Greek yogurt requires no draining.

Season the chicken with salt and pepper and keep refrigerated until shortly before serving.

In a saucepan, heat the ghee over medium heat. Add the onion and cook, stirring occasionally, for about 20 minutes, or until all the liquid the onion releases evaporates. Add the ginger, cumin, nutmeg, cinnamon, cardamom, and cloves and cook for about 2 minutes more, or until the spices are fragrant. Add the broth and boil down to reduce by half. Add the cream and continue to boil for about 3 minutes, or until slightly thickened.

Add the chicken and simmer gently for about 2 minutes, or until just cooked through. Stir in the yogurt, season with salt and pepper, and heat through before serving.

POACHED CHICKEN

Cooks often forget that whole chickens (and chicken parts for that matter) can be poached in savory broth with vegetables. A whole chicken can then be carved in the same way as a roast chicken—except the skin is pulled off and not served—and presented in soup plates surrounded by the savory broth and the vegetables. The result is light, beautiful to look at, and contains little fat.

Old recipes for poached chicken, especially in French cookbooks, call for a hen. But hens take a long time to cook and tend to dry out, so nowadays it is better to use a regular chicken. The vegetables are usually onions, carrots, and turnips, but almost any vegetable can be used. Leeks are tasty and look great on the plate, and if you are able to find baby vegetables, they create a handsome presentation. Larger vegetables should be cut into sections and can even be shaped.

Poached Chicken with Leeks and Root Vegetables

The chicken should be poached in chicken broth, which can then be served along with the chicken or saved and used again to poach another chicken. If you do the latter, the broth will become more concentrated with each use. For a richer version, add some heavy cream and chopped fresh tarragon, chervil, parsley, or chives, or a mixture, to the broth just before serving. This recipe can also be made by substituting baby vegetables for the adult vegetables called for here.

MAKES 4 MAIN-COURSE SERVINGS

> 4 leeks, white parts only
> 2 carrots, peeled
> 2 turnips, peeled
> 1 celeriac, peeled (optional)
> One 4-pound chicken, trussed as shown on page 245
> 3 to 4 quarts chicken broth, preferably brown chicken broth
> Bouquet garni
> 2 tablespoons finely chopped fresh parsley
> Salt
> Pepper

Halve the whites of the leeks lengthwise and clean as shown on page 293, and then tie together into a bundle with kitchen string. Cut the carrots into sections as shown on page 300. If you like, shape the turnip and celeriac wedges as shown on pages 305 and 299, or just leave whole.

Put all the vegetables in a pot just large enough to hold the chicken. The idea is to be able to cover the chicken with as little broth as possible. Put the chicken in the pot and pour over enough broth to cover. Nestle the bouquet garni in the center and bring to a gentle simmer over high heat. Immediately reduce the heat to maintain a gentle simmer and simmer for about 40 minutes, skimming off any froth that floats to the surface with a ladle.

To check for doneness, take the chicken out of the broth and insert an instant-read thermometer between the thigh and breast. The chicken is done when the thermometer reads 140°F. Or, stick a skewer into the joint where the drumstick meets the thigh. The juices should run clear, not bloody.

Pull the skin off the chicken and discard. Carve the chicken as shown on pages 248–249 and put the pieces in warmed soup plates. Discard the bouquet garni and add the parsley to the broth. Spoon the vegetables over the chicken, and then ladle some broth over each serving. Sprinkle each serving with salt and pepper, rather than seasoning the broth, as you may want to use it for something else or reduce it.

VARIATIONS

To create a luxury version of this dish, don't serve the vegetables you cooked in the broth. When the chicken is ready, put 2 cups of the broth in a saucepan with 1 cup heavy cream and 1 ounce dried morel or porcini mushrooms that you have reconstituted in warm water in advance. Bring to a simmer and season with salt and pepper and then serve the creamy broth over the chicken.

To make the poached chicken with baby vegetables, count on 2 carrots, 2 turnips, 2 onions (golf ball–sized boiling onions are perfect for this), and 1/2 leek per person. Don't put the vegetables in the pot at the beginning. Instead, wait until the chicken has been cooking for about 20 minutes, so the vegetables won't be overcooked.

Fresh tarragon and chives, chopped at the last minute and added to the broth, add a wonderful flavor. Heavy cream also helps tie the flavors of the broth, chicken, and vegetables together into a whole that is more exciting than the parts. You can use as little as 1/4 cup or as much as 1 cup for 4 servings.

GRILLED CHICKEN

Few dishes are as simple and satisfying as plain grilled chicken. There are only two pitfalls: if you overcook chicken, it will be dry, and if the grill flares up too much, the meat will taste sooty. The trick to avoiding flare-ups, at least with a charcoal fire, is to grill the chicken pieces on their flesh side first. That way, the fire will have died down somewhat by the time you grill the skin side, which contains fat that causes flare-ups. If you are using a gas grill, grill the flesh side over high heat and then turn down the heat a bit to grill the skin side. The chicken is done when it bounces back to the touch, usually after about 12 minutes on each side, but this can vary widely depending on your fire.

While the basic technique for grilling chicken is the same, variations are created with different marinades and rubs that are applied before the chicken goes on the grill and with various mixtures that are brushed on during grilling. The possibilities are countless, with tandoori chicken, which calls for a marinade of yogurt and spices; jerk chicken, in which the pieces are coated with chiles and spices; and various classic American barbecue recipes, in which sauces based on tomatoes are brushed on the chicken as it cooks, among the most famous.

There is also the question as to whether to cook the chicken in a covered grill, which results in it being in part smoked. This is more or less successful depending on the source of the smoke. As with all meats cooked over fire, if the smoke comes from the fat of the chicken dripping onto the coals, the meat is going to taste greasy and sooty. If it comes from wood chips, it will have a lovely smoked wood flavor. To get the best results, build a hot charcoal fire with the coals to one side in a grill with a cover, or preheat a gas grill to high and then turn off half of the burners. Grill the chicken skin side down directly over the fire until it is well browned and crispy but not cooked through, and then move the chicken to the side without the fire, and sprinkle the coals with a handful of wood chips. If using a gas grill, make a small sawdust-filled packet out of aluminum foil, and place the packet on one of the burners. Cover the grill, and "smoke" the chicken until it is done. For more on grilling, see pages 14–15.

Fried Chicken

The best fried chicken is made without batter. If you dust the chicken with flour only, it will absorb hardly any oil. The secret to success is to control the temperature of the oil so the chicken ends up golden brown and crispy at the same time that it is cooked through. An electric deep fryer or electric frying pan is a great help, because it eliminates the need to keep adjusting the temperature on your stove top. If you are cooking on the stove top, you will need a deep-frying thermometer. Try serving fried chicken with an assortment of different-flavored mayonnaises (see pages 359–361).

MAKES 4 MAIN-COURSE SERVINGS

One 4-pound chicken
Salt
Pepper
About 2 cups flour
About 3 cups vegetable oil

Cut up the chicken as shown on pages 248–249 and season the pieces on both sides with salt and pepper. Spread the flour on a plate and dredge the chicken pieces in the flour, patting off the excess. Place the pieces on a cake rack to dry at room temperature for 30 minutes. When dry, transfer the chicken pieces to a tray. Wash the cake rack thoroughly for later use.

Heat the oil in a deep cast-iron skillet, an electric deep fryer, or an electric frying pan to 350°F. The fat should be deep enough to cover the chicken, but keep in mind that some will be displaced when you add the chicken. Gently lower the chicken into the oil and deep-fry for about 10 minutes, or until well browned and when you take a piece out of the oil, it springs back to the touch. Using tongs, transfer to the cake rack to drain before serving.

TURKEY

Even though we can now buy turkey parts—breasts, thighs, and wings—at the supermarket, most of us still associate turkey with the whole roast bird served on holidays. And for many cooks, roasting a turkey is the only time they desperately reach for a cookbook for guidance on temperature and timing or to their grandmother's foolproof recipe for stuffing.

Turkey worries cooks for three reasons: they want to know when it is done, how long it is going to take to cook, and how to make good stuffing and gravy.

Five Tips for a Successful Roast Turkey

1. LEAVE THE TURKEY OUT OF THE REFRIGERATOR BEFORE ROASTING.

If you leave a turkey, or any roast, out of the refrigerator for about 3 hours before roasting, it will cook more quickly and evenly (see page 170). If you put an ice-cold bird into a hot oven, the outer part of the breast will overcook and dry out before the inside heats through.

2. DON'T STUFF THE TURKEY.

While this may sound heretical to some, stuffing a turkey can make cooking the turkey to the optimum temperature difficult. In order for the stuffing to reach a safe temperature, say, 145°F, the bird has to be considerably hotter, which means it will probably be overcooked. Stuffing can also be a health hazard if doesn't reach a sufficiently hot temperature, or if it is allowed to sit in the bird too long before it reaches the temperature that kills any bacteria. If you insist on stuffing the turkey, allow your bird to come to room temperature, and then stuff it just before it goes into the oven. Otherwise, the stuffing sits in the bird at a temperature that can favor the development of bacteria. Stuffing also absorbs juices from the turkey that would otherwise drip down onto the pan and provide flavorful gravy.

If you want to serve a stuffing, cook it in a separate roasting pan next to the turkey. Don't roast it in the same pan as the turkey, or it will absorb the juices you need for the gravy. Remember, the less stuffing, the more juices you will have for a flavorful gravy. If you want a flavorful stuffing, spoon gravy over it at the table.

HOW TO ROAST A TURKEY

1. Spread the turkey giblets in the roasting pan and place the turkey on top of the giblets.

2. Tie the two drumsticks together with a piece of kitchen string.

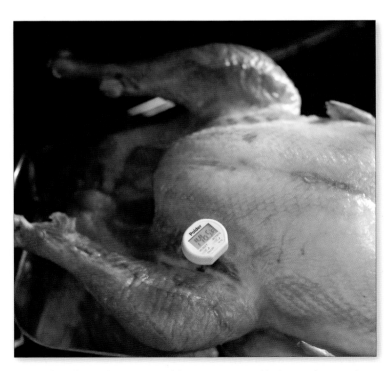

3. Butter one side a double-thick sheet of aluminum foil just large enough to cover the breast, and place buttered side down over the turkey breast.

4. Roast the turkey until the thighs are well browned and then remove the aluminum foil.

5. Roast the turkey until an instant-read thermometer inserted in the meat between the thigh and the breast reads about 147°F. Cover the turkey loosely with aluminum foil and let rest in a warm place for at least 20 minutes before carving.

3. DON'T USE A ROASTING RACK.

A roasting rack keeps the turkey above the roasting pan and will cause the juices to burn. A better trick is to put the giblets in the roasting pan and set the turkey on top of them. They will cook (you can chop them up for the gravy; see below) at the same time they prevent the turkey from sticking to the pan and the juices from burning.

4. COVER THE BREASTS WITH ALUMINUM FOIL.

For the turkey to get hot enough at the point where it cooks last—at the thigh joint—the heat has to be given plenty of time to penetrate through the breast and thigh. To keep the breast meat from drying out, cover the breast loosely with a triple-thick sheet of buttered aluminum foil. This insulates the breast, slowing down its cooking so it doesn't dry out.

5. CARVE THE TURKEY AT THE TABLE.

Many people have forgotten the old-fashioned ritual of carving at the table. Carving a big turkey makes a meal festive, a little more formal, and memorable. Carve the bird on a deep platter to catch juices. Be willing to be embarrassed the first few times, until you get the hang of it (see photos on page 267).

Roast Turkey and Gravy

When buying a turkey, buy at least a pound per guest and ideally a bit more so you will have leftovers. Unless you are stuffing your turkey, count on roasting about 8 minutes per pound. This is faster than most recipes recommend, but keep in mind this is based on the turkey being at room temperature before it goes in the oven.

The amount of juices you get for making gravy will depend on how long you cook the turkey and whether or not it is stuffed. If you don't overcook the turkey, you may find yourself with relatively few juices with which to make a jus or gravy, giving you two options: If you have few juices to work with, you will need to caramelize the juices in the way described here and shown on page 266 before you make the gravy. If the bird has been cooked longer and released more juices, you can pour the hot juices and fat into a glass pitcher or degreaser, spoon or pour off the fat, and then make the gravy as shown.

MAKES 12 MAIN-COURSE SERVINGS WITH LEFTOVERS

> One 20-pound turkey with giblets, rinsed under
>   cold running water and patted dry
> Salt and pepper
> 2 tablespoons butter

Turkey Gravy
> 2 tablespoons flour
> 2 cups chicken broth or more as needed
> Salt
> Pepper

Preheat the oven to 375°F. Season the turkey on the inside and outside with salt and pepper. Place the giblets in a roasting pan just large enough to hold the turkey and set the turkey, breast side up, on top of the giblets in the pan. Take a sheet of aluminum foil about 24 inches long and fold it to create a triple thickness. It will need to be vaguely trapezoidal to cover the breasts and not the thighs. Smear one side with the butter and place it, buttered side down, over the turkey breast. Tie the drumsticks together tightly with kitchen string.

Put the turkey in the oven and roast until well browned, about 1 hour. Remove the foil. Roast the turkey until an instant-read thermometer inserted in the meat between the thigh and the breast reads about 147°F. Remove the turkey from the oven, lift it out of the roasting pan, cover loosely with aluminum foil, and let rest in a warm place for at least 20 minutes before carving.

While the turkey is resting, make the gravy. Remove the giblets from the roasting pan and set aside. Look in the roasting pan to see if the juices have caramelized. If they have, the bottom of the pan will be coated with brown and a layer of clear fat will be floating on top. If they haven't caramelized, you will see brown liquid combined with the fat. The mixture of fat and juices may even be cloudy, meaning the juices have emulsified with the fat, which you want to avoid. If the juices haven't caramelized, put the roasting pan on the stove top and boil the juices until they caramelize on the bottom and separate from the fat, and then pour off all but 2 tablespoons of the fat. You now have a roasting pan with a layer of caramelized juices and a little fat. Sprinkle in the flour over medium heat and stir in for 1 minute. Whisk in the chicken broth, stirring over medium or medium-high heat until the gravy thickens as much as you like. Strain the gravy into a new saucepan and set over low heat. If using the giblets, strip the meat from the neck and chop it along with the heart, gizzards, and liver. Add the chopped giblets to the gravy, and transfer the gravy to a sauceboat.

Carve the turkey (see page 267) and serve with the gravy.

1. If you have roasted the turkey ahead of time and the juices are cold and congealed, skim off as much fat as you can with a spoon.

2. Boil down the juices by continually repositioning the roasting pan over the burner.

3. When all the juices have caramelized and formed a crust on the bottom of the roasting pan, pour off all but 2 tablespoons of the liquid fat.

4. Sprinkle the flour in the roasting pan and stir over medium heat.

5. Pour in the broth and stir over medium to medium-high heat.

6. Continue to stir until the gravy is the consistency you like.

7. Strain the gravy through a medium-mesh strainer.

8. If you are making giblet gravy, chop the meat from the neck, heart, gizzards, and liver. Add the chopped giblets to the gravy.

9. Taste the gravy and season with salt and pepper.

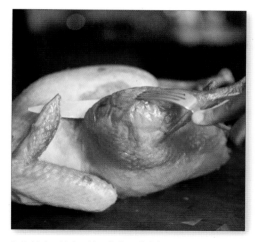

1. Hold the thigh with a fork and slide a carving knife along the inside of the thigh against the breast.

2. Continue sliding the knife down all the way to the joint. Pull the thigh away from the breast with a fork.

3. When the round end of the thigh bone is visible, cut through the joint and detach the thigh.

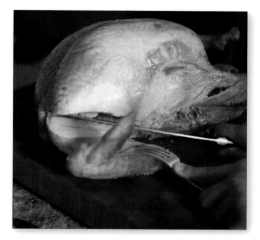

4. Slide the carving knife into the breast meat directly above the wing.

5. Slice off the breast meat down to the point where you cut above the wing and pull away the slices.

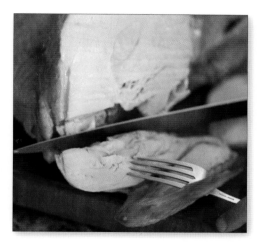

6. After slicing away several slices of breast meat, slide the knife into the cut above the wing and detach the wing.

7. Cut the drumstick away from the thigh (the first joint away from the second joint).

8. Slice the meat away from the thigh.

9. Slice the meat away from the drumstick.

DUCK AND SMALL BIRDS

Because of their petite size and, in the case of duck, because of the fat contained in their skin, these birds can't be roasted in the same way as a chicken or turkey—by prolonged exposure to dry heat. Ducks, unless you like the traditional "crispy" variety, need to be cut up to be cooked in the best way and small birds such as squabs and quail need to be browned on the stove before going into the oven.

DUCK

Unless you are lucky enough to have access to wild ducks, which are best when simply roasted rare or sautéed in the same way as the squabs on page 280, you will find only one or two varieties of duck in the market. The most common variety, found frozen in most supermarkets—fortunately, duck freezes well—is the Pekin (also called "Long Island") duck, which is not to be confused with the Peking duck, the famed roasted bird of the Chinese table. In fancier places, you are likely to find mullard (also spelled "moulard") ducks, which are giant hybrids used to make foie gras. They also happen to be especially delicious.

Lately, duck parts have begun to appear in markets. This makes cooking duck much simpler, since you can buy just the breast meat (often called magrets when they come from a mullard), which isn't much harder to cook than a steak, or just the thigh, which is easy to braise.

The inherent problem with American domestic ducks is that they have a thick layer of fat. If you roast a whole duck in the same manner as a chicken, you have to cook the duck for hours for the fat to render. You end up with so-called crispy duck that, while good in its own right, isn't nearly as exciting as a duck breast cooked rare or medium-rare. To cook duck successfully, you must break it down into its parts, since the breasts and thighs must be cooked differently. Duck breast meat is tender and cooks relatively quickly, while duck thighs are tougher and need to be braised or turned into confit. The ideal scenario is to braise the duck thighs, sauté the duck breasts, and use the braising liquid from the thighs to make a sauce for both.

(Clockwise) Squab, quail, poussin (baby chicken), duck.

269

1. With the duck breast side up, slide a large knife along the breastbone that runs along the top, keeping the knife pressed firmly against bone. Continue to slide the knife against the breastbone and ribs, always keeping the knife against bone, until you reach the base.

2. Cut through the joint attaching the thigh to the back.

3. Continue separating skin and meat from the underside of the duck until you reach the other side.

4. Turn the duck around and repeat on the other side.

5. Remove the rib cage.

6. When the duck is completely detached from the carcass, cut around the outline of the meat to separate the two breasts and two thighs.

7. Cut through the connective tissue to separate the breasts from the thighs.

8. The cut-up duck, ready for cooking.

Sautéed Duck Breasts

The secret to a successful sautéed duck breast is to get the thick layer of fat that coats it to render and turn crispy without overcooking the meat. You can always trim off the fat, but it is awfully flavorful, and your guests always have the choice of not eating it anyway. One trick to get the fat to render as quickly as possible, before the meat overcooks, is to make a series of slashes through the fat at 90-degree angles, stopping just short of the meat. The breast is then sautéed over medium heat, almost entirely on the skin side. If the heat is too low, the meat will overcook before the fat renders and the skin browns. If the heat is too high, the skin will brown before it has had a chance to render any fat and before the meat can cook. The fat released by duck breasts, especially mullard breasts, is delicious for sautéing, particularly eggs and poultry. If you want to save it, pour the fat out of the pan halfway through the sautéing and keep it in the refrigerator for weeks or in the freezer for months. Don't wait until the end of sautéing. By that time, the fat has started to burn.

MAKES 4 MAIN-COURSE SERVINGS

**4 Pekin duck breasts (about 7 ounces each) or
2 mullard duck breasts (about 1 pound each)**

Salt

Pepper

Use a thin, very sharp knife to make about 20 slashes through the fat covering the breasts. Hold the knife on an angle so you are cutting somewhat sideways through the skin and can cut more deeply without cutting through to the meat. Give the meat a 90-degree turn and make 20 more slashes going in the other direction. Season with salt and pepper.

Put the breasts, skin side down, in a nonstick or well-seasoned skillet just large enough to hold them in a single layer over medium heat. (There is no need to put oil in the pan.) Cook Pekin duck breasts for 8 to 10 minutes, and mullard breasts for 15 to 18 minutes. If halfway into the sautéing the meat is getting very brown, turn down the heat. If it shows no sign of browning, turn up the heat. Turn the breasts over and turn up the heat to high. Brown on the flesh side for 1 to 2 minutes.

You can serve Pekin breasts whole or sliced, but mullard breasts should be served sliced because they are so large. To slice duck breasts, put them skin side down on a cutting board (the skin otherwise can be hard to cut through) and slice them diagonally, with the knife held at an angle, into strips, each with maximal surface area when sliced. Arrange the breasts on warmed plates to serve.

1. Score the skin on the breasts at an angle as deeply as you can without cutting into the meat. Score again at a 90-degree angle to the first set of cuts.

2. Season the skin side of the breasts.

3. Put the breasts skin side down in a sauté pan over medium heat. Season the meat side.

4. After about 8 to 10 minutes for Pekin ducks and 15 to 18 minutes for mullards, turn the breasts over.

5. Sauté for 1 to 2 minutes on the meat side.

6. Slice the breasts and serve.

SAUCES FOR DUCK BREASTS

Most of us associate duck with fruit sauces, especially orange-based sauces. You can easily improvise almost any berry sauce: deglaze the pan used to sauté the breasts with broth or concentrated broth, add berries, simmer them until they soften, add a pinch of sugar and a few drops of vinegar to the sauce to create a sweet-and-sour effect, and then whisk in a little butter. Orange sauce is done a little differently.

Orange Sauce for Duck Breasts

Most recipes for duck à l'orange call for Grand Marnier, which is a delicious but expensive way to reinforce the flavor of oranges. You can get essentially the same result by combining orange zest and cognac. Cognac is expensive, too, but you need very little. Don't substitute generic brandy.

MAKES 4 MAIN-COURSE SERVINGS

> **3 navel oranges**
>
> **1 cup water**
>
> **1 teaspoon sugar**
>
> **2 teaspoons sherry vinegar or other good wine vinegar**
>
> **1 cup brown chicken broth or 1 tablespoon commercial meat glaze or 2 tablespoons homemade meat glaze (see page 177), softened in 3 tablespoons hot water**
>
> **2 tablespoons cognac or Grand Marnier**
>
> **2 tablespoons butter (optional)**
>
> **Salt**
>
> **Pepper**
>
> **Sautéed Duck Breasts (see page 271)**

Squeeze the juice from 1 orange and reserve the juice. Slice off the zest of the remaining 2 oranges and cut into fine julienne. Section the oranges and set aside (removing the peel as shown on page 90).

In a saucepan, combine the julienned zest and water and bring to a boil. Boil for 2 minutes and pour off the water.

Add the sugar and vinegar to the orange zest and simmer over high heat until dry. Pour in the orange juice and boil down until reduced by about half. Add the broth and simmer for about 5 minutes, or until the sauce is lightly syrupy. Add the cognac and simmer for 30 seconds. Whisk in the butter and season with salt and pepper.

Arrange the breasts on warmed plates with the orange segments and spoon the sauce over the meat and oranges.

Berry Sauce for Duck Breasts

Since all berries behave in the same way, you can use any type in this recipe, plus you can use cherries and fresh currants too. You will need to adjust the sweetness and sourness of the sauce to balance the flavor of the fruit.

> **2 teaspoons sugar, or as needed**
>
> **2 tablespoons sherry vinegar, or as needed**
>
> **1 cup brown chicken broth or 1 tablespoon commercial meat glaze or 2 tablespoons homemade meat glaze (see page 177), softened in 3 tablespoons hot water**
>
> **1 cup blueberries, raspberries, blackberries, fresh red or black currants, or pitted cherries**
>
> **Salt**
>
> **Pepper**
>
> **2 tablespoons butter**
>
> **Sautéed Duck Breasts (see page 271)**

In a small saucepan, heat the 2 teaspoons sugar over medium heat, stirring with a wooden spoon until the sugar melts and browns slightly. Add the vinegar and continue to cook until it evaporates. Then add the broth and boil down for about 5 minutes, or until the mixture is slightly syrupy and coats the back of a spoon.

Add the berries, cover the pan, and simmer over high heat for 4 minutes, or until they release their juices. Using a slotted spoon, gently remove the berries and reserve. Boil down the sauce, which will now be thinner because of the liquid released by the berries, until it has a syrupy consistency.

Taste the sauce and adjust with more sugar or vinegar. Season with salt and pepper and whisk in the butter. Return the berries to the sauce and reheat gently.

Arrange the sliced breasts on warmed plates and spoon the sauce over the top.

DUCK THIGHS

Duck breasts have become enormously popular in part because they are so easy to cook and take so little time. Now most of us can find boneless breasts at the supermarket, but if you have started out with a whole duck, you are going to have those extra thighs. Since thighs take a long time to cook, you may want to save them up in the freezer until you have enough to make it worth the effort to cook them. There are three ways to cook duck thighs: braising, slow roasting, and cooking into confit in their own fat.

Pekin thighs braise relatively quickly, in about 1 hour, while mullard thighs take about 2 hours. The advantage of braising is that you are left with a marvelous braising liquid that you can serve with the thighs, over duck breasts, or with both. If you are being ambitious, braise the thighs and serve part of the thigh and part of the breast on each plate. Slow roasting is the easiest method but leaves you with no sauce. Cooking the thighs in duck fat—not nearly as scary as it sounds because they end up absorbing very little fat—is the most time-consuming approach, but it may also be the way to get the most flavor out of the thighs.

Slow-Roasted Duck Thighs

You can serve 2 Pekin duck thighs or 1 mullard thigh per serving as a main course, or you can divide the thighs and breasts so everyone gets half of a Pekin duck breast and half of a thigh or, if you're serving mullards, half a breast or a whole thigh. If you are not serving thighs at the same time as the breasts, you can make these duck thighs a more complete dish by finishing them with sauerkraut, shredded red cabbage, or beans.

MAKES 6 MAIN-COURSE SERVINGS

> **12 Pekin duck thighs or 6 mullard duck thighs**
> **Salt**
> **Pepper**

Trim off excess fat if you're using mullard thighs (see page 276). Season the thighs on both sides with salt and pepper and put them, skin side up, in a heavy roasting pan that holds them in a single layer without a lot of extra space. Slide the pan into the oven, turn the oven to 350°F (there is no need to preheat), and roast Pekin thighs for 1½ hours or mullard thighs for 2½ hours, or until the skin is brown and crispy and a skewer or knife slides easily in and out.

Slow-Roasted Duck Thighs with Sauerkraut

Sauerkraut makes a tart and crispy foil for the rich thighs and is an easy addition: simply pile it on top of the thighs about 30 minutes before they are done.

MAKES 6 MAIN-COURSE SERVINGS

> **Slow-Roasted Duck Thighs (above)**
> **2 quarts sauerkraut, drained and rinsed in colander**

Roast the thighs as directed, using a roasting pan large enough to hold both the thighs and the sauerkraut. When the thighs are about 30 minutes away from being done, pour out all but about 3 tablespoons of the fat, and cover the thighs with the sauerkraut. Cover the pan and continue to cook for 30 to 45 minutes, or until the sauerkraut has the texture you like. (Don't worry about overcooking the duck.) Serve the thighs and sauerkraut on warmed plates.

Slow-Roasted Duck Thighs with Red Cabbage and Apples

The sweetness of the apples and the tartness of the vinegar make this a great combination. Use a sharp knife to shred the cabbage.

MAKES 6 MAIN-COURSE SERVINGS

Slow-Roasted Duck Thighs (opposite)

1 small red cabbage, shredded

10 juniper berries, crushed

4 tart apples, peeled, cored, and cut into $1/2$-inch dice

$1/4$ cup sherry vinegar or other good wine vinegar, or as needed

Salt

Pepper

Roast the thighs as directed, using a pot large enough to hold the cabbage, apples, and thighs. When the thighs are about 30 minutes away from being done, pour out all but about 3 tablespoons of the fat, and add the cabbage and crushed juniper berries and cook, covered until shrunk by half, about 20 minutes. Add the apples and vinegar. Cover the pan and continue to cook for 30 minutes more.

Before serving, season the cabbage and apples with salt and pepper and a little more vinegar if the mixture lacks tang. Arrange the thighs on top of the cabbage and apples to serve.

HOW TO MAKE SLOW-ROASTED DUCK THIGHS WITH RED CABBAGE AND APPLES

1. Roast duck thighs for about an hour. Remove from pan. Cook shredded red cabbage with crushed juniper berries in a small amount of duck fat until shrunk by half. Arrange the roasted duck thighs, skin side up, on the cabbage.

2. Sprinkle apples and vinegar over the thighs. Cover and place in the oven to continue cooking. Season with salt and pepper.

3. Serve the thighs on a mound of cabbage.

Duck Thighs Braised in Red Wine

Braised mullard thighs are one of the richest and most satisfying of all duck dishes. Look for mullard thighs in fancy grocery stores or check mail-order sources. They are usually relatively inexpensive, since most people don't know what to do with them. This recipe takes a long time, but involves very little real work, and the results are worth the effort. You can also make this dish a day ahead and reheat it just before serving.

MAKES 6 MAIN-COURSE SERVINGS

> 6 mullard duck thighs or 12 Pekin duck thighs

Salt

Pepper

1 large carrot, peeled and sliced

1 large onion, sliced

2 cloves garlic, crushed

1 cup red wine

1 quart chicken broth, preferably brown chicken broth, made without salt

Bouquet garni

Trim off excess fat as shown if you're using mullard thighs. Season the thighs on both sides with salt and pepper and put them, skin side up in a single layer, in a heavy pot with the carrot, onion, and garlic. Slide the pot into the oven, turn the oven to 400°F (there is no need to preheat), and roast Pekin

HOW TO MAKE BRAISED MULLARD DUCK THIGHS

1. Trim excess fat off the thighs.

2. Slide the knife along the fatty side of the thigh, leaving only a thin layer of fat.

3. Place a heavy knife over the thigh bone just in from the nub and give it a good tap with a hammer. (By doing this, instead of just hacking at the bone with a cleaver, you prevent splintering.)

7. Pour enough wine or broth into the pot to come about one-third up the sides of the thighs.

8. Cover the pot with aluminum foil and then with the lid and simmer very gently on the stove top or in the oven until the duck thighs are easily penetrated with a knife.

9. Take the thighs out of the pot, strain the braising liquid and discard the vegetables. If you have time, degrease the liquid by chilling and skimming off the fat as shown here or in a saucepan, over medium heat, with a spoon.

duck thighs for 1½ hours or mullard thighs for 2½ hours, or until the skin is golden brown.

Turn off the oven or, if you want to braise it, turn it down to 300°F. If you notice cloudy liquid in the pan, place the pan (still holding the thighs) over high heat and boil down the juices so they caramelize and you are left with a shiny layer of liquid fat floating on top. Pour off the fat. Add the wine and broth, nestle the bouquet garni in the center, and bring to a gentle simmer on the stove top. Cover the pot with a sheet of aluminum foil, pressing it down so the middle hangs over the thighs. (This causes moisture that condenses within the pot to baste the thighs from the inside.) Then cover with the lid and simmer very gently on the stove top or in the oven for 1½ hours for Pekin thighs or 2½ hours for mullard thighs, or until the thighs offer no resistance when you poke at one with a knife. (If you pull up the thigh when you pull out the knife, the thighs aren't ready.)

Transfer the thighs, still skin up, to a clean pot—or clean out the same pot—in which they fit as snugly as possible in a single layer. Strain the braising liquid into a saucepan, place the pan off center on a burner over medium heat so the liquid boils on only one side and pushes the fat to the other, and simmer, regularly skimming off any fat and froth with a ladle, for about 15 minutes, or until clear and free of fat.

Pour the degreased braising liquid over the thighs and slide the pot, uncovered, into the oven set at 400°F. Baste the thighs every 10 minutes for about 30 minutes, or until they are covered with a shiny glaze and the braising liquid is syrupy. Serve the thighs in warmed soup plates surrounded by the braising liquid.

4. Place a chopped onion and a chopped carrot in a pan just large enough to hold the thighs and add the thighs, fat side up. Season with salt and pepper. Roast in the oven until well browned and the pan is full of fat.

5. If you notice cloudy liquid in the pot, place the pot over high heat to evaporate the juices and cause them to caramelize.

6. Hold the duck in place with a pan lid and pour off the fat.

10. Strain the degreased braising liquid back over the duck thighs. Put the pot in the oven, and baste the thighs every few minutes with the braising liquid until the liquid becomes syrupy.

11. Serve the thighs with the braising liquid spooned on top. Here, the thighs are served with sautéed apple wedges.

1. Trim excess fat off the duck thighs and reserve the fat.

2. Chop garlic, thyme, and bay and make a paste.

3. Rub the paste on thighs, especially on the meat side, along with salt and pepper.

4. If you have time, store overnight in the refrigerator.

5. If using fat trimmings, puree the fat in a food processor.

6. Pureed duck fat.

7. Transfer the fat to a heavy, high-sided pot and render it over high heat for 10 minutes. If you're using already rendered fat, melt it in the pot.

8. Place the thighs, skin side down, in the pan. Initially the fat surrounding the thighs will be cloudy.

9. When the fat is clear and transparent and a knife slides easily in and out of the meat, the confit is ready.

Duck Confit

A generation ago, duck confit was an obscure regional dish from southwestern France, well on its way to being forgotten. Fortunately, it has not only been rediscovered, but also become enormously popular, especially in restaurants, where it is often added to other foods to contribute flavor.

A description of how to make duck confit might sound a little intimidating in this fat-conscious age. It is made by cooking duck parts very gently in rendered duck fat until the the duck flavor is concentrated in the meat and the meat is meltingly tender. The fat, while useful for cooking, is usually wiped off the duck parts before they are served, so very little of it is actually used. Once you have duck confit in hand, you can use it instead of the slow-roasted duck thighs in the sauerkraut and cabbage recipes (see pages 274 and 275, respectively), or you can use some of the suggestions that follow.

Thighs are the most practical cut to use for making confit for two reasons: if you have bought a whole duck to secure the breasts, you have the thighs left over, and if you buy thighs, they are less expensive than breasts. When made into confit, the meat is tastier than the breast meat. To make the project worthwhile, you need at least 12 Pekin thighs or 6 mullard thighs and some extra fat from a duck or two.

MAKES 12 OR 6 CONFIT THIGHS

> 12 Pekin duck thighs or 6 mullard duck thighs
>
> Salt
>
> Pepper
>
> 5 cloves garlic, minced and then crushed with the flat side of the knife
>
> 1 teaspoon fresh thyme leaves, chopped, or dried thyme
>
> 2 bay leaves, chopped
>
> 2 quarts duck fat trimmings or rendered duck fat

Trim off excess fat if you're using mullard thighs. Season the thighs liberally with salt and pepper. Chop the garlic, thyme, and bay into a paste on a cutting board, and rub the mixture on the thighs, especially on the flesh side. Cover the bowl and refrigerate the thighs overnight. (If you are in a rush, you can skip the overnight marinating.)

If you are using fat trimmings, puree them in a food processor for about 1 minute, and then put them in a heavy pot with high sides that's large enough to hold the thighs and the fat. Put the duck fat over medium heat on the stove top for about 10 minutes, or until it starts to render, and then nestle the duck thighs, skin side down, in the pot. If you are using already-rendered fat, put the fat in the pot and add the thighs. If the fat doesn't completely cover the thighs, don't worry. They will shrink and render fat of their own. Simmer the duck, uncovered, over low to medium heat—a bubble should rise in the pot every second or so—for 3 hours, or until the liquid fat is clear and the thighs are easily penetrated with a knife.

If you want to keep the confit for more than a few days, transfer it while it is still hot to sterile jars and ladle over the hot duck fat, making sure that no meat is sticking up above the fat. Seal the jars and store in a cool place or in the fridge for up to a month. If you are keeping for only a few days don't worry about covering all the meat.

Ideas for Duck Confit

Duck fat and confit can be used in small amounts to flavor vegetables, such as green beans, dried beans, cabbage, mushrooms, or spinach. Boil green beans, drain, and then reheat in a tablespoon or two of duck fat with some shredded confit. You can wilt spinach or sauté mushrooms, especially wild mushrooms, in duck fat and add a little shredded confit. You can nestle confit into partially cooked dried beans and then finish the cooking. Or, to make a cassoulet, see pages 331–332. Last, cook confit with shredded cabbage, vinegar, and maybe some apples to create the effect of a choucroute (substitute the confit for the duck thighs in the recipe on page 275)—the sauerkraut with meats served in every French brasserie.

Confit is also the base for a thick soup—recipes say that a spoon plunged into the soup should stay straight up—called a garbure, popular in southwestern France. It is essentially a vegetable soup, usually containing beans, made with plenty of confit—a kind of liquid cassoulet.

SQUAB AND QUAIL

Small birds must almost always be browned before they can be roasted, because by the time they brown in even a very hot oven, they are likely to be overcooked. This is especially true for birds with red meat, such as squab, which are roasted to a lower internal temperature than white-meat birds, such as quail, poussin (baby chicken), or pheasant.

SQUAB

Squab (pigeon) may be the most delicious farmed-raised bird and the one that tastes the most like wild game. It is best cooked simply—roasting is the classic technique—and served carved, unless your guests know what they are doing. Like duck, squab has red meat and should be cooked rare to medium-rare. Because of this and because squabs are small (each one is a single serving), they have to be browned very quickly—more quickly than most home ovens can manage. To avoid overcook-

HOW TO ROAST POUSSIN AND OTHER SMALL BIRDS

1. Red-meat birds, such as squab, should be browned on the stove top before roasting.

2. Put the browned birds (poussin are shown here), in a roasting pan just large enough to hold them, and season with salt and pepper.

3. Preheat the oven to its highest temperature. Cover the breasts with a double-thick layer of buttered aluminum foil.

4. Roast until the thighs brown, remove the foil, and continue roasting until the breasts brown.

ing them, preheat the oven to 500°F, brown the squabs on the stove top in some olive oil, clarified butter, or duck fat, and then immediately roast them for about 10 minutes.

A somewhat more elaborate approach, but one that lets you avoid the last-minute carving, is to cut up the squabs in advance and sauté only the breasts and thighs. If you are being ambitious, you can use the carcass to make a little broth, which in turn can be used to make a sauce or jus.

Sautéed Squab with Its Own Jus

Here, the breasts and thighs are taken off the squabs and a little jus is made out of the carcasses. The trick to extracting the flavor from the carcasses is not to simmer them for hours as though making a broth, but to roast them and deglaze the pan several times, letting the juices caramelize each time. It is best if you have homemade chicken or duck broth.

MAKES 4 MAIN-COURSE SERVINGS

> 4 squabs, about ³/₄ pound each, with giblets
> Salt
> Pepper
> 1 carrot, peeled and sliced
> 1 onion, sliced
> 2 cloves garlic, crushed
> 2 sprigs thyme (optional)
> ¹/₂ imported bay leaf
> 3 cups chicken broth or duck broth
> 2 tablespoons olive oil, duck fat, or clarified butter (page 341)
> 2 tablespoons unsalted butter (optional)

Preheat the oven to 500°F. Take the breasts and thighs off the squabs as shown. Take the small thighbone out of each of the thighs. Season the breasts and thighs on both sides with salt and pepper and refrigerate until needed.

Take out the giblets, which are usually in a little packet in the cavity, save the livers in the freezer for a civet recipe (pages 284 and 287) or cook them for the cat, and chop each carcass into 4 pieces with a cleaver. Put the carcasses, giblets, carrot, and onion in a roasting pan just large enough to hold everything in a single layer. Roast for about 45 minutes, or until well browned but not until the juices burn on the pan bottom. Put the roasting pan on the stove top, add the thyme and bay, and pour in 1 cup of the broth. Bring to a boil and boil down the juices until they caramelize on the bottom of the pan. Add another cup of broth and repeat. Add the final cup of broth

(continued)

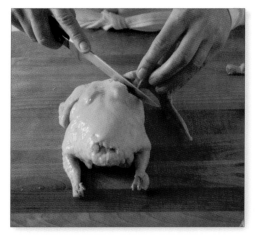

1. Place the bird, here a squab, breast side down and cut through the joint that attaches the wing to the body to remove the wing. Repeat with the other wing.

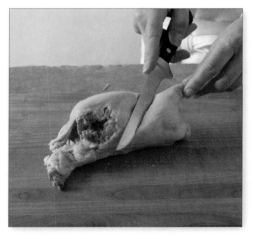

2. With the bird tilted so it is almost on its side, pull the thigh toward the end of the bird and cut through the skin along the edge of the thigh.

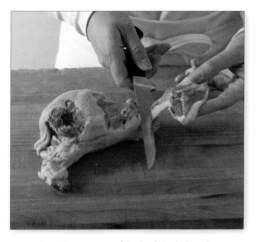

3. Cut along the contours of the back, including the oyster (the little nugget of meat nestled in the back), sliding the knife along until you detach the thigh.

4. Turn the bird on its side and remove the second thigh in the same way.

5. Slide the knife against the side of the breastbone nearest you, and cut all the way down, knife always against bone, until you hit cartilage.

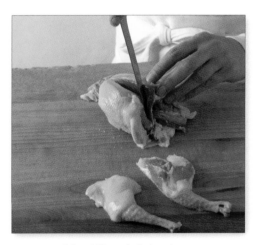

6. Cut around the wishbone (collarbone).

7. Cut the breast away from the bones.

8. Remove the second breast in the same way.

9. Remove the thighbone, but leave the drumstick bone intact.

Sautéed Squab, continued

and simmer for 1 to 2 minutes while scraping the bottom of thepan with a wooden spoon. Then pour the contents of the pan into a fine-mesh strainer set over a saucepan. Leave the pan off the heat until needed.

Ten minutes before serving, in a skillet large enough to hold the breasts and thighs in a single layer, heat the oil over high heat. When it begins to smoke, add the breasts, skin side down, and press down on them with the back of a spatula to keep them from curling. Cook for about 4 minutes, or until they stiffen. Add the thighs, turn the breasts over, and brown for about 2 minutes, or until the breast bounces back to the touch. Remove from the heat. If juices have caramelized on the bottom of the pan, pour out the burnt fat and deglaze the pan with the reserved jus. Then bring the jus to a simmer, whisk in the butter, and season with salt and pepper.

Arrange the breasts and thighs on warmed plates and spoon the jus over them.

HOW TO MAKE A JUS FROM A SMALL ROAST BIRD

1. Pour out any juices in the cavities of the birds into the roasting pan and put the pan over high heat.

2. Move the pan as needed so a brown crust forms over its entire surface.

3. Pour out and discard the fat in the roasting pan.

4. Deglaze the pan with wine or other liquid.

5. Stretch the jus with a little meat glaze (page 177) or reduced broth (optional).

6. Deglaze by scraping the bottom of the pan with a wooden spoon or spatula, and strain the jus unto a small pitcher for serving.

1. Hold the bird, here a squab, in place with a fork, pressing on the base of the cavity. Cut just above the wing until you reach the joint. Cut through the joint and remove the wing.

2. Slide the knife between the thigh and breast and continue down until you see the joint.

3. Slide the knife along the side of the breastbone where you removed the thigh. Continue separating the breast and eventually push it out, away from the bird.

4. Put the bird on its side and cut away the other thigh.

5. Cut away the second breast in the same way as the first. Prepare a jus as described (opposite) and serve either whole or sliced.

6. Sliced roast squab served with jus spooned over the top.

Squab Civet with Fava Bean Cassoulet

This is an elaborate and expensive dish that you can simplify by eliminating the fava bean cassoulet or the liver mixture for the sauce, or by forgetting about the sauce entirely. But if you decide to make the complete dish, it will be one of your most impressive. When buying your squabs, try to find birds with all the giblets, including the heart, gizzard, and liver, because you will need them for the sauce. The squabs for this dish are prepared exactly the same way as for Sautéed Squab with Its Own Jus, except that the jus is finished with giblet butter instead of plain butter. Most of the work for the elegant fava bean cassoulet can be done earlier the same day, and then the assembled cassoulet can be heated in the oven just before serving.

MAKES 4 MAIN-COURSE SERVINGS

Fava Bean Cassoulet

2 pounds fava beans in the shell, shucked

2 ounces foie gras

Salt

Pepper

2 tablespoons fresh bread crumbs

Salt

Pepper

Giblet Butter

Giblets from 4 squabs and any saved-up squab livers

3 tablespoons unsalted butter

Sautéed Squab with Its Own Jus (see pages 280–282)

To make the cassoulet, bring a saucepan three-fourths full of water to a rapid boil, add the fava beans, and blanch for 1 minute. Drain in a colander and rinse in cold water. Peel the fava beans, using a paring knife and your thumbnail to remove the tough skin.

Chop the foie gras and put it in a small sauté pan over medium heat. When it starts to melt, add the fava beans and stir them around to coat them with the foie gras fat. Season with salt and pepper and spread the beans in a small gratin dish or baking dish so they are about 1/2 inch deep. Sprinkle the bread crumbs evenly over the top.

Thirty minutes before serving, place the dish in a 400°F oven and bake for about 12 minutes, or until the bread crumbs turn golden.

To make the giblet butter, take the giblets, except the necks (you can add the necks to the roasting pan with the squab carcasses), from the 4 squabs, put them in a mini food processor with the butter, and process until smooth, stopping as needed to scrape down the sides of the processor. If you don't have a mini food processor, chop the giblets with the butter until very fine, and then force the mixture through a medium- or fine-mesh strainer or drum sieve with the back of a spoon. Cover and refrigerate until needed.

To prepare the sautéed squabs, make the jus as directed, and then sauté the squabs. Deglaze the pan with the jus, whisk the giblet butter into the jus, and season with salt and pepper.

To serve, arrange the squab breasts and thighs on warmed plates and pass the cassoulet at the table. Or, for a more elaborate restaurant-style presentation, arrange the cassoulet in mounds in the center of 4 warmed plates. Slice the breast meat lengthwise into thin strips and arrange these, in a rosette pattern, over the fava beans. Put the thighs in the center and spoon the sauce over the top.

VARIATIONS

Roast squab is rarely everyday fare, and if you go to the trouble to make a jus or a sauce, it is fairly labor-intensive. But since you are pulling out all the stops with this special bird anyway, you should consider adding sautéed wild mushrooms—especially morels or porcini—or even chopped truffles (see page 333 for more about truffles) to the sauce. If you don't want to bother with the fava bean cassoulet, you can use other foods to prop up the squab meat and augment the dish. Creamed spinach (see page 295), chopped mushroom duxelles (see page 318), or a round crouton, cooked in butter, are nice platforms. Or, try the ultimate extravagance: use a crouton and place a slice of foie gras terrine (see pages 24–25) between the crouton and the breast meat.

1. Slide a length of string under the quail, just slightly in front of the thighs.

2. Pull one end of the string over the drumsticks.

3. Pull the other end of the string over the drumsticks, and tuck the string under the drumsticks to form an X.

4. Pull the string tight to bring together the drumsticks.

5. Bring the string back along the sides of the quail over the unfolded wings.

6. Flip the bird over so the string is hooked in the wings.

7. Pull the string tight and then knot. Cut off the excess string.

8. Fold under the wings.

QUAIL

Because quail are small, about the size of a baby's fist, they can't be stuck into a hot oven to roast. The heat will penetrate and overcook them before they are crispy and brown on the outside. A better approach is to sauté them on the stove top until thoroughly browned and then finish them in the oven. You can adjust the oven temperature according to when you want to serve the quail: 400°F for 5 to 10 minutes; 250°F for 25 minutes or so.

If you don't want to roast the quail—perhaps you dread carving the little things or forcing it on your guests—you can take the breasts and thighs off the carcasses and sauté them. If you are ambitious, you can make a broth with the quail carcasses well ahead of time, reduce it to the consistency of hot maple syrup, and use it to deglaze the pan you used for sautéing the quail breasts and thighs. You can even puree the quail livers and hearts with butter and whisk the butter into the sauce at the last minute. Or, at the last minute, you can infuse

1. Season and truss the quail and brown them in oil over very high heat.

2. Roast in a 500°F oven for about 10 minutes, or until the breasts feel firm when squeezed.

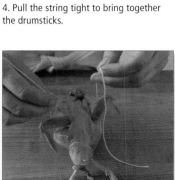

3. Cut off the breasts and thighs and arrange on plates, collecting any juices. Caramelize the juices in the roasting pan, deglaze the pan with the collected juices or broth, and strain the jus into a small container.

4. Serve with the jus.

the broth with a little finely chopped fresh chives or chervil and then whisk in a swirl of butter. Whatever your approach, keep the flavors simple, as the flavor of farm-raised quail is delicate.

Sautéed Whole Quail

If they bother you, cut off the little feet with shears or a knife. Trussing the quail as you would a chicken makes them compact and helps them cook more evenly, but this isn't essential. The best pan for browning is nonstick, but if you are using something else, get it good and hot with some olive oil in it, make sure the quail are patted perfectly dry, and shake the pan back and forth as you sauté, so the little birds don't have a chance to stick. Count on 1 quail per person for a first course and 2 quail for a main.

MAKES 8 FIRST-COURSE OR 4 MAIN-COURSE SERVINGS

> 8 quail
> Salt
> Pepper
> 3 tablespoons olive oil
> 1/2 cup quail, duck, or chicken broth (optional)

If the heads are still on, cut off and discard. If you like, trim the feet off the quail and then truss them as shown (see page 285). Preheat the oven according to your serving time, 500°F if you want to serve the quail within 5 to 10 minutes of putting them in the oven, or 250°F if you want to serve them after about 25 minutes. Choose an ovenproof sauté pan just large enough to hold the quail in a single layer.

Pat the quail dry with paper towels and season them liberally with salt and pepper. Pour the oil into the pan and heat over high heat. When the surface of the oil begins to ripple, add half of the quail and then move the pan back and forth on the burner as they brown. After 2 minutes or so, add the rest of the quail and sauté, turning the quail and moving the pan back and forth, for about 10 minutes, or until the quail are evenly browned. Slide the pan into the oven and roast for about 10 minutes more. Transfer the quail to a platter and slide the platter into the oven with the door open, to stay warm while you make the jus. Pour the fat out of the pan and set the pan aside. The quail are ready to serve or carve if the breasts feel firm when you squeeze them between your fingers.

If you are carving the quail, use a cutting board with a moat to catch any juices that run out. Then use the juices to deglaze the sauté pan, scraping up any caramelized juices, and serve a tablespoon of jus over each quail. If you don't have enough jus to deglaze the pan, just deglaze it with a little broth. Similarly, if you collect only a small amount of jus after deglazing the pan, you can extend it with a little broth.

VARIATION

Once you have deglazed the sauté pan, you should have about 1/2 cup jus. If you don't have that much, add broth until you have 1/2 cup. Put the jus in the smallest saucepan you have, and add 1 tablespoon chopped fresh parsley and 2 tablespoons cold butter. Puree the sauce with an immersion blender and season with salt and pepper with the pan over medium heat.

Sautéed Quail Breasts and Thighs en Civet

If you cut up the quail ahead of time, there is no last-minute carving. You can even brown the breasts, skin side down, ahead of time and then roast them in the oven just before serving. The "en civet" means that you are including the giblets in the sauce by pureeing them with butter in a food processor and working the butter through a strainer. If you don't want to bother with all the sauce-making advice, just sauté the breasts and thighs until they are firm to the touch (unlike squab, quail is a white meat and is cooked to the same doneness as chicken) and serve them as they are.

MAKES 8 FIRST-COURSE OR 4 MAIN-COURSE SERVINGS

8 quail, with giblets

Salt

Pepper

3 tablespoons olive oil

Optional Sauce

1 leek, white part only, cleaned, or onion, cut in half

1 carrot, peeled and thinly sliced

Bouquet garni

1 quart brown chicken broth, or more as needed to cover

4 tablespoons butter

1 tablespoon fresh parsley, finely chopped at the last minute

Cut the breasts and thighs off the bone as shown on page 281. Season on both sides with salt and pepper and refrigerate until needed. If the heads are still on, cut off and discard. Take the giblets—livers, hearts, gizzards—out of the cavities and reserve for the sauce, or sauté and give to the cat.

If making the sauce, preheat the oven to 400°F. Chop each carcass into a couple of pieces with a cleaver. Put the carcasses, leek, and carrot in an ovenproof sauté pan just large enough to hold everything in a single layer and roast for about 20 minutes, or until well browned but not until the juices burn on the pan bottom. Transfer the carcasses and vegetables to a saucepan and add the bouquet garni. Place the sauté pan on the stove top, add 1 cup of the broth, and deglaze the pan, scraping the bottom with a wooden spoon. Add to the

saucepan. Then add enough broth to cover the carcasses, bring to a simmer, and simmer gently for 3 hours. Strain through a fine-mesh strainer into a clean saucepan, and discard the bones and vegetables. Simmer the strained broth until reduced to about 1/2 cup. Set aside.

Put the reserved giblets and the butter in a mini food processor and process until smooth, stopping to scrape down the sides of the processor as needed. If you don't have a mini food processor, chop the giblets with the butter until very fine, and then force the mixture through a medium- or fine-mesh strainer or a drum sieve with the back of a spoon. Cover and refrigerate until needed.

Ten minutes before serving, select a sauté pan large enough to hold the quail breasts and thighs in a single layer, add the oil, and heat over high heat. When the surface of the oil begins to ripple, add the breasts and thighs skin side down and sauté for about 2 minutes, or until well browned. Turn and brown on the other side for about 1 minute, or until the meat feels firm to the touch. Transfer to a warmed platter or plates.

To finish the sauce, pour the burnt fat out of the pan, return to medium heat, and add the 1/2 cup reduced broth. Bring to a simmer and whisk in the giblet butter and parsley. Season with salt and pepper and spoon over the breasts and thighs.

VEGETABLES, BEANS, AND HERBS

Most vegetables are cooked in one of a number of simple ways. Green vegetables are cooked quickly in salted boiling water or steamed, either in a steamer or in their own moisture in a sauté pan. Root vegetables can be boiled in the same way as green vegetables, but they are usually taste best when cooked in a way that concentrates their flavors, such as braising or roasting. Some vegetable dishes, such as gratins, are sometimes simply baked or sometimes cooked in two stages.

GREEN VEGETABLES

While there are some good recipes for slow-cooked green vegetables, most of the time we want to cook them fast, so they keep their crunch, color, and freshness. Classic recipes insist on cooking green vegetables in a lot of rapidly boiling salted water. The purpose of so much water is to prevent the vegetables from cooling it down and thus slowing down the cooking. The faster the vegetables cook, the less color they lose. The salt also helps the vegetables keep their color, and it increases the temperature of the boiling water, which again shortens the cooking time. Some cooks prefer to steam green vegetables, believing that boiling leaches out nutrients, but many studies show that the loss of nutrients is about the same with both methods.

ASPARAGUS

It is a sad fact that asparagus has been banalized in this country into a ubiquitous, relatively tasteless green. In Europe, asparagus season is limited to spring, and the thick, meaty spears are sold for the price of good steak in the best restaurants. Until recently, Europeans preferred white asparagus spears, which are the same as green, except that sand is banked over the shoots to protect them from the sun and stop the development of chlorophyll. The difference in flavor between white and green is hard to detect, and most of the white asparagus spears sold in the United States are woody and expensive and not worth the bother. Buy asparagus in spring, when it is in season, and ideally from a local grower. Look for the thickest spears you can find, so that you get a meaty, satisfying flavor.

Asparagus tastes best when it is peeled. This is not a silly affectation, and if you are cooking thick asparagus, peeling won't take much time and it allows you to eat nearly the whole stalk. The asparagus will cook more evenly, too, so you don't have to worry about complicated methods found in some books that recommend submerging the asparagus in boiling water in increments. Like most green vegetables, asparagus is best cooked uncovered in lots of salted boiling water or steamed.

If you find really beautiful fresh asparagus spears, consider serving them as a first course. A sauce is always welcome. It can be as simple as a drizzle of melted butter or extra virgin olive oil, or it can be a hollandaise or one of its variations. Maltaise sauce, which is hollandaise flavored with orange (see page 346), is particularly popular in France. A more rustic variation is a fried egg on top, and a more urbane and extravagant one, some shaved white truffle slices. Feel free to eat asparagus with your fingers, dipping the spears in the sauce as you go.

Boiled or Steamed Asparagus

Asparagus is best steamed or cooked in a big pot of boiling water. As soon as it is cooked, toss it in a bowl to dry it slightly and then add cold butter and keep tossing to coat it. Whatever you do, don't heat the butter and asparagus in a sauté pan or the butter will turn oily. You can also just put a little butter or sauce on the asparagus as described in the recipe.

MAKES 4 FIRST-COURSE OR SIDE-DISH SERVINGS

- 1 pound thick asparagus
- 2 tablespoons salt, if boiling
- 3 tablespoons butter or extra virgin olive oil or
  1 cup Hollandaise Sauce (see page 345) or
  one of its variations

Cut 1 inch off the woody base of each asparagus spear and discard. Peel the stalks as shown below. Bring about 4 quarts

HOW TO PREPARE ASPARAGUS ────────

Trim an inch or two off the woody base of each stalk.

Peel the stalks from the base of the flower to the bottom of the stalk.

water to a rapid boil in a large pot and add the salt, or set up a steamer and bring the water to a boil.

Add the asparagus and boil or steam for 4 to 8 minutes, depending on its thickness, or just until it loses its crunch. Drain in a colander, or remove from the steamer rack.

Arrange the spears on warmed plates and top each serving with a thin slice of butter or a drizzle of olive oil or butter. If you are serving a sauce, pass it in a sauceboat at the table.

BROCCOLI AND BROCCOLI RABE

Other than being the same color and having the same name, broccoli and broccoli rabe are very different. Broccoli rabe has leaves and flowers and a pronounced bitter flavor that you either love or hate. Regular broccoli really only has leaves and flowers, sometimes called florets, that are green and, well, don't look that much like flowers. Broccoli should be quickly boiled or steamed, set to dry in a colander, and then tossed with a little butter and perhaps a chopped herb. Broccoli rabe is tastiest when sautéed with garlic.

Steamed or Boiled Broccoli

To steam or boil broccoli, cut it first into little bouquets by separating the florets from the stems. While there are those who insist steamed broccoli has more vitamins, it's virtually impossible to calculate the nutritional difference between steamed and boiled broccoli. Once cooked, broccoli can be tossed with cold butter or topped with a sauce such as hollandaise (see page 345).

MAKES 4 SIDE-DISH SERVINGS

- 1 head broccoli
- Salt
- 3 tablespoons butter
- Pepper
- 1 tablespoon finely chopped fresh parsley or chervil or
  1 teaspoon finely chopped fresh marjoram (optional)

Separate the head of broccoli into florets. Bring about 4 quarts water to a rapid boil in a large pot and add 2 tablespoons salt, or set up a steamer and bring the water to a boil.

Add the broccoli and boil or steam for 3 minutes, or until it turns a brighter green. Drain in a colander—shake it a little to rid the florets of any clinging water—or remove from the steamer. Place the florets in a warmed bowl, add the butter, and toss to coat. Season with salt and pepper and sprinkle with the parsley.

Sautéed Broccoli Rabe
with Garlic

If you like anchovies, you can do as the Italians do and include them here. Their saltiness nicely balances the bitterness of the broccoli rabe.

MAKES 4 SIDE-DISH SERVINGS

  1 large bunch broccoli rabe

  3 tablespoons extra virgin olive oil

  2 cloves garlic, minced and then crushed with the flat side of the knife

  9 anchovy fillets, or more to taste (optional)

  Salt

  Pepper

Cut the thick stems off the broccoli rabe and discard, so you are left with only the flower and leaves. In a large sauté pan, heat the oil over medium heat. Add the garlic and anchovies and stir for a couple of minutes to release their flavors into the oil. Add the leaves, turn the heat to high, and stir for about 3 minutes, or until the leaves are limp. Season with salt and pepper.

BRUSSELS SPROUTS

Brussels sprouts are in the same family as cabbage, so, like their cousins, they benefit from the addition of something meaty and smoky, such as bacon. If you like Brussels sprouts as they are, without adding meat, just halve them and boil or steam them for about 8 minutes and then toss them with butter, salt, and pepper.

Sautéed Brussels Sprouts
with Bacon

You can make this dish by cutting the Brussels sprouts in half through their stem end, or you can take the leaves off the sprouts and stir-fry them until they wilt. Use a large sauté pan or wok for this dish.

MAKES 4 SIDE-DISH SERVINGS

  1 pound Brussels sprouts

  1/4 pound thick-cut sliced bacon

  Salt

  Pepper

  1 tablespoon wine vinegar, or to taste

Trim off any wilted leaves from the Brussels sprouts, and then trim the base. Cut each sprout in half through the stem end, or cut off the base and pull away the leaves one by one. Cut the bacon slices crosswise into strips 1 inch long and about 1/4 inch wide.

In a large sauté pan or a wok, heat the bacon over medium heat for about 10 minutes, or until it just begins to turn crispy. Add the Brussels sprouts, turn the heat to high, and stir for about 5 minutes for halves or 2 minutes for leaves, or until the leaves wilt or the halves soften (bite into one to test). Season with salt, pepper, and vinegar.

HOW TO MAKE SATUÉED BRUSSELS SPROUTS WITH BACON ————————————————

1. Cut off the base of each sprout.

2. Pull away the leaves, separating them. Cook small strips of bacon until barely crispy and add the leaves. Stir over medium heat until leaves wilt.

3. Stir in wine vinegar and season with salt and pepper.

CABBAGE

Most cooks don't think of serving cabbage as a hot vegetable, perhaps because they don't realize that it must be cooked with meat, preferably pork and/or something smoky like bacon, to taste good. However you cook it, it is delicious served alongside rich meats such as pork or duck and is always best when livened up with vinegar. Juniper berries give it a distinctive martini flavor reminiscent of the sauerkraut served with sausages in France.

Cabbage with Bacon and Apples

Cabbage works well with sweet-and-sour and smoky flavors. Here, vinegar supplies the essential sour acidity while apples add a note of texture and sweetness.

MAKES 6 SIDE-DISH SERVINGS

> 1 head red, Savoy, or regular green cabbage
>
> 6 ounces thick-cut sliced bacon
>
> 6 juniper berries, crushed (optional)
>
> 3 tart apples such as Granny Smith, peeled, cored, and cut into ¹/₃-inch dice
>
> ¹/₄ cup wine vinegar
>
> Salt
>
> Pepper

Peel off and discard the outermost leaves from the cabbage. Quarter the cabbage through the core, and then cut the core out of each quarter. Slice each quarter as finely as you can with a vegetable slicer (below) or a chef's knife. Cut the bacon slices crosswise into strips 1 inch long and about ¹/₄ inch wide.

In a pot large enough to hold the cabbage, heat the bacon over medium heat for about 10 minutes, or until it just begins to turn crispy. Add the juniper berries and apples and stir for

HOW TO USE A PLASTIC VEGETABLE SLICER

Adjust the thickness of the slices with the nut on the back of the plastic vegetable slicer (commonly, a Benriner model).

Don't do what is shown here. Instead, use the guard or a towel to protect your hand.

2 minutes. Add the cabbage and the vinegar and cover the pot. Reduce the heat to low and simmer gently for 30 minutes.

Uncover the pot. If there is any liquid on the bottom of the pot, turn up the heat to high and boil the liquid until it evaporates, being careful not to scorch the cabbage. Season to taste with salt and pepper.

GREEN BEANS

Look for the thinnest green beans you can find. Slender, crisp French haricots verts are expensive, but are less costly today than they once were, as more farmers are now growing them. If you are a fanatic, you can also "french" regular green beans by halving or quartering them lengthwise.

Most of the time, it is best to cook green beans at the last minute and serve them hot. If you are cooking them ahead of time, or are serving them cold in a salad, drain them in a colander and immediately rinse them with cold water. When serving them hot, drain them in a colander and then shake the colander a bit so any clinging moisture evaporates. Put the beans in a warmed bowl and add slices of cold butter. Shake or stir the beans to coat them with the butter. Don't sauté the boiled beans in butter, or the butter will turn oily and leave a greasy coating on the beans.

Boiled or Steamed Green Beans

The trick to good buttered string beans is to drain them thoroughly or just take them out of the steamer and toss them in a bowl for a few seconds so the moisture clinging to them evaporates. Thin slices of cold butter should then be tossed with the beans, and not over any heat, or the butter will turn oily and greasy. Makes 4 side-dish servings

> 1 pound slender green beans, preferably haricots verts, ends trimmed
>
> Salt
>
> 2 tablespoons butter or extra virgin olive oil
>
> Pepper

Bring about 4 quarts water to a rapid boil in a large pot and add 2 tablespoons salt, or set up a steamer and bring the water to a boil. Add the green beans and boil or steam for 5 to 8 minutes, or until you bite into one and it has the texture you like. Drain in a colander—shake it a little to rid the beans of any clinging water—or remove from the steamer.

Place the beans in a warmed bowl, add the butter, and toss to coat. Season with salt and pepper.

LEEKS

Many cooks use leeks as components in soups and stews and other braised dishes. But leeks also make a wonderful vegetable side dish, hot or cold. One of the most delicious ways to serve them is to prepare the gratin on page 326. You can also steam or boil them and serve them cold with a mustardy vinaigrette, olive oil, or mayonnaise, or hot with butter, beurre blanc, extra virgin olive oil, or hollandaise sauce. They are also lovely served as a first course, arranged in neat rows on the plate.

Basic Leeks
for Serving Hot or Cold

Leeks have such a special finesse and flavor that, unlike other members of the onion family, merit being served on their own. Try just cooking them in boiling water or with steam and serving them hot with butter, olive oil, or a sauce, or serve them cold, tossed with vinaigrette. Makes 4 first-course or side-dish servings

10 leeks

Salt

Pepper

For Serving Hot

4 tablespoons butter, extra virgin olive oil, or Hollandaise Sauce (see page 341)

For Serving Cold

6 tablespoons Basic Vinaigrette (see page 69), made with 4 teaspoons mustard, or 3/4 cup Basic Mayonnaise (see page 359) or one of its variations

Trim, halve, and clean the leeks as shown. Bring about 4 quarts water to a rapid boil in a large pot and add 2 tablespoons salt, or set up a steamer and bring the water to a boil. Add the leeks and boil or steam for 12 to 20 minutes, or until a knife slides through a leek with no resistance. Drain in a colander, whether boiled or steamed. If serving the leeks cold, immediately rinse them with cold water. To extract excess water, press the leeks between your hands if they are cold or with the back of a spoon if they are hot.

Place the leeks in a bowl and toss gently with pepper, butter, olive oil, or vinaigrette. If serving with hollandaise or mayonnaise, pass the sauce at the table. Arrange the leeks, 5 halves per serving, on plates.

1. Cut off the greens, leaving about 1 inch of green attached to the white. Cut off the hairy root end.

2. Wittle off the outer green from the end of the leek white.

3. Cut the white in half lengthwise. Rinse under running water with the root end up. As you rinse, leaf through the membranes to release any sand.

4. Slice or julienne leeks.

Reheating Green Vegetables

The reason green vegetables are often tasteless in restaurants is because most chefs cook them in advance and then reheat them by plunging them into hot water or, even worse, keep them warm the length of the dinner service. If you have leftover green vegetables, don't reheat them in a pot of water, or they will lose most of their flavor and nutrients. Instead, put a few tablespoons of water in a skillet and put over high heat. Add the vegetables and toss or stir them until they are hot. If the water evaporates before the vegetables are heated through, add a couple more tablespoons of water.

FENNEL

Considering how versatile it is, fennel is oddly neglected. Used raw, it can be sliced paper thin with a vegetable slicer and then tossed with vinegar or lemon juice and extra virgin olive oil. To cook it, peel the fibrous stringy membrane from the outside as you would celery sticks and then cut the bulbs into wedges. Braise the wedges, in a single layer, in just enough water or broth to come about halfway up their sides.

HOW TO PREPARE FENNEL FOR BRAISING OR ROASTING

1. Cut the stalks off where they join the bulb. You can slice the stalks and use them in broths or freeze them for later use. Or, you can leave them whole and dry them by leaving them in the open air and then tossing them on the grill when grilling whole fish.

2. Peel the stringy outer layer off the bulb.

3. Cut the bulb in half, and then cut each half into wedges with some core attached.

PEAS

Fresh baby peas are such a rarity that most of us rely on frozen peas. In fact, most of the year frozen peas, especially baby peas, are sweeter and seem fresher than the overgrown woody peas commonly found at the supermarket. The trick to cooking frozen peas is to disobey the instructions that tell you to boil them. Boiling is unnecessary, since they are already lightly cooked at the factory. All you need to do is heat them up with a little water in a pan, and then toss them with butter and, if you like, some chopped herbs. In spring or early summer, you may find fresh baby peas at a local farmers' market. If you do, cook them in salted boiling water for about 1 minute, drain, and toss with butter.

Fresh Buttered Peas

If you're cooking fresh peas, they only need to be boiled for a minute or two before being drained and tossed with butter. If you're reheating frozen peas, don't follow the instructions on the package and boil them (they've already been boiled at the factory), but instead thaw them in a little water heated in a saucepan over high heat until they're heated through, toss with butter, and serve.

MAKES 4 SIDE-DISH SERVINGS

> 1¹/₂ **pounds fresh baby peas in the shell, shucked, or one 10-ounce package frozen petite peas**
>
> **Salt**
>
> **3 tablespoons butter or a compound butter (see pages 348–349)**
>
> **Pepper**
>
> **1 tablespoon chopped fresh parsley, chervil, mint, or tarragon (optional)**

If you are using fresh peas, bring about 4 quarts water to a rapid boil in a large pot and add 2 tablespoons salt. Add the peas, boil for 1 minute, and drain in a colander, shaking it a little to rid the peas of excess water. If you are using frozen peas, let them thaw—you can thaw them in the microwave—and put them in a sauté pan over medium heat. Stir them around just long enough to heat them through.

Put the hot peas in a warmed bowl with the butter and toss until the butter melts. Season with salt and pepper and sprinkle with parsley.

SPINACH

Nowadays, spinach is available in bags with most of the work—the stemming and washing—already done. There is nothing wrong with buying spinach in a bag. But you must inspect it carefully through the bag to make sure there are no wet spots or wilting or yellowing leaves. In theory, you shouldn't have to wash it again, but a quick rinse is a good idea. If you are fastidious, you may want to pick through it and pull off any stems that were left on when it was packed. If you are buying spinach in bunches, you will probably encounter (at different times of the year) one of two kinds: one with small, smooth leaves and the other with large, wrinkled leaves. The small-leaved spinach is best for salads. But if you are cooking spinach, those little leaves will shrink to nothing, so look for large leaves.

Like most green vegetables, spinach can be cooked in salted boiling water or steamed. It can also be stirred around in a sauté pan until it releases its water and then drained. Once the spinach is cooked and drained, you can mix it with a little butter or with some reduced cream. Or, you can give the spinach a more pronounced buttery flavor by cooking the butter in a pan until it caramelizes into beurre noisette, as shown on page 341, and then stirring in the spinach.

Basic Spinach

Spinach with beurre noisette is a classic combination. The trick to successful spinach is to squeeze excess water out of it before tossing it with butter or lightly creaming it. If the spinach is cold—you have cooked it ahead of time and reheated it—this just means wringing it out in your hands; if the spinach is hot, you'll need to compress it against the side of the saucepan you cooked it in or in a strainer to extract the excess liquid.

MAKES 4 SIDE-DISH SERVINGS

Two 10-ounce bunches or 14-ounce bags spinach
Salt
3 tablespoons butter or heavy cream
Pepper

Bring about 4 quarts water to a rapid boil in a large pot and add 2 tablespoons salt, or set up a steamer and bring the water to a boil. Add the spinach and boil for about 30 seconds or steam for 1 to 2 minutes, or until it wilts. You can also put the spinach in a large sauté pan with a couple of tablespoons

Hold the leaf with the sides folded down and the stem on top. Pull away the stem so it comes off the back of the leaf.

of water and stir it around over high heat for 1 to 2 minutes, or until it wilts. Drain the spinach in a colander and press on it with the back of a spoon to extract excess liquid.

In a sauté pan, heat the butter or cream over medium heat until the butter froths and the froth begins to subside, or the cream thickens. Stir in the spinach, mixing well. Season with salt and pepper.

Pureed Creamed Spinach

Spinach can be creamed without pureeing it, but most of us think of pureed spinach when we think of creamed spinach. You can cream spinach with a béchamel sauce or plain cream. Cream is easier but a bit rich.

MAKES 4 SIDE-DISH SERVINGS

Boiled or steamed spinach (left)
$1/2$ cup heavy cream or Béchamel Sauce (see pages 341–342)
Salt
Pepper

Prepare the spinach as directed, but omit the addition of butter or cream. Press the drained spinach well to eliminate any water.

If using cream, boil it over high heat until it thickens to about $1/4$ cup, then remove from the heat. In a blender, combine the cream (or béchamel) and the spinach and process for 1 minute, or until smooth. Season with salt and pepper.

SWISS CHARD

This relatively rugged green comes as red or white, both easily identifiable by the color of the stems. Red Swiss chard has a more pronounced beetlike flavor, so if you are cooking Swiss chard for the first time and are unsure about whether you will like it, use the white variety.

Swiss Chard with Garlic and Olive Oil

Swiss chard makes a great accompaniment to grilled or sautéed meats or seafood.

MAKES 4 SIDE-DISH SERVINGS

> 1 large bunch Swiss chard
>
> 2 cloves garlic, minced and then crushed with the flat side of the knife
>
> 1/4 cup extra virgin olive oil
>
> Salt
>
> Pepper

Using a paring knife, cut the green leafy part of the chard away from the stems. Wash the greens, spin dry, and reserve.

In a large sauté pan, combine the garlic and olive oil over medium heat. As soon as you see bubbles forming around the garlic, add the chard. Cook for about 10 minutes, or until any liquid released by the chard evaporates. Season with salt and pepper.

ARTICHOKES

Artichokes are cooked somewhat differently than most green vegetables, because they take a relatively long time to cook. They should be simmered uncovered in a nonaluminum pan, but with a plate set over them to keep them submerged. Most recipes call for adding lemon juice and oil (or sometimes even flour) to the water to keep the artichokes from turning dark. These in fact make little difference. If you are serving cold artichoke bottoms or hearts—you can make them very pale green by rubbing them with lemon juice *after* they are finished cooking.

Occasionally, baby artichokes are featured in markets, and after some trimming, they can be eaten whole because they haven't yet developed a choke. They can be cooked and served cold as a salad or in a salad (see page 83), or they can be sautéed with garlic and herbs (opposite) and served as a first course or side dish.

Basic Boiled Artichokes

You can serve artichokes with a simple sauce, such as melted butter, olive oil, vinaigrette, or mayonnaise. Aioli is especially good. A large artichoke, hot or cold, makes a lovely first course to a dinner or a satisfying side dish.

MAKES 4 FIRST-COURSE OR SIDE-DISH SERVINGS

> 4 large artichokes
>
> 1/2 cup melted butter, extra virgin olive oil, Hollandaise Sauce (page 345), Basic Mayonnaise (page 359), or Aioli (page 360)

Cut the stem off of each artichoke straight across the base, so the artichokes will stand upright on plates. Put the artichokes in a nonaluminum pot with enough water to cover by 1 inch and bring to a simmer. Put a plate on the artichokes to keep them submerged, but don't cover the pot. Simmer for about 25 minutes, or until a paring knife slides easily into the bottom of an artichoke.

Drain the artichokes in a colander and then arrange upside down. Let them drain this way for a minute or two before putting them on plates. Pass the butter, oil, or sauce at the table.

1. Cut off the stem, so the artichoke will stand upright on a flat surface.

2. Rotate the artichoke against a sharp paring knife to remove the outer leaves. Keep the knife perpendicular to the base.

3. Continue trimming until you see white on the side of the base.

4. Change the angle of the knife to about 45 degrees, and trim any green off the bottom of the artichoke.

5. Cut off the tops of the leaves.

6. Trim the top of the base where the leaves were attached.

7. Rub the artichoke bottom with lemon.

8. Simmer the artichokes until you can penetrate them with a skewer or paring knife. Scoop out the choke with a spoon.

Baby Artichokes with Garlic and Parsley

Once pre-cooked in the same way as large artichokes (but for less time), baby artichokes can be sautéed. They are especially good with garlic.

MAKES 4 FIRST-COURSE OR SIDE-DISH SERVINGS

- 1¹/₂ pounds baby artichokes (about 20)
- 2 tablespoons butter or olive oil
- 2 cloves garlic, minced and then crushed with the flat side of the knife
- 1 tablespoon finely chopped fresh parsley
- Salt
- Pepper

Trim the artichokes and put them in a nonaluminum pot. Add water to cover by about 2 inches, bring to a simmer, and simmer for about 15 minutes, or until a paring knife slides easily through the side of an artichoke. Drain in a colander and let cool just long enough to handle. Or, if cooking them in advance, rinse with cold water until cool.

Cut the artichokes in half through the stem end. In a large sauté pan, melt the butter over medium to high heat. Add the artichokes and sauté for 2 to 3 minutes, or until heated through. Sprinkle with the garlic, parsley, salt, and pepper and sauté, tossing or stirring, for 1 minute more. Serve on warmed plates.

Artichoke Bottoms

Fancy recipes for salads or hot dishes sometimes call for artichoke bottoms. There is indeed something luxurious about eating artichokes without fussing with the leaves, but also disturbing when one thinks of the waste. One obvious solution is to serve artichokes the night before and forbid everyone from eating the bottom. But this seems cruel and stingy. The professional way is to "turn" the artichoke by trimming off the leaves. The bottoms are then cooked, just like whole artichokes, and the choke pulled out with a spoon. Once you have the artichoke bottoms, you can cut them into wedges and sauté them (in the same way as the baby artichokes, left) or include them in salads with other ingredients. If you are being really old-fashioned, you can fill the bottoms with other vegetables, such as peas or sautéed mushrooms, and serve them around a roast on a platter, in the spirit of *Larousse Gastronomique*.

CHIFFONADE: Roll the leaves tightly and slice the rolls to make whispy slices of leafy vegetables. You can control the size of the chiffonade by controlling the thickness of your slices.

PAYSANNE: Cut carrot sections in half lengthwise. Cut each half into 3 lengthwise wedges. Slice the wedges into tiny triangles.

BRUNOISE: Cut tiny dice from julienned sticks.

RONDELLES: Slice cylindrical vegetables into rounds. Holding the knife facing slightly inward will keep the rondelles from running all over the cutting board.

JULIENNE: Slice the vegetable, here a cleaned leek sheaf is shown, 1/16 inch thick.

BÂTONNETS: Slice a root vegetable, such as a turnip, about 1/8 inch thick, and then cut the slices into sticks of the same width.

ROOT VEGETABLES

Root vegetables are cooked differently than green vegetables, because the purpose is to concentrate their flavors and natural sugars in a way that's different than for green vegetables. Occasionally, a root vegetable will be old or overgrown and will need to be blanched in boiling water to take away bitterness. But for the most part, exposing root vegetables to water robs them of some of their good flavors.

BEETS

For those who have only had beets out of a can, a fresh beet right out of the oven is a revelation. If you want to dramatize the presentation, buy the largest beets you can find and carve them at the table. The best way to cook beets is to roast them in their skin—wrapped in aluminum foil or on a sheet pan so they don't drip on the oven floor—and then peel them afterward. If you are cooking only one or two beets, consider using the microwave, either by itself or in conjunction with the oven (see page 306).

Roast Beets with Wine Vinegar, Butter, and Parsley

Because beets take a long time to roast—about an hour— it is worthwhile to roast more than you need and then serve some of them cold in salads or as part of a crudité plate (see page 77) later in the week. Beets are great with vinegar, especially wine vinegar with a full woody flavor, such as sherry vinegar, good balsamic vinegar, or homemade vinegar.

MAKES 6 MAIN-COURSE SERVINGS

> **6 beets**
> **1/4 cup wine vinegar**
> **4 tablespoons butter, sliced**
> **Salt**
> **Pepper**
> **1 tablespoon finely chopped parsley**

Cut off any greens where they join the bulb. Put the beets on a sheet pan or wrapped in foil, slide the pan into the oven, turn on the oven to 400°F. (There is no need to preheat.) Bake for about 1 hour, or until a knife slides easily in and out. Peel the beets while they're still hot by holding them in a kitchen towel and by pulling away the peel with your thumb and the edge of a paring knife.

If serving the beets hot, cut a thin slice off the top and bottom of each beet and, using an old kitchen towel that you don't mind staining, slip off the skin.

Slice the beets into rounds about 1/8 inch thick—use a fork to hold the hot beet in place while slicing—and put the slices into a warmed bowl. Boil the vinegar down by about half and whisk in the butter, a piece at a time. Keep whisking the butter until it completely emulsifies with the vinegar, season with salt and pepper, and toss with the beets. Sprinkle the parsley over and serve immediately.

VARIATION

Serve the beets cold, leaving them in rounds or cutting them into sticks the size of small French fries. Toss them with 3 tablespoons walnut oil, 1/4 cup sherry vinegar, and 1/4 cup toasted walnuts. Season with salt and pepper.

CELERIAC

This hairy-looking root vegetable, also known as celery root, owes much of its obscurity to its appearance, not its taste. It can be cooked like a turnip—roasted, shaped, and glazed—but its flavor is reminiscent, though more subtle and somehow more alluring than the green branch kind. Other than using it to make mashed potatoes or celeriac rémoulade, it is worth trimming, shaping, and glazing it as a root vegetable.

CELERIAC MACÉDOINE

1. Peel celeriac with a knife, not a vegetable peeler.

2. Trim off the sides of the celeriac so you have a perfect cube.

3. Cut the cube into slices 1/8 to 1/4 inch thick. Cut the slices into bâtonnets.

4. Cut the sticks into cubes, or macédoine.

CARROTS

The poor carrot is rarely served as a vegetable, and when it is, it is often so badly cooked that it has no flavor. Never boil carrots unless you want their flavor to go into the surrounding liquid, such as when making soup or broth. Instead, glaze them in a small amount of water or broth, or roast them, ideally surrounding a meat roast so the flavors of the meat and

HOW TO PREPARE CARROTS FOR GLAZING OR ROASTING

1. Cut off the stem end.

2. Peel the carrots.

3. Cut into sections the length you want.

4. Cut the sections into wedges according to their size. For example, large sections may need to be cut in 5 wedges, while the thin end may only need to be halved.

5. If the carrots are old, cut out the tough core from each wedge.

6. If you want to round the edges, rotate them against a paring knife.

carrots mingle and the fat from the roast prevents the carrots from drying out.

When preparing carrots for cooking, you can slice them or cut them into sections and then cut each of the sections into wedges. If you are being particular, you can remove the woody cores from the wedges with a paring knife, as shown. You can also turn the carrots into little football shapes.

If you have purchased stem-on baby carrots (not from a bag), scrape them with a knife to remove the thin peel, rather than use a vegetable peeler, which will take too much of the carrot with the peel.

Glazed Baby or Sectioned Carrots

The secret to glazing carrots and other root vegetables is to braise the vegetables in just enough liquid and over just the right heat, so the complete evaporation of the liquid coincides with the vegetables being done. In this way, all of the flavor released into the liquid ends up coating the vegetables in the form of a glaze. Classic recipes call for cooking the vegetables with the pan uncovered, but with the vegetables covered with a round of parchment paper. This system allows the glazing liquid to evaporate while trapping enough steam so that the part of the vegetable above the liquid cooks at the same rate as the part that is submerged. You can skip the parchment paper and just partially cover the pan with its lid, quickly moving the pan back and forth on the burner every few minutes so the vegetables cook evenly.

MAKES 4 SIDE-DISH SERVINGS

> **2 large carrots, 4 medium carrots, or 16 baby carrots with greens attached, or one small bag baby carrots without greens**
>
> **$3/4$ cup water or broth, or as needed**
>
> **2 tablespoons butter**
>
> **Salt**
>
> **Pepper**

If using large or medium carrots, trim, peel, and cut into sections about 1 inch long as shown at left. Cut the sections lengthwise according to their thickness. For example, near the tip of the carrot, where the section is narrow, you may want only to cut the section in half, while sections from the stem end, which are thicker, may call for as many as 5 wedges. The wedges can be any size you choose, but they should be uniform. If you like, cut out the tough cores. If using baby carrots, scrape them with a knife, leave about $1/2$ inch of the green attached, and leave the carrots whole.

1. Put the carrot wedges in a pan just large enough to hold them in a single layer. Add enough broth or water to come halfway up their sides and a little butter.

2. Cook, partially covered, until the carrots can be penetrated with a skewer and the cooking liquid is evaporated.

Put the carrots in a sauté pan just large enough to hold them in a single layer, and pour in enough water to come halfway up the sides of the carrots. Add the butter and put the pan over high heat. When the liquid comes to a simmer, turn the heat down to medium and partially cover the pan. Cook, quickly moving the pan back and forth on the burner every 5 minutes or so to make sure the carrots are cooking evenly, for about 20 minutes, or until the carrots offer only a little resistance when you poke one with a paring knife.

If the liquid is threatening to evaporate before the carrots are done, add more liquid and turn down the heat. If the opposite is true and the carrots are done and swimming in liquid, uncover and raise the heat to high to evaporate the liquid. Season with salt and pepper. There should be no liquid remaining in the pan when the carrots are done.

Baked Carrots with Parsley

Traditionally, this dish is made with Vichy water, a very minerally mineral water appreciated in France as a hangover cure. If you want to be authentic and manage to track down Vichy water, it will give your carrots a distinct flavor. But this dish is also nice without it.

MAKES 6 SIDE-DISH SERVINGS

> **4 tablespoons butter**
>
> **3 large or 5 medium carrots, peeled and sliced between 1/16 and 1/8 inch thick**
>
> **2/3 cup Vichy water, broth, or tap water**
>
> **1 tablespoon finely chopped fresh parsley**
>
> **Salt**
>
> **Pepper**

Preheat the oven to 425°F. Using 1 tablespoon of the butter, grease a baking dish large enough to hold the carrots in a layer between 1/2 and 1 inch thick. Spread the carrots in the dish and pour in the water. Thinly slice the remaining 3 tablespoons butter, and lay the slices evenly over the top. Cover the dish loosely with aluminum foil.

Bake the carrots for 30 minutes. Check the carrots—a paring knife should slide easily in and out—and notice the liquid in the dish. If the liquid is gone and the carrots are done, they are ready to serve. If there is liquid in the dish and the carrots are done, take off the foil, turn up the oven to 450°F, and bake until all the liquid evaporates. If there is liquid in the dish and the carrots aren't done, turn up the oven to 450°F but leave the foil on the dish, and bake until the carrots are done and all the liquid evaporates.

Sprinkle the carrots with the parsley, salt, and pepper and serve.

Roast Carrots

One of the simplest dinners is a roast surrounded with root vegetables. The vegetables get coated with the juices and fat from the roast, and when all goes well, they lightly caramelize. If you are not making a roast, you can still roast root vegetables. You just have to coat them with fat, such as butter or oil, to keep them from drying out.

MAKES 4 SIDE-DISH SERVINGS

> **3 large or 5 medium carrots**
>
> **2 tablespoons olive oil or melted butter**
>
> **Salt**
>
> **Pepper**

Preheat the oven to 400°F, or if you are roasting meat, leave it at the temperature you are using for your roast. Trim and peel the carrots, cut into 1-inch sections, and then into wedges as shown on opposite page. Toss the carrots with the oil and season with salt and pepper.

If serving the carrots with a roast, put them around the roast about 1 hour before you think it will be ready. Otherwise, arrange them in a baking dish in which they fit in a single layer and roast for about 45 minutes, or until a knife slides easily in and out.

ONIONS

Even though it is hard to imagine a more versatile vegetable than the onion, they are rarely served as a side dish. There are several varieties, of course, from the standard large yellow onion and the fresher white onion to the sweeter red onion and the very sweet Vidalia. They also come in various sizes, from gigantic to walnut-sized boiling onions to miniature pearl onions. Large onions end up in all manner of soups and sauces, but can also be halved and baked and served as a vegetable. Smaller onions can be glazed or roasted.

Glazed Pearl or Boiling Onions

This dish, which calls for glazing onions in a little water or broth, is most impressive when made with the little pearl onions sold in pint boxes, but because they are tedious to peel, some cooks opt to use larger boiling onions. Onions can be "white" glazed or "brown" glazed. When white glazed, the onions are glazed just until the surrounding liquid evaporates and coats them. When brown glazed, the evaporated liquid is allowed to caramelize on the bottom of the pan and then a little more liquid is added to dissolve the brown glaze so that it can coat the onions. Traditional recipes call for covering the pan with a sheet of parchment paper, but this isn't absolutely necessary. This recipe makes 4 side-dish servings,

but if you are combining the onions with other vegetables, it will make twice that number.

MAKES 4 SIDE-DISH SERVINGS, OR 8 IF COMBINED WITH OTHER VEGETABLES

> **1 pint pearl onions or 1 pound walnut-sized boiling onions**
> **About $^3/_4$ cup broth or water**
> **2 tablespoons butter (optional)**
> **Salt**
> **Pepper**

Bring about 4 quarts water to a rapid boil in a large pot and add the onions. Boil for 1 minute, drain in a colander, and rinse with cold water. Slip off the skins.

Place the onions in a sauté pan just large enough to hold them in a single layer and add enough broth to come halfway up their sides; add the butter. Bring to a simmer over high heat, turn the heat down to medium, and partially cover the pan. Simmer, quickly moving the pan back and forth on the burner every 5 minutes or so, for about 15 minutes for pearl onions or 25 minutes for boiling onions, or until a knife easily slides through an onion. If the liquid evaporates before the onions are done, add 2 or 3 tablespoons more liquid. If the onions are done and there is liquid in the pan, uncover the pan and turn up the heat to high to evaporate the liquid.

If you want the onions to be white or you are using them

HOW TO PEEL AND CHOP ONIONS

1. Slice stem and root ends off each onion, being careful not to cut too deeply.

2. Cut the onion in half through the root end.

3. Pull the peel away from each half. Slice the onion with the knife perpendicular with the base of the onion, keeping the slices attached at the root end.

4. Make 2 or 3 horizontal slices into the onion almost to the root end.

5. Keep the onion compact as you finish horizontal slices.

6. Cut across the slices.

7. Continue to chop as finely as you like.

to make creamed onions, serve them as soon as they are done and the liquid has evaporated, seasoning them with salt and pepper. If brown-glazing them, leave the pan over medium heat until the liquid browns and caramelizes on the bottom of the pan. Then add 3 tablespoons water or broth, raise the heat to high, and quickly move the pan back and forth on the burner to dissolve the glaze and coat the onions. When the liquid evaporates, season with salt and pepper and serve.

CREAMED ONIONS

Prepare the Glazed Pearl or Boiling Onions, white-glazing them. When they are ready, pour 1/2 cup heavy cream into the pan, put the pan over medium heat, and simmer until the cream thickens and coats the onions. Season with salt and pepper.

Roast Onions

If you are roasting a piece of meat, you can surround it with boiling onions, carrot sections, and turnip sections— a complete meal in one pan.

MAKES 4 SIDE-DISH SERVINGS

> **1 1/2 pounds walnut-sized boiling or pearl onions**
> **2 tablespoons melted butter or olive oil**
> **Salt**
> **Pepper**

Preheat the oven to 400°F, or if you are roasting meat, leave it at the temperature you are using for your roast. Bring about 4 quarts water to a rapid boil in a large pot and add the onions. Boil for 1 minute, drain in a colander, and rinse with cold water. Slip off the skins. Toss the onions with the butter and season with salt and pepper.

If serving the onions with a roast, put them around the roast about 45 minutes before you think it will be ready. Otherwise, arrange them in a baking dish just large enough to hold them in a single layer and roast for about 45 minutes, or until a knife slides easily in and out.

Toss the onions with butter or oil, season them with salt and pepper, and arrange them around the roast or put them in a baking dish just large enough to hold them in a single layer. Bake until a knife slides easily in and out, about 45 minutes.

HOW TO MAKE GLAZED PEARL ONIONS

1. Cut out a round of parchment paper the diameter of the pan.

2. Fold the parchment in half, then in half again repeatedly.

3. Put the peeled onions in a pan just large enough to hold them in a single layer. Add a chunk of meat glaze (page 177), optional, and enough water or broth to come halfway up the sides. Cut the round of parchment to fit over the onions.

4. Cook over medium heat with the parchment covering.

5. If the onions are done before all the liquid has evaporated, take off the paper and boil over high heat.

6. Continue until the onions are coated with a shiny glaze.

PARSNIPS

The poor ignored parsnip fortunately keeps well during its long wait for takers. A parsnip looks like a yellow carrot, usually a large yellow carrot, and rarely shows up with its greens. When roasted, it has a surprising sweetness and texture reminiscent of sweet potatoes, but earthier and not as sweet. Parsnips should be cooked until they are tender, like potatoes, and then served in sections or pureed and served alone or mixed with an equal amount of potatoes. For parsnips at their best, peel them, cut them into sections an inch or two long, and arrange them around a roast about an hour before the roast is ready.

Roast Parsnips

This dish will yield more than 4 servings if there are other vegetables on the evening's menu.

MAKES 4 SIDE-DISH SERVINGS

> 3 parsnips, peeled and cut into 1½-inch sections
> 3 tablespoons melted butter or olive oil
> Salt
> Pepper

Toss the parsnips with the butter, salt, and pepper. Arrange them in a baking dish just large enough to hold them and slide them into the oven. Turn the oven to 350°F (there is no need to preheat) and roast for about 1 hour, until a knife slides through the thickest pieces with no resistance.

Glazed Parsnips

Parsnips take well to glazing since their natural sugars caramelize along with butter and broth.

MAKES 4 SIDE-DISH SERVINGS

> 3 parsnips, peeled and cut into 1½-inch sections
> About 1 cup chicken broth or water
> 2 tablespoons butter
> 2 teaspoons sugar
> Salt
> Pepper

Put the parsnips in a sauté pan just large enough to hold them in a single layer, and pour in enough broth to come halfway up the sides of the parsnips. Add the butter, sugar, salt, and pepper and put the pan over high heat. When the liquid comes to a simmer, turn the heat down to medium and partially cover the pan. Cook, quickly moving the pan back and forth on the burner every 5 minutes or so to make sure the parsnips are cooking evenly, for about 20 minutes, or until the parsnips offer only a little resistance when you poke one with a paring knife.

If the liquid is threatening to evaporate before the parsnips are done, add more liquid and turn down the heat. If the opposite is true and the parsnips are done and swimming in liquid, uncover and raise the heat to high to evaporate the liquid.

SHALLOTS

Shallots are like miniature onions, with a particularly clean, direct flavor. They are especially delicious in sauces, or sprinkled on sautéed vegetables near the end of cooking so they remain a little raw, thus delivering a little bite. Shallots are minced like regular-sized onions, just in miniature.

HOW TO MINCE SHALLOTS

1. Cut the peeled shallot in half through the stem end.

2. Slice the shallot with the knife perpendicular to the base as thinly as you can, keeping the slices attached at the root end.

3. Make horizontal slices into the onion almost to the root end.

4. Slice across the slices.

TURNIPS

The much maligned turnip is more likely to evoke an image of a Dickensian boarding-school dining room than a picture of anything tasty. True, when made into a puree without the mollifying effects of potato, turnips can be bitter and aggressive. But when glazed or roasted, they have a depth of flavor that makes them a great accompaniment, especially to roasts or sautéed meats. When shopping for turnips, select those that feel heavy in your hand. As they age, they get spongy and bitter.

Turnips can be sliced and baked in a gratin (page 327), or they can be cut into sections and glazed in the same way as carrots.

Glazed Turnips

This recipe yields 4 servings, but if you are roasting other vegetables, it will make twice that number.

MAKES 4 SIDE-DISH SERVINGS

> **4 turnips**
> **About 3/4 cup broth or water**
> **2 tablespoons butter**
> **Salt**
> **Pepper**

Peel and section the turnips as shown. Put the turnips in a sauté pan just large enough to hold them in a single layer, and pour in enough broth to come halfway up the sides of the turnips. Add the butter and put the pan over high heat. When the liquid comes to a simmer, turn the heat down to medium and partially cover the pan. Cook, quickly moving the pan back and forth on the burner every 5 minutes or so to make sure the turnips are cooking evenly, for about 20 minutes, or until the turnips offer only a little resistance when you poke one with a paring knife.

If the liquid is threatening to evaporate before the turnips are done, add more liquid and turn down the heat. If the opposite is true and the turnips are done and swimming in liquid, uncover and raise the heat to high to evaporate the liquid. Season with salt and pepper.

1. Cut off the root end with a knife.

2. Peel with a vegetable peeler.

3. To cut into half moons, cut in half lengthwise and slice the halves crosswise.

4. To turn turnips, cut the turnip into wedges and rotate each wedge against a paring knife.

CHESTNUTS

Chestnut vendors were once a common sight on American city streets in winter, but their popularity has waned since the turn of the twentieth century. America used to have its own native chestnuts, but they were wiped out by a blight during the early part of the twentieth century and now all chestnuts in the United States are imported. We forget to serve them (they should be thought of as a starch), which is a pity because they're particularly satisfying when pureed or when glazed like carrots. They can also be peeled and used to surround a roast. Perhaps the reason we don't cook them more is that they're difficult to find peeled and expensive when you do find them. Plus peeling them is laborious, at least when compared to peeling the equivalent weight of potatoes. However, peeling chestnuts is a lovely ritual, not as mysterious as it might seem, and—like preparing fava beans—especially rewarding.

HOW TO PEEL CHESTNUTS

1. Make a slit through the flat side of the chestnut. Spread the chestnuts in a single layer in a pan and bake in a 375°F oven for 20 minutes.

2. Before the chestnuts cool completely (use a towel if they are too hot to touch), break open the peel and strip away from the nut meat.

POTATOES

In the early nineteenth century, potatoes were virtually unknown in the Old World and in parts of the New World as well. They had been planted in France in the eighteenth century, but because they were judged by the flavor of their greens, they failed to become popular. By the end of the nineteenth century, classic French cookbooks contained close to a hundred recipes for cooking potatoes.

Until relatively recently, cooks in the United States found only three types of potatoes in the market: russets, sometimes called Idaho potatoes, used for baking; white waxy potatoes; and red waxy potatoes. Now, we find everything from Yukon Golds, which are perfect for mashing, and fingerling potatoes, sometimes called rattes, to exotic purple potatoes. Waxy potatoes remain firm when cooked and are best in gratins or stews when you don't want the potatoes to fall apart. Irish stew (see page 224) is sometimes made with both russets, which dissolve and give body to the sauce, and waxy potatoes, which hold their shape.

Potatoes can be prepared by virtually every cooking technique: boiling, frying, roasting, baking, steaming, sautéing, and braising (in a gratin). When they are pureed for serving as mashed potatoes, very little is better to eat.

Cooking Root Vegetables in the Microwave

It seems like a waste to turn on the oven for an hour if you are baking root vegetables for only one or two people. A microwave can be used to cook 1 or 2 potatoes or beets in a little more than a few minutes. When using the microwave, keep in mind that the speed at which the vegetable cooks diminishes as the number of vegetables increases. If you put 5 potatoes in the microwave, they will take longer to cook than they would in the oven. On the other hand, whether you cook 1 potato or 10 potatoes in the oven, the timing is the same.

If you cook a potato in the microwave for, say, 12 minutes, you need to reposition it every couple of minutes to make sure the heat is penetrating it more or less evenly. It is also helpful to let the vegetable rest every 5 minutes or so, to give the heat time to spread out evenly within the vegetable. If you are in a hurry, you can use both methods: start the vegetable in the microwave and finish it in the oven.

Mashed Potatoes

The best mashed potatoes are made with Yukon Gold or fingerling potatoes. Yukon Golds are more practical because they are bigger and you will have fewer to peel. If you can't find either of these, use russet potatoes, preferably labeled Idaho. (Russets from other places often turn dark when exposed to air.)

Once you have peeled your potatoes, cut them into quarters—or even smaller if you are in a rush—and put them in a pot with just enough water to come about halfway up the sides of the potatoes. Don't cover them completely with water. You want their flavor to concentrate in the water, so you can use the water to thin the puree, and then simmer for 20 minutes. At this point, cooks disagree about what to do next. Some insist that the potatoes must be beaten with the whip attachment of a stand mixer to make them fluffy, while others claim that excessive working makes them gummy and gluey. (This seems to be true only with waxy potatoes.) Then there is the debate over whether to use a masher, a ricer, a food mill, or the more exotic drum sieve. A drum sieve provides the ideal method. With its sheet of fine screen stretched over a round metal or wooden frame, this handy tool in fact looks a little like a drum. Solid mixtures are worked through the screen to make them perfectly smooth. A ricer is a good second choice, as is a food mill with the finest attachment. The old-fashioned masher, which allows too many lumps to escape, comes in last.

Mashed potatoes can be made as rich or as lean as you like, but adding more cream or butter after a certain point just makes them richer without really improving their flavor. If you have already added a shocking amount of cream and/ or butter and the potatoes are still stiffer than you like, add some of their cooking liquid.

MAKES 6 SIDE-DISH SERVINGS

> 6 large Yukon Gold potatoes or 3 pounds
>   fingerling potatoes, peeled
> 1/2 cup butter, or to taste
> 1 to 2 cups hot milk, heavy cream, or half-and-half
> Salt
> Pepper

Cut large potatoes into quarters. Put the potatoes into a pot and add water to reach halfway up their sides. Cover the pot, bring to a gentle simmer, and simmer gently for about 30 minutes, or until the potatoes are falling apart. Check the potatoes every 10 minutes to make sure the water is not running dry, and if it threatens to, add a little more.

Drain the potatoes in a colander over a bowl to save the cooking liquid. Work the potatoes through a drum sieve, ricer, or food mill over a bowl, or mash the potatoes in a bowl with a potato masher. Work in the butter with a whisk or wooden spoon until it melts and then add enough liquid, including some of the cooking liquid, until the potatoes are the consistency you like. Season with salt and pepper.

VARIATIONS

Potatoes have such a mild yet satisfying flavor that they make a perfect foil for other vegetables that would be too aggressive or wouldn't have the right texture if pureed alone. Celeriac, fennel, and garlic are particularly good when cooked and pureed along with the potatoes. Or, stir truffle butter into the potatoes just before serving,

MASHED POTATOES WITH FENNEL: Cut the stalks off the top of a large fennel bulb. Peel off the stringy outer layer of the bulb, then cut in half, cut out the tough core portion, and chop the bulb. Cook the fennel with the potatoes as directed above. Don't puree the potatoes with a masher, because it won't crush the fennel.

MASHED POTATOES WITH GARLIC: Cut 1 head of garlic in half crosswise and cook it with the potatoes as directed above. Work through a drum sieve, ricer, or food mill.

MASHED POTATOES WITH CELERIAC: Peel and chop 1 large celeriac. Cook it with the potatoes as directed above. Work through a drum sieve, ricer, or food mill.

MASHED POTATOES WITH TRUFFLES: Replace the butter in the Mashed Potatoes with an equal amount of Truffle Butter (see page 350), which can be made without having to use any of the truffles.

Baked Potatoes

Few foods are better than a baked potato with plenty of butter and sour cream. But even though that classic combination is hard to improve on, it is fun to experiment with compound butters made from different herbs, mushrooms, truffles, or Parmesan cheese (see pages 348–349). You can even make a few and pass them at the table. If you want a low-fat topping, try a little yogurt, broth, or a sprinkle of cheese. The one mistake people often make when baking potatoes is wrapping them in aluminum foil. This keeps their skin from getting crispy, a tragedy for those of us who like the skin.

Wash each potato well and dry. Poke each potato in several places with a knife or skewer to keep them from exploding. There is no need to preheat the oven—just stick the potatoes in, turn the oven to 375°F, and bake for about 1 hour, or until a knife slides easily in and out. If you are only cooking a couple of potatoes or you are in a rush, you can use the microwave (see page 306).

"Raw" Sautéed Potatoes

It is easy to assume that sautéing a potato is one of the easiest things to do in the kitchen, but in fact it is a little tricky. Yet when done perfectly, the results are worth it, with each slice containing a melting puree between two disks of golden crust.

There are two approaches to sautéing potatoes, one that starts with raw potatoes and one that starts with cooked potatoes. The raw approach gives the best results but takes longer. The second approach is good to keep in mind when you have leftover baked potatoes. In fact, it is a good idea to bake a few extra potatoes to have for sautéing on the following days.

Ideally, you have two large sauté pans with sloping sides for cooking the potatoes. The pans must be large because you don't want to crowd the potatoes. If you do, the ones on top will steam, release starch into the pan, and cause the rest of the potatoes to gum together into a messy mass.

You need to peel the potatoes, slice them $1/8$ inch thick, soak the slices in water to eliminate starch, and then carefully dry the slices to prevent steaming and sticking. The sautéing must begin over very high heat to seal the potatoes, and the potatoes should be cooked in butter. To reconcile these two necessities, you can sauté the potatoes in clarified butter (which can be heated very hot without burning), or you can sauté them in oil, and then transfer them to a second pan and finish them with butter.

4 large Yukon Gold potatoes

4 tablespoons clarified butter (see page 341) or olive oil

Salt

Pepper

4 tablespoons butter if sautéing with oil

Preheat the oven to 200°F. Peel the potatoes and cut them into 1/8-inch-thick slices. A mandoline is handy here. Put the slices in a bowl, cover with cold water, and let soak for 30 minutes. Drain off the water, cover the potatoes again with water, immediately drain off the water, cover again with water, and then drain again. Continue in this way until the potato slices no longer cloud the water. Drain the slices in a colander and then spin them, in batches, in a salad spinner to rid them of most of the liquid. Pat them dry on kitchen towels—not paper towels, which will stick and tear.

In 2 large sauté pans (or 1 large pan, if that is all you have), heat the clarified butter or oil over high heat. When it just begins to smoke, add enough of the potato slices to form

HOW TO MAKE "RAW" SAUTÉED POTATOES ─────

Heat clarified butter in a wide sauté pan large enough to hold the potatoes in a single layer. Brown over high heat, turning gently with a spatula so as not to break through the crust and release starch into the pan.

Pat dry, season with salt and pepper, and serve immediately.

a single layer. Shake the pans for the first couple of minutes, quickly moving them back and forth on the burners to keep the potatoes in motion and prevent them from sticking. After about 5 minutes, still over high heat, when the potatoes are well browned on the first side, start to gently turn them over with a long, thin spatula. Don't use tongs or a fork, which can tear through the crust and release starch. Cook for about 5 minutes more on the second side, or until well browned.

Transfer the browned slices to a sheet pan, pat them dry to remove surface fat, and keep them warm in a 200°F oven while you continue cooking additional batches of potatoes. If you used clarified butter, sprinkle the potatoes with salt and pepper and serve. If you used oil, put the butter in one of the sauté pans, melt over medium heat, add the potatoes, toss the potatoes with the butter, and sauté for 2 minutes. Season with salt and pepper and serve.

"Cooked" Sautéed Potatoes

This is a convenient method of accommodating leftover baked potatoes. If you are starting from scratch, peel waxy potatoes and boil them, starting in cold water so they cook through evenly. Let cool before slicing.

MAKES 4 SIDE-DISH SERVINGS

> **4 large potatoes, baked or boiled**
> **4 tablespoons butter**
> **Salt**
> **Pepper**

Preheat the oven to 200°F. If the potatoes are not already peeled, peel them. Cut the potatoes into 1/4-inch-thick slices. In 2 large sauté pans, preferably nonstick, melt the butter over medium heat. Add the potato slices in a single layer and sauté for about 12 minutes, or until golden brown on the first side. Using a long, thin spatula, turn the slices and cook for about 5 minutes on the second side, or until golden brown. Don't use tongs or a fork for turning, as both can tear through the crust and release starch.

Transfer the browned slices to a sheet pan and keep warm in the oven while you sauté the remaining slices. Season with salt and pepper just before serving.

Roasted Fingerling or Shaped Potatoes

Fingerling potatoes can be roasted whole, with the skin on, so that guests can crush their own serving with the back of a fork and slip in a pat of butter. For a more elegant presentation and for even browning, peel fingerling potatoes or peel and shape large potatoes into elongated footballs. Unless you are cooking the potatoes for a long time with a roast to ensure they brown, they should be sautéed in oil and then put in the oven with butter. If you are shaping whole large or medium potatoes into something smaller, peel the potatoes first and then save the trimmings, immersed in water, for making mashed potatoes. If you are cooking the potatoes with a roast, put them—peeled or unpeeled—around the roast about 1 an hour before you think it will be ready.

MAKES 4 SIDE-DISH SERVINGS

> **1¹/₂ pounds fingerling potatoes or 4 medium to large Yukon Gold or russet potatoes**
> **3 tablespoons vegetable oil**
> **3 tablespoons butter**
> **Salt**
> **Pepper**

Preheat the oven to 400°F, or if you are roasting meat, leave it at the temperature you are using for your roast. If using fingerling potatoes, you can leave the peel on and just toss them with the oil to coat them before roasting, so they don't dry out when first exposed to the hot oven. If using Yukon Golds or russets, peel and shape them into egg shapes.

In an ovenproof skillet, heat the oil over high heat. When it begins to smoke, add the potatoes and sauté for about 5 minutes, or until evenly browned. Pour off the oil, let the pan cool for a couple of minutes, and add the butter. Slide the pan into the oven and bake for 25 minutes, or until a knife slides easily in and out of the potatoes. Season with salt and pepper before serving.

1. Peel 7 large waxy potatoes and cut into thin sticks with the julienne attachment of a mandoline.

2. In a nonstick sauté pan, heat olive oil over high heat until it begins to smoke.

3. Heap the potatoes in the pan.

4. With a spatula, press the potatoes down into a flat cake.

5. Cut up butter and scatter the pieces around the pan.

6. Cook over medium heat. When the potatoes are brown around the edges, press a plate over them to hold them in place and drain the butter into a heatproof bowl; save the butter.

7. Invert the pan and plate, set the plate on the counter, and lift off the pan, transferring the potatoes to the plate.

8. Slide the potatoes back into the pan, browned side up.

9. Pour the reserved butter back into the pan and cook the potatoes on the other side.

10. Drain off the butter a second time and slide the pancake onto a plate.

Sautéed Straw Mat Potatoes

This straw mat makes a dramatic presentation, plus its buttery crunchiness is hard to resist. It is remarkably quick to make, too, finished in little more than 30 minutes.

MAKES ABOUT 6 SIDE-DISH SERVINGS

7 large waxy potatoes, peeled

3 tablespoons olive oil

8 ounces (16 tablespoons) butter, cut into $1/4$-inch-thick pieces

Salt

Pepper

Just before you are ready to begin cooking, julienne the potatoes as shown. Don't do it any sooner or they will turn dark. It's unnecessary to soak them in water to prevent discoloration.

Heat the oil in a 10- or 12-inch skillet, preferably nonstick. When the oil begins to smoke, heap the julienned potatoes in the center of the pan and press them down into a flat cake. Keep the pan over high heat for about 1 minute to cook the starch, and then turn the heat down to low. Give the pan handle a few quick clockwise-counterclockwise movements to keep the cake from sticking. Press down on the cake with the back of a spatula.

Scatter the pieces of butter around the pan and turn up the heat to medium. Season with salt and pepper. Sauté for about 7 minutes, pressing down on the cake with the spatula and pushing in any stray potatoes around the edges. When the first side is golden brown, press on the cake to hold it in place, and tilt it over a heatproof bowl to drain off the butter.

If you are feeling brave, give the pan a quick forward jerk while tossing upward, to get the cake to flip over, and then promptly catch it in the pan. If caution prevails, flip the cake out onto a plate and then return it, browned side up, to the pan. Pour the drained-off butter back into the pan and sauté in the same way for about 7 minutes on the second side. Season the second side with salt and pepper. Drain off the excess butter, slide onto a plate, and serve cut into wedges.

Potato Pancakes

If you find yourself with leftover mashed potatoes or baked potatoes, just work in a little egg, season with salt and pepper, shape the mixture into patties, and cook gently in butter for 3 to 5 minutes on each side. If you are starting from scratch, boil the potatoes and combine them with the egg and some chives.

MAKES 6 SIDE-DISH SERVINGS

2 pounds Yukon Gold or russet potatoes, peeled and quartered

4 eggs, beaten

$1/2$ cup heavy cream

2 tablespoons finely chopped fresh chives

Salt

Pepper

2 tablespoons butter

Sour cream or crème fraîche for serving

Put the potatoes into a pot and add water to reach halfway up their sides. Cover the pot, bring to a simmer, and simmer gently for about 30 minutes, or until the potatoes are falling apart. Check the potatoes every 10 minutes to make sure the water is not running dry, and if it threatens to, add a little more.

Drain the potatoes in a colander. Work the potatoes through a drum sieve, ricer, or food mill over a bowl. Add the eggs, cream, and chives, season with salt and pepper, and stir to mix. Let the mixture cool at room temperature for 1 hour, and then cover and refrigerate for at least 3 hours or up to overnight.

Shape the mixture into patties about 4 inches in diameter and $1/4$ inch thick.

In a large nonstick sauté pan, melt the butter over medium heat. When it froths, add the patties and cook, turning once, for about 5 minutes on each side, or until golden brown. Pass the sour cream at the table.

Potatoes Anna

This elegant cakelike concoction is made with sliced pota-toes, rather than the julienned potatoes used for the straw mat on page 311. If you are lucky, you have a pommes Anna pan. Its two-piece construction allows you to turn the cake over without spilling the butter out of the pan. In its absence, you can use a nonstick sauté pan, pour off the butter, invert the potato cake onto a plate, and then slide the cake back into the pan, return the butter to the pan, and brown the second side.

MAKES 6 SIDE-DISH SERVINGS

> 1 tablespoon butter, room temperature, plus 3/4 cup
> (12 tablespoons)
>
> 4 large waxy potatoes (about 2 1/2 pounds), peeled
> and shaped into perfect cylinders (opposite)
>
> Salt
>
> Pepper

Preheat the oven to 400°F. Brush the bottom of a straight-sided 8-inch sauté pan, preferably nonstick, with soft butter. Line the sauté pan with an 8-inch round of parchment paper. Brush the paper with the softened butter. Using a mandoline, slice the potatoes about 1/16 inch thick. For a dramatic effect, cut the first two potatoes into perfect cylinders before slicing, as shown. Arrange a layer of potato slices, overlapping them, in concentric circles on the paper. This layer will eventually be the top of the potato cake. Season with salt and pepper and add slices of butter or melt the butter and dribble it over. Arrange a second layer of potatoes on top, season with salt and pepper, and add or sprinkle with butter. Continue to make layers until you have used up all the potatoes and butter. Place a second round of parchment paper, the same size as the first, over the cake. Set a smaller pot or lid over the potatoes to weight them down.

Bake for 25 minutes, or until the cake shrinks slightly and the sides are golden brown.

While holding the potatoes in place with the back of a spatula, pour out the excess butter into a heatproof bowl. Peel off the paper. Place a plate, ideally one that just fits into the pan over the potatoes, on top of the cake. Invert the pan and plate together and lift off the pan. Peel off the paper. Gently slide the potatoes back into the pan and then pour the butter back into the pan.

Return the pan to the oven and bake the potatoes for 15 minutes longer, or until brown on the sides. To serve, pour off the excess butter from the pan and then slide the cake out onto a large plate. Cut into wedges at the table.

1. Peel large waxy potatoes. Shape the first two potatoes into perfect cylinders.

2. Brush the bottom of a sauté pan with soft butter. Fold and cut parchment to line pan.

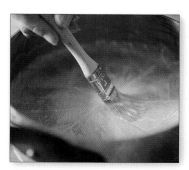

3. Place the round of parchment in the buttered pan. Brush the parchment with butter.

4. Using a mandoline, slice 1 shaped potato into rounds the thickness of a quarter.

5. Arrange the slices, overlapping them, in concentric circles in the pan.

6. Thinly slice butter and place evenly over the potatoes. Season with salt and pepper.

7. Slice the remaining shaped potatoes and arrange in layers in the same way, topping each layer with thin butter slices, salt, and pepper. Cover the top with a round of parchment paper.

8. Place a pan or lid over the potatoes and weight it down with another pan.

9. Bake at 400° for 25 minutes, remove the weight, and cook for 15 minutes. When the surface of the potatoes is brown around the edges, take off the parchment.

10. Run a knife around the inside edges of the pan to detach any potatoes that have stuck. Place an ovenproof serving plate over the pan and invert both to dislodge the potatoes from the pan and onto the plate.

11. Gently peel away the parchment.

12. Return the potatoes to the oven to brown the top, or invert them into another pan with butter to brown the top on the stove top. Serve cut into wedges.

Potatoes Noisette

You will need a melon baller to make these marble-sized potatoes. This Franglish title alludes to the actual French name, which is pommes noisettes.

MAKES 4 SIDE-DISH SERVINGS

> **5 large waxy potatoes, peeled**
> **3 tablespoons olive oil**
> **4 tablespoons butter**
> **Salt**
> **Pepper**

Using the large end of a melon baller, carve the potatoes into balls. Soak the balls in cold water to cover for 30 minutes, drain, and pat dry with kitchen towels.

In a skillet, heat the oil over high heat. When it begins to smoke, add the potatoes and sauté, tossing gently every 60 seconds, for about 7 minutes, or until the potatoes are golden brown. Turn down the heat, place the potatoes in a strainer to drain off the oil, and add the butter to the pan. Continue to sauté over medium heat for about 15 minutes, or until cooked through. Season with salt and pepper and serve right away.

1. Peel waxy potatoes and cut out little balls with the large end of a melon baller.

2. In a large sauté pan, heat oil over high heat. Add the potatoes and brown well, quickly moving the pan back and forth on the burner to prevent sticking.

3. Drain the potatoes in a strainer and put them back in the pan.

4. Cook the potatoes in butter over medium heat until cooked through.

5. Season with salt and pepper. Serve immediately.

Fried Potatoes

There may be no more universally revered food than the French fry, but sadly French fries are rarely made at home. This is easy to understand, given both the large amount of hot oil and the general mess.

French-fry connoisseurs are divided into two camps: thick and thin. Choosing sides is important since different techniques apply to each. The very thinnest French fries, matchstick potatoes, are cooked in one step: a quick plunge in almost-boiling oil. Slightly thicker French fries (still classified as thin) and thick French fries must be cooked in two separate steps: The first step is slow-frying in hot, but not fiery hot, oil for a relatively long time—3 minutes or so—to cook the potatoes through. The second step, done just before serving, requires submerging the precooked fries in the very hottest oil to reheat them and create the delicate, crusty crust. Fortunately, the first step can be done hours in advance.

How Hot to Fry

If you don't have a deep-fry thermometer, you will have to judge the temperature of the oil by how it behaves. For the low-temperature first stage, a single potato stick should sink to the bottom of the pot and be immediately surrounded by bubbles and then take about 15 seconds to rise to the surface. For the high-temperature second stage, a potato stick should immediately float on the surface and be surrounded by an abundance of bubbles.

Matchstick Potatoes

Because these potatoes are so thin, they cook within a minute or two of being dropped in hot oil. Start by cooking just a few sticks and diagnosing any problems, so you can adjust the temperature of the oil accordingly. If the potatoes brown quickly but are limp and soggy when you bite into one, the oil is too hot. If the potatoes are greasy and/or dry, the oil isn't hot enough.

MAKES 4 SIDE-DISH OR APPETIZER SERVINGS

1 pound russet or Yukon Gold potatoes, peeled
About 3 quarts pure olive oil, vegetable oil, or rendered duck fat
Salt

Using the finest attachment on a mandoline, or using a chef's knife as shown on page 310, step 1, cut the potatoes into julienne sticks $1/16$ inch wide and a couple of inches long. Soak the sticks in cold water to cover for 20 minutes. Drain them in a colander and then spin them, in batches, in a salad spinner to rid them of most of the liquid. Pat them dry on kitchen towels—not paper towels, which will stick and tear.

Pour the oil into a deep, heavy pot large enough so that it comes no more than halfway up its sides, and heat to 360°F, or until a potato stick dropped into the oil floats immediately on the surface and is surrounded with bubbles. Add a handful of the potatoes and fry for about 3 minutes, or until golden brown. If the potatoes brown sooner, turn down the heat. If they brown too quickly, they will turn golden but remain limp. Using a spider or skimmer, transfer the potatoes to paper towels to drain briefly. Fry the remaining potatoes in the same way, adding as many as you can at once without the oil boiling over. Sprinkle with salt and serve immediately.

Classic Thin French Fries

The most flavorful fat for frying potatoes is rendered beef kidney fat, which is brittle and snow white when cold. But because of cholesterol fears, most cooks now use vegetable oil or pure, not extra virgin, olive oil.

These French fries are cooked in two stages, low temperature and high temperature, so if you are cooking a lot of fries, you can set up two pots and use a spider to move the potatoes from one to the other. If you are not making too many, you can finish the preliminary frying ahead of time.

The best potatoes for frying are russets that have been sitting around for a while, losing moisture. If you would like to cook French fries often, get a big bag of potatoes and keep them in a cool place.

MAKES 4 SIDE-DISH SERVINGS

> **4 russet potatoes, peeled**
> **About 4 quarts pure olive oil or vegetable oil**
> **Salt**

Using a mandoline, or using a chef's knife as shown on page 310, step 1, cut the potatoes into julienne sticks 1/8 inch wide and the length of the potato. Soak the sticks in cold water to cover for 20 minutes. Drain them in a colander and then spin them, in batches, in a salad spinner to rid them of most of the liquid. Pat them dry on kitchen towels—not paper towels, which will stick and tear.

At this point you can fry the potatoes ahead of time, and then fry them in hot oil just before serving. Pour the oil into a deep, heavy pot large enough so that it comes no more than halfway up its sides, and heat to 320°F, or until a potato stick dropped into the oil sinks to the bottom of the pot and then rises to the surface. Add a handful of the potatoes and fry for about 5 minutes, or until cooked through but not browned. Using a spider or skimmer, remove the potatoes from the oil and put them on a sheet pan. Continue to fry the remaining potatoes, adding as many at once as you can without the oil boiling over.

Increase the temperature of the oil to 360°F. Add a handful of the potatoes—they should stay on the surface rather than sink—and fry for 1 to 2 minutes, or until golden brown. Using a spider or skimmer, transfer the potatoes to paper towels to drain briefly. Continue to fry the remaining potatoes, adding as many at once as you can without the oil boiling over. Sprinkle with salt and serve immediately.

1. Cut the potatoes with a mandoline or knife into 1/8-inch-thick sticks for thin fries and 1/2-inch-thick sticks for thick fries.

2. Fry until potatoes are soft and pureelike when you pinch one.

3. The fries should look limp and droopy when you take them out of the first-stage oil.

4. Drain the fries on paper towels, and then increase the oil temperature.

5. Fry the second time until golden brown and crispy when you bite into one.

6. Thick and thin French fries.

Thick French Fries

These potatoes are fried in the same way as thin French fries; the cooking times are just longer. Remember that the first-stage frying or baking can be done earlier the same day.

MAKES 4 SIDE-DISH SERVINGS

> **4 large russet potatoes, peeled**
> **About 4 quarts pure olive oil or vegetable oil**
> **Salt**

Cut the potatoes lengthwise into sticks 1/2 wide and thick. Soak the sticks in cold water to cover for 20 minutes. Drain them in a colander and then spin them, in batches, in a salad spinner to rid them of most of the liquid. Pat them dry on kitchen towels—not paper towels, which will stick and tear.

To fry the potatoes for the first stage, proceed as directed for Classic Thin French Fries, opposite, and fry for 10 minutes at 320°F, or until cooked through but not browned. If the potatoes start to brown, reduce the heat slightly.

For the second stage, increase the oil temperature to 360°F and fry the potatoes for 1 to 2 minutes, or until golden brown. Drain as directed, sprinkle with salt, and serve immediately.

Steamed Potatoes

Often served as an accompaniment to seafood, steamed potatoes contain no fat, which makes them a good counterpoint to rich sauces or seafood. Use fingerling potatoes, shaped russets, or Yukon Golds.

MAKES 4 SIDE-DISH SERVINGS

> **8 fingerling potatoes or 2 large Yukon Gold or russet potatoes, peeled**

If using Yukon Gold or russet potatoes, quarter them lengthwise and shape each quarter into an elongated football. Bring the water to a boil in a steamer, add the potatoes, and steam for 12 to 20 minutes, depending on their size, or until a knife penetrates them easily. Serve right away.

MUSHROOMS

As hard as it is to imagine these days, with several kinds of cultivated mushrooms and an extravagant assortment of wild mushrooms in the market, a generation ago mushrooms were considered exotic.

The most common mushroom is the cultivated white mushroom. But in recent years, cremini mushrooms, which are brown instead of white and are popular in Europe, have become more widely available, usually at the same price. They contain less water than white mushrooms, so you get more mushroom per pound.

When cooking any cultivated mushrooms and most wild mushrooms, always keep in mind that they contain a lot of water. For example, if you are making a quiche and put raw mushrooms in the shell before pouring over the custard mixture, the mushrooms will release water during baking and end up surrounded by little puddles. For most recipes in which mushrooms are used as a garnish, in a sauce, or in a stuffing, the mushrooms are sautéed first to brown them and to evaporate their moisture and concentrate their flavor. But you can also steam them with a little water and capture the liquid they release for adding to sauces.

The first question many cooks ask about mushrooms is whether they should be washed or just brushed clean, as many cookbooks suggest. Cultivated mushrooms should be washed by putting them in a big bowl of cold water, swirling them around, and then lifting them out with your fingers splayed. Even if you allow them to sit in the water, they absorb virtually no liquid. Most wild mushrooms can be washed the same way, but some, such as morels and porcini (also called cèpes), absorb water, so it is best to rinse them quickly and pat them dry.

Small button mushrooms look attractive in a sauce on top of a piece of meat or seafood, but if you are using larger mushrooms, they should be sliced or quartered through the stem end. Wild mushrooms can usually be sliced, or sometimes you can follow their contours with a knife so that they retain their shape.

Mushroom "duxelles" is simply a filling or stuffing made of chopped mushrooms that have been cooked down until all the water they contain evaporates. In some versions cream is added to help bind the mushrooms and make them a little richer.

1.Slice mushrooms.

2. Finely chop the slices.

3. Cook the mushrooms in butter or olive oil over high heat, adding only a small handful at a time to the pan, until all the liquid evaporates and the mushrooms are browned.

4. If you like, add heavy cream and cook until thick.

HOW TO MAKE MUSHROOMS TARTUFATI ————————

1. Add very thinly sliced mushrooms, a few at a time, to hot butter or olive oil in a very hot sauté pan.

2. Stir over high heat until the mushrooms curl and brown. Add to sauces or pasta for a trufflelike flavor.

Sautéed Mushrooms with Garlic and Parsley

Feel free to substitute shallots for the garlic, or tarragon for the parsley. Get the pan very hot and then add the mushrooms, starting a few at a time, so they don't release water and boil in their own juices. If they do release water, just keep the pan over high heat and boil the juices until they evaporate. You can serve these mushrooms as a side dish, or over steaks, chops, or seafood, either by themselves or warmed in a sauce.

MAKES 4 SIDE-DISH SERVINGS OR TOPPINGS FOR 6 STEAKS, CHOPS, OR SEAFOOD

$1^1/_2$ pounds cultivated mushrooms, preferably cremini

3 tablespoons butter or olive oil

Salt

Pepper

2 cloves garlic, minced and then crushed with the flat side of the knife

2 tablespoons finely chopped fresh parsley

Put the mushrooms in a bowl filled with cold water and slosh them around with your hands. Lift them into a colander with your fingers splayed, so the water drips off of them. If the bottoms of the stems are dark or wizened, cut off about $1/_8$ inch. If the mushrooms are very small, leave them whole. If they are medium-sized, cut them into quarters through the stem end. If they are large, cut them into slices. Be sure to cut all the mushrooms the same way.

In a large sauté pan, heat the butter or oil over high heat. When the butter froths and then the froth begins to subside, or the oil ripples, add a handful of mushrooms. Stir or toss for a couple of minutes with a wooden spoon and then add another handful of mushrooms. Continue in this way until you have added all the mushrooms and they have browned and smell fragrant. This will take about 10 minutes total. (If there is liquid in the pan, keep sautéing until all the liquid evaporates and the mushrooms have browned.) Season with salt and pepper. Add the garlic and parsley and stir for about 1 minute, or until the garlic is fragrant. Serve right away in a warmed bowl.

Mushroom Varieties

With the exception of morels and porcini, wild mushrooms are better fresh than dried. Dried morels and porcini can be reconstituted and used to flavor sauces and soups.

Porcini

Also known as cèpes, these classically shaped Alice-in-Wonderland mushrooms have a meaty texture, deep, rich flavor, and can grow quite large—some caps are a foot in diameter. When dried, the texture is lost but the flavor remains, and is sometimes even enhanced. When buying fresh porcini, avoid any with patches of wetness and check under the caps and on the stems for evidence of worms. When buying dried porcini, check the bag carefully to make sure it holds large, unbroken slices. Take a whiff, too. You should be able to detect an earthy aroma. If you have bought fresh porcini and are worried they may carry worms—they are often wormy—put them in a 175°F oven for about 30 minutes, or until the worms crawl out and die. (Say nothing to the guests.) When using dried porcini, soak them in a minimum amount of warm water, squeeze out the water they absorb, and use this liquid, leaving any grit behind, in sauces, stews, or soups.

Morels

Don't confuse morels with gyromitra (see below). Morels are dark brown, almost black, and have a distinct Christmas-tree shape, while gyromitra, which have a similar weblike surface, are irregularly shaped. When buying fresh morels, avoid

any that are wet or smell like mildew. When morels sit on the shelf, they do one of two things: they get soggy and moldy and should be avoided, or they dry out, which enhances their flavor and also makes them lighter and cheaper per pound. Pick through them and choose the driest ones. When buying dried morels, look for large ones with the classic shape. Rehydrate in just enough hot water to wet them, not cover.

Chanterelles

You may sometimes see this mushroom called a *girolle,* the French name. There are many varieties of chanterelle, but the golden chanterelle, named for its bright orange color, is the most commonly available type. Chanterelles contain a relatively small amount of water, so they are easy to sauté. You may encounter them dried, but pass them up, as they have little flavor and a very hard texture.

Black Trumpets

In French, these are called *trompettes de la mort,* or "death trumpets," phrasing that American marketing people don't seem to have picked up. These mushrooms are in fact shaped like little cornucopias and are jet black. They are best sautéed.

Gyromitra (False Morels)

Occasionally, dried gyromitra are sold as morels because of their similar shape and texture. While it's possible to see how one could confuse the two, morels are always conical while gyromitras are irregular and more amorphous in shape. Fresh gyromitras can even be poisonous (only some people are sensitive to their toxicity) but since the poison is volatile and evaporates when the mushrooms are dried or cooked, the mushrooms have only proven dangerous when eaten fresh and raw. Despite being poisonous when fresh and raw, they do sometimes show up dried in shops as dried morels. Avoid them by always looking for the distinctive cone shape of true morels.

Sautéed Wild Mushrooms for Seafood or Meat

You can serve wild mushrooms as a side dish—they look great passed in a nice bowl—but since they generally shrink a lot when cooked, this can get very expensive. By spooning them over a piece of sautéed meat or fish, you can get by with fewer.

MAKES ENOUGH TO TOP 6 SERVINGS OF MEAT OR SEAFOOD

1 pound fresh wild mushrooms such as porcini, morel, chanterelle, or black trumpet, alone or in combination

3 tablespoons butter or olive oil

Salt

Pepper

Inspect the mushrooms for dirt. Give them a quick rinse in a colander, pat them dry, and look inside the hollow stem to make sure nothing is hiding there.

If the porcini are large, cut them into 1-inch-thick slices. The slices are thick because they shrink a lot in the pan and you don't want to compromise the meaty texture. The other mushrooms are usually small enough to leave whole, but if you have giant chanterelles, cut them in half or into quarters, following their contours so the pieces maintain their shape.

In a large sauté pan, heat the butter or oil over medium-high to high heat. Add the mushrooms and sauté for about 7 minutes, or until the mushrooms are browned and fragrant and any liquid they may have released evaporates. Season with salt and pepper. Spoon directly onto servings of seafood or meat, or stir into a sauce.

EGGPLANT

The best kept secret for cooking eggplants is to buy the bright purple eggplant sold in Asian markets. These eggplant have fewer seeds and a milder flavor than regular bulb eggplant. Another trick is to avoid sautéing eggplant because it simply absorbs too much liquid. A better method is to brush it lightly with olive oil—you can slice it lengthwise or in rounds—and bake it until tender. It can then be served as is or used in other dishes such as eggplant parmigiano. To make eggplant parmigiano, follow the lasagne recipe on page 385, but substitute lengthwise slices of eggplant, baked until tender, for the lasagne noodles. Use 3 to 4 eggplants to substitute for the noodles.

SQUASHES

There are two basic kinds of squash: winter squash, which starts to appear in the fall, and summer squash, of which zucchini is the best known member. Zucchini, both green and yellow, can be sautéed, baked, or grilled to rid them of their water and bring out their flavor. Winter squashes, however they are served, are almost always baked at least as a preliminary step.

Sautéed Zucchini

Most of the zucchini we encounter end up a watery, insipid mess because they release water when they cook and then boil in their own juices. They are best sautéed like mushrooms: add just a few slices at a time until they heat through and start to brown. When all the slices are well browned, toss them with garlic or shallots and an herb such as parsley, thyme, marjoram, or oregano.

MAKES 4 SIDE-DISH SERVINGS

4 zucchini

3 tablespoons olive oil

Salt

Pepper

2 cloves garlic, minced and then crushed with the flat side of the knife

1 tablespoon finely chopped fresh parsley, 1 teaspoon finely chopped fresh thyme, 2 teaspoons chopped fresh marjoram or oregano, or 1/2 teaspoon dried thyme or oregano

Trim the ends off the zucchini. Slice the zucchini, ideally with a plastic vegetable slicer, into rounds the thickness of a quarter.

In your largest sauté pan, heat the oil over high heat. When the oil begins to ripple, toss in a handful of the zucchini. Quickly stir or toss, wait for a couple of minutes, or until you see the first hint of browning, and then toss in another handful. Continue in this way for about 15 minutes, or until all the zucchini slices are browned. Season with salt and pepper, sprinkle with the garlic and herbs, and toss or gently stir for 1 minute longer. Serve immediately.

Grilled Zucchini

When grilling zucchini, fire up your largest grill. It takes up a lot of room. It is best to slice zucchini lengthwise, as round slices are harder to turn and can slip through grill racks. The trick to tasty grilled zucchini is to cook it until it is a pronounced brown, almost burnt. A preliminary marinating with oil and herbs also contributes flavor.

MAKES 4 SIDE-DISH SERVINGS

- 4 zucchini
- 3 tablespoons olive oil
- Salt
- Pepper
- 1 teaspoon finely chopped fresh thyme, 2 teaspoons coarsely chopped fresh marjoram or oregano, or ½ teaspoon chopped dried thyme or oregano

Trim the ends off the zucchini. Slice the zucchini lengthwise into slices the thickness of a quarter. Spread the slices on a sheet pan and rub them on both sides with oil. Sprinkle on both sides with salt, pepper, and thyme and let sit for at least 30 minutes or up to 2 hours before grilling.

Build a hot fire in a charcoal grill, or preheat a gas grill to high. Lay the zucchini slices on the grill rack directly over the fire and grill for 3 to 7 minutes, depending on the distance from the fire, or until you see dark brown grill marks on the first side. Turn with tongs and grill until well browned on the second side. Serve immediately.

Winter Squashes

Most winter squashes, such as acorn or butternut, are cooked by cutting them into two or more pieces, pulling out the seeds, adding a little butter to the cavity of each piece, and then baking the pieces in a moderate to hot oven.

Once the pieces are lightly caramelized and are easily penetrated with a knife, you can serve them as they are, or you can scoop out the flesh with a spoon, combine it with butter, cream or coconut milk, and herbs or spices and puree it or leave rough and chunky. You can also thin this same puree with milk, broth, or water to convert it to a soup, and then swirl a compound butter (see pages 348–349)—butter flavored with curry is especially good—on top of each serving.

BELL PEPPERS AND CHILES

Bell peppers are typically used as ingredients in other dishes, such as salads or stews, as a garnish for seafood or meats, or as part of an antipasto platter. They taste best when they have been charred and their skin and seeds have been removed, a process that not only cooks them but also takes away some of their aggressive flavor. Bell peppers and some thick-skinned chiles such as poblanos can be charred right on the gas burner, as shown below, or can be slid under the broiler until blackened and then the skin peeled off in the same way.

HOW TO PEEL PEPPERS

1. Put the peppers over the flame of a gas stove. Turn the peppers every couple of minutes so they blacken evenly. Cook until covered with black but not white, which indicates too much cooking.

2. Place the peppers in a paper bag or plastic wrap–covered bowl to cool and steam, which aids with peeling.

3. Rinse the peppers with cold water to cool them and pull away the peel with your fingers. Scrape away any stubborn patches with a knife.

4. Cut out the cores and scrape the seeds out of the inside.

Bell Peppers with Herbs and Anchovies

You can serve this salad alone, as part of an antipasto platter, or as part of a selection of crudités.

MAKES 4 FIRST-COURSE SERVINGS OR 6 SERVINGS WHEN PART OF A CRUDITÉ OR ANTIPASTO PLATTER

- 4 bell peppers, preferably of different colors except green, charred, peeled, and seeded (see page 321)
- 1/4 cup extra virgin olive oil
- One 2-ounce jar anchovies, drained and anchovies separated (optional)
- 1 tablespoon freshly chopped fresh marjoram, basil, or parsley
- 1 small clove garlic, minced and then crushed with the flat side of the knife
- Salt
- Pepper

Cut the peppers lengthwise into 1/4-inch-wide strips and place in a bowl. Add the oil, anchovies, marjoram, garlic, salt, and pepper and toss to mix.

Poblano Chiles

These mildly hot, dark green chiles have more flavor, or at least a more distinctive flavor, than bell peppers and can be used in recipes that call for bell peppers or when you want the flavor, not just the heat, of chiles. They are charred and peeled the same way as bell peppers and are delicious stuffed for chiles rellenos.

Chiles Rellenos with Tomatillo Sauce

The secret to great chiles rellenos is to use poblano chiles, which have more flavor than the bell peppers sometimes used. Here, the batter is lightened by separating the eggs, beating the whites and yolks separately, and then folding them together. The chiles are lightly floured before they are coated with batter to help the batter stick, and then the stuffed chiles are gently sautéed in butter. This recipe calls for goat cheese, but if you want to stuff the chiles with something milder and more traditional, you can use Monterey Jack or another cheese.

MAKES 4 MAIN-COURSE SERVINGS OR 8 FIRST-COURSE SERVINGS

- 8 poblano chiles, charred and peeled with stems intact (see page 321)
- 3/4 pound fresh goat cheese, crumbled, or Monterey Jack cheese, grated
- Tomatillo Sauce (opposite)
- 6 eggs, separated
- Pinch of salt
- Tiny pinch of cream of tartar
- 1/2 cup flour
- 4 tablespoons butter
- Sour cream for serving

Carefully make a small incision—about 1 inch long—next to where the stem end enters each chile, being careful not to damage or cut through the rest of the chile. Leave the stem on. Pull out the seeds that cling to the inside of the stem end and rinse out the remaining seeds. Pat the chiles dry. Slip about one-eighth of the cheese through the slit in each chile.

About 10 minutes before serving, bring the sauce to a bare simmer and set up 2 sauté pans large enough to hold the chiles in a single layer without them touching one another. In a bowl, combine the egg whites, salt, and cream of tartar (you can skip the cream of tartar if you are using a copper bowl). Using an electric mixer, beat on low speed for about 1 minute, or until the whites are frothy. Then beat on high speed for about 2 minutes, or until the egg whites are fluffy but not stiff. In a separate bowl, using a fork or whisk, beat 4 of the egg yolks for about 1 minute, or until blended. Using a rubber spatula, fold the egg yolks into the beaten whites.

Spread the flour on a plate. Coat the stuffed chiles with the flour and pat off any excess. Melt 2 tablespoons butter in each sauté pan over medium heat until the butter froths. When the froth subsides, one at a time, dip the chiles in the batter, using your hands to heap the batter on top so they are well coated, and then gently place them in a pan. Cook the chiles for about 6 minutes, or until golden brown on the first side. Gently turn them over and cook for about 6 minutes on the second side, or until golden brown.

Spoon the sauce onto warmed plates—use enough to cover the plate—and put a chile or two on top. Serve immediately. Pass the sour cream at the table.

TOMATILLOS

Don't confuse tomatillos with green tomatoes. Tomatillos are related to gooseberries and have the same papery sheath, which must be peeled off.

Tomatillo Sauce

A tomatillo sauce is simply a puree of stewed tomatillos. By cooking the tomatillos with the pot covered, they steam and soften in their own juices. After pureeing, the sauce can be worked through a food mill if you prefer to remove the seeds.

MAKES 2 CUPS

1 white or yellow onion, peeled and chopped

2 cloves garlic, minced

2 tablespoons olive oil or canola oil

1 chipotle chile, soaked in hot water for 30 minutes to soften if dried or rinsed if canned, seeded and chopped, or 2 jalapeño chiles, seeded and finely chopped

2 poblano chiles, charred, peeled, and seeded (see page 321) and then chopped

2 pounds tomatillos, sheaths removed and coarsely chopped or two 24-ounce cans, drained

$1/4$ cup water

$1/2$ bunch cilantro, large stems removed and leaves and small stems finely chopped

Salt

2 tablespoons fresh lime juice, or to taste

To make the sauce, in a small saucepan, cook the onion and garlic in the oil over medium heat, stirring every minute or so, for about 10 minutes, or until the onion turns shiny but doesn't brown. Add the chipotle and poblano chiles, tomatillos, and water, cover, and simmer gently for 15 minutes. Add the cilantro and simmer for 2 minutes more. Let cool slightly, then transfer to a blender and process to a smooth puree, or puree in the pan with an immersion blender. Season the sauce with salt and lime juice and keep warm for immediate use, or cool and store in an airtight container in the refrigerator for up to 5 days.

TOMATOES

Most of the time, tomatoes end up as components in sauces, salsas, stews, salads, or sandwiches in which they provide moisture and flavor. Slow baking brings out their flavor, as does grilling and stewing.

Slow-Baked Tomatoes

Most recipes for baked tomatoes call for a relatively high oven temperature. This recipe calls for a low oven temperature, so the tomatoes lose their moisture and their flavor concentrates without burning the edges or scalding the bottoms.

MAKES 6 SIDE-DISH SERVINGS

> **6 tomatoes, stemmed**
>
> **1 tablespoon olive oil**
>
> **3 cloves garlic, minced and then crushed with the flat side of the knife**
>
> **30 fresh basil leaves**
>
> **1/3 cup extra virgin olive oil**
>
> **1 1/2 cups grated Parmigiano-Reggiano cheese**

Cut the tomatoes in half through the equator and squeeze the seeds and juices out of each half as shown on page 85. Select a baking dish just large enough to hold the tomatoes in a single layer and rub with the 1 tablespoon olive oil. Arrange the tomatoes, flat side up, in the baking dish. Slide the dish into the oven and turn the oven to 275°F. Bake for 2 to 3 hours, or until any liquid released by the tomatoes completely evaporates.

While the tomatoes are baking, combine the garlic, basil, extra virgin olive oil, and cheese in a food processor and process until smooth.

When the tomatoes are ready, divide the basil mixture evenly among them—push it into the cracks in the tomatoes—and bake for 10 minutes more. Serve immediately.

VARIATIONS

You can prepare cherry tomatoes using this same technique. Substitute 2 pints cherry tomatoes for the regular-sized tomatoes and bake in the same way. You can pass the cherry tomatoes as they are as hors d'oeuvres, or you can crush them on toasted thin baguette slices for bruschetta.

Smoke the tomatoes before baking, using the indirect method described for barbecuing pork spareribs on page 240.

Tomato Tartar

Make this lovely first course when tomatoes are at their peak and beautifully ripe. The effect and the analogy are more dramatic if you use blood red tomatoes, but any color will work.

MAKES 6 FIRST-COURSE SERVINGS

> **6 large or 12 medium tomatoes, peeled**
>
> **2 tablespoons coarse salt**
>
> **Pepper**

Cut the tomatoes in half through the equator and squeeze out the juices and seeds (as shown on page 85). Coarsely chop the halves and toss them in a bowl with the salt. Stir gently for about 1 minute, or until the salt dissolves and no longer feels gritty. Put the tomatoes in a large strainer or colander set over a bowl. Let sit in the refrigerator until just before you are ready to serve, up to overnight.

Just before serving, chop the tomatoes medium-fine and season them with pepper and, if necessary, more salt. Spoon or scoop them with an ice cream scoop and place on chilled plates, serving one scoop per person.

VEGETABLE GRATINS

The best-known gratin is a potato gratin, with au gratin pronounced *oh grahtin*, instead of the French *grahtan*, with the n at the end silent. However you pronounce it, the original meaning of the word *gratin* is crust, or especially the upper crust (as in society). A gratin is made by pouring a sauce, typically a béchamel sauce, or just cream over vegetables, sprinkling over cheese, and baking. For some gratins, such as turnip, the vegetables are blanched to start the cooking or to take away bitterness.

Potato Gratin

Most gratins call for béchamel sauce, which of course is thickened with flour. Because potatoes have enough starch of their own, you can simply use half-and-half, cream, or a combination of cream and milk over the layers of sliced potatoes. Some recipes insist that you rinse the potatoes after slicing them. Others say that the starch adhering to the slices is essential for the gratin to hold together. In fact, it doesn't make much difference whether you rinse or not. If you want to slice the potatoes ahead of time, they have to be soaked, as they will turn gray if they are exposed to air. If you are assembling the gratin while you are slicing, don't bother rinsing the slices. The secret to success is to use the best cheese you can afford. Gruyère, aged Gouda, Parmigiano-Reggiano, and good American or English Cheddar are just a few of the possibilities.

MAKES 6 SIDE-DISH SERVINGS

1 clove garlic, minced and then crushed with the flat side of the knife

1 tablespoon butter, room temperature

2¹/₂ pounds white or red waxy potatoes, peeled

2 cups half-and-half or 1 cup each milk and heavy cream

2¹/₂ cups (about 8 ounces) grated Gruyère or other flavorful cheese

Salt

Pepper

¹/₄ teaspoon ground nutmeg (optional)

Preheat the oven to 375°F. Smear the bottom of an oval gratin dish or square baking dish with the garlic and butter. Slice the potatoes about ¹/₈ inch thick, and spread a single layer in the prepared dish. At this point, estimate how many layers your gratin will have, and pour over the appropriate amount of half-and-half, scatter over the appropriate amount of cheese, and sprinkle with salt, pepper, and nutmeg. You want to make sure you have enough of these ingredients to cover each layer, including the top.

Bake for about 1 hour, or until a knife slides easily through the gratin and no excess liquid is floating around the potatoes. The gratin may seem runny when it comes out of the oven, but it will stiffen up if you let it sit for about 15 minutes before serving.

Cauliflower Gratin

Cauliflower makes a good gratin because it doesn't lose flavor during the long cooking.

MAKES 6 SIDE-DISH SERVINGS

1 tablespoon butter, room temperature

1 head cauliflower

Béchamel Sauce (see pages 341–342)

1¹/₂ cups grated Gruyère or other flavorful cheese

Salt

Pepper

Preheat the oven to 375°F. Rub a medium-sized baking dish with the butter. Peel away the green leaves at the base of the cauliflower, and break it up into florets as shown. Put the florets in a pot, add cold water to cover, and bring to a rapid boil. Immediately drain in a colander and then pour into the prepared dish. Pour the sauce evenly over the cauliflower, scatter the cheese over the top, and sprinkle with salt and pepper.

Bake for about 45 minutes, or until bubbling and golden brown on top. Let sit for 10 minutes, and then serve.

HOW TO CUT UP CAULIFLOWER

1. Cut around the center of the base of the cauliflower.

2. Remove a cone-shaped section that holds together the florets.

3. Separate the larger florets with your fingers.

4. Break larger florets into smaller florets with a knife.

Leek Gratin

Don't tell your guests how you make this—it requires a horrifying amount of heavy cream—until they have eaten it. It's so good that they will no doubt ask for the recipe. If you want to avoid using so much cream, you can also make it with béchamel sauce (see pages 341–342).

MAKES 4 SIDE-DISH SERVINGS

> **6 leeks**
> **1¹/₂ cups heavy cream or more as needed**
> **Salt**
> **Pepper**

Preheat the oven to 375°F. Prepare the leeks as shown. Place the leek halves, flat side up, in a gratin dish or baking dish in a single layer and pour over enough cream to come halfway up the sides.

Season with salt and pepper and cover loosely with aluminum foil.

Bake for about 30 minutes, or until the cream begins to thicken. Remove the foil and bake for 5 to 10 minutes more, or until the cream is very thick but not oily and is lightly browned. Serve right away on warmed plates.

HOW TO MAKE LEEK GRATIN

1. Cut off the greens, leaving about 1 inch of green attached to the white. Cut off the hairy root end.

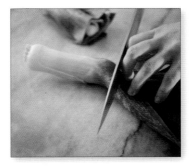

2. Wittle off the outer green from the end of the leek white.

3. Cut the white in half lengthwise. Rinse under running water with the root end up.

4. As you rinse, leaf through the membranes to release any sand.

5. Arrange leek halves in a baking dish in a compact but single layer and pour over the cream. Season with salt and pepper.

6. When you press on the leeks with a fork, the cream should barely cover the leeks. Cover with foil and slide the dish into a 375°F oven.

7. As the leeks brown, push the brown parts down into the cream (shown without foil).

8. When there is no liquid cream left, the leeks are ready. Serve from the baking dish.

Turnip and Potato Gratin

Turnips can be a bit strong if used alone in a gratin, so they are best combined with an equal amount of potatoes. Follow the recipe for Potato Gratin on page 325, substituting 2 turnips (about 1 1/2 pounds total) for half of the potatoes.

Tomato Gratin with Bacon

A good tomato gratin is a little like a pizza without the crust. The trick is to use the largest baking dish or roasting pan you have, so you can spread the tomato slices in a single layer. You can make the simplest version with a little Parmigiano-Reggiano and olive oil, or you can be a little more extravagant and use cream, instead of the oil, and bacon along with the cheese. However you approach this gratin, the point is the same: you want the tomatoes to release their liquid and then that liquid to concentrate around them. Serve the gratin with crusty French bread.

MAKES 6 FIRST-COURSE OR SIDE-DISH SERVINGS

- 1/4 pound thick-cut sliced bacon, cut into 1/3-inch cubes (optional)
- 1/4 cup extra virgin olive oil or 2/3 cup heavy cream
- 6 large tomatoes (about 5 pounds total), peeled and cut crosswise into 1/4-inch-thick slices
- 3/4 cup (about 3 ounces) grated Parmigiano-Reggiano cheese
- Salt
- Pepper

Preheat the oven to 400°F. In a sauté pan, cook the bacon over medium heat for about 10 minutes, or until it renders its fat and just starts to turn crispy. Using a slotted spoon, transfer to paper towels to drain. Pour the oil (if using only the cheese) or the cream (if using the bacon and the cheese) into a large baking dish and arrange the tomato slices on top in a single layer. Scatter the bacon and then the cheese over the tomatoes. Sprinkle with salt and pepper, going easy on the salt because the cheese is salty.

Bake the gratin for 25 minutes, or until the cheese turns golden brown. If at this point the tomatoes are swimming in liquid, you can continue to bake until the liquid evaporates, or you can tilt the gratin into a saucepan, drain off most of the liquid, boil it down until it starts to thicken or get syrupy, and then pour it back over the gratin and bake for 5 minutes more. Serve right away on warmed plates.

HOW TO MAKE TOMATO GRATIN WITH SAGE

1. Seed tomato halves with the peel on.

2. Arange, flat side up, in a gratin dish.

3. Put minced garlic and cheese into the openings left by the seeds.

4. Lay 2 sage leaves over each tomato half, and drizzle the tomatoes with olive oil. Bake until the tomatoes are soft and all the liquid they released has evaporated.

Endive Gratin

Some people are put off by Belgian endive because of its bitterness, but if you include bacon in this gratin, the smokiness will balance the bitterness. In fact, bacon works great with many vegetables in the cabbage family, such as turnips and Brussels sprouts.

MAKES 4 SIDE-DISH SERVINGS

2 slices thick-cut bacon, cut crosswise into strips 1 inch long and 1/4 inch wide

4 Belgian endives

1 cup chicken broth or 1/2 cup heavy cream

Salt

Pepper

Preheat the oven to 375°F. In a sauté pan, cook the bacon over medium heat for about 10 minutes, or until it renders its fat and just starts to turn crispy. Using a slotted spoon, transfer to paper towels to drain. Trim the stem ends and cut the endives in half lengthwise. Place them, flat side down, in a gratin dish or baking dish just large enough to hold them in a single layer. Pour the broth over the endives and sprinkle with the bacon, salt, and pepper.

Bake, basting the endives with the surrounding liquid every 5 to 10 minutes, for about 40 minutes, or until the endives are tender and the liquid has thickened. Serve right away on warmed plates.

Mushroom and Sausage Gratin

Here, the fennel notes found in sweet Italian sausage perfectly accent fresh mushrooms. If you can find cremini mushrooms, use them, as they contain less water than white mushrooms.

MAKES 6 SIDE-DISH SERVINGS

2 pounds cultivated mushrooms, preferably cremini

3 tablespoons olive oil

2 shallots, minced

Salt

Pepper

3/4 pound sweet Italian sausages

Béchamel Sauce (see pages 341–342)

1 cup (about 4 ounces) grated Gruyère cheese

Wash and dry the mushrooms. Cut the end off the bottom of each mushroom stem if dried out or dirty, and then slice the mushrooms as thinly as you can. In a large sauté pan, heat the oil over high heat. When the oil ripples, add a handful of mushrooms. Stir or toss for a couple of minutes with a wooden spoon and then add another handful of mushrooms. (If you add them all at once, they will boil in their own liquid.) Continue in this way until you have added all the mushrooms and they have browned and smell fragrant. This will take about 15 minutes total. (If there is liquid in the pan, keep sautéing until all the liquid evaporates and the mushrooms have browned.) Sprinkle with the shallots, salt, and pepper and sauté for 1 minute more, or until the shallots are fragrant. Let cool.

Preheat the oven to 375°F. Cut the sausages into 1/4-inch-thick slices and arrange in a single layer in a gratin dish or baking dish just large enough to hold the slices in a single layer. Or, remove the sausages from their casings and crumble the meat into the dish. Spread the mushrooms evenly on top, cover with the sauce, and sprinkle with the cheese.

Bake for about 30 minutes, or until the sauce is bubbling and the top is crusty. Let sit for 10 minutes, and then serve.

Zucchini and Tomato Gratin

The secret to making this gratin especially tasty is to sauté the zucchini ahead of time, to evaporate the water they contain and to concentrate their flavor. If you can't find fresh marjoram, thyme will do, but marjoram is marvelous and worth the search. If you can't find good, ripe fresh tomatoes, you can use canned (see Linguine with Tomato Sauce head-note, on page 384).

MAKES 6 SIDE-DISH SERVINGS

> 3 zucchini
>
> 2 teaspoons coarse salt
>
> 6 tomatoes
>
> 2 tablespoons olive oil
>
> 2 cloves garlic, minced and then crushed with the flat side of the knife
>
> 2/3 cup (about 2 generous ounces) grated Parmigiano-Reggiano cheese

Trim the ends off the zucchini. Slice the zucchini, ideally with a plastic vegetable slicer, into rounds the thickness of a quarter. In a bowl, sprinkle the salt over the zucchini and then toss and rub the salt into the rounds for about 2 minutes, or until the salt dissolves and no longer feels gritty. Transfer the zucchini to a colander, set it in the sink or over a bowl, and let drain for about 30 minutes.

Meanwhile, cut the tomatoes in half through the equator and squeeze out the juices and seeds. Chop the halves coarsely, put them in a saucepan, and cook over medium-high to high heat for about 15 minutes, or until the liquid they release evaporates and the mixture stiffens. Remove from the heat and, using the back of a spoon or ladle, work the mixture through a fine-mesh strainer held over a bowl.

Preheat the oven to 375°F. Working with a little at a time, squeeze the zucchini in your fists to extract as much liquid and salt as possible. In a sauté pan, heat the oil over high heat. When the oil ripples, add the zucchini and sauté, tossing regularly, for about 10 minutes, or until they turn pale brown. Sprinkle in the garlic and sauté for 1 minute more, or until the garlic is fragrant. Let cool.

Arrange the zucchini slices, overlapping them slightly, in a single layer in a gratin dish or baking dish. Spoon the tomato coulis evenly over the top, and then sprinkle with the cheese.

Bake for about 25 minutes, or until pale brown and crusty on top. Serve right away on warmed plates.

Spaghetti Squash Gratin

You can bake the squash the day before or earlier the same day you make the gratin.

MAKES 6 SIDE-DISH SERVINGS

> One 2- to 3-pound spaghetti squash
>
> Salt
>
> Pepper
>
> 1 tablespoon butter, room temperature
>
> 2 cups heavy cream or Béchamel Sauce (see pages 341–342)
>
> 3/4 cup (about 3 ounces) grated Gruyère or other flavorful hard or semi-hard cheese

Put the squash on a sheet pan in the oven and turn the oven to 375°F (there is no need to preheat). Bake for about 40 minutes, or until a knife slides easily into the squash. Let cool. Leave the oven on.

Cut the squash in half lengthwise. Using a fork, pull out the flesh so that it forms long strands and you end up with a bowl of what looks like spaghetti. You should have about 4 cups. Season with salt and pepper.

Select a gratin dish or a baking dish just large enough to hold the "spaghetti" in a layer 1/2 to 1 inch thick and rub it with the butter. Spread the squash in the dish, pour the cream evenly over the top, and sprinkle with the cheese.

Bake for about 40 minutes, or until crispy brown on top and no excess liquid is surrounding the squash. Let sit for 10 minutes, and then serve.

BEANS

Most beans, with the exception of green beans (see page 292), are available either dried or canned. However, some beans that many cooks typically think of as only dried or canned are showing up fresh nowadays, too. They are sometimes labeled as shell or shelling beans, and lima, fava, and cranberry are among the most common. Fresh lima and cranberry beans are cooked in simmering liquid for anywhere from 10 minutes to 1 hour, depending on how fresh they are, while fava beans need to be peeled twice, and once peeled they require only a few minutes of simmering.

But beans don't really get interesting until we consider dried beans, which come in an enormous variety of sizes, shapes, and colors. Indeed, the diversity is so appealing that you may find yourself picking up dozens of little packets of exotic-looking beans at a gourmet store or farmers' market. But beans are also appealing for the same reason cooks often avoid them: their long cooking time. The advantage to long cooking is that the beans absorb the flavors of the surrounding liquid and contribute a flavor of their own. The disadvantage, of course, is that you need to be on hand while the beans cook. You can reduce your time commitment with a pressure cooker—even the densest, driest beans will cook in 30 minutes—or with a little forethought.

Most recipes for dried beans call for soaking them first to shorten their cooking time by anywhere from 30 minutes to 1 hour and to help them keep their shape. Cooks argue over which method is best for soaking. Putting them in a pot of cold water, bringing the water to a simmer, removing the pot from the heat, and letting the beans cool completely seems to be the favorite method. Even easier is to cover the beans with hot tap water and let them soak for 4 hours. In both cases, the result is the same: the beans will about double in size. And if time is not an issue, soaking the beans overnight in cold water to cover will yield the same result.

But more important than soaking is the mineral content of the water. Beans take forever to cook in hard water, that is, water with a lot of calcium in it. So you are best off cooking beans in bottled water, though not bottled mineral water. If you have only hard tap water, add a pinch—no more—of baking soda. It will help neutralize the effect of the calcium.

Because beans absorb the flavor of the surrounding liquid, spices, herbs, and other flavorings should go into the pot near the same time as the beans, so the beans will be flavored all the way through. However, never add salt or wine until the beans have softened, as both of them will keep the beans from softening.

Bean Varieties

Beans come in so many varieties that it is impossible to name them all. The cooking time for most beans is a function of the age of the bean, not the variety. In general, dried beans cook in 45 to 90 minutes. Here are a few of my favorites:

Black-eyed pea: Really a bean, not a pea, these beans have a little spot of black on one end and should be gently simmered in soups and stews for 40 to 60 minutes, depending on the age of the bean and on whether they have been soaked.

Calypso: You can use these white and orange beans in any recipe calling for white beans or black beans. They will cook in about 30 minutes.

Cannellini: These popular white, kidney-shaped beans can be used in any recipe calling for white beans. They will cook in about 1 hour.

Cranberry: White beans mottled with burgundy, cranberry beans are among the few beans that show up both fresh and dried. The fresh beans will cook in 15 minutes to 1 hour, depending on their freshness, while dried cranberry beans will take about $1^1/_2$ hours.

Fava: Don't bother with dried fava beans, which have a strong flavor. Serve fresh fava beans, peeled twice: split open pods and remove beans, then slip off outer skin on the beans. Boil beans for 1 minute and butter or drizzle with olive oil.

Flageolet: These small, pale green beans are adored by the French, who often serve them with roast lamb. They cook in about 1 hour.

Great Northern: These large, white beans can be used in any recipe calling for cannellini or other white beans. They will cook in about the same amount of time as cannellini beans (1 hour) but lack their delicacy.

Kidney: Named for their oval, curved shape, kidney beans come in shades ranging from red to pink to nearly brown. When simmered in a flavorful liquid for about $1^1/_2$ hours, they put their canned cousins to shame.

Scarlet runner: These large, flat, pretty purple and black beans are great in salads, stews, and soups. They cook in about $1^1/_2$ hours.

Tongue of Fire: Delicately flavored, these mottled beige beans are one of the best choices for cassoulet. For cassoulet, they are simmered with meat stew, but if cooked alone, they are simmered in water with a bouquet garni for about 1 hour.

Bean Casseroles

You can turn any stew into a casserole by adding enough beans to absorb the stewing liquid, and then baking the beans and the rest of the stew ingredients, topped with bread crumbs, until a crust forms. The bean casserole par excellence is of course the cassoulet of southwestern France, which varies according to both cook and region but is essentially a meat stew with enough beans added to absorb all the liquid. The beans are then spread out in a baking dish, goodies such as duck or goose confit and/or sausages are added, bread crumbs are sprinkled on top, the surface is treated to a healthy drizzle of duck fat or goose fat, and the whole thing is slowly baked. The particular genius behind cassoulet is the formation of multiple crusts: as the bread crumbs form a crust, the crust is folded back into the melting interior of the casserole, fresh bread crumbs and fat are spread over the new surface, and the process is repeated. This topping, browning, and folding are repeated, sometimes as many as 7 times, until the interior of the mixture is a study in contrasts between the melting beans and the crunchy crust.

Cassoulet

It may be fair to say the French are an argumentative people, but Americans can be as vehement about what defines a New England clam chowder as the French are about what defines the true cassoulet. While each point of view has its own refined definition, cassoulet aficionados can be divided into three general groups: the Castelnaudary (don't bother trying to pronounce it) school, whose cassoulet contains mostly pork; the Carcassonne camp, whose cassoulet is made with lamb, and the Toulouse version, which seems to contain everything.

Unless you are a cook interested in replicating something tasted in a distant place—an effort often doomed to fail—you are best off understanding the principles behind a good cassoulet, as one might a bouillabaisse, and then adapting both the principles and your cassoulet to what is at hand. Essential, of course, are beans, but they can be any of a number of varieties (just make sure they are large and plump), and some kind of meat. Ideally, the meat should take plenty of time to cook, so it can cook simultaneously with the beans. If you are making your cassoulet with lamb or pork, stew the meat with the beans until both are done. If you are making your cassoulet with confit, simmer the beans in broth with aromatic vegetables and a bouquet garni, as well as something meaty to provide flavor, such as a blanched ham

hock, a piece of bacon rind, or a ham bone. If you have good sausages, nestle them in the beans in the oven about 30 minutes before you think the whole concoction will be done.

MAKES 8 MAIN-COURSE SERVINGS

> **4 cups dried beans such as cranberry, navy, Tongue of Fire, or cannellini, soaked and drained**
>
> **2 carrots, peeled and cut into 1-inch sections**
>
> **1 large onion, halved**
>
> **1 stalk celery**
>
> **Bouquet garni**
>
> **About 2 quarts broth or water**
>
> **Salt**
>
> **8 confit mullard duck thighs or 16 confit Pekin duck thighs (see page 274)**
>
> **1¹/₂ cups fresh bread crumbs made from 6 slices white bread (see page 255)**
>
> **¹/₃ cup melted duck fat from the confit, or as needed**

In a large pot, combine the beans, carrots, onion, celery, bouquet garni and enough broth to cover by 3 to 4 inches. Bring to a gentle simmer and simmer uncovered, adding more broth or water as needed to keep the beans covered, until the beans are soft. The timing will vary depending on the type and age of the beans (older beans take longer), but it will range from about 60 to 90 minutes. (If you have an extra confit thigh, nestle it in the pot to flavor the beans.) If you are in a hurry, you can use a pressure cooker, which will take only about 30 minutes.

(continued)

Cassoulet, continued

Preheat the oven to 350°F. Drain the beans in a colander set over a large saucepan to collect any liquid the beans didn't absorb. If it is more than 1 cup, boil the liquid down to 1 cup.

Discard the bouquet garni, then spread the beans and vegetables in a baking dish, forming a layer about 2 inches thick, and season generously. Nestle in the duck thighs and sprinkle with half of the bread crumbs and drizzle with half of the duck fat.

Bake for about 30 minutes, or until a crust forms. Gently fold the crust into the beans, and then sprinkle the surface with the rest of the bread crumbs and drizzle with the rest of the fat. Bake for another 30 minutes, or until a crust forms again. Serve directly from the dish.

Lentils

Unlike dried beans, which need to be soaked before cooking, lentils only need a quick sorting on a sheet pan to eliminate pebbles. Lentils come in many colors: pink, orange, bright red, black, brown, yellow, and greenish and need only be simmered for 20 to 30 minutes to soften. They make a great base for soups and can be dressed cold with vinaigrette to make salads. Hot lentils are best when cooked with something smoky such as bacon or a ham hock, and rich foods such as duck confit are delicious simmered with lentils. Lentils absorb about triple their volume in liquid.

GARLIC

This mysterious little plant behaves according to how you cook it (or don't): When cloves are slowly simmered in a stew or pot roast, the flavors of the garlic meld with the herbs and other vegetables into a subtle whole, but if this same amount of garlic, or even far less, were minced and added to the stew at the end, all the ingredients would be completely overwhelmed. For the most subtle effect, simmer garlic in its peel; for a more forthright effect, peel and mince the garlic and cook it in oil before combining it with other ingredients; and for the most dramatic effect, chop, mince and crush it to a paste and add it to soups and sauces at the last minute. Garlic can also be roasted in its peel and then worked through a food mill to create a mild puree that can be spread on toast or whisked into soups and sauces.

HOW TO PEEL, MINCE, AND CRUSH GARLIC TO A PASTE

1. Separate the garlic head into cloves.

2. Lightly crush the garlic by placing a knife blade over it and pounding with your fist.

3. Pull away the peel.

4. Cut off the small root end.

5. Slice the clove in one direction.

6. Slice the clove crosswise, mincing as finely as possible.

7. Chop the garlic very fine.

8. Crush the garlic, a little at a time, by smearing it with the flat side of the knife.

Roast Garlic Puree

Make a batch and keep it for a week or so in the refrigerator or in the freezer for several months.

MAKES 1 CUP PUREE

> **12 heads garlic**
> **3 tablespoons olive oil**

Peel off and discard the excess peel from the garlic heads, and break the heads into cloves. Don't peel the cloves. Toss the cloves with the oil and spread them in a roasting pan. Slide the pan into the oven, turn the oven to 325°F, and bake for about 45 minutes, or until the cloves offer no resistance when you pinch a few in a towel.

Work the cloves through a food mill or coarse-mesh strainer and then again through a drum sieve or fine-mesh strainer. Store tightly sealed.

TRUFFLES

Nearly everyone is fascinated by truffles, both how they are hunted and what they really are. Some say they are a mushroom, others say a fungus but not a mushroom, and still others describe them as most closely related to yeast, which is both a plant and an animal. In any case, truffles grow underground, attached to roots of trees, usually oaks. Truffle hunters rely on pigs or dogs to detect the truffle's pungent aroma. Hunters without pigs or dogs look for unhealthy trees, worn down by the truffle parasite, and then search the ground around them for flies. Flies it seems are drawn to the same odor as pigs and dogs.

Once unearthed, some truffles sell for a small fortune. Others, less expensive, appear regularly on menus in Italy for not much more money than anything else. (In Rome, a few casual places make truffle pizzas.) Most truffles look a little like a golf ball and range in size from a marble to a large fist. The two best-known and most expensive truffles are winter truffles, white from northern Italy and black from France and Umbria. White truffles are usually eaten raw, shaved over pasta, veal, or just about anything the cook desires. Black truffles are usually cooked. Summer truffles, both black (from Tuscany) and white (from the south of France) are more common and less expensive than winter truffles, and are often a good value. Be sure when buying a winter truffle that you are not buying a summer truffle. When you look at a cross section of a black winter truffle, you should see white filigree. A cross sec-

Black winter truffles should reveal a filigree of white when sliced.

Slice truffles with a plastic vegetable slicer or a truffle slicer.

tion of a summer truffle is an even dark brown or black. White winter truffles smell a little like garlic or a gas leak, while white summer truffles have a moldy smell, like a good Brie.

The flavor of truffles is somewhat similar to that of morels, especially truffles that have been sautéed to bring out their aroma. But more mysterious is the truffle's tendency to make foods taste more like themselves. An ordinary egg suddenly becomes the best egg ever. A supermarket chicken suddenly tastes like the finest organic free-range bird on the planet.

If you decide to splurge on a truffle or two, use it within a couple of days or freeze it. Store it in a large jar with a stick or more of unwrapped butter and, if you like truffle omelets, a few eggs in their shells. Overnight the truffle aroma will permeate the eggs and butter. You can use the butter in sauces and gravies, in mashed potatoes, or just spread it on bread. If you are not using the butter right away, wrap it tightly and freeze it. You can make truffle oil by storing your truffles covered in oil and then just saving the oil. Usually a night or two is long enough to flavor the oil.

Truffles complement rich, fatty foods, such as cream, butter, and eggs, all of which seem to trap the flavor better than, say, broth. In other words, eating truffles is not an occasion for dieting.

HERBS

Herbs are the spices of Western cooking and add vitality and variety to many a dish that would otherwise be bland. Much is made about using fresh herbs, and for some herbs, such as tarragon, parsley, or chervil, freshness is imperative, but many herbs take well to drying while other herbs such as basil can be pureed with oil and stored in the freezer or refrigerator as pestos. Most herbs fall into one of two categories: fines herbes (pronounced "feens erbe"), which include parsley, chervil, tarragon, and chives, and herbes de Provence, which include thyme, marjoram, oregano, savory, and lavender. Fines herbes are best used fresh while herbes de Provence can be used fresh or dried, separately or altogether.

How to Preserve and Store Fresh Herbs

Different kinds of herbs call for different preserving methods. Oily herbs, such as thyme, rosemary, marjoram, hyssop, lavender leaves and flowers, and oregano, should be tied into small bundles with string and hung in a dry, breezy place until fully dried. These same herbs can also be preserved in oil or vinegar. Sage is an oily herb that doesn't take well to drying, but is easily preserved in oil. Watery herbs, such as chives, basil, parsley, tarragon, cilantro, and chervil, don't dry well. Tarragon is delicious in vinegar, and keeps its flavor intact, but the others should be pureed with olive oil to make a pesto of sorts, and then immediately packed into an airtight container and frozen. Any fresh herb can also be preserved by using it to make a compound butter, which can then be stored in the refrigerator for a month or longer in the freezer.

Once you have dried oily herbs, you can store them, still hung by their string, in a cool spot in the kitchen for a couple of months. To store watery herbs, submerge their stems in water in a large tumbler and then cover the tops of the sprigs with a plastic bag, attaching it to the sides of the glass with a rubber band. If you change the water every couple of days, the herbs will keep in the refrigerator for as long as 2 weeks. If you leave any fresh herbs closed up in plastic bags in the refrigerator, they will quickly go bad.

How to Chop Herbs Efficiently

Some cooks, especially novices or anyone who hasn't worked in a restaurant, will spend the better part of an hour carefully removing the individual leaves from a bunch of parsley or cilantro, when in fact the delicate stems, once chopped, are indistinguishable from the leaves. When chopping bunches of parsley, chervil, or cilantro, just cut off the bulk of the stems—the part with no leaves on them—then chop the leaves with the small stems.

Cut off the leaves where they join the bulk of the stems. Don't bother removing the smaller stems. Chop a lot at once.

Tarragon and basil have hardier stems, which should be removed. When removing tarragon leaves, don't pick off the leaves one by one. Instead, pull downward on the stem, pinching gently with your thumb and forefinger so you pull away the leaves as you slide down the stem. This method also works with such oily herbs as thyme, marjoram, rosemary, and oregano.

Unlike parsley or cilantro, which is chopped randomly, chives require a chopping method all their own. Take about 8 blades at a time, align them carefully, and then pinch them together with the thumb and fingers of one hand while slicing with the other. Slice them as thinly as you can, as no one likes little strips of chive stuck in their teeth.

Substituting Dried Herbs for Fresh

The flavor of some herbs intensifies when they are dried, while the flavor of others weakens. For example, the flavor of dried thyme is about four times stronger than the same volume of fresh, and the flavor of dried oregano is about ten times stronger than the same amount of fresh. Dried parsley, chervil, chives, tarragon, and cilantro not only get weaker in flavor, the flavor changes into something unpleasant. Just throw them in the trash.

BOUQUET GARNI

A bouquet garni is a bundle of fresh herbs or a packet of dried herbs used to flavor broths, sauces, stews, beans, and soups. The herbs are tied together so they are easier to pull out of the liquid at the end. Also, when making broths, a bundle isn't as likely to interfere when you are skimming off the froth and fat. If you put the herbs in the bottom of the pot and cover them with bones, or if the liquid is not being skimmed and is going to be strained, just put the herbs in loose.

Bouquet garnis are ideally made by tying up sprigs of fresh thyme with parsley stems or whole parsley (stems with leaves), bay leaves, and the greens from leeks. But you can use any herbs you like, as long as they release their flavors slowly, allowing them to meld with the other ingredients. Chervil and basil are best left out of bouquet garnis since they release their flavor very quickly. Tarragon, in general, is best added near the end of cooking, but it does lend a subtle delicacy to chicken broth when included in the bouquet garni.

If you have fresh thyme or thyme that has been dried on the sprigs, make the bouquet garni by just wrapping it in a short length of string or in unflavored dental floss. If you only have dried thyme leaves (don't bother with powdered thyme) use cheesecloth or leek greens to make little packets to encase the thyme. Most of us make bouquet garnis too small. A bouquet garni for a large pot of broth should be as thick as a man's wrist and a bouquet garni for a pot roast twice the thickness of a thumb.

HOW TO MAKE A BOUQUET GARNI

For a large bouquet garni, cradle the herbs in a washed leek green.

Tie with kitchen string to secure the bundle.

Which Herbs Go with What?

While there is no easy answer—this is a bit like asking what notes go with what instruments—the question can be discussed in terms of the two types of herbs already introduced, watery and oily, which behave in somewhat predictable ways. Water-based herbs have a relatively fleeting aroma, don't dry well, and grow stale quickly. In contrast, oily herbs, whose aroma is contained in their oils, release their aroma and flavor slowly into surrounding liquids and dry well. In fact, it may be that their natural oils are designed to prevent them from drying out in the hot climates where they usually flourish. Oily herbs are ideal for simmering in slow-cooked dishes such as stews and soups or for adding to a bouquet garni, while watery herbs are better suited to sprinkling on meats and seafood before grilling or for adding to sauces and soups at the last minute.

Basil

Is any herb more versatile or more seductive? Nowadays, basil is abundant in the summer, from our gardens and from local markets. In fact, it is so abundant that we are even a little stuck with it and feel guilty if we don't use it. Fortunately, any excess can be pureed with olive oil in a food processor (a pesto minus the garlic, the pine nuts, and the hand working of the authentic version), frozen, and then whisked into sauces or soups (especially vegetable and seafood soups) to provide a burst of summer in the cool months. When chopped with butter, it becomes a bit French and a perfect candidate to finish a subtle sauce or soup. It is marvelous with garlic, tomatoes, and saffron, and a swirl of the pestolike puree, next to a dollop of aioli and a dribble of saffron with its soaking liquid, is unforgettable atop a fish soup or the French version of minestrone known as pistou. You can also whisk it into a fresh tomato soup or tomato sauce at the last minute. In fact, basil should always be used at the last minute—its aroma and flavor are fleeting—rather than simmered, as you would thyme.

Although it is an herb, basil is also a green, and in the summer months it is great in a salad. Try using equal parts basil leaves and arugula.

Cilantro

To the uninitiated, and they are increasingly few, cilantro, the leaves of the coriander plant, taste vaguely of soap suds. To dispel this impression, and to show off cilantro at its best, use it, along with chiles, to flavor hot, spicy dishes, especially Indian and Mexican recipes. It is also magnificent in Thai and other Southeast Asian dishes, marrying well with fish sauce, lemongrass, and kaffir lime leaves. In any dish calling for curry powder, add a little chopped cilantro at the end, and the flavors of the spices will come into focus.

Chervil

At the moment, chervil is almost impossible to find and not that easy to plant. It is delicate and shade loving and very fussy. This delicacy translates into its appearance and flavor. A tiny filigree-like chervil sprig often provides the necessary final flair to a salad or a piece of shellfish. The flavor of chervil is vaguely like tarragon but much more delicate and fleeting. It shares with parsley a subtle freshness that can be used at the last minute in sauces for seafood, chicken, veal, and pork. It is also often combined with parsley, chives, and tarragon in the mixture known as fines herbes. While the idea of such a mixture is brilliant, the inclusion of tarragon, which is about four times more strongly flavored than the other three partners, poses a problem. The solution, of course, is to use only one-fourth the amount of tarragon as the other herbs.

Lavender

While we think of lavender as a flower best suited to flavor soap, it is actually an herb that's included in herbes de Provence mixtures. Lavender adds a note of complexity when rubbed on foods for grilling or when sprinkled on sautéed mushrooms or zucchini. It is best when combined with garlic.

Chives

Unlike most herbs, which can be chopped haphazardly until fine, chives must be approached with a certain precision, or they will look careless and feel raw in the mouth. Chop them as described in "How to Chop Herbs Efficiently" (see page 334). Do your best to slice them microscopically thin.

Chives are of course a member of the onion family and can be used to flavor sauces and steaming liquid from shellfish and as a final garnish for soups. They are also part of the iconic fines herbes mixture.

Mint

Some mint varieties are stronger flavored than others. The robust ones can be chopped and added to a vinaigrette for a salad, while the milder types, usually with larger leaves, can be used as salad greens along with basil and arugula. Lightly chopped mint is always a pleasant surprise on top of fruity summer tomatoes, and is a classic addition to the French salad of cucumbers and crème fraîche, or to the Indian salad of cucumbers and yogurt known as raita. Mint can also be snuck into any sauce or salsa that might otherwise call for cilantro, especially when chiles are part of the mix.

Marjoram

Somewhat hard to find and often confused with oregano, marjoram is worth tracking down. It has a distinctive, clean aroma that asserts itself without dominating. It is best used fresh, though drying doesn't actually harm it, but just weakens it a little. Chop marjoram with a little olive oil (the oil helps trap its flavor and keep it from turning black) and rub it on fish or meats before grilling or sautéing. It is wonderful with lamb—sprinkle it chopped on the meat itself or add it to a sauce—and if you have more than you need, you can hang it in a cool spot to dry or infuse it in olive oil. It doesn't do much in vinegar.

Parsley

Because parsley is so widely available and inexpensive, it is often taken for granted. Many cooks put a parsley sprig on a plate without really thinking about what it adds. A sprig, in fact, doesn't add much except for a little clichéd color. But when parsley is chopped, finely and at the last minute, and added to seafood and meat sauces, it contributes an ineffable complexity and nuance. Indeed, it is often the missing element in a long-cooked sauce that has lost some of its vitality and freshness for having spent so many hours on the stove.

When buying parsley, look for the flat-leaf variety, sometimes called Italian parsley. It. has a bit more punch than the frizzy variety, though the latter still has plenty to offer. Cut off the large stems, then wash the leaves, with the smaller stems attached, and dry them in a salad spinner. It is important that the leaves are dry when you chop them, or their flavor will stay in a puddle of liquid on the cutting board.

Chop parsley, as you should all herbs, with a razor-sharp knife that will cut, rather than crush. When crushed, herbs release their flavor, which ends up embedded in the cutting board. Also, chop the parsley at the very last minute. If this isn't practical, chop it about three-fourths of the way ahead of time, and then give it a final chop at the last minute, so it releases its flavor then. If you fully chop it ahead of time, it will smell like lawn clippings when you go to use it.

Oregano

One of the few herbs that intensifies in flavor as it dries, oregano comes in several varieties of which Mexican and Greek are the most popular. Use dried oregano on grilled meats—spread it, chopped, on the meat before grilling—and fresh oregano in more subtly flavored dishes such as beans.

Rosemary

You need to be judicious with rosemary. It is aggressive and can take over the taste of whatever it is supposed to complement. Some cooks automatically think of rosemary when cooking lamb, but it has a nasty habit of making lamb taste gamy. To use it in the most subtle way, shove sprigs on the charcoal fire you use for grilling. Its smoke is gentle, imparting just a hint of the herb. Rosemary is good mixed with garlic, too, but make sure it is finely chopped to eliminate the prick of its sharp needles.

Tarragon

Tarragon has an unmistakable flavor that the uninitiated describe as reminiscent of anise or licorice. But it soon acquires its own identity. It is one of the fines herbs that especially complements fish and chicken, and, along with shallots, flavors béarnaise sauce. It goes beautifully with tomatoes, much like basil but more intricate, and when cream is included, the aniselike tarragon notes are brought stunningly into relief.

Once hard to find, tarragon now appears in such large bunches that cooks are often stuck with more than they can use. Shoving the extras down the neck of a bottle of vinegar is one obvious solution. But you can also finely chop it with butter to make tarragon butter that keeps, tightly wrapped, for months in the freezer. The butter can be used to finish seafood sauces—especially the steaming liquid from shellfish—or it can be whisked into a deglazed pan used to sauté chicken. It is not bad on grilled corn either. Don't try to dry tarragon, as it just turns stale. If your tarragon sprigs have thick stems, remove the leaves (see "How to Chop Herbs Efficiently," page 334).

Thyme

Thyme may be second only to parsley in usefulness in the kitchen, though it is employed very differently. It can be used in three ways: slowly simmered in liquids so that its flavor is integrated with the flavors of the aromatic vegetables; chopped and added to sauces or other liquids just before serving for a sudden burst of direct flavor; or chopped and sprinkled on meats or seafood headed for the grill. Until recently, thyme was rarely available fresh, but now you can find it in the market year-round. You will seldom need a whole bunch, but since it dries easily without losing its character, this isn't a problem. Use only what you need and tie the rest of the bunch on one end with string and hang it in a cool spot in the kitchen to dry. When it is thoroughly dried, rub the sprigs between your palms, letting the leaves sprinkle down over a steak or chop to season it. You may also want to slip fresh thyme sprigs down the neck of an olive oil bottle to give your salads a little herbal flavor. Several thyme varieties are available, including lemon thyme. Don't substitute lemon thyme for regular thyme. Its aggressive lemon flavor is mildly reminiscent of furniture polish.

SAUCES, SALSAS, AND CHUTNEYS

Sauces, salsas, and chutneys are designed either to underline the intrinsic flavor of an ingredient or to accent it by juxtaposing it with other flavors. Sauces that accent by juxtaposing are accompaniments that are often passed at the table and are usually called condiments. A sauce can be derived from the juices released as certain foods cook, or it can be made with completely separate ingredients. A salsa is usually a combination of chopped raw ingredients, such as tomatoes, avocados, mangoes, or cucumbers, often mixed with some olive oil, yogurt, cream, or other liquid. A chutney usually contains cooked ingredients, often salty, and often has sweet-and-sour elements (such as vinegar and sugar).

SAUCES

French cooks have long talked about the mother sauces, but sauces can also be broken down into two basic types: integral sauces that are derived from cooking a particular food, and nonintegral sauces that are made from foods cooked separately. Nonintegral sauces are more or less related to what they're being served with. For example, a gravy or a pan-deglazed sauce is an integral sauce, while a sauce made from chicken broth is a nonintegral sauce. Some nonintegral sauces are made to mimic integral sauces, such as thickened chicken broth trying to replace a gravy, while others have no relationship to the food at all.

Most home cooks think in terms of whether the sauce is hot, whether it contains butter or cream, whether it is thickened with flour, or whether it's a salsa—not whether it's an integral or nonintegral sauce. But understanding the distinctions and uses of the most common sauces is one surefire way to elevate your home cooking.

Nonintegral sauces are usually broken down into brown sauces and white sauces. Brown sauces are typically put together by combining very concentrated broth with some kind of flavoring, such as wine, and then whisking in butter. White sauces usually contain cream that has been cooked down so it functions as a thickener. Traditional recipes for both white and brown sauces call for flour, cooked with butter into a roux, to be used as a thickener, but more modern recipes rely on the thickening power of butter and cream.

Ragù sauces are based on broth, often include tomatoes, and include shredded or chopped meat. The best ragù sauces are made by making a stew and then shredding the stew meat and combining it with the cooked-down stewing liquid. Salsas often contain raw ingredients such as tomatoes, tomatillos, avocados, and chiles. Some sauces are emulsified—beurre blanc, mayonnaise, hollandaise—while others such as salsas are simply stirred to combine.

The famous mother sauces are hollandaise, an egg-butter sauce; espagnole, which is essentially beef broth thickened with flour; velouté, or white broth thickened with flour; béchamel, milk thickened with flour; mayonnaise; and tomato sauce. A seventh sauce, beurre blanc, should also be added. All the classic French sauces are based on one of these sauces and are given fanciful names, depending on their individual ingredients.

HOW TO THICKEN A SAUCE

Until the 1970s, cooks insisted that a sauce be thick enough to coat and stay on top of a piece of meat or fish. In medieval times in Europe, toasted bread and egg yolks were used for thickening. In the sixteenth century, roux—flour cooked usually with butter—was discovered and replaced the bread.

In the 1970s, cream, butter, egg yolks, and vegetable purees replaced the flour. But the 1970s also brought another big change: cooks realized that a sauce could be served around or under a food—usually in a soup plate—which eliminated the need for any thickener. Instead of using an enormous amount of reduced cream, butter, or egg yolks, cooks found they needed only enough fat to bring together the flavors of a sauce. This enabled them to make extremely savory sauces without flour or any extra fat.

BUTTER, CREAM, AND EGG YOLKS IN SAUCE MAKING

Sauces, especially French sauces, have a reputation for being overly rich—or at least far from dietetic. This is partly true, especially for traditional sauces and for the sauces based on butter and cream that were popular in the last two decades of the twentieth century. But many cooks have since eliminated these fats from their cooking, replacing them with lighter brothlike sauces held together with vegetable puree or not thickened at all. However, fats, especially emulsified fats such as butter, cream, and egg yolks, unite and bring into focus otherwise disparate flavors and make what would otherwise be just a flavorful liquid into a suave and deeply satisfying sauce. Fats carry flavor and deliver them to our palates like nothing else. The bright side is that very little of these calorie-laden fats is needed. For example, traditional cream soup recipes call for about 1 cup cream for each quart of soup. Many cooks overreact and eliminate the cream altogether, ending up with a pleasant pureed soup. But that soup would have been enhanced enormously with the addition of just $1/4$ cup cream for each quart, or about 1 tablespoon for each serving.

Also keep in mind that most of the time you don't need to add enough butter, cream, or egg yolk to thicken a sauce, only enough to flavor it. Nor is it necessary to serve a large amount of sauce: 3 tablespoons per serving or even less is usually about right. People who blithely eat a crème brûlée or a bowl of ice cream for dessert but recoil at a sauce that contains a teaspoon of butter need to rethink their fat-intake worries.

Why Cream and Not Milk or Half-and-Half?

Beginning cooks sometimes try to lighten recipes by replacing the cream with milk or half-and-half. The problem with this approach is that the emulsifiers in milk and half-and-half lose their ability to emulsify when they are exposed to heat or to various foods, including acidic ingredients and especially certain vegetables such as artichokes. Cream, on the other hand, is relatively stable and can be boiled, uncovered, until it reduces and thickens. To replace cream in a recipe with milk, the milk has to be stabilized with an emulsifier, like flour (in the form of roux), or with a vegetable puree, such as potato.

What Is an Emulsion?

Most sauces that contain fat, such as egg yolks, butter, cream, or oil, are emulsions. In the simplest terms, an emulsion is produced on a microscopic level when particles of fat are surrounded with molecules of an emulsifier, such as the protein in cream or egg yolks. The emulsifier has one side that is soluble

HOW TO MAKE A ROUX

1. Combine equal parts flour and butter in a heavy saucepan.

2. Stir over medium heat until smooth.

3. Stir until the roux smells toasty. To make a brown roux, continue to cook the mixture until caramel colored with a nutty aroma.

1. The homestyle method for clarifying butter is the same as for making ghee. Melt butter in a heavy-bottomed saucepan over medium heat.

2. The butter will foam up at first.

3. After about 5 minutes, the foam will subside and you will see white particles floating in the butter.

4. When the milk solids form brown particles that cling to the bottom of the pan, the ghee is ready for straining through a fine-mesh strainer.

in fat and the other that is soluble in water. The fat-soluble side embeds itself into the fat particle, while the water-soluble side protrudes out. These protruding molecules keep the particles of fat from touching one another and coalescing from two particles into one ad infinitum, which is what happens when an emulsion such as a mayonnaise "breaks" and separates into oil and liquid. An emulsion can be broken by increasing the concentration of fat so much that the fat particles are forced into one another, despite the surrounding coating of emulsifier, and coalesce. Breaking can also occur when certain emulsions are overheated and the emulsifier (usually a protein) loses its structure and stops working as an emulsifier. The reason that cream is a common component of sauces is because it can be boiled (to a degree) without losing its emulsifying properties (see "Why Cream and Not Milk or Half-and-Half?" opposite).

WHITE SAUCES FOR FISH, MEAT, AND VEGETABLES

For centuries, the two basic white sauces have been béchamel, made differently over the centuries but now basically milk thickened with flour, and velouté, which is essentially white broth thickened with flour. In the 1970s, when nouvelle cuisine hit France, flour became taboo in sauces in most fine restaurants. The broth was sometimes thickened by being heavily reduced—occasionally to a glaze—and then finished with egg yolks, cream, and/or butter and whatever ingredients gave the sauce its identity. Another approach, still popular today, is to reduce the broth less, finish it with a modest amount of cream, butter, or egg yolks—the amounts of these used in the 1970s were prodigious—and serve it as a rich, flavorful broth that surrounds the food, rather than coats it. It is also possible to compromise and thicken a broth lightly with flour or other starch, such as cornstarch, rice flour, arrowroot, or potato flour, and a small amount of the rich ingredient.

HOW TO MAKE BÉCHAMEL SAUCE

1. Make a roux, as shown opposite. Pour milk into the hot roux.

2. Stir until thick and smooth.

Béchamel Sauce

Sometimes simply called white sauce, béchamel is essentially milk thickened with a roux made by cooking together flour and butter. Older recipes were somewhat more elaborate and contained mirepoix—diced celery, carrots, and onions— cooked in butter before the flour was added and sometimes a bit of unsmoked bacon or air-cured ham. A bouquet garni, rarely called for in modern recipes, was also included. Depending on how you are using the sauce, these are still worthwhile additions. But if your béchamel will be used as the base for a cheese soufflé, for example, these extra ingredients are probably more bother than they are worth.

Béchamel is made in different thicknesses, depending on how it will be used: very thick for a soufflé base, somewhat thinner for a vegetable gratin, and thinner still for a soup base.

MAKES 2 CUPS

- 1 to 4 tablespoons butter
- 3 tablespoons finely diced onion (optional)
- 3 tablespoons finely diced carrot (optional)
- 1 tablespoon finely diced celery (optional)
- 1 tablespoon finely diced prosciutto end or pancetta (optional)
- 1 to 4 tablespoons flour
- 2 cups milk
- Bouquet garni (optional)
- Pinch of cayenne pepper (optional)
- Tiny pinch of ground nutmeg (optional)
- Salt
- White pepper

In a small saucepan, melt the butter over low to medium heat. Add the vegetables and prosciutto and cook for 5 minutes, stirring almost constantly, or until the onion turns translucent. (This technique is called sweating.) Add the same amount of flour as you did butter and cook, stirring constantly, for 2 minutes longer, or until the flour smells toasty. If you are not using vegetables and/or prosciutto, just cook the flour in the butter for 2 minutes.

Add the milk all at once and bring to a simmer while whisking constantly. Whisk until smooth, add the optional bouquet garni, and simmer for 5 to 20 minutes. If the sauce is being cooked in something else, such as a soup, soufflé, or gratin, simmering for 5 minutes is enough. The longer cooking time is to cook the starchy taste out of the flour or infuse the bouquet garni. Discard the bouquet garni and season with cayenne, nutmeg, salt, and pepper.

VARIATIONS

CLASSIC CREAM SAUCE: A traditional cream sauce is simply a béchamel with heavy cream added. Add 1/2 to 1 cup heavy cream with the milk and cook the sauce down to the consistency you like. While still rich, cream sauce is not as rich as heavy cream used alone, and can replace heavy cream in vegetables gratins, such as the Leek Gratin on page 326.

VELOUTÉ, CREAM SAUCES, AND WHITE WINE SAUCE: Say, for example, you are making a tarragon sauce for chicken or fish. A traditional approach would be to thicken chicken or fish broth with a roux to create a velouté, add cream and/or egg yolks, and finish it with chopped tarragon. Modern versions would leave out the flour, reduce the broth to deepen its flavor, and, if the sauce is meant to be thick, thicken it with a little starch, and then finish it with cream. If you want the sauce to coat the fish or chicken, it is further reduced with the cream until it thickens and then the tarragon is added. Lighter versions contain less cream or egg yolk, reduce the broth less, and are served around the fish or chicken. White wine sauces come in two varieties: one is simply a béchamel or veloute that contains wine, the other, a hollandaise in which the egg yolks are beaten with wine before the butter is added.

Cream Sauce Base
for Fish, Chicken, or Veal

The flavor of this sauce is going to depend on the quality of the broth. The ideal broth would be brown chicken broth, reduced by three-fourths, perhaps used to finish cooking the chicken. But this isn't always practical, so straight broth or slightly reduced broth can be used instead. Concentrated broth can also be made by dissolving chicken, veal, or fish glaze in water (see "Meat Glaze" box on page 177). If you want the sauce to be thick enough to coat the chicken, use the roux and the larger amount of cream; otherwise omit the roux and use the lesser amount of cream. The thick version for this recipe calls for reducing $1^1/_2$ cups of broth down to $1/_2$ cup; if you already have very concentrated broth, use $1/_2$ cup and skip the reduction.

MAKES ENOUGH FOR 6 MAIN-COURSE SERVINGS

> **2 teaspoons flour, if making thick sauce**
>
> **2 teaspoons butter, if making thick sauce**
>
> **$1^1/_2$ cups concentrated flavorful fish, chicken, or veal broth**
>
> **$1/_2$ cup heavy cream, if making thin sauce, or 1 cup heavy cream, if making thick sauce**
>
> **Salt**
>
> **Pepper**

If you are making a thick sauce, melt the butter in a small saucepan over medium heat, add the flour, and cook, stirring constantly, for about 2 minutes, or until the flour smells toasty. Add the broth and bring to a simmer while whisking constantly. If you are not using the roux, just bring the broth to a simmer.

If making a thick sauce, boil down the broth to about $1/_2$ cup, add 1 cup cream, and simmer while stirring with a whisk, for about 5 minutes, or until the sauce is thick enough to coat a spoon. If making a thin sauce, don't boil down the broth. Instead, add the $1/_2$ cup cream and bring to a simmer. Season with salt and pepper, unless you will be flavoring the sauce with salty ingredients.

VARIATIONS

TARRAGON: Finely chop 1 tablespoon fresh tarragon at the last minute and stir into the sauce 3 minutes before serving.

FINES HERBES: Finely chop 1 tablespoon each fresh chives and parsley and 1 tablespoon fresh chervil or 1 teaspoon tarragon at the last minute and stir into the sauce 3 minutes before serving.

CREMINI OR FRESH PORCINI MUSHROOMS: Wash and dry 12 cremini or porcini mushrooms, cut off the stem ends, and then cut into quarters through the stem end. Add the mushrooms to the sauce about 10 minutes before serving. Because the mushrooms release liquid, you may need to boil down the sauce slightly to thicken it.

MOREL MUSHROOMS: Soak 1 ounce dried morel mushrooms in $1/_2$ cup Madeira, sherry, or water for about 30 minutes, or until soft. Squeeze the mushrooms over the bowl, saving all the soaking liquid, and simmer the morels in the sauce for 5 minutes. Pour the soaking liquid into the sauce—leave any grit behind in the bowl—and reduce the sauce, if necessary, to thicken it.

SPRING VEGETABLES: Assorted miniature vegetables, such as pearl onions, baby carrots or turnips, full-sized carrot or turnip pieces, peas, or thin green beans such as haricots verts, can be precooked and reheated in the sauce at the last minute.

TRUFFLES: To get the most flavor and aroma from truffles, chop a truffle—as large as you dare—with 6 tablespoons butter, wrap in plastic wrap, and refrigerate overnight. When the base sauce is the consistency you like, whisk in the truffle butter.

Mushroom Cooking Liquid

The reduced liquid released by mushrooms when they are steamed adds enormous complexity and flavor to a variety of sauces. Depending on whether you use regular cultivated mushrooms or cremini mushrooms, you'll end up with different amounts of liquid, but to make mushroom cooking liquid, put a pound of quartered mushrooms in a pot with a half cup of water, cover the pot, and bring to a boil. Turn down the heat and steam the mushrooms, still covered, over medium heat for about 10 minutes. They'll release from $1/_2$ to a full cup of liquid. This liquid can be cooked down to a tenth its volume and added to virtually any savory sauce. Serve the mushrooms, tossed with vinaigrette, as a cold salad.

WARM EGG YOLK–THICKENED SAUCES

There are two kinds of warm egg yolk–thickened sauces. The first is made by combining egg yolks with flavorful liquids and cooking them gently, stirring constantly and taking care not to let the liquid boil, which would cause the yolks to curdle. The crème anglaise on page 497 is an example of this type. The second kind is made by whisking egg yolks with a small amount of water until a frothy emulsion, called a *sabayon*, forms, and then adding clarified butter in a steady stream until the sauce thickens.

The first method is often used in conjunction with other thickeners, such as cream, flour, or butter. Old-fashioned recipes called for a large number of egg yolks and were very rich, but it is possible to make a sauce with the distinctive silky consistency that egg yolks contribute by using relatively few yolks—as few as 2 yolks for each cup of liquid.

Sauce Marguery, one of the most famous hollandaise-style sauces for fish, is an example of the second, or sabayon, type. It is made by whisking together egg yolks and white wine–based fish broth until the mixture is frothy and stiff, and then whisking in clarified butter as you do for a classic hollandaise. The sauce can be served as is or flavored with herbs. For a more pronounced flavor, you can use shellfish steaming liquid or the liquid from braised fish in place of the wine-based broth.

A sabayon sauce is essentially a hollandaise-style sauce without the butter or with much less butter. The word *sabayon* can be confusing because in French cooking the term can mean one of two things: a sweet sauce, similar to zabaglione, made by whisking egg yolks, sugar, and white wine over medium heat until they thicken, or the foamy frothy mixture of beaten egg yolk that's the prelude to making hollandaise and related sauces.

Seafood "Crème Anglaise"

Of course, real crème anglaise is a sweet liquid custard made by gently cooking milk, sugar, egg yolks, and usually a vanilla bean over gentle heat while stirring steadily. A seafood crème anglaise is derived from what used to be called a sauce allemande, velouté sauce (stock thickened with flour) cooked with egg yolks. The difference between a seafood crème anglaise and a sabayon is that the egg yolks aren't aerated with a whisk. They are simply stirred. For a lighter version, use only 2 egg yolks instead of 3.

MAKES ENOUGH FOR 4 MAIN-COURSE SERVINGS

> 1/2 cup shellfish steaming liquid from mussels or cockles (see pages 108 and 113), mushroom cooking liquid (see page 343), or fish broth, or a combination
>
> 1/4 cup heavy cream
>
> 3 egg yolks
>
> Salt
>
> Pepper

Bring the liquid to a simmer in a small saucepan. In a bowl, whisk together the cream and egg yolks until blended. Slowly pour the hot liquid into the cream mixture while whisking constantly. Off the heat, stir the mixture with the whisk—don't beat it—for about 2 minutes to stabilize the egg yolks, and then pour the mixture back into the saucepan.

Place the pan over low heat and stir the sauce with a wooden spoon. Be sure to reach into the corners of the saucepan so the egg yolk doesn't hide there and curdle. As you stir the sauce, you will see little ripples at first. As the sauce thickens, the ripples will disappear and you will see silky, undulating waves, at which point the sauce is ready. This will take about 3 minutes. Remove from the heat and season with salt and pepper.

VARIATIONS

You can add the same flavors and garnishes as those for Cream Sauce Base for Fish, Chicken, or Veal (see page 343). Because the crème anglaise is specifically for seafood, you can garnish it with oysters (heated in a separate pan in their own juices so their juices don't dilute the sauce) or other shellfish, infuse it with lemon zest (preferably from Meyer lemons), or puree it with caviar, sea urchin roe, or salmon roe and strain it.

Emulsified Seafood Sabayons

This sauce is closer to the Sauce Marguery, described on page 344. A sabayon is an emulsion, technically a foam (an emulsion of a gas with a liquid), made by beating egg yolks with liquid over just enough heat to stiffen the foam without curdling the yolks. A Windsor pan, which has sloping sides that allow you to reach into the corners with a whisk, is the best kind of saucepan to use for this technique. In a regular saucepan, the yolks can hide in the corners, out of reach of the whisk, and scramble. You can also use a bowl set over a saucepan of barely simmering water. Make sure the bowl is wider than the top of the saucepan, so you can grab it quickly with a towel and get it off the steaming water the instant the mixture stiffens.

Once you have your sabayon, you can serve it as is—despite the egg yolks, it is very light because it contains so much air—or you can add butter to it (clarified if you want a very stiff sauce; whole butter for a more liquid sauce) to convert it into a traditional emulsified butter sauce. The latter calls for a lot of butter, though you can compromise and add less.

MAKES ENOUGH FOR 4 TO 6 MAIN-COURSE SERVINGS, DEPENDING ON HOW MUCH BUTTER YOU ADD

> 1/2 cup shellfish steaming liquid from mussels or cockles (see pages 108 and 113) or fish broth
>
> 3 egg yolks
>
> 4 to 16 tablespoons butter, cut into 1-tablespoon slices, or clarified (see page 341)
>
> Salt
>
> Pepper

In a Windsor pan (see headnote) or a metal bowl set over a saucepan of barely simmering water, combine the liquid and egg yolks. Whisk rapidly for about 3 minutes, or until the mixture froths up, loses a little volume, and you see deep traces on the bottom of the pan. Immediately remove the sabayon from the heat.

Whisk in the butter 1 tablespoon at a time. If using clarified butter that you just made, it shouldn't be too hot—you should be able to hold your knuckle in it—or it will curdle the yolks. The sauce will thicken as you add butter. Season with salt and pepper.

VARIATIONS

This sauce is delicious seasoned with saffron (soak saffron threads in 1 tablespoon water for 30 minutes), curry powder (first cooked briefly in a little butter), herbs, chopped reconstituted dried wild mushrooms such as morels or porcini, truffles, Tomato Coulis (see page 366) cooked down until stiff, or vegetable purees such as fennel, pea, fava bean, or winter squash.

HOLLANDAISE AND BÉARNAISE SAUCES

This is a whole family of classic sauces made by whisking water with egg yolks and adding clarified butter. The flavoring added to the emulsion is what gives the sauce its particular identity: lemon juice produces hollandaise, while an infusion of wine vinegar, pepper, tarragon, and shallots turns it into a béarnaise sauce. More classic variations follow.

Blender or Food Processor Hollandaise-Style Sauces

While you won't get the same airiness as when you make a hollandaise by hand, you can make hollandaise and related sauces in a blender or food processor by slowly pouring melted or clarified butter into the egg yolks with the motor of the blender or processor engaged. The butter should be hot enough to cook the yolks but not hot enough to curdle them. Melt the butter in a saucepan and continue heating until it registers 165°F on an instant-read thermometer. Put the egg yolks and the water in the blender or food processor, turn it on, and pour in the butter in a thin, steady stream.

Basic Emulsified
Egg Yolk–Butter Sauce

The French classic repertoire is filled with recipes for variations on hollandaise and béarnaise sauces—mousseline is hollandaise with whipped cream, palloise is béarnaise with mint, choron is béarnaise with tomato puree, and the list goes on. Fortunately, all these sauces are based on the same emulsified base sauce that, once mastered, allows you to make all the derivatives.

**MAKES ABOUT 1¹/₄ CUPS, OR ENOUGH
FOR 6 MAIN-COURSE SERVINGS**

> **3 tablespoons water**
>
> **3 egg yolks**
>
> **¹/₂ pound butter, clarified (about ²/₃ cup clarified, see page 341)**
>
> **Salt**
>
> **Pepper**

Combine the water and egg yolks in a Windsor pan (see sabayon headnote page 345) or metal bowl set over a saucepan of barely simmering water. Whisk rapidly until the mixture froths up, loses a little volume, and you see deep traces on the bottom of the pan. Immediately remove the mixture from the heat. Whisk in the butter 1 tablespoon at a time. Season with salt and pepper.

VARIATIONS

HOLLANDAISE SAUCE: Whisk 1 tablespoon fresh lemon juice into the finished sauce.

BÉARNAISE SAUCE: Combine ¹/₃ cup white wine vinegar; 1 shallot, minced; 5 peppercorns, crushed with a saucepan; and 3 tarragon sprigs and simmer until reduced to 2 tablespoons liquid. Strain through a fine-mesh strainer into the finished sauce and whisk to combine.

TOMATO BÉARNAISE SAUCE (SAUCE CHORON): Cook ¹/₂ cup Tomato Coulis (see page 366) down over medium heat until very stiff (about ¹/₄ cup). Whisk into Béarnaise Sauce.

MINT BÉARNAISE SAUCE (SAUCE PALOISE): Prepare Béarnaise Sauce as directed, substituting mint for the tarragon.

ORANGE HOLLANDAISE (SAUCE MALTAISE): This is the classic sauce used for asparagus. Remove one-fourth of the zest from a navel orange and cut into very thin julienne (see page 298). Blanch

1. Combine egg yolks with cold water, using 1 tablespoon water for each yolk.

2. Whisk off the heat for just a few seconds until fluffy.

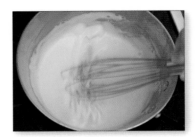

3. Whisk over medium heat until stiff.

4. Whisk in clarified butter 1 tablespoon at a time.

5. Whisk in lemon juice. Season with salt and pepper.

in boiling water for 30 seconds and drain. Squeeze juice from the orange and strain it into a saucepan. Add the julienned zest to the juice and boil until the juice is reduced to about 2 tablespoons. Whisk the reduced juice and zest into the finished sauce.

HOLLANDAISE SAUCE WITH WHIPPED CREAM (SAUCE MOUSSELINE): This luxurious sauce is delicious on asparagus and seafood. If using it for seafood, you can replace the water in the base sauce with shellfish steaming liquid or fish broth. Whip ¹/₂ cup heavy cream to medium peaks. Just before serving, fold the cream into the finished sauce.

BUTTER SAUCES

Butter, like egg yolks, works as an emulsifier, albeit one that needs to be handled carefully to keep it from separating. Butter contains about 25 percent water and about 5 percent protein, and the balance is fat. The protein is what keeps the fat and water in an emulsion. If you heat butter in a pan, the proteins are "denatured" and lose their ability to emulsify, and the butter separates into frothing proteins, water, and clear butterfat. But if butter is whisked into liquid, especially a liquid that is already an emulsion, such as a sauce thickened with flour, the emulsion is preserved. Keep two things in mind when making butter sauces: the sauce must never boil and the butter must be cold and whisked continuously until it emulsifies into the sauce.

Beurre Blanc

Until the 1970s, the most famous butter sauce, beurre blanc, was an obscure regional sauce made in Brittany and in a few famous restaurants in Paris. It was considered nearly impossible to make and was said to require an almost mythical action of the wrist to produce the creamy, buttery sauce with only butter as the emulsifier. Any restaurant that tried to pass off an egg yolk sauce as a beurre blanc received bad press. But in the late 1960s, a few inventive chefs discovered that beurre blanc required no magic after all, just care not to let the sauce boil and constant whisking until all the butter was incorporated. It became the darling of nouvelle cuisine chefs and soon appeared flavored with every conceivable herb or spice. When red wine was added, it was labeled beurre rouge, a pour substitute for a bordelaise sauce.

Monter au Beurre

Monter au beurre is a classic technique for finishing a sauce with butter. The discovery that beurre blanc was an easy sauce to make, and that a pure emulsion of butter allowed flavors to shine through in a unique way, led chefs to experiment with whisking butter into sauce bases that were analogous to the wine, vinegar, and shallot base used for beurre blanc. Classic sauces, originally based on beef or veal broth thickened with roux, were instead based on concentrated unthickened broth and given a silky consistency by the addition of butter at the end. When high-butterfat butter is used, such as European-style butters which have more butter fat, butter also acts as a thickener.

Beurre blanc is almost identical to a béarnaise sauce without the egg yolks, tarragon, and pepper. A simple infusion of white wine and white wine vinegar is boiled down with minced shallots, sometimes a little cream is added to help stabilize the emulsion (while considered heretical, it is virtually impossible to detect its presence), and then cold butter is whisked in. Most recipes insist that the butter be cut into little cubes and be whisked into the infusion one at a time, over low or at most medium heat, with the next cube not added until the previous one is incorporated. But all you actually need to do once you have the infusion is throw all the cut-up butter into the pot at once, turn the heat to high, and whisk until all the butter emulsifies and you have a creamy, almost white sauce.

Of course, because beurre blanc contains virtually nothing but butter, it is profoundly rich. But the acidity of the wine and sometimes wine vinegar cuts through the richness, making it a satisfying sauce.

Beurre Blanc

This basic beurre blanc can be flavored with herbs, spices, mushrooms, or other ingredients in the same way you flavor white sauces thickened with cream, flour, or egg yolks.

MAKES 1 CUP, OR ENOUGH FOR 6 TO 8 MAIN-COURSE SERVINGS

- **2 shallots, minced**
- **1/2 cup dry white wine**
- **1/2 cup white wine vinegar**
- **2 tablespoons heavy cream**
- **1/2 pound cold butter, cut into 1/2-inch cubes**
- **Salt**
- **White pepper**

In a small saucepan, combine the shallots, wine, and vinegar over medium heat. Simmer until only 2 to 3 tablespoons remain. Add the cream, simmer for 1 minute more, and add the butter all at once.

Raise the heat to high and whisk constantly until all the butter has melted. If the sauce starts to look oily or waxlike—beurre blanc is never very thick—add a tablespoon or two of water or cream to keep it from breaking. Season with salt and pepper.

VARIATIONS

Beurre blanc can be flavored with saffron threads (soaked in 1 tablespoon of water for 30 minutes) and other spices, herbs, chopped reconstituted dried mushrooms, truffles, lobster roe,

(continued)

Beurre Blanc, continued

caviar, sea urchin roe, tomatoes, and almost any ingredient that is used to flavor a white sauce. It can also be lightened by whisking in some broth or other flavorful liquid shortly before serving. The initial reduction of shallots and wine can be replaced with fish broth, shellfish steaming liquid, garlic, ginger, meat broth, reduced tomato coulis, dashi, or soy sauce. Flavored or infused olive oil can also be whisked into the sauce and will stay emulsified by the butter. After infusing, the added ingredients can be strained out or left in for color and texture.

HOW TO MAKE BEURRE BLANC

1. Combine white wine and wine vinegar, along with minced shallots, in a saucepan. Boil down the wine until only a couple of tablespoons of liquid are left.

2. Add a small amount of heavy cream.

3. Whisk in chunks of cold butter.

4. Whisk until smooth and creamy.

5. Flavor the beurre blanc with (clockwise) tomatoes, curry, herbs, or saffron.

Lightened Beurre Blanc

If cold butter is whisked into too large a proportion of hot liquid, it will separate after a few minutes and end up as oil floating on top. For this reason, the obvious method of using more liquid as the base for a beurre blanc doesn't work. A better way to lighten a beurre blanc—beurre blanc can be kept in a pan of warm water for up to a couple of hours before serving—is to combine it with a flavorful liquid, such as vegetable broth or fish broth, just before serving. The result is a buttery brothlike sauce with less richness than a traditional beurre blanc but with the same satisfying butteriness.

This lightened version is excellent with pieces of sautéed or poached fish, scallops, lobster tails, or assorted seafood.

MAKES ENOUGH FOR 8 MAIN-COURSE SERVINGS

> **Beurre Blanc (see page 347)**
> **1 cup vegetable broth, fish broth, or shellfish steaming liquid from mussels or cockles (see pages 108 and 113)**

Make the beurre blanc as directed. Shortly before serving, bring the broth to a simmer and remove from the heat. Whisk the hot broth into the sauce, and immediately ladle the sauce over or around seafood in warmed soup plates.

COMPOUND BUTTERS

A compound butter is cold butter with some kind of flavoring mixed with it, such as herbs or reconstituted dried mushrooms. Maître d'hôtel butter, made by working butter with chopped parsley and a little lemon juice, is the best-known traditional version. It is ubiquitous on steak frites in restaurants in France.

The value of compound butters is their versatility—they can be made with nearly any flavoring—and their ability to preserve the flavor of whatever ingredients are used. For example, if you have extra fresh tarragon on hand, chop it with butter and freeze it. You can then serve it atop a piece of fish or chicken, or whisk it into another sauce just before serving. When making herb butters, chop the herbs coarsely and then finish more finely by chopping them with the butter. This method is better than chopping them by themselves and then combining them with the butter, which causes them to turn dark. Chopping them with the butter keeps them from turning dark and losing flavor. Use the largest knife you have or are comfortable using so that you're cutting more at a time and the process goes more quickly. Keep tightly wrapped in plastic wrap or parchment paper until ready to use.

1. Coarsely chop parsley leaves.

2. Add the butter.

3. Chop until finely chopped and completely combined.

4. Add lemon juice.

5. Bring the butter together into a cylinder with the side of the knife.

6. Put the butter near the end of a sheet of parchment paper.

7. Fold over and roll up the parchment.

8. Twist the ends in opposite directions until tight.

Maître d'hôtel Butter: Coarsely chop the leaves from 1 small bunch parsley and then chop with ¹/₄ pound cold butter until the parsley is finely chopped and evenly incorporated in the butter. Work in juice of ¹/₂ lemon.

Tarragon Butter: Unlike most herbs, which can be coarsely chopped before combining with butter, tarragon should be chopped entirely while combining with butter to prevent blackening. Combine the leaves from about 20 tarragon sprigs—about ¹/₄ cup leaves—with ¹/₄ pound cold butter and chop until the tarragon is finely chopped and evenly incorporated in the butter.

HOW TO MAKE TARRAGON BUTTER

Chop cold butter with fresh tarragon leaves.

Chop until the tarragon is fully chopped and incorporated.

Chervil Butter: Replace the tarragon in Tarragon Butter with chervil leaves.

Fines Herbes Butter: The combination of herbs called "fines herbes" contains as much tarragon as it does the other three herbs, chives, parsley, and chervil. But because tarragon is so much stronger than these other three, leave it out for more delicate sauces. Combine 2 tablespoons coarsely chopped parsley leaves (preferably flat-leaf parsley) 2 tablespoons thinly sliced chives (don't chop the chives with the butter; thinly slice them first), and the leaves from 1 bunch chervil with ¹/₄ pound cold butter, and chop until the parsley and chervil are finely chopped and all the herbs are evenly incorporated in the butter.

Morel or Porcini Butter: Soak ¹/₂ ounce dried morel or porcini mushrooms in ¹/₄ cup warm water for about 30 minutes, or until soft. Turn the mushrooms around in the liquid and squeeze them every few minutes to get them to soften without having to use too much liquid. Chop the mushrooms with ¹/₄ pound cold butter until the mushrooms are finely chopped and evenly incorporated in the butter.

Foie Gras Butter: Chop 2 ounces diced foie gras with 4 tablespoons butter. Work the mixture through a fine-mesh strainer with the back of a ladle or wooden spoon. The butter can be frozen and used in small amounts to finish white and brown sauces.

Truffle Butter: Coarsely chop 1 fresh truffle and combine it with $1/4$ pound cold butter. Chop until the truffle is finely chopped and evenly incorporated into the butter. Make the truffle butter the day before you plan to use it to give the truffle time to permeate the butter.

HOW TO MAKE TRUFFLE BUTTER

1. Slice the truffle with a vegetable slicer or truffle slicer as shown here.

2. Chop the truffle and butter together.

3. Roll up in parchment paper.

Shellfish Butter Sauce Model

This model uses beurre blanc as the base and combines it with fish broth or shellfish steaming liquid to lighten the effect and make the sauce less rich and more brothlike. The beurre blanc itself can be made with part herb, mushroom, or truffle butter.

MAKES ENOUGH FOR 6 MAIN-COURSE SERVINGS

Beurre Blanc (see page 347)

$1/2$ cup shellfish steaming liquid from mussels or cockles (see pages 108 and 113), shrimp broth (see page 40), or vegetable broth

Optional Finishes

3 tablespoons Crustacean Butter (opposite), or to taste

3 tablespoons herb butter such as Tarragon Butter (see page 349)

3 tablespoons Mushroom Butter (see page 349) or Truffle Butter (at left)

2 tablespoons raw sea urchin roe, worked through a fine-mesh strainer and combined with 2 tablespoons heavy cream

3 tablespoons raw lobster roe, worked through a fine-mesh strainer and combined with 2 tablespoons heavy cream

Salt

Pepper

Make the beurre blanc as directed. Shortly before serving, bring the liquid to a simmer and remove from the heat. Whisk the hot liquid into the sauce and whisk in one or more of the optional finishes. If you use the lobster roe, do not let the sauce simmer and add some of the sauce to the roe before returning the mixture to the bulk of the sauce. Season with salt and pepper and ladle over seafood in warmed soup plates.

Crustacean Butters

Crustacean butters are often called for finishing bisques and seafood sauces to add color and flavor. They're especially delicious in sauces based on the cooking liquid from shellfish. These butters, which are used primarily to underline the flavor of seafood sauces and contribute a bright orange color, are made differently than most compound butters because they are cooked. They are made from lobster or crayfish shells or shrimp heads. In fact, it is almost impossible to tell which crustacean the butter is made from. One caveat: since the crustacean shells are ground in a food processor, don't use very hard shells, such as lobster claws or crab claws.

MAKES ABOUT ¹/₂ CUP

1 quart lobster or crawfish tail shells or shrimp heads
¹/₂ pound cold butter, sliced

In a food processor, combine the shells and butter and grind, stopping as needed to scrape down the sides of the processor, for about 2 minutes, or until the mixture is pink and finely ground. Put this pink shell butter in a small saucepan over low to medium heat and cook for about 30 minutes, or until the butter turns deep orange. If the shells start to sizzle in the butter before 30 minutes has passed, turn down the heat and add a few tablespoons water to keep the butter from burning.

When the butter is bright orange, add enough water to the saucepan to cover the shells completely. Bring the water to a gentle simmer, remove from the heat, and let cool at room temperature for 1 hour. Cover and refrigerate overnight.

The next day, pull off the bright orange disk of congealed butter and transfer it to a small saucepan. Melt the butter over low to medium heat and cook for about 5 minutes, or until any liquid is cooked off. Strain through a fine-mesh strainer into a clean container. Cover tightly and refrigerate for several weeks or freeze for up to several months.

HOW TO MAKE LOBSTER SAUCE WITH LOBSTER SHELLS

1. Grind lobster shells from 6 lobsters (which can be saved up in the freezer), except hard claw shells, in a food processor.

2. Add 4 chopped tomatoes.

3. Add ground shells and processed tomatoes to a mixture of 1 each chopped carrot, small onion, and celery stalk, all sautéed.

4. Add tarragon sprigs, 1 cup cream, 2 cups broth, and ¹/₂ cup white wine and simmer for 20 minutes.

5. Work through a fine-mesh strainer.

6. Return strained sauce to the pan. Finish with strained lobster roe and tomalley. Heat without simmering.

BROWN SAUCES

Most brown sauces are served with meat and are, in fact, brown. Traditionally, they were made by combining veal and beef broth, adding tomatoes, and thickening the mixture with a brown roux. The sauce was then reduced, to yield sauce espagnole, which was usually reduced again, to yield demi-glace, the base for virtually every meat sauce.

When nouvelle cuisine chefs took the flour out of their sauces in the 1970s, demi-glace was replaced with the even more dramatically reduced glace de viande, a syrupy glaze made from bones. It was added to flavorful bases, often made with wine, to give the sauce its body, and the sauce was finished with butter (see Monter au Beurre on page 347). The extreme reduction of the meat glaze and the use of European butter give these sauces their thickness. A more modern, lighter approach calls for reducing the sauce less, leaving it more like a broth, and finishing it with little or no butter.

Making traditional meat sauces at home requires a highly concentrated broth or glaze. Meat glazes are now sold commercially and are often of high quality, making it possible to throw together a complex sauce in minutes. Meat glaze can be made at home—a good winter weekend project—kept for months (at least) in the freezer, and used in tiny amounts as needed. The ideal meat glaze is made with meat, but this is expensive unless you figure out a way to serve the meat to family or friends without the broth or braising liquid. An alternative is to use bones, or bones and meat. (For making basic beef broth, see pages 38–39.)

To make your own brown sauces, it is helpful to examine how classic brown sauces are constructed. Typically, a flavorful liquid such as white or red wine, Madeira, or vinegar is infused with aromatic ingredients such as shallots or mushrooms. This flavor base is then boiled down in the same way the wine, vinegar, and shallot base is reduced for a beurre blanc (see page 347). Next, concentrated broth or meat glaze is added to the base, the mixture is reduced or thinned with liquid to get it close to the desired final consistency, and then butter is whisked into the sauce at the last minute.

Here are several classic meat sauces that can be made up to a couple of hours in advance or at the last minute by deglazing the pan with wine, broth, or water and adding the rest of the ingredients to the pan juices.

Cooking with Red Wine

When beurre blanc–derived sauces were all the rage in the '70s and '80s, a popular derivative was beurre rouge, made simply by replacing the white wine with red. The sauces were often harsh and acidic. Red wine needs to cook with protein (and ideally herbs and aromatic vegetables) to soften and round out its flavor. Rather than simply reducing red wine and combining with concentrated broth to make a sauce, reduce the broth and wine together so the proteins in the broth neutralize the tannins in the wine. The broth can even be made with wine instead of water (see Red Wine Broth on pages 354–355), or best of all, cook meat with red wine as though making a stew and then use the stewing liquid reduced and/or thickened as a sauce base. Another trick is to brown a few meat trimmings with a little onion and carrot and then simmer these with the broth or glaze used to make the sauce.

HOW TO MAKE A BROWN MUSTARD SAUCE

1. Combine 2 minced shallots and 1/2 cup white wine and simmer to reduce by three-fourths.

2. Add 2 tablespoons commercial meat glaze or 4 tablespoons homemade meat glaze (see page 177) and enough broth to thin to the consistency you like. Simmer to dissolve the meat glaze.

3. When the sauce is the consistency you like, add mustard to taste.

4. Whisk in butter and parsley or herb butter.

Bordelaise Sauce

Bordelaise sauce is best atop beef, particularly steaks. You can also make it for roasts such as tenderloin that provide very little in the way of drippings. Most recipes for borde-laise sauce—red wine sauce—call for reducing red wine down to a glaze and then adding meat glaze. A better system is to combine the red wine and broth or glaze before reduc-ing (see "Cooking with Red Wine," opposite) and then reduce the two together. This allows the proteins in the glaze to soften the tannins and acidity in the wine.

Bordelaise sauce is traditionally finished with sliced or diced beef marrow, swirled into the sauce at the last minute because it melts very quickly. To get perfect rounds of marrow, buy marrow bones. If the bones are shaped right, you can just push the marrow out with your thumb. If they aren't, you have to crack the bones in two places with a cleaver. Stand a bone on end and with a quick hacking motion, crack one side; repeat on another side and pull away the broken bone. The marrow should just pop out. To take the blood out of the mar-row (so the marrow doesn't turn gray when you heat it), and soak it overnight in salty water in the refrigerator.

MAKES ABOUT 1¹/₄ CUPS, OR ENOUGH FOR 6 MAIN-COURSE SERVINGS

- 1 cup full-bodied red wine
- 2 shallots, minced
- 2 sprigs thyme
- ¹/₂ bay leaf
- 4 tablespoons commercial meat glaze or ¹/₂ cup homemade meat glaze (see page 177), 1 cup concentrated brown beef broth, or 1 cup liquid from a stew or drippings from a roast (see page 169)
- 5 black peppercorns, crushed
- 6 tablespoons cold butter, preferably French or European-style butter, sliced (optional)
- Salt
- 2-inch section marrow (at right), cut into 6 slices or into ¹/₃-inch cubes, soaked overnight in very salty water to remove blood (optional)

In a saucepan, combine the wine, shallots, thyme, bay leaf, and meat glaze. Place the pan off center on the burner over medium heat so that the liquid simmers on only one side and pushes the fat to the other. Simmer, regularly skimming off any fat or froth that forms on the top, until the mixture is the consistency and flavor you like or, for a classic consistency, is lightly syrupy and coats the back of a spoon. If you want to incorporate pan drippings in the sauce, use this base to deglaze the pan.

Add the peppercorns, simmer for 1 minute, and whisk in the butter over medium heat. Season with salt and strain through a fine-mesh strainer into a clean saucepan. Add the marrow cubes or slices, bring to a simmer, and serve.

VARIATIONS

A bordelaise sauce is a perfect example of a classic sauce made in a systematic way. Many similar sauces can be made by substituting other wines for the red wine, different herbs for the thyme and bay leaf, and other aromatic vegetables for the shallots.

MADEIRA SAUCE: Substitute Rainwater or Malmsey Madeira for the red wine. Omit the marrow.

WHITE WINE BORDELAISE SAUCE: Substitute white wine for the red wine. Omit the marrow. Serve with chicken or veal.

Tricks for Enhancing Brown Sauces

It often happens that a cook will have labored over a sauce only to find that it lacks vitality and tastes flat. To liven up a brown sauce without changing its identity, make sure it has enough salt, and then add a few drops of wine vinegar and 1 to 2 teaspoons cognac. To freshen it, add 1 or 2 tea-spoons chopped fresh parsley or chervil and simmer for 30 seconds. Adding 1 tablespoon butter that has been stored overnight in a jar with a truffle will do wonders, as will 1 to 2 teaspoons Foie Gras Butter (see pages 349–350) whisked in the last minute.

The standard method of using reduced broth or meat glaze for making a brown sauce is convenient and reliable, but because the broth is cooked for so long, it loses some of its freshness and vitality during the long simmering. To give a brown sauce a more immediate meaty flavor, a little like the natural drippings (jus) from a roast, caramelize a few trimmings

GETTING MARROW OUT OF BONES

1. Soak marrow overnight in salted water.

2. Slice soaked marrow and use as needed.

of meat—whatever meat you are making the sauce for—with a little chopped onion or shallot on top of the stove. Add some broth, caramelize by reducing to dryness, add more broth, and so on, in much the same way you make the fake jus on page 170.

Chasseur Sauce

This is a mushroom sauce, usually served with chicken, that is based on Bordelaise Sauce (see page 353).

MAKES 1 CUP

4 ounces cremini or white mushrooms, sliced

5 tablespoons butter

1 shallot, minced

1/2 cup dry white wine

2 tablespoons cognac

2 cups concentrated brown chicken broth or 4 tablespoons commercial meat glaze or 1/2 cup homemade meat glaze (see page 177) dissolved in 1 cup water

1 tablespoon chopped fresh tarragon

Salt

Pepper

Sauté the mushrooms in 2 tablespoons of the butter over medium heat until browned. Sprinkle the shallot over the mushrooms and sauté for 1 minute, or until fragrant. Add the wine, cognac and boil down until reduced by three-fourths. Add the stock or meat glaze and water and boil down until reduced by one-half. Simmer until the sauce has a slightly syrupy consistency. Stir in the tarragon. Whisk in the remaining 3 tablespoons of butter. Season with salt and pepper.

Improved Brown Sauce

If you are making Bordelaise Sauce or one of the sauces that follows it, you can enhance the flavor of the sauce by making it with meat trimmings.

MAKES 1¼ CUPS, OR ENOUGH FOR 6 MAIN-COURSE SERVINGS

Ingredients for Bordelaise Sauce (see page 353) or variations

2 tablespoons butter

1½ pounds beef, veal, chicken, pork, lamb, or game trimmings or stew meat, depending on the meat the sauce will accompany, cut into ½-inch cubes

Have the sauce ingredients ready. In a sauté pan, melt the butter over medium-high to high heat. Add the meat trimmings and whatever aromatic ingredients, such as shallot, carrot, onion, and/or celery, are called for in the recipe and sauté for about 8 minutes, or until browned. Add half of the wine or vinegar (some sauces call for vinegar) called for in the recipe, if any, raise the heat to high, and boil while stirring with a wooden spoon until the pan runs dry and a layer of caramelized drippings forms on the bottom. Repeat with the remaining wine or vinegar and then repeat again with half of the broth. (If you are using a meat glaze, dissolve the glaze in 1 cup hot water to make broth.) When the broth caramelizes on the bottom of the pan, add the rest of the broth, turn down the heat, and simmer gently for 10 minutes. Strain through a fine-mesh strainer and continue as directed in the recipe.

Burgundy-Style Red Wine Sauce (Sauce Meurette)

This sauce is served in Burgundy with poached eggs (a delightful brunch item, by the way), but it can also be used for chicken, meat, or fish. Its greatest advantage is that it requires no broth—just a piece of prosciutto end, which some grocers will give you or at least sell for far less than the typical cost of sliced prosciutto. It is traditionally thickened with a little flour, but not cooked in a roux. The flour is instead worked into a paste with a little softened butter (called beurre manié) and whisked into the sauce at the end. An alternative is to add meat glaze to give the sauce body and finish it with 3 tablespoons butter.

MAKES ³/₄ CUP SAUCE

- **6 tablespoons butter**
- **3 ounces prosciutto end, cut into ¹/₄-inch cubes**
- **1 onion, minced**
- **2 carrots, peeled and minced**
- **¹/₄ fennel bulb or fennel stalks, thinly sliced (optional)**
- **2 cloves garlic, crushed, peeled, left whole**
- **3 sprigs thyme or ¹/₂ teaspoon dried thyme**
- **1 bay leaf**
- **2 cups full-bodied red wine**
- **2 tablespoons meat glaze (see page 177), optional**
- **1 tablespoon finely chopped fresh chives or parsley (optional)**
- **Salt**
- **Pepper**

In a small saucepan, melt 2 tablespoons of the butter over medium heat. Add the prosciutto, onion, carrots, fennel, and garlic and cook, stirring every few minutes, for about 10 minutes, or until any liquid released by the vegetables evaporates and caramelizes into a crust on the sides and bottom of the saucepan. Continually scrape the crust that forms in the saucepan back into the mixture with a wooden spoon.

Add the thyme, bay leaf, and ¹/₂ cup wine and boil down the wine until it evaporates and a crust forms. Add the meat glaze and the remaining 1¹/₂ cups wine and simmer gently for 20 minutes, until the flavor of the ingredients is well infused. Strain through a fine-mesh strainer into a clean saucepan. Simmer until reduced to about ¹/₂ cup, or until lightly syrupy. Whisk in the remaining 4 tablespoons butter, add the chives, and season with salt and pepper.

HOW TO MAKE SAUCE MEURETTE

1. Gently cook prosciutto and vegetable mixture in butter.

2. When a crust forms on the bottom of the pan, scrape it off with a wooden spoon. Add the herbs, and dissolve the crust with wine and let evaporate while scraping.

3. Continue to scrape and cook until the wine has evaporated.

4. Add the rest of the wine and simmer.

5. Strain into a new saucepan.

6. Simmer down until lightly syrupy and then whisk in cold butter.

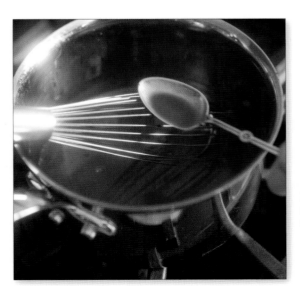

7. The sauce should coat a spoon.

SWEET-AND-SOUR BROWN SAUCES MADE WITH FRUIT

The best-known fruit sauce is orange sauce for duck, but fruit-based brown sauces are good with all sorts of game, such as deer and hare. There are several approaches to serving meat with fruit and fruit sauce. For example, when flavoring a sauce with a citrus fruit, the juice of the fruit can be used, but a better source of flavor is the zest—the thin, shiny colored part of the rind—which is usually blanched first to eliminate bitterness. Berries can be lightly cooked in the appropriate broth and the broth reduced and used in the sauce. Or, fruits such as apples can be cooked separately from the meat and served with the meat, while the apple or other fruit character is added directly to the meat through the addition of a brandy or liqueur made from the fruit, such as Calvados (apple brandy) for apples, Grand Marnier for oranges, and kirsch (dry, clear, cherry brandy) for cherries.

Fruit sauces, and for that matter most brown sauces, benefit from a subtle sweet-and-sour accent. The juxtaposition of an acidic element, such as vinegar, with sugar or the sweetness of fruit brings the other flavors in the sauce into relief. The traditional component added to sweet-and-sour sauces is called a gastrique and is essentially caramel made with vinegar. If you don't want to bother, just use sugar and vinegar alone.

For recipes for orange sauce and berry sauce, see page 273.

RAGÙ-TYPE SAUCES

The words *ragout* and *ragù* are, to the American ear at least, homonyms. This observation leads to the secret of the best ragù. Make a ragout, or stew, reduce and degrease the braising liquid as though you were making a classic French brown sauce, and then—here is where the similarity with French sauces ends—shred or dice the meat (for example, beef, rabbit, duck, veal, hare) and stir it back into the reduced braising liquid. Your stew becomes sauce with tiny pieces of meat dispersed throughout—in other words, stew and braising liquid have become one. This method—make a stew and then dice, chop, or shred the meat—is far better than what most recipes recommend: chop or dice raw meat, brown it, and simmer it in liquids such as tomatoes, wine, or broth.

Duck Ragù

This sauce, made from braised duck thighs, has the deep complexity of a French brown sauce but delivers the rustic satisfaction of the best ragù in Italy. This method applies to anything you can braise. In other words, if you have leftover stew or pot roast, simply separate the meat, chop, shred or dice it, and combine it with its braising liquid. Serve this sauce with fresh pappardelle.

MAKES 4 MAIN-COURSE SERVINGS OR 6 FIRST-COURSE SERVINGS

1/2 recipe Slow-Roasted Duck Thighs (see page 274)
Salt
Pepper

You need half of the duck thighs recipe. When basting the duck thighs during their final phase of cooking, baste only until the braising liquid becomes lightly syrupy. If you have already cooked the thighs and they are cold, remove any congealed fat with a spoon.

Shred the meat by pulling it off the thighs with your fingers. Combine the shredded meat with the braising liquid in a pot large enough to hold the noodles. Season with salt and pepper.

Bolognese Sauce

Most Bolognese sauce recipes call for browning chopped meat with aromatic vegetables and then simmering the meat with tomatoes. In this method, you slowly simmer larger pieces of meat, which allows the sauce to develop a deeper, more complex flavor and makes it possible to eliminate every trace of fat.

MAKES ABOUT 5 QUARTS

> 5 pounds beef stew meat, cut into 1-inch cubes
>
> Salt
>
> Pepper
>
> 6 tablespoons olive oil
>
> 3 cloves garlic, finely chopped
>
> 1 large onion, finely chopped
>
> 2 large carrots, peeled and finely chopped
>
> Nine 14$\frac{1}{2}$-ounce cans tomatoes, drained, seeded, and chopped or 20 tomatoes, peeled, seeded, and chopped (see page 85)
>
> Bouquet garni
>
> 2 cups full-bodied red wine
>
> $\frac{1}{2}$ cup red wine vinegar, or to taste
>
> Sugar, if needed

Season the meat with salt and pepper. In a pot large enough to hold the stew, heat 3 tablespoons of the oil over high heat. Working in batches, brown the meat on all sides. This should take about 20 minutes for each batch.

Pour the burnt oil out of the pot, return the pot to medium heat, and add the garlic, onion, and carrots. Sweat (cook gently to release the juices) for about 10 minutes, or until the vegetables brown slightly. Return the meat to the pot and add the tomatoes, bouquet garni, wine, and $\frac{1}{2}$ cup wine vinegar, bring to a simmer, and simmer gently, uncovered, for 3 hours. Remove from the heat and let cool. Ideally, refrigerate overnight. Spoon off and discard any fat that has congealed on top.

Remove the meat from the sauce and let cool until cool enough to handle. Using your fingers, break up the meat into shreds. Return the sauce to high heat and simmer to thicken slightly. Discard the bouquet garni. Stir the shredded meat into the sauce.

Season the sauce with salt and pepper. Taste and adjust with a little sugar and with more vinegar if needed. Strangely, if the sauce tastes acidic, vinegar helps attenuate the acidity. Store for up to 5 days in the fridge or several months in the freezer.

Rabbit Sauce

This is a great way to use a large rabbit—5 pounds or more—that would otherwise need to be larded and braised for hours to become tender. Here, larding isn't necessary because it is irrelevant if the rabbit dries out. The meat will be distributed throughout the sauce, making any dryness imperceptible. Serve this sauce with flat egg noodles such as pappardelle, fettucinne, or linguini.

MAKES ABOUT 6 CUPS

> 6 tablespoons olive oil
>
> 1 large rabbit, cut up
>
> Salt
>
> Pepper
>
> 1 large onion, finely chopped
>
> 2 large carrots, peeled and finely chopped
>
> 3 cloves garlic, chopped
>
> 1 cup dry white wine
>
> 3 cups chicken broth
>
> Bouquet garni
>
> 4 large tomatoes, peeled, seeded, and chopped (see page 85)
>
> $\frac{1}{2}$ cup heavy cream (optional)

In a large sauté pan, heat 3 tablespoons of the olive oil over high heat. Working in batches, add the rabbit pieces and season with salt and pepper. Cook, turning as needed, for about 8 minutes on each side, or until well browned on all sides.

Pour the burnt oil out of the pan, return the pan to medium heat, and add the onion, carrots, and garlic. Sweat (cook gently to release the juices) for about 10 minutes, or until lightly browned. Return the rabbit pieces to the pan, pour in the wine and broth, and nestle the bouquet garni in the center of the pan. Sprinkle the tomatoes over the rabbit, reduce the heat to low, cover, and braise at a bare simmer for 3 hours, or until a knife slides easily in and out of one of the pieces.

Remove the rabbit pieces from the sauce and let cool. Simmer the sauce over low heat to thicken slightly, then discard the bouquet garni. Pull the rabbit meat away from the bones and shred the meat. Discard the bouquet garni. Stir the shredded meat into the sauce.

Add the cream to the sauce and season with salt and pepper. Store for up to 5 days in the fridge or several months in the freezer.

MAYONNAISE

Mayonnaise is one of the most underrated sauces. Most of us get it out of a jar and forget how much better a simple homemade mayonnaise is, and how versatile mayonnaise is as a medium for flavors and as the base for salsalike sauces.

Made by working oil slowly into egg yolks, homemade mayonnaise intimidates beginning cooks because it can separate if you don't approach it right. Directions are overly complicated with warnings about this and that. If you add the oil to the egg yolks too quickly, especially at the beginning, the mayonnaise won't pull together and the yolks and oil will stay separate. The mayonnaise can also separate if you let it get too thick and the particles of emulsified oil are forced together (see more about emulsions on page 341).

You can make mayonnaise by hand—usually the easiest method if you are just making a small amount—or in a food processor or blender. Once you have made a basic mayonnaise, you can flavor it easily.

What about Raw Egg Yolks?

While contracting salmonella from raw egg yolks is highly unlikely—your odds become even with the consumption of about 20,000 raw egg yolks—many people still worry about the danger. Some cooks recommend purchasing pasteurized egg yolks. But you can pasteurize your own egg yolks by cooking them as though you were making a hollandaise sauce (see page 345). Combine the yolks with 1 tablespoon cold water per yolk in a medium metal mixing bowl and whisk until frothy. Holding the edge of the bowl with a towel, hold the bowl over low to medium heat and whisk the yolks until they froth up and stiffen. Whisk in the oil as you would if making the mayonnaise with raw eggs. Once the sabayon made from the yolks begins to stiffen, it has reached close to 180°F, which is far higher than the 140°F needed to kill salmonella.

Olive Oil in Mayonnaise

For some inexplicable reason, extra virgin olive oil turns bitter when beaten with a whisk, and even more so when worked in a blender or food processor. If you are making mayonnaise with extra virgin olive oil, such as aioli, avoid using a whisk. Traditionally, aioli was made by grinding the garlic in a mortar with a pestle and then working the oil in with the pestle. This is still a great method, but is only practical if you have a mortar that is too large to lift and that costs more than a high-end food processor. You can mince and then crush the garlic with the side of a knife, combine it with the egg yolks, and then work the olive oil in with a wooden spoon, but this takes time, because a spoon integrates the oil much more slowly than a whisk. Another approach is to use half pure olive oil, which doesn't turn bitter when whisked into egg yolks. Then, once the emulsion is established and you can add oil more quickly, you can use a wooden spoon to work in the extra virgin olive oil.

Quick Fix for Bottled Mayonnaise

If you don't want to bother making mayonnaise from scratch, but you want to create the effect of homemade mayonnaise, work some extra virgin olive oil or other oil into a few tablespoons of bottled mayonnaise. You can even add an egg yolk to give the mayonnaise a homemade color.

MAKES 1 CUP

> 1/4 cup bottled mayonnaise
> 1 tablespoon fresh lemon juice
> 1 tablespoon Dijon mustard
> 1 egg yolk (optional)
> 3/4 cup canola or safflower oil, pure olive oil, extra virgin olive oil, or nut oil
> Salt
> Pepper

In a bowl, whisk together the mayonnaise, lemon juice, mustard, and egg yolk. Whisk in the oil in a steady stream. If the mayonnaise starts to get thicker than bottled mayonnaise, add 1 to 2 teaspoons water to keep it from breaking. Season with salt and pepper.

Basic Mayonnaise

Classic basic mayonnaise calls for both mustard and lemon juice, but you can leave out the mustard or use vinegar instead of the lemon juice.

MAKES 1 CUP

> **2 egg yolks**
> **1 tablespoon Dijon mustard**
> **1 tablespoon fresh lemon juice**
> **³/₄ cup vegetable oil**
> **Salt**
> **Pepper**

To make the mayonnaise by hand, in a bowl, whisk together the egg yolks, mustard, and lemon juice until blended. Spoon about 1 tablespoon of the oil into the egg yolks next to the side of the bowl. Using a whisk, and working from the side opposite the oil, whisk to incorporate the oil a small amount at a time by moving the whisk in circles and taking a little of the oil with each turn. It should take about a minute to work in the first tablespoon, and 30 seconds each for the subsequent tablespoons. (You can also add the oil drop by drop, but this is tedious.) Repeat until you have incorporated 4 tablespoons of the oil and the mixture is emulsified but has not yet thickened, and then start working in the oil in larger amounts. If the mayonnaise starts to look stiffer than bottled mayonnaise, add 1 to 2 teaspoons water. Season with salt and pepper.

To make the mayonnaise in a blender or food processor, combine the egg yolks, mustard, and lemon juice in the blender or processor container and process briefly to blend. Then, with the motor running, add the oil in a thin, steady stream. If the mayonnaise gets too stiff to turn with the blades, add 1 to 2 teaspoons water to thin it. Transfer to a bowl and season with salt and pepper.

VARIATIONS

To impress your guests, serve an assortment of different mayonnaises with barbecued chicken or fish. Put the mayonnaises in small, attractive bowls and pass them at the table.

Mayonnaise can be flavored with nearly any herb, curry powder or other spice mixtures, vegetable purees such as tomato or pea, mushrooms, truffles, horseradish, diced apples, capers, pickles, or diced vegetables. You can also add or substitute 1 tablespoon extra virgin olive oil or a nut oil (hazelnut, walnut, pistachio, and so on) to the recipe for Basic Mayonnaise.

Chlorophyll for Green Mayonnaise

You can give your mayonnaise a green hue by using Maille brand herb mustard, which is green, or you can extract the chlorophyll from spinach and use it.

MAKES 2 TABLESPOONS

> **3 cups tightly packed spinach leaves (from about 10 ounces spinach leaves, typically the size of bags of prewashed leaves)**
> **1¹/₂ cups cold water**
> **About ¹/₄ cup olive oil for preserving**

In a blender, combine the spinach and water and puree for 1 minute. Strain through a strainer lined with a triple layer of cheesecloth held over a small saucepan. Discard the contents of the strainer. Line the strainer with a coffee filter or a paper towel and set aside.

Place the saucepan over medium heat and heat, watching closely, for about 2 minutes, or until the green in the liquid coagulates into little pieces. Immediately strain through the coffee filter. Let it take its time—don't push down on it—and use a spoon to scoop out what doesn't go through the cloth. This is the pure chlorophyll. Use it in small amounts to color cold sauces. To save what you don't use, put it in a small ramekin or jar and add just enough oil to cover the surface with a thin film. It will keep refrigerated for up to 5 days. Use 1 teaspoon to flavor 1 cup Basic Mayonnaise.

Classic and Improvised Mayonnaises

Classic French cookbooks list about two dozen mayonnaises, from tartar to gribiche sauce. In these classic recipes, a relatively small amount of flavoring, such as an herb or capers, is added. Contemporary versions call for larger amounts because modern palates have grown used to more assertive sauces. Also, more intense flavoring has the effect of making a mayonnaise less rich and more salsalike. These mayonnaises can also be used to make salads out of diced cold meat, seafood, or vegetables. Each of the following mayonnaises makes about 1 1/2 cups.

Aioli Sauce

Aioli is delicious on grilled chicken, fish, or meat and can be whisked into soups for a last-minute burst of flavor. Make Basic Mayonnaise as directed, omitting the mustard and adding 1 egg yolk, 2 teaspoons water, and 2 cloves garlic, minced and then crushed with the flat side of the knife. Using a wooden spoon, slowly incorporate 1/2 cup extra virgin olive oil. Makes about 1 1/2 cups.

Andalouse Sauce

This sauce is a little bit like a salsa because it contains tomatoes and peppers. If you want it to have a little heat, replace 1 or both bell peppers with 1 or 2 poblano chiles. Char, peel, and seed 2 red bell peppers or 1 yellow and 1 red pepper, as directed on page 321, and cut into 1/4-inch dice. Chop 2 tomatoes and cook in a small saucepan over medium heat until a stiff paste forms. Work the paste through a strainer with the back of a small ladle. Stir the diced peppers and the paste into Basic Mayonnaise. Use on cold or hot grilled meats or fish. Makes about 1 1/2 cups.

Chantilly Sauce

This is mayonnaise lightened with whipped cream. Whip 1/2 cup heavy cream until stiff peaks form. Fold into Basic Mayonnaise and season with salt and pepper. If you like, color the sauce green with 1 teaspoon chlorophyll (see page 359). Serve with cold seafood. You can also fold whipped cream into any of the flavored mayonnaises. Makes about 1 1/2 cups.

Curry Mayonnaise

Cook 1 tablespoon curry powder in 1 tablespoon oil for 30 seconds. Thin Basic Mayonnaise with 2 teaspoons water (the curry thickens the mayonnaise and may otherwise cause it to break), and then work in the curry mixture. Makes about 1 1/4 cups. Curry mayonnaise is great as the base for chicken salad.

Green Sauce

Add 1 recipe chlorophyll (see page 359) to Basic Mayonnaise. This sauce looks great served with cold salmon. Makes about 1 cup.

Gribiche Sauce

Make Basic Mayonnaise as directed, using white wine vinegar instead of lemon juice and increasing the mustard to 2 tablespoons. Chop 3 tablespoons drained capers and 4 sour gherkins (cornichons) to the consistency of relish. Chop 2 hard-boiled eggs (see page 95) to the same consistency. Stir the capers, gherkins, eggs, 2 tablespoons finely chopped fresh parsley, and 1 tablespoon finely chopped fresh tarragon into the mayonnaise. This sauce complements deep-fried fish or vegetables. Makes about 1 1/2 cups.

Herb Mayonnaise

Stir 2 tablespoons finely chopped fresh chives, parsley, chervil, or tarragon, alone or in combination, into Basic Mayonnaise. Allow the mayonnaise to stand for at least an hour or two for the herb flavor to infuse. Color it green, if you like, with 1 teaspoon chlorophyll (see page 359). Makes about 1 cup. Herb mayonnaise is delicious with cold seafood and chicken.

Hazelnut Mayonnaise

Prepare Basic Mayonnaise as directed, using canola, grape seed, or other flavorless oil; white wine vinegar instead of lemon juice; and omitting the mustard. Work in 1 tablespoon hazelnut oil or more to taste. Season with salt and pepper and, if you like, color green with 1 teaspoon chlorophyll (page 359). Makes about 1 cup.

Saffron Mayonnaise

Soak 1 teaspoon saffron threads in 2 teaspoons water for 20 minutes. Stir the saffron and its soaking liquid into aioli or Chantilly Sauce (at left). Makes about 1 cup.

Mushroom Mayonnaise

You can make this mayonnaise by reconstituting dried mushrooms or with cultivated fresh mushrooms that have been chopped and have had all the water cooked out of them. To use dried mushrooms, soak 1/2 ounce dried morel or porcini mushrooms in the least amount of warm water needed, usually a couple of tablespoons, for about 30 minutes, or until softened. Squeeze them every few minutes to get them to soften. Chop finely and add to Basic Mayonnaise. To use fresh cultivated mushrooms, wash, dry, and chop 10 ounces cremini or white mushrooms to the consistency of hamburger relish. (If using a food processor, don't overdo it and turn the mushrooms into a paste.) In a sauté pan, cook the mushrooms in butter or olive oil over high heat until all the liquid they release runs dry. Let cool and stir into Basic Mayonnaise. Season with salt and pepper. Makes about 1 1/2 cups.

Mustard Mayonnaise

Make Basic Mayonnaise as directed, using 2 tablespoons Dijon or whole-grain mustard instead of 1 tablespoon. When the mayonnaise is ready, taste and adjust with more mustard if desired. Confusingly, this is the mustard mayonnaise used to make celeriac remoulade (see page 78), not remoulade sauce. Makes about 1 cup.

Suédoise Sauce

This mayonnaise contains a peculiar-sounding combination—horseradish and apples—but the mixture is irresistible. Dice 1 tart apple, place in a saucepan with 2 tablespoons fresh lemon juice, cover, and cook over low heat, stirring occasionally, for about 15 minutes, or until the apple is soft. Uncover the pan, raise the heat to medium, and cook until any liquid evaporates. Work the apple through a medium-mesh strainer and stir the pureed apple and 1 teaspoon grated fresh horseradish into Basic Mayonnaise. Taste and adjust with more horseradish. Season with salt and pepper. Serve with cold meats, such as pork, veal, chicken, or turkey.

Tartar Sauce

Some recipes for tartar sauce contain anchovies, but the choice is yours. Make Basic Mayonnaise as directed, using white wine vinegar instead of lemon juice and increasing the mustard to 2 tablespoons. Combine 2 shallots, minced; 3 tablespoons minced cornichons; 4 anchovy fillets, chopped and crushed to a paste (optional); and 2 tablespoons finely chopped fresh chives, and stir into the mayonnaise. Tartar sauce should be tangy, so you may want to add a teaspoon or two more vinegar.

Serving Mayonnaise Hot

Most people think of mayonnaise as a cold sauce, but for generations aioli has been used to flavor fish soup in the south of France (see the recipe for Bourride on page 56). To serve mayonnaise as a heated sauce, whisk an appropriate hot liquid, such as fish broth, shellfish steaming liquid, chicken or meat broth, soup, or a braising liquid, into a relatively small amount of flavored mayonnaise and return the mixture to the heat for just a few seconds to warm it. Do not warm it too long or the yolks will curdle and the oil will separate.

Warm Saffron Mayonnaise Sauce for Seafood

For 6 servings, bring 3/4 cup shellfish steaming liquid from mussels or cockles (see pages 108 and 113) or white wine–based fish broth to a simmer in a small saucepan. Put 6 tablespoons saffron mayonnaise into a bowl and whisk in the hot liquid. Pour the mixture back into the saucepan and heat over low heat, stirring constantly, for about 1 minute. Don't allow it to boil. Serve over and around seafood in warmed soup plates.

Warm Morel Mayonnaise for Chicken or Seafood

For chicken, prepare the Poached Chicken with Leeks and Root Vegetables on page 262. Whisk 1 cup of the poaching liquid into 3/4 cup Mushroom Mayonnaise made with dried morels. Pour the mixture into a small saucepan, place over low heat, and heat, stirring constantly, for about 1 minute. Season with salt and pepper and serve over and around the chicken in soup plates.

For seafood, whisk 1 cup poaching or braising liquid from any recipe into 3/4 cup Mushroom Mayonnaise made with dried morels. Finish and serve as directed for chicken.

Warm Sea Urchin Roe Mayonnaise

Work 3 tablespoons raw sea urchin roe through a fine-mesh strainer into about 1/4 cup Basic Mayonnaise (see page 359), and then whisk in 2/3 cup simmering seafood poaching liquid or braising liquid. Pour the mixture into a small saucepan, place over low heat, and heat, stirring constantly, for about 1 minute to cook the roe gently but not curdle the egg yolks. This same method can be used with a mixture of raw crab roe and tomalley or with lobster roe, worked through a strainer and into the mayonnaise.

MEDITERRANEAN PASTE SAUCES

The word *pesto* refers to the verb *pestare*, which means to crush or pound together the ingredients for these pastes in a mortar. Most people have heard of pesto, the Ligurian basil paste tossed with pasta, but fewer are aware of rouille and romesco. Rouille sauce is a garlicky pastelike sauce served atop bouillabaisse (see pages 54–55), either spread on bread for eating with the soup or spread on bread that is placed in the soup plate with the soup ladled over it. It can also be whisked into or spooned over a variety of fish stews. Romesco is a chile-based sauce, made more substantial with ground almonds and bread. It is ubiquitous in Spain.

Making pestolike sauces seems to be a fundamentally Mediterranean habit. In dozens of variations, garlic is worked to a smooth paste in a mortar, is often bulked up with bread (softened in broth) or potatoes (a post-Columbus addition), gets heat and color (rouille means "rust" and is that color) from peppers (another New World addition), has the flavor of fennel from Pernod or one of its cousins, and has an added dimension of flavor with saffron. Nuts often enter the mixture—pine nuts in pesto, hazelnuts and almonds in Catalonia's romesco—and egg yolks are usually added before the olive oil to turn the mixture into a mayonnaise. Coriander or caraway seeds are sometimes added to Moroccan harissa (see page 50), which is used to flavor couscous or tagines or as a marinade and sauce for grilled toasts. Purists of some versions of these pasty sauces, such as Catalans, leave out the egg yolks when making their version of aioli, and rely on the garlic alone to hold together the (very fragile) emulsion.

Pesto

Essentially a puree of fresh basil leaves, authentic pesto, from Genoa and the rest of Liguria where pesto is said to have originated, also contains Parmigiano-Reggiano cheese, garlic, olive oil, and pine nuts. Arguments arise more often over technique than exact ingredients. Purists insist pesto be made by hand, starting leaf by leaf, in a large, very heavy mortar. The rest of us make pesto in a food processor or blender. The purists are right: pesto made by hand is better. Olive oil can become bitter when beaten, and the basil loses a certain floral quality when worked in a machine. But few of us opt to sacrifice an afternoon and accept less-than-perfect pesto. The garlic must be minced and crushed by hand or it will never be ground finely enough in the machine. All the other ingredients except the oil can be added whole (toasting the nuts first is a good touch). To retain the flavor of the best olive oil, start with pure olive oil, adding just enough for the mixture to turn freely and become a smooth puree, and then turn the puree out into a bowl and add extra virgin olive oil by hand until the proper consistency is reached.

MAKES ENOUGH FOR 4 PASTA SERVINGS

> 1/2 cup pine nuts or blanched almonds
>
> 4 cloves garlic, minced and then crushed with the flat side of the knife
>
> Leaves from 1 large bunch basil
>
> 1/2 cup pure olive oil
>
> 1/2 cup extra virgin olive oil
>
> 1/2 cup grated Parmigiano-Reggiano cheese
>
> Salt
>
> Pepper

Preheat the oven to 350°F. Spread the nuts on a sheet pan and toast in the oven, stirring occasionally, for 10 to 15 minutes, or until they are fragrant and have taken on color. Pour onto a plate and let cool. In a small food processor, pulse the nuts until ground to a paste.

In a blender or food processor, combine the garlic, basil, and nuts. With the motor running, add the pure olive oil in thin, steady stream until the mixture turns on the blades and a smooth paste has formed.

Transfer the paste to a bowl, and stir in the remaining pure olive oil, the extra virgin oil, and the cheese and season with salt and pepper.

Storing Pesto

Once made, pesto should be kept tightly sealed in lock-top bags and frozen. No air should be allowed to reach the pesto or it will turn brown. To use it, just break off a chunk, thaw it, and toss it with hot pasta. You can also brush it on grilled meats, seafood, or vegetables; toss it with cooked potatoes and serve hot or cold as potato salad; fold it into ratatouille or another vegetable "stew" at the last minute; whisk it into a vegetable soup just before serving; or swirl it atop servings of seafood soup.

Rouille

Rouille sauce is a garlicky pastelike sauce served atop bouillabaisse (see pages 54–55), spread on bread for eating with the soup, or spread on bread that is placed in the soup plate and the soup is ladled over it. It can also be whisked into or spooned over a variety of fish stews. Once you have made a few of these sauces and get into the habit of using them to flavor and accompany fish and vegetable soups and stews, you will be able to make up your own mixtures. Here is a respectable rouille for whisking into soups or spreading on bread. Because it has egg yolks, remember never to let it get close to a boil.

**MAKES ABOUT 1$\frac{1}{2}$ CUPS SAUCE, OR ENOUGH
FOR 6 MAIN-COURSE BOUILLABAISSE SERVINGS**

> 3 ancho chiles, soaked in warm water for 30 minutes to soften, then drained
>
> 1 red bell pepper, charred, peeled, and seeded (see page 321) and then coarsely chopped
>
> 3 cloves garlic, minced and then crushed with the flat side of the knife
>
> 2 egg yolks
>
> $\frac{1}{2}$ teaspoon saffron threads, soaked in 1 tablespoon water for 20 minutes
>
> 2 teaspoons red wine vinegar, or to taste
>
> $\frac{1}{2}$ cup pure olive oil
>
> Salt
>
> Pepper
>
> $\frac{1}{2}$ cup extra virgin olive oil

Remove the seeds from the chiles, tear the chiles into pieces, and add them to a food processor or blender along with the bell pepper, garlic, egg yolks, saffron and its soaking water, and vinegar. With the motor running, add the pure olive oil in a thin, steady stream. If the mixture gets too thick and the blades don't move, add about 2 teaspoons water. Season with salt and pepper. Transfer the puree to a bowl and add the extra virgin olive oil in a thin, steady stream, stirring constantly until fully incorporated. The sauce should be thick and unctuous.

Romesco Sauce

This Catalan classic comes from the city of Tarragona, the old Roman capital (of what's now Spain) about 60 kilometers south of Barcelona. For the sauce to be perfectly authentic, it must contain a chile almost never seen in the United States, a medium-hot little pepper called the nora. (Mulattos make a good substitute.) Here is a version I adapted from Colman Andrews's authoritative book Catalan Cuisine.

MAKES 1$\frac{1}{4}$ CUPS

> 4 mulatto chiles, seeded, soaked for 30 minutes in hot water, then drained and minced
>
> 2 jalapeños, stemmed, seeded, and minced
>
> 2 tablespoons olive oil
>
> 2 tomatoes, peeled, seeded, and chopped
>
> 24 blanched and roasted almonds
>
> 24 roasted hazelnuts
>
> 3 cloves garlic, minced
>
> 8 tablespoons extra virgin olive oil
>
> 3 slices good quality white bread, crusts removed
>
> 1 tablespoon red wine vinegar
>
> Salt

Combine the chiles and cook them in a sauté pan in 2 tablespoons olive oil over medium heat for about 5 minutes, or until they release their aroma. Add the tomatoes and cook while stirring until the mixture is stiff. Grind the nuts with the garlic in a food processor or with a mortar and pestle and combine with the tomato mixture. Use your hands to work the extra virgin olive oil with the bread to form a paste and work this into the tomato mixture. Add the vinegar and season to taste with salt.

Improvising Mediterranean Paste Sauces

By understanding the ingredients you can use and the order you need to add them, you can improvise sauces for topping grilled foods, whisking into soups or stews, or spreading on bread.

To make by hand, use the largest mortar and pestle you can find. Crush the garlic to a paste, then the nuts, and then the remaining solid ingredients. Work in the liquids a little at a time.

To make in a food processor or blender, combine the garlic, chiles, peppers, egg yolks, ground nuts, herbs, and spices in the machine. With the motor running, add the pure olive oil in a thin, steady stream, processing until all the oil is absorbed. Transfer the puree to a bowl and work in the extra virgin oil and starchy ingredients such as bread or potatoes (which can get gummy in the machine) by hand.

Garlic: An essential ingredient, garlic should be minced with a chef's knife and then crushed to a paste with the side of the knife (see page 332), even if you are making the sauce in a machine.

Egg yolks: Egg yolks will make the sauce more spreadable, and any soup the sauce goes into a bit creamy. They also emulsify the sauce and help carry flavor.

Fresh peppers and chiles: Char, peel, and seed peppers or chiles (see page 321) and chop coarsely.

Dried chiles: An amazing assortment of chiles is available, and whatever you choose will flavor your sauce in innumerable ways. All dried chiles should be soaked in warm water for about 30 minutes, drained, seeded, and chopped before using.

Bread: Stretch the sauce and temper its heat or its intense garlic flavor by soaking bread in an appropriate broth (such as the fish soup you are serving) and working it into the other ingredients.

Potatoes: Cook and peel a potato and work it into the sauce for bulk. Don't use waxy potatoes, which can make the sauce gluey. Yukon Golds or Yellow Finns are good choices; russets will also do in a pinch, though their texture is not as fine.

Nuts: Toasting the nuts in a 350°F oven for 10 to 15 minutes brings out their flavor. It is also a good idea to grind the toasted nuts in a food processor separately and then combine them with the other ingredients.

Herbs: Basil is the best-known herb for pestolike sauces, but cilantro, parsley, and mint can also be used, alone or in combination.

Spices: Cumin is the most popular spice in harissa, but mojos, the Canary Islands cousins of moles, also use paprika or smoked paprika (pimentón), nutmeg, and cinnamon. For the best results, start with whole spices and toast them in a dry pan before grinding to release their flavor. If using ground spices, cook them in a little oil for 1 minute to release their flavor before adding to the sauce.

Citrus juices: Boil down fruit juice with a strip of the blanched zest from the fruit to reinforce its flavor.

Vinegar and lemon juice: Acidulate the mixture with good vinegar or fresh lemon juice.

Oils: Extra virgin olive oil is the universal oil for pesto sauces, but it is worth adding nut oils (see page 3) to bring out the flavor of the nuts. If you are making the sauce in a blender or food processor, use half pure olive oil and half extra virgin olive oil. Process the pure oil into the pesto and then work in the extra virgin oil by hand.

VINAIGRETTES

A vinaigrette is much like a mayonnaise, in that it is the emulsion of an acidic ingredient with oil. While mayonnaise is emulsified with egg yolk, a vinaigrette is emulsified with mustard—at least traditionally. Because mustard is a less stable emulsifier than mayonnaise, a vinaigrette can separate if made too far in advance or if stored overnight in the refrigerator.

The secret to a successful vinaigrette is to use the best possible oils and vinegars. Homemade vinegar is great if you have it (see page 70), but you can also use good-quality commercial vinegar, such as sherry vinegar or balsamic vinegar. Extra virgin olive oil equals wine in variety and complexity of flavor, so it is worth experimenting to find your favorites. Some vinaigrettes are made with bland oils, such as canola oil or grape seed oil, when they are being used for dishes so delicate that a stronger oil would interfere. Nut oils are delicious in vinaigrettes used on bitter greens, but they are so strongly flavored (at least good ones) and expensive that it is usually best to combine them with a flavorless oil. (See page 70 for more information on oils, vinegars, and vinaigrette for salads.)

To make a basic vinaigrette, simply whisk together mustard, vinegar, salt, and pepper, and then whisk in oil in a steady stream. Mustard turns extra virgin olive oil bitter, so if you want to use extra virgin olive oil, leave out the mustard and just pour the vinegar and oil separately over the salad and toss. You can also make a creamy vinaigrette by making mayonnaise and thinning it with vinegar (see page 70).

Expanded Basic Vinaigrette

Other than the choice of oil or acid, the character of a vinaigrette comes from flavorings, such as shallots, garlic, and herbs.

MAKES ENOUGH TO COAT 2 CUPS COOKED VEGETABLES OR FOR 6 FIRST-COURSE SALADS OR 4 MAIN-COURSE SALADS

> 2 teaspoons Dijon mustard
>
> 1 shallot, minced
>
> 1/2 teaspoon salt
>
> 1/4 teaspoon pepper
>
> 2 tablespoons red wine vinegar
>
> 5 tablespoons canola oil, grape seed oil, or other vegetable oil

In a small bowl, whisk together the mustard, shallot, salt, pepper, vinegar. Ideally, this mixture should sit for a couple of hours to infuse the flavor of the shallot. Whisk in the oil a couple of teaspoons at a time.

One tablespoon finely chopped fresh chives, parsley, chervil, or tarragon, or 1 teaspoon finely chopped stronger-flavored herbs, such as fresh marjoram, oregano, lavender, or thyme, can also be added. These stronger herbs are good in conjunction with garlic; replace the shallot in the Basic Vinaigrette with a small garlic clove minced and then crushed with the flat side of the knife. You can use truffle oil (see how to make your own on page 383) or add finely chopped truffles to the sauce. If the vinaigrette is being served with cold seafood, raw sea urchin roe or cooked lobster roe can also be added to the sauce.

Because mustard doesn't go well with extra virgin olive oil, it is useful to know that you can replace it with another emulsifier, such as an egg yolk (which actually turns your vinaigrette into a mayonnaise), a couple of tablespoons heavy cream that have been lightly reduced, or a little Tomato Coulis (see page 366) made with cream, Roast Garlic Puree (see pages 332–333), or onion puree made by roasting onions and then working them through a food mill.

Citronette

A citronette is a vinaigrette in which the vinegar has been replaced with lemon, lime, or other citrus juice. You can make a citronette by just substituting lime juice for the vinegar in a basic vinaigrette (see page 70 and at left), or you can make this creamy version, in which heavy cream replaces the oil. The acidity in the lime juice thickens the cream, so the mustard, which is no longer needed as an emulsifier, is optional. Citronette is particularly good on hot fish.

MAKES ABOUT 2/3 CUP

> 3 tablespoons fresh lime juice
>
> 1/2 cup heavy cream
>
> 2 teaspoons Dijon mustard (optional)
>
> Salt
>
> Pepper

In a small bowl, whisk together the lime juice, cream, and mustard and season with salt and pepper. Refrigerate for at least 15 minutes before serving to allow the lime juice to thicken the cream slightly. If the cream refuses to thicken, beat it until it barely begins to whip.

VEGETABLE PUREE–BASED SAUCES

Sometimes you may need a vinaigrette with no mustard in it, such as when using your best extra virgin olive oil, or you may want to thicken a sauce without using flour and an excess of cream or butter. Some cooked vegetable purees act as emulsifiers or, when used with other emulsifiers, add body to a sauce. They also provide flavor and character, whereas thickeners like flour or cream add little. The best-known and most often used vegetable puree (well, fruit actually) is thick tomato sauce, but potato also works well (just as it does in cream soups), as do garlic, onion, and certain green and root vegetables. Vegetable purees can also be used in conjunction with other thickeners to help them along.

It is easiest to puree vegetables in a food processor—the puree is usually too stiff for a blender—and then ideally to work them through a drum sieve or fine-mesh strainer, to create a puree that is as smooth as possible.

Tomato Sauces

Cooked tomato sauces are made either as a coulis or a concassée. A coulis has been strained to yield a smooth liquid, while a concassée remains more or less chunky. Making a coulis is actually easier, of course, because straining eliminates the need to peel the tomatoes.

To make the simplest tomato sauce, just cook tomato coulis or concassée on the stove top until it thickens. French versions often call for cooking aromatic vegetables such as onion and carrot, adding broth, a bouquet garni, and tomatoes, and then simmering to the desired consistency, while Italian versions put shredded or chopped meat in the sauce (see Ragù-Type Sauces, pages 356–357). In general, the better the tomatoes, the simpler the method should be. When tomatoes are at their best, serve a raw concassée or coulis for cold seafood, meat, or poultry.

Raw Tomato Concassée and Coulis

To make a raw tomato concassée, peel and seed the tomatoes as shown on page 85 and season with salt and pepper. To make a raw coulis, don't bother seeding and peeling the tomatoes, just chop them and work them through a food mill, using the finest mesh grid attachment, or through a strainer.

Tomato Coulis

A coulis is simply a puree that has been strained. To make the simplest tomato coulis, chop the tomatoes—don't bother with peeling—simmer them until softened, work them through a food mill or strainer, and then cook them down until they thicken. If your tomatoes are less than perfect, you may prefer a more elaborate approach—given here—that includes cooking the tomatoes with aromatic vegetables and herbs.

MAKES ABOUT 1 1/2 CUPS SAUCE

- **2 tablespoons butter or olive oil**
- **1 small onion, minced**
- **1 small carrot, peeled and finely chopped**
- **2 cloves garlic, minced and then crushed with the flat side of the knife**
- **3 ounces prosciutto end, cut into 1/3-inch dice (optional)**
- **1/4 cup dry white wine (optional)**
- **1 cup chicken broth**
- **Bouquet garni with 3 sprigs tarragon**
- **8 tomatoes, stemmed**
- **1 to 2 tablespoons wine vinegar**
- **1 to 2 teaspoons sugar**
- **1/2 cup heavy cream (optional)**
- **Salt**
- **Pepper**

In a saucepan, melt the butter over medium heat. Add the onion, carrot, garlic, and prosciutto and cook, stirring occasionally, for about 10 minutes, or until the onions are translucent. Add the wine, broth, and bouquet garni and bring to a gentle simmer.

While the vegetables are cooking, cut the tomatoes in half crosswise and squeeze out and discard the seeds from each half, easing them out with a fingertip if necessary. Chop the tomato halves coarsely and add them to the simmering broth. Cook for 30 minutes, or until thickened.

Pass the sauce through a food mill or medium-mesh strainer—if you want it perfectly smooth, strain it a second time through a fine-mesh strainer—into a clean saucepan or, if you are in a hurry, into a sauté pan. Place the sauce over medium heat and simmer until it has the consistency you like. Add the vinegar to taste (it will bring out the flavor of the tomatoes), a little sugar (start with 1 teaspoon), and the cream. Simmer again to the consistency you like and season with salt and pepper.

Cooked Tomato Concassée

Always make a tomato concassée—chunky tomato sauce—with the best possible tomatoes and cook them as little as possible to preserve their texture while concentrating their flavor. The usual approach is to cook the raw tomatoes until their liquid evaporates, but this can turn the tomatoes into mush. One alternative is to cook the concassée just long enough for the tomatoes to release their liquid, drain them in a strainer, boil the liquid they released down to a syrup, and then add it back to the tomatoes. The pulp cooks very little with this method. Another method, which involves long cooking but concentrates the flavor, is to bake the tomatoes gently, essentially drying them out, and then scoop out the pulp. Both methods are given here. (For raw tomato concassée, see the opposite page.)

MAKES ABOUT 2 CUPS

Stove-Top Method

12 tomatoes, peeled, seeded, and chopped

Salt

Pepper

Oven Method

12 tomatoes

1 tablespoon olive oil

Salt

Pepper

For the stove-top method, put the tomatoes in a saucepan and bring to a simmer over high heat. Turn down the heat and simmer gently for 10 minutes. Set a large strainer over another pan and pour in the tomatoes. Let drain—hit the strainer with a wooden spoon to encourage draining—and then return the tomatoes to the original pan. Boil down the liquid they released until you have only a couple of tablespoons of syrup. Pour this into the tomatoes. Season with salt and pepper and simmer.

For the oven method, stem the tomatoes and cut them in half crosswise. Select a roasting or baking pan with at least 3-inch sides and brush with the oil. Arrange the tomato halves, cut side up, in a single layer in the prepared pan, slide the pan into the oven, and turn the oven to 300°F. Bake for 30 minutes, remove the pan from the oven, and turn the oven down to 200°F.

Gently transfer the tomatoes to a second roasting pan and pour the liquid in the first roasting pan into a saucepan. Return the tomatoes to the oven and bake for 2 to 3 hours, or until they wrinkle on the edges and barely begin to brown. Boil the liquid they released down to a couple of tablespoons of syrup and reserve.

Spoon the tomato pulp out of the skins and transfer it to a saucepan. Add the reduced tomato liquid. Bring to a simmer—simmer until it has the right consistency—and season to taste with salt and pepper.

Smoked Tomatoes

To give your salsas an added dimension of smokiness, smoke the tomatoes in the same way you smoke the ribs on page 240, by putting sawdust on the coals pushed to one side of the barbecue and leaving the barbecue covered. After smoking the seeded tomato halves for about 60 minutes, take the tomatoes out of the smoker, let cool, scoop out the pulp, and use it in your salsa (see page 371).

Barbecue Sauce

This is a good basic sauce that you can use for brushing on pork or chicken.

MAKES ABOUT 3 CUPS

2 cups ketchup

1 large clove garlic, minced, and then crushed to a paste with the flat side of the knife

1-inch-fresh ginger, minced

1/4 Worcestershire sauce

1/4 cup soy sauce

1/4 cup light brown sugar

1 chipotle chile, soaked in hot water for 30 minutes to soften, if dried or rinsed if canned, seeded and minced

In a bowl, combine all the ingredients, stir well, and let stand at room temperature for 1 hour before using. Store in the refrigerator.

Dried Chile Sauces

Dried chiles come in dozens of varieties and can be used alone or in combination to make delicious sauces. By pureeing the softened chiles with hot heavy cream, the chiles act as a thickener, so the sauce doesn't need to be reduced. You can vary the sauce by using different combinations of chiles or by using just one chile. Or, you can make several sauces, using a different chile for each one, and serve them separately at the table so everyone can appreciate the distinctive character of each chile. Use a roast or grilled chicken or fish as a foil for the sauces.

This recipe is very simple—you just puree the soaked chiles, combine with simmered cream, puree again, and strain—but you can make it more elaborate by cooking aromatic vegetables in a little butter, adding little cubes of bacon or prosciutto, and then adding the cream and simmering the chiles. If you're interested in trying a classic chile-based sauce, try the simple mole sauce recipe on page 252.

MAKES 1 CUP

> 2 large dried mild chiles such as ancho, guajillo, mulatto, or chilhuacle negro
>
> 1 dried smoked hot chile such as chipotle or pasilla de Oaxaca
>
> 1 poblano chile, charred, peeled, and seeded (see page 321) and then coarsely chopped
>
> 1 cup heavy cream
>
> Salt
>
> Pepper

Put the dried chiles in a skillet over medium heat and stir them around for about 5 minutes, or until they smell aromatic. Cut off the stems and soak the chiles in a bowl of hot water for about 30 minutes, or until they are pliable and feel like leather. Cut them in half lengthwise and rinse out the seeds. Chop all chiles coarsely and place in a blender or food processor.

In a small saucepan, bring the cream to a simmer. Remove from the heat and add to the chiles. Process for about 1 minute, or until a smooth puree forms, and then strain through a fine-mesh strainer. Adjust the consistency by adding a little water to thin it, or boiling the sauce for a few minutes to thicken it. Season with salt and pepper.

ASIAN SAUCES

Many of Asia's best sauces come about from stir-frying or quickly stewing meats or seafood with liquids such as coconut milk or dashi. The genius of such sauces is that they go together quickly, are inexpensive to make, and seldom require long simmering. They also rarely call for broth, much less the long-reduced glazes found in European cooking. This makes Asian sauces convenient last-minute preparations, provided you set yourself up with the ingredients, most of which keep almost indefinitely. For a sweet-and-sour stir-fry sauce, see page 241.

Brown Sauce for Stir-Fries

Other than using the technique of stir-frying, stir-fries are also characterized by certain ingredients, particularly garlic, ginger, sesame oil, various bottled Chinese sauces, spices, and corn starch, which are added at different stages during the stir-frying. Typically, dry ingredients are first added to hot oil in a wok and then stirred over high heat. Liquid ingredients are then added, often the same ingredients used to marinate meat or seafood. Last, the thickener, usually corn starch, dissolved in a small amount of liquid, is stirred in, which pulls together the ingredients in the sauce that will coat the ingredients in the stir-fry.

MAKES ABOUT 1/2 CUP

> 1 tablespoon canola oil
>
> 1 tablespoon grated fresh ginger
>
> 1 clove garlic, minced, crushed to a paste
>
> 1 teaspoon Asian dark sesame oil
>
> 1/4 cup sake, Chinese rice wine, or dry sherry
>
> 1 cup brown chicken broth (see page 36)
>
> 2 teaspoons corn starch dissolved in 2 tablespoons cold water
>
> Salt
>
> Pepper

Heat the oil in a wok or in a saucepan and stir in the ginger and garlic. When you smell the garlic and ginger, add the sesame oil and rice wine and simmer for about 1 minute. Add the broth and simmer to reduce by about one-fourth. Whisk in the corn starch mixture and bring to the simmer. Season to taste with salt and pepper. The sauce can be tightly covered and refrigerated for up to 1 week.

Japanese Sauces

Most Japanese sauces are more like soups or broth and are served around foods, rather than clinging on top of them. To make these sauces, Japanese cooks rely on a relatively small number of ingredients, used in various combinations to create different effects. The heart and soul of most Japanese sauces is dashi, a broth made from seaweed and dried bonito, a type of tuna. There are many instant dashi mixes on the market, or you can make your own batch of dashi (see page 40). Other common ingredients are sake, mirin (sweet rice cooking wine), soy sauce, miso, lime juice (or actually yuzu juice, squeezed from a small citrus fruit hard to find in the United States), rice vinegar, ginger, and sesame oil. For a Japanese salad sauce, see page 82.

Ponzu Sauce

This tart and refreshing sauce can be used for dipping pieces of raw fish or for spooning over hot seafood. Using Ponzu Sauce is much like using lemon juice, except for the smokiness of the bonito flakes and the sweet-and-sour flavor provided by the vinegar and mirin. For a decorative touch, use the julienned lime zest. This sauce is made a day ahead.

MAKES ABOUT 1 CUP

> 5 limes
> 1/3 cup fresh lemon juice (from about 5 lemons)
> 3 tablespoons rice vinegar or sherry vinegar
> 1/3 cup dark Japanese soy sauce
> 2 tablespoons mirin
> 1 cup bonito flakes

Trim away the zest from 1 lime and reserve. Squeeze the juice from all 5 limes and put the juice into a saucepan with the lemon juice, vinegar, soy, mirin, and bonito flakes. Cover and let stand at room temperature for 24 hours.

Strain through a fine-mesh strainer into a bowl. Cut the lime zest into fine julienne, blanch in boiling water for 1 minute, and drain. Add the zest to the sauce. The sauce can be tightly covered and refrigerated for about 2 weeks or frozen for up to a few months.

Tosa Sauce

Sweetened with mirin and given a little kick with sake, this sauce is used for dipping raw or cooked fish and grilled or deep-fried vegetables. You can also serve it as a sauce for tofu: just put tofu cubes in a serving dish and surround them with the cold sauce. The ginger isn't used in traditional recipes, so if you don't like it, leave it out.

MAKES 1/2 CUPS

> 1 cup dashi
> 1-inch piece fresh ginger, peeled and grated
> 1/2 cup dark Japanese soy sauce
> 1 cup bonito flakes
> 6 tablespoons mirin
> 6 tablespoons sake
> 1 scallion

In a small saucepan, bring the dashi to a simmer. Remove from the heat and add the ginger, soy, bonito flakes, mirin, and sake. Cover and let stand at room temperature for 24 hours.

Strain though a fine-mesh strainer into a bowl. Just before serving, slice the scallion, white and green parts, as thinly as possible and add it to the sauce. The sauce can be tightly covered and refrigerated for up to 1 week or frozen for up to several months.

Yakitori Sauce

While yakitori refers literally to chicken, the term can be used more generically to refer to little skewers of grilled meats found everywhere in Japan. You can also use the sauce to glaze sautéed fish and meats. The shallot is not traditional. This sauce makes enough for about 8 yakitori. For another yakitori recipe, see the Chicken Skewers on page 31.

MAKES 3/4 CUP

> 1/2 cup sake
> 1/2 cup dark Japanese soy sauce
> 3 tablespoons mirin
> 1 shallot, minced

In a saucepan, combine the sake, soy, mirin, and shallot, bring to a boil, and boil for about 5 minutes, or until reduced by half and syrupy. Remove from the heat and let cool. The sauce can be tightly covered and refrigerated for several months.

Thai and Vietnamese Sauces

It is not fair to lump these two cuisines together, but their sauces share an approach and many ingredients. The heart and soul of both cuisines is fish sauce, made by letting small anchovy-like fish ferment in the sun and then draining off the juices, which become the sauce. While fish sauce isn't very appetizing-sounding or appealing on its own, it is what gives the best Southeast Asian cuisines their savor. It is to Southeast Asia what broth and meat glazes are to France.

Basic Thai Curry Paste

Combine this paste, a simplified version of a classic green Thai curry, with a can of coconut milk to provide a sauce for chicken or shrimp. The cashews are more typical of Indian cooking but give the curry body; leave them out if you want more authenticity.

MAKES 1 CUP

- 3 stalks lemongrass, white bulb part only, tough outer layer discarded and very thinly sliced
- Zest of 1 lime
- 3 shallots, peeled and minced
- 3 cloves garlic, peeled and minced
- Leaves from 1 bunch cilantro
- 6 serrano or 12 jalapeño chiles, stemmed, seeded, and minced
- 1/2 cup cashew nuts, roasted

Puree all the ingredients together in a food processor for 5 minutes. If you have a large mortar and pestle, grind the mixture again by hand.

Vietnamese Fish Dipping Sauce (Nuoc Cham)

This sauce is familiar to most of us since it contains the essential elements of Asian dipping sauces—fish sauce, lime juice, and something to provide heat. Serve this with grilled chicken or fish.

MAKES 3/4 CUP

- 2 cloves garlic, minced
- 4 Thai chiles or 2 serrano chiles, stemmed, seeded, and minced
- 2 tablespoons sugar
- 6 tablespoons lime juice
- 4 tablespoons Thai or Vietnamese fish sauce

Combine all the ingredients and stir long enough to dissolve the sugar.

SALSAS

Most salsas are made only with raw ingredients, chopped more or less coarsely, and flavored with herbs, often chiles, and such acidic ingredients as lime juice. They may be held together with a little olive oil, yogurt, cream, or mayonnaise, and are usually simple stirred mixtures. They are light, healthy, and bright accents to all sorts of foods, hot or cold, grilled or deep-fried.

When creating your own salsas or when following recipes, keep in mind that harder ingredients, such as onion, or very strong-flavored ingredients, such as chiles or garlic, should be very finely chopped, while softer ingredients, such as tomatoes or ripe mangoes, can be left on the coarse side. Usually salsas are informal affairs that allow you to chop the ingredients randomly, but you can also make refined salsas by dicing the ingredients uniformly. For a green salsa, use the Tomatillo Sauce (see page 323) for a base and convert it into salsa by adding diced avocado or red onion.

Many salsas are spicy hot, typically from the addition of raw or dried chiles, which are available in a wide variety. The best salsa makers will often use a mix of chiles, with some added for complexity, some for heat, and some for smokiness. For additional smokiness, add smoked tomatoes (see page 367) to your salsas.

Tomato Salsa

When making a salsa, keep in mind the principle that the better the ingredients, the simpler the treatment should be. If in the middle of September you find yourself with gorgeous ripe heirloom tomatoes, you won't need much more. Just peel and chop the tomatoes, season them with salt, and let them drain in a strainer for an hour or so. If they release a lot of liquid, you can boil it down and add some or all of it (be careful, as it will be salty) back to the raw tomatoes.

If your tomatoes are good but not wonderful, make the salsa a little more elaborate with finely minced onion, chiles, and cilantro.

MAKES ABOUT 3 CUPS

6 tomatoes, peeled, seeded, and chopped
   medium-coarse

Salt

1 small red onion, minced

1 clove garlic, minced and then crushed with the
   flat side of the knife

1 dried smoked hot chile such as chipotle or pasilla
   de Oaxaca, soaked in warm water for 30 minutes to
   soften, drained, seeded, and finely chopped

1 fresh flavorful chile such as poblano, charred,
   peeled, and seeded (see page 321) and then chopped
   medium-fine

2 dried mild chiles such as ancho, mulatto, guajillo, or
   chilhuacle negro, soaked in warm water for 30 minutes
   to soften, drained, seeded, and finely chopped

2 tablespoons finely chopped fresh cilantro, chopped
   at the last minute

Season the tomatoes with salt and place in a large strainer or colander over a bowl to catch the liquid they release. Let drain for 1 to 12 hours—the longer the better but it's not terribly important.

In a bowl, combine the tomatoes, onion, garlic, chiles, and cilantro. This is best done a couple of hours ahead of time, so the flavors of the chiles meld with one another and the tomatoes. Boil down the liquid released by the tomatoes until you have a couple of tablespoons of salty syrup. Stir it, a little at a time and tasting as you go—you don't want to risk oversalting the tomatoes—into the salsa. Serve cool but not refrigerator cold.

Tropical Fruit Salsa

If you make this whole recipe, you will have enough to feed a crowd, plus you will have half of a pineapple and perhaps half of a papaya left over. Or, you may want to make a half batch of salsa and save the rest of the fruit for a round or two of tropical daiquiris. The salsa is especially good atop grilled chicken or fish.

MAKES 5 CUPS

2 dried chipotle chiles or chipotle chiles in adobo sauce,
   2 pasilla de Oaxaca chiles, or 4 jalapeño chiles

2 poblano chiles, charred, peeled, and seeded (see
   page 321) and then chopped medium-fine

1 mango, about 1 pound

1/2 pineapple, preferably Golden

1 Hawaiian or 1/2 Mexican papaya

1 red onion, finely chopped

3 tablespoons finely chopped fresh cilantro, chopped
   at the last minute

3 tablespoons fresh lime juice

Salt

If you are using dried chipotle or pasilla de Oaxaca chiles, soak them in warm water for 30 minutes to soften, then drain, seed, and finely chop them. If using canned chipotles, rinse, seed, and finely chop them. If using jalapeño chiles, seed and finely chop them. Ready the poblano chiles. Set all the chiles aside.

Halve the mango lengthwise, remove the pit, scoop out the flesh from each half with a spoon, and cut into 1/2-inch dice. Twist the stem off the pineapple half and stand the pineapple upright. Cut downward on all sides to remove the peel. Then, with a paring knife, remove the "eyes" by making diagonal cuts across the flesh just deep enough to lift them out. Cut the pineapple lengthwise into quarters, and cut away the strip of core that runs along each wedge. Cut the quarters crosswise into wedges about 1/4 inch wide, and cut the wedges into 1/4-inch dice. Peel the papaya, cut it in half lengthwise, and spoon out the seeds. Cut the halves lengthwise into wedges about 1/2 inch wide, and cut the wedges into 1/2-inch dice.

In a bowl, combine the chiles, mango, pineapple, papaya, onion, cilantro, and lime juice. Toss together to mix well and then season with salt.

Guacamole

There are two secrets to outstanding guacamole: chop the avocados instead of mashing them, and include a smoke-flavored chile. The richest and most flavorful avocados are the rough-skinned Hass variety. Because avocados turn dark when exposed to air, store guacamole in a bowl with plastic wrap pressed directly onto the surface. Make it within hours of serving.

MAKES 3 CUPS WITHOUT THE TOMATOES,
OR 4 CUPS WITH THE TOMATOES

- 3 tomatoes, peeled, seeded, and chopped medium-coarse (optional)
- 1 small red onion, minced
- 1 clove garlic, minced and then crushed with the flat side of the knife
- 1 dried smoked hot chile such as chipotle or pasilla de Oaxaca, soaked in warm water for 30 minutes to soften, drained, seeded, and finely chopped
- 1 fresh flavorful chile such as poblano, charred, peeled, and seeded (see page 321) and then chopped medium-fine
- 2 dried mild chiles such as ancho, mulatto, guajillo, or chilhuacle negro, soaked in warm water for 30 minutes to soften, drained, seeded, and finely chopped
- 3 ripe avocados, preferably Hass
- 2 tablespoons finely chopped fresh cilantro, chopped at the last minute
- Salt

Season the tomatoes with salt and place in a large strainer or colander to drain. Let drain for 2 hours or overnight.

In a bowl, combine the tomatoes, onion, garlic, and all the chiles. This is best done a couple of hours ahead of time, so the flavors of the chiles meld with one another and the tomatoes.

Shortly before serving, halve, pit, and peel the avocados and then chop them medium-coarse. Add the avocados and cilantro to the tomato mixture, season with salt, and stir to mix.

CHUTNEYS

Indian cooks are geniuses at accenting their dishes with assorted condiments known as chutneys. Made of various fruits, vegetables, and spices, they heighten the complexity of the dishes they accompany. Chutneys often include dramatic contrasts, such as extreme saltiness next to sweetness, or fruit next to spice. Some of them are extremely simple, while others can be highly complex. Fortunately, most chutneys keep well, so you can make one or two to have on hand to serve alongside stews, grilled meats or seafood, deep-fried dishes, or roasts—and not just Indian dishes.

Sweet, Sour, and Salty Fruit Chutney

This chutney is best made with underripe fruit or hard fruit, such as pears, apples, peaches, apricots, mangoes, or papayas. You can also substitute dried fruit, such as apricots and raisins. Almonds, pine nuts, or other nuts are included to create a contrasting texture, but they are not essential. Serve the chutney with stews, especially stews that have been finished with Indian spices. This chutney keeps in the refrigerator for months.

MAKES 2 CUPS

- 1/2 cup slivered blanched almonds
- 3 pounds underripe fruit or hard fruit (see headnote)
- 1 tablespoon canola or safflower oil
- 1-inch piece fresh ginger, peeled and grated
- 3 jalapeño chiles, seeded and minced
- 1 tablespoon curry powder or garam masala
- 1/2 cup white wine vinegar
- 1/4 cup sugar, or to taste
- Salt
- Pepper

Preheat the oven to 350°F. Spread the almonds on a sheet pan and toast in the oven, stirring occasionally, for 10 to 15 minutes, or until they are fragrant and have taken on color. Pour onto a plate and let cool.

Core the fruit and cut into 1/2-inch dice. In a saucepan large enough to hold the fruit, heat the oil over medium heat and add the ginger, chiles, curry powder, and garam masala. Cook for about 1 minute, or until you smell the spices. Add the vinegar and 1/4 cup sugar and simmer for 1 minute, or until the sugar has dissolved Add the fruit, cover the pan, and simmer over medium heat for 10 minutes, or until the fruit releases its liquid.

Remove from the heat and pour off the liquid into another saucepan. Place the liquid over high heat and boil it down until it forms a thick syrup, then pour it over the fruit.

Season the fruit with salt and pepper and add more sugar and/or vinegar if it seems too sweet or too sour. Stir in the almonds just before serving (they get soggy if put in too early).

Herb Chutney

Anyone who has eaten in an Indian restaurant will recognize the ubiquitous green cilantro sauce served with crunchy flat bread before the meal. Few sauces are easier to make: the cilantro is combined with onion; chiles; liquid such as water, coconut milk, or yogurt (either thick or thin); citrus juice; and sometimes a little sugar. While this method works especially well with cilantro, you can also use parsley, chervil, mint, or basil, and serve the light liquid sauce around and over fish fillets or chicken. This sauce is best made just before serving, but since everything can be set up in advance, it only takes a few minutes to finish the sauce.

MAKES ABOUT 1 CUP

1 cup tightly packed fresh herb leaves such as mint, cilantro, basil, parsley, or chervil, or a mixture

1/2 onion, chopped

1/2 cup liquid such as water, plain yogurt, or coconut milk

2 jalapeño chiles, seeded and finely chopped

2 tablespoons fresh lime juice, or to taste

Salt

Pepper

In a blender, combine the herb, liquid, chiles, and 2 tablespoons lime juice and process on high speed for 1 minute, or until smooth. Pour into a bowl and season with additional lime juice, if needed, and salt and pepper.

Sweet-and-Sour Chutney for Deep-Fried Foods

This chutney is a great accompaniment not only to deep-fried foods but grilled shrimp and chicken as well. It's traditionally served with Indian samosas, stuffed and fried dumplings.

MAKES ABOUT 1 CUP

1/4 teaspoon ground cardamom

1/4 teaspoon ground cinnamon

1/8 teaspoon ground cloves

1/2 teaspoon ground cumin

1/2 teaspoon ground coriander

2 tablespoons butter

6 ounces dried apricots, diced

1/2 cup golden raisins

3/4 cup sugar

1 cup sherry vinegar

3 jalapeno chiles, stemmed, seeded, and finely chopped

1/2 teaspoon salt or more to taste

Combine the spices with the butter in a small saucepan and heat over low heat while stirring with a wooden spoon until fragrant, about 1 minute. Remove from the heat. Add the apricots, raisins, sugar, vinegar, chiles, and salt and simmer gently stirring occasionally for 15 minutes or until lightly syrupy. Let cool. Adjust the sweetness or sourness if necessary with sugar and vinegar. Serve cold.

PASTA, RICE, COUSCOUS, AND POLENTA

We typically round out a meal with a starch such as potatoes, pasta, rice, or sometimes even couscous. These starches are perfect meal-stretchers and an important component of honest home cooking. In the age of prepared and boxed foods, it is tempting to rely exclusively on the quick-cook versions we find at the market, but the building block recipes in this chapter are easily mastered with a little practice. Learning to make these foods from scratch is an essential step in feeling confident in the kitchen (and calm whenever you want to feed an extra guest).

PASTA

Pasta comes in two forms: fresh pasta, made from eggs and relatively low-gluten flour (all-purpose flour generally works fine for this kind of pasta), which is typically cooked shortly after making, and dried pasta, made from high-gluten flour (usually from durum wheat) and water and suitable for long storage. Fresh egg pasta can also be dried, but it becomes brittle and breaks easily.

Flat pasta ribbons, such as fettuccine, linguine, and pappardelle, are made with fresh egg pasta dough that is ideally rolled out by hand with a rolling pin and gently stretched to the appropriate thickness. This hand method yields a better result than a pasta machine, because it creates a slightly rougher surface texture that encourages sauces to cling.

That said, rolling and stretching fresh pasta dough can be difficult and frustrating for inexperienced pasta makers, especially if the flour has a high gluten content that makes the dough elastic. A hand-crank machine with rollers that you set to decreasing thicknesses as you roll the dough through simplifies the task. Once you have the sheets of dough, you can cut them to the desired width with the cutter on the machine or by hand.

We Americans have the habit of serving pasta in gargantuan portions as a main course, whereas in Italy pasta is served in relatively small portions as a first course. To serve your meal in true Italian fashion, precede the pasta with an antipasto course.

Fresh pasta can now be found in most supermarkets, but it often has a raw, doughy texture because it is seldom kneaded enough. Dried pasta from Italy is generally a better buy. Most dried pasta is made without eggs, which is particularly traditional for tubular pastas such as spaghetti, ziti, and macaroni. The best dried egg pasta, which rivals the best homemade, is manufactured by Cipriani and comes in lovely, long pastel boxes. It can be hard to find but is worth its rather hefty price. When cooked according to the package directions, for 2 minutes only, it is perfectly al dente.

Making Pasta Dough by Hand

There are those who swear that pasta dough kneaded by hand and rolled out with a pin instead of kneaded in a food processor and rolled out in a machine has a better texture. While there may be subtle differences in texture, the differences in the amount of work required aren't subtle at all. Kneading the dough by hand takes about 20 minutes. If it's being rolled, it should be rolled out one-fourth at a time with long rests—keep the dough covered with a moist towel or plastic wrap—in the refrigerator, as it gets elastic and difficult to roll.

Fresh Egg Pasta Noodles

You can make pasta dough by combining the ingredients together by hand, but it is easier to mix it in a food processor. The number of eggs you will need can vary—the more gluten in the flour, the more eggs you will need—so you must learn to recognize when the dough has the right amount of egg. It should feel just moist to the touch but not sticky. If it is too wet, it will stick to the rolling pin or in the pasta machine when you begin to roll it out. If this happens, you can flour it as you roll it and it will absorb some of the flour, reducing the stickiness.

MAKES ABOUT 2½ POUNDS DOUGH, ENOUGH FOR 8 FIRST-COURSE SERVINGS OR 6 MAIN-COURSE SERVINGS

> 6 large eggs, or as needed
> 4 cups all-purpose flour
> 2 tablespoons extra virgin olive oil

To make the dough in a food processor, make it in two batches to avoid straining the processor. Process 3 eggs with 2 cups of flour and 1 tablespoon of oil and repeat with the remaining ingredients. Process until the dough forms a ragged mass around the sides of the processor. If the dough doesn't come together in a loosely cohesive mass, add another egg yolk (save the white) and process a little longer. If it still doesn't come together, add the egg white. Turn the dough out onto a floured work surface and knead a few times with the heel of your hand until the dough comes together in a cohesive mass.

To make the dough by hand, mound the flour on a work surface, make a well in the center, and add 5 eggs and the oil to the well. Lightly break up the eggs with your fingers, and then gradually pull the flour into the well. Work the ingredients together with one hand until the dough comes together in a cohesive mass. Or, you can use this same method, but form the well of flour in a large bowl, rather than on a work surface. If the dough remains crumbly, add an extra egg yolk, and then the white if necessary. If the dough sticks to your hands, add a handful of flour.

Knead the dough, one-third at a time, on the widest setting, repeating until the dough is perfectly smooth and has the texture of suede. When you are ready to roll out the dough, roll it once again through the widest setting, adjust the knob to the next narrower setting, and roll the dough through again. Continue in this way, setting the machine to the next narrower setting each time, until you reach the narrowest or the second-to-narrowest setting. If the dough becomes long and unwieldy, cut it in half to make it easier to roll. You have two 3-foot long segments. The dough should be thin enough for light to pass through it. Use the sheets for making ravioli, tortellini, lasagna, or hand-cut ribbon-width noodles or to run through the machine for machine-cut ribbon-width noodles.

If you are cutting the dough by hand, dust the sheet liberally with flour (to keep it from sticking to itself), roll it up jelly-roll fashion, and then cut crosswise into the width desired, about ⅛ inch wide for linguine, ¼ inch wide for fettuccine, or ¾ inches wide for pappardelle.

To cut the rolled-out dough on the machine, set the cutters to the narrower setting for linguine and to the wider setting for fettuccine, dust the dough sheet with flour, and pass it through the cutters.

Arrange the pasta ribbons in large mounds on a sheet pan and dust liberally with flour. Toss the mound around every 10 minutes or so for an hour, to let the noodles dry a little, which helps to keep them from sticking together while they cook.

Cooking Fresh Pasta

Bring a large pot of water to a boil, and add a couple of tablespoons of olive oil and salt to keep the noodles from sticking to one another as they cook. Toss the mounds of pasta to eliminate most of the flour clinging to them, and then toss them into the water. Bite into the pasta after about 30 seconds—fresh pasta cooks quickly—to see if it is ready. Continue testing in this way until there is no rawness but you still sense a little resistance to the bite, a quality known as al dente. Drain the noodles until dripping, but not totally dry.

1. Form the flour into a well and break in the eggs. Add olive oil.

2. Stir the eggs around with your fingers, breaking up the eggs and eroding the inside walls of the flour.

3. Drag more flour from the walls into the eggs.

4. Continue to pull flour from the walls until a dough starts to form.

5. Use a cleaver blade or a pastry scraper to pull up the dough and work it together. If there is still loose flour on the board, add another egg yolk or and then the white if necessary.

6. Continue to work the dough until it comes together in a ball.

1. Divide the dough according to how much you've made. For the recipe on page 376, divide it into thirds or fourths. Set the rollers at the widest setting. Work a portion of the dough through the rollers.

2. Fold the dough over on itself and work through the rollers.

3. Again fold and roll.

4. Continue in this way until the dough has the feel of suede.

5. Adjust the knob to the next-narrowest setting and pass the dough through the rollers.

6. Continue to pass the dough through rollers, setting the machine down another notch after each roll. If the dough becomes too long to handle, cut it in half.

7. Dough at the fifth narrowest setting.

8. Dough after rolling on the sixth or seventh narrowest setting appears transparent.

9. Roll the dough down to the last or second-to-the-last notch. To keep it for up to 3 days, put it on a sheet pan with waxed paper between each layer, cover the sheet pan tightly with plastic wrap, and refrigerate.

1. To cut fettuccine on a pasta machine, pass a sheet of pasta through the wider cutter.

2. Shape the pasta into a mound as it comes out of the machine. Sprinkle with flour to prevent sticking.

3. To cut pasta noodles by hand, dust the pasta sheet with flour.

4. Roll the floured pasta sheet into a cylinder, and cut crosswise into the width you want.

5. Shape the noodles into mounds and sprinkle with flour to prevent sticking.

6. To cut pasta into rounds for tortellini or other stuffed pastas, put the pasta sheets on a floured kitchen towel, which allows the cutter to sever the pasta without fusing it with the work surface. Cut out rounds with a cookie or biscuit cutter.

Ravioli with Basil-Ricotta Filling

**MAKES 48 RAVIOLI (6 MAIN-COURSE SERVINGS OR
8 FIRST-COURSE SERVINGS)**

Leaves from 1 bunch basil

1 tablespoon olive oil

1 clove garlic, minced, crushed to a paste

1 cup finely grated Parmigiano-Reggiano

1 1/2 cups ricotta

Salt

Pepper

1/2 recipe dough for Fresh Egg Pasta Noodles
(see page 376)

Sprinkle the basil with the olive oil and chop fine. Combine with the rest of the ingredients. Divide the pasta in two and roll it out as described on page 376. Cut the long strip in half and keep one half on a sheet pan covered with plastic wrap. Arrange mounds of the filling about an inch in from the sides and 3 inches apart on one of the strips of pasta. Brush in between the mounds with cold water and unroll the second strip of pasta over the mounds. Press in between the mounds to seal in the filling. Cut the ravioli with a ravioli cutter (2 inches is the best size) or just cut between them with a knife.

Store on sheets of waxed paper in stacks in the refrigerator.

HOW TO MAKE RAVIOLI

1. Place a sheet of pasta on a floured work surface, and put the filling, in 2-teaspoon-size mounds in rows along each side of the pasta.

2. Brush between the mounds with water.

3. Lay a second sheet of pasta over the first sheet, covering the mounds.

4. Press around each mound to seal in the filling.

5. Cut between the mounds with a ravioli cutter.

1. Place a mound of filling off-center on a round of pasta. Fold the pasta over the mound, sealing the top edge of the round about 1/8 inch in from the edge of the bottom half.

2. Fold the exposed bottom edge of the pasta up over the top edge of the round to form a seal.

3. Bend the two ends of the pasta around and pinch them together to finish forming the tortellini.

Tortellini with Mascarpone-Parmigiano Filling

Because the filling for these tortellini is very rich, it's best to avoid rich sauces and serve the pasta in a light broth instead.

MAKES ABOUT 100 (8 MAIN-COURSE SERVINGS OR 12 FIRST-COURSE SERVINGS)

Dough for Fresh Egg Pasta Noodles (see page 376)

1 cup mascarpone

1 cup finely grated Parmigiano-Reggiano

1/4 pound prosciutto, sliced very thin, chopped (optional)

Salt

Pepper

8 cups brown chicken broth or 2 cups other sauce such as tomato sauce

Roll out the dough into thin strips. Cut out rounds with a 3-inch cookie cutter. Brush the rounds with water as you work. Combine the ingredients for the filling. Place 1/2 teaspoon of filling just off-center on the circle of dough, fold the top flap of dough over, creating a half-moon, and pinch together all around. You can serve the pasta like this, in half-moons, or you can seal the edge by folding the sealed edge over itself and then bringing the tips of the dough around and pinching to connect them as shown.

Heat broth or sauce over medium heat. Just before serving, boil the tortellini for about 5 minutes and drain in a colander. Serve in soup plates with broth.

PASTA SAUCES

Pasta, both fresh and dried, serves as a medium for an almost infinite variety of sauces. The most famous pasta sauces are in the ragù family, which are often, but not always, slow cooked and contain meat (see pages 356–357). Simpler sauces can be based on fresh tomatoes, peeled, seeded, and chopped and cooked down to a sauce, or on cream, which is typically flavored with cheese, mushrooms, truffles, or seafood.

Stuffed pasta such as ravioli or tortellini should be served with either broth or a simple sauce that doesn't compete with the filling or, when the filling is rich, that make the dish too filling. Count on using between $1/3$ and $2/3$ cup of sauce per first-course serving. In some cases, such as when serving a meaty ragù sauce, you may use as much as 1 cup for a first-course serving.

Tortellini with Pesto

If you are making tortellini for a small group of people, say, four, making pesto by hand takes not much more time than making it in a blender, plus there is a primal satisfaction to it. The hardest part to pull off is locating the mortar and pestle. The giant marble mortars once found in any pharmacy have become scarce, and if you find one in some faraway place, you are stuck with carrying a very heavy object onto an airplane. It is critical that the mortar be large and heavy. Otherwise, it will wobble around and it will take forever to crush whatever is at hand.

MAKES 4 FIRST-COURSE OR LIGHT MAIN-COURSE SERVINGS

> Tortellini (see page 381)
> Pesto Sauce (see page 362)
> Parmigiano-Reggiano for serving

Boil and drain the tortellini.

Toss the tortellini with the pesto to coat and pass the remaining pesto and the cheese at the table.

Fettuccine or Linguine with Dried Porcini Mushroom Sauce

This is one of the most delicious pasta dishes and one of the easiest to make. When buying dried porcini, look for large, flat slices, not little broken pieces. They should be slightly flexible and leathery and have a heady aroma.

MAKES 4 FIRST-COURSE SERVINGS

> Small handful of dried porcini mushrooms
> 1$1/2$ cups heavy cream
> Salt
> Pepper
> 12 ounces dried or 1$1/2$ pounds fresh fettuccine or linguine
> About 1 cup grated Parmigiano-Reggiano cheese

In a bowl, soak the porcini in warm water just to cover for about 30 minutes, or until softened. Lift the mushrooms out of the water, squeeze them over the bowl to capture the soaking liquid, and then chop.

In a saucepan large enough to hold the cooked pasta, combine the porcini and cream and carefully pour in the soaking liquid, leaving any grit behind in the bowl. Bring to a gentle simmer over low to medium heat and simmer for about 5 minutes, or until thickened very slightly. Remove from the heat and season with salt and pepper and reserve.

Cook the pasta as directed (page 376) or according to package directions if using dried pasta.

Add the pasta and half of the cheese to the sauce, toss to coat, and serve. Pass the rest of the cheese at the table.

Fettuccine or Linguine with Mushrooms Tartufati

This dish takes its name from the fact that the mushrooms are sliced very thin, as though they were truffles. Oddly, cutting the mushrooms this way also gives them a trufflelike flavor and aroma. If you are uncomfortable slicing this finely with a knife, use a plastic vegetable slicer, but be careful not to slice your fingers. If you can find them, use cremini mushrooms instead of white mushrooms.

MAKES 4 FIRST-COURSE SERVINGS

1 pound cultivated mushrooms, preferably cremini

3 tablespoons butter or olive oil

Salt

Pepper

1/2 cup heavy cream

12 ounces dried or 11/2 pounds fresh fettuccine or linguine

About 1 cup grated Parmigiano-Reggiano cheese

Wash and dry the mushrooms. Cut the end off the bottom of each mushroom stem if dried out or dirty. Slice the mushrooms paper-thin.

In a sauté pan, heat the butter or oil over high heat. When the butter froths and then the froth begins to subside, or the oil ripples, add a handful of mushrooms. Stir or toss for a couple of minutes with a wooden spoon and then add another handful of mushrooms. Continue in this way until you have added all the mushrooms and they have browned and shrunk and smell fragrant. This will take about 10 minutes. Season with salt and pepper, pour in the cream, and simmer over low heat for about 5 minutes, or until just slightly thickened. Reserve off the heat.

Cook the pasta as directed (page 376) or according to package directions if using dried pasta.

Add the pasta and half of the cheese to the sauce, toss to coat, and serve. Pass the rest of the cheese at the table.

Fettuccine, Linguine, or Elbow Pasta with Peas and Pesto

Unless fresh baby peas are in the market, thawed, frozen petite peas are your best choice here. By combining virtually any vegetable with pasta, you turn it into a polished first or main course. If you toss the pasta with good extra virgin olive oil or fresh cold butter, you will be pleased with the dish no matter which vegetable you use.

**MAKES 6 FIRST-COURSE SERVINGS OR
4 MAIN-COURSE SERVINGS**

11/2 pounds fresh baby peas in the shell, shucked, or one 10-ounce package frozen petite peas

1 tablespoon olive oil

12 ounces dried or 11/2 pounds fresh fettuccine or linguine

About 1 cup grated Parmigiano-Reggiano cheese

Pesto Sauce (see page 362) or 1 stick of butter, sliced

Salt

Pepper

If using fresh peas, bring a large pot of salted water to a boil, add the peas, boil for 1 minute, and drain. If using frozen peas, just let them thaw. There is no need to cook them.

Cook the pasta as directed (page 376) or according to package directions if using dried pasta.

Place the pasta in a warmed bowl, add the peas, half of the cheese, and the pesto or butter, and toss to coat. Season with salt and pepper and serve. Pass the rest of the cheese at the table.

Ravioli with Spinach-Ricotta Filling

Follow the directions for the Ravioli with Basil-Ricotta Filling on page 380, but substitute the leaves from 1 large bunch of spinach for the basil. Plunge the spinach leaves in a pot of boiling salted water and as soon as they wilt, after about 30 seconds, drain them in a colander and rinse with cold water. Squeeze out the water and finely chop the leaves. Combine the spinach with the ricotta and other ingredients.

Ravioli with Butter, Walnuts, and Sage

The secret to this sauce, which is popular in Tuscany, is to cook the butter until it browns but not until it burns, which gives the sauce a nutty flavor. You can use any kind of nuts you like—pine nuts are wonderful but cost a fortune, and pistachios look great—and you can substitute different herbs, such as chopped marjoram or thyme, for the sage. This ravioli filling is traditionally flavored with nutmeg, but you can instead flavor it with an herb, such as chives, chervil, or thyme.

MAKES 6 FIRST-COURSE SERVINGS OR 4 MAIN-COURSE SERVINGS

Ravioli with Basil-Ricotta Filling (see page 380)

$1/4$ pound butter

$1/2$ cup coarsely chopped walnuts

6 fresh sage leaves

Grated Parmigiano-Reggiano or grana padano cheese for serving

Try to time the cooking of the ravioli so you are ready to add them to the sauce just as the butter browns. But if you have started the ravioli too soon, drain them in a colander, turn them into a bowl, and toss them with a little butter to keep them from sticking.

In a large sauté pan, combine the butter, walnuts, and sage over high heat and heat for about 3 minutes, or until the butter melts and begins to brown and the nuts brown and the sage turns bright green and both release their flavor. Add the ravioli and toss them in the hot sauce (if the ravioli were made in advance and are cold, give them a couple of minutes to heat through) until well coated.

Serve on warmed plates. Pass the cheese at the table.

Linguine with Tomato Sauce

If tomatoes are out of season, substitute canned: 1 medium tomato yields about $1/2$ cup chopped, seeded tomato.

MAKES 6 FIRST-COURSE SERVINGS OR 4 MAIN-COURSE SERVINGS

Dough for Fresh Egg Pasta (see page 376) or 12 ounces dried linguine

Tomato Sauce

2 tablespoons olive oil

I yellow onion, diced

4 cloves garlic, minced

12 tomatoes, peeled, seeded, and chopped (see page 85)

Salt

Pepper

Leaves from 1 bunch basil

Parmigiano-Reggiano for serving

Make the pasta dough as directed, and then roll out and cut into linguine (page 376).

To make the tomato sauce, heat the olive oil in a large saucepan. Add the onion and garlic and sauté until soft. Add the tomatoes and simmer, stirring occasionally, until they have cooked down into a smooth sauce with a few small chunks, about 30 minutes. Season to taste with salt and pepper. Mince the basil and stir into the sauce. Keep the sauce warm while you cook the pasta.

Cook the pasta as directed (page 376) or according to package directions if using dried pasta.

In a large mixing bowl, toss the noodles with the sauce. Serve grated Parmigiano on the side.

HOW TO MAKE RAVIOLI WITH BUTTER, WALNUTS, AND SAGE

1. Cook the butter, walnuts, and sage.

2. The nuts and butter will brown, the sage will brighten.

3. Toss ravioli with sauce and serve.

Pappardelle with Chicken Liver Ragù Sauce

Remember, a ragù is basically a meat sauce with the shredded or chopped meat in the sauce, rather than served separately, as in a French sauce. For example, you can make a delicious ragù by combining equal parts peeled, seeded, and chopped tomatoes and turkey giblet gravy. Or, you can improvise with leftover stew (shred the meat and combine it with the braising liquid), leftover roast (shred the meat and combine the juices from the roast with tomato as for the turkey gravy), or even leftover meat loaf (break it up and simmer it with chopped tomatoes). Here is an equally easy ragù made with chicken livers and tomatoes that goes together quickly.

MAKES 6 FIRST-COURSE SERVINGS OR 4 MAIN-COURSE SERVINGS

> **Dough for Fresh Egg Pasta (see page 376) or 12 ounces dried pappardelle**
>
> **³/₄ pound chicken livers, any membranes removed**
>
> **Salt**
>
> **Pepper**
>
> **2 tablespoons olive oil**
>
> **¹/₂ cup concentrated chicken broth or 1 tablespoon commercial meat glaze or 2 tablespoons homemade meat glaze (see page 177), optional**
>
> **8 tomatoes, peeled, seeded, and chopped (see page 85)**
>
> **Parmigiano-Reggiano for serving**

Make the pasta dough as directed, and then roll out and cut into pappardelle (see page 376).

Season the chicken livers with salt and pepper. In a sauté pan, heat the oil over high heat. When the oil ripples, add the chicken livers and cook, turning once, for about 8 minutes total, or until browned on both sides and firm to the touch. Transfer to paper towels to drain, and then let rest for 10 minutes.

In a small saucepan, combine the broth and tomatoes and bring to a simmer. Finely chop the chicken livers, add them to the tomato mixture, and simmer for about 10 minutes, or until the sauce thickens to the consistency you like.

Meanwhile, cook the pasta as directed (page 376) or according to package directions if using dried pasta.

In a large mixing bowl, toss the noodles with the sauce. Served grated Parmigiano on the side.

Lasagne

The secret to the best lasagne is simply using the ingredients. If you use a homemade ragu sauce (see pages 356–357 and 384–385), the best mozzarella, and real Parmigiano-Reggiano, your lasagne will be extraordinary.

MAKES 12 MAIN-COURSE SERVINGS

> **Dough for Fresh Egg Pasta (see page 376) or 1 pound dried lasagne noodles**
>
> **Three 15-ounce containers ricotta cheese**
>
> **2¹/₂ pounds mozzarella, sliced**
>
> **3 quarts Duck Ragù, Bolognese, or Rabbit Sauce (see pages 356–357) or Tomato Sauce (opposite) or Chicken Liver Ragù Sauce (at left)**
>
> **1 pound Parmigiano-Reggiano, finely grated**

Make the pasta dough as directed, and then roll out and cut into lasagna-width noodles.

Butter a 10-by-14-inch baking dish with high sides (a roasting pan often works well).

Cook the pasta as directed (see page 376) or according to package directions if using dried pasta.

Place one-third of the cooked noodles in the bottom of the baking dish. Layer the first noodles with one-third of each of the ricotta, mozzarella, sauce, and Parmigiano-Reggiano. Repeat for the second and third layers, finishing the lasagne with a layer of sauce and a generous sprinkling of Parmigiano. Bake in a 350°F oven—there's no need for preheating—until you see the lasagne bubbling, about 1 hour 15 minutes.

Let cool for at least 15 minutes before serving or better yet, let cool completely so the layers settle and become easier to portion out, and then reheat to serve.

RICE

Rice dishes are usually of two types: risotto, made from short-grain rice, in which the rice is cooked slowly over the stove while stirring, and pilaf, in which the rice is cooked in a little oil or butter, usually with onion, before all the liquid is added. In addition to these two dishes, there is what European cooks call "Indian-style" rice, which describes rice cooked in an abundance of boiling water just as pasta is cooked. This method is excellent for making perfectly fluffy rice that doesn't stick to itself.

One reason risotto, the classic rice dish of Italy, has not been fully appreciated in the United States, at least until recently, is because it has often been presented as a side dish to a main course, much as one might serve rice pilaf. Risotto should always be served as a first course or a light main course. Like pasta, the possibilities for improvisation are limitless. You just need to keep in mind the logic of how ingredients cook and add them at the right time during the cooking of the rice.

Much is made about the constant stirring required for successful risotto, but in fact you can get away with letting it simmer for a few minutes, unattended, while you work on other things. You can also get it halfway done, let it cool, cover it, and then finish it at the last minute. This will cut down on the time you spend in the kitchen while family or guests wonder where you are.

If your risotto includes slow-cooking vegetables, such as onions or garlic, cook them gently in butter or olive oil to soften them, but not brown them, before the rice is added. Also, keep the butter or oil you use at this point to a minimum, especially if you are adding more butter or olive oil at the end. The delicate flavor of the fat added early on will be lost by the time the risotto is cooked.

Once you have cooked the onion, garlic, or other aromatic vegetables, add the rice and cook it gently in the fat for a couple of minutes before adding about one-fourth of the anticipated amount of cooking liquid (the actual amount will vary according to the kind of rice you use and how flowing or dry you like your risotto). When adding liquid to a risotto, the liquid should be near or at the simmer so the cooking doesn't slow when you add it. If you have a flavorful liquid, such as the steaming liquid from clams, good broth, soaking liquid from dried wild mushrooms, or wine, add it to the rice near the beginning, to be sure it is completely absorbed by the time the rice is cooked. Continue adding liquid, about one-fourth at a time, and stir until it is almost fully absorbed by the rice before pouring in the next addition.

After about 20 minutes, you will have added all or nearly all of the liquid and the rice should be creamy and look a little like tapioca. Taste a grain for doneness. It should have just lost any dry, raw texture at its heart but still be firm to the bite. If it still tastes dry, add more liquid, or hot water if you have used all your liquid, and cook, stirring, for a few minutes longer. In some parts of Italy, the finished risotto is relatively dry, while in others, such as Venice, it has a consistency almost like soup. A soupy consistency is especially delightful for guests who are not used to eating risotto as a first course.

Shellfish Risotto with Saffron

You can make this risotto with as many or as few different shellfish as you like. The trick to creating a particularly delicious dish is to use the liquid from cooking the shellfish in the risotto. If you have extra time, you can make a broth from the shells of crustaceans (page 124) to use in place of the chicken broth or water.

MAKES 4 FIRST-COURSE OR LIGHT MAIN-COURSE SERVINGS

20 littleneck clams

20 mussels, preferably green New Zealand

1 cup dry white wine

2 cloves garlic, minced

2 tablespoons butter or oil

1 cup Arborio, Carnaroli, or Vialone Nano rice

2 cups chicken broth or water, or as needed, brought to a simmer

1/2 teaspoon saffron threads, soaked in 2 tablespoons water for 30 minutes

12 large or jumbo shrimp, peeled and then deveined if desired

4 sea scallops, small muscle removed (see page 119) and halved crosswise

4 tablespoons butter or extra virgin olive oil for finishing (optional)

Salt (if needed)

Pepper

Scrub the clams and mussels, push the sides in opposite directions to identify dead ones, and rinse thoroughly.

Select a pot large enough so that the mussels and clams will reach no higher than two-thirds up the sides. Add the wine and garlic, cover, bring to a simmer over low heat, and simmer for 5 minutes. Add the clams, cover, raise the heat to medium, and simmer for 5 minutes. Add the mussels, re-cover, and simmer for 5 minutes longer, or until all the shellfish have opened. Discard any mussels that failed to open, but use a knife to force open any clams that don't open. Scoop out the clams and mussels in their shells and set aside in a warm place.

In a large saucepan, melt the 2 tablespoons butter over medium heat. Add the rice and cook, stirring, for about 5 minutes, or until the rice turns slightly opaque. Add about 1 cup of the simmering steaming liquid from the clams and mussels and cook, stirring, just until the liquid is absorbed. Add the remaining steaming liquid (being careful to leave behind any grit that may be in the bottom of the pot) and continue to cook and stir just until the liquid is absorbed. Then begin to add the broth, again about 1 cup at a time, adding more only after the first batch has been absorbed. When the rice is almost done, stir in the saffron and its soaking liquid, the shrimp, and the scallops and continue to cook over medium heat for 3 to 5 minutes, or until the shrimp is pink and the scallops have lost their translucency.

Stir in the 4 tablespoons butter and season to taste. Spoon the risotto into warmed soup plates. Divide the clams and mussels among the plates, arranging them on top, and serve immediately.

HOW TO MAKE SHELLFISH RISOTTO

1. Stir the rice in butter or oil until opaque.

2. Stir in shellfish cooking liquid.

3. Continue to add liquid, adding more as the rice absorbs it.

4. Stir in the saffron with its soaking liquid.

5. Continue to cook until the risotto has the consistency you like and the rice is just cooked through.

6. Arrange the risotto on heated plates and add the shellfish.

Risotto Milanese

This is a classic risotto and one of the easiest to make. Traditional recipes call for capon broth, but good homemade chicken broth can be used.

MAKES 4 FIRST-COURSE OR LIGHT MAIN-COURSE SERVINGS

> **2 tablespoons butter**
> **1 small onion, minced**
> **1 cup Arborio, Carnaroli, or Vialone Nano rice**
> **4 cups chicken broth, brought to a simmer**
> **1/2 teaspoon saffron threads, soaked in 2 tablespoons water for 30 minutes**
> **1 1/2 cups grated Parmigiano-Reggiano cheese**
> **Salt**
> **Pepper**

In a large saucepan, melt the butter over medium heat. Add the onion and cook, stirring often, for about 10 minutes, or until translucent. Add the rice and cook, stirring, for about 3 minutes, or until slightly opaque.

Add 2 cups of the broth and cook, stirring, just until the broth is absorbed. Add 1 cup of the broth and cook, stirring, just until the broth is absorbed. Add the remaining 1 cup broth a little at a time so that the risotto is the creamy consistency you like at the same time that the rice grains lose any hint of dryness at their center.

Stir in the saffron and cheese, season with salt and pepper, and spoon into warmed soup plates to serve.

Fluffy Rice

The secret to making light, fluffy rice is to use the right kind of rice—look for basmati or jasmine, which both have a rich, nutty flavor—and to cook it in a large amount of boiling water, in the same way you cook pasta.

MAKES ABOUT 3 CUPS, OR 4 SIDE-DISH SERVINGS

> **1 cup long-grain rice such as basmati or jasmine**

In a large pot, bring about 6 quarts water to a boil. Meanwhile, pour the rice into a strainer and rinse under cold running water until the water runs clear.

When the water is boiling, add the rice and boil for about 12 minutes, or until just tender (taste a grain; it should be tender but still slightly firm). Drain in a large strainer and let rest for about 10 minutes before serving.

Rice Pilaf

A rice pilaf is simply rice flavored with a little onion cooked in olive oil.

MAKES ABOUT 3 CUPS, OR 4 SIDE-DISH SERVINGS

> **1 cup long-grain rice such as basmati or jasmine**
> **2 tablespoons butter or olive oil**
> **1 onion, chopped**
> **2 cups chicken broth or water**

Pour the rice into a strainer and rinse under cold running water until the water runs clear. Set aside.

In a saucepan large enough to hold the cooked rice, melt the butter over medium heat. Add the onion and cook, stirring, for 3 to 5 minutes, or until translucent. Add the rice and cook, stirring, for 3 to 5 minutes, or until the rice turns white. Pour in the broth, reduce the heat to low, cover, and cook for 15 to 20 minutes, or until the rice is tender (taste a grain; it should be tender but still slightly firm).

COUSCOUS

The word *couscous* refers to both the uncooked pellet-sized spheres of semolina flour and to the finished steamed dish, a staple of the North African table that is usually paired with vegetables and lamb, chicken, or other meat. You can make couscous yourself by moistening semolina flour, shaping it into the tiny grains, and then steaming it, but it is time-consuming and requires considerable practice. Nowadays, the couscous we find boxed and in bulk in the market is presteamed and dehydrated. It is quickly made at home by combining the dehydrated pellets with boiling water or broth and letting them stand for 5 to 10 minutes until they swell, at which point they are ready to fluff with a fork and serve as a quick and easy side dish. Israeli couscous consists of larger pellets and can be cooked like pasta in a big pot of boiling water until tender, about 10 minutes.

Basic Couscous

Couscous varies depending on the brand, so follow the directions on the package. If there are none, use the amounts here.

MAKES 6 SIDE-DISH SERVINGS

> 2¹⁄₄ cups dried couscous
> 3¹⁄₂ cups chicken broth or water
> Salt

Put the couscous in a heat-proof bowl and pour over the boiling broth or water. Let sit for 5 minutes and then fluff the couscous with a fork while sprinkling with salt.

VARIATIONS

Consider adding toasted pine nuts and raisins or dried apricots to your couscous. Couscous is also good served cold with olive oil and vinegar.

POLENTA

Essentially cornmeal, polenta, a specialty of northern Italy, comes in fine and coarse grind. Coarse-ground polenta is harder to locate—it may require a trip to a specialty-foods store—but it has a more robust flavor that justifies the effort. In a pinch, however, fine-ground polenta is a satisfactory substitute.

Like risotto, most polenta recipes call for stirring polenta on the stove top almost constantly for it to achieve its characteristic smooth, thick texture. Sally Schneider, in her estimable book *A New Way to Cook,* recommends starting the polenta on the stove top and then finishing it in the oven, which eliminates nearly all of the stirring.

Basic Polenta

This simple unflavored polenta is a good starchy backdrop for stews and braised dishes. To use Sally Schneider's oven method mentioned above, use 3³⁄₄ cups water, instead of 4 cups, and as soon as the mixture comes to a simmer, slide the saucepan, uncovered, into a 350°F oven and bake for 40 minutes, stir, and then bake for 10 minutes longer.

MAKES 4 SIDE-DISH SERVINGS

> 1 cup polenta, preferably coarse grind
> 1 teaspoon salt
> 4 cups water

In a heavy saucepan, combine the polenta, salt, and water and bring to a simmer over high heat. Stir every minute or so over low to medium heat—a bubble should break on the surface every few seconds for about 35 minutes, or until the mixture is thick and smooth and pulls away from the sides of the pan. Serve hot.

VARIATIONS

If you are serving polenta with a stew or braised meats, keep it simple, as you want it to enhance, rather than upstage, the main dish. If you are serving polenta as a separate course, pass a wedge of Parmigiano and a grater at the table along with some good olive oil for guests to add to taste. Or, enrich the polenta by stirring in brown butter, cheese such as crumbled Roquefort or Gorgonzola, or lightly crisped strips of pancetta or bacon. You can also spread hot polenta ¹⁄₄ to ¹⁄₂ inch thick on an oiled sheet pan, let it cool until set, cut it into squares, and sauté the pieces in butter or olive oil until golden or brush them with butter or olive oil and grill them until piping hot and golden.

QUICK BREADS AND FLAT CAKES

This chapter includes all sorts of wonderful things to do with flour—popovers, muffins, crepes, pancakes, waffles, and French toast. These are recipes for foods that, for the most part, contain no yeast and hence aren't really breads in the traditional sense. There are quick breads, essentially muffins, biscuits, and breakfast "breads," which are leavened with baking powder and eggs. I also include popovers, whose only leavening triggers when egg is suddenly exposed to a lot of heat. All of the flat cakes are similar. The difference between crepes and pancakes is that crepes are thin and unleavened, while pancakes are thicker and leavened. Waffles are made from a pancakelike batter that includes melted butter and beaten egg whites to make them light and crispy, and blini are pancakes made by adding yeast to crepe batter. These are simple foods, achievable for even beginning bakers who are looking for reliable master recipes.

Blueberry Muffins

Muffins are a delightful cross between bread and cake, richer than one and lighter and less sweet than the other. They are usually leavened with baking powder, but eggs and butter also play a role in keeping them light and tasty. Muffins are especially good spread with sweet butter. Here is a traditional recipe for blueberry muffins, but keep in mind that muffins lend themselves to improvisation and you should feel free to substitute various fruits and coarsely chopped nuts. The best muffins are made with plenty of butter. You can use berries other than blueberries, such as blackberries, raspberries, or quartered strawberries in this recipe.

MAKES 12 MUFFINS

> **2 cups plus 2 tablespoons flour**
> **1/4 cup granulated sugar**
> **2 teaspoons baking powder**
> **1/2 teaspoon salt**
> **1/4 cup butter, melted**
> **2 eggs, lightly beaten**
> **1 cup milk**
> **2 cups blueberries**
> **Confectioners' sugar (optional)**

Preheat the oven to 375°F. Butter a 12-cup muffin tin and then coat with flour, tapping out the excess.

In a bowl, stir together the 2 cups flour, granulated sugar, baking powder, and salt until well mixed. Add the butter, eggs, and milk and stir until just combined, just long enough to form a smooth thick paste, but no longer or you'll overwork it. Don't worry if the batter contains a few lumps.

In a separate bowl, toss the berries with the remaining 2 tablespoons flour—this keeps them from sinking to the bottom of the muffins—and then fold them into the batter.

Fill the prepared muffin cups three-fourths full of batter. Bake for 25 minutes, or until golden brown and a knife or toothpick inserted into the center of a muffin comes out clean. Let cool in the pan for 10 minutes, then turn out onto a rack. If you like, sift over confectioners' sugar.

Buttermilk Biscuits

Making a basic biscuit dough is similar to making a pie dough. The difference is that biscuit dough calls for more liquid and for baking powder, which makes the biscuits rise in the heat of the oven. These biscuits are leavened with baking soda instead of baking powder because of the acidity of the buttermilk, which makes the tartaric acid in the baking powder superfluous.

MAKES 12 BISCUITS

> **2 cups flour**
> **$1/2$ teaspoon baking soda**
> **$1^1/2$ teaspoons baking powder**
> **$1/4$ teaspoon salt**
> **6 tablespoons cold butter, cut into 12 slices**
> **$3/4$ cup buttermilk, or as needed**

Preheat the oven to 400°F.

In a bowl, stir together the flour, baking soda, baking powder, and salt until well mixed. Put the butter slices on top of the flour mixture, and then cut through the mixture with a pastry blender until the butter is about the size of peas. Add the $3/4$ cup buttermilk and, using a wooden spoon, combine the mixture just until the liquid has been absorbed and there is no loose flour in the bottom of the bowl. If you still see loose flour, mix in another
2 tablespoons buttermilk to absorb it. Be careful not to overstir the dough; overworking it produces tough biscuits.

Dump the dough out onto a work surface and gather it together into a mound with your hands. Knead it just long enough to flatten it into a disk that holds together in a shaggy mass. Flour the work surface and roll out the disk to $2/3$ inch thick. Using a $2^1/2$-inch round biscuit or cookie cutter, cut out as many disks as possible and arrange them on an ungreased sheet pan, spacing them about 1 inch apart. If you like, pull together the trimmings and roll them and cut them out in the same way.

Turn down the oven to 375°F and bake the biscuits for about 20 minutes, or until golden brown. Let cool on a rack for 10 minutes and serve while still warm.

Scones

Scone dough, like biscuit dough, is similar to pie dough except that it has more liquid, a leavening agent, and is lightly sweetened. This basic recipe can be adapted to incorporate nearly any kind of dried fruit.

MAKES 8 SCONES

> **2 cups flour**
> **3 tablespoons sugar**
> **1 tablespoon baking powder**
> **$1/4$ teaspoon salt**
> **$1/4$ cup plus 2 tablespoons cold butter, cut into 10 slices**
> **$3/4$ cup milk or heavy cream, or as needed**
> **$3/4$ cup raisins, dried currants, dried cranberries, dried cherries, or diced dried apricots, soaked in water to cover for 30 minutes, drained, and patted dry**

Preheat the oven to 375°F.

In a bowl, stir together the flour, sugar, baking powder, and salt until well mixed. Put the butter slices on top of the flour mixture, and then cut through the mixture with a pastry blender until the butter is about the size of peas. Add the $3/4$ cup milk and, using a wooden spoon, combine the mixture just until the liquid has been absorbed and there is no loose flour in the bottom of the bowl. If you still see loose flour, mix in another 2 tablespoons of milk to absorb it. Fold in the raisins. Be careful not to overwork the dough.

Dump the dough out onto a work surface and gather it together into a mound with your hands. Knead it just long enough to flatten it into a disk that holds together in a shaggy mass. Flour the work surface and roll out the disk into a round $3/4$ inch thick. Cut the round into 8 wedges and arrange the wedges on an ungreased baking sheet, spacing them about 1 inch apart.

Turn down the oven to 350°F and bake the scones for about 30 minutes, or until pale brown. Let cool on a rack and serve while still warm.

Popovers

Popovers are fascinating to watch since they begin to puff almost as soon as you add the batter to the pan. This is all the more amazing when we consider that they contain no leavening other than egg. You need a special pan for baking popovers. It looks somewhat like a muffin pan, except that it is traditionally made of heavy metal, so that it retains heat well. The intense heat is then delivered quickly to the batter the moment it is poured into the pan, which causes the popovers to rise. The melted butter is important, not only for flavor but also to ensure the popovers are light. For the best result, make sure the batter is at room temperature when you pour it into the pan.

MAKES 12 POPOVERS

> 1$\frac{1}{2}$ cups flour
> $\frac{1}{2}$ teaspoon salt
> 3 eggs
> 2 cups milk
> 6 tablespoons butter, melted
> 3 tablespoons vegetable oil

Preheat the oven to 500°F. In a bowl, stir together the flour and salt until well mixed. Add the eggs and 1 cup of the milk and whisk until smooth. Stir in the rest of the milk and the melted butter and then let the batter sit for 30 minutes at room temperature. Transfer the batter to a pitcher to make filling the pan quicker and easier.

Put a 12-mold popover pan in the oven for 5 minutes to get hot. Then, as quickly as possible, slide the oven rack out slightly, brush the inside of each mold generously with the oil, and fill each mold two-thirds full with the batter. Push the rack back in and immediately close the oven door. Within minutes you should see the popovers rising through the oven window. Don't open the oven door again until the popovers are ready. When the popovers are golden brown, after about 15 minutes, turn the oven down to 300°F and bake for 10 minutes longer, or until the popovers are cooked all the way through.

Remove from the oven—they should pop right out of the pan. Encourage guests and family to break open the popovers as soon as they come out of the oven and spread them with butter and honey or jam.

French Toast

French toast is a clever way of making use of stale bread. In France, where it is known as pain perdu, it is served with a little sugar and jam, but in America we are lucky to have maple syrup. This recipe calls for stale bread, but fresh bread right out of the package will do well also. Avoid using sourdough bread, which conflicts with the sweet theme of the whole recipe.

MAKES 4 BREAKFAST SERVINGS

> 6 eggs
> 1 cup milk
> 12 slices stale white bread
> Butter for cooking
> Butter and warmed maple syrup for serving

In a shallow bowl, whisk the eggs until blended, and then whisk in the milk. Dip the bread slices, one at a time, in the egg mixture, and press down on them so they absorb some of the egg mixture.

In a large, heavy skillet, melt about 3 tablespoons of butter over medium heat. When the butter froths, add as many bread slices as will fit without crowding. Cook for about 4 minutes, or until well browned on the first side. Then turn and cook for about 3 minutes longer, or until well browned on the second side. Serve right away with butter and maple syrup. Repeat with the remaining bread slices, adding more butter to the pan as needed.

Crepes

In the past, cooking crepes was considered difficult because the thin cakes always seemed to stick to the pan. But nowadays we have nonstick pans, eliminating the problem. To make crepes efficiently, you will need more than one pan. Since most of the time you can get by without all your crepes being the same size, you can use whatever nonstick pans you have on hand. If you are buying pans to make crepes, you may want to buy slope-sided omelet pans, rather than traditional crepe pans with a flat bottom and angled sides, or virtually no sides at all, because they are more versatile. But if you like crepes and find yourself making them often, you may want as many as four pans going at once. Crepes can be made ahead—each one must be on its own sheet of waxed paper, but the sheets can be stacked—and then frozen in an airtight container for up to several months.

MAKES EIGHTEEN 7-INCH CREPES

> **2 cups flour**
> **4 eggs**
> **2¹⁄₄ cups milk, or as needed**
> **About 4 tablespoons butter, room temperature**
> **or melted, for cooking**

In a bowl, whisk together the flour, eggs, and ¹⁄₂ cup of the milk. Work the batter until it is smooth and free of lumps, and then whisk in the remaining milk. The batter should be the consistency of cold heavy cream, so add additional milk, a little at a time as necessary to achieve the correct consistency. Ideally, let the batter sit for 1 hour before you use it to keep the crepes from shrinking in the pan.

Heat an 8-inch nonstick sauté pan over medium heat. If this is your first time, just cook 1 crepe at a time, rather than trying to manage 2 pans. When the pan is hot, brush it with a little of the butter. Use a 1- or 2-ounce ladle to add the batter to the pan. A 7-inch crepe requires about 3 tablespoons of batter. Add the ladle of batter all at once and then quickly rotate the pan so the batter spreads evenly over the bottom. You want just enough batter to create a thin layer. If you have added too much batter, just pour the excess back into the bowl of batter. If you haven't added enough, just ladle in more to cover the bare spots of the pan. As you work, always notice the level of batter in the ladle, so that after a couple of crepes, you will add just the right amount to the pan.

As you practice, you will get the feel for the right temperature of the pan. If the pan is too hot, not only will the butter smoke when you brush it on—with a nonstick pan you don't have to butter the pan for each crepe—but the batter will seize where you first add it and make a thick patch. If the pan isn't hot enough, it is not a problem (in the old days it made the crepes stick), but it will take forever to make a batch of crepes. The ideal temperature is when you hear a faint sizzle as the batter hits the surface.

Once the batter is spread evenly in the pan, leave the pan over medium heat for about 3 minutes, or until the batter loses its sheen and the very edges of the crepe start to brown. Pinch the edge of the crepe and lift to look under it. When the crepe is pale brown on the bottom, using the thumb and index finger of each hand, pinch it in two places at the edge farthest from you and flip it over. If the crepe is thin, the heat shouldn't be a problem. If it is, slide a rubber spatula under the crepe and flip it with that. Cook on the second side for about 1 minute, or until pale brown on the second side.

As each crepe is ready, slide it off the pan onto a plate. If you're storing the crepes and not serving them within a few hours, stack them on sheets of waxed paper.

HOW TO MAKE CREPES

1. Whisk together flour, eggs, and milk until smooth. Whisk in remaining milk.

2. Pour or ladle the batter onto the hot pan and spread evenly.

3. Cook until pale brown, then flip and cook the other side.

4. Cook until the second side has browned, and then slide out of the pan onto a plate.

Crepes Suzette

We have come a long way since the days when crepes suzette epitomized the pinnacle of luxury, and tuxedo-clad waiters spent their evenings fiddling with chafing dishes. But unlike similar dishes, where much ado is made about relatively little, crepes suzette is one of the great desserts of the world and is remarkably easy to make.

Traditional recipes, in one of French cuisine's cleverest little tricks, call for extracting the essence of orange zest by rubbing the orange with a sugar cube until the oil is absorbed into the cube. Several such cubes are then worked with butter, and this butter is combined with various combinations of cognac and Grand Marnier, flambéed or not, and used to heat up the rolled or folded crepes, which absorb the heady combination of orange, butter, and alcohol. Theoretically one could cook off nearly all of the alcohol, but unlike savory cooking, in which raw alcohol always clashes, a little alcohol in a sweet dish is often just what's needed.

Many cooks are put off before they even begin by the elaborate preparation of the sugar cubes, the expense of a small bottle of Grand Marnier, and the scary-sounding flambéing. But the sugar cubes and Grand Marnier can be circumvented with some grated orange zest and boiled-down orange juice, and an inexpensive cognac (authentic cognac, but the least expensive bottle in the shop) is all that's needed for the alcohol.

MAKES 6 DESSERT SERVINGS

2 oranges

1 tablespoon fresh lemon juice

1/2 cup butter, sliced

6 tablespoons cognac, 3 tablespoons each cognac and Grand Marnier, or 6 tablespoons Grand Marnier

18 crepes, each 6 to 8 inches in diameter, folded into triangles or rolled

If you want to serve your crepes on fire, be sure the dessert plates are well heated in the oven. Grate the zest off one of the oranges. Squeeze the juice from both oranges, and combine the juice with the zest in a small saucepan. Boil the juice down by about half and add the lemon juice.

Just before serving, bring the orange mixture to a simmer and whisk in the butter.

Arrange the crepes in a single layer in a chafing dish or sauté pan. Add the alcohol to the orange mixture and, working carefully, tilt it over the flame to ignite it or light it with a long match. Wait for the flames to die down and then pour the orange sauce over the crepes. Set the sauté pan on the stove over high heat or the chafing dish pan over an ingnited sterno canister. Spoon the flaming sauce over the crepes and serve, still afire if you are feeling up to it.

What to Do with Crepes

Once you have made a batch of crepes, they can be used many ways. You can serve them as you would pancakes, with butter and maple syrup or fruit preserves. You can use them for rolling up creamed turkey or chicken or a similar mixture that you might otherwise bake into a casserole. You can make soufflé crepes by rolling them around a soufflé mixture, such as the cheese soufflé on page 102, and baking them in a 375°F oven for about 15 minutes. To make sweet crepes, you can fill them with chocolate mousse or ice cream and serve them drizzled with chocolate sauce. Or, best of all, you can make my favorites, crepes suzette.

Blini

A blini is a pancake made with yeast and is most famous as an accompaniment to caviar. Blini also happen to be delicious with smoked salmon or just about anything that might be good with a pancake. Just as with bread, the slower the rise, the more flavorful the blini. This is not to say that quickly leavened blini, inspired by a sudden whim, aren't worth the effort, which they definitely are. Most recipes for bread (and blini) slow the rise by refrigerating the dough, but because refrigerators nowadays are generally colder than they were in the past, time in the refrigerator too often just paralyzes the whole project. A more cunning approach is to use a minute amount of yeast, or at least to correlate the amount of yeast with the anticipated rising time in a cool place (but not in the refrigerator). This may take a little fussing around to get right, but once you do, you can use the same formula every time you make blini. Blini are traditionally made with buckwheat flour, but standard all-purpose flour works just as well. If you have buckwheat flour and want to try using it, substitute it for $^3/_4$ cup of the all-purpose flour.

MAKES SIXTEEN 4-INCH BLINI FOR 4 HORS D'OEUVRE OR
LIGHT BREAKFAST SERVINGS

> **2 cups flour**
>
> **2 cups milk, at cool room temperature**
>
> **$^1/_2$ teaspoon active dry yeast, soaked in 1 tablespoon warm water with 1 teaspoon flour**
>
> **4 eggs, separated**
>
> **$^1/_2$ teaspoon salt**
>
> **Room-temperature or melted butter for cooking**

In a bowl, whisk together the flour and 1$^1/_2$ cups of the milk until smooth, then whisk in the remaining $^1/_2$ cup milk and the yeast mixture. Cover and let rise at room temperature for about 3 hours, or until double in volume.

Add the egg yolks and salt to the batter and whisk until smooth. In a separate bowl, using an electric mixer or a whisk, beat the egg whites until stiff peaks form. Using a rubber spatula, fold the egg whites into the batter just until combined. Heat a nonstick or seasoned sauté pan or skillet over medium heat. Brush with butter and ladle in enough batter to make the size blini you want. You will need about 2 tablespoons to make 4-inch blini. Cook for about 2 minutes, or until bubbles form on the surface and then break. Flip with a spatula and cook for a couple of minutes on the second side, or until set and no longer doughy. Serve right away. Cook the remaining batter in the same way.

Pancakes

A pancake is similar to a crepe, but the batter includes some type of leavening to make it fluffy. The usual leavening is baking powder, well combined with the flour before any liquid is added. Once liquid is added to the dry ingredients, the pancakes should be made right away, so the baking powder doesn't wear itself out producing gas—carbon dioxide—that just escapes into the atmosphere.

Like many everyday things, pancakes can be improved on by using a leavening other than baking powder. Yeast-leavened pancakes have a lovely bready flavor, and pancakes leavened with egg whites (the recipe is identical to the waffle recipe, opposite) are especially light. When both yeast and egg whites are used, pancakes become ethereal blini suitable for caviar and other such treats. Perhaps most recherché, but also the best, are sourdough pancakes made with a starter that needs as much care and attention as a pampered cat. For sourdough pancakes make the bread starter on page 409 and add it to crepe batter (see page 394).

This basic pancake recipe can be multiplied as many times as you like. The consistency of your pancakes will depend on the flour you use—on the East Coast and in the South, White Rose brand is a good choice because of its low gluten content—so if they come out tough, experiment with a different flour or substitute half cake flour. Two or three tablespoons of melted butter will also soften the pancakes by interfering with gluten development. Serve the pancakes with butter and hot maple syrup or jam.

MAKES ABOUT TWELVE 4- TO 5-INCH PANCAKES

> **2 cups flour**
>
> **2 teaspoons baking powder**
>
> **$^1/_4$ teaspoon salt**
>
> **3 eggs**
>
> **2 cups milk**
>
> **Room-temperature or melted butter for cooking**

In a bowl, stir together the flour, baking powder, and salt until well combined. Just before you are ready to start cooking the pancakes, whisk in the eggs and just enough of the milk (approximately 1 cup) to form a thick paste. Work the batter until it is smooth and free of lumps, and then whisk in the remaining milk.

Heat a nonstick or seasoned sauté pan or skillet over medium heat. Brush with butter and ladle in enough batter to make the size pancakes you want. You will need about

3 tablespoons of batter to make a 5-inch pancake. Cook for about 5 minutes, or until bubbles form on the surface and then break. Flip with a spatula and cook for a couple of minutes on the second side, or until browned on the second side. Serve right away. Cook the remaining batter in the same way.

VARIATIONS

Fold about 1/2 cup berries into the batter if you like. If it is your child's birthday, add about 1/3 miniature chocolate chips and 1 teaspoon vanilla extract to the batter. If you want to put a little tang in your pancakes, substitute sour cream or buttermilk for the milk and replace the baking powder with 1/2 teaspoon baking soda, added along with the dry ingredients.

Waffles

You can use pancake batter to make waffles, but they will be a little on the heavy side. For a better result, separate the eggs, beat the egg whites until stiff peaks form, and then fold the whites into the batter just before you cook it. Butter also makes waffles lighter and crispier.

MAKES EIGHT 8-INCH-SQUARE WAFFLES

> **2 cups flour**
> **1/2 teaspoon baking powder**
> **1/4 teaspoon salt**
> **11/2 cups milk**
> **8 tablespoons butter, melted**
> **4 eggs, separated**
> **Room-temperature or melted butter for cooking**

HOW TO MAKE WAFFLES

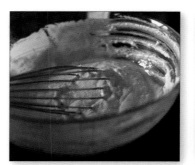 

1. Combine the dry ingredients. Mix milk, butter, and egg yolks. Whisk wet ingredients into dry ingredients.

2. Beat the whites to stiff peaks. Fold the egg whites into the batter.

In a bowl, stir together the flour, baking powder, and salt until well combined. If the baking powder is lumpy, crush the lumps with your fingers. If you think lumps may have gotten through, work the mixture through a fine-mesh strainer. Whisk in 1 cup of the milk, the 8 tablespoons of butter, and the egg yolks. Work the batter until it is smooth and free of lumps, and then whisk in the remaining 1/2 cup milk.

In a separate bowl, using an electric mixer or a whisk, beat the egg whites until stiff peaks form. Using a large rubber spatula, fold the egg whites into the batter just until combined. Preheat a nonstick waffle iron according to the manufacturer's directions. Brush the grid with the room-temperature butter; it should sizzle immediately. Ladle in the batter, spreading it to the edges. Close the waffle iron and cook according to the manufacturer's directions, or until crisp and browned. Serve right away. Cook the remaining batter in the same way. Sprinkle the waffles with confectioners' sugar, or serve with maple syrup, butter, or jam.

STAGES OF WHIPPED EGG WHITES

Soft peaks

Medium peaks

Stiff peaks

BREADS

Beware of bread making. During the winter months it will be especially hard to resist some therapeutic kneading, and a loaf in the oven makes every home seem more snug. But if you like to experiment, you may find yourself trying artisanal breads made with tricky natural starters. In short order, matters can get out of hand and you'll find yourself spending more time making bread than you had imagined.

Most bread is a mixture of water, flour, salt, and yeast. Some bread has oil, butter, eggs, or milk added, or sometimes bits of other ingredients, such as olives or prosciutto, but the essential elements are invariably the same. The process used to transform these ingredients into a variety of different types of breads varies little from recipe to recipe as well. Virtually all bread is made by kneading together flour, water, salt, and yeast to form a supple dough, letting the dough rise until doubled or so, and then punching down the dough, shaping it, letting it rise again, and finally baking it. But the same recipe seldom yields the same result every time. Fortunately, the baker seldom screws up so badly that the bread is inedible. Usually, the worst that happens is that your loaf turns out looking a little funny.

While the simplest way to make bread calls for combining all the ingredients and letting the dough rise, many home bakers like to do as professional bakers do and ferment a small portion of the flour with some or all of the liquid and all of the yeast, separately, in what is called a sponge, and then combine the sponge with the rest of the dough ingredients and let the whole batch rise. Dough that is fermented in this way develops a better flavor and has a crispier crust. You can control the rising time of the sponge by altering the amount of yeast it contains and the temperature at which it rises: the less yeast and the lower the temperature, the slower the rise and the better the flavor.

Yeast and bacteria are highly sensitive to temperature. Yeast is active between just above freezing (albeit barely) and 130°F. Bread that is allowed to rise slowly, in a relatively cool environment—even the refrigerator—will develop better flavor. If the temperature is too high—above 80°F—the dough will ferment very quickly and may develop off-flavors and odors.

Professional bakers have the advantage of having ovens that produce steam during baking. Steam keeps the surface of a loaf moist, so that a crust doesn't form right away and prevent the bread from rising. Some manufacturers are now making ovens for home cooks that produce steam, but in the absence of that kind of luxury, you can put a sheet pan filled with water to a depth of about $1/2$ inch on the lower rack or floor of the oven and then preheat the oven. You can also crack open the oven door once or twice during the first 10 minutes of baking—and often just during the first minute—and using a clean plastic spray bottle, quickly spray the oven walls with water.

Yeast Amounts and Approximate Rising Times for Straight Dough Method

FIRST RISE	YEAST	WATER TEMPERATURE	SECOND RISE
About 24 hours	1/64 teaspoon yeast per cup of flour	Cold water (soften yeast in warm water)	4 hours at room temperature, remaining time in the refrigerator
About 12 hours	1/64 teaspoon yeast per cup of flour	Warm water	Rise at room temperature
About 7 hours	1/16 teaspoon yeast per cup of flour	Warm water	Rise at room temperature
4 to 6 hours	1/4 teaspoon yeast per cup of flour	Room temperature water	Rise at room temperature
4 to 6 hours	1/2 teaspoon yeast per cup of flour	Room temperature water	Rise for 30 minutes at room temperature, remaining time in the refrigerator
1 1/2 to 2 hours	1/2 teaspoon yeast per cup of flour	Warm water	Rise at room temperature

Working with Small Amounts of Yeast

When a recipe calls for a small amount of yeast, say 1/64 teaspoon, it becomes impossible to measure. To work around this problem, knead 1/4 teaspoon of yeast with 1/2 cup flour and 1 tablespoon water, or more as needed, to form a dough. Then take this dough and cut it into quarters (so each quarter now contains 1/16 teaspoon yeast) and then each of these quarters can be halved (to 1/32 teaspoon yeast) or quartered to yield 1/64 teaspoon.

How to Know When Dough Has Been Kneaded Enough

There two ways to tell when dough has been kneaded well. The first is the so-called baby's bottom test, which refers to how the surface of a neatly formed ball of dough should feel. The second is the windowpane test, which is done by positioning the thumb and index finger of each hand a few inches apart and pulling upward and outward to stretch the dough as thinly as possible. If the dough has been sufficiently kneaded, the sheet will be nearly translucent.

How to Know When Bread Is Done

Professional bakers are able to give a quick tap to a hot loaf and immediately know whether it is done or not (it should emit a hollow sound). The rest of us may judge by how much the bread has risen or by the color of the loaf, but both of these methods can be deceiving. An easy and accurate method is to insert an instant-read thermometer through the bottom of the loaf into its center; it should register 205°F when it is done.

Paddle or Dough Hook

Most recipes for bread recommend using the dough hook attachment for the mixer, but when there is too little dough, the hook doesn't grasp enough of the dough at a time and the dough just sits on the bottom of the bowl. In cases like these, it's best to start with the paddle and then when the dough comes together, switch to the dough hook. The main disadvantage to the paddle is that using it to mix and knead a dough can strain the mixer's motor; the main disadvantage to the dough hook is that the dough may just flop around and fail to really get kneaded.

Steps of Bread Making

Mixing: The ingredients are loosely mixed, covered with plastic wrap, and allowed to rest for 20 minutes or so to give the liquid, usually water, time to penetrate the flour. If you are in a rush, you can skip this resting step. In many situations, this mixing is done with a portion of the flour to make what's called a "sponge."

Kneading: The dough is worked to activate the gluten—the protein in the flour—which traps the carbon dioxide released by the yeast and causes the bread to rise. When kneading by hand, knead until the dough pulls away from your hands and the work surface. When kneading in a mixer, use the paddle or dough hook, and knead until the dough pulls away from the bowl and collects on the paddle or dough hook. For large amounts of dough, use the dough hook.

Everyone has their favorite style of kneading dough by hand, but the essential thing to remember is to keep the dough in motion by continually pushing it away and folding it over itself toward you. Try pushing it away from you with the heel of your hand and then folding it over itself toward you before pushing it away again.

First rise (fermentation): The dough is covered with plastic wrap or a damp towel to prevent a crust from forming and allowed to rise. The cooler the rising environment, the slower the dough will rise and the more flavor the bread will develop. For this reason, bakers sometimes "retard" the dough.

Retarding: Some bakers let bread dough rest for a period, sometimes overnight, in the refrigerator. This helps the dough develop flavor and also creates greater flexibility in the baking schedule. In other words, you can make the dough, let it rise overnight in the refrigerator, and then bake it when you have time the following day.

Punching down: When the dough has at least doubled in volume, it is pressed, or literally punched, to force out the carbon dioxide and to rearrange the yeast within the dough so that it is in contact with more nutrients.

Dividing: If you have made enough dough to yield more than a single loaf, now is when you divide the dough into portions.

Shaping: The dough or each portion of dough is shaped.

Proofing (second rise): The shaped dough is allowed to rise a second time, with the timing depending on temperature, the amount of dough, and the shape of the dough.

Baking: The shaped dough is baked. Ideally, steam is introduced in the oven to help prevent a crust from forming on the bread too soon, which can keep it from rising.

Cooling: The bread is usually allowed to cool on a rack, so air circulates around the loaf as it cools.

Basic White Bread

This bread is made in the most direct way: the ingredients, including the yeast, are simply combined and the dough is allowed to rise. The way to vary the flavor and texture when using this so-called straight dough method is to use different amounts of yeast added at the beginning. It may take some experimentation to get both the dough and the finished bread to follow your schedule, but ideally give the dough as slow a rise as you can accommodate.

MAKES ONE 9-BY-5-INCH (8-CUP) LOAF, 2 BAGUETTES,
1 LARGE ROUND LOAF (BOULE), 1 BÂTARD, OR 10 ROLLS

- 3 cups flour
- 1 cup plus 2 tablespoons barely warm or cold water, depending on desired rising time
- $1/4$ teaspoon active dry yeast, softened in 1 tablespoon barely warm water for 3 minutes
- 1 teaspoon salt

Review the steps for bread making on page 401 before beginning. Combine the flour, water, and yeast in a bowl if you are mixing the dough by hand or in the mixing bowl if you are using a stand mixer, or in a food processor (see the specific directions for combining the ingredients by each method, below). For the fastest rise, use the maximum amount of yeast, warm water, and let the dough rise in a warm place. For a slower rise, use cold water—add the yeast only after first mixing the flour and water or the cold water, will kill it—and let the dough rise in a cool place and/or retard it in the refrigerator.

To mix and knead by hand: Mix and knead for 3 minutes and let rest, covered with a bowl or plastic wrap, for 20 minutes. Sprinkle the salt over the dough and knead for 10 to 15 minutes, or until the dough is smooth and passes the windowpane test (see page 401).

To mix and knead in a stand mixer: Fit the mixer with the paddle or dough hook and mix on low speed (no. 2 on a Kitchen-Aid) for 2 minutes to moisten the flour. Cover the bowl with a damp towel or with plastic wrap and let rest for 20 minutes. Sprinkle the salt over the dough and mix for 3 minutes on low speed, or until well combined. Increase the speed to medium (or to the minimum speed required to get the dough to slap against the inside of the bowl) and knead for about 7 minutes, or until the dough is smooth and passes the windowpane test (see page 401).

To mix and knead in a food processor: Put the flour in the food processor bowl and pour over room-temperature water. Sprinkle over the yeast and let stand for 3 minutes, or until the yeast softens. Turn the processor on for 10 seconds to moisten the flour. Remove the top of the food processor bowl and cover tightly with plastic wrap, sealing the surface of the dough; let rest for 20 minutes. Remove the wrap, add the salt, and process for 30 seconds. Touch the dough. If it feels very warm, put the food processor bowl in the freezer for 15 minutes. If the dough feels cool, let it rest at room temperature for 5 minutes. Process the dough for 30 seconds longer. At this point, the dough may have formed little pellets. These are fine. Let the dough rest for 5 minutes longer and then process again for 30 seconds. You will notice that the dough will come together in a single smooth mass when you lift it out of the processor. Knead it for a few seconds on the work surface (you do not need to flour the surface).

For the first rise: Cover the dough and let rise at warm room temperature for 4 to 6 hours or until doubled in volume.

If making a standard loaf, oil a 9-by-5-inch loaf pan; if making a boule, batard, or baguettes, oil a sheet pan; if making rolls, oil a 9-inch cake pan. Punch down the dough, shape as you wish (see right) and place in the prepared pan. Cover with plastic wrap and let rise at room temperature for about 2 hours, or until doubled in volume.

Preheat the oven to 425°F. Place a sheet pan on the floor or the bottom rack of the oven and heat for 5 minutes. Slide the loaf into the oven and pour in enough hot water to just cover the sheet pan. Immediately spray the oven walls with water and quickly close the oven door. Wait for 30 seconds, spray again, and again quickly close the oven door. Bake for 50 minutes, or until the loaf sounds hollow when tapped. Turn out onto a cooling rack.

1. Press the dough into a rectangle.

2. Fold the right side of the rectangle into the center.

3. Fold the other side over.

4. With the flap facing you, roll the top of the dough toward you to form a cylinder.

5. Press down along the front of the cylinder to firm it up.

6. Roll on the cylinder to elongate it.

7. Fold down the ends of the cylinder.

8. Place the dough in an oiled loaf pan.

9. Cover with plastic wrap and let rise until slightly above the rim of the pan.

1. First, begin to stretch the dough mass into an oblong shape.

2. Form the dough into a baguette by shaping it into a sausage.

3. Fold the sides in toward the middle and press down.

4. Arrange the loaves on nonstick sheet pans, cover with oiled plastic wrap, and let rise.

5. Just before baking, make 2 or 3 diagonal slashes across the top of each loaf.

HOW TO SHAPE ROLLS

1. Force the dough into a cylindrical shape by folding the top down over the rest of the dough as though making a baguette (above).

2. Continue rolling the cylinder until it has the shape of a large baguette.

3. Use a knife or bench scraper to cut the dough into slices.

4. Roll each slice in your hands to form a ball.

5. Pull the dough down the sides of the ball and pinch it at the bottom to form a tight ball.

6. Cover the rolls with plastic wrap and let rise in a warm place.

HOW TO SHAPE A BOULE (LARGE ROUND)

1. Flatten the dough out into a disk.

2. Pull the edges of the disk into the center and press them together.

3. Turn the dough over and press around the dough with the flats of your hands until it is smooth on top.

4. Form the dough into a ball shape.

5. Cover with plastic wrap and let rise.

HOW TO SHAPE A BÂTARD

1. Use your fingertips to press the dough into a rectangle that runs horizontally in front of you.

2. Fold the top of the triangle down from both ends so a triangle forms in the middle.

3. Roll the dough toward you to form a cylinder.

4. Cover the batard with plastic wrap and let rise.

5. The bread is ready when it has increased in size by about 50 percent.

6. Make three slashes across the bread and bake.

White Sandwich Bread

In an effort to get the most flavor from flour in the shortest time, bakers often use what is known as a sponge, which is what is used for this bread. A sponge contains part of the flour called for in the recipe and may contain all or most of the liquid and some or all of the yeast. Because this bread is meant for sandwiches, milk is added, which makes the crust softer and easier to bite through.

MAKES ONE 9-BY-5-INCH LOAF

> **3 cups flour**
> **1/2 cup barely warm water**
> **2/3 cup milk, barely warmed**
> **1 teaspoon sugar**
> **1/2 teaspoon active dry yeast**
> **11/2 teaspoons salt**

Review the steps for bread making on page 401 before beginning. To make the sponge, put 1 cup of the flour in a bowl and pour the warm water and milk over it. Whisk in the sugar until combined and then sprinkle the yeast over the top. Wait for about 3 minutes for the yeast to soften, and then stir again until the mixture has the consistency of a thick batter. Cover the bowl with plastic wrap and let rise for about 3 hours, or until doubled or even tripled in volume.

Add the remaining 2 cups of flour and the salt to the sponge in a bowl if you are mixing the dough by hand or in the mixing bowl of a stand mixer.

Knead for 3 minutes by hand or in a stand mixer with a dough hook, until there is no loose flour and the dough pulls away from the work surface or sides of the bowl. Cover with plastic wrap, and let rest for 20 minutes. Knead the dough for about 7 minutes more, or until smooth.

For the first rise: Cover the dough and let rise until doubled in volume, at warm room temperature for the fastest rise or overnight in the refrigerator for the slowest rise.

For proofing: Punch down the dough, shape it into a pullman loaf (see page 403), and put it in an oiled 9-by-5-inch loaf pan. Cover and let rise for about 2 hours, or until doubled in volume.

Preheat the oven to 400°F. Bake the loaf for about 40 minutes, or until nicely risen and golden brown and an instant-read thermometer inserted into the bottom of the loaf registers 205°F. Turn out onto a cooling rack.

USING A SPONGE TO MAKE BREAD DOUGH

1. The ready-to-use sponge.

2. Combine the flour and salt with the sponge (shown here, mixed on work surface).

3. Knead the dough until there is no loose flour.

4. Pile the dough in a mound, cover with plastic wrap, and let rest.

5. Knead the dough until it pulls away from the work surface.

6. Cover dough and let rise until doubled.

7. Punch down risen dough and shape into pullman loaf (see page 403).

Baguettes

Much is made about baguettes, the long, thin loaves that typify Paris and all things French. Nowadays, most baguettes are light, with flaky crusts and not a whole lot of flavor. Old-fashioned baguettes are smaller, denser, and have thicker crusts and a delicate flavor sometimes reminiscent of hazelnuts ("sometimes" because each bakery's baguette has its own flavor nuances). To make a modern baguette, use a simple bread dough made with yeast, such as Basic White Bread (see page 402). For an old-fashioned baguette, use a starter (White Sandwich Bread made with a sponge starter, opposite). Make your baguettes small (see pages 404–405) because most ovens aren't large enough to accommodate traditional-length baguettes, unless you bake them one at a time and set them diagonally in the oven.

Ciabatta

Ciabatta is a slipper, flat and full of holes. To get the holes, the dough has to be very wet and must rise very slowly. Because it is so wet, it will run off the sides of a sheet pan, so it is best to bake ciabatta in a square or round cake pan or similar pan. While a little unorthodox, this method makes beautiful bread.

You start this recipe by making a very wet sponge that triples in volume before it is combined with the rest of the ingredients. The dough is too wet to knead in a food processor and is hard to knead by hand because it is sticky, so a stand mixer is the ideal tool.

MAKES ONE 1¹/₄-POUND LOAF (8 CUPS)

- 3 cups flour
- 1 cup plus 6 tablespoons barely warm water
- ¹/₄ teaspoon active dry yeast, softened in 1 teaspoon barely warm water
- ¹/₄ cup extra virgin olive oil
- ³/₄ teaspoon salt

Review the steps for bread making on page 401 before beginning. To make the sponge, put ³/₄ cup of the flour, ¹/₂ cup of the warm water, and the yeast mixture in a bowl and whisk until the consistency of a thick batter. Cover the bowl with plastic wrap and let rise for about 4 hours, or until doubled or even tripled in volume.

To mix and knead the dough, combine the sponge, the remaining 2¹/₄ cups flour, and the oil, in the bowl of a stand mixer fitted with the dough hook and mix on low speed for 2 minutes to moisten the flour. Cover the bowl with a damp towel or with plastic wrap and let rest for 20 minutes.

Sprinkle the salt over the dough and mix for 3 minutes on low speed, or until well combined. Increase the speed to medium (or to the minimum speed required to get the dough to slap against the inside of the bowl) and knead for about 10 minutes, or until the dough is smooth.

For the first rise, cover the dough and let rise for about 1¹/₂ hours at warm room temperature for the fastest rise or overnight in the refrigerator for the slowest rise, or until doubled in volume.

Because it is so wet, this dough is difficult to shape. Transfer the dough gently—don't punch it down—into a baking pan about 10 inches square. Cover with plastic wrap and let rise at room temperature for about 2 hours, or until about doubled in volume.

Preheat the oven to 450°F. Place a sheet pan on the floor or the bottom rack of the oven and heat for 5 minutes. Slide the loaf into the oven, and pour in enough hot water to just cover the sheet pan. Immediately spray the oven walls with water, and quickly close the oven door. Wait for 30 seconds, spray again, and again quickly close the oven door. Turn the oven down to 425°F and bake for about 35 minutes, or until the loaf sounds hollow when tapped or an instant-read thermometer inserted into the loaf registers 205°F. Let cool in the pan for 5 minutes and then turn out onto a rack to cool completely.

Sourdough Breads Made from a Natural Starter

Sourdough Breads Made from a Natural Starter

Most bread is made from a single strain, a clone, of yeast—the kind we buy at the supermarket—while artisanal breads are made from a natural starter that encourages the growth of bacteria and wild yeasts that live in the flour and in the environment. Bread made with a natural starter has a deeper flavor because it contains many strains of yeast. These strains are less aggressive than strains in commercial yeast, so they ferment more slowly and allow more time for the flavor to be extracted from the flour. During this slow fermentation, beneficial bacteria in the air or in the flour take up residence next to the yeasts and create the tangy flavor we recognize in sourdough bread. When the bread is finally fermented, the sourness is controlled by regulating the rising time—the shorter the rise, the less tangy the bread.

To make a natural starter, begin by combining a small amount of organic flour and water and let the mixture ferment for a day or so. You then add more flour and water, let ferment again, repeat, and so on for at least a week. By the end of the week you will have more starter than you know what to do with. Fortunately, flour is cheap, so you don't have to feel guilty about pouring excess starter down the sink. By starting with a small amount of flour and gradually increasing it, you select the yeast strains that are robust enough to live in the acids produced by the bacteria. By letting the starter tire out, but not die completely, before adding more flour, you are selecting yeasts that can live in the harsh conditions of a dying starter, filled with the waste products of their fellow residents (namely, alcohol).

To make a sourdough starter, wait until all activity dies down before adding flour. For a less sour starter, feed the yeast as soon as the starter froths up from the last addition. The starter can be kept indefinitely and can be slowed down in the refrigerator, so you are not feeding it for half of your life and relying on neighbors to take care of it while you are on vacation. After a week or so, your culture should be robust enough to make bread.

From Seed to Starter (the seed culture)

From Seed to Starter (the seed culture)

To make 2 cups seed culture, the foundation for a starter, follow this day-by-day plan:

Day one: Combine 1 teaspoon organic rye or whole-wheat flour and 2 teaspoons water in a small bowl, cover with plastic wrap, and leave at room temperature.

Day two: Often the starter does nothing for the first 24 hours but then suddenly froths up and is usually ready for the second feeding after 36 hours. When the starter has frothed up, stir in 1 tablespoon organic rye or whole-wheat flour and 2 tablespoons water. Re-cover with plastic wrap.

Day three: Stir in 2 tablespoons flour and 4 tablespoons water and re-cover with plastic wrap. You now have about 5 teaspoons seed culture.

Day four: Stir in 3 tablespoons flour—at this stage, and from now on it can be any flour and doesn't have to be organic rye or whole-wheat flour—and 3 tablespoons water. Re-cover with plastic wrap.

Day five: Stir in 6 tablespoons flour and 6 tablespoons water and re-cover again. You now have about 11 tablespoons seed culture.

How a Sourdough Starter Works

The reason that making a natural sourdough starter takes so long is because time is needed to develop a strain of yeast that can survive in the acidic environment produced by the bacteria. In essence, the yeast and bacteria need time to battle it out and coexist peacefully, at least until we bake them to death. This strain of yeast must also be vigorous enough to make your loaf rise. By repeatedly fermenting a small amount of flour and water and letting the yeasts tire themselves out, weaker strains are gradually eliminated, while more vital strains—the naturally selected ones—take over.

When you first mix flour, especially untreated organic flour, natural yeasts clinging to the grains of flour begin to transform starches and sugars into alcohol and carbon dioxide. At the same time, bacteria start fermenting the flour, but instead of producing alcohol, they produce lactic and acetic acids, which create the characteristic tang.

Day six and beyond: Stir $1/2$ cup water and $1/2$ cup any type of flour into the seed culture. At this stage, you will have almost 2 cups seed culture, which you can feed each day (or three times a week if you keep the culture in the refrigerator) by throwing away about half of the culture and stirring in 1 cup each flour and water.

A day before baking: When you anticipate making bread, begin by building the seed culture into a finished starter by adding flour and water. If your starter isn't as vigorous as you would like—it takes longer than 8 hours to double in volume—consider adding a small amount of yeast to the dough you are making (see the chart on page 400) to hurry things along. This recipe calls for 2 cups seed culture, so if you want to have some left over, feed it the day before without throwing any out.

Natural or Sourdough Starter

This is both the natural starter and the sourdough starter called for in the recipe that follows, depending on whether you feed the seed culture after it froths or before it almost dies.

MAKES SLIGHTLY MORE THAN 2 CUPS STARTER

$1^1/2$ cups flour
1 cup finished seed culture (opposite)
$1/2$ cup barely warm water
$1/4$ teaspoon active dry yeast, softened in 1 tablespoon barely warm water and 1 tablespoon flour (optional; to help expedite rising and attenuate sourness)

Put the flour in a bowl, pour the seed culture over it, and stir to combine. Pour the water over the mixture and stir to combine (mixed method only). Add the yeast mixture if you're using it and mix until all the flour is moistened. Using a stand mixer fitted with the paddle blade, knead for 2 minutes to moisten the flour further. Cover with plastic wrap and let rise at room temperature for about 6 hours, or until doubled in volume.

Sourdough Bread

When the starter is ready, it needs to be combined with more flour and water to make bread. This recipe yields about 2 pounds of dough.

MAKES 1 LARGE ROUND LOAF (BOULE) OR 2 OR 3 BAGUETTES

$2^1/4$ cups flour
1 cup barely warm water
Sourdough starter (left)
1 teaspoon salt

Review the steps for bread making on page 401 before beginning. Combine the flour, water, starter, and salt in a bowl if you are mixing the dough by hand or in the mixing bowl if you are using a stand mixer.

To mix and knead by hand: Mix the ingredients until the dough comes together. Knead for 7 minutes and let rest, covered with plastic wrap, for 20 minutes. Knead for 12 minutes, or until the dough is smooth and passes the windowpane test (see page 401).

To mix and knead in a stand mixer: Fit the mixer with the dough hook and mix on low speed for 2 minutes to moisten the flour. Cover the bowl with a damp towel or with plastic wrap and let rest for 20 minutes. Sprinkle the salt over the dough and mix for 3 minutes on low speed, or until well combined. Increase the speed to medium (or to the minimum speed required to get the dough to slap against the inside of the bowl) and knead for about 7 minutes, or until the dough is smooth and passes the windowpane test (see page 401).

Cover the dough with plastic wrap and let rise at room temperature for about 6 hours (the timing depends on the strength of your starter), or until doubled in volume. At this point, the dough is ready to be punched down and shaped into 1 large round loaf or 2 or 3 baguettes as shown on pages 404-405, which are then covered with a clean kitchen towel and set aside for approximately $1^1/2$ hours or until puffed and risen.

Preheat the oven to 425°F. Place a sheet pan on the floor or the bottom rack of the oven and heat for 5 minutes. Slide the loaf into the oven and pour in enough hot water to just cover the sheet pan. Immediately spray the oven walls with water and quickly close the oven door. Wait for 30 seconds, spray again, and again quickly close the oven door. Bake for 50 minutes, or until the loaf sounds hollow when tapped. Turn out onto a cooling rack.

Rye Bread

There are many ways to make rye bread. Every recipe seems to contain varying proportions of medium or pumpernickel (dark rye) flour and bread flour. Like most other bread recipes, rye bread can be made with a wet (sponge) or dry starter or with a sourdough starter. But however you approach it, rye bread made with authentic rye flour and given a slow rise will have more flavor than anything you are likely to have tasted. One tip: Leave out the caraway seeds, unless you just can't resist them. They dominate the flavor of the bread so much that most of us have to come to think of the flavor of rye bread and caraway as synonymous.

This recipe has a deep rye flavor and is designed to conform to your schedule and enthusiasm. The quickest and easiest approach—doable in an afternoon—is to make a sponge out of some of the flour, water, and yeast and let it and, eventually, the bread rise at room temperature. The middle road is the same, except that the risings are colder and slower—doable over 2 days—and the tastiest method uses a sourdough starter.

MAKES 1 LARGE ROUND LOAF (BOULE)

> 1¼ cups medium rye flour
>
> ¾ cup bread flour
>
> ¾ cup barely warm water
>
> ½ teaspoon salt
>
> 1 cup starter (see page 409) or ½ teaspoon active
>   dry yeast

Review the steps for bread making on page 401 before beginning. Combine both flours, the water, the salt, and the starter in a bowl if you are mixing the dough by hand or in the mixer bowl if you are using a stand mixer.

To knead by hand: Mix the ingredients until the dough comes together. Knead for 7 minutes and let rest, covered with plastic wrap, for 20 minutes. Then knead for about 8 minutes, or until the dough is smooth and passes the windowpane test (see page 401).

To mix and knead in a stand mixer: Fit the mixer with the dough hook and mix on low speed for 2 minutes to moisten the flour. Cover the bowl with a damp towel or with plastic wrap and let rest for 20 minutes. Then mix for 3 minutes on low speed, or until well combined. Increase the speed to medium (or to the minimum speed required to get the dough to slap against the inside of the bowl) and knead for about 8 minutes, or until the dough is smooth and passes the windowpane test (see page 401).

Cover with plastic wrap and let rise at room temperature for about 2 hours (the timing depends on the strength of your starter), or until doubled in volume.

Punch down the dough, shape into a round loaf (see page 44–45), place in a pan, cover with plastic wrap, and let rise at room temperature for about 1½ hours, or until doubled in volume.

Preheat the oven to 450°F. Place a sheet pan on the floor or the bottom rack of the oven and heat for 5 minutes. Slide the loaf or loaves into the oven and pour in enough hot water to just cover the sheet pan. Immediately spray the oven walls with water and quickly close the oven door. Wait for 30 seconds, spray again, and again quickly close the oven door. Turn down the oven to 350°F, and bake for about 45 minutes, or until nicely risen and golden brown and an instant-read thermometer inserted into the bottom of the loaf registers 205°F. Let cool on a rack.

Controlling Sourness

When using a natural starter to make bread (such bread is often called "levain" bread or "pain levain"), you can control the sourness by varying when you add fresh flour to the starter. If you add fresh flour as soon as the starter froths, the bread will be less sour. Conversely, if you wait until the starter almost dies before adding fresh flour, you will favor the growth of bacteria and the yeasts that thrive in an acidic environment, which will make your starter and your bread more sour.

Sourdough Whole-Wheat Bread

Buy whole-wheat flour where the stock turns over often—a popular health-foods store perhaps—so the flour is fresh. Because whole-wheat flour contains the germ, which is oily, it turns rancid quickly.

MAKES 1 LARGE ROUND LOAF (BOULE)

1¼ cups whole-wheat flour

¾ cup bread flour

¾ cup barely warm water

2 cups Sourdough Starter (see page 400)

½ teaspoon salt

Review the steps for bread making on page 401 before beginning. Combine both flours, the warm water, and the starter in a bowl if you are mixing the dough by hand or in the mixing bowl if you are using a stand mixer.

To mix and knead by hand: Mix the ingredients until the dough comes together. Knead for 7 minutes and let rest, covered with plastic wrap, for 20 minutes. Sprinkle the salt over the dough and knead for 8 minutes, or until the dough is smooth and passes the windowpane test (page 401).

To mix and knead in a stand mixer: Fit the mixer with the dough hook and mix on low speed (no. 2 on a KitchenAid) for 2 minutes to moisten the flour. Cover the bowl with a damp towel or with plastic wrap and let rest for 20 minutes. Sprinkle the salt over the dough and mix for 3 minutes on low speed, or until the dough pulls away from the sides of the bowl. Increase the speed to medium (or to the minimum speed required to get the dough to slap against the inside of the bowl) and knead for about 12 minutes, or until the dough is smooth and passes the windowpane test (see page 401).

Cover with plastic wrap and let rise at room temperature for about 6 hours or in the refrigerator for about 15 hours, or until doubled in volume. Punch down the dough and shape into 1 large round loaf (see page 405) and place on a sheet pan. Cover with plastic wrap and let rise at room temperature for 2 hours, or until doubled in volume. Slash the loaf with a razor blade (see page 405) to create vents for the bread as it bakes.

Preheat the oven to 500°F. Place a sheet pan on the floor or the bottom rack of the oven and heat for 5 minutes. Slide the loaf into the oven and pour in enough hot water to just cover the sheet pan. Immediately spray the oven walls with water and close the oven door. Wait for 30 seconds, spray again, and close the oven door. Turn the oven down to 425°F and bake for about 45 minutes, or until nicely risen and golden brown and an instant-read thermometer inserted into the bottom of the loaf registers 205°F. Let cool on a rack.

Pumpernickel Bread

Pumpernickel flour, sometimes labeled dark rye flour, is a coarse, especially dark, flavorful form of rye flour. To make a pumpernickel loaf, follow the directions for rye bread (opposite), but substitute pumpernickel flour for the rye flour. Pumpernickel bread is best made with a natural starter, but you can also make it with yeast. Use a stand mixer for this dough. It is quite sticky and unpleasant to make by hand.

MAKES TWO 1-POUND LOAVES OR TWO 1½-POUND LOAVES

2 cups pumpernickel flour

1 cup all-purpose flour

1 cup plus 2 tablespoons warm water

1¼ teaspoons salt

1 cup Sourdough Starter (see page 409) or
   1 teaspoon active dry yeast, softened in
   2 teaspoons barely warm water

¼ cup unsweetened cocoa powder (optional)

Review the steps for bread making on page 401 before beginning. Combine both flours, the water, the salt, and the starter or yeast in the bowl of a stand mixer fitted with the paddle. If you like your pumpernickel bread very dark, add the cocoa powder as well. Mix on low speed (no. 2 on a KitchenAid) for 2 minutes to moisten the flour. Cover the bowl with a damp towel or with plastic wrap and let rest for 20 minutes. Then mix for 3 minutes on low speed, or until well combined. Increase the speed to medium (or to the minimum speed required to get the dough to slap against the inside of the bowl) and knead for about 8 minutes, or until the dough is smooth and passes the windowpane test (see page 401).

Cover with plastic wrap and let rise at room temperature for about 2 hours (the timing depends on the strength of your starter), or until doubled in volume.

Oil two 9-by-5-inch loaf pans or three 8½-by-4½-inch loaf pans. Punch down the dough and divide into 2 or 3 equal portions. Shape each portion into a rectangular loaf and place in the prepared pans. Cover with plastic wrap and let rise for 1 to 2 hours, or until increased by 50 percent.

Preheat the oven to 450°F. Place a sheet pan on the floor or the bottom rack of the oven and heat for 5 minutes. Slide the loaf into the oven and pour in enough hot water to just cover the sheet pan. Immediately spray the oven walls with water and quickly close the oven door. Wait for 30 seconds, spray again, and again quickly close the oven door. Bake for about 30 minutes, or until nicely risen and an instant-read thermometer inserted into the bottom of the loaf registers 205°F. Let cool on a rack.

Pizza Dough

This basic dough is made with a yeast or a starter. It contains olive oil, which provides flavor and makes the crust not quite as hard. The dough is quite sticky. If it is too difficult to manage, sprinkle a little extra flour over it, but avoid this if you can.

MAKES ENOUGH DOUGH FOR TWO 11-INCH PIZZAS

4 cups flour

1 cup room-temperature water if using yeast

$1/2$ teaspoon active dry yeast, softened in 2 tablespoons barely warm water or 2 cups starter (see page 409)

$1/2$ cup extra virgin olive oil

$3/4$ teaspoon salt

Review the steps for bread making on page 401 before beginning. Combine the flour, water (if using yeast), yeast or starter, and the oil in the bowl of a stand mixer. Fit the mixer with the dough hook and mix on low speed for 2 minutes to moisten the flour. Cover the bowl with a damp towel or with plastic wrap and let rest for 20 minutes. Sprinkle the salt over the dough and increase the speed to medium (or to the minimum speed required to get the dough to slap against the inside of the bowl). At this point, the dough should be moist, cling to the sides of the mixer, and be sticky but not actually stick to your finger. If it is too dry, add a little water; if it is too sticky, add flour a small handful at a time. Knead for about 7 minutes. During this time you should see (and hear) the dough slapping against the bowl. If it clings stubbornly to the dough hook, increase the speed of the mixer so the centrifugal force pulls the dough away from the attachment. You can also pull it off the hook once or twice to ensure it mixes evenly. The dough is ready when it is smooth.

Transfer the dough to a bowl and cover with plastic wrap. Let rise for about 4 hours at room temperature or 1 hour at room temperature and then overnight in the refrigerator, or until doubled in volume. Punch down and shape.

Shaping a Pizza Crust

Much of the trick to making a good pizza is shaping the dough into a large, thin round. While most of us are unable to send the dough twirling toward the ceiling, everyone can roll dough with a rolling pin or stretch it with fingers. The dough made here is dry enough to roll with a rolling pin, but if your dough is sticky, it is easier to press and stretch it into a round with your fingers, let the dough rest for 15 minutes, and then repeat the stretching until the dough covers the pizza pan. You can also alternate between stretching the dough and rolling it with a pin.

Pizza Margherita

In Italy, pizza margherita is on the menu in virtually every restaurant that serves pizza. It's simple and ubiquitous, and often the most satisfying pizza there is.

MAKES TWO 11-INCH PIZZAS

Pizza Dough (at left)

2 tablespoons extra virgin olive oil

4 tomatoes, sliced

$3/4$ pound fresh mozzarella cheese, sliced

6 large fresh basil leaves (optional)

Preheat the oven to 500°F. Brush two 11-inch pizza pans with half of the oil. Divide the dough in half and round each half into a ball. Shape each dough portion with your fingers, pressing and turning, until the dough is at least somewhat round, and about 11 inches in diameter, and then place each portion on a prepared pan. Put the pans in the refrigerator for 15 minutes.

Remove the pans from the refrigerator and shape the dough again on the work surface, either pressing it and stretching it with your fingers or using a rolling pin. You may have to press and stretch the dough 2 or 3 times, with a 15-minute rest between each attempt, to get it to cover the pans. Once it fills the pans, press up against the edges of the round from the inside to create a shallow rim around the crust.

Brush each round with 1 tablespoon of the oil. Top each crust with the tomato and then cheese slices, dividing them evenly.

Slide the pizzas into the oven and bake for about 15 minutes, or until the crusts are golden brown. Just before the pizzas are ready, stack the basil leaves, roll up lengthwise, and cut finely crosswise to create thin strips.

Remove the pizzas from the oven, sprinkle the basil evenly over each pizza, and serve immediately.

Pizza with Roquefort and Walnuts

American pizza joints—even "upscale" places—often fail with their version of this pizza because they use generic blue cheese. Be sure to use authentic Roquefort, Gorgonzola, or Stilton and your pizza will stand out.

MAKES TWO 11-INCH PIZZAS

> **Pizza Dough (opposite)**
> **2 tablespoons extra virgin olive oil**
> **6 ounces Roquefort, Stilton, or Gorgonzola cheese**
> **1 cup walnuts, coarsely chopped**

Preheat the oven to 500°F. Brush two 11-inch pizza pans with half of the oil. Divide the dough in half and round each half into a ball. Shape each dough portion with your fingers, pressing and turning, until the dough is at least somewhat round, and about 11 inches in diameter, and then place each portion on a prepared pan. Put the pans in the refrigerator for 15 minutes.

Remove the pans from the refrigerator and shape the dough again on the work surface, either pressing it and stretching it with your fingers or using a rolling pin. You may have to press and stretch the dough 2 or 3 times, with a 15-minute rest between each attempt, to get it to cover the pans. Once it fills the pans, press up against the edges of the round from the inside to create a shallow rim around the crust.

Brush each round with 1 tablespoon of the oil. Crumble the cheese over the pizzas, dividing it evenly. Sprinkle the walnuts evenly over the top.

Slide the pizzas into the oven and bake for about 15 minutes, or until the crusts are golden brown. Serve immediately.

HOW TO MAKE PIZZA WITH ROQUEFORT AND WALNUTS

1. Stretch and roll the dough on the work surface.

2. Set dough on an oiled pan. Again, press and stretch dough to cover pan.

3. Brush with olive oil.

4. Top with Roquefort and walnuts.

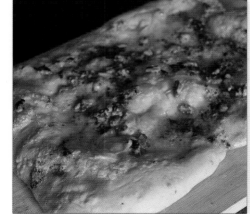

5. Bake until golden brown.

Focaccia with Morocccan Olives and Onions

Like pizza, focaccia takes well to all manner of improvisation. Some recipes call for mixing flavorful ingredients, such as olives and herbs, into the dough, while other versions, such as the one that follows, put the ingredients on top. Just about any topping you might use for a pizza will also work for focaccia.

The focaccia dough is made with leftover dough and a small amount of yeast for extra lift. If you are in a hurry, adjust the yeast upward as shown in the chart on page 400.

MAKES ONE 13-BY-17-INCH FOCACCIA

- 4 cups flour
- 1 cup water
- 1/2 teaspoon active dry yeast, softened in 1 tablespoon barely warm water for 3 minutes or 1 cup sourdough starter (see page 409), combined with 1/2 cup flour
- 1/2 cup plus 1 tablespoon extra virgin olive oil
- 1 cup leftover dough (optional)
- 3/4 teaspoon salt
- 2 pounds red or white onions, sliced paper-thin
- 1 cup pitted Moroccan or other flavorful black olives, halved

To mix and knead by hand: Mix all the ingredients, except the salt, onions, and olives, until the dough comes together. Let rest for 15 minutes. Knead in the salt and continue kneading for 7 minutes. Cover the bowl with a damp towel or with plastic wrap and let rise until doubled in volume.

To mix and knead in a stand mixer: Fit the mixer with the dough hook and mix all the ingredients, except the salt, onion, and olives, until the dough comes together. Let rest for 15 minutes. Knead in the salt and continue kneading for 7 minutes. Cover the bowl with a damp towel or with plastic wrap and let rise until doubled in volume.

In a heavy sauté pan, heat 3 tablespoons of the oil over medium heat. Add the onions and cook, stirring every couple of minutes, for about 30 minutes, or until the onions soften and turn pale brown. Remove from the heat, transfer to a bowl, and cover with plastic wrap. (Be sure to cover them or they will turn gray.)

Brush a 13-by-17-inch sheet pan with olive oil. Depending on the stickiness of the dough, you can either roll it on an oiled work surface or press it into shape in the pan. It should cover the bottom of the pan. You may have to work in 2 or 3 stages, letting the dough rest for about 10 minutes between each stage, before you can get it to cover the pan. Press up against the edges of the rectangle from the inside to create a shallow rim around the entire edge. Then press on the dough with your fingers to make dimples about 1/4 inch deep, spacing them about 1/2 inch apart. Cover with plastic wrap and let rest at room temperature for about 1 hour, or until at least doubled in volume.

Preheat the oven to 450°F. Spread the onions and olives over the dough, leaving a 1-inch border around the edge. Sprinkle the entire surface with the remaining oil. Don't press on the dough. Bake for about 25 minutes, or until the edges are golden brown. If the focaccia is browning unevenly, rotate the pan 180 degrees halfway through the baking. Let cool in the pan on a rack.

Pita Bread

The dough for pita bread is made in the same way as virtually all bread dough except that it is best to make by hand, rather than by mixer. Pita is unique in that it has a naturally formed pocket that can be used for fillings.

MAKES EIGHT 6-INCH ROUNDS

> **3 cups flour**
> **3/4 teaspoon salt**
> **2/3 cup barely warm water**
> **3/4 teaspoon active dry yeast**
> **6 tablespoons extra virgin olive oil, plus additional for bowl**

Review the steps for bread making on page 401 before beginning. In a bowl, stir together the flour and salt and pour over the water. Sprinkle the yeast over the water and let stand for 3 minutes, or until the yeast softens. Pour over the olive oil and mix with a wooden spoon.

Knead the mixture for about 7 minutes, or until it is smooth and passes the windowpane test (see page 401). Brush a bowl with oil and place the dough in it. Cover with plastic wrap and let the dough rise at room temperature for about 3 hours, or until tripled in volume.

Place a pizza stone on the bottom of the oven or a floured sheet pan on the middle rack of the oven and preheat the oven to 500°F. Punch down the dough and, using a bench scraper, divide it in half, then into quarters, and then divide each quarter into 2 pieces. Roll each piece into a ball between your palms. One at a time, roll out each ball into a 6-inch round. Because the dough is elastic, you may have to let the rounds rest once or twice before you they reach their full size and hold their shape.

Working quickly, so you don't let too much heat out of the oven, slide 2 dough rounds onto a floured sheet pan. Slide the pans onto the pizza stone and bake for about 10 minutes on the first side, or until puffed. Turn and bake on the second side for about 2 minutes, or until browned. Repeat with the remaining dough rounds. Cool the pita breads on a rack.

Bread Sticks

One of the great things about making bread sticks—known as grissini in Italy—is how little dough you need to make a lot of them. Any bread dough will do as long as it is stiff enough to hold its shape. The dough used here is flavored with olive oil and Parmigiano-Reggiano cheese.

MAKES ABOUT THIRTY-FOUR 12-INCH-LONG BREAD STICKS

> **3 cups flour**
> **1/2 teaspoon salt**
> **1/4 pound Parmigiano-Reggiano cheese, grated**
> **1 cup barely warm water**
> **3/4 teaspoon active dry yeast**
> **1/2 cup extra virgin olive oil, plus additional for bowl**

Review the steps for bread making on page 401 before beginning. Combine the flour, salt, and cheese in a bowl if you are mixing the dough by hand or in the mixer bowl if you are using a stand mixer. Pour over the water. Sprinkle the yeast over the water and let stand for 3 minutes, or until the yeast softens. Pour over the olive oil.

To mix and knead by hand: Mix the ingredients until the dough comes together, about 5 minutes, and let rest for 20 minutes. Knead the mixture for about 7 minutes, or until it is smooth and passes the windowpane test (see page 401).

To mix and knead in a stand mixer: Fit the mixer with the dough hook and mix on low speed for 2 minutes to moisten the flour. Let rest for 20 minutes. Knead the mixture for about 7 minutes, or until it is smooth and passes the windowpane test (see page 401).

Brush a bowl with oil and place the dough in it. Cover with plastic wrap and let the dough rise at room temperature for 4 to 6 hours, or until tripled in volume. (The rising time is slow because of both the salt and the salt in the cheese.)

Preheat the oven to 450°F. Punch down the dough and, using a bench scraper, divide it into fourths, and then divide each third into 6 pieces. Working with 1 piece at a time, place it on a floured work surface and, starting from the middle, roll outward with both hands until each piece is about 12 inches long. Arrange the sticks crosswise on floured sheet pans.

Bake for about 12 minutes, or until pale brown and crispy. Let cool on racks.

Brioche

Because brioche gets its character mostly from butter and eggs, it can be made directly, without a starter, and still have plenty of flavor. Most recipes for brioche start out the same— eggs are worked into the dough—but some call for as little as 20 percent butter to flour and others as much as equal amounts butter and flour. The usual axiom is the more butter the better, but if you are using the brioche for something that is already rich, such as French toast, use less butter. Because this dough contains a lot of liquid, it may seem like it needs more flour. Avoid using any more flour than necessary for shaping, and shape the dough when it is cold, so the cold butter will keep the dough firm.

MAKES ENOUGH FOR 1 BRIOCHE LOAF, 2 LARGE BRIOCHE TÊTES (BALLS), OR 8 SMALL BRIOCHES

- $1/3$ cup heavy cream, at room temperature
- $1/2$ teaspoon active dry yeast or 1 cup starter (see page 409)
- 4 eggs if using starter or 5 eggs if using yeast
- 1 egg yolk, or more if needed
- 3 cups flour
- $1/2$ teaspoon salt
- $1/2$ pound cold butter, cut into $1/2$-inch slices
- 1 egg, beaten, with 1 teaspoon salt, for egg wash

In a bowl, combine the cream and the yeast or the starter, let stand for yeast to soften, and set aside. In the bowl of a stand mixer, combine the eggs and the egg yolk, flour, and salt. Fit the mixer with the dough hook and mix on low speed for 3 minutes to moisten the flour. Increase the speed to medium and beat for 3 minutes, or until well combined. Add the cream mixture and mix for 1 minute longer. At this point, the dough should adhere to the hook and also to the sides of the bowl. If the dough is dry, add another egg yolk and beat for 1 minute more. Cover the bowl with a damp towel and let the dough rest for 15 minutes.

Knead the dough on medium speed for about 7 minutes, or until it no longer adheres to the sides of the bowl but instead gathers around the blade or hook. If the dough doesn't pull away from the sides, add a handful of flour and mix for 1 minute more. Add the butter and continue to mix on medium

HOW TO MAKE BRIOCHE DOUGH

1. Combine the flour and salt on a work surface, make a well in the center, and add the eggs to the well.

2. Gradually erode the flour from inside the well, mixing the ingredients to make the dough. Let rest for 20 minutes, and then knead until smooth.

3. Cover the kneaded dough and let rise until doubled in volume.

4. Uncover the dough.

5. Punch down the dough.

6. Soften butter with the heel of your hand.

7. Work the softened butter into the brioche dough.

1. Form balls by pulling down on the sides of a piece of brioche.

2. Place the larger of 2 balls in well-buttered brioche molds and make an impression with your finger.

3. Place small balls on the impression. Cover with plastic wrap and let rise.

4. Brush with egg wash.

speed for about 15 minutes, until the butter disappears and the dough no longer adheres to the sides of the bowl—it will have started to adhere to the sides again when you added the butter—but instead clumps around the dough hook.

Transfer the dough to a bowl, cover with plastic wrap, and let rise at room temperature for about 3 hours, or until increased in volume by 50 percent. Transfer the dough—leave it in the bowl and don't punch it down—to the refrigerator and let rise for 3 to 6 hours, or until double its original volume. This last cool rising helps to firm up the dough, making it easier to handle.

To make a brioche loaf, butter an 9-by-5-inch (8-cup) loaf pan. Using a bench scraper, divide the dough into 8 equal portions (each will weigh about 3 ounces) and roll each portion into a ball. Arrange the balls in the prepared pan in 2 rows of 4 balls each. Cover the loaf pan with oiled plastic wrap and let the balls rise at room temperature for about 2 hours, or until doubled in volume. They should rise up to the rim of the pan.

You can also use this dough to make 8 small brioche têtes (boules) or 2 large brioche têtes. To make small brioche têtes, brush eight 3½-inch (the diameter at the top) fluted brioche molds with room-temperature butter. Using a bench scraper, divide the dough into 8 equal portions (each will weigh about 3 ounces) and round each piece into a ball. Use the side of your hand to form the tête, or "head": Place the side of your hand two-thirds of the way from one end of the ball and roll while pressing gently down. Don't go all the way through the dough.

HOW TO SHAPE A BRIOCHE LOAF

Form brioche dough into 8 equal balls, and arrange them in 2 rows in a well-buttered loaf pan. Let rise until doubled in volume and bake.

Finished brioche loaf.

Place the ball with the smaller end up, in a prepared mold. Press around the small end—the tête—with your fingertips to make the tête poke above the rest of the dough. Repeat with the rest of the dough portions. Cover with plastic wrap and let rise at room temperature for about 2 hours, or until doubled in volume. Shape large brioche têtes the same way, using 6-inch molds and letting them rise the same amount of time.

Preheat the oven to 425°F. Brush the brioche(s) with the egg wash. Bake the single large loaf and large têtes for 1 hour and the small têtes for about 35 minutes, or until golden brown. Let cool in the molds for 5 minutes and turn onto a cooling rack.

Coffee Cake

A coffee cake is kind of a cross between cake and bread. The cake part contains butter, sugar, eggs, and flavorings, while the bread part contains the flour and yeast. Before baking, these two mixtures are combined. A third mixture, a streusel, tops the cake.

MAKES TWO 10-INCH SQUARE OR ROUND CAKES

Sponge

2 teaspoons active dry yeast

2 cups milk, barely warmed

1/2 cup flour

Batter

3/4 cup butter, at room temperature

1/4 cup granulated sugar

1/2 teaspoon salt

2 eggs

2 egg yolks

2 cups flour

2 cup raisins, soaked in just enough water to cover until plumped and then drained

2 teaspoons grated lemon or orange zest

1 teaspoon vanilla extract

Streusel

1 cup flour

2 cups firmly packed dark brown sugar

1/2 pound butter, melted

1/2 cup chopped walnuts

To make the sponge, in a small bowl, sprinkle the yeast over the milk and let soften for 3 minutes. Put the flour in another bowl, pour the yeast mixture over the flour, and whisk to combine. Cover with plastic wrap and let rise at room temperature for about 45 minutes, or until at least doubled in volume.

While the sponge is rising, make the batter. Using a stand mixer fitted with the paddle blade, or a bowl and a wooden spoon, cream together the butter, granulated sugar, and salt until smooth. Work in the eggs and the egg yolks one at a time, mixing well after each addition. Add the flour and mix for about 30 seconds in the mixer or 1 minute by hand, or just long enough to create a smooth mixture.

Add the sponge, raisins, lemon zest, and vanilla to the egg mixture and knead for about 3 minutes, or until smooth. Transfer to a bowl, cover with plastic wrap, and let rise at room temperature for 1 to 1 1/2 hours, or until increased in volume by about 50 percent.

To make the streusel, in a bowl, stir together the flour, brown sugar, melted butter, and walnuts until evenly moistened. Set aside.

Brush two 9-inch square baking pans or 10-inch round cake pans with rom-temperature butter.

Divide the dough in half and, using your hands or a rolling pin, shape each half to fit the pan. Set the dough in the prepared pans and cover evenly with the streusel topping. Let rise at room temperature for about 1 1/2 hours, or until increased in volume by about 50 percent.

Preheat the oven to 350°F. Bake the cakes for about 50 minutes, or until a toothpick inserted in the center comes out clean. Let cool in the pans on racks.

Cinnamon Rolls

Cinnamon rolls are made much like coffee cake, but instead of scattering streusel on top, the dough is rolled out into a rectangle, a filling is spread on it, and then the dough is rolled up and sliced.

MAKES 16 ROLLS

Dough

2 teaspoons active dry yeast

2 cups milk, barely warmed

6 cups flour

1/2 cup butter, melted

1/2 cup granulated sugar

1/2 teaspoon salt

2 eggs

1 egg yolk

1 teaspoon vanilla extract

1 tablespoon grated orange zest

1 teaspoon ground cinnamon

Filling

1/2 pound butter

1/2 teaspoon salt

1 1/2 cups firmly packed dark brown sugar

1 1/2 cups firmly packed light brown sugar

1/4 cup honey

1 egg, beaten, with a pinch of salt, for egg wash

To make the dough, first make a sponge. In a small bowl, sprinkle the yeast over the milk and let stand for 3 minutes, or until softened. Put 2 cups of the flour in another bowl, pour the yeast mixture over the flour, and stir to combine. Cover with plastic wrap and let rise at room temperature for about 30 minutes, or until increased in volume by about 50 percent.

In another bowl, stir together the melted butter, granulated sugar, and salt. If the butter is hot, let it cool until warm. Then whisk in the eggs, egg yolk, vanilla, orange zest, and cinnamon. Put the remaining 4 cups flour in the bowl of a stand mixer or other bowl large enough to hold all of the dough and add the sponge and the butter mixture. Stir until all of the ingredients are well combined. Fit the mixer with the dough hook and then knead the mixture for about 7 minutes, or until smooth. Or, knead by hand on a floured surface for about the same amount of time. Cover the dough with plastic wrap—or slip into a resealable plastic bag—and let rise at room temperature for about 2 hours or overnight in the refrigerator, or until increased in volume by about 50 percent.

To make the filling, in a heavy saucepan, combine the butter, salt, both brown sugars, and the honey over medium heat. Stir until the butter has melted and the mixture is bubbling. Turn down the heat to low and stir for 5 minutes, or until the mixture smells like butterscotch.

Oil a smooth work surface. To make the rolls, punch down the dough, place it on the oiled surface, and stretch and press it into a rectangle 16 by 18 inches. If the dough is very elastic and won't hold its shape, transfer it to a large sheet pan, cover it with plastic wrap, let it rest in the refrigerator for 15 minutes, and then try again. Using an offset spatula, spread the filling over the dough, leaving a 1/2-inch border around the edge. Starting from a long side, first pinch the border to help create a tight roll, and then roll up the dough into a tight cylinder. Using unflavored dental floss, cut the log into 1-inch-thick rounds by sliding a length of the floss under one end of the log and pulling the two ends together at the top at regular intervals.

Oil a large sheet pan or line it with a nonstick baking liner. Arrange the slices on the prepared pan, spacing them at least 2 inches apart to allow room for them to expand. (Or, you can leave them closer together so they merge during baking.) Cover with oiled plastic wrap and let rise at room temperature for about 30 minutes, or until slightly puffed.

Preheat the oven to 400°F. Brush the rolls gently with egg wash, slide them in the oven, and turn down the oven temperature to 350°F. Bake for about 35 minutes, or until golden brown. Cool slightly on racks and serve warm or at room temperature.

Sticky Buns

These popular buns are similar to cinnamon rolls, except the filling is simpler and the buns rest on a sweet nut mixture as they bake. After baking, the buns are turned out of the pan so the sticky nut mixture becomes the topping.

MAKES 16 SMALL BUNS

1/2 recipe Cinnamon Rolls Dough (opposite)

Filling
4 tablespoons butter, melted
3/4 cup walnuts, chopped

Topping
1/2 cup butter
1/2 cup firmly packed dark brown sugar
3/4 cup walnuts, coarsely chopped

Oil a smooth work surface. Punch down the dough, place it on the oiled surface, and stretch and press it into a rectangle 11 by 16 inches. If the dough is very elastic and won't hold its shape, cover it with plastic wrap, let it rest in the refrigerator for 15 minutes, and then try again.

For the filling, brush the dough with the butter and then sprinkle evenly with the nuts, leaving a 1-inch border uncovered around the perimeter. Starting from a long side, roll up the dough as tightly as you can into a cylinder. Wrap the roll in plastic wrap and chill for 30 minutes to make the dough easier to slice.

To make the topping, in a heavy saucepan, combine the butter, sugar, and nuts over medium heat. Stir until the butter has melted and the mixture is bubbling. Turn down the heat to low and stir for 5 minutes, or until the mixture smells like butterscotch. Immediately pour the mixture into a 9-inch square baking pan (making sure you use a metal pan, not a glass baking dish).

Remove the roll from the refrigerator and, using unflavored dental floss, cut the roll into 9 rounds each about 1 3/4 inches thick. Arrange the slices on the topping in 3 rows of 3 slices each. Cover with oiled plastic wrap and let rise at room temperature for about 1 hour, or until puffed and swollen.

Preheat the oven to 375°F. Place the baking pan on a sheet pan and slide it onto the center rack in the oven. Bake for 40 minutes, or until a toothpick inserted in the center comes out clean. Let cool in the pan on a rack for about 15 minutes, and then turn the buns out onto a large flat plate. Don't wait too long, or the topping will congeal and cause the buns to stick to the pan. Serve warm.

CAKES

It may seem that there is little logic to the enormous number of cake recipes, but in fact most cakes can be broken down into two basic types: butter cakes, which are made by emulsifying butter in various ways, and foam cakes, which are generally lighter and leavened by beaten eggs.

The most common butter cake is the pound cake, made by whipping butter with sugar, beating in eggs one at a time, and then working in flour just long enough to rid the batter of lumps. Butter cake recipes generally include some kind of chemical leavener, such as baking powder or baking soda, or sometimes call for separating eggs to incorporate air. Another kind of butter cake, called a dump cake or high-ratio cake, contains a high percentage of sugar to other ingredients (hence the name high-ratio) and is made by working sliced butter into flour until the butter breaks up into small pieces and then adding the liquid ingredients, which always include eggs, one-third at a time.

Foam cakes, such as sponge cake, are made by beating whole eggs with sugar and then folding in flour and melted butter, or by separating the eggs, beating the yolks and whites separately, each with sugar, and then folding them together while sifting in flour. The latter is also the batter used for ladyfingers.

Other cakes include angel food cake, which is essentially meringue with flour mixed in; chiffon cakes, which contain oil; and cheesecakes, which are really custards.

Cakes also come in various shapes, including the classic round layered cake and the rectangular sheet cake. European cakes tend to be shorter than American cakes and are often made by cutting a single cake into two layers and then stacking the layers. American cakes achieve their height by cutting two cakes into at least two layers each and then stacking

the layers. Most round cakes are baked in a classic cake pan, which is 9 inches across. The cake usually shrinks a little in the oven and ends up slightly less than 9 inches in diameter and about $1^1/_2$ inches high.

The amount of batter you need for a 9-inch round cake is the same amount you need for a $^1/_2$-inch-thick sheet cake baked in a classic 13-by-17-inch sheet pan, dubbed a half sheet pan by professional bakers. A sheet cake is easily cut into rectangles and the rectangles layered—a rectangular cake is a nice break from the usual round—or, if the cake is moist, it can be covered with frosting and rolled. If you want to make a sheet cake but don't want to layer it, double the amount of cake batter needed for a 9-inch round cake and your sheet cake will come out of the oven 1 inch thick. If you want to make a small round cake—small European-style cakes make an elegant impression—keep in mind that the amount of cake batter needed for one 9-inch cake pan is enough for two 6-inch round cake pans. You can cut these two cakes crosswise into layers and stack them high.

How to Layer a Cake

Most of us just wing it when it comes to layering and icing a cake, but there are a few tricks that make it easier to do a professional-looking job. You can construct it in a cake ring or springform pan and then unmold it, you can assemble it on a cardboard round that enables you to hold the cake at eye level, or you can use a revolving cake stand.

If you bake your cake in a springform pan, you can remove it once it has cooled, cut it into layers, and then stack the layers in the pan again, frosting each one as you add it to the stack. Use what was the bottom of the cake, which will have even edges and a flat surface, for the top layer. You then frost the top.

The sides are frosted when the cake is unmolded. Refrigerate the cake for an hour or so, and then run a thin knife between the cake and the sides of the pan before you release the clap and lift off the sides. Frost the sides.

If you are not using a mold, you can layer the cake on a revolving cake stand that allows you to rotate the cake as you spread the frosting on the sides and top. The stand makes applying the frosting evenly easier, especially on the sides. Or, you can cut a piece of stiff cardboard the size of your cake, and then layer the cake on the cardboard. You can then hold the cardboard round at eye level with one hand while applying the frosting with the other. If the cardboard is the same size as the cake or just slightly larger, nothing blocks the spatula as you apply frosting to the sides.

Guaranteeing a Moist Cake

To make your cake moist, even wet, generously brush each cake layer as you stack it with a light sugar syrup flavored with rum, Cognac, whiskey, kirsch, framboise (raspberry), poire Williams (pear), mirabelle (plum), or other fruit brandy. These brandies, which are made by distilling wines made from the different fruits, are dry and colorless yet full of fruit flavor. Don't confuse them with fruit-flavored brandies, which are grape brandies flavored with fruit and lots of sugar that tend to taste like cough syrup. The purpose of this method is not to make your cake reek of alcohol—very little spirit is used—but to moisten it. For a non-alcoholic option, use fruit juice instead of syrup flavored with spirrits. The moistening is so effective that you can use even stale cake and no one will know the difference. It means you can freeze cakes and break them out as you need them.

AMOUNTS OF FROSTING, GLAZE, AND SYRUP NEEDED FOR CAKES

Frosting for a 9-inch round layer cake: 1 to $1^1/_2$ cups frosting per layer and top; $2/_3$ cup frosting per inch of height (for the sides only). Total frosting for a 4-inch-tall cake: $6^2/_3$ to $8^2/_3$ cups

Glaze for a 9-inch round layer cake: After you have constructed your cake and coated the outside with frosting, you may want to glaze the cake with melted chocolate ganache (see page 438) or cover it with marzipan (see page 428). Brush any errant crumbs off the top and sides of the cake as best you can and refrigerate it for an hour before pouring over the glaze. Some bakers like to add the glaze in two steps, allowing the first covering to harden in the refrigerator, thus creating a smooth surface for the final glazing. You will need these amounts for a 4-layer, 4-inch-tall, 9-inch round cake: $3/_4$ cup glaze for the top (if applied in two stages of 6 tablespoons for each stage, half to seal the cake and half to finish it); $2/_3$ cup glaze per inch of height for the sides (if applied in two stages of $1/_3$ cup for each stage, half to seal the cake and half to finish it).

Syrup for a 9-inch round layer cake: Brushing cake layers with a light sugar syrup is more of a European tradition than an American one, but it will ensure that your cake is moist (see "Guaranteeing a Moist Cake," left). Usually $1/_4$ to $1/_3$ cup syrup is needed for each layer.

Frosting for a 13-by-17-inch sheet cake: 4 to 5 cups frosting makes a layer about $1/_4$ inch thick.

Glaze for a 13-by-17-inch sheet cake: $2^1/_2$ to 3 cups for the top (if applied in two stages of $1^1/_4$ to $1^1/_2$ cups for each stage, half to seal the cake and half to finish it.

Syrup for a 13-by-17-inch sheet cake: 2 cups.

Frosting, glaze, and syrup for a 3-layer rectangular cake made from a sheet cake: Use the same amounts as for an unstacked sheet cake (4 to 5 cups frosting, $2^1/_2$ to 3 cups glaze, and 2 cups syrup).

Classic Sponge Cake (Genoise)

This is one of the easiest foam cake recipes to remember because the steps are very simple. A stand mixer is almost essential for this making cake, because it takes about 30 minutes of beating by hand and almost 20 minutes with a handheld mixer to get the eggs to fluff up sufficiently. Make sure the eggs are warm—body temperature or so—before beating, or they will take twice as long to beat.

MAKES ONE 9-INCH CAKE

Room-temperature butter and cake flour for
   preparing pan

3 eggs in their shells, soaked in warm water
   to cover for 10 minutes

6 tablespoons sugar

1/2 cup plus 2 tablespoons cake flour

3 tablespoons butter, melted (optional)

Preheat the oven to 350°F. Brush a 9-inch round cake pan with butter. Put a small handful of flour in the pan, tap the pan while rotating it at all angles to coat the bottom and sides completely, and then tap out the excess. If you want to be certain the cake doesn't stick—this cake rarely does—butter the pan, cover the bottom with a round of parchment paper, butter the parchment, and then coat the sides of the pan and the parchment with flour, tapping out the excess.

Crack the eggs into the mixer bowl, add the sugar, and beat at high speed to the ribbon stage: when the beater is lifted, the mixture falls in a wide band onto the surface, forming a figure eight that stays for 5 seconds before dissolving. This will take about 4 minutes with a stand mixer and 20 minutes with a handheld mixer.

Transfer the egg mixture to a large bowl to make folding easier. Sift the flour over the egg mixture while folding it in with a rubber spatula. In a smaller bowl, fold together the melted butter and about one-fifth of the egg mixture, and then fold this mixture into the egg mixture. Transfer the batter to the prepared pan and gently smooth the top with an offset spatula.

Bake for about 25 minutes, or until the top springs back when pressed with a fingertip and a toothpick inserted in the center comes out clean. Let cake cool in the mold until cool enough to handle and then turn out onto a cake rack. Peel away the parchment and let cool completely.

Ladyfingers

Use a variation on Classic Sponge Cake batter to make ladyfingers for nibbling one at a time or for lining cakes and dessert terrines: Preheat the oven to 400°F. Line a sheet pan with floured and buttered parchment. Separate 3 room-temperature eggs. Beat the yolks with 1/4 cup sugar until pale. Beat the whites to stiff peaks (see page 397), add 1/4 cup sugar, and beat 2 minutes more. Fold together the two mixtures while sifting over 1/2 cup flour. Using a pasty bag, fitted with a 3/4-inch tip, pipe out rows of ladyfingers close enough to touch as they bake and expand—about 1/4 inch apart. Pipe rows the length of the terrine or the circumference of the cake you plan to line and wide enough to come up the sides. Sprinkle with confectioners sugar and bake for 12 minutes or until puffed and pale brown. Let cool before removing from the pan.

Sponge Cake for Rolling

If you are baking a cake in a sheet pan and rolling it up, it must be quite moist or it will crack.

To make a rolled cake, preheat the oven to 400°F. Brush a 13-by-17-inch sheet pan with room-temperature butter and then cover the bottom with a sheet of parchment paper. Brush the parchment with butter and then coat the parchment and the pan sides with flour, tapping out the excess. Assemble the ingredients for Classic Sponge Cake (left), but don't melt the butter, and add 1/4 cup heavy cream. Combine the butter with the cream in a small saucepan and heat just until the butter melts. Combine the butter-cream mixture with one-fifth of the egg mixture and proceed as directed in the genoise recipe at left to finish the batter. Transfer the batter to the prepared sheet pan, smoothing the top with an offset spatula. Bake for about 12 minutes, or until the top springs back when pressed with a fingertip and the edges pull in from the sides of the pan.

Dust a sheet of parchment paper slightly larger than the cake with confectioners' sugar, and turn the hot cake out onto it (the sugar will prevent it from sticking). Peel off the parchment from the bottom of the cake, and then place the removed parchment over the cake to keep it moist while it cools. As soon as the cake is cool—don't wait any longer or it may dry out and crack—cover it with filling and roll up jellyroll-style. Because of their thinness, rolled cakes are not brushed with syrup.

Individual Chocolate Fondant Cakes

These cakes, half cake and half soufflé, should be cakelike on the outside and melting in the middle and must be served as soon as they come out of the oven. The secret to success is to freeze the cakes once you put them in their ramekins. This gives the outside plenty of time to bake and keeps the center molten. Freezing is also convenient, because you can make these cakes days ahead of time and bake them at the last minute.

These cakes use the same principle as the Classic Sponge Cake on page 423—you will need a stand mixer to beat the eggs—except that a mixture of melted chocolate and butter is folded with the eggs just before baking.

MAKES 6 INDIVIDUAL CAKES

- 1 tablespoon room-temperature butter for preparing ramekins
- 1 tablespoon unsweetened cocoa powder, sifted, for preparing ramekins
- 1/2 cup butter
- 8 ounces bittersweet chocolate, coarsely chopped
- 4 eggs, soaked in warm water to cover for 10 minutes
- 1/3 cup granulated sugar
- 3 tablespoons flour
- Confectioners' sugar for dusting

Butter six 2/3- or 3/4-cup ramekins and then coat them with the cocoa powder.

Combine the 1/2 cup butter and chocolate in a heatproof bowl and set over a saucepan of simmering water. Stir with a rubber spatula until melted and smooth, and then immediately remove from the heat and set aside.

Crack the eggs into a bowl, add the granulated sugar, and beat at high speed to the ribbon stage: when the beater is lifted, the mixture falls in a wide band onto the surface, forming a figure eight that stays for 5 seconds before dissolving. This will take about 5 minutes with a stand mixer fitted with the whisk attachment and 20 minutes with a handheld mixer.

Pour the egg mixture over the chocolate mixture. Sift the flour over the combined mixtures while folding it in with a rubber spatula. Transfer the batter to the prepared molds, dividing it evenly. Cover with plastic wrap and freeze for at least 2 hours or up to several days.

Preheat the oven to 425°F. Arrange the ramekins on a sheet pan and bake for 17 to 20 minutes, or until they have risen by almost half. Dust the cakes with confectioners' sugar and serve immediately in the ramekins. Or, unmold the cakes onto individual plates, dust with confectioners' sugar, and serve immediately.

Angel Food Cake

If you are watching your fat intake, this is the ideal cake. It calls for no butter, and egg whites are the only leavening. Angel food cakes are traditionally baked in tube pans, which help them to bake evenly, and they are cooled upside down. Some pans have small "feet," so you can invert the pan and it will stand above the counter, eliminating the problem of trapped moisture as the cake cools. But if your pan doesn't, slipping the tube of the pan over the neck of a wine bottle works well, too.

MAKES ONE 10-INCH CAKE

- 15 egg whites (2 cups)
- 1 teaspoon cream of tartar, if not using a copper bowl
- 1 cup sugar
- 1 tablespoon fresh lemon juice
- 1 1/4 cups cake flour

Preheat the oven to 350°F. In a large bowl, combine the egg whites and cream of tartar. Beat on high speed for about 5 minutes with a stand mixer fitted with the whisk attachment or 12 minutes with a handheld mixer, or until medium peaks form (see page 397). Add the sugar in a slow, steady stream while continuing to beat for about 5 minutes longer with a stand mixer or 12 minutes longer with a handheld mixer, or until medium to stiff peaks form. Sprinkle the lemon juice over the whites, and then sift the flour over the whites while folding it in with a rubber spatula. Transfer the batter to an ungreased 10-inch tube pan.

Bake for 40 minutes, or until the top springs back when pressed with a fingertip and a toothpick inserted in the center comes out clean. Invert the tube pan onto the neck of a wine bottle or similar bottle to cool. Cooling the cake upside down helps loosen the sides and keeps the cake tall. After an hour, lift the pan off the bottle and roll it on its side once or twice. Then slide a knife along the inside of the pan sides and the tube to detach the cake.

Carrot Cake

Cakes like this carrot cake or banana bread are different than most cakes in that they call for oil, rather than butter. While the oil doesn't contribute much flavor, especially if you use vegetable oil, it does allow you to serve the cakes cold without them hardening, as they would if they were made with butter. Grate the carrot on the finest holes of a box grater that won't turn it to mush, or use the finest grater attachment on your food processor.

**MAKES ONE 9-BY-5-INCH OR
4¹/₂-BY-8¹/₂-INCH (1 QUART) LOAF CAKE**

Cake

Room-temperature butter and flour for preparing pan
²/₃ cup flour
¹/₂ cup granulated sugar
1 teaspoon baking soda
³/₄ teaspoon baking powder
1 teaspoon ground cinnamon
¹/₄ teaspoon ground cloves
¹/₄ teaspoon freshly grated nutmeg
¹/₄ teaspoon ground allspice
¹/₄ teaspoon salt
¹/₃ cup vegetable oil, hazelnut oil, or walnut oil
2 eggs
1 cup chopped walnuts
¹/₂ cup chopped, drained pineapple
1 cup finely grated carrot (from about 1 large carrot)

Cream Cheese Frosting

One 8-ounce package cream cheese
6 tablespoons butter
1 teaspoon vanilla extract
1³/₄ cups confectioners' sugar

Preheat the oven to 350°F. Butter a 9-by-5-inch or 4¹/₂-by-8¹/₂-inch loaf pan. Coat the pan with flour, tapping out the excess. In a bowl, whisk together the flour, granulated sugar, baking soda, baking powder, spices, and salt, and then sift them into a second bowl to make sure the spices are well combined. In a small bowl, whisk together the oil and eggs until blended, and then stir the egg mixture into the flour with a rubber spatula. Fold in the walnuts, pineapple, and grated carrot. Transfer the batter to the prepared pan and smooth the top with an offset spatula.

Bake for 50 minutes, or until a toothpick inserted in the center comes out clean. Let cool until easy to handle, and turn out onto a cake rack.

While the cake is cooling, make the frosting. In a bowl, combine the cream cheese, butter, vanilla, and confectioners' sugar. Using a stand mixer fitted with the paddle attachment or a handheld mixer, beat on medium speed until well combined and fluffy, about 10 minutes or until smooth. Spread the frosting on the top of the loaf.

Pound Cake

It took 20 tries to make this pound cake successfully without adding chemical leavening. The only aeration this cake gets is the air beaten into the butter at the beginning, so the secret to success is not to scrimp on this step. In other words, don't stop even when the butter looks fluffy and ready to go. If you do it correctly, the cake will still be dense, as pounds are by nature, but it will also be wonderfully buttery. A stand mixer is almost essential for making this cake successfully, but if you're using a handheld, count on 20 minutes of beating.

MAKES 1 LOAF CAKE

Room-temperature butter and flour for preparing pan
³/₄ pound cold butter, cut into ¹/₂-inch slices
1¹/₃ cups sugar
¹/₄ teaspoon salt
5 eggs
6 tablespoons milk
1 teaspoon vanilla extract
1¹/₂ cups flour

Preheat the oven to 350°F. Butter a 9-by-5-inch loaf pan. Line the bottom with parchment paper or waxed paper, and then flour the sides of the pan, tapping out the excess.

In a stand mixer fitted with the paddle attachment, combine the butter, sugar, and salt and beat on high speed for about 8 minutes, or until fluffy and well aerated. Don't be tempted to shorten the beating time, or your cake will be heavy. Stop and scrape down the sides of the bowl every minute or so with a rubber spatula.

In a separate bowl, combine the eggs, milk, and vanilla and beat by hand to combine well. Add the egg mixture to the butter mixture in a steady stream while beating on medium speed for about 2 minutes, or until the mixture has the consistency of sour cream or small-curd cottage cheese (the exact consistency depends on the temperature of the ingredients).

(continued)

Pound Cake, continued

Turn off the mixer and add all the flour. Turn the mixer on low speed and beat for only 5 seconds, or just long enough to mix in the flour with no leftover lumps. Stop, scrape down the sides of the bowl, and beat for 5 seconds longer. Scrape the batter into the loaf pan and smooth the top with an offset spatula.

Bake for about 1 hour and 15 minutes, or until a toothpick inserted in the center comes out clean. Let cool for 10 minutes and then turn out onto a cake rack and let cool completely. Slice and serve out of the pan, or run a knife around the edges of the cake and invert the pan to unmold onto a serving plate.

Classic American Butter Cake

This cake shares certain characteristics with pound cake—butter is beaten with sugar—but is leavened by separating the eggs and beating the whites and by using a small amount of baking powder. It is a great standby white cake with plenty of buttery flavor. Egg whites are ideally beaten in a copper bowl (copper chemically interacts with the protein in egg whites to create a particularly stable, satiny, high-volume foam). If you don't have such exotic accessories, just add a pinch of cream of tartar to the whites before beating.

MAKES ONE 9-INCH CAKE

Room-temperature butter and flour for preparing pan
1¼ cups cake flour
1¼ teaspoons baking powder
½ teaspoon salt
¾ cup butter, at room temperature
¾ cup plus 3 tablespoons sugar
3 eggs, separated
⅔ cup milk
1 teaspoon vanilla extract
Pinch of cream of tartar, if not using a copper bowl

Preheat the oven to 350°F. Butter a 9-inch springform pan. Coat the pan with flour, tapping out the excess.

In a bowl, sift together the flour, baking powder, and salt. In a separate bowl, beat the butter on high speed with a stand mixer fitted with the paddle attachment or a handheld mixer or with a wooden spoon until soft and fluffy. This will take about 10 minutes by mixer or 20 minutes by hand. Switch to the whisk attachment or a hand whisk and beat in ¾ cup of the sugar. Add the egg yolks one at a time, beating well after each addition until the mixture is smooth. Whisk in the milk, the vanilla, and then the flour mixture ½ cup at a time. Don't overwork the mixture. You want to stop whisking the moment you see no lumps of flour.

In a bowl, combine the egg whites and cream of tartar and beat on high speed for about 2 minutes with a stand mixer fitted with the whisk attachment or 5 minutes with a handheld mixer, or until soft peaks form. Add the remaining 3 tablespoons sugar and beat until medium peaks form. Whisk one-fourth of the beaten whites into the butter mixture to lighten it. Using a rubber spatula, fold in the remaining beaten whites just until combined. Transfer the batter to the prepared pan and smooth the top with an offset spatula.

Bake for about 40 minutes, or until the top springs back when pressed with a fingertip and a toothpick inserted in the center comes out clean. Let cool in the pan and then turn out onto a cake rack to cool completely.

1. Brush a springform pan with room-temperature butter. Put flour in the cake pan and rotate the pan to coat it with flour. Tap the pan on the surface to loosen any extra flour and turn it out of the pan.

2. Sift together the dry ingredients.

3. Beat together butter and sugar with the paddle attachment of a stand mixer. When the mixture softens, attach the whisk attachment and continue beating.

4. Separate eggs and beat the yolks, one by one, into the butter mixture. Whisk in milk and vanilla.

5. Quickly beat the flour mixture into the butter mixture, beating just until smooth.

6. Beat egg whites to soft peaks. Beat sugar into the egg whites and beat until medium peaks form.

7. Whisk about one-fourth of the beaten egg whites into the butter-flour mixture.

8. Fold the rest of the egg whites into the butter-flour mixture.

9. Pour the mixture into the cake pan. Use an offset spatula to level the batter in the cake pan. Bake the cake until it springs back to the touch.

1. When the baked cake is cool, unmold it and cut into thin layers: With your hand on top of the cake, using a serrated knife, saw laterally through the cake to slice off the top layer.

2. Slip a cardboard round under the top layer to lift it off the cake without cracking. Repeat to cut and remove a second layer.

3. Continue, removing a third thin layer of cake.

4. Put a layer back into the spring-form pan, brushing the layer with flavored simple syrup (opposite).

5. Spread buttercream or other filling over the layer.

6. Keep stacking the layers, brushing each with syrup and covering each with filling. Use a cardboard round to transfer each layer to the springform pan.

7. Spread frosting over the top of the cake, smoothing it well.

8. Chill the cake, and then release the clamp and lift off the sides. At this point, the cake layers should be perfectly even.

9. While the cake is chilling, work a few drops of food coloring into marzipan. Knead the marzipan to work in the color evenly.

10. Pound and roll the marzipan into a disk.

11. Roll out the marzipan into a thin sheet, roll it onto the rolling pin, and then unroll it evenly over the cake.

12. Tuck the marzipan around the edges of the cake.

13. Trim off the excess marzipan.

Devil's Food Cake

The secret to making a devil's food cake that is better than the next person's is to use the best chocolate you can find. Valrhona chocolate made in France and Scharffen Berger chocolate made in Berkeley, California, are two excellent choices. Callebaut chocolate from Belgium is also good.

MAKES ONE 9- OR 10-INCH CAKE

Room-temperature butter and flour for preparing pan
1 cup cake flour
1 1/2 teaspoons baking soda
1/2 teaspoon baking powder
1/4 teaspoon salt
1/2 cup butter, sliced, at room temperature
6 ounces bittersweet chocolate, chopped
1 cup sour cream
3/4 cup sugar
3 eggs, beaten

Preheat the oven to 350°F. Butter a 9-inch round cake pan. Coat the pan with flour, tapping out the excess.

In a bowl, whisk together the flour, baking soda, baking powder, and salt and set aside. Combine the butter, chocolate, and sour cream in a heatproof bowl and set over a saucepan of simmering water. Stir with a rubber spatula until melted and smooth, and then immediately remove from the heat.

In a large bowl, whisk together the sugar and eggs until well blended. Stir the chocolate into the egg mixture. Sift the flour mixture over the egg mixture while folding it in with a rubber spatula. Transfer the batter to the prepared pan and smooth the top with an offset spatula.

Bake for about 40 minutes, or until the top springs back when pressed with a fingertip and a toothpick inserted in the center comes out clean. Let cool for 10 minutes and then turn out onto a cake rack.

Simple Syrup

Dissolve 1 cup sugar in 1 1/2 cups boiling water by volume. Let cool and then flavor with 2 to 4 tablespoons spirit, such as kirsch. Makes 2 cups syrup.

Vanilla Butter Cake

This cake is an example of a high-ratio cake, in which the dry ingredients are combined with the butter and the liquid is added last. This is a delicious cake, rich and buttery yet still light.

MAKES ONE 9-INCH CAKE

Room-temperature butter and cake flour for preparing pan
2 1/2 cups cake flour
1 1/2 cups sugar
4 teaspoons baking powder
1/2 teaspoon salt
2 eggs
3 egg yolks
1 1/2 cups milk
2 teaspoons vanilla extract
1 3/4 cups cold butter, cut into thin slices

Preheat the oven to 350°F. Butter a 9-inch round cake pan. Coat the pan with flour, tapping out the excess.

In a mixing bowl or large bowl, whisk together the flour, sugar, baking powder, and salt. In another bowl, whisk together the eggs, egg yolks, 1/2 cup of the milk, and the vanilla.

Add the remaining 1 cup milk and the butter to the flour mixture. Beat on low speed with a stand mixer fitted with the paddle attachment or on high speed with a handheld mixer for about 2 minutes, or until well combined. Add the egg mixture one-fourth at a time and beat until smooth after each addition. Transfer the batter to the prepared pan and smooth the top with an offset spatula.

Bake for about 35 minutes, or until the top springs back when pressed with a fingertip and a toothpick inserted in the center comes out clean. Let cool for 10 minutes and then turn out onto a cake rack.

Cheesecake

This classic Jewish American cheesecake is essentially sweetened cream cheese held together, like a custard, with eggs. The only thing that sometimes goes wrong is that the top of the cake cracks. You can cover any fissures with a layer of sour cream, but you can also prevent the cracking by baking the cake in a water bath, which ensures that it bakes slowly and evenly.

MAKES ONE 10-INCH CAKE

> Room-temperature butter for preparing pan
>
> Two 8-ounce packages cream cheese, at room temperature
>
> $3/4$ cup sugar
>
> 1 teaspoon fresh lemon juice
>
> 3 eggs
>
> 1 egg yolk
>
> $1^1/_2$ cups sour cream
>
> $1^1/_2$ teaspoons vanilla extract
>
> $1/_4$ teaspoon salt

Preheat the oven to 350°F. Butter a 10-inch springform pan and wrap the outside of the pan with aluminum foil (to prevent leaks from the water bath).

In a bowl, combine the cream cheese and sugar and beat on medium speed with a stand mixer fitted with the paddle attachment or a handheld mixer or by hand with a wooden spoon until smooth. This should take about 5 minutes by mixer or 10 minutes by hand. With the mixer on low to medium speed, or with the spoon, beat in the lemon juice and the eggs and egg yolk one at a time, beating well after each addition. Then beat in the sour cream, vanilla, and salt until incorporated. Transfer the batter to the prepared pan and smooth the top with an offset spatula.

Place the springform pan in a baking pan or roasting pan that is at least as deep as the cake pan. Pour the hottest tap water into the baking pan to reach halfway up the sides of the springform pan. Bake for $1^1/_2$ hours, or until only a 1-inch-wide bull's-eye at the center of the cake moves when you jiggle the pan. Remove the cake from the water bath and let cool on a rack for 1 hour. Remove the foil, cover the cake, and refrigerate for at least 1 hour or up to 24 hours before serving. To serve, release the clamp, lift off the sides, and place on a serving plate.

Baba au Rhums and Savarins

The difference between a baba and a savarin is that babas contain raisins and are made in cylindrical $1/2$-cup molds called dariole molds, and savarins traditionally have no raisins and are baked in large ring molds. They are both soaked in a flavored sugar syrup, which means they are ideal for making ahead of time because they won't dry out. They are leavened with yeast, and before they are soaked, they are more like a bread than a cake. But once the sweet syrup is introduced, all thoughts of bread disappear. Babas and savarins like to stick to their molds, so if you are buying molds, buy nonstick or silicone ones.

**MAKES 20 BABAS OR 1 LARGE
(6 CUPS, 9 INCHES IN DIAMETER) SAVARIN**

Dough

1 teaspoon active dry yeast, softened in 1 tablespoon barely warm water and 1 teaspoon flour for 10 minutes, or 1 cup starter (see page 409)

4 cups flour

1 teaspoon salt

1 tablespoon granulated sugar

4 eggs

$1^{1}/_{2}$ cups milk, barely warm

$1/2$ pound cold butter, cut into $1/2$-inch cubes

About $1/2$ cup butter, at room temperature, for preparing mold(s)

Syrup

5 cups granulated sugar

5 cups hot water

3 tablespoons to 1 cup dark rum, kirsch, or cognac, depending on the amount of alcohol preferred

Filling

2 cups heavy cream

2 tablespoons confectioners' sugar

2 teaspoons vanilla extract

To make the dough, in a stand mixer fitted with the paddle attachment, combine yeast or starter, flour, salt, granulated sugar, eggs, and milk and beat on medium speed for about 8 minutes, or until the dough pulls away from the sides of the bowl and clings to the blade. Add the butter cubes and continue to beat at medium speed. As the butter is worked into the dough, the dough will again cling to the sides of the bowl. But continue beating for about 5 minutes, or until all the butter is absorbed and the dough once again pulls away from the sides of the bowl and clings to the blade.

Cover with plastic wrap and let rise at room temperature for about 3 hours, or until doubled in volume.

Thickly butter twenty $1/2$-cup baba molds or one 10-cup savarin mold. Punch down the dough and divide among the baba molds or put into the savarin mold. The mold(s) should be about half full. Cover with plastic wrap and let rise at room temperature for 1 to 2 hours, or until the dough has risen to about three-fourths of the way up the sides of the mold(s).

Preheat the oven to 350°F. Bake for about 30 minutes for babas or 45 minutes for the savarin, or until nicely risen above the rim of the mold(s) and golden brown. Immediately turn out of the mold(s) onto a rack and let cool. If a hard crust has formed on the savarin (the eventual bottom), trim it off with a bread knife.

While the babas or savarin is baking, make the syrup. In a saucepan, combine the granulated sugar and the hot water (be sure to let your tap water heat up to its hottest point before you combine it with the sugar) and stir until all the sugar dissolves. If the sugar doesn't dissolve, heat it over high heat. Let the syrup cool until just slightly warm and then add the rum. Transfer the syrup to a bowl large enough to hold all the babas or savarin.

If you have round metal tart rings (small ones for the babas and large ones for the savarin), put one on the top and one on the bottom of the babas or savarin to make them easier to turn. One at a time, press the babas or savarin down into the syrup for 1 minute on each side, or until well soaked.

To make the filling, in a large bowl, combine the cream, confectioners' sugar, and vanilla. Using a mixer on high speed or with a whisk, whip until stiff peaks form. Spoon the cream into a pastry bag fitted with a $1/2$-inch fluted decorating tip and pipe into the center of the savarin, or simply spoon the cream into the center. If you have made babas, slice them in half vertically, pipe or spoon the whipped cream over the insides, and then press them together slightly. Refrigerate the babas or savarin until ready to serve.

CAKE FROSTINGS, FILLINGS, AND COVERINGS

Layer cakes can be filled with a single frosting, or they can have as many different fillings as there are layers. Buttercream is the most popular frosting for cakes, and justifiably: what could be better than butter and sugar? Buttercream is a smooth mixture of butter, sugar, flavoring, and egg yolks or egg whites. The simplest approach is to beat together confectioners' sugar with butter and add flavoring. The only disadvantage to this method is that the sugar sometimes leaves a slight grainy texture. Professional bakers make buttercream by cooking egg yolks or egg whites with hot sugar syrup and then working the butter and flavoring into the egg-syrup mixture.

Other cake fillings include whipped ganache, which is chocolate melted in cream, allowed to cool, and then whipped in the mixer; fruit curds, such as the Lemon Curd on page 469; chocolate (dark or white) mousses (see pages 502–503); Bavarian creams (see pages 498–499); and mousseline, made by beating pastry cream with butter (see page 437). Once the layers have been stacked, the cake can be covered with more frosting and then finished with a layer of marzipan.

Frosting Versus Icing

Often these terms are used interchangeably. A frosting is something fluffy and thick that's used to fill and cover cakes. An icing is usually thinner and, when hot, often in liquid form and is often shinier than a frosting. Royal icing and ganache are examples of icings. Buttercream and whipped ganache are examples of frostings.

Strawberry Shortcakes

Cake in name only, shortcake dough is similar to savory biscuit dough. Be careful not to overwork the dough, or you will end up with tough biscuits.

MAKES 8 SHORTCAKES

2 cups flour

1/4 cup sugar, plus 2 tablespoons for sprinkling

1 1/2 teaspoons baking powder

1/2 teaspoon salt

1/2 cup cold butter, cut into 1/3-inch cubes

1 egg, beaten

3/4 cup milk, or as needed, plus 2 tablespoons for brushing

4 cups strawberries, hulled, sliced, and tossed with 1 tablespoon sugar, or to taste

Sweetened Stabilized Whipped Cream (see page 437) for serving

Preheat the oven to 375°F.

In a bowl, stir together the flour, 1/4 cup sugar, baking powder, and salt until well mixed. Put the butter cubes on top of the flour mixture, and then cut through the mixture with a pastry blender until the butter is about the size of peas. Add the egg and 3/4 cup milk and, using a rubber spatula, combine the mixture just until the liquid has been absorbed and there is no loose flour in the bottom of the bowl. If you still see loose flour, mix in another 2 tablespoons milk to absorb it.

Dump the dough out onto a floured work surface, and shape it into eight rounds, each 3 inches in diameter and 1 inch thick. Be careful not to overwork the dough, handling it just enough to shape it and no more. Arrange the rounds on an ungreased sheet pan, spacing them about 2 inches apart. Brush the tops of the shortcakes with the 2 tablespoons milk and sprinkle with the 2 tablespoons sugar.

Bake the shortcakes for about 20 minutes, or until pale brown. Transfer to a rack to cool. Just before serving, using a serrated knife, cut each shortcake in half horizontally. Place the bottom halves on individual plates, cut side up. Spoon the strawberries over the bottom halves, dividing them evenly. Top each serving with a dollop of whipped cream. Replace the tops and serve at once.

Miniature Cake Petits Fours

A petit four can be virtually any miniature sweet thing—never more than a bite or two—usually served after dinner with coffee. Professional pastry chefs divide petits fours into two types: so-called dry petits fours, which are just miniature cookies, and so-called fresh petits fours, which are miniature tartlets and cakes.

These luxurious miniature cakes are time-consuming to make, but elegant to look at and to eat. This recipe makes enough for a party—the most likely reason to make them. Here, a sponge cake is used; the finished cake should be about 3/8 inch thick. Traditionally, fondant is used for icing the squares and apricot glaze is used to fill them. Butter-cream is sometimes spread over the tops and sides of the petits fours to seal them before they are coated with fon-dant. You can ice them by dipping them one at a time in the fondant, or you can arrange them all on a wire rack set over a sheet pan and pour the fondant over them. Classic recipes for petits fours call for brushing the cake with a simple syrup that has been flavored with some kind of spirit, but this isn't essential.

MAKES 80 PETITS FOURS

- 1/2 cup sugar, dissolved in 1/2 cup hot water and cooled, for simple syrup (optional)
- 1/4 cup kirsch or other spirit, or to taste (optional)
- 1 cup apricot preserves
- 2 tablespoons water
- One 16-by-12-inch Classic Sponge Cake (see page 423)
- 1/2 cup buttercream (see pages 434–435), optional
- 3 cups Liquid Fondant (see page 489), liquid enough to flow in a steady stream off a spoon
- Food coloring (optional)
- 2 tablespoons tinted Royal Icing (see page 510), optional

If using the simple syrup, flavor it with the kirsch to taste and set aside.

In a saucepan, combine the apricot preserves and water over medium heat and stir until smooth. Strain through a fine-mesh strainer and let cool slightly before using as a glaze.

Trim the cake so it measures 16 by 10 inches, and then cut it into two 8-by10-inch rectangles. Set one of the rectangles on a large piece of parchment paper. If using the simple syrup, brush half of it on the rectangle that isn't resting on the parchment, which will become the bottom layer of the petits fours. Spread the apricot glaze over the bottom rectangle and, using the parchment paper as a sling, place the other rectangle on top, sliding out the parchment as you scoot the top rectangle into position on top of the bottom rectangle. Brush the top rectangle with the remaining simple syrup.

Spread the buttercream in a thin layer over the top of the cake. Cut the cake into 1-inch-wide strips. If you have any buttercream left, use it to coat the sides of each strip. Cut across the strips to make 1-inch cubes, so there are two sides with buttercream and two sides without.

Thin the fondant by heating it in a bowl set over a saucepan of simmering water. If it is still too thick, thin it with water, a teaspoon at a time. Color the fondant with food coloring. If using the Royal Icing, choose a different color for the fondant.

Coat the petits fours with fondant by dipping them in the bowl of fondant, or by setting them on a cooling rack set over a sheet pan and pouring the fondant over them. If pouring the fondant, return the fondant that drips onto the sheet pan to the bowl and then pour it again. Let the petits fours sit for 20 minutes for the fondant to harden. If the coating is too thin, you can coat them again. Use a paper cone (see page 439) with a small hole cut in the end to pipe on decorative icing, or a fork, tines dipped in icing and waved over to create decorative striping. Serve within 1 day after assembling.

Professional-Style Buttercream Made with Egg Yolks

This is the buttercream recipe used by most professionals. You make a sugar syrup and cook it to the soft-ball stage, and although it isn't difficult, you do need to arm yourself with a small metal spoon and a bowl of cold (but not iced) water. As the sugar syrup boils, you dip the spoon handle in the syrup and then immediately into the water. When the syrup hardens to the texture of chewing gum that has been chewed a bit, soft-ball stage on a candy thermometer (234°F to 240°F), the syrup is ready. You can also use a thermometer and cook the syrup until it reads 235°F. Once it reaches this stage, it quickly goes to the next stage, firm ball, so it is important to work fast. Fortunately, if you do go too far, all is not lost. You can reverse the process for a while by adding 1 tablespoon cold water to the syrup. When the syrup is ready, you simultaneously pour it into beaten egg yolks and beat the mixture with the whisk attachment. The trick is to pour the syrup between the whisk and the sides of the bowl so it doesn't hit either one. If it does hit one or the other, it will harden into little lumps that will end up distributed throughout your buttercream. If you need your buttercream to be perfectly white, make it with egg whites (opposite) instead of yolks.

MAKES ABOUT 4 CUPS, OR ENOUGH FROSTING FOR ONE 4-LAYER 9-INCH CAKE

- 1¹/₂ cups sugar
- ¹/₂ cup water
- 6 egg yolks, eggs soaked in their shells in warm water to cover for 10 minutes before cracked and separated
- 1 pound cold butter, cut into ¹/₂-inch cubes

In a heavy saucepan, combine the sugar and water and bring to a boil over low to medium heat. While the syrup is heating, put the egg yolks in a stand mixer fitted with the whisk attachment and beat on high speed for about 8 minutes, or until quadrupled in volume and very pale. Doing this by hand or with a handheld mixer will take about twice as long.

Meanwhile, begin checking the syrup with the spoon handle as described above. If the syrup is ready before the egg yolks, add 1 tablespoon of water to reverse the process slightly and keep boiling.

When both the syrup and yolks are ready, with the mixer still on high speed, pour the syrup into the yolks, carefully aiming between the whisk and the side of the bowl. Once all the syrup is added, continue beating until the mixture is just slightly warmer than room temperature when you put your hand on the bottom of the bowl.

Turn the mixer speed down to medium and add the butter a small handful at a time, waiting until each batch is absorbed before adding more. Beat for about 10 minutes once all the butter has been added, or until smooth and fluffy. Use immediately, or set aside in a cool place (not the refrigerator).

HOW TO TEST SOFT-BALL STAGE FOR SUGAR SYRUP

Combine sugar with one-third as much water by volume and bring to a boil.

Verify that the syrup is ready with a candy thermometer—it should register 234°F to 240°F—or by dipping a metal spoon handle into the syrup and then immediately into a glass of cool water. The syrup should harden to the consistency of chewed chewing gum.

HOW TO MAKE BUTTERCREAM WITH EGG YOLKS

1. Beat egg yolks until pale and fluffy and quadrupled in volume.

2. Pour syrup cooked to the soft-ball stage (above) into the yolks while beating. Don't let the syrup hit the whisk or the sides of the bowl.

3. Continue beating until the mixture is a little warmer than room temperature.

4. Add butter a handful at a time and beat for about 10 minutes, or until fluffy.

Professional-Style Buttercream Made with Egg Whites

If you need a buttercream that is very pale, you will need to make it with egg whites instead of yolks, or use the quick method on page 436 that contains no eggs at all. To make it with egg whites, you first make an Italian meringue by combining beaten egg whites and hot sugar syrup, and then when it has cooled, you beat in the butter. You can also use Italian meringue by itself as a cake frosting, or you can make a light buttercream by using half the butter called for in the recipe.

MAKES 5 CUPS, OR ENOUGH FROSTING FOR ONE 4-LAYER 9-INCH CAKE

> **Italian Meringue (right), cooled**
> **3/4 pound cold butter, sliced**

Using the whisk attachment, beat the butter into the cooled meringue one small handful at a time and beat on medium speed, waiting until each batch is absorbed before adding more. Beat for about 10 minutes after adding all the butter, or until smooth and fluffy. This buttercream keeps for 1 to 2 days in a cool place.

Italian Meringue

This meringue is made by beating hot sugar syrup into beaten egg whites and then continuing beating until the mixture is stiff and fluffy. Italian meringue can be used as a filling or frosting by itself, or it can be combined with fruit purees and frozen into frozen soufflés.

MAKES ABOUT 4 CUPS, OR ENOUGH FROSTING FOR ONE 4-LAYER 9-INCH CAKE

> **1 3/4 cups sugar**
> **1/2 cup water**
> **6 egg whites, eggs soaked in their shells in warm water to cover for 10 minutes before cracked and separated**
> **Pinch of cream of tartar, if not using a copper bowl**

In a small saucepan, combine the sugar and water and bring to a boil over high heat. While the syrup is heating, put the egg whites and cream of tartar in a stand mixer fitted with the whisk attachment and beat on medium speed for 1 minute. Then increase the speed to high and beat for about 5 minutes, or until stiff peaks form. (If instead you use a handheld mixer or a whisk, this will take about 10 minutes.)

Meanwhile, begin checking the syrup with the spoon handle: dip the handle of a metal spoon into the syrup and then immediately dip the handle into a bowl of cool (but not iced) water or measure with a thermometer, which should read 235°F. When the syrup hardens to the texture of chewing gum that has been chewed a bit, soft-ball stage on a candy thermometer (234°F to 240°F), the syrup is ready. If the syrup is ready before the eggs, add a tablespoon of water to reverse the process slightly and keep boiling.

When both the syrup and whites are ready, with the mixer on high speed, pour the syrup into the whites, carefully aiming between the whisk and the side of the bowl. Once all the syrup is added, continue beating until the mixture is at room temperature. The frosting keeps for up to 5 days, covered at room temperature.

Quick-and-Easy Buttercream

This is the easiest buttercream to make because there is no fussing with egg yolks or whites. All you do is beat together confectioners' sugar and butter.

MAKES ABOUT 5 CUPS, OR ENOUGH FROSTING FOR ONE 9-INCH LAYER CAKE

> 1 1/2 pounds cold butter, sliced
> 2 1/2 cups confectioners' sugar

In a bowl, combine the butter and sugar. Using a stand mixer fitted with the paddle attachment or a handheld mixer, start on low speed and then gradually increase the speed to high. Beat for about 5 minutes, or until smooth and fluffy. Use the frosting immediately or store in a cool place for 1 day.

How to Flavor Buttercream

Once the buttercream is made, it is easy to flavor it.

CHOCOLATE BUTTERCREAM: Melt 2 ounces bittersweet chocolate or 1 ounce unsweetened chocolate per cup of buttercream and beat in until smooth.

COFFEE BUTTERCREAM: Dissolve 2 to 4 teaspoons instant coffee granules or powder in 2 to 4 teaspoons hot water per cup of buttercream and beat in until smooth.

NUT BUTTERCREAM: Add 1/4 cup nut praline, such as hazelnut, almond, or pistachio, per cup of buttercream and beat until smooth.

CITRUS BUTTERCREAM: Add the grated zest of 1 orange or the grated zest of 2 lemons (preferably Meyer) or 2 limes per 4 cups of buttercream and beat until smooth.

SPIRIT-FLAVORED BUTTERCREAM: Usually, about 1 tablespoon of any spirit per cup of buttercream does the trick, depending on the quality of the spirit. Beat in until smooth.

FRUIT-FLAVORED BUTTERCREAM: Fresh or frozen fruit can be pureed, strained and cooked until soft, strained, and then cooked down, stirring constantly with a spatula to prevent burning, until thick. Once it has cooled, it can be beaten into the buttercream until smooth. About 1 pound fresh or frozen fruit can be cooked down to 2/3 cup, which will flavor 4 to 5 cups of buttercream. Beat in until smooth.

Pastry Cream

Essentially a semisolid custard you cook on the stove top, pastry cream is the traditional filling for chocolate éclairs. It can also be used to fill cake layers. But it is much tastier and has a much better texture when it is beaten with butter and turned into what French cooks call crème mousseline (opposite). You can flavor the mousseline with virtually any fruit puree that has been strained and cooked down until thick.

MAKES ABOUT 5 CUPS

> 4 cups milk
> 1 vanilla bean, split lengthwise
> 1 cup sugar
> 2 eggs
> 5 egg yolks
> 6 tablespoons cornstarch
> 2 teaspoons vanilla extract to substitute for vanilla bean if not using bean

In a heavy saucepan, bring the milk and vanilla to a simmer over high, then low heat.

Meanwhile, in a bowl, whisk together the sugar, eggs, egg yolks, and cornstarch for about 4 minutes, or until smooth. When the milk reaches a simmer, slowly whisk about half of it into the egg mixture. Then pour the egg mixture into the saucepan with the remaining milk and cook over medium heat, stirring with a whisk or wooden spoon, for about 3 minutes, or until the mixture comes to a boil and thickens dramatically. As you stir, be sure to reach into the corners and across the bottom of the pan so the mixture doesn't hide there and scorch.

Remove from the heat. If you have used the vanilla bean, remove it from the pan and, with a knife tip, scrape the little seeds from each half of the pod back into the pan. If you are using vanilla extract, add it now.

Pour into a bowl, straining it first if there are lumps, and cover with plastic wrap, pressing it directly onto the surface to prevent a skin from forming. Let cool and refrigerate until needed. It will keep for up to 4 days.

Crème Mousseline

Mousseline is one of the best fillings for a cake and surprisingly underrated. It is also easy to flavor with thick fruit purees, nut pralines, spirits, coffee, chocolate, and vanilla.

MAKES 4 CUPS

> 2¹/₂ cups Pastry Cream (opposite), cooled
> ³/₄ pound cold butter, sliced

In a bowl, combine the pastry cream and butter. Using a stand mixer fitted with the paddle attachment or a handheld mixer, beat on medium speed for about 10 minutes, or until all the butter is incorporated and the mixture is light and fluffy.

Mousseline can be stored in a cool place for up to 24 hours or in the refrigerator for 3 days. If stored in the refrigerator, beat it with a paddle attachment to fluff it up before using.

VARIATIONS

COFFEE MOUSSELINE: Dissolve 2 teaspoons instant coffee powder or granules in 2 teaspoons hot water and beat into the mousseline until smooth. Taste and add more if desired.

CHOCOLATE MOUSSELINE: Melt 8 ounces bittersweet chocolate or 6 ounces unsweetened chocolate and beat into the mousseline until smooth.

STRAWBERRY OR RASPBERRY MOUSSELINE: Puree 1 pint fresh berries or one 12-ounce package frozen berries in a blender and work the mixture through a fine-mesh strainer into a saucepan. Boil down the puree, stirring with a rubber spatula until it stiffens. Let cool and beat into the mousseline until smooth.

HAZELNUT OR PISTACHIO MOUSSELINE: Beat 1 cup hazelnut or pistachio praline into the mousseline until smooth.

Stabilized Whipped Cream

Cakes aren't often frosted with whipped cream because it separates quickly and can leave the cake a soggy mess. The trick is to add just enough gelatin to keep the whipped cream from separating but not enough to make it rubbery.

Cream should always be very cold before you try to whip it. Put the cream in a bowl along with the whisk you will be using and then put the bowl in the freezer for 5 minutes. If you are making sweetened whipped cream, put 1 to 2 tablespoons sugar and 1 teaspoon vanilla extract per cup of cream into the cold cream before you begin beating it. When cream is this cold, it beats quickly, in about 1 minute by hand, a little faster with a stand mixer, and a little slower with a handheld mixer. It takes proportionately longer the more cream you beat. When beating the cream to medium peaks, the cream should sag off the end of the whisk when you hold it sideways. If it calls for stiff peaks, the cream should stick straight out.

MAKES ABOUT 4 CUPS WHIPPED CREAM, OR ENOUGH FROSTING FOR ONE 4-LAYER 9-INCH CAKE

> 2 cups heavy cream, very cold
> 2 teaspoons gelatin (two-thirds of a packet)
> 2 tablespoons water
> 2 to 4 teaspoons sugar
> 1 teaspoon vanilla extract

Combine 6 tablespoons of the cold cream with the gelatin and water in a heatproof bowl. Let stand for 10 minutes to soften the gelatin. Then place the bowl over a pan of simmering water and stir with a rubber spatula just until the gelatin dissolves. Remove from the heat. Meanwhile, beat the rest of the cream, the sugar, and the vanilla until medium peaks form (see page 397). Whisk the gelatin mixture into the cream and continue beating just until stiff peaks form.

HOW TO MAKE PASTRY CREAM

1. Split a vanilla bean in half lengthwise. Bring milk and vanilla bean to a simmer. Scrape the pulp out of the bean into the milk, or add the vanilla extract.

2. Whisk together sugar, eggs, egg yolks, and cornstarch until smooth and pale.

3. Pour half of the milk into the egg mixture while whisking constantly.

4. Pour the milk-egg mixture back into the saucepan and cook until thick, whisking or stirring constantly to prevent lumps from forming.

GANACHE

Ganache is made by melting chocolate in hot heavy cream and stirring the mixture until smooth. Depending on the proportion of cream to chocolate—a classic version contains equal parts by weight—the ganache will become more or less hard as it cools. Because ganache is dense, it is usually poured over a cake, rather than spread like a frosting. When chilled and whipped, it becomes light and fluffy and makes the perfect chocolate frosting. In fact, one approach is to make a batch of ganache, whip half of it for spreading between the layers of the cake, and then pour warm, still-molten ganache over the cake as a glaze.

You can also make ganache with white chocolate, but don't use boiling cream as you do when using dark chocolate. Let the cream cool until it is no longer hot to the touch. If the cream is too hot, the white chocolate will clump up. You also need a higher proportion of white chocolate to cream to get the same stiffness you get with dark chocolate. And you will need to beat dark chocolate ganache for about 5 minutes on high speed, while white chocolate ganache whips up in just 20 seconds or so.

Dark Chocolate Ganache

This is the classic ganache recipe and it makes just enough to cover a 4-layer 9-inch cake. This same ganache can also be used hot as a sauce for ice cream. If you want a very thick chocolate sauce, add half as much butter as chocolate when melting the chocolate.

MAKES 1 1/2 CUPS

> **1 cup heavy cream**
> **8 ounces bittersweet chocolate, coarsely chopped**

In a small saucepan, bring the cream to a boil over high heat, and then turn off the heat. Add the chocolate to the cream and let stand for 5 minutes. Stir with a rubber spatula until you have a perfectly smooth dark sauce. When you can barely hold your hand against the bottom of the saucepan because of the heat, the ganache is ready to pour over your cake.

For whipped dark chocolate ganache, whip the ganache for 5 minutes or so on high speed, or until fluffy, and use to fill a cake.

PASTRY BAGS

A pastry bag is essential for decorating cakes and cookies with frosting. If you are new to cake decorating, you'll find it is easy to improvise a pastry bag by using a plastic food storage bag—just cut off one corner, insert a decorating tip through the hole, fill, and pipe. Once you have decorated a birthday cake or two, you will likely upgrade to reusable pastry bags, which come in various sizes and are plastic-lined for easy hand-washing.

If the reusable pastry bag is new, cut the end off with a pair of scissors so the base of the tip will stick about 1/2 inch through the opening. Start by cutting just a little bit (if you cut too much the bag is ruined), testing the hole with the tip until the cut is just the right size. Push the tip into the end of the bag.

Twist the bag a couple of times just above the tip and push the twisted material into the back of the tip with your thumb to clog the hole, so the contents won't leak out as you fill the bag. Fold the top of the bag down about 3 inches to create a cuff. Slip one hand under the cuff to hold the bag, and use the other hand to fill the bag one-half to three-fourths full with a rubber spatula, scraping the spatula along the rim of the bag to detach the excess filling.

Close the end of the bag by bringing the two corners together like an accordion. Twist the top of the bag so the filling can't escape while you are piping. Untwist the material clogging the tip to open the tip. As you pipe, make sure the bag is always taut with filling, not flaccid, or you won't be able to control the flow while you are piping.

HOW TO MAKE A DISPOSABLE PASTRY BAG

1. Cut the corner off a plastic food storage bag.

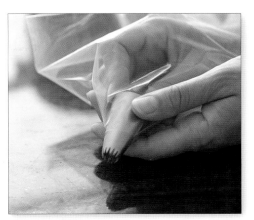

2. Insert a decorating tip into the corner and fill the bag.

3. Pipe as if using a reusable pastry bag.

HOW TO FILL A PASTRY BAG

1. Cut off the end of the pastry bag with scissors, making a hole just large enough for you to insert the base of the tip.

2. Slide the tip firmly into the end of the bag.

3. Twist the bag a couple of times just above the tip and push the twisted material into the back of the tip to prevent filling from leaking out as you fill the bag.

4. Fold down the top of the bag to form a cuff.

5. Hold the bag under the cuff with one hand, and use the other hand to fill the bag with a rubber spatula.

6. Unfold the cuff and let the filling settle down near the tip.

7. Seal the top of the bag by folding it like an accordion.

8. Twist the top end of the bag to seal in the filling. The bag should be taut. Untwist the material clogging the tip to open the tip.

HOW TO DECORATE A CAKE

A lot can go wrong with the inside of a cake and no one will know the difference if it is well decorated. If the cake is dry, brush it with sugar syrup (ideally flavored with a little brandy or whiskey). If it is lopsided, rotate one of the uneven layers to compensate. If it is a real mess, cover the whole thing with a sheet of colored marzipan and it will look professional. Here are some easy ways to decorate a cake to give it a finished look.

Pipe a decorative border around the perimeter of the top of the cake: To pipe, hold the filled pastry bag with one hand underneath for stability and control and the other hand on top, squeezing and guiding the bag, which is held at an angle to the surface of the cake.

Make berry-filled rosettes on the top of the cake: Using a pastry bag fitted with a $1/4$-inch star tip, pipe little rosettes of frosting around the perimeter of the top of the cake and put a berry in each one.

Surround the cake with a sheet of ladyfingers: Line a sheet pan with buttered and floured parchment paper. To make ladyfingers, see page 423. Once cool, trim one edge of the sheet of ladyfingers so it is straight, and, with this side on the bottom, wrap the ladyfingers around the cake.

Roll the cake: The same amount of batter you use for making a 9-inch cake can be baked into a thin sheet cake in a 13-by-17-inch sheet pan. Brush the pan with butter and then cover the bottom with a sheet of parchment paper. Brush the parchment with butter and then coat the parchment and the pan sides with flour, tapping out the excess. Set the oven 50 degrees hotter than called for in the recipe for a standard round cake, and bake the sheet cake for about 12 minutes, or until it springs back when pressed with a fingertip or a toothpick inserted in the center comes out clean. Dust a sheet of parchment paper slightly larger than the cake with confectioners' sugar, and turn the cake out onto it (the sugar will prevent it from sticking). Peel off the parchment from the bottom of the cake, and then rest the removed parchment over the cake to keep it moist while it cools. As soon as the cake is cool—don't wait any longer or it may dry out and crack—lightly brush it with a simple sugar syrup (see page 429), which will keep it from cracking as you roll it, and then spread it with a filling, such as buttercream, pastry cream, whipped cream, or whipped ganache. Starting from one side, roll up as tightly as possible. Slice crosswise to serve.

Cover the cake with a sheet of marzipan: Marzipan is essentially almond paste that has been mixed with corn syrup to make it easy to roll. Since most stores that sell almond paste also sell marzipan, it makes sense just to buy the marzipan, rather than buy the paste and make it yourself. Marzipan is easy to color and roll out. Just knead in a drop or two of food coloring until the marzipan is evenly colored, roll the marzipan out into a thin sheet (use confectioners' sugar while rolling to keep the sheet from sticking to the surface or the rolling pin), roll the sheet around the rolling pin, and then unroll the marzipan over the cake. Brush off any stray sugar, tuck the marzipan neatly around the cake, and trim off the excess around the base of the cake. One pound of marzipan is just enough to cover a 3- or 4-layer 9-inch cake.

Make a pattern in the frosting on the top of the cake with a serrated knife: To give a frosted cake a professional-looking swirled top, pull a serrated knife across the surface while gently swerving the knife left and right to create a wavelike pattern.

Make a colored mirror for the top of the cake: To make a shiny, colored mirror for the top of a frosted cake, combine 2 teaspoons of gelatin with 2 tablespoons water and let stand for 10 minutes to soften the gelatin. In a small saucepan, combine $1/3$ cup strained fruit puree and $2/3$ cup strained apricot or other fruit preserves and heat almost to a simmer. Remove from the heat and immediately add the gelatin and its soaking liquid, stirring until the gelatin dissolves. Let cool until just slightly warm. Meanwhile, place a cake ring or a strip of doubled aluminum foil on the top of the cake to contain the mirror. When the fruit mixture has cooled, but is still pourable, pour it on the top of the cake inside the ring. Let stand for about 25 minutes, or until the mirror has set, and then remove the ring.

Make a chocolate strip to wrap around the cake: Buy a piece of flexible acetate at a baking-supply store or hobby store. Make sure it is long enough to wrap around the cake. Cut it to the width you want the strip—the strip looks dramatic if it covers the cake and extends an inch or so above the top of the cake—and melt bittersweet chocolate. Using an offset spatula, spread the chocolate in a thin layer on the acetate, and then weight both ends of the acetate until the chocolate is cool. As soon as the chocolate loses its sheen, wrap the acetate, chocolate side in, around the cake and refrigerate for 15 minutes. Peel away the acetate.

Make chocolate curls and arrange on the cake: For small curls, scrape a block of chocolate with the wide end of a pastry bag tip. For larger curls, use a vegetable peeler. If the chocolate is too brittle and doesn't curl, heat it for a few seconds in a microwave. If the curls are too soft and won't hold their shape, let the chocolate cool or stick it in the refrigerator a few minutes.

Decorate the cake with burnt sugar: Dust the top of the cake liberally with confectioners' sugar. Heat a metal skewer until almost red hot on the stove top of a gas stove or in the flame of a propane kitchen torch and then burn lines or a crisscross pattern in the sugar as shown on page 481.

CAKE DECORATIONS

To create a wavy effect drag a serrated knife over the surface of the cake while moving it from side to side.

Decorate the sides of cakes with ground nuts or cake crumbs as shown here.

Pipe around the edge of the cake, lifting and pulling back on the bag at regular intervals to create a wave-like effect.

Encircle the cake with a strip of foil to keep the mirror mixture in place. Pour the liquid over the cake and allow to set.

Set mirror.

Pipe rosettes around the cake.

Place a blueberry in the center of each rosette.

Cake finished with a strip of ladyfingers.

Spread melted chocolate over a strip of acetate.

Wait until the chocolate looses its sheen and takes on a matte appearance.

Wrap the strip around the cake.

Peel off the acetate.

PIES AND TARTS

Some of the best cooks and cake bakers are intimidated by the thought of making a pie or tart crust, so homemade pies and tarts are too often left out of th`eir repertoire. True, some of the techniques take practice, and if you live in a hot climate, rolling out pastry dough full of butter can be challenging. But all of the techniques can be mastered with a little repetition, so that even once-intimidated bakers will soon feel confident making everything from an apple pie to a berry tart.

PIE AND TART DOUGH

More is written about pie and tart dough, some of it frighteningly complicated, than any other component of dessert. Books are filled with minute details, intricate techniques, and measurements to the gram. First, exact measurements are impossible to give since much depends on the brand of flour and kind of butter you use and the temperature of the room. It is also hard to pin down the perfect technique—you will feel your way through and develop your own—though one rule always holds true: you need to use a light touch so you work the dough as little as possible.

The tricky thing about the best dough, which is made with butter, is that butter melts at close to body temperature. It is precisely this characteristic that makes the dough so good—that gives it that melt-in-your-mouth quality. But the temperature range in which dough is neither too hard to roll out nor melting and falling apart is very narrow. If your room is cool, rolling out buttery pastry dough will be relatively easy. But as soon as a room feels hot, butter and pastry melt.

Cutting Butter into Cubes

To cut butter into cubes the perfect size for most pie or tart doughs, cut each cube lengthwise into thirds. Stack the resulting rectangles three high and slice the stack into thirds lengthwise. This will leave you with 9 sticks. Cut crosswise the same width as the sticks to create cubes. The cubes are between 1/3 and 1/2 inch; for flaky pastry they can be larger.

Many books debate the advantages of using different fats, such as vegetable shortening, lard, and butter. Shortening is easy to use and rolls out smoothly even if you let it get too warm, but it tastes ghastly. There may have been a time when lard was delicious—it still is in some places in the world—but American lard, sold in blocks, typically tastes like soap. Butter has the best flavor but is somewhat harder to work with and must be kept cool. An American pie crust is traditionally meant to be flaky, while Europeans favor tart crusts that are crumbly, like butter cookies. Crusts made with butter will be crumbly, but there are techniques that will yield flaky butter crusts if that is what you prefer.

Myths about pie and tart dough abound. Most books warn against overworking the dough and insist on chilling it before you roll it out. The only danger to overworking is that you can melt the butter in the dough, which will make the dough tough when you bake it. If the dough keeps breaking apart, you will need to work it together, which may mean keeping it cold by moving it in and out of the freezer. In a cool kitchen, working the dough sufficiently to get it to hold together is rarely a problem, and there is no need to chill it before you roll it out. If your kitchen is hot, a short chill—15 minutes—is enough. Don't chill it longer or the butter will harden and the dough will be impossible to roll out, or will require that you hammer it repeatedly with a rolling pin to make it malleable.

How to Measure Flour

The best way to measure flour is by weight. A small pastry scale is inexpensive and will guarantee that the amount of flour you use will be constant. The only ingredient that is tricky—in other words, it doesn't always weigh the same for a given volume—is flour. If you just measure flour by weight, you will standardize your recipes and be able to tweak them. The recipes given here use volume measurements that are based on the scoop-and-sweep method: you reach into a bag of flour with a measuring cup, scoop up the flour, and sweep the top level with a knife. If you sift the flour before measuring, the flour will take on more volume, so that you will end up using less than the recipe calls for. But unlike cakes, which often call for sifted flour, most pie and tart doughs don't require sifting. If you want to weigh your flour, keep in mind that the recipes in this chapter are based on 1 cup of flour weighing $5^1/_2$ ounces.

Flour

The elasticity of dough and the eventual possible toughness of the crust is determined by the amount of gluten, a kind of protein, in the flour. All-purpose flour has varying amounts of gluten depending on what part of the country you're from; flour from the South typically has less gluten and is more suitable for baking pastry than Northern flour, which is considered "harder." If you're uncertain of your flour, try using equal parts all-purpose flour and cake flour, which contains virtually no gluten. Flour with a higher gluten content will also absorb more liquid.

PIES AND TARTS

A pie can have a top and a bottom crust or just a bottom crust and is baked in a pie pan with sloping sides. A tart almost always has no cover, is baked in a pan with fluted or plain straight sides, often with a removable bottom, and is not as deep as a classic pie.

Most pie crusts, though not all, are fitted into the pan, the filling is added to the unbaked crust, and the pie is baked. Tart crusts are often prebaked partially or fully, known as baking blind, before the filling is added.

What If the Dough Is Too Dry or Too Wet?

Because gluten varies in different brands of flour and especially if amounts are being measured by volume rather than by weight, different amounts of liquid are required to make dough. If when you've added all the liquids, the dough doesn't come together when you pinch it, it's too dry and you should work in more liquid. If the dough is sticky and too wet, you need to roll it out with a generous dusting of flour to dry it out.

Basic Pie and Tart Dough

There are three ways to make this basic dough: by hand, in a food processor, and in a stand mixer fitted with the paddle attachment. The key to success in every case is to keep the butter cold and not to overwork the dough. If you are using a food processor, the butter will be very finely chopped into the dough, but if you are making the dough by hand or in a mixer, you will probably see butter chunks dispersed throughout the dough. Resist the compulsion to work in every little piece of butter. The butter pieces help break up the gluten in the flour, yielding a more tender crust. If you are making a double-crust pie, double the ingredient amounts.

MAKES ONE 9- OR 10-INCH PIE OR TART CRUST (ABOUT 2 POUNDS)

> 10 tablespoons cold butter, cut into small cubes (see "Cutting Butter into Cubes," page 443)
>
> 2 cups (5½ ounces) all-purpose flour or a mixture of equal parts all-purpose and cake flour
>
> 2 eggs
>
> ½ teaspoon salt

By food processor: The food processor method is the most foolproof, so if you have never made pie dough before, try it first. If your kitchen is warm, put the butter cubes in the freezer for 15 minutes while you measure the flour. Then put the flour in the processor and add the butter cubes, eggs, and salt. Process until the dough comes together in a ragged mass. If after 30 seconds or so it doesn't come together, add a tablespoon of cold water to it and continue processing. Shape the dough into a ball and then flatten it into a disk.

If the kitchen is warm, wrap the dough in waxed paper and chill for 15 minutes before you roll it out. Don't chill for longer than that or it will be hard to roll out. Roll out the dough as shown on page 448.

By hand: If you want to have a real feel for pie dough, make the dough by hand. If your kitchen is warm, put the butter cubes in the freezer for 15 minutes while you measure both flours. Then dump the flour onto a work surface (or into a work bowl) and sprinkle the butter cubes and the salt over the top. Chop the butter into the flour using a pastry cutter (either a bench knife as shown on page 446, step 1, or an old-fashioned pastry blender with wires) to chop the mixture, lifting it up and over itself to combine the liquid until you see no loose flour and the butter looks like gravel. Pull the mixture together into a pile, and use your fingers to make a well in the middle of the flour. Put the eggs in the well and, with the fingertips of one hand, move around the inside of the flour wall, gradually eroding away the flour and combining it with the eggs. When all of the liquid and flour are loosely combined. If you keep chopping and still see loose flour, add 1 tablespoon of cold water and continue to work the dough until all the loose flour is absorbed. You might want to try a different brand of flour the next time you make the dough to avoid having to add the water.

If the kitchen is warm, put the mixture in the freezer for 15 minutes and then continue. Bring the mixture together in a mound near you on the work surface and, with the heel of one hand, smear it, about one-eighth at a time, away from you, until it comes together in a shaggy mass. Shape the dough into a disk. If the kitchen is warm, wrap the dough in waxed paper and chill for 15 minutes before you roll it out. Don't chill for longer than that or it will be hard to roll out. Roll out the dough as shown on page 448.

By stand mixer: This is the method most often used in restaurants, since it can be mixed in large amounts. If your kitchen is warm, put the butter cubes in the freezer for 15 minutes while you measure the flour. Then put the flour and salt in the mixer fitted with the paddle attachment, sprinkle the butter over the top, and add the eggs. Start on low speed and then gradually increase the speed to run the mixer as fast as possible without flour flying all over the place. Beat the mixture for about 3 minutes, or until the mixture comes together in a ragged mass. Shape the dough into a disk.

If the kitchen is warm, wrap the dough in waxed paper and chill for 15 minutes before you roll it out. Don't chill for longer than that or it will be hard to roll out. Roll out the dough as shown on page 448.

1. Chop the butter cubes into the flour until they are the size of baby peas.

2. Make a pile with the mixture, and then make a well in the center with your fingertips.

3. Add the eggs to the well.

4. Stir around with your fingers, gradually eroding the insides of the flour walls.

5. As the liquid gets absorbed, chop it into the mixture with a plastic pastry scraper. The mixture should end up the consistency of grated Parmesan cheese.

6. Pinch a piece of the dough. It should come together and not crumble. If it crumbles, work in a little cold water.

7. Pile up the dough and then smear the pile away from you, a small amount at a time, crushing the dough with the heel of your hand.

8. Bring the dough together and begin to shape it.

9. Press on the sides and top to form a disk.

HOW TO MAKE BASIC PIE AND TART DOUGH IN A FOOD PROCESSOR

Combine all the ingredients in a food processor and process until it comes together in a ragged mass.

When the dough comes together, it is ready. Turn out and gather into a disk.

HOW TO MAKE BASIC PIE AND TART DOUGH IN A STAND MIXER

1. Combine all the ingredients in a stand mixer fitted with the paddle attachment.

2. Turn the mixer on to its lowest speed, then medium, and mix for a few minutes, until the dough is the consistency of gravel.

3. Continue to beat for a bit more, or until the dough comes together into a shaggy mass.

1. Hammer on the dough with a rolling pin to soften it and roll it out. If it cracks or is difficult to roll, fold it over onto itself, wrap, refrigerate for 15 minutes, and then roll again.

2. Roll out the disk into a round, always rolling the third of the disk the farthest from you and rotating the dough 90 degrees after each rolling.

3. When the dough round is 4 inches larger in diameter than the tart pan, fold it in half and place it in the tart pan with the fold in the center. Unfold it.

How to Roll Out Pie or Tart Dough

Flouring the work surface: When rolling out dough, try to keep the work surface and the top of the dough covered with a very thin layer of flour. If possible, avoid sprinkling flour over from above, which can cause clumps to form. Instead, hold a tablespoon or so of flour in one hand, hold your hand back, and then with a quick motion toward the dough, release the flour about a foot away from the dough, so it forms a cloud of fine particles that lightly coat both the dough and the work surface. Admittedly this trick takes a little practice. If it defeats you, sprinkle the flour from overhead.

Rolling the dough: Using a rolling pin, roll the third of the disk that is farthest away from you until the disk stretches out a few inches. Slide the dough around a bit—this coats the bottom of the dough with flour and keeps it from sticking to the surface—and give the disk a quarter turn. Again roll out the third of the disk that is farthest away from you, move the dough in a circle—reflour as necessary—and give the disk a quarter turn and repeat. Keep working in this way until you have a dough round that is large enough to cover the pie or tart pan with some excess to form a border or wall.

Transferring the dough round to the pan: There are two ways to transfer the dough easily. You can fold the dough in half, quickly slide your splayed hands underneath it, lift it and place it in the pan so the fold is at the center, and then unfold the dough. You can also roll the dough loosely around the rolling pin and unroll it over the pan. If the dough falls apart while you are transferring it, it is probably too warm. Refrigerate it for about 20 minutes, pull it together into a mound, shape it into a disk, and roll it out again. If the dough cracks in the pie or tart pan, press the cracks together with your fingers.

Sweet Pie and Tart Dough

For some pies and tarts, especially those with tart fillings such as lemon curd, you will need a sweet crust. There are several ways to make a sweet crust. The simplest way is to make the basic dough, adding sugar to the flour and cutting down the liquid by 1 tablespoon: whisk 1 of the eggs in a small bowl and then add it a bit at a time. (The sugar keeps the flour from absorbing liquid, so you need less.) You can also make a classic pâte sucrée, which is a delicate, brittle sweet crust that is made almost like a cake. You cream together the butter and sugar, work in the eggs, and then work in the flour all at once. Last, you can make a buttery, rich sweet dough that is almost like cookie dough. For Basic Sweet Pie and Tart Dough, add $1/2$ cup sugar with the flour in Basic Pie and Tart Dough (page 445) and use only 1 tablespoon of egg.

4. Press the dough into the corners of the pan with the side of your index finger. Fold the overhanging dough inward and press firmly to form a small, overlapping lip.

5. Press down on the dough, cutting away the excess by pressing on the edge of the tart pan. Or roll the pin over the rim of the tart to completely detach the excess dough.

6. Press around the sides of the dough and along the lip to form a border that reinforces the sides of the tart shell.

Classic French Sweet Pie and Tart Dough (Pâté Sucrée)

This dough calls for a completely different method than most pie and tart dough. A stand mixer works best for this.

MAKES ONE 9- OR 10-INCH TART OR PIE CRUST (ABOUT 2 POUNDS)

> 10 tablespoons cold butter
> 2/3 cup sugar
> 2 eggs
> 2 cups flour
> 1/2 teaspoon salt

By stand mixer: Slice the butter, put it the stand mixer fitted with the paddle attachment, and add the sugar. Cream together on medium, then high, speed for about 4 minutes, or until the mixture is smooth. Add 1 egg and beat on high speed for a minute or so. Separate the remaining egg and reserve the egg white. Add the yolk to the butter mixture and beat for about 2 minutes, or until the mixture looks like cottage cheese or is smooth. (Sometimes the whole thing emulsifies into a smooth mixture, but usually it doesn't.) Turn off the mixer.

Add the flour and salt, cover the mixing bowl with a towel—hold the towel around the sides of the mixer bowl to keep flour from flying out and to keep the towel from getting caught in the blade—and turn the mixer on high. As soon as

you hear the motor begin to strain, turn off the mixer. If after 30 seconds you don't hear anything, stop the mixer, add the reserved egg white, and beat again. The dough is ready when it looks shaggy.

Shape the dough into a disk. If the dough is soft or your kitchen is warm, wrap the dough and refrigerate for 15 minutes, and then roll out as shown.

By food processor: Slice the butter and put it in the food processor with the sugar. Process until the butter is creamed and the mixture is smooth and forms a ball. You may have to stop the processor a few times and scrape down the sides of the bowl with a rubber spatula. Add 1 egg to the processor. Separate the remaining egg and reserve the egg white. Add the yolk to the processor and process for about 30 seconds, or until the mixture looks like cottage cheese. Add the flour and salt and process for about 30 seconds, or until the mixture looks like lumpy mashed potatoes. If the mixture doesn't come together, add the reserved egg white and process until it does.

Shape the dough into a disk. If the dough is soft or your kitchen is warm, wrap the dough and refrigerate for 15 minutes, and then roll out as shown.

By hand: Slice the butter thinly and put it on the work surface. Pour over the sugar and knead the mixture with the heel of your hand until it is smooth and creamy. Transfer to a bowl and add 1 egg. Separate the remaining egg, add the yolk to the bowl, and reserve the white. Whisk the eggs and egg yolk into the butter mixture until combined.

(continued)

Pour the flour into the bowl and combine the flour with the butter mixture by cutting into the mixture with a rounded plastic pastry scraper or a pastry blender. When the mixture comes together into a shaggy mass, it is ready to roll. If it doesn't come together, add the reserved egg white and continue cutting the mixture until it comes together.

Pull the dough together into a mound and shape it into a disk. If the dough is soft or your kitchen is warm, wrap the dough and refrigerate for 15 minutes, and then roll out as shown on pages 445 and opposite.

Buttery Cookielike Pie and Tart Dough (Pâté Sablée)

This dough can be somewhat hard to work, especially if it gets too cold (in which case it cracks) or too warm (in which case it falls apart). The good news is that it is difficult to go wrong as long as you keep the dough relatively cool. Because of the butter it contains, reworking this dough to bring it together causes no harm. You can use this same dough to make butter cookies called sablées (see page 505).

MAKES ONE 9- OR 10-INCH PIE OR TART CRUST (ABOUT 2 POUNDS)

- 1/2 **pound cold butter, sliced**
- 2 **cups all-purpose flour or 1 cup all-purpose flour combined with 1 cup cake flour**
- 3/4 **cup sugar**
- 1 **egg**
- 1/2 **teaspoon salt**

By food processor: Put the butter in the food processor with the flour, sugar, eggs, and salt. Process just until the mixture looks like lumpy mashed potatoes. If you fail to stop soon enough and the dough forms a ball, don't worry about it. This buttery dough is very hard to toughen. Just try not to let it get warm.

Shape the dough into a disk. If the dough feels sticky or your kitchen is warm, wrap the dough and refrigerate for 15 minutes, and then roll out as shown on pages 445 and opposite.

By hand: If your kitchen is warm, put the butter slices in the freezer for 15 minutes while you measure the flour. Then dump the flour onto a work surface (or into a work bowl) and sprinkle the butter cubes over the top. Pull the mixture together into a pile, and use your fingers to make a well in the middle of the flour. Put the sugar, egg, and salt in the well and, with the fingertips of one hand, move around the inside of the flour wall, gradually eroding away the flour and combining it with the sugar and eggs. When there is no loose flour on the work surface or in the bowl, chop the dough with a plastic pastry scraper, if using a work surface, or a pastry blender, if using a bowl, until the dough comes together in a shaggy mass.

Pull the dough together into a mound and shape it into a disk. If the dough feels sticky or your kitchen is warm, wrap the dough and refrigerate for 15 minutes, and then roll out as shown on pages 445 and opposite.

By stand mixer: Combine the butter and the dry ingredients with the paddle attachment on low speed. Add the egg and while holding a towel over the top of the bowl to keep flour from flying out, turn the mixer to high and wait for about 15 seconds until you hear the motor begin to strain and the dough comes together into a shaggy mass. The dough is ready to roll out.

1. Roll out the dough into a long rectangle and fold the ends in to almost meet in the center.

2. Fold one half over the other to make a square packet with four layers.

3. Roll out the packet into a rectangle. Transfer the rectangle to a baking sheet, cover with plastic wrap and refrigerate. When chilled, fold the dough again into a packet, hammer with a rolling pin, and then roll out for the pie.

How to Make Flaky Pastry

American pie dough recipes traditionally yield flaky crusts, while their European equivalents, which are like the recipes included in this chapter, turn out crusts that crumble in the mouth almost like sand. To achieve a flaky crust, older American recipes call for lard and newer American recipes call for vegetable shortening. Although both ingredients create the desired flaky layers, neither results in a pastry that tastes as good as a butter-based pastry. To make an all-butter pastry that is flaky, rather than crumbly, requires a little manipulation.

To make the flakiest pastry, make the Puff Pastry on page 476. But to make a dough that is just slightly flaky and layered, make the Basic Pie or Tart Dough (see page 445) by hand, but cut the butter into $1/2$-inch cubes (you want cubes of butter dispersed in the dough) and don't blend the dough any more than necessary to get it to come together. Once the dough is made, roll it out into a rectangle about 2 feet long and 8 inches wide, and then fold in both ends so they almost meet in the middle, with about 1 inch between them. Then fold over one end to create a square of dough made up of 4 layers. Roll this square out into a rectangle about 2 feet long and 8 inches wide, put it on a sheet pan, cover with plastic wrap, and refrigerate for at least 2 hours or up to overnight. Fold the dough into a square in the same way, hammer it with the rolling pin to make it malleable enough to roll, and then roll it out for your tart or pie. Or, if you are going for even more flaki-

ness, roll it out again into the rectangle, fold it into the 4-layer square, and then roll it out. If at any point the dough is getting hard to roll and keeps shrinking, it means you have activated the gluten and you need to let the dough rest for a few hours in the refrigerator before you try rolling it again. If you force the dough, it will shrink when you bake it.

Constructing Fruit Pies and Tarts

A fruit pie is typically a straightforward affair made by enclosing the fruit between two layers of pastry and baking. The inherent problem is that most fruits (apples are the exception) release a lot of liquid as they cook and can make the crust soggy. Many recipes call for tossing the fruit with cornstarch or flour to thicken any liquid that is released and to prevent the pie from being a runny mess. Another more exacting approach is to cook the fruit ahead of time, reduce the liquid it releases, thicken it with a little cornstarch, recombine the liquid with the fruit, chill the mixture, and then bake it in the pie.

Traditional fruit tarts approach the same problem in different ways. One method calls for leaving the fruit raw—this works especially well with berries—and for baking the tart shell separately as shown on page 458. The prebaked tart shell is usually lined with some kind of filling, such as lemon curd or pastry cream, and the raw fruit is arranged on top. Another approach is to cook the pastry shell and the fruit together with a layer of filling under the fruit—often a kind of pastry cream containing almonds, called frangipane—to absorb liquid that is released by the fruit. Apple tarts are the exception to this approach. They don't release liquid as they bake, so they can be spread in an uncooked tart shell and the two baked together. In a classic French apple tart, some of the apples or the apple trimmings are used to make a stiff applesauce. The unbaked tart shell is spread with the applesauce and thinly sliced apples are arranged on top. The whole thing is then baked and glazed.

Apple Pie

A classic apple pie is made with unsweetened pie dough, but a sweetened pie dough also works well. If you have access to tart local heirloom apples, use them. Otherwise, Granny Smith or Golden Delicious is the best choice.

MAKES ONE 10-INCH PIE

> **Double recipe Basic Pie and Tart Dough (see page 445) or Basic Sweet Pie and Tart Dough (see page 448)**
>
> **7 large Granny Smith or Golden Delicious apples**
>
> **1¹/₂ cups sugar, plus extra for sprinkling (optional)**
>
> **1 tablespoon cornstarch**
>
> **4 tablespoons butter, thinly sliced**
>
> **1 egg yolk or 3 tablespoons heavy cream**
>
> **Pinch of salt**

Have ready a 9- or 10-inch glass or metal pie plate. Roll out half of the dough into a round about 4 inches larger in diameter than the pie plate and line the plate by simply pressing the dough against the bottom and sides. Refrigerate the pie crust while you prepare the apples. Preheat the oven to 375°F.

Peel, halve, and core the apples, and then cut each half into 5 wedges. Put the wedges in a large bowl and add the 1¹/₂ cups sugar and the cornstarch. Using your hands with your fingers splayed, toss gently until all the apples are evenly coated with the sugar and cornstarch.

Mound the apples in the pie pan and cover evenly with the butter slices. Roll out the remaining dough, roll it loosely around the rolling pin, and unroll it over the pie. Trim the edges of the top and bottom crust so they both extend ¹/₂ to 1 inch beyond the rim, and then pinch them together, fold them under, and flute decoratively around the rim as shown (opposite).

In a small bowl or cup, beat together the egg yolk and salt to make an egg wash, and then brush the top of the pie with the wash. Or, for a slightly lighter effect, brush the top of the pie with the cream. Using a sharp knife, make about 5 slits in the top of the pie so steam can escape. If you like the effect of sparkly sugar on top of the pie, sprinkle liberally with sugar.

Bake for about 1¹/₂ hours, or until golden brown and a knife slid through one of the slits into the filling encounters no resistance. If the pie browns before the apples soften, turn the heat down to 300°F. Let cool on a rack.

1. Press the pie dough into a glass pie dish or a pie pan.

2. Heap the apples in a mound in the pie crust.

3. Unroll a second round of dough on top of the pie and cut around the edges of the top and bottom crusts with scissors, so both rounds of dough stick out about $1/2$ inch beyond the rim of the pie plate.

4. Pinch the edges together.

5. Fold the edges of the dough under.

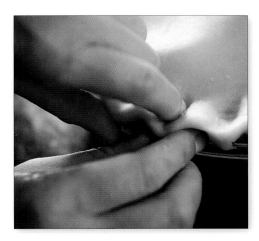

6. Press the rim of the dough between two fingers to form a fluted rim.

7. Make about 5 slits in the top of the pie.

8. Brush with egg wash or heavy cream. Sprinkle with sugar (optional). Bake in a moderate oven.

Classic French Apple Tart

A classic apple tart differs from an American apple pie in three ways: it has no top, the pastry is lined with a layer of applesauce, and the apples are very thinly sliced. When you slice the apple halves, leave a tiny strip uncut near one end, so the slices are still attached to one another. Then before you arrange the slices in the tart shell, cut away the tiny strip that holds them together. This allows you to more easily shape small groups of the slices in the pastry shell.

MAKES ONE 9-INCH TART

> 8 large Golden Delicious or tart baking apples, peeled, halved, and cored
>
> 1/2 lemon
>
> 1/2 cup plus 1 tablespoon sugar
>
> 1/2 cup water
>
> 1 vanilla bean, split lengthwise (optional)
>
> Basic Pie and Tart Dough (see page 445)
>
> 3 tablespoons butter, melted
>
> 2 tablespoons apricot glaze (see page 470), optional

How to Use a Tart Ring

Professional bakers, especially European bakers, often bake tarts in simple rings with no bottoms. These give the tart elegant smooth sides. There's no trick to using tart rings but be careful not to forget that there's no bottom support. If you try to lift the tart by lifting on the sides, it will fall apart. A tart with no bottom plate can be moved with two wide spatulas or by sliding the round disk that fits in the traditional fluted rings under the tart.

Peel, halve, and core the apples and rub the halves with the lemon. Then squeeze the juice from the lemon half and set aside. Cut half of the apples into 1/3-inch cubes (don't spend a lot of time doing this precisely) and put them in a wide saucepan with the lemon juice, 1/2 cup of the sugar, the water, and the vanilla bean. Place over medium heat, bring to a simmer, and cook, stirring with a rubber spatula, for about 15 minutes, or until the apples have softened, all the liquid has evaporated, and the mixture has stiffened. Remove from the heat and let cool. Scrape the tiny seeds out of the vanilla bean and add them to the applesauce. Dry the vanilla bean and save to store with sugar to make vanilla-flavored sugar.

Using a plastic vegetable slicer or a chef's knife, thinly slice the remaining apple halves crosswise. If you're using a knife, leave the slices attached to one another by a thin strip at one end. Cut off the strip where the slices are attached, so you detach the slices from each other.

Preheat the oven to 375°F. Line a 9- or 10-inch tart ring (see "How to Use a Tart Ring," left) or fluted tart pan with removable bottom with the dough (see page 448). Spread the cooked apple mixture in the tart shell. One at a time, press the sliced apple halves between your palms so they fan out slightly, and arrange them around the sides of the tart shell, setting them on the cooked apple mixture. Fit in extra slices here and there to make the arrangement even. Place some apple slices—use the small end pieces—in the middle of the tart to elevate the apples that will be arranged in the middle, and then fan out a second row of apples around the center of the tart. Use a few apple slices for the tiny round in the middle of the tart. Brush the apples generously with the butter and then sprinkle them with the 1 tablespoon of sugar.

Bake for about 1 hour and 15 minutes, or until the apples are deep golden brown. Transfer to a rack. Brush the top of the tart with the glaze while it is still hot and then let cool.

1. Spread the cooked apple over a tart pan or ring lined with basic tart dough.

2. Thinly slice the remaining apple halves crosswise, leaving the slices attached by a thin strip at one end, then cut off that strip. Gently press the sliced apple halves between your palms to fan out.

3. Arrange thinly sliced apples over the layer of cooked apple.

4. Brush with butter and sprinkle with sugar.

5. You can also dot liberally with butter and bake.

6. While the tart is still hot, brush the apples with apricot glaze.

1. Line a pie plate with dough. Leave about 1 inch of dough overhanging the sides, then fold it outward over itself, and pinch together to make a raised rim.

2. Flute the edge of the dough by pressing it between two separated fingers (see step 6 on page 453, "How to Make Apple Pie"). Refrigerate the shell until time to fill it.

3. Cook the blueberries with sugar and lime juice in a covered sauté pan until they release their liquid.

4. Drain the berries in a strainer set over a small pan. Boil down the liquid and then let cool. Combine the reduced liquid with the berries.

5. Pour the blueberry mixture into the pie shell and bake.

6. Serve in wedges. Top with crème fraîche or whipped cream if you wish.

Berry Pies with and without Lids

The most direct method for making a berry pie is to toss the berries with cornstarch and sugar and bake them in the pie crust. But because berries release an enormous amount of liquid and thus require a large amount of cornstarch, the pie ends with a sticky, gluey consistency. A better technique is to cook the blueberries with a little liquid to get them to release their juices, drain them in a strainer—you don't want to cook the berries any more than necessary—boil down the liquid they released, and then thicken the liquid with a little cornstarch and recombine the liquid with the berries. The technique for cooking pies without lids is essentially the same as for with lids, except that the filling must be cool before you construct a covered pie. If it is hot, the top crust dough will just melt.

Blueberry Pie

There is no cornstarch in this recipe to thicken the liquid the berries release. Instead, the berries are held together by the natural pectin they contain, which binds them up nicely if the pie is served cold. They are also precooked, as described above.

MAKES ONE 9- OR 10-INCH PIE

> **Basic Pie and Tart Dough (see page 445) or Sweet Basic Pie and Tart Dough (see page 448)**
> **4 pints blueberries**
> **1 cup sugar, or to taste**
> **1/4 cup fresh lime juice**

Have ready a 9- or 10-inch glass or metal pie plate. Roll out the dough into a round about 4 inches larger in diameter than the pie plate and line the plate by simply pressing the dough against the bottom and sides. Fold the edge under to create a double thickness and then flute the edge as shown in step 6 for "How to Make Apple Pie," on page 453. Refrigerate the pie crust until you are ready to fill it.

Preheat the oven to 350°F. In a large sauté pan, combine the blueberries, sugar, and lime juice over medium heat. Cover and cook for about 10 minutes, or until the berries release their liquid. Remove from the heat and pour the berries into a strainer set over a saucepan large enough to hold the juice with plenty of room to spare. Boil down the liquid over high heat until you have about 2 cups. Remove from the heat, let cool, and combine with the blueberries.

Put the blueberries in the pie shell and bake for 1 1/2 hours, or until the filling is bubbling and the crust is golden brown on the edges. Let cool on a rack at room temperature for 2 hours, and then refrigerate for at least 2 hours before serving.

Cherry Pie

In this version of an American favorite, the cherries are pre-cooked, the liquid they release is thickened with cornstarch, the thickened liquid is recombined with cherries, and the mixture is baked in a covered pie.

MAKES ONE 9- OR 10-INCH PIE

> **Double recipe Basic Pie and Tart Dough (see page 445) or Sweet Basic Pie and Tart Dough (see page 448)**
> **3 pints fresh Bing or sour cherries, pitted, or three 12-ounce bags frozen pitted cherries, thawed (about 5 cups)**
> **1/2 cup sugar for Bing cherries, or 3/4 cup sugar for sour cherries, plus extra for sprinkling**
> **1/4 cup water**
> **3 tablespoons cornstarch**
> **2 tablespoons fresh lime juice (optional)**
> **Egg wash for Pie Pastry (see page 470)**

Have ready a 9- or 10-inch glass or metal pie plate. Roll out half of the dough into a round about 4 inches larger in diameter than the pie plate and line the plate by simply pressing the dough against the bottom and sides. Refrigerate the pie crust until you are ready to fill it. Preheat the oven to 375°F.

In a saucepan, combine the cherries, sugar, and water over medium-high heat. Cover and cook for about 10 minutes, or until the cherries release their liquid. Remove from the heat and pour the cherries into a fine-mesh strainer set over a bowl, and then return the liquid to the saucepan.

In a small bowl or cup, stir together the cornstarch and lime juice and then stir the mixture into the cherry liquid. Bring to a boil, remove from the heat, and stir in the cherries. Let cool.

Put the cherries with their cooking liquid in the pie shell. Roll out the remaining dough, roll it loosely around the rolling pin, and unroll it over the pie. Trim the edges of the top and bottom crust so they both extend 1/2 to 1 inch beyond the rim, and then pinch them together, fold them under, and flute decoratively around the rim as shown in "How to Make Apple Pie," page 453.

Brush the top of the pie with the egg wash. Using a sharp knife, make 5 slits in the top of the pie so steam can escape.

Bake for about 1 hour, or until you see steam and juices coming out of the slits. Let cool on a rack.

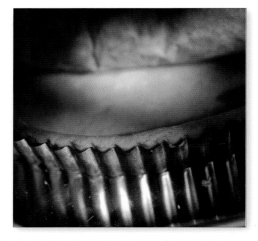

1. Line the crust with a sheet of parchment paper—leave extra paper around the sides to make it easier to remove—and pour in dried beans or rice saved for this purpose. Spread the beans so they cover the entire surface of the crust.

2. Bake in a hot oven until the edge is no longer translucent. Remove the paper and beans.

3. Continue baking until the bottom of the tart is pale brown.

Tools for Spreading

Many of us lack some of the tools that make spreading mixtures and filling easy and efficient. When bakers refer to a spatula, they mean a long thin flat strip of metal with a handle on it, not the wide pancake-turning variety of spatula that most of us have in a kitchen drawer. Professional bakers also use offset spatulas, which are made with a similar strip of metal that steps down at an angle from the handle and then flattens out. Offset spatulas are convenient for spreading mixtures that are surrounded with a ring or border that makes getting to the center area with a regular spatula almost impossible. If you don't have these spatulas, improvise by using a rubber spatula or a large spoon.

PREBAKING PASTRY SHELLS

Some of the most delightful tarts and pies are filled with raw fruit, such as berries, kiwifruits, grapefruits, or bananas. To make them, the pastry shell is fully baked with no filling (called baking blind) allowed to cool, and covered with a creamy filling such as lemon curd or pastry cream, and then the fruit is arranged on top.

To prebake the pastry shell, roll out the dough, line the pan or ring, and chill for 30 minutes to 2 hours while you prepare the filling and fruit. Preheat the oven to 400°F. Line the pastry-lined pan with a sheet of parchment paper (aluminum foil leaves specks, waxed paper leaves wax), making sure it extends beyond the rim so it is easy to remove, and then fill with something heavy like rice or dried beans (you can reuse them for prebaking other crusts) to hold the pastry down (otherwise it will puff up). After about 15 minutes, when the edges of the pastry lose their sheen and take on a matte appearance, remove the weights and parchment and bake the shell for about 10 to 15 minutes longer, or until the shiny center loses its sheen and the edges barely begin to brown.

HOW TO LINE A TART MOLD OR PIE PLATE

First, tart molds come in different forms. The most popular and easiest to use is a metal pan with a removable bottom. This makes it easy to take the ring off the finished tart and allows you to serve the tart right on the metal base of the tart pan, eliminating the potential hazard of trying to transfer the tart, bottomless, to a serving plate. There are also tart molds made of porcelain, but these are designed for serving the tart directly from the mold and are usually reserved for quiches or country-style savory dishes. The third type is a tart ring, which is a simple metal ring that supports only the sides of the tart. Lining a pie pan is straightforward: simply roll over the dough and press it into the corners and against the walls. Trim off the edges, leaving at least $1/2$ inch of extra dough around the sides to form a fluted edge. If you're making a pie without a top cover, simply fold under this extra $1/2$ inch of dough and press it between the thumb of one hand and the fingers of another to form a fluted edge (see step 6, "How to an Make Apple Pie," page 453). If the pie has a cover, simply pinch together the top and bottom crusts to form the fluted edge.

To line a tart mold with pastry, set the mold beside you and roll the dough out as directed on pages 448–449, constantly sliding the dough around so that it gets floured from underneath to prevent it from sticking. The dough should end up as a disk about 4 inches greater in diameter than the tart ring or pie pan. In other words, if you set the ring on it, it would be surrounded by a 2-inch border of dough. Then fold the dough disk in half (or even quarters), transfer it to the mold, placing the fold in the center, and unfold. Or, loosely roll the dough around the pin and unroll it over the mold. Once the dough is centered over the tart mold, work around the sides of the mold, first pushing the dough in and then down to get it into the corners. Next, again working around the mold, push down on the dough with one hand while using the fingers of the other hand to push the dough firmly into the corners at the base of the ring. When you have completed this, go around the ring again and push the dough against the outside rim to cut off the excess. Before you press down on the dough to cut it, push the dough in a bit, so a little extra dough is left attached that you can use to form a border. When you have gone all around the tart, roll the rolling pin over the rim to cut off any remaining dough. Form the border by pressing the excess dough both together and down, so it forms a ridge that goes up above the tart ring and also a little dough is forced down to reinforce the sides of the tart. Chill the tart for 15 minutes before baking.

Banana Cream Pie

This American classic is simply a prebaked pie shell filled with American-style pudding (essentially pastry cream but with less cornstarch) and layered with banana slices. The nutty-flavored browned butter adds a touch of richness and flavor to the pudding.

MAKES ONE 9- OR 10-INCH PIE

> **Basic Pie and Tart Dough (see page 445)**
> **3 cups milk**
> **1 teaspoon vanilla extract**
> **3/4 cup sugar**
> **2 eggs**
> **2 egg yolks**
> **6 tablespoons cornstarch**
> **6 tablespoons Brown Butter (see page 471), optional**
> **4 bananas**

Preheat the oven to 400°F. Have ready a 9- or 10-inch glass or metal pie plate. Roll out the dough into a round about 4 inches larger in diameter than the pie plate and line the plate by simply pressing the dough against the bottom and sides. Fold the edge under to create a double thickness and then flute the edge as shown in step 6 for "How to Make an Apple Pie," on page 453. Refrigerate the pie shell for 30 minutes.

Prebake the pie shell (see opposite): Line the pastry-lined pan with a sheet of parchment paper that extends beyond the rim, and then fill with rice or dried beans). Bake for 15 minutes, or until the edges of the pastry lose their sheen and take on a matte appearance. Remove the weights and parchment and bake the shell for 10 to 15 minutes longer, or until the shiny center loses its sheen and the edges of the crust barely begin to brown. Let the shell cool completely.

In a heavy saucepan, bring the milk and vanilla to a simmer over high heat. (Watch it like a hawk; it boils over in a half a second.) Meanwhile, in a bowl, whisk together the sugar, eggs, egg yolks, and cornstarch for about 4 minutes, or until smooth. When the milk reaches a simmer, slowly whisk about half of it into the egg mixture. Then pour the egg mixture into the saucepan with the remaining milk and cook over medium heat, stirring with a wooden spoon, for about 5 minutes, or until it bubbles and thickens. As you stir, be sure to reach into the corners and across the bottom of the pan so the mixture doesn't hide there and scorch. Whisk in the brown butter and remove from the heat. Pour into a bowl and cover with plastic wrap,

(continued)

pressing it directly onto the surface to prevent a skin from forming. Let cool to room temperature.

Using an offset spatula, spread one-third of the cooled pudding over the bottom of the pie shell. Peel all the bananas except one and cut into slices 1/8 to 1/4 inch thick. Arrange one-third of the banana slices in a single layer over the pudding. Spread half of the remaining pudding over the banana slices, and top with half of the remaining banana slices. Spread the remaining pudding over the banana slices. Chill for at least 1 hour before serving. Shortly before serving—any sooner and the banana will turn dark—peel and slice the last banana and finish with a layer of banana slices.

Coconut Cream Pie

Here is another American classic, this one filled with pastry cream–like pudding laced with sweetened shredded coconut. To give this pie an intense coconut flavor, use coconut milk to make the pudding. Don't buy the sweetened coconut milk that goes into a pina colada. Look for unsweetened coconut milk, usually from Thailand. The cans typically hold about 14 ounces, so you will need to buy 2 cans for this recipe.

MAKES ONE 9- OR 10-INCH PIE

Basic Pie and Tart Dough (see page 445)

3 cups milk or unsweetened coconut milk

1 teaspoon vanilla extract

3/4 cup plus 2 tablespoons sugar

2 eggs

2 egg yolks

6 tablespoons cornstarch

One 14-ounce package (4 cups) sweetened shredded coconut]

1 cup heavy cream

Preheat the oven to 400°F. Have ready a 9- or 10-inch glass or metal pie plate. Roll out the dough into a round about 4 inches larger in diameter than the pie plate and line the plate by simply pressing the dough against the bottom and sides. Fold the edge under to create a double thickness and then flute the edge as shown in step 6 for "How to Make Apple Pie," on page 453. Refrigerate the pie shell for 30 minutes.

Prebake the pie shell (see page 458): Line the pastry-lined pan with a sheet of parchment paper that extends beyond the rim, and then fill with rice or dried beans. Bake for 15 minutes, or until the edges of the pastry lose their sheen and take on a matte appearance. Remove the weights and parchment and

bake the shell for 10 to 15 minutes longer, or until the shiny center loses its sheen and the edges of the crust barely begin to brown. Let the shell cool completely.

In a heavy saucepan, bring the milk and vanilla to a simmer over medium heat. Meanwhile, in a bowl, whisk together 3/4 cup of the sugar, the eggs, egg yolks, and cornstarch for about 4 minutes, or until smooth. When the milk reaches a simmer, slowly whisk about half of it into the egg mixture. Then pour the egg mixture into the saucepan with the remaining milk and cook over medium heat, stirring with a wooden spoon, for about 5 minutes, or until it bubbles and thickens. As you stir, be sure to reach into the corners and across the bottom of the pan so the mixture doesn't hide there and scorch. Pour into a bowl and cover with plastic wrap, pressing it directly onto the surface to prevent a skin from forming. Let cool to room temperature.

Fold three-fourths of the shredded coconut into the cooled pudding. Using an offset spatula, spread the cooled pudding over the bottom of the pie shell. Cover and chill for at least 1 hour or up to 3 days.

In a bowl, combine the cream and the remaining 2 tablespoons sugar. Using a mixer on high speed or a whisk, beat to stiff peaks. Using a spatula, spread the whipped cream over the pie. Sprinkle the top with the remaining shredded coconut and serve.

Lemon Meringue Pie

A traditional lemon meringue pie is made by filling a pre-baked pie crust with cornstarch-thickened lemon curd, topping it with a soft meringue, and then baking it. In this version, a hard meringue shell is filled with a tangy lemon curd made without cornstarch, topped with a soft meringue, and then finished with whipped cream. Much of the pleasure of eating this pie comes from experiencing the different textures of the meringues, the curd, and the whipped cream.

You will need to make meringue twice for this recipe. The amount of sugar needed for the meringue for the crunchy shell will vary depending on what kind of day it is. Classic French meringue, which is made with relatively little granulated sugar, works fine on dry, cool days, but if the day is humid, you will need to fold in confectioners' sugar at the end to keep the shell crunchy. The second meringue, for the soft topping, calls for only a small amount of granulated sugar, so that it remains soft after baking. Most recipes for lemon curd use at least some whole eggs, but here only egg yolks are called for, because they have been left over from making the meringues.

Meringue Shell

Room-temperature butter and confectioners' sugar for preparing pan

6 egg whites

Pinch of cream of tartar, if not using a copper bowl

$^3/_4$ cup plus 2 tablespoons granulated sugar

1$^1/_3$ cups confectioners' sugar, if the day is humid

Lemon Curd

8 egg yolks

$^2/_3$ cup granulated sugar

Grated zest of 1 lemon

$^2/_3$ cup fresh lemon juice

6 tablespoons butter, sliced (optional)

Meringue Topping

4 egg whites

Pinch of cream of tartar, if not using a copper bowl

6 tablespoons granulated sugar

Whipped Cream

1 cup heavy cream

2 tablespoons granulated sugar

1 teaspoon vanilla extract

Butter a 10- or 11-inch pie plate. Coat with confectioners' sugar, tapping out the excess.

To make the meringue shell, preheat the oven to 250°F. In a large bowl, combine the egg whites and cream of tartar. Beat on medium speed for about 1 minute with a stand mixer fitted with the whisk attachment or with a handheld mixer, and then on high speed for about 4 minutes longer with a stand mixer or 10 minutes longer with a handheld mixer, or until medium peaks form. Add the granulated sugar in a slow, steady stream while continuing to beat on high speed for about 2 minutes longer with a stand mixer or 4 minutes longer with a handheld mixer, or until the whites are stiff and shiny white. If it is a humid day, fold the confectioners' sugar into the beaten egg whites. Using a spatula, spread the meringue over the prepared pie plate, leaving an indentation in the middle to hold the lemon curd.

Bake for about 3 hours, or until the shell is hard and dry to the touch. If it starts to brown, turn the oven down to 200°F. Let cool on a rack.

To make the lemon curd, in a heatproof bowl that fits over a saucepan, whisk together the egg yolks and granulated sugar for about 2 minutes, or until smooth and slightly pale. Whisk in the lemon zest and juice. Bring a few inches of water to a simmer in the saucepan and rest the bowl in the rim of the pan over, but not touching, the water. Make sure that no flame wraps around the bottom of the saucepan and overheats the edge of the bowl. Continue whisking the mixture for about 7 minutes, or until it thickens.

Alternatively, in a saucepan with sloping sides, whisk together the egg yolks and granulated sugar for about 2 minutes, or until smooth and slightly pale. Whisk in the lemon zest and juice. Place over medium heat and whisk the mixture for about 3 minutes, or until it thickens. If there is the slightest hint that the mixture might boil, remove the pan from the heat. (See page 469, "How to Make Lemon Curd.")

Remove the curd from the heat and whisk in the butter until melted. Cover with plastic wrap, pressing it directly onto the surface to prevent a skin from forming. Let cool and refrigerate until needed.

When both the meringue shell and lemon curd are ready, preheat the oven to 350°F. To make the meringue topping, in a bowl, combine the egg whites and cream of tartar. Beat on medium speed for about 1 minute with a stand mixer fitted with the whisk attachment or with a handheld mixer, and then on high speed for about 4 minutes longer with a stand mixer or 7 minutes with a handheld mixer, or until medium peaks form. Add the granulated sugar in a slow, steady stream while continuing to beat on high speed for about 2 minutes longer with a stand mixer or 4 minutes longer with a handheld mixer, or until stiff peaks form.

Using a spatula, spread the lemon curd over the indented part of the meringue shell, and then spread the meringue topping over the whole pie. Bake for 15 minutes, or until the topping is medium brown. Let cool on a rack for 1 hour before serving.

Just before serving, whip the cream: In a bowl, combine the cream, granulated sugar, and vanilla. Using a mixer on high speed or a whisk, beat to stiff peaks. Using a spatula, spread the whipped cream over the pie.

Pecan Pie

A pecan pie is basically a very sweet custard with pecans baked into it. Both chopped pecans and whole pecan halves are used for this recipe, the former mixed into the filling and the latter used to decorate the top. While you can buy only pecan halves and chop some of them, you will spend less money if you buy halves for the decorative finish and chopped pecans for the custard. Because the filling is very sweet, you will probably want to use an unsweetened dough for the crust.

MAKES ONE 9- OR 10-INCH PIE OR 11-INCH TART

> **Basic Pie and Tart Dough (see page 445)**
>
> 1³/₄ **cups pecan halves**
>
> **3 eggs**
>
> ¹/₂ **cup sugar**
>
> ¹/₂ **cup dark corn syrup**
>
> **5 tablespoons butter, melted, plus 2 tablespoons melted for brushing pie (optional)**
>
> ¹/₂ **teaspoon salt**
>
> **1 teaspoon vanilla extract**

Preheat the oven to 400°F. Have ready a 9- or 10-inch glass or metal pie plate. Roll out the dough into a round about 4 inches larger in diameter than the pie plate and line the plate by simply pressing the dough against the bottom and sides. Fold the edge under to create a double thickness and then flute the edge as shown in step 6 for "How to Make Apple Pie," on page 453. Refrigerate the pie shell for 30 minutes.

Prebake the pastry shell (see page 458): Line the pastry-lined pan with a sheet of parchment paper that extends beyond the rim, and then fill with rice or dried beans. Bake for 15 minutes, or until the edges of the pastry lose their sheen and take on a matte appearance. Remove the weights and parchment and bake the shell for 10 to 15 minutes longer, or until the shiny center loses its sheen and the edges of the crust barely begin to brown. Let the shell cool completely.

Preheat the oven to 350°F. Coarsely chop ³/₄ cup of the pecans. In a bowl, whisk together the eggs, sugar, and corn syrup for about 2 minutes, or until the sugar is dissolved. Whisk in the 5 tablespoons butter, salt, and vanilla. Stir in the chopped pecans. Pour the mixture into the prebaked shell. Arrange the pecan halves on top of the pie. Brush the pecans with the 2 tablespoons melted butter.

Bake for about 40 minutes, or until the center no longer moves when you gently move the pan back and forth. If the edges of the crust start to get too brown before the pie is ready, place a foil ring (see below) over the edge of the pie to prevent further browning. Let cool on a rack.

How to Make a Pie Shield

If you're baking a tart and the crust starts to get too brown before the inside of the tart is cooked, cover the edge of the tart with a foil ring. To make the ring, fold a square of foil at least as wide as the diameter of the tart in half and then half again. Fold the foil like a paper airplane with the point where the folds meet at the front of the plane. Place this tip over the center of the tart and with a pair of scissors cut the foil where it covers the rim of the tart. Unfold and you'll have a ring that you can rest over the tart as it finishes baking.

Pumpkin Pie

The filling for a pumpkin pie is a custard in which the eggs set the pumpkin puree. Here, the puree is seasoned with spices and given a luxurious texture with cream before it goes into a prebaked pie or tart shell. If you keep in mind that you need about 1 egg to set each ²/₃ cup puree, it is easy to use this recipe as a model for making sweet pies from similar purees, such as winter squash or sweet potato puree. Savory versions, based on purees such as spinach or mushroom, are made in the same way, minus, of course, the sugar and spices.

MAKES ONE 9- OR 10-INCH PIE

> Basic Sweet Pie and Tart Dough (see page 448), Classic French Sweet Pie and Tart Dough (see page 449), or Buttery Cookielike Pie and Tart Dough (see page 450)
>
> One 15-ounce can (2 cups) pumpkin puree
>
> ³/₄ cup firmly packed light or dark brown sugar
>
> 3 eggs
>
> ¹/₂ teaspoon ground cinnamon
>
> ¹/₂ teaspoon ground ginger
>
> ¹/₄ teaspoon ground cloves
>
> Scant ¹/₄ teaspoon freshly grated nutmeg
>
> 1¹/₂ cups heavy cream
>
> ¹/₄ teaspoon salt

Preheat the oven to 400°F. Have ready a 9- or 10-inch glass or metal pie plate. Roll out the dough into a round about 4 inches larger in diameter than the pie plate and line the plate by simply pressing the dough against the bottom and sides. Fold the edge under to create a double thickness and then flute the edge as shown in step 6 for "How to Make Apple Pie," on page 453. Refrigerate the pie shell for 30 minutes.

Prebake the pastry shell (see page 458): Line the pastry-lined pan with a sheet of parchment paper that extends beyond the rim, and then fill with rice or dried beans. Bake for 15 minutes, or until the edges of the pastry lose their sheen and take on a matte appearance. Remove the weights and parchment and bake the shell for 10 to 15 minutes longer, or until the shiny center loses its sheen and the edges of the crust barely begin to brown. Let the shell cool completely.

Preheat the oven to 325°F. In a bowl, whisk together the pumpkin puree and sugar. Whisk in the eggs one at a time, beating well after each addition. Stir in all the spices, the cream, and the salt until well mixed. Pour the mixture into the prebaked shell.

Put the plate on a sheet pan—in case it leaks—and bake for about 45 minutes, or until the center no longer moves when you gently move the sheet pan back and forth. If the crust starts to get too brown, place a foil ring (see opposite) over the edge to prevent further browning. Let cool on a rack.

Cherry Cobblers

A cobbler is fruit baked with crumbled-up biscuit dough on top. Cherries or berries are two good choices for cobblers because they release liquid when they cook, making the dessert deliciously moist. Here, either sweet cherries, such as Bing, or sour cherries, such as Montmorency, can be used. Just adjust the sugar accordingly.

MAKES 6 INDIVIDUAL COBBLERS

> ¹/₂ recipe Buttermilk Biscuit dough (see page 392)
>
> 4 cups pitted and halved fresh or frozen cherries
>
> ¹/₂ cup sugar if using sweet cherries or ³/₄ cup if using sour cherries, plus 2 tablespoons for sprinkling
>
> Whipped cream (see page 437), ice cream, or Crème Anglaise (see page 497) for serving

Preheat the oven to 375°F. In a bowl, toss the cherries with the sugar and distribute them evenly among six ³/₄-cup, 3- to 4-inch ramekins. Crumble the biscuit dough evenly over the tops and then sprinkle each top with 1 teaspoon sugar.

Bake for about 30 minutes, or until the biscuit dough is golden brown and the fruit is bubbling. If the dough is ready but the fruit isn't bubbling, turn the oven down to 300°F and bake for about 10 minutes longer. Cool on a rack. Serve warm with whipped cream.

Hot Berry Compotes

A compote is a small ramekin of cooked fruit covered with a sheet of pastry and baked. You can make compotes with regular pie dough, but puff pastry is more dramatic.

MAKES 6 COMPOTES

> One 12-ounce package frozen fruit to complement fruit filling, thawed and pressed through a fine-mesh strainer to yield 3/4 cup puree
>
> 1 1/2 pints (3 cups) assorted whole raspberries, blackberries, blueberries, sliced strawberries, or halved and pitted cherries, in any combination
>
> 3 tablespoons butter, cut into 6 equal slices
>
> 2 tablespoons sugar
>
> 1 pound Puff Pastry dough (see page 476) or Basic Pie or Tart Dough (see page 445)
>
> Egg wash (see page 470)
>
> Crème fraîche or whipped cream for serving (optional)

Put 2 tablespoons fruit puree in each of six 3/4-cup ramekins. Divide the berries evenly among the ramekins. Don't fill the ramekins to the rim, as you don't want the fruit to touch the pastry. Lay a slice of butter on the fruit in each ramekin. Then spoon 1 teaspoon sugar on top of each ramekin.

On a floured work surface, roll out the pastry between 1/8 and 1/4 inch thick. Cut into rounds 2 inches larger in diameter than the ramekins. Brush the rounds on the top side with the egg wash. Top each ramekin with a dough round, egg wash side down. Gently press the dough against the sides of the ramekins, first pressing the dough with your fingertips and then with the sides of your hands to seal the pastry securely to the ramekins. Brush the tops of the pastry with the egg wash. Refrigerate or freeze the compotes for 30 minutes. If you like, decorate the surface of the pastry with a paring knife.

Preheat the oven to 425°F. Arrange the ramekins on a sheet pan and slide into the oven. Bake for about 25 minutes, or until the pastry is golden brown and slightly mounded. Serve hot with crème fraîche.

HOW TO MAKE HOT RASPBERRY COMPOTES

1. Combine raspberry puree or preserves, raspberries, butter, and sugar in ramekins.

2. Roll out a sheet of puff pastry and cut out fluted rounds about 2 inches larger than the ramekins.

3. Brush the rounds with egg wash.

4. Place the rounds, egg wash side down, over the ramekins and press them onto the sides. Brush the tops of the pastry with egg wash.

5. Using a sharp paring knife, decorate the top of the pastry with spokes.

6. Bake until the pastry is golden brown. Serve hot.

1. Prebake a tart shell as directed on page 458.

2. Spread lemon curd (page 469) over the tart shell.

3. Start arranging the raspberries by placing 1 berry in the middle and then work outward in concentric circles.

Fresh Berry Tart

If you are an insecure pie and tart maker, start here. This one is simple to put together and so beautiful that the reward will inspire you to try more difficult recipes.

MAKES ONE 9- OR 10-INCH TART

> **Basic Pie and Tart Dough (see page 445) or Basic Sweet Pie and Tart Dough (see page 448) or Classic French Sweet Pie and Tart Dough (see page 449)**
>
> **1 cup Lemon Curd (see page 469), Pastry Cream (see page 436), or Crème Mousseline (see page 437)**
>
> **3 cups berries**
>
> **2 tablespoons apricot glaze (page 471), optional**

Preheat the oven to 400°F. Line a 9- or 10-inch tart ring or fluted tart pan with removable bottom with the dough (see page 459). Prebake the tart shell (see page 458): Line the pastry-lined tart ring with a sheet of parchment paper that extends beyond the rim, and then fill with rice or dried beans. Bake for 15 minutes, or until the edges of the pastry lose their sheen and take on a matte appearance. Remove the weights and parchment and bake the shell for 10 to 15 minutes longer, or until the shiny center loses its sheen and the edges of the crust barely begin to brown. Let the crust cool completely.

Using an offset spatula, spread the curd over the tart shell in an even layer. Arrange the berries on top so they cover the filling. Brush with the glaze.

4. If you want the berries to have a sheen, brush them with apricot glaze (page 471).

1. Roll out the dough and cut a square or round of pastry slightly larger than the tartlet ring.

2. Roll out the pastry cutout to expand it slightly.

3. Line the rings with the pastry cutouts.

4. Press the dough down into the ring and then press in slightly to form a lip.

5. Press on the rim of the ring with your thumb to begin cutting off the dough. Roll the rolling pin over the rim of the tart ring to fully sever the excess dough.

6. Slide a knife around the inside of the ring to detach the pastry and make the ring easier to remove.

HOW TO MAKE TARTS WITH COOKED FRUIT

Just as with pies, if you put raw fruit in a tart shell and bake it, the fruit will release its juice and you will end up with a pastry shell full of fruit soup. You can solve this problem by using one of two methods. The first method, used for plums, apricots, peaches, or other stone fruits, is to cut the fruit into wedges and bake the wedges on a sheet pan at 375°F until the liquid they release evaporates. The cooked fruit can then be arranged on a tart shell lined with creamy filling, just as it is for fresh Raspberry-Lemon Tart shown on page 465. The second approach is to line the unbaked tart shell with a mixture that you can cook—a nut cream called frangipane is the most popular choice—and that will absorb the liquid released by the fruit.

Plum, Apricot, or Peach Tart

This system of surrounding fruit with frangipane (almond cream) in a tart during baking can also be used for tartlets.

MAKES ONE 9- OR 10-INCH TART

> Basic Sweet Pie or Tart Dough (see page 448), Classic French Sweet Pie or Tart Dough (see page 449), or Buttery Cookielike Pie or Tart Dough (see page 450)
>
> 2 cups Frangipane (see page 470)
>
> 5 large plums, 7 medium apricots, or 5 medium peaches
>
> 2 tablespoons butter, cut into tiny cubes
>
> 1 tablespoon sugar
>
> Apricot glaze (see page 471) or confectioners' sugar (optional)

Line a 9- or 10-inch tart ring (as shown) or fluted tart pan with removable bottom with the dough (see page 448). Using an offset spatula, spread the Frangipane over the tart shell in an even layer. Refrigerate the shell while you prepare the fruit.

Preheat the oven to 400°F. If using plums or apricots, halve and pit them and cut each half into 3 or more wedges, depending on the size of the fruit. If using peaches, halve and pit them and cut each half into 6 or 8 wedges. Arrange the fruit wedges in the tart shell, dot with the butter, and sprinkle with the sugar.

Bake for about 40 minutes, or until the tart crust is golden brown. Brush while still hot with the glaze, or wait until just before serving and dust with confectioners' sugar.

VARIATION

To make tartlets, construct as shown above and at right, using kiwis, blueberries, or stonefruits, and bake at 425°F for 35 minutes.

1. Line a tart or tartlet ring with pastry and spread over a thick layer of frangipane.

2. Cut plums, apricots, or peaches into wedges and arrange them around the tart, working from the outside.

3. Cover with thin slices or little cubes of butter. Sprinkle the top liberally with sugar.

4. Bake the tart until the crust is golden brown, and then brush the fruit with apricot glaze.

5. Or, instead of the glaze, dust the cooled tart with confectioners' sugar.

HOW TO MAKE COOKED FRUIT AND FRANGIPANE TARTLETS

1. Spread a thick layer of Frangipane over an unbaked pastry-lined tartlet ring.

2. Cover with fruit such as kiwifruits, peaches, plums, or berries.

3. Sprinkle sugar over the fruit and then cover with very thin slices of butter. Bake until the crust is golden brown.

COOKING

1. Grate the zest from 1 lemon.

2. Combine the eggs and sugar in a saucepan with sloping sides. Whisk together, then add the lemon juice and zest.

3. Whisk over medium heat. The lemon curd will gradually thicken.

4. Remove from heat and stir in the butter, if using.

FILLINGS FOR TARTS

Three fillings are most often used for lining the bottom of a prebaked pastry shell: pastry cream (see page 436), crème mousseline (see page 437), and lemon curd (see page 469). Pastry cream, which is essentially milk and eggs sweetened with sugar and thickened with cornstarch, is also the classic filling for chocolate éclairs and for many layer cakes. Mousseline, made by beating a large amount of butter into pastry cream, is also a popular filling for layer cakes and some pastries, and it too appears in the chapter on cakes. Lemon curd, which follows here, is made by cooking together eggs, sugar, and lemon juice until the mixture thickens. Sometimes butter is added to give the curd more flavor and so that is it thicker when it cools. Other fruit juices and purees can be used in the same way to make a curd for lining pastry shells, but you can turn to other sources for those once you have mastered the basics. Frangipane (see page 470), which also follows here, is the most popular choice for lining unbaked pastry shells.

Lemon Curd

Lemon curd makes a refreshing contrast to very sweet ingredients, such as berries and other fillings, such as when used in a cake. You can cook the curd two ways: in a bowl over simmering water or in a saucepan with sloping slides. In both cases, make sure the curd does not boil, or it will curdle.

MAKES ABOUT 2 CUPS WITHOUT BUTTER, OR ABOUT 2½ CUPS WITH BUTTER

> **4 eggs or 10 egg yolks**
> **²/₃ cup sugar**
> **Grated zest of 1 lemon**
> **²/₃ cup fresh lemon juice**
> **4 to 8 tablespoons butter (optional)**

In heatproof bowl that fits over a saucepan, whisk together the eggs and sugar for 2 minutes, or until smooth and slightly pale. Whisk in the lemon zest and juice. Bring a few inches of water to a simmer in the saucepan and rest the bowl in the rim of the pan over, but not touching, the water. Make sure that no flame wraps around the bottom of the saucepan and overheats the edge of the bowl. Continue whisking the mixture for about 2 minutes, or until it thickens.

Alternatively, in a saucepan with sloping sides, whisk together the eggs and sugar for about 3 minutes, or until smooth and slightly pale. Whisk in the lemon zest and juice. Place over medium heat and whisk the mixture for about 2 minutes, or until it thickens. If there is the slightest hint that the mixture might boil, remove the pan from the heat and lower the heat before continuing.

Remove the curd from the heat and whisk in the butter until melted. Cover with plastic wrap, pressing it directly onto the surface to prevent a skin from forming. Let cool and refrigerate until needed. It will keep for up to 3 days.

Frangipane

Frangipane is a simple almond cream used for lining unbaked tart shells before topping with fruit. It provides flavor and texture of its own, but also absorbs the liquid released by the fruit, so the pastry won't become soggy.

MAKES ABOUT 2 CUPS

> **2 cups slivered blanched almonds**
>
> **1/3 cup sugar**
>
> **2 tablespoons cornstarch**
>
> **4 tablespoons cold butter, sliced**
>
> **2 eggs**

Preheat the oven to 350°F. Spread the almonds on a sheet pan and toast in the oven, stirring occasionally, for about 15 minutes, or until they are fragrant and have taken on color. Pour onto a plate and let cool.

In a food processor, combine the almonds, sugar, and cornstarch and process, stopping and scraping down the sides of the processor every minute or two, for 5 minutes, or until the mixture is the consistency of sandy peanut butter. Add the butter and process until smooth. Add the eggs and process for 2 minutes longer, or until creamy. Use immediately, or store in a tightly covered container in the refrigerator for up to 3 days.

Egg Wash for Pie Pastry

Brushing pie pastry with an egg wash gives it an attractive golden sheen. A classic egg wash is made with an egg yolk, a whole egg, and salt, but you can play around with the ingredients, adding another yolk if you want a darker glaze, or another white if you want a lighter glaze. For convenience, a single whole egg beaten with 1/2 teaspoon salt will work well on most pastries.

HOW TO MAKE FRANGIPANE

1. Combine almonds, sugar, and cornstarch in a food processor and process until the mixture is the consistency of sandy peanut butter.

2. Add sliced butter and process until smooth.

3. Add eggs and process until creamy.

Apricot Glaze

You can dramatically improve the appearance of fruit tarts and give them a professional finished look by brushing them with a glaze made from fruit preserves and water. As a general rule, cool glaze should be brushed on hot fruit tarts as soon as they come out of the oven, and hot glaze should be used on tarts made with uncooked fruit. Tarts that are brushed with glaze while they are hot can be brushed a second time once they have cooled. Apricot glaze is the traditional choice for apples and other pale fruits, but you can make glaze out of virtually any jam or preserves, from raspberry to red currant to any clear jelly. When using a glaze, don't get carried away. Err on the side of too little or too thin. A tart with too much glaze looks artificial—almost shellacked.

MAKES 1 1/2 CUPS

> **One 12-ounce jar apricot or other fruit preserves or jam**
> **3 tablespoons water**

In a small saucepan, combine the preserves and water over medium heat and heat, stirring constantly, until well combined. Remove from the heat and strain through a fine-mesh strainer placed over a small bowl. The glaze should have the consistency of hot maple syrup. If it is too thin, return it to the pan and boil it down. If too thick, thin with a little water. Store in a tightly covered container in the refrigerator for up to 3 weeks. To reheat for brushing on room-temperature tarts, simply stir in a small saucepan and add water if needed.

Brown Butter

Brown butter, also known as beurre noisette, is butter that has been cooked until all of its water has evaporated and its milk solids have coagulated and browned. The solids are then strained out, and what is left is a form of clarified butter with an intense nutty, butterscotch flavor. Ghee, the common Indian cooking fat, is made the same way. Brown butter is added to pastry doughs and batters and fillings to intensify their flavor. Its advantage is that you need only a small amount to deliver a lot of flavor, so you are not mixing in large amounts of butter. Because it contains no water, brown butter is also sometimes added to fillings and other mixtures to make them stiffer when they are cold. It will keep for months in the refrigerator.

MAKES 3/4 CUP

> **1/2 pound butter**

Put the butter in a heavy saucepan with a shiny bottom so you can easily see the milk solids when they coagulate, and place over medium heat. The butter will foam at first, but gradually, after about 5 minutes, the foam will subside. As the foam subsides, the milk solids will coagulate in tiny specks. Watch the specks closely: They will start out white, turn pale brown, and finally deep brown. This will take about 10 minutes. As soon as they are deep brown, immediately strain the butter through a fine-mesh strainer or a strainer lined with a paper towel into a bowl or other container. Use immediately, or let cool, cover tightly, and refrigerate.

Linzertorte

A linzertorte is sometimes considered a cake even though it's really much more like a tart. A linzertorte has a lattice top that allows the moisture on the inside of the torte to evaporate. A traditional linzertorte is made with linzer dough, which has almond flour in it and ends up being very delicate and fragile to the tooth. The problem is that linzer dough can be almost impossible to roll and the requisite almond flour impossible to find without a mail-order source. So this version is made with the Basic Tart and Pie Dough. Because the filling (frangipane and raspberry preserves) is fairly dry and won't make the crust soggy, there is no need to prebake the crust. This recipe uses more frangipane and less raspberry jam than most versions, yielding a less sweet result.

MAKES ONE 9- OR 10-INCH TORTE

> 1 recipe Basic Tart and Pie Dough (see page 445)
> 2 cups Frangipane (see page 470)
> 1 cup raspberry jam
> Egg Wash for Pie Pastry (see page 470)
> Confectioners' sugar

On a floured work surface, roll out the dough into a round slightly thicker than 1/8 inch and use to line a 9- or 10-inch tart ring or fluted tart pan with a removable bottom (page 458). When you press the dough into the ring and cut off the excess dough to make a border, save the excess dough for making the lattice top.

Preheat the oven to 400°F. Using an offset spatula, spread the frangipane over the tart shell in an even layer. Then spread the preserves evenly on top. Place the tart in the refrigerator.

Gather the dough scraps, shape into a disk, and roll out into a rectangle large enough to provide 12 strips for the lattice. Cut the strips about 1/2 inch wide and arrange 6 evenly across the tart. Arrange 6 more at a diagonal angle to the first strips. Trim off the edges where they hang over the tart.

Brush the strips with the egg wash, being careful not to let any drip down the sides onto the filling. Bake for about 1 hour, or until the lattice is golden brown and the filling is puffed up slightly (don't worry, it will settle back down as the torte cools). Let cool on a rack.

To decorate the rim of the torte with confectioners' sugar, place a cardboard disk, the same size as the torte, on top of the torte, with just a sliver of the edge exposed. Dust the exposed portion with confectioners' sugar. Then continue to move the cardboard, exposing a bit of the rim with each move and dusting as you go, until the entire rim has a light dusting of sugar.

Crisp Puff Pastry Apple Tart

This tart combines a fragile crispiness with a butterscotch sweetness and the tang of apples. If you are making puff pastry for this tart, you can get by giving it only 4 turns, since the point is to end up with a flaky, crispy pastry, rather than one that rises.

MAKES ONE 14-BY-11-INCH TART

> Puff Pastry (see page 476; no more than 4 turns needed) or Quick Puff Pastry (see page 478)
> 3 large apples such as Golden Delicious or Macintosh or tart baking apple, peeled, cored, and sliced as shown opposite
> 2/3 cup sugar
> 1/2 cup butter, very thinly sliced

Preheat the oven to 425°F. On a floured work surface, roll out the puff pastry into a 12-by-15-inch rectangle between 1/8 and 1/16 inch thick. Sprinkle cold water on a 13-by-17-inch sheet pan. The water will keep the bottom of the tart from burning. Roll the dough loosely around the rolling pin and unroll it over the pan. Trim the edges of the rectangle so they are even.

Arrange the apple slices in 4 rows along the length of the tart, overlapping the slices so that each slice covers about half of the one before it. Sprinkle the tart evenly with the sugar, and cover evenly with the butter slices.

Bake for about 1 hour, or until the edges are a deep golden brown. Twenty minutes into the baking, start checking the tart to make sure it isn't puffing and forcing off the apples. If it is puffing, poke the puffed part with the tip of a paring knife to deflate it and use the tip of the knife to rearrange gently any slices that have moved. Let cool on a rack.

Use a long, wide spatula to get the tart off the sheet pan. It always sticks a little, and often the very edges of the tart burn slightly. If this is true of your tart, trim off the edges. Cut into 8 rectangles to serve.

1. Peel, halve, and core the apples.

2. Thinly slice the apple halves crosswise, leaving the slices attached by a thin strip at one end, and then cut off that strip.

3. Gently press the sliced apple halves to fan out.

4. Unroll very thin puff pastry on a sheet pan sprinkled with cold water.

5. Arrange the apple slices in overlapping rows on the pastry.

6. Sprinkle with sugar.

7. Cover with thin slices of butter. Bake until golden brown.

8. Trim off the edges.

9. Cut the tart into rectangles. Serve with whipped cream if you like.

PASTRIES

The enormous variety of pastries, from napoleons to croissants to turnovers, comes from manipulating butter, flour, eggs, and often sugar using different techniques. The secret to the best pastry is butter. Pastries made from shortening or margarine may look as nice—sometimes they even look better—but they will never have the taste of butter-based pastry.

As you practice making basic pastries, you will start to recognize that flour behaves differently from brand to brand. Flour from the South tends to contain less gluten than other flours and will absorb less liquid. The recipes included here work with everyday all-purpose flour. If you are using southern flour, you will find you need less liquid, and in fact that certain kinds of dough, such as puff pastry, will roll out easier.

Pastries are made from a wide variety of doughs. The various doughs used for making pies and tarts in the preceeding chapter are a type of pastry, as is cream puff pastry dough (not to be confused with puff pastry), which is used for cream puffs and éclairs and is made by cooking together flour, water, and butter and then adding eggs. Some doughs are laminated, in other words, butter is sealed up in them and they are repeatedly folded like a letter so that the layers multiply. Puff pastry is the purest example of this. Other doughs, such as those used to make croissants or Danish pastry, are laminated like puff pastry but also contain yeast, which helps lighten them and give them flavor.

Storing, Refrigerating, and Freezing Dough

Since most doughs contain butter, they get very hard when cold. For this reason, it's not always a good idea to conform to the conventional wisdom of chilling dough before rolling it out. Cold dough cracks when rolled and has to warm up some to become workable. On the other hand, as soon as dough gets to the melting point of butter (around 85°F) it is ruined. We often stick dough in the refrigerator to give it time to rest and the gluten to lose some of its tenacity. An ideal environment would be warmer, around 55 degrees, so the dough would rest without the butter becoming so terribly hard. Most doughs can be kept in the refrigerator, tightly wrapped, for several days and in the freezer for several months. It's essential that dough you freeze be first tightly wrapped in plastic wrap and then again in aluminum foil to hold the plastic wrap in place. While it may seem counterintuitive, dough doesn't rest in the freezer, but instead the whole process of the gluten relaxing is arrested; so don't assume that simply because your dough has been in the freezer for 3 months that it's ready to roll out. If it was elastic when it went into the freezer, it will be elastic when it comes out. Dough is best thawed in stages—first transfer it to the refrigerator, then to a cool place such as on a windowsill, and finally to cool room temperature.

Puff Pastry

Most people are terrified by the thought of making puff pastry because they have never seen it made. True, it takes a little practice to roll out the dough and get the butter to behave, but once you have mastered the systematic rolling and folding, it is a satisfying exercise that will make you an expert with a rolling pin.

Classic puff pastry is made by enclosing butter in a square or rectangle of plain dough made with water and flour, and here, oil. The packet is rolled out into a long rectangle, folded over itself like a letter, rolled out again, allowed to rest, rolled out again, and so on until six "turns," or series of folds, have been completed. The recipe and method given here differ from classic recipes (and create much more dramatic results) in two ways: the addition of oil and the kneading of the dough before it is used. The oil helps relax the dough, and though the kneading requires a 12-hour rest, it creates a smoother dough that forms thin layers that don't break. And instead of the classic six turns, seven turns are completed, yielding an even lighter effect.

There are several tricks to success. Never force the dough. If it becomes elastic and shrinks as you are rolling it, wrap it in plastic wrap and put it in the refrigerator for an hour. It must never get warm. If the kitchen is hot, keep putting it in the refrigerator or freezer to chill it. The butter must be worked before you use it, so that it rolls out with the dough. The time needed to make puff pastry will depend on the kind of flour you use. If the flour has a lot of gluten, the dough will start to shrink with less rolling than it will with low-gluten flour, and will require more resting time between the rollings.

MAKES 1¹/₂ POUNDS DOUGH

- 1 cup all-purpose flour
- 1 cup cake flour
- ¹/₂ cup water
- 3 tablespoons vegetable oil
- 1 teaspoon salt
- ³/₄ pound cold butter, each stick cut into 4 cubes

In a food processor, combine both flours, the water, the oil, and the salt and process for 1 minute, or until the dough looks like gravel. Pull the dough out of the food processor and knead it on a work surface (no need for flouring) with the heel of your hand for 2 to 3 minutes, or until it pulls together into a single mass. Shape into a disk, wrap in plastic wrap, and refrigerate for at least 12 hours.

The next day (or the evening of the first day), on a clean work surface, crush the butter with the heel of your hand and work it with your fingers until you feel no lumps. It should be smooth, spreadable, and have the consistency of buttercream. Wrap in plastic wrap and refrigerate for 15 minutes.

On a floured work surface, roll out the dough into a rectangle about 18 inches long and 9 inches wide. Shape the butter into an 8-inch square and place it on one end of the rectangle, leaving a small border around the edges. Fold the uncovered half of the rectangle over the butter, covering it completely. Press around the edges to seal in the butter. Wrap in plastic wrap and refrigerate for 15 minutes. Don't refrigerate for longer, or the butter will harden and you won't be able to roll it out.

Gently hammer on the package with a rolling pin and, when it softens, roll it, to spread it out into a rectangle about 18 inches long and 9 inches wide with the butter sealed inside. Run your hand along the surface of the rectangle to make sure the butter is spreading out evenly. Now, fold the rectangle as if you are folding a business letter: starting from a narrow end, fold the bottom third of the rectangle up, and then fold the opposite end down.

If the dough is still easy to work, roll it out into a rectangle and fold in the same way. If it's not easy to roll, wrap it and refrigerate it for 30 minutes or up to 12 hours and fold it in the same way. Make two imprints with your fingers to indicate that it has had 2 "turns." Wrap in plastic and refrigerate for at least 1 hour. Give the dough 1 to 3 turns—as many as you can get by with without it turning elastic—wrap and refrigerate for at least 30 minutes. Continue in this way until the dough has had a total of 7 turns.

1. Combine all the ingredients except the butter in a food processor and process until the dough looks like gravel.

2. Pull the dough out of the food processor and knead it with the heel of your hand for a few minutes. Wrap in plastic wrap and refrigerate for at least 12 hours.

3. The next day, crush the butter with the heel of your hand.

4. Work it with your fingers until you feel no lumps. It should be smooth, spreadable, and have the consistency of buttercream. Refrigerate for 15 minutes.

5. Roll out the dough into a rectangle about 18 inches long and 9 inches wide.

6. Shape the butter into an 8-inch square and place it on one end of the rectangle, leaving a small border around the edges. Fold over the other half of the rectangle to cover the butter.

7. Press around the edges to seal in the butter. Refrigerate for 15 minutes. Don't chill it longer, or it will harden and be difficult to roll out.

8. Gently hammer on the package to spread it out into a long rectangle with the butter sealed inside. Switch to rolling as the dough becomes more malleable.

9. Run your hand along the surface of the rectangle to make sure the butter is spreading out evenly.

10. Starting at a narrow end, lift up the end of pastry nearest you over half the remainder of the rectangle.

11. Fold the end of the rectangle farthest away from you over the first fold.

12. If the dough is still easy to work, roll it out again into a rectangle and fold in the same way. Make two imprints with your fingers to indicate that you have completed 2 "turns." Wrap in plastic wrap and refrigerate for at least an hour before giving the dough any more turns. Continue in this way until you have completed 7 turns.

Quick Puff Pastry

Many of us don't have the foresight or want to take the time to make classic puff pastry. Quick puff pastry rises almost as dramatically and can be made in only a couple of hours. However, it is trickier to make than the classic pastry because large chunks of butter are distributed in the dough and can stick to the pin and to the work surface, while in the classic method, no butter ever touches the pin or surface because it is sealed in the layers of dough. The quick version is especially difficult to make if you are working in a hot kitchen and may require sliding it in and out of the freezer or fridge to keep it cool.

MAKES 1½ POUNDS DOUGH

> **2 cups flour**
> **³/₄ pound cold butter, each stick cut into 4 cubes**
> **²/₃ cup water**
> **1 teaspoon salt**

Combine the flour and butter and assemble the mixture in a mound on a work surface. Make a well in the middle with your fingers. Pour the water into the well and then add the salt. With the fingertips of one hand, move around the inside of the flour wall, gradually eroding away the flour and combining it with the liquid. When all of the liquid and flour are loosely combined, use a plastic pastry scraper to fold the dough over itself until there is no loose flour.

Dust the dough with flour and, using a rolling pin, hammer on the butter and dough to form the dough in a rectangle about 18 inches long and 9 inches wide. Fold the rectangle over itself to form a square, and with the rolling pin and the pastry scraper, form the dough-butter mixture into a rectangle about 20 inches long and 8 inches wide. This may require a lot of hammering and frequent dusting of the surfaces with flour to prevent sticking. Now, fold the rectangle as if you are folding a business letter: starting from a narrow end, fold the bottom third of the rectangle up, and then fold the opposite end down. If the kitchen is warm, wrap the dough in plastic wrap and refrigerate for 15 minutes.

Pound on the squarish rectangle with the rolling pin to form another rectangle about 20 inches long and 8 inches wide. Keep flouring the surfaces to prevent sticking (see below). Fold the narrow ends of the rectangle toward the middle so they nearly meet, leaving about 1 inch between them. Fold the two ends together so they meet in the middle and then fold the two ends together to form a square with 4 layers. Hammer out this square with the rolling pin, roll out again into a rectangle of the same size, and fold again with the two ends meeting in the middle. Wrap and refrigerate for 1 hour before using. When the dough is folded in this way—so the two ends meet in the middle and then the two ends of the dough are folded together—it is called a "double turn," even though it doesn't really double the number of layers but multiplies the layers by 4 instead of by 3.

Flouring Surfaces to Prevent Sticking

When dusting a work surface and/or pastry with flour, the point is to create as thin a layer as possible to prevent sticking while adding very little additional flour. Most beginning cooks sprinkle the flour from above and it lands in clumps that do little to prevent sticking and add considerable flour to the dough. The "professional" technique is to grab a large pinch of flour, pull your hand back, and with a throwing motion swing the hand toward the dough and release the flour just at the edge of the table so it releases in a cloud over and around the dough. To flour underneath the dough, simply hold the dough and move it over the work surface in a circular motion. As you're rolling the dough and it wants to stick to the surface, don't make the mistake of repositioning yourself to accommodate the dough but instead move the dough. The idea is to dust with flour and move the pastry almost constantly. This will prevent sticking and use very little flour. While you're learning, you might make a mess and dust anyone who happens to be standing around.

1. Roll out a sheet of puff pastry on a sheet pan (so the cutouts stay round when you pull away the excess dough) and cut out rounds with a fluted cutter.

2. Pull away the excess dough.

3. Place a small mound of filling slightly off center on each pastry round.

4. Rub the edges of the round with cold water.

5. Fold over the round to make a half-moon and press the edges together.

6. Brush tops with egg wash.

7. Make slits along the surface without cutting through.

8. Bake until golden brown.

Blueberry Turnovers

You can put virtually any cooked mixture on one-half of a round of puff pastry, fold over the pastry, and press the two edges together. Don't be tempted to put too much filling into each turnover, or it will leak out during baking.

MAKES 10 TURNOVERS

> **2 cups blueberries**
> **1/4 cup water**
> **1/4 cup granulated sugar, or more as needed**
> **Puff Pastry (see page 476) or Quick Puff Pastry (opposite)**
> **Cold water for sealing turnovers**
> **1 egg**
> **Salt**
> **Confectioners' sugar for dusting (optional)**

In a saucepan, combine the blueberries, water, and granulated sugar over medium heat. Cover and simmer for about 4 minutes, or until the berries release all their liquid. Uncover and cook down over medium heat for about 15 minutes, or until the mixture thickens. Stir every minute or so to prevent sticking and burning. You should end up with about 1/2 cup. Let cool to room temperature, taste and adjust with more sugar if needed, cover, and refrigerate until cold.

Cut the pastry dough in half to make it easier to roll out and roll each half on a floured work surface, so that it's slightly thicker than 1/8 inch. Cut out 10 rounds with a 4-inch fluted cookie cutter.

Preheat the oven to 425°F. Place about 1 tablespoon of the berry mixture slightly off center on each pastry round. Brush half of the edge of the pastry rounds with cold water, using your fingers or a brush. Fold over the pastry, enclosing the filling, and gently pinch the edge of the turnover to seal it. Beat the egg with a good pinch of salt until dark and runny. Brush the tops of the turnovers with the egg wash. Don't let any egg wash drip down the sides because the drips will create a seal and prevent rising. Place the turnovers on a sheet pan sprinkled with cold water. Make a series of decorative slashes across each turnover.

Bake for about 25 minutes, or until golden brown. For a shiny glaze, sift a little confectioners' sugar over the turnovers about 5 minutes before they come out of the oven. Serve warm or cold.

Napoleons

Napoleons are rectangular pastries made by sandwiching a filling, traditionally pastry cream, between two, or sometimes three, thin sheets of cooked puff pastry. The pastry is rolled very thin and baked between two sheet pans to keep it from puffing, and it is baked to a very deep brown for maximum flavor and crispiness. By definition, napoleons are rectangular, but the principle (sandwiching filling between sheets of brittle puff pastry) can be used to make large round or square pastries with virtually any filling, provided it is stiff enough that it doesn't ooze out when you cut through the layers.

MAKES 6 PASTRIES

Puff Pastry (see page 476) or Quick Puff Pastry (see page 478)
2 cups Pastry Cream (see page 436)
Confectioners' sugar for dusting

Preheat the oven to 400°F. On a floured work surface, roll out the pastry dough into a 13-by-17-inch rectangle. Loosely roll it around the rolling pin and unroll it on a sheet pan covered with a sheet of parchment paper or sprinkled with cold water. Trim the sides if necessary to make the sheet fit. Using a fork, lightly prick the pastry to create holes (this is called docking) at regular intervals all over the surface. This will keep it from puffing in the oven.

Cover the pastry with a sheet of parchment paper, top with another sheet pan, and bake for 20 minutes. Remove the top sheet pan and the parchment and continue to bake for 20 minutes longer, or until deep golden brown. Let cool completely in the pan on a rack. Turn the rectangle out onto the work surface.

Using a bread knife, trim the edges so the rectangle is perfectly even. Measure the rectangle and cut it crosswise into 3 rectangles of equal size. Because the pastry shrinks in the oven (to be expected), each rectangle will be about 5 by 12 inches.

Cut a piece of cardboard the same size as the rectangles. Set aside about 1/3 cup of the pastry cream to finish the sides of the pastries. Put the first pastry rectangle on the cardboard, and spread it with half of the remaining pastry cream. Press the second rectangle on top of the filling, and spread over the remaining pastry cream. Put the last rectangle, flat bottom side up, on top. Using a small metal spatula, smooth the reserved pastry cream evenly over the sides of the rectangle. Cover and chill the rectangle for at least 1 hour to make it easier to cut.

Sprinkle the top of the stacked rectangles liberally with confectioners' sugar. If you like, heat a metal skewer until almost red hot on a gas stove top or with a kitchen blowtorch and burn a crisscross pattern in the sugar. Cut into 2-by-5-inch rectangles to serve.

1. Roll out puff pastry into a thin sheet and place it on a sheet pan sprinkled with cold water. Poke the surface evenly with a fork to prevent it from puffing up. Cover with a sheet of parchment paper and a sheet pan, and bake until golden brown.

2. Trim the edges to make the rectangle perfectly even.

3. Measure the sheet so you can cut 3 rectangles of equal size.

4. Cut the rectangles evenly.

5. Trim the edges off the rectangles so they are all the same size.

6. Spread a layer of pastry cream over the first rectangle.

7. Place another rectangle on top.

8. Spread over another layer of pastry cream.

9. Place the final rectangle on top.

10. Spread pastry cream over the sides to cover evenly. Cover and chill to make cutting easier.

11. After refrigerating, sprinkle liberally with confectioners' sugar.

12. If you like, burn a crosshatch pattern with a red-hot skewer over the top. Then cut into rectangles and serve.

Pithiviers (Almond Galette)

Sometimes called galette du roi, this round puff pastry cake is sometimes fitted with a gilded paper crown meant to be worn by whoever bites into the "feve," a bean meant to bring good luck, embedded in the galette. This cake is also a good vehicle for showing off your puff pastry since the rise can be dramatic.

MAKES 10 DESSERT SERVINGS

Puff Pastry (see page 476) or Quick Puff Pastry (see page 478)

1 cup Frangipane (see page 470)

1 egg, beaten with 1 large pinch of salt

Preheat the oven to 425°F. Cut the pastry dough in half. On a floured work surface, roll out each half into a square slightly larger than 10 inches and slightly thicker than 1/8 inch. Transfer one half to a sheet pan sprinkled with cold water. Using a 10-inch pie pan, tart ring, or similar template, cut out a 10-inch round.

Dollop the frangipane on the center of the round. Then, using a spatula, smooth it out into an even layer, leaving a 2-inch border uncovered. Brush the uncovered border with water. Loosely roll the remaining pastry around the rolling pin, and unroll it over the bottom round, covering the filling. Use a bowl or something the same diameter as the round on the bottom to cut the top round where it comes to the edge of the bottom round. Trim the edges as needed create an even round. Press around the edges to create a seal. Brush the top with the egg wash. Use a paring knife to create spokes that arc from the center to the outside edge.

Bake for about 25 minutes, or until well puffed and golden brown. Turn down the oven to 300°F and bake for 20 to 30 minutes longer, or as long as possible without overbrowning the pastry. The second half of the baking is to cook any raw dough left on the inside of the pastry. Let cool on a rack.

HOW TO MAKE PITHIVIERS

1. Roll out a sheet of puff pastry and use a pie pan or other template to cut out a large disk.

2. Spread frangipane over the center, leaving a 2-inch border. Brush the border with water.

3. Unroll another sheet of puff pastry and place it over the bottom round to cover the filling.

4. Use a bowl that matches the diameter of the galette to trim away the excess pastry and create an even round. Press around the edges to seal.

5. Brush the top with egg wash, and make a series of spokes, starting from the center and working toward the outside.

6. Bake until well puffed and golden brown. Turn down the oven and bake as long as possible without overbrowning to cook the dough through on the inside. Serve in wedges.

Croissant Dough

There are few pastries more satisfying to make at home than croissants. The dough is made much like puff pastry, with the butter sealed in the dough and the packet rolled out and folded over itself to make layers. Unlike puff pastry, the dough for croissants also contains yeast, which helps it rise and gives it its delicate flakiness.

You can't be quite as leisurely when making croissant dough as when making puff pastry, because if the dough is out too long, the yeast will overproof and wear itself out before the final rise. Refrigerating the dough or the shaped croissants during the whole process can slow down the process but never stops the action completely. Freezing is an option, but it significantly weakens the yeast.

MAKES 2 POUNDS, ENOUGH FOR 18 CROISSANTS

2 cups cake flour

1¹/₃ cups all-purpose flour or more as needed

1 teaspoon salt

1¹/₃ cups milk, barely warm

2 tablespoons sugar

1 teaspoon active dry yeast

3 sticks cold butter

Combine the flour and the salt in a mound on a work surface or in a bowl, and make a well in the middle with your fingers. Pour the milk into the well and add the sugar and yeast. If on a work surface, using the fingertips of one hand, move around the inside of the flour wall, gradually eroding away the flour and combining it with the liquid. If in a bowl, stir with a wooden spoon, gradually pulling the flour wall into the liquid.

When the milk is almost completely combined, flour the work surface and knead the dough for about 10 minutes, or until smooth and elastic. If the dough sticks to your hands, knead in extra flour until it pulls away from your hands. You may also knead the dough with a mixer, using the dough hook. Shape the dough into a disk, wrap with plastic wrap, and refrigerate for at least 1 hour or up to 3 hours. Don't refrigerate it longer than that or it may overferment.

Cut the butter into ¹/₂-inch-thick slices and either flatten the slices with the heel of your hand or work the slices in a

stand mixer fitted with the paddle blade until smooth. Spread the butter into an 8-inch square, and wrap in plastic wrap. Refrigerate the square.

On a floured work surface, flatten the dough with the heel of your hand and roll it into a rectangle about 16 inches long and 8 inches wide. The rectangle must be twice as long as it is wide. Place the butter on one end of the rectangle. Fold the uncovered half of the rectangle over the butter, covering it completely. Press around the edges to seal in the butter. Press gently on the square with one hand while firming up the sides with the other hand to even out the square. Gently hammer on the pastry square with the rolling pin to stretch the pastry and the butter in it and then roll the pastry into a rectangle 16 inches long and 8 inches wide. Now, fold the rectangle as if you are folding a business letter. This is the first turn. (At this point the dough may become difficult to roll.) Wrap the dough and refrigerate for 1 hour before continuing.

As if it were a book, position the packet on the work surface with the "spine" on your left, and roll out again into a rectangle 16 inches long and 8 inches wide. Again, fold the rectangle like a letter. This is the second turn. Wrap the dough and refrigerate it for at least 30 minutes, then repeat the rolling and folding. This is the third turn. If the dough is elastic or the butter threatens to ooze out, refrigerate the dough for 1 hour before continuing.

Roll out the dough and fold it for the fourth and final turn. Let rest for at least 1 hour in the refrigerator before rolling out for croissants or other pastries.

(continued)

1. Combine the salt and flours, pile them on the work surface, and make a well in the center.

2. Pour in warm milk and add the sugar and the yeast.

3. Work the milk with the flour, gradually eroding the sides of the well.

4. Knead the dough with the heel of your hand until smooth and elastic. Wrap in plastic wrap and refrigerate for 3 hours.

5. Roll out the dough into a rectangle.

6. Knead the butter until smooth.

7. Shape the butter into a square, wrap in plastic wrap, and refrigerate.

8. Place the butter square on one end of the pastry rectangle.

9. Fold the dough over the butter.

10. Pinch around the sides to seal in the butter.

11. Gently hammer and roll the sealed-in butter into a rectangle.

12. Continue hammering and rolling...

13. ...until you have a rectangle.

14. When you have a long rectangle, fold the top third down.

15. Fold the bottom third up, like folding a business letter. Wrap in plastic wrap and let rest in the refrigerator. Let rest and repeat 3 times, for a total of 4 turns.

Croissants

How long it takes for shaped croissants to rise before baking depends on the temperature of their environment. You can shape them the night before, let them rise a little bit at room temperature, and then refrigerate them so they are ready to bake when you get up in the morning, or you can let them rise at room temperature in just about 2 hours. If you don't want to make the full batch of 18 croissants, use only part of the dough and freeze the rest. But don't freeze it for too long. The yeast will start to lose its potency in about 2 weeks.

MAKES 18 CROISSANTS

> **Croissant Dough (see page 483)**
> **1 egg**
> **Salt**

On a floured work surface, roll out the dough into a rectangle 20 inches long by 12 inches wide and 1/8 to 1/4 inch thick. Trim any uneven edges off the rectangle. Starting at the edge, measure 5 inches along one long side of the first rectangle, and make a tiny notch to mark the base of the first triangle. Continue in this way until you have made 3 notches each 5 inches apart the length of the rectangle. One side of the rectangle will now be marked off into four 5-inch sections.

On the other long side of the rectangle, make a notch 2 1/2 inches in from the end. Make a second notch 5 inches farther along, a third notch 5 inches farther along, and the last notch another 5 inches farther along. This second side will now be marked into 5 sections, with the first section at either end 2 1/2 inches long and the 3 sections in the middle each 5 inches long. While the notches of the first long side mark the bases of the triangles, the notches on the second side mark the tips of the triangles. Repeat with the second rectangle.

Use a large knife to cut out the triangles by connecting the notches on the first side with those on the second side. You will end up with 7 full triangles, each 5 inches along the base and 6 inches on the sides, and two 1/2 triangles on the ends.

(continued)

HOW TO MAKE CROISSANTS

1. Roll the croissant dough into a long rectangle and make notches every 5 inches on one side.

2. Do the same on the other long side, but start the notches 2 1/2 inches in from the end.

3. Cut from point to point so you cut the dough into triangles.

4. Pull the apex of the triangles to stretch them.

5. Make a slit in the center of the bottom of each triangle.

6. Roll up from the base of the triangle, working away from the slit in the center and curling the triangle ends downward.

7. Curl the ends inward to make the classic shape. Make sure the end of the triangle is tucked underneath. Cover with plastic wrap and let rise in a moderately warm place until doubled in size.

8. Brush with egg wash. Bake until golden brown.

Croissants, continued

Make a 1/4-inch slit in the center of the base of each triangle. As you begin to roll up each triangle to form a croissant, curl the two sides of the cut away from each other. Continue rolling with one hand on each half of the triangle, pointing your hands away from each other as you roll. When you have finished rolling, the tip of triangle should be underneath. Now, bend the 2 ends toward each other, forming a small crab shape. You should see 3 distinct layers of dough on the croissant.

Arrange the croissants on a sheet pan, spacing them about 2 inches apart, and cover with plastic wrap (they should be well covered, but don't tuck the plastic under the pan). Put the pan in a warm, though not hot, place. The croissants should never get hotter than 85°F, or the butter will melt and ooze out. When they have doubled in size, they are ready to bake. This should take about 2 hours at 75°F.

Preheat the oven to 375°F. Beat the egg with a big pinch of salt until dark and runny. Brush the croissants with this egg wash and bake for about 35 minutes, or until puffed and golden brown. Place on a rack and let cool on the pan to room temperature before serving.

The croissants should pull apart in layers.

Danish Pastries

Real Danish pastries, unlike the breadlike imitations so often sold by the same name, are made with dough that is similar to croissant dough. Indeed, it is so similar that you can use croissant dough to make Danish pastries without compromising quality. Here, the dough is rolled out, sprinkled with raisins and nuts, and spread with frangipane, but almost any filling—fruit preserves and cream cheese, shredded apple, currants, and nuts—will work.

MAKES 12 DANISH PASTRIES

> **Croissant Dough (see page 483)**
> **1 1/2 cups Frangipane (see page 470)**
> **1/2 cup golden raisins, soaked in water to cover for 30 minutes, drained, and patted dry**
> **1 cup walnuts or natural almonds, coarsely chopped**
> **1 egg, beaten with 1 large pinch salt until dark and runny**
> **4 tablespoons Apricot Glaze (see page 470), optional**
> **Royal Icing (see page 510), optional**

On a floured work surface, roll out the dough into a rectangle about 18 inches long, 10 inches wide, and 1/8 to 1/4 inch thick. Using an offset spatula, spread the frangipane over the rectangle in an even layer. Sprinkle evenly with the raisins and nuts.

Brush a nonstick sheet pan with oil (this is important because the pastries will be expanding sideways as they proof and must not be held in place by a sticky pan). Starting from a 10-inch side, begin rolling the dough by pinching the edge and then continue rolling as tightly as you can into a log.

Slice the log into 12 equal disks. Tuck the little flap of dough on the outside of each disk under the center to hold it in place. Arrange the disks, cut side down, on the sheet pan, spacing them at least 2 inches apart to allow for expansion, and cover with plastic wrap (they should be well covered, but don't tuck the plastic under the pan). Put the pan in a warm, but not hot, place, and let proof until each layer of dough is about 50 percent thicker. This should take about 1 hour.

Preheat the oven to 400°F. Brush the pastries with the egg wash and bake for about 35 minutes, or until golden brown. If they start to get too brown, turn the oven down to 325°F to finish baking. Remove from the oven and brush with the apricot glaze while still hot. Drizzle with the royal icing, either with a paper cone (see page 439) or by dipping a fork into the icing and waving it back and forth over the pastries.

1. Roll out the dough into a rectangle and spread it with Frangipane.

2. Sprinkle with nuts and raisins and start rolling it as tightly as possible.

3. Continue to roll, tucking the roll under as you go.

4. Cut the log into slices about 3/4 inch thick. Tuck under the end of the roll of each Danish, and place the pastries on an oiled nonstick sheet pan, cut side down.

5. Cover loosely with plastic wrap and let rise at room temperature.

6. Brush with egg wash and bake until golden brown.

1. Combine butter, water, and salt and bring to a simmer over medium-high heat until the butter melts. Add the flour all at once.

2. Stir vigorously over high heat to eliminate lumps.

3. Continue to stir until the dough comes together in a solid mass and pulls away from the sides of the pan. Remove from the heat, transfer to a bowl, and stir until it cools slightly.

4. Work in eggs one at a time until a groove drawn through the middle of batter slowly folds in on itself, or the batter droops from the spoon when it is held sideways.

Cream Puff Pastry

Don't confuse this pastry with puff pastry, which is made by rolling butter in a packet of dough. This one, also called choux paste or pâté à choux, is used for making cream puffs, éclairs, and more exotic delicacies such as swans. It is made differently from most other pastry doughs: flour is added to boiling water and butter, the mixture is stirred until it no longer clings to the sides of the pan, and eggs are beaten in one at a time until the dough, which is more like a batter, is the correct consistency.

MAKES 3 CUPS

> 1 cup water
> 1/2 teaspoon salt
> 8 tablespoons butter, sliced
> 1 1/4 cups flour, sifted
> 7 eggs, or more as needed

In a saucepan, combine the water, salt, and butter and bring to a simmer over medium-high heat just until the butter melts. Add the flour all at once. Stir with a wooden spoon for about 2 minutes, or until the mixture forms a cohesive mass and pulls away from the sides of the pan, leaving a white film of flour on the pan sides.

Transfer the dough to a bowl or a stand mixer and work it with a wooden spoon or the paddle for about 1 minute, or until it has cooled slightly. Then work in the eggs one at a time, beating well after each addition. Check the consistency of the batter by pulling a wooden spoon through it. When the groove it makes slowly closes in on itself, you have added enough eggs. Or, the batter is ready if it droops from the spoon when the spoon is held sideways. It must be stiff enough to hold its shape when it is piped or spooned onto a sheet pan. Add more eggs one half at a time as needed to achieve this consistency. Use the dough right away.

Éclairs

To make éclairs, you pipe out strips of cream puff pastry batter, bake them in a hot oven, and then fill the cooled pastries with pastry cream or another filling. There are two ways to get the filling into the éclair: You can cut the éclair in half horizontally, put the cream on the bottom, and replace the top. Or, you can make a little hole in each end of the bottom of an éclair and pipe the filling through holes with a pastry bag fitted with a star tip, which is done here. The classic topping for éclairs is fondant. It can be messy to work with, however, making a dusting of confectioners' sugar a good solution when you are in a hurry. This recipe describes piping the batter onto parchment paper to prevent sticking, but if you have nonstick pans just pipe the batter right onto them (no buttering or flouring is needed).

MAKES 16 ÉCLAIRS

Cream Puff Pastry (opposite)

Egg wash (see page 470)

2½ cups Pastry Cream (see page 436), flavored with coffee, chocolate, or fruit brandy as desired

2 cups chocolate, coffee, or vanilla Liquid Fondant (at right, and see page 490)

Preheat the oven to 500°F. Cut two 13-by-17-inch sheets of parchment paper. Use a pencil to make 8 evenly-spaced lines, each 4½ inches long and 1¼ inches wide, on each sheet of parchment. Spoon the pastry batter into a pastry bag fitted with a ½-inch plain tip, and pipe a tiny dollop of dough into each corner of a 13-by-17-inch sheet pan. Lay the parchment paper, marks side down, in the pan, pressing the corners of the parchment onto the dollops of batter to anchor it in place.

Using the pencil marks as guides, pipe 8 strips of the pastry batter onto the parchment paper. Brush each strip with the egg wash.

Slide the sheet pan into the oven and immediately turn down the oven to 400°F. Bake for 20 minutes, or until the pastries are golden brown. If the éclairs start to look too brown, turn down the oven to 200°F. At no point should you open the oven door. When the éclairs are done, they should feel feather light. Let cool on the pan on a rack.

Fill the éclairs when you are ready to serve them, or plan to serve them within a few hours. To fill the éclairs, use a ⅓-inch star decorating tip to make a hole in the bottom of each end of an éclair. Then fit the pastry bag with a ⅓-inch plain tip, spoon the pastry cream into the bag, and squeeze a little cream into each hole until the éclairs are filled and you can't fit any more in (using about a scant 3 tablespoons filling).

Warm the fondant to slightly warmer than body temperature (it should feel barely warm when you touch the bottom of the bowl), or until it has the consistency of cold maple syrup. You can do this in a heatproof bowl over a pan of simmering water or in a microwave. One at a time, dip the éclairs, top down, in the fondant. Lift them out of the fondant without turning them upright immediately, so any excess fondant drips off. Allow the fondant to set for at least 30 minutes before serving.

Liquid Fondant

Liquid fondant is the glaze used on éclairs. Until the secret behind making it in a food processor was discovered, making fondant was such a nuisance—it required interminable kneading of sugar syrup on a marble surface—that most bakers just bought it. Unfortunately, it is hard to buy in amounts smaller than 5 pounds, so making it in a food processor has become a great solution. Fondant will keep in a tightly sealed container, in or out of the refrigerator, for months. If it hardens, add a tiny bit of water to it and heat it in a metal bowl set over a pan of simmering water or in a microwave.

MAKES 4 CUPS

3 cups sugar

2 cups water

½ cup light corn syrup

In a heavy saucepan, combine the sugar, water, and corn syrup and stir over low heat until the sugar has dissolved. Increase the heat to medium and heat, without stirring, until the mixture comes to a boil and registers 234°F to 240°F on a candy thermometer, or the soft-ball stage. If you don't have a candy thermometer, have ready a teaspoon and a bowl of cold (but not iced) water. As the sugar syrup boils, dip the spoon handle in the syrup and then immediately into the water. When the syrup hardens to the texture of chewing gum that has been chewed a bit, the syrup is ready. Pour the syrup into the food processor and let stand until the temperature drops to 143°F on an instant-read thermometer. Process for about 5 minutes, or until the fondant is milky and opaque. Don't overprocess or the friction overheats the fondant and breaks down the emulsion.

Flavoring Semisolid Glazes and Fillings

Some mixtures such as fondant, pastry cream, mousseline, and royal icing allow for a great deal of improvisation when it comes to flavoring them with coffee, vanilla, chocolate, fruit purees, or fruit brandies, but these flavors have to be added with a certain amount of caution so that the filling or icing does not become too liquid. The surest way to deal with chocolate is to melt chocolate with a high cacao content, even unsweetened chocolate, and whisk it into the glaze or filling until the color and flavor are what you want. The milk used to make pastry cream can be infused with ground coffee, which is then strained out before the milk is added to the egg mixture, but this is a convoluted approach that's usually avoided by using a very concentrated mixture of water and instant coffee instead. Vanilla extract is very concentrated, as are the best fruit brandies from France or Switzerland, so a small amount of liquid added rarely makes the mixture too liquidy. Fruit purees should be strained and cooked down until stiff and very concentrated and then stirred in according to taste and color. In general, count on 1/2 teaspoon vanilla extract per cup of icing or glaze, 2 teaspoons instant coffee combined with 1 tablespoon hot water per cup of icing or glaze, 2 tablespoons concentrated fruit puree per cup of icing or glaze, 2 tablespoons bitter or semisweet chocolate per cup of icing or glaze, and 2 tablespoons fruit brandy per cup of icing or glaze. Increase any of these amounts as needed.

Cream Puffs

Many people prefer cream puffs to éclairs because they are filled with whipped cream instead of pastry cream, so the effect is lighter. The secret to fabulous cream puffs is baking them at the last minute and then piping or spooning in the whipped cream just before serving. If you have nonstick pans, you don't need to use the parchment paper called for in the directions.

MAKES 8 LARGE PUFFS

> **Cream Puff Pastry (see page 488)**
> **Egg wash (see page 470)**
> **2 cups heavy cream**
> **4 tablespoons granulated sugar**
> **2 teaspoons vanilla extract**
> **Confectioners' sugar for dusting**

Preheat the oven to 500°F. Fit a pastry bag with a 3/4-inch fluted decorated tip and spoon the pastry batter into the bag. If your pastry bag isn't big enough, you may have to pipe out the cream puffs in two stages. Pipe a tiny dollop of batter into each corner of a sheet pan, and line the pan with a sheet of parchment paper, pressing the corners of the parchment onto the dollops of batter to anchor it in place.

Pipe 8 rounds of batter onto the lined or nonstick sheet pan. Start by holding the pastry bag about 3/4 inch above the sheet pan and squeezing. If the pastry bag tip is too close, the cream puffs won't be thick enough. If it is too far away, the cream puffs won't be wide enough. As the round of pastry takes shape, lift the pastry bag so it is about 1 1/2 inches above the sheet pan. Each mound should be about 3 1/2 inches across and about 1 1/2 inches high in the center. Brush with the egg wash, lightly smoothing the surface of each puff with the brush at the same time.

Slide the sheet pan into the oven and immediately turn down the oven to 400°F. Bake for 20 minutes, or until the pastries are golden brown. If the puffs start to look too brown, turn down the oven to 200°F. At no point should you open the oven door. When the puffs are done, they should feel feather light. Let cool on the pan on a rack for at least 20 minutes before filling.

1. Put a dollop of the pastry batter in each corner of the sheet pan to hold down a sheet of parchment paper.

2. Pipe out round dollops about 3$\frac{1}{2}$ inches in diameter and 1$\frac{1}{2}$ inches high in the center.

3. Brush the mounds with egg wash.

4. Bake until puffed and golden brown, and let cool.

5. Cut the puffs in half horizontally with a serrated knife.

6. Pipe whipped cream flavored with sugar and vanilla into the bottom of each puff.

In a bowl, combine the cream, granulated sugar, and vanilla. Using a mixer on high speed or a whisk, whip until stiff peaks form. Use a serrated knife to cut each cream puff in half horizontally. Pull away and discard any undercooked dough from the top and bottom. Spoon the whipped cream into the pastry bag fitted with a fluted decorating tip and pipe generously onto the bottom of each puff. Or, generously spoon the cream into the bottom halves. Replace the tops and dust with confectioners' sugar.

CUSTARDS, SOUFFLÉS, AND MOUSSES

A custard is simply a liquid that has been combined with eggs or part of the egg, the yolk or the white, and then cooked until set or thickened. Variations abound: a crème anglaise is a liquid custard cooked by stirring constantly on the stove; a Bavarian cream is a crème anglaise folded with whipped cream and set with gelatin; panna cotta is a simple custard held together in part with gelatin, much like a Bavarian cream but without the whipped cream; crème caramel and crème brûlée differ in that crème caramel is made with milk and whole eggs while crème brûlée is made with cream and egg yolks. Crème brûlée of course has the crystalline sugar crust. Mousses and soufflés are related to custards in that they're held together with eggs; soufflés and some mousses are lightened with beaten egg whites.

CUSTARDS

Crème caramel and crème brûlée lead the list of favorite custard desserts. Both contain caramel, but it is applied in different ways. For crème caramel, it is poured into the mold and allowed to set before the custard mixture is added. During baking, the caramel dissolves and creates a sauce for the custard when you unmold it. Crème brûlée is covered with granulated sugar, which is then melted into a brittle, glassy cap with a kitchen torch or under a broiler. A pot de crème is made the same way as a crème brûlée, except the caramel crust is absent and the custard is cooked in small covered ramekins (or, more traditionally, in special little pots with lids).

Basic Caramel

Many recipes for caramel insist that you combine the sugar with water before heating it. But because the water has to evaporate completely for the sugar to caramelize, this is a waste of time. Instead, put the sugar in the pan, put it directly on the heat, and stir until it turns deep red. Caramel syrup and caramel sauce are easily fashioned from this basic caramel.

MAKES 1 CUP

> **2 cups sugar**

Put the sugar in a heavy saucepan, place over high heat, and heat, stirring constantly with a wooden spoon, for about 5 minutes, or until the sugar has turned a deep red-brown. Initially, the sugar will become lumpy but then you'll see that it has liquefied. Stir until the mixture is perfectly smooth. Often the moment when all the lumps disappear is the moment when the caramel is ready. Plunge the pot in a bowl of cold water for 1 second to stop the cooking. Use immediately to line ramekins or a baking dish with caramel.

VARIATIONS

CARAMEL SYRUP: Make the basic caramel using 1 cup of sugar as directed, but instead of plunging the pot into a bowl of cold water, add 1/2 cup water to the hot caramel and stand back—it spatters. Bring it back to a boil and simmer while stirring until all the caramel has dissolved into the syrup. Makes 1 cup.

CARAMEL SAUCE: Stir 1 cup heavy cream into hot caramel to make caramel sauce.

1. Pour the hot caramel in the bottom of porcelain ramekins, creating a thin layer.

2. Pour the custard mixture into the ramekins and bake gently.

3. When the custards are cold, run a knife along the inside edge of each ramekin to loosen the sides.

4. Invert a plate over the top of the ramekin.

5. Invert the plate and ramekin together.

6. Give the plate and ramekin a quick up and down shake and lift off the ramekin.

Crème Caramel

A crème caramel makes a nice alternative to a crème brulee because it is less rich; it is made with milk and whole eggs instead of cream and egg yolks.

MAKES EIGHT 5-OUNCE SERVINGS

> 2¼ cups sugar
>
> 3 cups milk
>
> 4 eggs
>
> 2 egg yolks
>
> 2 teaspoons vanilla extract

Preheat the oven to 325°F. Have ready eight 5-ounce or 6-ounce ramekins. Using 1½ cups of the sugar, prepare the caramel as directed on page 493. Pour enough of the caramel onto the bottom of each ramekin to create a thin layer; rotate the molds to allow the caramel to spread over the entire surface. Avoid getting any caramel on the sides of the ramekins.

In a saucepan, bring the milk to a simmer over medium heat. Meanwhile, in a bowl, whisk together the eggs, egg yolks, and sugar for about 2 minutes, or until the mixture is slightly pale. Remove the milk from the heat, add the vanilla, and then gradually pour the hot milk into the egg mixture while whisking constantly. If a lot of froth forms on the surface, skim it off with a pastry scraper. If you see specks of cooked egg in the mixture, strain it through a fine-mesh strainer.

Arrange the lined ramekins in a baking pan or sheet pan that is at least as deep as the ramekins. Divide the custard mixture evenly among the ramekins. Pour the hottest tap water into the baking pan to reach halfway up the sides of the ramekins.

Bake for 50 minutes, or until the surface of the custard doesn't jiggle when you gently move a ramekin back and forth. Remove the ramekins from the water bath and let cool on a rack for about 1 hour, or until they are at room temperature. Then cover and refrigerate for at least 2 hours or up to 2 days before serving.

To unmold each custard, run a thin knife blade along the inside of each ramekin. Invert a plate over the top of the ramekin, invert the plate and ramekin together, shake up and down once, and lift off the ramekin. A small pool of caramel will surround the custard. Serve cold.

Crème Brûlée

For crème brûlée, a vanilla bean is infused in the hot cream and each custard is finished with a layer of crunchy caramel.

MAKES SIX 4-OUNCE SERVINGS

> 2 cups heavy cream
>
> 1 vanilla bean, split lengthwise, or 2 teaspoons vanilla extract
>
> 6 egg yolks
>
> 1 cup sugar

Preheat the oven to 300°F. Pour the cream into a saucepan. If you are using the vanilla bean, add the halves to the pan. Place over medium heat and bring to a simmer. Meanwhile, in a bowl, whisk together the egg yolks and ½ cup of the sugar for about 2 minutes, or until slightly pale.

Remove the cream from the heat. If you have used the vanilla bean, remove it from the pan and, with a knife tip, scrape the little seeds from each half of the pod back into the pan. Or, if you are using the vanilla extract, stir it in. Gradually pour the hot cream into the egg mixture while whisking constantly. Continue stirring until no yolk clings to the sides of the bowl. If you see specks of cooked egg, strain the mixture through a fine-mesh strainer.

Arrange six 4-ounce crème brûlée dishes or ramekins in a baking pan or sheet pan that is at least as deep as the dishes. Divide the custard mixture evenly among the molds. Pour the hottest tap water into the baking pan to reach halfway up the sides of the molds.

Bake for 40 minutes, or until the surface of the custard doesn't jiggle when you gently move a mold back and forth. Remove the molds from the water bath and let cool on a rack for about 1 hour, or until they are at room temperature. Then cover and refrigerate for at least 1 hour or up to 3 days before serving. (Don't be tempted to stick them, still warm, in the refrigerator or moisture will condense on the underside of the foil and drip down on the custards.)

No more than 1 hour before serving, sprinkle the remaining ½ cup sugar evenly over the tops of the custards, covering them with a thin layer. Tilt a kitchen torch over each custard so the flame is about 2 inches from the surface, and move the torch around until the sugar melts and caramelizes, forming a thin sheet. Alternatively, preheat the broiler and position the rack about 3 inches from the heat source. Top the custards with the sugar, slide them under the broiler, and broil for about 1 minute, or until the sugar caramelizes.

Serve immediately or refrigerate until you're ready to serve.

Ginger Pots de Crème

Pots de crème (poe de krem) get their name from the little pots with lids that are traditionally used to bake them. The molds are expensive, however, and have only one use, so the custards are baked in small ramekins here. Because pots de crème call for a mixture of milk and cream, they are halfway in richness between crème caramel and crème brûlée. Here, the custards are flavored with ground ginger.

MAKES SIX 4-OUNCE SERVINGS

> 1 cup heavy cream
>
> 1 cup milk
>
> 7 egg yolks
>
> $1/2$ cup sugar
>
> 2 tablespoons ground ginger
>
> 6 pieces crystallized ginger (optional)

Preheat the oven to 300°F. In a saucepan, combine the cream and milk and bring to a simmer over medium heat. Meanwhile, in a bowl, whisk together the egg yolks, sugar, and ground ginger for about 2 minutes, or until the mixture is slightly pale.

Remove the cream mixture from the heat and gradually pour the hot cream mixture into the egg mixture while whisking constantly. Continue stirring until no yolk clings to the sides of the bowl, and then strain through a fine-mesh strainer.

Arrange six 4-ounce ramekins or pot de crème pots in a baking pan or sheet pan that is at least as deep as the molds. Divide the custard evenly among the molds. If using ramekins instead of traditional pot de crème molds with lids, cover each ramekin with a small sheet of aluminum foil. This prevents a crust from forming on top of the custards. Pour the hottest tap water into the baking pan to reach halfway up the sides of the molds.

Bake for 40 minutes, or until the custards have set. To check if they are ready, take the foil or lid off 2 custards—choose them from different positions in the baking pan—and gently move them back and forth. If the surface doesn't jiggle, the custards have set.

Remove the molds from the water bath and let cool on a rack for 1 hour uncovered, or until they are at room temperature. Then cover and refrigerate for at least 2 hours or up to 3 days before serving. (Don't be tempted to stick them, still warm, in the refrigerator or moisture will condense on the underside of the foil and drip down on the custards.) Just before serving, decorate each custard with a piece of crystallized ginger.

VARIATIONS

For chocolate pots de crème, melt 8 ounces bittersweet chocolate, chopped, with the cream and milk, or whisk 4 tablespoons unsweetened cocoa powder with the egg yolks. For coffee pots de crème, infuse 3 tablespoons espresso-grind dark roast coffee in the hot milk mixture and let stand for 10 minutes before straining. For spice-flavored pots de crème, add $1/4$ to $1/2$ teaspoon ground spice, such as cinnamon or cloves, to the cream mixture, or add $1/4$ teaspoon ground cardamom and a pinch of saffron threads.

Zabaglione and Sauce Sabayon

Zabaglione is a frothy custard usually served as a stand-alone dessert, while sauce sabayon, which is tangy and sweet at the same time, is usually served as a sauce for berries or fruit tarts. But the technique for making both is the same, only zabaglione is made with Marsala, sherry, or Madeira wine and sauce sabayon is made with dry white wine.

MAKES 4 DESSERT SERVINGS OR 6 SAUCE SERVINGS

> $1/2$ cup sugar (if using sweet wine) or $3/4$ cup (if using dry wine)
>
> 1 cup dry sherry, Madeira or Marsala (for Zabaglione) or dry white wine (for sabayon sauce)
>
> 4 egg yolks
>
> 1 whole egg

Whisk together all the ingredients in a saucepan with sloping sides or in a metal bowl set over a pan of simmering water. Continue whisking until the mixture stiffens and you see bubbles coming up (the mixture can boil without curdling because the boiling point of alcohol is below the temperature at which eggs curdle). If you're serving the mixture cold, continue beating off the heat until it is at room temperature and then refrigerate.

Vanilla Panna Cotta

A panna cotta is a custard made with milk or cream and gelatin and little if any egg. The gelatin ensures the custard will set when cold. Keep in mind that half of a packet of gelatin—a scant 1^1/$_2$ teaspoons—barely sets a cup of liquid, or half the amount called for on the package. (The amounts to use given on the package are more generous than necessary and will make things rubbery with a Jello-like consistency, when in most cases you want something that has barely any resistance to the tooth.) Make a custard as you would a crème caramel, with or without the caramel, and simply add gelatin, soaked first in cold water, to the hot custard mixture before baking.

MAKES EIGHT 4-OUNCE SERVINGS

> 3 cups heavy cream
>
> 2 vanilla beans, split lengthwise, or
>   4 teaspoons vanilla extract
>
> 1 packet powdered gelatin
>
> ^{1}/$_4$ cup water
>
> ^{1}/$_2$ cup sugar

In a saucepan, combine the cream and vanilla beans and bring to a simmer over medium heat. (If you are using vanilla extract, don't add it yet.) Meanwhile, in a small bowl or cup, sprinkle the gelatin over the water and let stand for about 10 minutes to soften.

Remove the cream from the heat. If you have used the vanilla beans, remove them from the pan and, with a knife tip, scrape the little seeds from each half pod back into the pan. Or, if you are using the vanilla extract, stir it in. Stir the sugar and the gelatin mixture into the hot cream until both are fully dissolved, and then strain through a coarse-mesh strainer.

Pour into eight 4-ounce ramekins and let cool for about 1 hour, or until they are at room temperature. Then cover and refrigerate for at least 1 hour or up to 2 days before serving. Serve cold.

Crème Anglaise

Crème anglaise is a so-called stirred custard. It is cooked on the stove top until it thickens into a silky sauce, rather than slowly baked in an oven until set. It is most commonly flavored with a vanilla bean or vanilla extract, as it is here, but it can be infused with coffee, chocolate, or fruit puree, or flavored with a fruit brandy, whiskey, or rum. It can be used as a sauce, hot or cold, for fruit tarts and cakes, or as the base for the world's best eggnog. It is a base for other similar recipes, such as the Bavarian creams that follow.

Recipes for crème anglaise vary in the number of egg yolks used per quart of milk—the range is 8 to 20—which you can adjust according to how rich and thick you want your sauce. The version here calls for 12 yolks.

MAKES ABOUT 6 CUPS

> 1 quart milk
>
> 1 vanilla bean, split lengthwise, or
>   1 teaspoon vanilla extract
>
> 12 egg yolks, whites reserved for another use
>
> ^{3}/$_4$ cup sugar

In a saucepan, combine the milk and vanilla bean, if you are using, and bring to a simmer over medium heat. Meanwhile, in a bowl, whisk together the egg yolks, vanilla extract if you're using it, and sugar for about 2 minutes, or until slightly pale.

Remove the milk from the heat and gradually pour about one-third of the hot milk into the egg yolk mixture while whisking constantly. Return the combined mixtures to the saucepan and stir until well mixed.

Return the pan to medium-low heat, and cook, stirring constantly with a wooden spoon, for about 2 minutes, or until the ripples disappear and are replaced by smooth, silky waves. Don't ever let the mixture come to a boil or it will curdle. Remove from the heat and continue to stir for a couple of minutes so the heat retained in the pan doesn't cause the yolks to curdle.

If you have used the vanilla bean, remove it from the pan and, with a knife tip, scrape the little seeds from each half of the pod back into the pan. Use the sauce immediately, or pour into a bowl. If you notice any lumps, pass it through a fine-mesh strainer and cover with plastic wrap, pressing it directly onto the surface to prevent a skin from forming. Let cool and refrigerate until needed. It will keep for up to 2 days.

BAVARIAN CREAMS

Once you know how to make crème anglaise, making a Bavarian cream is a snap. You need only to flavor the custard, add gelatin, and fold in whipped cream. The trick is to soften the gelatin in water, add it to the crème anglaise while the crème anglaise is still hot—so the gelatin dissolves—and then to let the crème anglaise cool just enough so that it won't melt the whipped cream, but not so much that the gelatin sets. To make getting cream out of the mold easier, rinse the mold with cold water before you fill it.

Coffee Bavarian Cream

The secret to making coffee custard is to infuse the ground beans directly in the custard, instead of adding brewed coffee. You then just strain the coffee out before you combine the milk with the egg yolks.

MAKES SIX 5-OUNCE SERVINGS

> **2 cups milk**
> **1/4 cup espresso-grind ground dark roast coffee**
> **5 egg yolks**
> **1/3 cup sugar**
> **2 tablespoons plus 2 teaspoons powdered gelatin**
> **1/4 cup water**
> **1 cup heavy cream**

In a saucepan, combine the milk and coffee and bring to a simmer over medium heat. Meanwhile, rinse a 1-quart mold or six 5-ounce ramekins with cold water. In a bowl, ready an ice bath with cold water and ice for cooling the custard. In another bowl, whisk together the egg yolks and sugar for about 2 minutes, or until slightly pale. In a small bowl or cup, sprinkle the gelatin over the water and let stand for about 10 minutes to soften.

Remove the milk from the heat and gradually pour about half of the hot milk into the egg yolk mixture while whisking constantly. Return the combined mixtures to the saucepan and stir until well mixed. Return the pan to medium-low heat, and cook, stirring constantly with a wooden spoon, for about 2 minutes, or until the ripples disappear and are replaced by smooth, silky waves. Don't ever let the mixture come to a boil or it will curdle. Remove from the heat and continue to stir for a couple of minutes so the heat retained in the pan doesn't cause the yolks to curdle.

Strain through a fine-mesh strainer into a bowl, and stir in the gelatin mixture. Cover the bowl with plastic wrap, pressing it directly onto the surface to prevent a skin from forming, and nest the bowl in the ice bath until the custard is cool. Don't let it stand until cold or the gelatin will have set. While the custard is cooling, in a bowl, using a mixer on medium speed or a whisk, whip the cream until soft peaks form.

Fold the whipped cream into the cooled custard mixture just until combined and then pour into the mold(s). Cover and refrigerate for at least 3 hours or up to 12 hours before unmolding and serving.

To unmold, invert a plate over the top of the mold, invert the plate and mold together, shake up and down once, and lift off the mold. If it resists unmolding, run a knife around the inside of the mold and try again. Serve cold.

Fruit Bavarian

The traditional approach for making fruit Bavarians is to make a crème anglaise, as you do for the Coffee Bavarian (opposite). But for a lighter, less fussy method, you can combine whipped cream with a fruit coulis (strained puree) and gelatin. Simply puree ripe berries, melon, or stonefruits such as apricots or peaches in a blender or food processor and force them through a fine-mesh strainer. If you are using a tropical fruit, such as pineapple, papaya, or mango, bring the puree to a boil at some point before you add the gelatin. Otherwise, the protease enzymes present in the fruit will break down the gelatin and the Bavarian will never set.

MAKES 6 SERVINGS

$1/2$ cup sugar or more as needed
$1/4$ cup plus 3 tablespoons water
$1^1/2$ cups strained fruit puree
1 packet powdered gelatin
1 cup heavy cream
Whipped cream for serving

Rinse a 1-quart mold or six 5-ounce ramekins with cold water. In a small saucepan, combine the sugar and $1/4$ cup of the water over medium heat, stir until the sugar is dissolved, and remove from the heat. Gradually add this syrup to the fruit puree, tasting as you go. If you have added all of it and the fruit still isn't sweet enough, make more syrup. Keep in mind that the fruit will be less sweet after you add the whipped cream, plus chilling the mixture will diminish the effect of sweetness. Make sure the fruit puree is at room temperature before you combine it with the cream.

In a small heatproof bowl, sprinkle the gelatin over the 3 tablespoons water and let stand for about 10 minutes to soften. Meanwhile, in a bowl, using a mixer on medium speed or a whisk, whip the cream until medium peaks form.

Place the bowl holding the gelatin over simmering water in a saucepan and heat for about 5 minutes, or until the gelatin dissolves. Remove from the heat and whisk the gelatin into the fruit puree. Immediately fold the whipped cream into the fruit puree, and transfer the mixture to the mold(s). Cover and refrigerate for at least 3 hours or up to 12 hours before unmolding and serving.

To unmold, invert a plate over the top of the mold, invert the plate and mold together, shake up and down once, and lift off the mold. If it resists unmolding, run a knife around the inside of the mold and try again. Serve cold with a dollop of whipped cream.

DESSERT SOUFFLÉS

There are two kinds of dessert soufflés: hot and frozen. You can also put chocolate or another kind of mousse in collar-lined soufflé dishes, with the mousse coming halfway up the collar, sprinkle the top with confectioners' sugar, and then remove the collar just before serving. The effect is that of a soufflé, but the true content remains a mousse.

The traditional approach to all sweet soufflés is to flavor pastry cream—essentially eggs and sugar thickened with cornstarch—and fold in beaten egg whites, and then bake. Lighter, more "modern" soufflés are sometimes made by starting with a sabayon—the yolks are beaten with sugar and liquid until frothy and hot—or a curd. Whether improvising or following a recipe, remember that you are essentially folding together a flavorful mixture and beaten egg whites and then baking the whole thing.

If the prospect of last-minute hot soufflés is terrifying, keep in mind a couple of principles. First, wrap the soufflé dishes with a collar. This prevents the soufflés from running over the rim of the dish before they set. Don't overcook them. To test if they are done, just dig into them with a spoon and peek to see how the inside is doing. With a little practice, you will be able to skip the spoon and tell by jiggling the dishes if the soufflé is stiff enough. If the soufflés are overcooked, they will fall the instant they come out of the oven. If undercooked, they won't fall, your guests will go "ooh," and you will just put them all back in the oven.

Frozen soufflés aren't really soufflés. They are frozen mousses made by folding a fruit puree with Italian meringue and freezing the mixture. You can also make a parfait mixture—not to be confused with what Americans call a parfait—by folding whipped cream into egg yolks that have been beaten with sugar syrup (an exact parallel to Italian meringue, which is made by beating egg whites with syrup), and then freezing the mixture in the molds.

These soufflés are particularly good when made with the juice of Meyer lemons. Or, you can substitute lime juice for the lemon juice.

MAKES 6 INDIVIDUAL SOUFFLÉS

> **Room-temperature butter and superfine sugar for preparing dishes and collars**
> **3 or 4 lemons**
> **6 eggs, separated**
> **Pinch of cream of tartar if not using copper bowl**
> **1/4 cup plus 5 tablespoons granulated sugar**
> **2 teaspoons cornstarch**
> **Confectioners' sugar for dusting**

Preheat the oven to 350°F. Brush the bottom and sides of six 8-ounce soufflé dishes with the butter. Coat the bottom and sides of the dishes with the superfine sugar, tapping out the excess. Cut 6 strips of aluminum foil wide enough to stand 2 inches above the rim of the dish when folded in half and long enough to wrap around the dish with a little overlap. Fold the foil in half lengthwise, butter one side and dust with superfine sugar, and set aside until you are ready to bake the soufflés.

Grate the zest from 1 lemon. Squeeze as many lemons as needed to yield 6 tablespoons juice. In a heatproof bowl or in a saucepan with sloping sides, whisk together the egg yolks, lemon zest, and 1/4 cup of the granulated sugar for about 2 minutes, or until slightly pale. Whisk in the 6 tablespoons lemon juice and the cornstarch until well combined. Place the bowl over a saucepan of simmering water, or put the pan over medium heat, and heat, stirring with a whisk, for about 4 minutes, or until the mixture thickens. Remove from the heat. Let cool.

In another bowl, using a mixer, beat the egg whites on high speed for about 5 minutes, or until stiff peaks form. Add the remaining 5 tablespoons sugar in a slow, steady stream and continue to beat for about 2 minutes, or until the sugar has dissolved and the whites are shiny.

Stir about one-fourth of the beaten whites and the cream of tartar, if using, into the lemon mixture, and then fold in the remaining whites with a rubber spatula just until no white streaks are visible. Fill the prepared molds with the mixture, smoothing the tops with a rubber spatula. Run your thumb around the rim of each dish to form a moat about 1/2 inch wide along the edge of the soufflé mixture. This keeps the top of the soufflé mixture from attaching to the rim. Wrap a collar, buttered side in, around the rim of each dish, and pinch together the ends to hold the collar in place.

Bake for about 20 minutes, or until the soufflés have risen and are lightly browned. Dust with confectioners' sugar and pull away the collars. Serve immediately.

VARIATION

GRAND MARNIER SOUFFLÉS: To make Grand Marnier soufflés, boil down the grated zest and juice of 1 orange to 3 tablespoons and substitute for 3 tablespoons of the lemon juice in the Lemon Soufflés. Whisk 2 tablespoons Grand Marnier into the egg yolk mixture before folding in the whites and then proceed as directed. For a real punch of flavor, sprinkle 1/2-inch cubes of sponge cake (see page 424) with a little Grand Marnier and fold them into the soufflé mixture with the beaten whites.

HOW TO MAKE LEMON SOUFFLÉS

1. Fold together lemon curd with egg whites that have been beaten with sugar to make them very stiff.

2. Put the mixture into buttered and sugared molds and smooth the tops with a spatula.

3. Make a little moat around the edge of each soufflé with your thumb. Bake until risen and browned.

4. Dust confectioners' sugar over the finished soufflés and serve immediately.

Raspberry or Strawberry Soufflés

The method used here for thickening a strained fruit puree with cornstarch and then combining it with beaten egg whites can be used for fruits such as berries, peaches, apricots, persimmons, and nectarines.

MAKES 6 INDIVIDUAL SOUFFLÉS

> **Room-temperature butter and superfine sugar for preparing dishes and collars**
>
> **One 12- or 14-ounce package frozen raspberries or strawberries (not packed in syrup), thawed**
>
> **1 rounded tablespoon cornstarch, dissolved in 2 tablespoons water**
>
> **6 egg whites**
>
> **Pinch of cream of tartar if not using copper bowl**
>
> **1/4 cup granulated sugar**
>
> **Confectioners' sugar for dusting**

Preheat the oven to 350°F. Brush the bottom and sides of six 1-cup soufflé dishes with the butter. Coat the bottom and sides of the dishes with the superfine sugar, tapping out the excess. Cut 6 strips of aluminum foil wide enough to stand 2 inches above the rim of the dish when folded in half and long enough to wrap around the dish with a little overlap. Fold the foil in half lengthwise, butter one side and dust with superfine sugar, and set aside until you are ready to bake the soufflés.

Using the back of a small ladle, work the fruit through a fine-mesh strainer placed over a saucepan. Add the cornstarch mixture, place over medium heat, and bring to a simmer while stirring constantly. Remove from the heat and let cool slightly. You should have about 1 cup.

In a bowl, using a mixer, beat the egg whites and the cream of tartar, if using, on high speed for about 5 minutes, or until stiff peaks form. Add the granulated sugar in a slow, steady stream and continue to beat for about 2 minutes, or until the sugar has dissolved and the whites are shiny.

Stir about one-fourth of the beaten whites into the berry mixture, and then fold in the remaining whites with a rubber spatula just until no white streaks are visible. Fill the prepared molds with the mixture, smoothing the tops with a rubber spatula. Run your thumb around the rim of each dish to form a moat about 1/2 inch wide along the edge of the soufflé mixture. This keeps the top of the soufflé mixture from attaching to the rim. Wrap a collar, buttered side in, around the rim of each dish, and pinch together the ends to hold the collar in place.

Bake for about 20 minutes, or until the soufflés have risen and the tops are lightly browned. Serve immediately. Sprinkle with confectioners' sugar and pull away the collars.

MOUSSES

Mousses are made from a variety of ingredients, both sweet and savory, and are typically distinguished by their light, fluffy texture, the result of incorporating air into the mixture. A chocolate mousse is the easiest type to make because the chocolate hardens when it cools, which helps hold the mousse together. Fruit mousses are usually bound with gelatin.

The simplest chocolate mousse is made by melting together chocolate and butter and then folding in beaten egg whites (which should include a little sugar to make them stiff and smooth) or whipped cream. Sometimes egg yolks are added as well, beaten with the melted chocolate before the egg whites or cream is added. The more butter used to make the mousse, the denser its texture will be. If the mousse contains a lot of butter and is served as a terrine, it is called a marquise.

Fruit mousses are made by folding fruit purees with cooked egg white (Italian meringue, see page 435), or by adding fruit puree to crème anglaise (custard sauce), combining it with whipped cream, and holding the whole thing together with gelatin.

Basic Chocolate Mousse

There are many variations on chocolate mousse, but the basic approach is always the same: the chocolate is melted, often with butter, and then often combined with egg yolks. The mixture is folded together with sweetened whipped cream or beaten egg whites. Variations in the kind of chocolate used, the amount of butter added, and whether cream or egg whites are used create the subtle differences in texture. Flavoring ingredients—vanilla extract, cognac, whiskey, grappa (marc), kirsch—are often added, usually to the initial chocolate mixture. Because chocolate mousse isn't cooked, a little flavoring goes a long way, so be careful that you don't add too much.

MAKES TEN 4-OUNCE SERVINGS

8 ounces bittersweet chocolate, coarsely chopped

4 tablespoons butter, sliced, at room temperature

1 teaspoon vanilla extract

4 eggs

2 tablespoons sugar

Combine the chocolate and butter in a heatproof bowl and set over a saucepan of simmering water. Stir with a rubber spatula until melted and smooth, and then immediately remove from the heat. Stir in the vanilla extract. Let cool slightly.

Meanwhile, separate the eggs and set the whites aside. In a large bowl, beat the egg yolks until blended. Whisk the melted chocolate into the egg yolks, beating until smooth.

In another bowl, using a mixer, beat the egg whites on high speed for about 5 minutes, or until stiff peaks form (see page 397). Add the sugar in a slow, steady stream and continue to beat for about 2 minutes, or until the sugar has dissolved and the whites are shiny.

Stir about one-fourth of the beaten whites into the chocolate mixture to lighten it. Then, using a rubber spatula, fold in the remaining whites just until no white streaks are visible. Divide evenly among six 4-ounce ramekins and smooth off the tops. Chill and serve with little spoons.

Marquise

A marquise is a chocolate terrine served in slices, like a pâté. The basic chocolate mixture is made like a mousse, but with more butter, so that the mixture is firm enough to slice once it has been chilled. The secret to success is to use the best chocolate you can find.

MAKES 10 SERVINGS

About 30 small ladyfingers or 3 strips the length of the terrine, for lining the mold (see page 423)

12 ounces bittersweet chocolate, coarsely chopped

1/2 pound butter, sliced, at room temperature

2 eggs

2 tablespoons cognac, Grand Marnier, or bourbon (optional)

1/4 cup sugar

Line a 4-cup terrine with plastic wrap, allowing the edges to overhang the sides by a few inches. If using homemade ladyfingers, cut the strips to fit the walls of the terrine, and place the strips in the mold with the rounded ends down, the curved sides against the mold, and the flat sides facing the center. Cut both ends off the third strip of ladyfingers and press this strip into the bottom of the mold, with the rounded sides down. (This will become the top of the marquise.)

Combine the chocolate and butter in a heatproof bowl and set over a saucepan of simmering water. Stir with a rubber spatula until melted and smooth, and then immediately remove from the heat. Let cool slightly.

Meanwhile, separate the eggs and set the whites aside. In a large bowl, beat the egg yolks until blended. Whisk the melted chocolate into the egg yolks, beating until smooth. Whisk in the cognac. If you are not using spirits, whisk in enough water to create a perfectly smooth mixture. The exact amount will depend on the type of chocolate you're using, so add the water 2 tablespoons at a time and stir.

In another bowl, using a mixer, beat the egg whites on high speed for about 5 minutes, or until stiff peaks form. Add the sugar in a slow, steady stream and continue to beat for about 2 minutes, or until the sugar has dissolved and the whites are shiny.

Stir about one-fourth of the beaten whites into the chocolate mixture to lighten it. Then, using a rubber spatula, fold in the remaining whites just until no white streaks are visible.

Pour the chocolate mixture into the prepared terrine, smoothing the top (the eventual bottom) even with the rim, and cover with the overhanging plastic. Chill for at least 5 hours or up to 3 days before unmolding and serving.

To unmold, turn the marquise out onto a platter and gently pull away the mold. Peel away the plastic wrap. Serve in 1-inch-thick slices by slicing gently with a very sharp knife, using a sawing motion with very little downward force.

HOW TO MAKE MARQUISE

1. Line the terrine with plastic wrap and ladyfingers.

2. Fill with the chocolate mixture. Cover with the overhanging plastic wrap and chill.

3. To unmold, unfold the plastic wrap on top of the marquise. Invert onto a platter and pull away the terrine.

4. Gently remove the plastic wrap.

COOKIES

Cookies are shaped by a variety of different methods: the dough can be rolled and cut out, molded by hand, dropped from a spoon, piped through a pastry bag, or spread with an offset spatula. Most cookies are baked only once, but some, known as rusks—biscotti are the best known of the group—are baked twice. Still others, known as bar cookies, are made by spreading batter in a pan, baking it, and then cutting it into rectangles or squares.

BAKING, COOLING, AND STORING

If you have a convection oven, use it for baking cookies. Just keep in mind that a convection oven behaves as though it is 50 degrees hotter than the temperature on the dial. So if the recipe calls for baking at 400°F, bake at 350°F when using a convection oven. A convection oven is especially handy if you have more than one sheet of cookies to bake at a time. With a regular oven it's a good idea to swap the positions of the two sheet pans so the cookies bake evenly. Often the cookies in the back bake more quickly than those in front, so much more quickly that you should give the sheet pans a 180-degree turn halfway through baking to even out the cookies' doneness.

When cookies come out of the oven, let them cool a couple of minutes on the sheet pan before transferring them to a rack. If you transfer them too soon, some cookies can fall apart. Store cookies in a covered container at room temperature, not in the refrigerator (which desiccates them). Most cookies will keep at room temperature in an air-tight container for up to one week.

Basic Butter Cookies (Sablées)

These cookies, known in France as sablées, are made out of the same dough—a basic pie dough with extra measures of butter and sugar—that is used for making sweet crusts for pies and tarts. Here, the dough is rolled into logs, which are then sliced into cookies. Store unused dough, tightly wrapped, in the refrigerator for up to 2 weeks.

MAKES ABOUT 50 COOKIES

Buttery Cookielike Pie and Tart Dough (see page 450)

Cut the dough in half. On a floured work surface, roll half of the dough into a log about 8 inches long and 1½ inches in diameter, using the palms of your hands. Repeat with the remaining dough. Wrap the logs separately in plastic wrap and chill for 30 minutes.

Preheat the oven to 350°F. Line two sheet pans with parchment paper, or use nonstick sheet pans. Slice the logs into ⅓-inch-thick rounds, and arrange the rounds on the prepared pans, spacing them about ½ inch apart.

Bake for about 12 minutes, or until only the very slightest bit of browning is visible on the edges of the cookies. When set, transfer to a cooling rack or cool on the pans set on racks.

Checkerboard Butter Cookies

To make these cookies, you need two different kinds of dough, one chocolate and one plain. Each dough gets rolled into ropes that are then pressed together to make the checkerboard pattern.

MAKES ABOUT 40 COOKIES

> Confectioners' sugar for dusting
> 1/2 recipe Buttery Cookielike Pie and Tart Dough (see page 450)
> Unsweetened cocoa powder for dusting
> 1/2 recipe Chocolate Butter Cookies dough (opposite)
> 1 egg white, lightly beaten

On a work surface dusted with confectioners' sugar, roll the two doughs with the flats of your hands into sausage shapes each having the same diameter of about 1 1/2 inches. Wrap in plastic wrap and chill for 30 minutes.

Line 2 sheet pans with parchment paper, or use 2 nonstick sheet pans. Return the ropes to the work surface, and cut each rope in half crosswise. Arrange the 4 halves side by side, alternating the chocolate and plain dough. Tap the tops of the ropes with a rolling pin while pushing on the sides with a ruler or pastry scraper to force them into a square shape. Cut the length of 4 strands in half lengthwise so you have 2 pieces the same length. Brush the top of 1 piece with the egg white, and then turn over the other piece, so the colors alternate, and place it on top. Tap the top of the stacked pieces with the rolling pin to press the strands together. Cut the strands in half again crosswise. Again brush 1 piece with egg white, and then turn over the other piece, so the colors alternate, and place it

Better with Butter

The best cookies are made with butter. The more butter the cookie contains, the better its flavor, but cookies made with too much butter will spread or even melt and become so fragile that they break apart at the slightest touch. If your cookies are too crumbly, follow Shirley Corriher's advice and sprinkle in a little water to activate the flour's gluten. Some cookies get browner than others with the same amount of baking. For browner cookies, use flour with a higher protein content (or a mixture of all-purpose and bread flours) or substitute a tablespoon of corn syrup for a tablespoon of the sugar in the recipe.

on top. Press the squares together and tap them lightly with the rolling pin to make sure they hold together. Cut crosswise into 1/3-inch-thick squares, and arrange on the prepared pans. Cover and chill for 30 minutes before baking.

Preheat the oven to 375°F. Bake for about 12 minutes, or until only the very slightest bit of browning is visible on the edges of the cookies. Let cool until set and then transfer to cooling racks or cool on the pans set on racks. Store tightly sealed in an airtight container for up to 1 week.

VARIATIONS

MARBLED SABLÉE COOKIES: Work plain and chocolate dough together in a random pattern, shape that dough into a log, and then slice and bake to create cookies with a charming marbled pattern as shown at right.

PINWHEEL COOKIES: Roll out a rectangle of each dough 1/8 to 1/4 inch thick, lay one rectangle on top of the other, roll up tightly, chill, slice, and bake.

Chocolate Butter Cookies

This easy dough can be used to make simple chocolate-flavored butter cookies, or it can be combined with plain butter cookie dough to make checkerboard, pinwheel, or marbled cookies.

MAKES ABOUT 40 COOKIES

> 2 cups flour
> 2/3 cup confectioners' sugar
> 6 tablespoons unsweetened cocoa powder
> 1/2 teaspoon salt
> 1/2 cup cold butter, sliced
> 1 egg

In a food processor, combine the flour, sugar, cocoa powder, and salt and process for 15 seconds, or until well mixed. Add the butter and egg and process for about 20 seconds, or until the dough comes together in a lumpy mass. Remove the dough from the processor and shape into a sausage about 1 1/2 inches in diameter and about 15 inches long. Chill the dough for 45 minutes in the refrigerator and slice it between 1/3 and 1/2 inch thick. Arrange the cookies in rows on a nonstick or parchment-lined sheet pan.

Preheat the oven to 375°F. Bake for 20 minutes until firm but not hard. Let cool until set and then transfer to cooling racks or cool on the pan set on racks. Store tightly sealed in an airtight container for up to 1 week.

1. Roll the plain dough into two ropes.

2. Roll the chocolate dough into two ropes.

3. Align the ropes next to each other and roll over them gently to press them together and square them off. Cut the band of ropes in half crosswise to make two pieces the same length.

4. Brush the top of one band with beaten egg white.

5. Turn the other band around and place it on the bottom section of the band so the colors alternate to create a checkerboard effect. Cut the combined sections in half crosswise and repeat the brushing and layering.

6. Slice into cookies and arrange on sheet pans.

7. For marbled cookies, work the chocolate and plain doughs together, form into a log and slice.

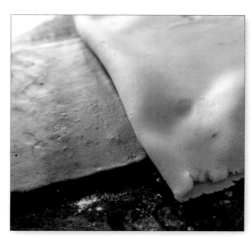

8. For pinwheel cookies, unroll a sheet of plain dough over a sheet of chocolate dough and roll up.

9. Slice the roll.

Shortbread Cookies

This is the shortest of all pastry doughs because it contains no liquid at all, just butter, sugar, flour, and a somewhat generous amount of salt that tastes delicious next to the sugar. If you have some turbinado, a coarse-grained brown sugar, on hand, finish the cookies with it. Its pale brown color, slightly crunchy texture, and mild molasses flavor complement the shortbread dough. The dough is baked uncut, and is then cut into attractive lozenge shapes when it comes out of the oven.

MAKES ABOUT 20 COOKIES

> 1/2 pound butter, at room temperature, cut into
> 1/2-inch cubes
> 3/4 cup granulated sugar
> 1 teaspoon salt
> 1 3/4 cups flour
> 1/4 cup turbinado sugar or additional granulated sugar (optional)

In a bowl with a wooden spoon, or in a stand mixer fitted with the paddle blade on medium speed, beat together the butter, 3/4 cup sugar, and the salt for about 7 minutes by hand or 5 minutes with the mixer, or until smooth and creamy. Add the flour and work by hand or on low and then medium speed with the mixer until the dough comes together in a cohesive mass. Flatten the dough, wrap it in waxed paper, and chill it about 15 minutes but not too long or it will harden the dough, making it too hard to handle.

Line a sheet pan with parchment paper or use a nonstick sheet pan. On a floured work surface, using a rolling pin or your fingers, roll or press the dough into a rectangle about 1/3 inch thick. Sprinkle with the turbinado sugar. Transfer to the prepared pan, cover, and chill for 1 hour.

Preheat the oven to 375°F. Bake for about 20 minutes, or until pale brown on top. Remove from the oven, transfer the log to a cutting surface, and immediately cut the rectangle into 1-inch-wide strips. Then cut across the strips at about a 30-degree angle every 2 inches to make lozenges. Let cool completely on cooling racks and then pull apart the cookies.

Old-Fashioned Butter Cookies

This is the traditional butter cookie dough long used in American bakeries. Because the recipe contains baking powder, these cookies have a lighter texture than the Holiday Butter Cookies (opposite).

MAKES ABOUT 20 COOKIES

> 2 cups flour
> 3/4 teaspoon baking powder
> 1/4 teaspoon salt
> 1/2 pound cold butter, sliced
> 3/4 cup superfine or granulated sugar
> 1 teaspoon vanilla extract
> 1 egg
> Room-temperature butter for preparing pan

In a bowl, sift together the flour, baking powder, and salt. In a large bowl, using a wooden spoon or a mixer, gradually building up speed from low to high, cream together the butter, sugar, and vanilla for about 7 minutes by hand or 5 minutes with the mixer, or until smooth and creamy. Beat in the egg. Add the flour mixture and work it in with a wooden spoon or with the mixer on low then medium speed just until there is no loose flour, the dough comes together in a shaggy mass, and you hear the motor straining, about 30 seconds. This dough may also be made in a food processor, following the directions for Buttery Cookielike Pie and Tart Dough, on page 450. Don't work it any more than necessary to make it come together. Chill the dough for 15 minutes and then, with the flats of your hands, roll it into a sausage about 2 inches in diameter and 10 inches long. Wrap in plastic and chill for 45 minutes.

Preheat the oven to 350°F. With a knife or bench scraper, slice the sausage, using a series of rapid movements, into 1/2-inch-thick cookies. Put the cookies on sheet pans (you'll need two), leaving about 1 inch between each cookie.

Bake for 20 minutes, or until the cookies lose their sheen and become pale blond on the edges, repositioning the pans 10 minutes into the baking. Let cool until set and then transfer to cooling racks or cool on the pans set on racks. Store tightly sealed in an airtight container for up to 1 week.

VARIATION

JAM-TOPPED BUTTER COOKIES: After arranging the cookies on a sheet pan, make an indentation in the center of each one with your finger and fill the dent with 1/2 teaspoon of your favorite jam or jelly.

Holiday Butter Cookies

The dough used here is almost identical to the dough used to make the Old-Fashioned Butter Cookies (opposite) except this recipe includes an additional $1/2$ cup flour to make it easier to roll out with a pin. Without the extra flour, the dough would be too soft to roll out.

MAKES ABOUT 20 COOKIES, DEPENDING ON SIZE AND SHAPE

$2^1/_2$ **cups flour**
$3/_4$ **teaspoon baking powder**
$1/_4$ **teaspoon salt**
$1/_2$ **pound cold butter**
$3/_4$ **cup superfine or granulated sugar**
1 teaspoon vanilla extract
1 egg
1 egg yolk
Room-temperature butter for preparing pan
Colored sugar(s) or Royal Icing (see page 510) for decorating (optional)

In a bowl, sift together the flour, baking powder, and salt. In a large bowl, using a wooden spoon or a mixer, gradually building up speed from low to high, cream together the butter, sugar, and vanilla for about 7 minutes by hand or 5 minutes with the mixer, or until smooth and creamy. Beat in the egg and egg yolk. Add the flour mixture and work it in with a wooden spoon or with the mixer on low then medium speed just until there is no loose flour, the dough comes together in a shaggy mass and you hear the motor straining, about 30 seconds. Don't work it any more than necessary to make the dough come together.

Preheat the oven to 325°F. Line 2 sheet pans with parchment paper, or use nonstick pans. Place the dough between 2 large sheets of parchment paper. Pound it to flatten it slightly and then roll out into a rectangle about $1/_4$ inch thick. Rolling the dough between sheets of parchment paper eliminates the need to dust the work surface with flour (which the cookies absorb during cutting, and make for less tender baked cookies) and makes it easier to move the dough in and out of the refrigerator if it gets too warm and starts to get too soft. Move the dough in and out of the refrigerator as needed to keep it cool and easy to roll. Make sure the dough is cold when you cut out the cookies. Using decoratively shaped cutters, cut out the cookies, and pull away the excess dough. Transfer the cookie cutouts to the prepared pans, spacing them about 1 inch apart. Gather up scraps and reroll once to cut out more cookies. (Rerolling more than once makes for tough cookies.) Decorate the cookies with colored sugar if you wish.

Bake for 15 to 20 minutes, or until very pale brown. Let cool until set and then transfer to cooling racks or cool on the pans set on racks. Store tightly sealed in an airtight container for up to 1 week or first decorate with royal icing as shown on page 510, let icing set, and then store.

How to Decorate Cookies with Colored Sugar

Using colored sugars, also known as sanding sugars, is an easy way to decorate cookies. You can create different designs by covering parts of the cookies with waxed paper as you sprinkle on the sugar. If you are decorating the cookies all the same color, you can decorate them right on the sheet pan. If you are decorating them with different colors or in different ways, take them off the sheet pan and decorate them on the work surface one at a time, so you don't accidentally spill the wrong-colored sugar on a cutout. Make sure the dough is very cold—stick the cutouts in the freezer as needed—so the cookies don't lose their shape as you move them to and from the work surface. Brush them with lightly beaten egg white before sprinkling on the sugar, to help the sugar adhere.

Royal Icing

There are several ways to use this simple icing to decorate baked and cooled cookies: You can spread the icing in a shallow baking dish and dip the cookies, face down, into it; you can pipe it on with a pastry bag or paper cone (see page 439); you can paint it on with a brush; you can spread it with an icing spatula; or you can dip fork tines into the icing and wave the tines back and forth over the cookies, allowing the icing to drizzle over them. You can also tint the icing with food coloring.

Lemon oil, which is extracted from the rind of lemons and is highly aromatic, lightens the sweetness of the icing. Or, you can flavor the icing with other citrus oils but not liqueurs or eaux de vie because they're too liquid and will make the icing runny.

MAKES ABOUT 2¹/₂ CUPS, OR ENOUGH TO ICE ABOUT 60 COOKIES

> 4 cups confectioners' sugar
> 3 egg whites or 6 tablespoons heavy cream
> 1 teaspoon lemon oil (optional)
> Food coloring (optional)

In a bowl, combine the sugar, egg whites, and lemon oil and beat with a wooden spoon for about 2 minutes, or until smooth and snowy white. If the mixture is too thick for how you want to apply it (see above), thin it with 1 teaspoon of cold water. If it is too thin, add more sugar.

To color the icing, mix in the food coloring a drop at a time until you have the desired shade. Or, you can divide the icing into 2 or more bowls and tint each portion a different color.

Pecan Mounds

These cookies are light and rich at the same time. They are light because their texture is more fragile than most other cookies (any more fragile and they would fall apart), and rich because they contain so much butter. Sometimes they are called Russian tea cookies or Mexican wedding cookies, and they can be made with hazelnuts, walnuts, or pecans. You can make them by hand, with a mixer (stand or handheld), or in a food processor. The secret to success is never to let the dough get warm or the butter will melt and the cookies will not keep their shape and will lose their delicacy. If your kitchen is warm, keep moving the dough in and out of the freezer or refrigerator as you work with it.

MAKES ABOUT 24 COOKIES

> 2 cups flour
> ¹/₂ teaspoon salt
> ¹/₂ pound cold butter, cut into 1-inch cubes
> ²/₃ cup granulated sugar
> 2 teaspoons vanilla extract
> 2 cups pecans
> Confectioners' sugar for coating

To make the dough by hand, in a bowl, stir together the flour and salt. In another bowl, using a wooden spoon, cream together the butter and granulated sugar for about 8 minutes, or until smooth. Work in the vanilla. In a food processor, process the pecans for about 30 seconds, or until finely ground but not oily. Work the ground nuts into the butter mixture until evenly distributed, and then work in the flour mixture just long enough to eliminate lumps. Cover and chill for at least 20 minutes or up to 2 hours, or until the dough is firm enough to roll into balls.

To make the dough with a mixer, in a bowl, stir together the flour and salt. In another bowl, using a stand mixer fitted with the paddle attachment or a handheld mixer, cream together the butter and granulated sugar on medium speed for about 5 minutes, or until smooth. Add the vanilla and beat until combined. In a food processor, process the pecans for about 30 seconds, or until finely ground but not oily. With the mixer on medium speed, work in the ground nuts until evenly distributed, and then work in the flour mixture just long enough to eliminate lumps and until the dough comes together in a cohesive mass. Cover and chill for at least 20 minutes or up to 2 hours, or until the dough is firm enough to roll into balls.

To make the dough in a food processor, combine the pecans and granulated sugar in the processor and process for 1 minute, or until the nuts are finely ground. Add the flour and butter and process for about 45 seconds, or until it forms a paste with no lumps. Stop and scrape down the sides of the processor with a rubber spatula halfway through the processing, or more often as needed to get the mixture to combine. Scrape down the sides of the processor and process for about 10 seconds longer, or until the mixture clumps together. Chill in the freezer for 20 minutes or up to 2 hours, or until the dough is firm enough to roll up into balls.

Scoop up 2 rounded tablespoons of the dough, roll into a 1¼-inch-diameter ball between the palms of your hands, and place on a sheet pan (there's no need for buttering). Repeat with the remaining dough, spacing the cookies about 1 inch apart. Chill for 20 minutes.

Preheat the oven to 350°F. Bake for about 30 minutes, or until pale brown on the bottom. Cool first on the pan for about 10 minutes and then transfer to a rack. Once completely cool, roll in confectioners' sugar. Store tightly sealed in an airtight container for up to 1 week.

Chocolate Chip Cookies

Most bakers make chocolate chip cookies with the chocolate chips sold at the supermarket. To take your cookies up a notch, chop a piece of high-quality bittersweet chocolate for the chips. This recipe contains more butter and walnuts than the classic Toll House recipe.

MAKES ABOUT 16 COOKIES

> **1 cup flour**
> **¹/₂ teaspoon baking soda**
> **¹/₂ teaspoon salt**
> **³/₄ cup butter, at room temperature, sliced**
> **¹/₄ cup firmly packed brown sugar**
> **¹/₄ cup granulated sugar**
> **1 egg yolk**
> **¹/₂ teaspoon vanilla extract**
> **³/₄ cup coarsely chopped walnuts**
> **6 ounces bittersweet chocolate, chopped by hand or in a food processor into ¹/₄-inch chunks**
> **Room-temperature butter for preparing pans (optional)**

In a bowl, sift together the flour, baking soda, and salt. In a large bowl, using a wooden spoon or a stand mixer (fitted with paddle blade) on medium speed or handheld mixer on high speed, cream together the butter and both sugars for about 7 minutes by hand or 5 minutes with the mixer, or until smooth and creamy. Beat in the egg yolk and vanilla. Add the flour mixture and work it in with a wooden spoon or with the mixer on low to medium speed just until there is no loose flour. Stir in the nuts and chocolate. Cover and chill for 30 minutes.

Preheat the oven to 375°F. Brush 2 sheet pans with butter, or line 2 sheet pans with nonstick baking liners. For the first cookie, scoop up 2 tablespoons dough—a 1-ounce (2-tablespoon) ice cream scoop works great for this—and roll it into a ball between the palms of your hands. Don't handle the dough more than necessary or you will warm the butter too much, or it will make the cookies hard when baked. Set the ball on a prepared pan and press into a 2- to 3-inch round with a glass (if it sticks, dip the glass in cold water) or the heel of your hand. Repeat with the remaining dough, spacing the rounds about 1 inch apart.

Bake for about 20 minutes, or until the edges of the cookies are slightly browned. Let cool until set and then transfer to cooling racks or cool on the pans set on racks. Store tightly sealed in an airtight container for up to 1 week.

Madeleines

Madeleines are made like a sponge cake: whole eggs are beaten with sugar, and then flour is folded in. But they are denser and more buttery than genoise, the classic sponge cake (see page 423), because the recipe calls for more butter and browns it, which gives these delicate cakelike cookies a deep nutty flavor.

MAKES 18 COOKIES

> Room-temperature butter for preparing molds
> 3 eggs in their shells, soaked in warm water
>   for 10 minutes
> 1/2 cup sugar
> 1/2 cup plus 1 tablespoon cake flour
> 6 tablespoons Brown Butter (see page 471), cooled
>   to room temperature but not hard

Preheat the oven to 400°F. Generously brush eighteen 1-ounce madeleine molds with butter.

Crack the eggs into a bowl, add the sugar, and beat on high speed to the ribbon stage: when the beater is lifted, the mixture falls in a wide band onto the surface, forming a figure eight that stays for 5 seconds before dissolving. This will take about 6 minutes with a stand mixer and 15 minutes with a handheld mixer.

Transfer the egg mixture to a large bowl to make folding easier. Sift the flour over the egg mixture while folding it in with a rubber spatula. In a smaller bowl, fold together the brown butter and about one-fourth of the egg mixture, and then fold this mixture into the egg mixture.

Spoon the batter into a pastry bag fitted with a 2/3-inch plain decorating tip and pipe the batter (see page 439) into the prepared molds, or spoon the batter into the prepared molds.

Bake for about 20 minutes, or until puffed and lightly browned around the edges. Turn the madeleines out of the molds onto a cooling rack. Store tightly sealed in an airtight container for up to 1 week.

Almond Butter Cookies

Slightly chewy and wonderfully rich, these little butter cookies are made with brown butter, almond flour, and cake flour. You can use any small molds—round, boat-shaped, square—you have on hand, such as the tartlet molds used for the miniature tartlet shells on page 22. Each mold should hold about 1 tablespoon batter.

MAKES 25 TO 30 COOKIES

> 2/3 cup blanched almonds
> Room-temperature butter for preparing molds
> 1 cup confectioners' sugar
> 3 tablespoons cake flour
> 1/4 teaspoon salt
> 3 egg whites
> 6 tablespoons Brown Butter (see page 471), cooled
>   to room temperature but not hard

Preheat the oven to 350°F. Spread the almonds on a sheet pan and toast in the oven, stirring occasionally, for about 15 minutes, or until they are fragrant and have taken on color. Pour onto a plate and let cool. Transfer to a food processor and process for about 30 seconds, or until finely ground. You should have 1/2 cup.

Raise the oven heat to 400°F. Brush 20 to 25 small molds (see above) with butter and chill. Add the sugar, flour, and salt to the almonds in the processor and process until well combined. Add the egg whites and process until smooth. Then add the brown butter and process until smooth.

Spoon the batter into a pastry bag fitted with a 2/3-inch plain decorating tip and pipe the batter (see page 439) into the prepared molds, spoon the batter into the prepared molds, or pour the batter in with a small measuring cup.

Set the molds on a sheet pan and bake for about 15 minutes, or until pale brown. Let cool in their molds for 5 minutes and then unmold and let cool on a rack. Store tightly sealed in an airtight container for up to 1 week.

Almond Tuiles

Shaping these thin, crisp cookies, named after the curved roof tiles used in Mediterranean countries, takes a little work. The key to success is to spread the batter very thinly on the pan—it should seem as if there is not enough to hold together as a cookie—and then to shape the cookies—on a rolling pin or bottle—within seconds of being removed from the oven. If the tuiles darken around the edges but are raw in the middle, your oven is too hot.

MAKES ABOUT 30 COOKIES

Room-temperature butter for preparing pan

1 cup flour

1¹/₃ cups confectioners' sugar

1 tablespoon grated orange zest

4 egg whites

1 teaspoon vanilla extract

¹/₂ cup plus 1 tablespoon butter, melted and cooled

1¹/₃ cups sliced almonds

Preheat the oven to 350°F. Brush 2 or 3 sheet pans with butter, or line the pans with nonstick baking sheets.

In a bowl, stir together the flour, sugar, and orange zest. Whisk in the egg whites until smooth. Add the vanilla and butter and again whisk until smooth. Gently stir in the sliced almonds.

Drop a level tablespoon of batter onto a prepared pan and, using a small offset spatula or the back of a spoon, spread it into a 4-inch round. Repeat to make 6 rounds in all on the pan.

Bake for 13 to 15 minutes, or until the edge of each tuile is deep brown and the inside is pale brown. Remove from the oven and let stand for about 15 seconds, or until the cookies are just firm enough to handle. Then, working quickly, lift the still-flexible rounds off the sheet pan with a spatula one at a time and immediately place, top side up, over a rolling pin and/or clean wine bottle. If they don't droop on their own, press them gently against the pin. Let cool completely and then remove the cookies from the pin. As each batch is baking, shape the tuiles on another sheet pan, always making sure the pan is cool before you add the batter.

French-Style Macarons

Don't confuse macarons—a single o—with macaroons, which are coconut cookies. Macarons are made by folding almond flour—it is best to buy almond flour, rather than grinding almonds to make your own because the milled flour is finer—into meringue, shaping the meringue into cookies, and then sticking two cookies together with a little jam. The cookies should have a fragile crunch on the outside but a melting interior. To achieve this, leave the macarons at room temperature for about 20 minutes before baking.

MAKES ABOUT 24 FILLED MACARONS

¹/₂ cup almond flour

³/₄ cup plus 2 tablespoons confectioners' sugar

3 egg whites

1 pinch cream of tartar, if not using a copper bowl

1 to 5 drops food coloring in color of choice

3 tablespoons jam, any kind

2 teaspoons kirsch (optional)

In a bowl, combine the almond flour, ¹/₂ cup of the sugar, and 1 egg white and whisk until smooth. Don't try to beat this mixture to make it fluffy. In another bowl, combine the remaining egg whites and the cream of tartar and whisk until medium peaks form. Add the remaining 6 tablespoons sugar and whisk until stiff peaks form. Whisk enough of the food coloring into the beaten egg white until the mixture is the color you like. Fold the colored egg white into the almond mixture.

Preheat the oven to 375°F. Line 2 sheet pans with parchment paper. Spoon the mixture into a pastry bag fitted with a ¹/₂-inch plain decorating tip. Pipe rounds about 1¹/₄ inches in diameter and ¹/₈ inch high on the prepared sheet pans (see page 491). Hold the tip of the pastry bag no more than ¹/₂ inch above the pan, so the rounds stay flat. Also, move the tip quickly in a spiral motion as you pull away, so you don't leave a little peak (like a Hershey's kiss) in the center. If you make the rounds too high, they will crack in the oven. Let the rounds sit out at room temperature for 20 minutes, so a thin skin forms on the surface.

Bake for 10 minutes, or until the surface loses its sheen. Let cool on the pans set on racks, and then peel the rounds off the parchment paper. If the macarons still feel soft to the touch, allow them to dry at room temperature or in a 200°F oven.

In a small bowl, stir together the jam and kirsch. Using a small spoon or a paper cone (see page 439) with a ¹/₄-inch opening, put about ¹/₄ teaspoon jam on the bottom of half of the cookies. Top with the remaining cookies, bottom sides down.

Coconut Macaroons

Coconut macaroons are sometimes made with almond paste, or sometimes, as shown here, as simple mounds of baked meringue with shredded coconut folded into it.

MAKES ABOUT 24 COOKIES

>   **4 egg whites**
>   **1 pinch cream of tartar if not using a copper bowl**
>   **³/₄ cup sugar**
>   **One 12-ounce package sweetened shredded coconut (about 4 cups)**

Preheat the oven to 200°F. Line 2 sheet pans with parchment paper. In a bowl, beat the egg whites with the creme of tartar on high speed for about 5 minutes with a stand mixer fitted with the whisk attachment or with a handheld mixer, or until medium peaks form. Add the sugar in a slow, steady stream while continuing to beat for about 2 minutes longer with a stand mixer or 3 minutes longer with a handheld mixer, or until stiff peaks form. Set aside ¹/₂ cup of the shredded coconut and fold the remaining coconut into the egg whites.

Spoon the meringue into a pastry bag fitted with a ¹/₂-inch star decorating tip and pipe rounds 2 inches in diameter and 1 inch high onto the prepared pans (see page 439). Or, use 2 spoons to form the rounds on the pans, scooping up batter with one and shaping and scraping it off onto the baking sheet with the other.

Bake for about 3 hours, or until the cookies feel hard and dry to the touch. If they start to brown, turn the oven down to 200°F. Let cool until set and then transfer to cooling racks or cool on the pans set on racks. Store tightly sealed in an airtight container for up to 1 week.

Palmiers

Crisp and buttery, these cookies are made by rolling out puff pastry on a work surface dusted with granulated sugar, rather than flour. They will keep for days in an airtight container, but like most pastries taste best when eaten right away.

MAKES 30 TO 35 COOKIES

>   **Sugar for rolling and sprinkling**
>   **Puff Pastry (see page 476) or Quick Puff Pastry (see page 478)**

Dust a work surface liberally with sugar, and then roll out the pastry into a rectangle 9 by 14 inches and about ¹/₄ inch thick. Trim the edges so the rectangle measures about 8 by 13 inches. Sprinkle the rectangle with sugar. Fold over 1 inch along a 13-inch side of the rectangle. Repeat on the opposite side. Sprinkle the folds with sugar and again fold over the sides 1 inch, so they meet in the center of the rectangle. Pressing gently on the rolling pin, roll over the entire surface of the rectangle. This will help it hold its shape and will also lengthen it by about 1 inch. Fold the two sides of the rectangle together, folding the long sides in to meet in the center. Press gently along the sides of the rectangle to even them out, and roll over the now long, thin rectangle with the rolling pin. Cover and chill for 30 minutes.

Preheat the oven to 400°F. Line a sheet pan with parchment paper. Slice the rectangle crosswise into ¹/₄-inch-wide slices. Coat the slices with sugar and arrange the slices on the prepared pan, spacing them about 2 inches apart.

Bake for about 25 minutes, or until golden brown. Flip each cookie over and bake for about 5 minutes longer, or until brown on both sides. Let cool on the pan. Store tightly sealed in an airtight container for up to 1 week.

1. Sprinkle a long rectangle of puff pastry with sugar and fold in the long sides so they form a 1-inch border. Sprinkle the borders with sugar.

2. Fold the borders in toward the center and again sprinkle with sugar.

3. Fold the two sides together, and then press the whole log together.

4. Slice the rectangle into palmiers and coat them with sugar.

5. Bake until golden brown.

Biscotti

Biscotto and biscuit both mean "twice cooked"; the closest equivalent in English is a rusk. Here, a basic dough is mixed in a stand mixer or food processor, and then hazelnuts, dried fruit, and candied orange rind are stirred into it. The spices used to flavor these biscotti are similar to those used to flavor panforte, the dense medieval cake sold at Christmastime in Italy.

MAKES ABOUT 35 COOKIES

> **2 cups flour**
>
> **3/4 cup sugar**
>
> **1 teaspoon baking powder**
>
> **1/2 teaspoon salt**
>
> **1/4 teaspoon ground cloves**
>
> **1/2 teaspoon ground cinnamon**
>
> **1/8 teaspoon freshly grated nutmeg**
>
> **2 eggs**
>
> **3/4 cup butter, melted and cooled**
>
> **1/2 cup dried currants, cherries, or cranberries, soaked in water to cover for 30 minutes, drained, and patted dry**
>
> **1 1/2 cups hazelnuts, coarsely chopped**
>
> **1/4 cup diced candied orange rind (optional)**

Preheat the oven to 350°F. Line a sheet pan with parchment paper. In a stand mixer fitted with the paddle blade or in a food processor, combine the flour, sugar, baking powder, and spices and beat on slow to medium speed for 1 minute with the mixer or process for 15 seconds in the processor, or until well mixed. Add the eggs and butter and beat on medium speed for 2 minutes or until well combined, or process for 1 minute or until the mixture clumps together and there are no lumps. Add the currants, nuts, and orange rind to the mixer and beat on medium speed for 2 minutes, or until evenly distributed. If using a processor, transfer the dough to a bowl and work in the currants, nuts, and orange rind with a wooden spoon. Or, you can mix the dough completely by hand: stir together the dry ingredients, beat in the eggs and butter until the mixture clumps together, and then work in the currants, nuts, and orange rind.

Divide the dough in half. Shape each half into an 11-inch-long log on the prepared pan, spacing the logs well apart. With your palms, flatten each log so it is about 3 inches wide.

Bake for about 35 minutes, or until the tops of the logs are pale brown. Remove the pan from the oven, and turn the oven down to 300°F. Let the logs cool for 15 minutes on the pan.

Carefully transfer the logs to a cutting board. Using a serrated knife, cut each log on the diagonal into slices 1/2 inch thick. If the dough is soft and tears as you cut, let the logs cool for 5 minutes longer. Arrange the slices, a cut side down, on the sheet pan (you may need a second parchment-lined sheet pan for all of them to fit) and bake for 30 minutes longer. Let cool until set and then transfer to cooling racks or cool on the pans set on racks. Store tightly sealed in an airtight container for up to 1 week.

Brownies

Brownie aficionados are divided into two camps: cakey and fudgy. At the risk of pleasing no one while trying to please everyone, these brownies fall in between. They are rich, very chocolatey, and not too sweet—the definitive bar cookie. Use the best chocolate you can find. It will make all the difference.

MAKES 8 BROWNIES

> **1 cup walnuts**
>
> **Room-temperature butter for preparing pan**
>
> **8 ounces bittersweet chocolate, chopped**
>
> **3/4 cup butter, sliced**
>
> **3 eggs**
>
> **1/2 cup sugar**
>
> **1/2 teaspoon salt**
>
> **1 teaspoon vanilla extract**
>
> **1/2 cup flour**

Preheat the oven to 350°F. Spread the walnuts on a sheet pan and toast in the oven, stirring occasionally, for about 8 minutes, or until they are fragrant and have taken on color. Pour onto a plate, let cool, and then coarsely chop.

Turn down the oven to 325°F. Brush a 7-by-11-inch baking pan with butter.

Combine the chocolate and 3/4 cup butter in a heatproof bowl and set over a saucepan of simmering water. Stir with a rubber spatula until melted and smooth, and then immediately remove from the heat. Let cool slightly.

In a bowl, whisk together the eggs, sugar, salt, and vanilla for about 2 minutes, or until frothy. Stir in the chocolate mixture. Sift over the flour and fold in with a rubber spatula just until there are no lumps. Fold in the nuts. Spread the mixture in the prepared pan, smoothing the top.

Bake for 25 minutes, or until a knife inserted in the center comes out clean. Let cool on a wire rack and then cut into rectangles.

Lemon Bars

These classic bar cookies are made by pressing a buttery sweet pastry dough into a baking pan, baking it, letting it cool, and then spreading lemon curd on top. Most lemon curd is made with whole butter. Here, brown butter is used for a more pronounced butter flavor and a stiffer curd, but whole butter works fine, too.

MAKES 8 TO 10 BARS

Dough

2/3 **cup all-purpose flour**

2/3 **cup cake flour**

1/2 **cup confectioners' sugar**

1/4 **teaspoon salt**

1/2 **cup plus 3 tablespoons cold butter, cut into 1/3-inch cubes**

1 egg

Lemon Curd

3 eggs

3/4 **cup sugar**

1 tablespoon grated lemon zest

3/4 **cup fresh lemon juice**

6 tablespoons Brown Butter (see page 471) or 1/2 **cup butter, sliced**

To make the dough, combine both flours, the sugar, and the salt in a food processor and process for 15 seconds, or until well mixed. Add the butter and egg and process for about 20 seconds, or until the dough comes together in a ragged mass. Remove from the processor, shape into a disk, wrap in plastic wrap, and chill for 15 minutes.

Preheat the oven to 400°F. Have ready a 7-by-11-inch baking pan or similar-sized pan.

To make the lemon curd, in a heatproof bowl that fits over a saucepan, whisk together the eggs and sugar for about 2 minutes, or until smooth and slightly pale. Whisk in the lemon zest and juice and the brown butter. If using regular butter, don't add it yet. Bring a few inches of water to a simmer in the saucepan and rest the bowl in the rim of the pan over, but not touching, the water. Make sure that no flame wraps around the bottom of the saucepan and overheats the edge of the bowl. Continue whisking the mixture for about 5 minutes, or until it thickens.

Alternatively, in a saucepan, ideally with sloping sides, whisk together the eggs and sugar for about 2 minutes, or until smooth and slightly pale. Whisk in the lemon zest and juice and the brown butter. If using regular butter, don't add it yet. Place over medium heat and whisk the mixture for about 5 minutes, or until it thickens. If you are using a saucepan that doesn't have sloping sides, switch to a rubber spatula so you can reach into the corners. If there is the slightest hint that the mixture might boil, remove the pan from the heat and lower the heat before continuing.

Remove the curd from the heat. If you are using regular butter, whisk it in until melted. Cover with plastic wrap, pressing it directly onto the surface to prevent a skin from forming. Place in the refrigerator to cool while you make the crust.

On a floured work surface, roll out the dough into a square or rectangle about 1 inch wider and longer than your baking pan. Loosely roll the dough around the rolling pin, unroll it over the pan, and press it onto the bottom. Then, with the side of your finger, press the edge of the dough against the sides of the pan to form a 1-inch-high rim. Trim the edges so the rim is even. Bake for about 30 minutes, or until pale brown. Let cool on a rack for 15 minutes.

Spread the lemon curd over the still-warm pastry and let cool at room temperature for 30 minutes. Cover the pan with plastic wrap—don't allow the plastic wrap to touch the surface of the curd this time or it may leave marks when you remove it—and refrigerate for at least 2 hours before serving. Cut into rectangles.

INDEX

CONVERSIONS

VOLUME

FORMULAS:

1 teaspoon = 4.93 milliliters

1 tablespoon = 14.79 milliliters / 3 teaspoons

1 cup = 236.59 milliliters / 16 tablespoons

1 liter = 202.88 teaspoons / 67.63 tablespoons / 4.23 cups

U.S.	IMPERIAL	METRIC
1 tablespoon	1/2 fl oz	15 ml
2 tablespoons	1 fl oz	30 ml
1/4 cup	2 fl oz	60 ml
1/3 cup	3 fl oz	90 ml
1/4 cup	4 fl oz	120 ml
2/3 cup	5 fl oz (1/4 pint)	150 ml
3/4 cup	6 fl oz	180 ml
1 cup	8 fl oz (1/3 pint)	240 ml
1 1/4 cups	10 fl oz (1/2 pint)	300 ml
2 cups (1 pint)	16 fl oz (2/3 pint)	480 ml
2 1/2 cups	20 fl oz (1 pint)	600 ml
1 quart	32 fl oz (1 2/3 pint)	1 l

WEIGHT

FORMULAS:

1 ounce = 28.35 grams

1 pound = 453.59 grams / 16 ounces

1 kilogram = 2.2 pounds

U.S./IMPERIAL	METRIC
1/2 oz	15 g
1 oz	30 g
2 oz	60 g
1/4 lb	125 g
1/3 lb	150 g
1/2 lb	225 g
3/4 lb	350 g
1 lb	450 g

LENGTH

FORMULAS:

1 inch = 2.54 cm

1 foot = .3 m / 12 inches

1 cm = .39 inch

1 m = 3.28 feet / 39.37 inches

INCH	METRIC
1/4 inch	6 mm
1/2 inch	1.25 cm
3/4 inch	2 cm
1 inch	2.5 cm
6 inches (1/2 foot)	15 cm
12 inches (1 foot)	30 cm

TEMPERATURE

FORMULAS:

$9/5 \ C + 32 = F$

$(F - 32) \times 5/9 = C$

FAHRENHEIT	CELSIUS/GAS MARK
250°F	120°C / gas mark 1/2
275°F	135°C / gas mark 1
300°F	150°C / gas mark 2
325°F	160°C / gas mark 3
350°F	180 or 175°C / gas mark 4
375°F	190°C / gas mark 5
400°F	200°C / gas mark 6
425°F	220°C / gas mark 7
450°F	230°C / gas mark 8
475°F	245°C / gas mark 9
500°F	260°C

COOKING TERMS

A

Al dente: Literally, "to the tooth"; describes a cooked food, most commonly pasta, that is tender but still offers some resistance to the bite.

B

Bain-marie: A hot-water bath; used to ensure even, gentle cooking on the stove top or in the oven.

Bake: To cook uniform pieces of food uncovered in an oven, usually with a little fat or a small amount of liquid; also, to cook cakes, breads, pastries, pies, and other baked goods in an oven.

Barbecue: To cook food slowly over a charcoal or gas fire in a covered grill, usually with smoke.

Bard: To wrap meat in a thin sheet of fat to keep it moist.

Baste: To brush, pour, or spoon liquid over food as it cooks to prevent it from drying out.

Béarnaise sauce: Classic emulsified butter sauce made from clarified butter and egg yolks and flavored with shallots, tarragon, and vinegar.

Béchamel sauce: Classic white sauce made from butter, flour, and milk.

Beurre blanc: Classic emulsified butter sauce made by beating cubed butter into a white wine and vinegar reduction.

Beurre manié: A paste of butter and flour used to thicken braising and other liquids.

Blanch: To immerse food in boiling liquid as a preliminary cooking step, to be followed by a second cooking method; also, to immerse certain fruits and vegetables, such as peaches and tomatoes, in boiling water briefly to ease peeling.

Boil: To cook food by immersing it in boiling liquid.

Bouquet garni: A bundle of herbs added to soup, stews, and braises to infuse them with flavor.

Braise: To simmer food, such as a pot roast or whole chicken, in a small amount of liquid.

Broil: To cook food, usually relatively thin, small pieces, under—and usually quite close—to a heat source; the cooking equipment, known as a broiler, is often, but not always, part of the oven.

Broth: The flavorful liquid that results from cooking meat, poultry, seafood (fish bones and parts and/or crustacean shells), or vegetables and seasonings in water for varying amounts of time depending on the type of broth and the desired concentration.

Brown: To cook food, such as meat or poultry, over medium-high or high heat on the stove top or in a hot oven until the surface darkens to a rich brown.

Brown sauce: Classic French sauce made by reducing rich beef and/or veal broth to concentrate its flavor, combining it with tomatoes, and then thickening with a brown roux.

Butterfly: To cut a food, such as a boned leg of lamb or a peeled shrimp, nearly in half so it lies flat.

C

Caramelize: To cook foods over medium-high or high heat until their natural sugars are converted to a rich brown caramel; also, to heat sugar until it melts and turns brown.

Chiffonade: To cut a leafy vegetable into thin little strips by rolling the leaves tightly and slicing the rolls, controlling the size of the chiffonade by varying the thickness of the slices.

Chop: To cut food into pieces, from fine to large depending on the recipe; when no indication of size is given, cut into about 1/4-inch pieces.

Chutney: A traditional Indian condiment made from fruits and/or vegetables and spices that may be sweet, sour, tart, and/or hot; nowadays, the term is also used for similar preparations originating in other countries.

Clarify: To melt butter and reserve the clear golden liquid for cooking, while discarding the milk solids; also, to create a crystal-clear broth by adding egg whites that trap scum and sediment and then straining the broth through cheesecloth.

Concassée: A chunky sauce made from a vegetable.

Confit: Poultry, primarily duck and goose, or meat slowly cooked in a generous amount of fat until tender and then stored covered in the fat; nowadays, the term is also used for vegetables, usually onions, slowly cooked in oil until softened.

Coulis: A strained pureed sauce made from a fruit or vegetable.

Cube: To cut food into uniform pieces that are of equal size on all six sides; when no indication of size is given, cut into 1/4-inch cubes.

Curdle: To clump; can refer to the lumps that result when eggs in a sauce get too hot, causing the sauce to separate, or to the desirable curds that are produced when cooking scrambled eggs or making cheese or crème fraîche.

D

De-fat: To remove the fat, as is done for broths and jus, usually by skimming off the fat with a small ladle as the fat floats to the surface. Another method, commonly used for jus, is to use a degreasing cup that has a spout coming from the bottom of the cup instead of at the top, which pours off the jus below the surface of the fat. Last, broths and jus can be de-fatted by chilling them and then lifting off the congealed fat when cold.

Deep-fry: To cook food by immersing it in hot fat.

Deglaze: To use liquid to dissolve the caramelized juices on the bottom of a pan in which meat, poultry, or seafood has been sautéed, panfried, or roasted.

Degrease: To remove the fat from drippings, broth, braises, and the like.

Demi-glace: A highly reduced brown sauce used as a base for meat sauces.

Dice: To cut food into uniform squares, from fine to large (1/8 to 1/2 inch) depending on the recipe.

Drain: To separate a solid food from the liquid in which it has been cooked or soaked, often by means of a colander or strainer, with the liquid usually discarded.

Drippings: The juices that collect in the pan when meat or poultry is roasted; also, the fat rendered from bacon.

E

Egg wash: A light coating of whisked egg or egg yolk beaten with a pinch of salt that is brushed on some pastries and breads to enhance their baked appearance. The salt is added to thin the egg, making it easier to apply evenly.

Emulsify: To create a mixture of two or more ingredients that are held together by the presence of an emulsifier, such as egg yolks or cream.

Emulsion: A stabilized mixture produced when particles of fat are surrounded with molecules of an emulsifier, such as when the protein in egg yolks combines with oil to make a mayonnaise; a vigorously whisked vinaigrette of oil and vinegar is a temporary emulsion.

En papillote: To cook food in a parchment-paper package, usually resulting in it simultaneously steaming and braising.

F

Fillet: To remove the bones from meat, poultry, or fish; also, a piece of boneless meat, poultry, or fish.

Forcemeat: Seasoned ground mixture of meat, poultry, or fish used for pâtés, terrines, and as a stuffing.

French: To trim off the meat and fat from the last two inches or so of the bones on a rack of lamb or pork, a crown roast of pork, or a prime rib of beef, or chops.